T0180409

Lecture Notes in Computer Science　13142

More information about this series at https://link.springer.com/bookseries/558

Björn Þór Jónsson · Cathal Gurrin ·
Minh-Triet Tran · Duc-Tien Dang-Nguyen ·
Anita Min-Chun Hu · Binh Huynh Thi Thanh ·
Benoit Huet (Eds.)

MultiMedia Modeling

28th International Conference, MMM 2022
Phu Quoc, Vietnam, June 6–10, 2022
Proceedings, Part II

 Springer

Editors
Björn Þór Jónsson (iD)
IT University of Copenhagen
Copenhagen, Denmark

Cathal Gurrin (iD)
Dublin City University
Dublin, Ireland

Minh-Triet Tran (iD)
University of Science, VNU-HCM
Ho Chi Minh City, Vietnam

Duc-Tien Dang-Nguyen (iD)
University of Bergen
Bergen, Norway

Anita Min-Chun Hu (iD)
National Tsing Hua University
Hsinchu, Taiwan

Binh Huynh Thi Thanh (iD)
Hanoi University of Science and Technology
Hanoi, Vietnam

Benoit Huet (iD)
Median Technologies
Valbonne, France

ISSN 0302-9743   ISSN 1611-3349 (electronic)
Lecture Notes in Computer Science
ISBN 978-3-030-98354-3   ISBN 978-3-030-98355-0 (eBook)
https://doi.org/10.1007/978-3-030-98355-0

This Springer imprint is published by the registered company Springer Nature Switzerland AG
The registered company address is: Gewerbestrasse 11, 6330 Cham, Switzerland

Preface

These two-volume proceedings contain the papers accepted at MMM 2022, the 28th International Conference on MultiMedia Modeling.

Organized for more than 25 years, MMM has become a respected and well-established international conference bringing together excellent researchers from academic and industrial areas. MMM is considered a core-B conference. During the conference, novel research works from MMM-related areas (especially multimedia content analysis; multimedia signal processing and communications; and multimedia applications and services) are shared along with practical experiences, results, and exciting demonstrations. The 28th edition of the conference was organized in Vietnam during June 6–10, 2022. Due to the COVID-19 pandemic, the conference date had been shifted back by a number of months from the original scheduled dates. Despite the pandemic, MMM 2022 received a large number of submissions organized in different tracks.

Specifically, 212 papers were submitted to MMM 2022 tracks. Each paper was reviewed by at least three reviewers from the Program Committee, while the TPC chairs and special event organizers acted as meta-reviewers and assisted in the decision-making process. Out of 163 regular papers, 71 were accepted for the proceedings. In particular, 35 papers were accepted for oral presentation (acceptance rate of 21%) and 36 papers for poster presentation (acceptance rate of 22%). Regarding the remaining tracks, 23 special session papers were submitted with 13 accepted for oral presentation. Additionally, one paper was accepted (from three submitted) for a new Brave New Ideas track and six demonstration papers were accepted. Finally, there were 16 papers accepted for participation at the Video Browser Showdown 2022.

The special sessions are traditionally organized to extend the program with novel challenging problems and directions. The MMM 2022 program included four special sessions:

- MAPTA - Multimedia Analytics Perspectives, Tools and Applications
- MULTIMED - Multimedia and Multimodal Analytics in the Medical Domain and Pervasive Environments
- MACHU - Multimedia Analytics for Contextual Human Understanding
- MDRE - Multimedia Datasets for Repeatable Experimentation

Besides the four special sessions, the 11th Video Browser Showdown represented an important highlight of MMM 2022 with 16 participating systems in this exciting (and challenging) competition. In addition, three highly respected speakers were invited to MMM 2022 to present their impressive talks and results in multimedia-related topics.

Last but not least, we would like to thank all members of the MMM community who contributed to the MMM 2022 event. We also thank all authors of submitted papers, all reviewers, and all members of the MMM 2022 organization team for their great work and support. They all helped MMM 2022 to be an exciting and inspiring international event for all participants!

June 2022

Björn Þór Jónsson
Cathal Gurrin
Minh-Triet Tran
Duc-Tien Dang-Nguyen
Anita Min-Chun Hu
Binh Huynh Thi Thanh
Benoit Huet

Organization

General Chairs

Björn Þór Jónsson   IT University of Copenhagen, Denmark
Cathal Gurrin   Dublin City University, Ireland
Minh-Triet Tran   University of Science, VNU-HCM, Vietnam

Community Direction Chairs

Tat-Seng Chua   National University of Singapore, Singapore
Jan Zahálka   Czech Technical University in Prague,
                             Czech Republic
Maria Eskevich   CLARIN, The Netherlands

Technical Program Chairs

Duc-Tien Dang-Nguyen   University of Bergen, Norway
Anita Min-Chun Hu   National Tsing Hua University, Taiwan
Huynh Thi Thanh Binh   Hanoi University of Science and Technology,
                             Vietnam

Technical Program Coordinator

Benoit Huet   EURECOM, France

Demo Chairs

Aaron Duane   IT University of Copenhagen, Denmark
Binh Nguyen   University of Science, VNU-HCM, Vietnam

Local Arrangement Chairs

Tien Dinh   University of Science, VNU-HCM, Vietnam
Vu Nguyen   University of Science, VNU-HCM, Vietnam
Vu Lam   University of Science, VNU-HCM, Vietnam

Video Browser Showdown Chairs

Klaus Schoeffmann	University of Klagenfurt, Austria
Werner Bailer	JOANNEUM RESEARCH, Austria
Jakub Lokoč	Charles University, Czech Republic
Cathal Gurrin	Dublin City University, Ireland

Publication Chair

Vinh-Tiep Nguyen   University of Information Technology,
                                VNU-HCM, Vietnam

Steering Committee

Phoebe Chen	La Trobe University, Australia
Tat-Seng Chua	National University of Singapore, Singapore
Kiyoharu Aizawa	University of Tokyo, Japan
Cathal Gurrin	Dublin City University, Ireland
Benoit Huet	EURECOM, France
Klaus Schoeffmann	University of Klagenfurt, Austria
Richang Hong	Hefei University of Technology, China
Björn Þór Jónsson	IT University of Copenhagen, Denmark
Guo-Jun Qi	University of Central Florida, USA
Wen-Huang Cheng	National Chiao Tung University, Taiwan
Peng Cui	Tsinghua University, China

Web Chairs

Omar Shahbaz Khan	IT University of Copenhagen, Denmark
Mai-Khiem Tran	University of Science, VNU-HCM, Vietnam
Viet-Tham Huynh	University of Science, VNU-HCM, Vietnam

Organizing Agency

Minh-Hung Nguyen-Tong   CITE, Vietnam

Special Session Organizers

Multimedia Datasets for Repeatable Experimentation (MDRE)

Cathal Gurrin	Dublin City University, Ireland
Duc-Tien Dang Nguyen	University of Bergen, Norway
Björn Þór Jónsson	IT University of Copenhagen, Denmark
Klaus Schoeffmann	University of Klagenfurt, Austria

Multimedia Analytics: Perspectives, Tools and Applications (MAPTA)

Björn Þór Jónsson	IT University of Copenhagen, Denmark
Stevan Rudinac	University of Amsterdam, The Netherlands
Xirong Li	Renmin University of China, China
Cathal Gurrin	Dublin City University, Ireland
Laurent Amsaleg	CNRS-IRISA, France

Multimedia Analytics for Contextual Human Understanding (MACHU)

Duc-Tien Dang-Nguyen	University of Bergen, Norway
Minh-Son Dao	NICT, Japan
Cathal Gurrin	Dublin City University, Ireland
Ye Zheng	South Central University for Nationalities, China
Thittaporn Ganokratanaa	KMUTT, Thailand
Hung Tran-The	Deakin University, Australia
Zhihan Lv	Qingdao University, China

MULTIMED: Multimedia and Multimodal Analytics in the Medical Domain and Pervasive Environments

Georgios Meditskos	Centre for Research and Technology Hellas, Information Technologies Institute, Greece
Klaus Schoeffmann	University of Klagenfurt, Austria
Leo Wanner	ICREA – Universitat Pompeu Fabra, Spain
Stefanos Vrochidis	Centre for Research and Technology Hellas, Information Technologies Institute, Greece
Athanasios Tzioufas	National and Kapodistrian University of Athens, Greece

Program Committee and Reviewers (Regular and Special Session Papers)

Esra Açar Çelik	Fortiss Research Institute, Germany
Naushad Alam	Dublin City University, Ireland
Ahmed Alateeq	Dublin City University, Ireland
Laurent Amsaleg	IRISA, France
Evlampios Apostolidis	Centre for Research and Technology Hellas, Information Technologies Institute, Greece
Ognjen Arandjelovic	University of St Andrews, UK
Werner Bailer	JOANNEUM RESEARCH, Austria
Kai Uwe Barthel	HTW Berlin, Germany
Ilaria Bartolini	University of Bologna, Italy
Christian Beecks	University of Münster, Germany

Jenny Benois-Pineau	LaBRI, University of Bordeaux, France
Richard Burns	West Chester University of Pennsylvania, USA
Benjamin Bustos	University of Chile, Chile
Ying Cao	City University of Hong Kong, Hong Kong
Annalina Caputo	Dublin City University, Ireland
Angelos Chatzimichail	Hellenic Electricity Distribution Network Operator S.A., Greece
Edgar Chavez	CICESE, Mexico
Chien-Wen Chen	National Cheng Kung University, Taiwan
Wen-Cheng Chen	National Cheng Kung University, Taiwan
Zhiyong Cheng	Shandong Artificial Intelligence Institute, China
Wei-Ta Chu	National Cheng Kung University, Taiwan
Claudiu Cobarzan	Alpen-Adria-Universitaet Klagenfurt, Austria
Tuan Linh Dang	Hanoi University of Science and Technology, Vietnam
Duc-Tien Dang-Nguyen	University of Bergen, Norway
Minh-Son Dao	National Institute of Information and Communications Technology, Japan
Mihai Datcu	DLR/UPB, Germany
Cem Direkoglu	Middle East Technical University - Northern Campus Cyprus, Cyprus
Aaron Duane	ITU Copenhagen, Denmark
Athanasios Efthymiou	University of Amsterdam, The Netherlands
Mehdi Elahi	University of Bergen, Norway
Fabrizio Falchi	ISTI - CNR, Italy
Marc Gallofré Ocaña	University of Bergen, Norway
Thittaporn Ganokratana	HMUTT, Thailand
Ralph Gasser	University of Basel, Switzerland
Negin Ghamsarian	University of Klgagenfurt, Austria
Ilias Gialampoukidis	Centre for Research and Technology Hellas, Greece
Nikolaos Gkalelis	Centre for Research and Technology Hellas, Information Technologies Institute, Greece
Ziyu Guan	Xidian University, China
Gylfi Gudmundsson	Reykjavik University, Iceland
Cathal Gurrin	Dublin City University, Ireland
Graham Healy	Dublin City University, Ireland
Silvan Heller	University of Basel, Switzerland
Shintami Chusnul Hidayati	Institut Teknologi Sepuluh Nopember, Indonesia
Nhat Hoang-Xuan	University of Science, VNU-HCM, Vietnam
Frank Hopfgartner	University of Sheffield, UK
Min-Chun Hu	National Tsing Hua University, Taiwan

Zhenzhen Hu	Hefei University of Technology, China
Jen-Wei Huang	National Cheng Kung University, Taiwan
Lei Huang	Ocean University of China, China
Benoit Huet	EURECOM, France
Tran-The Hung	Deakin University, Australia
Ichiro Ide	Nagoya University, Japan
Konstantinos Ioannidis	Centre for Research and Technology Hellas, Information Technologies Institute, Greece
Bogdan Ionescu	Politehnica University of Bucharest, Romania
Adam Jatowt	UIBK, Austria
Peiguang Jing	Tianjin University, China
Hyun Woo Jo	Korea University, South Korea
Björn Þór Jónsson	IT University of Copenhagen, Denmark
Yong Ju Jung	Gachon University, South Korea
Anastasios Karakostas	Centre for Research and Technology Hellas, Greece
Ari Karppinen	Finnish Meteorological Institute, Finland
Omar Shahbaz Khan	IT University of Copenhagen, Denmark
Tran Thuong Khanh	University of Oulu, Finland
Koichi Kise	Osaka Prefecture University, Japan
Markus Koskela	CSC - IT Center for Science Ltd., Finland
Calvin Ku	National Tsing Hua University, Taiwan
Yu-Kun Lai	Cardiff University, UK
Minh-Quan Le	University of Science, VNU-HCM, Vietnam
Tu-Khiem Le	Dublin City University, Ireland
Andreas Leibetseder	Alpen-Adria-Universität Klagenfurt, Austria
Jiatai Lin	Guangdong University of Technology, China
Yu-Hsun Lin	National Tsing Hua University, Taiwan
Xueting Liu	Caritas Institute of Higher Education, Hong Kong
Jakub Lokoc	Charles University, Czech Republic
Stephane Marchand-Maillet	Viper Group - University of Geneva, Switzerland
Lux Mathias	University of Klagenfurt, Austria
Mitsunori Matsushita	Kansai University, Japan
Thanassis Mavropoulos	Centre for Research and Technology Hellas, Greece
Georgios Meditskos	Aristotle University of Thessaloniki, Greece
Frank Mejzlik	Charles University, Czech Republic
Robert Mertens	BHH University of Applied Sciences, Germany
Vasileios Mezaris	Centre for Research and Technology Hellas, Greece
Weiqing Min	ICT, China
Phivos Mylonas	Ionian University, Greece

Binh Nguyen	University of Science, VNU-HCM, Vietnam
Hien Nguyen	University of Information Technology, VNU-HCM, Vietnam
Manh-Duy Nguyen	Dublin City University, Ireland
Thao-Nhu Nguyen	Dublin City University, Ireland
Thi Oanh Nguyen	Hanoi University of Science and Technology, Vietnam
Thu Nguyen	SimulaMet, Norway
Nguyen Nhung	University of Manchester, UK
Tu Van Ninh	Dublin City University, Ireland
Naoko Nitta	Osaka University, Japan
Noel E. O'Connor	Dublin City University, Ireland
Vincent Oria	NJIT, USA
Tse-Yu Pan	National Tsing Hua University, Taiwan
Jian-Wei Peng	National Cheng Kung University, Taiwan
Ladislav Peska	Charles University, Czech Republic
Yannick Prié	LS2N - University of Nantes, France
Athanasios Psaltis	Centre for Research and Technology Hellas, Greece
Georges Quénot	Laboratoire d'Informatique de Grenoble, France
Fazle Rabbi	University of Bergen, Norway
Miloš Radovanović	University of Novi Sad, Serbia
Amon Rapp	University of Turin, Italy
Benjamin Renoust	Osaka University, Japan
Luca Rossetto	University of Zurich, Switzerland
Stevan Rudinac	University of Amsterdam, The Netherlands
Mukesh Saini	Indian Institute of Technology Ropar, India
Shin'ichi Satoh	National Institute of Informatics, Japan
Klaus Schoeffmann	University of Klagenfurt, Austria
Heiko Schuldt	University of Basel, Switzerland
Jie Shao	University of Electronic Science and Technology of China, China
Xi Shao	Nanjing University of Posts and Telecommunications, China
Ujjwal Sharma	University of Amsterdam, The Netherlands
Koichi Shinoda	Tokyo Institute of Technology, Japan
Hong-Han Shuai	National Chiao Tung University, Taiwan
Mei-Ling Shyu	University of Miami, USA
Vassilis Sitokonstantinou	National Observatory of Athens, Greece
Tomas Skopal	Charles University, Czech Republic
Alan F. Smeaton	Dublin City University, Ireland
Natalia Sokolova	University of Klagenfurt, Austria

Thanos Stavropoulos	Centre for Research and Technology Hellas, Information Technologies Institute, Greece
Li Su	University of Chinese Academy of Sciences, China
Lifeng Sun	Tsinghua University, China
Shih-Wei Sun	Taipei National University of the Arts, Taiwan
Mario Taschwer	University of Klagenfurt, Austria
Georg Thallinger	JOANNEUM RESEARCH, Austria
Diego Thomas	Kyushu University, Japan
Christian Timmerer	University of Klagenfurt, Austria
Ly-Duyen Tran	Dublin City University, Ireland
Minh-Triet Tran	University of Science, VNU-HCM, Vietnam
Thanh-Hai Tran	TU Wien, Austria
Thy Thy Tran	Technische Universität Darmstadt, Germany
Ngo Thanh Trung	Osaka University, Japan
Wan-Lun Tsai	National Cheng Kung University, Taiwan
Athina Tsanousa	Centre for Research and Technology Hellas, Information Technologies Institute, Greece
Shingo Uchihashi	FUJIFILM Business Innovation Corp., Japan
Habib Ullah	Norwegian University of Life Sciences, Norway
Tiberio Uricchio	University of Florence, Italy
Lucia Vadicamo	ISTI-CNR, Italy
Guido Vingione	Serco, Italy
Muriel Visani	University of La Rochelle, France
Stefanos Vrochidis	Centre for Research and Technology Hellas, Information Technologies Institute, Greece
Qiao Wang	Southeast University, China
Xiang Wang	National University of Singapore, Singapore
Xu Wang	Shenzhen University, China
Zheng Wang	University of Tokyo, Japan
Wolfgang Weiss	JOANNEUM RESEARCH, Austria
Tien-Tsin Wong	Chinese University of Hong Kong, Hong Kong
Marcel Worring	University of Amsterdam, The Netherlands
Xiao Wu	Southwest Jiaotong University, China
Sen Xiang	Wuhan University of Science and Technology, China
Yingqing Xu	Tsinghua University, China
Ryosuke Yamanishi	Kansai University, Japan
Toshihiko Yamasaki	University of Tokyo, Japan
Keiji Yanai	University of Electro-Communications, Japan
Gang Yang	Renmin University of China, China
Yang Yang	University of Electronic Science and Technology of China, China

Mei-Chen Yeh   National Taiwan Normal University, Taiwan
Zhaoquan Yuan   Southwest Jiaotong University, China
Jan Zahálka   Czech Technical University in Prague,
                                 Czech Republic
Bo Zhang   Dalian Maritime University, China
Hanwang Zhang   Nanyang Technological University, Singapore
Bingchao Zhao   Xi'an Jiaotong University, China
Liting Zhou   Dublin City University, Ireland
Lei Zhu   Shandong Normal University, China

Contents – Part II

Demonstration Papers

Video Browser Showdown 2022

Contents – Part I

Multimedia Applications - Perspectives, Tools and Applications (Special Session) and Brave New Ideas

Activities and Events

Multimedia Datasets for Repeatable Experimentation (Special Session)

Learning

Multimedia for Medical Applications (Special Session)

Applications 2

Image Analytics

Speech and Music

Multimodal Analytics

Poster Papers

Long-Range Feature Dependencies Capturing for Low-Resolution Image Classification

Sheng Kang, Yang Wang$^{(\boxtimes)}$, Yang Cao, and Zheng-Jun Zha

Department of Automation, University of Science and Technology of China,
Hefei 230027, China
ksc@mail.ustc.edu.cn, {ywang120,forrest,zhazj}@ustc.edu.cn

Abstract. Recognition of images with low-resolution is extremely challenging, due to the feature smoothness caused by the loss of structural details. Specifically, after losing the structural details, low-resolution image patches with different structural properties tend to have a uniform distribution in the specific channels of deep representation space, which will introduce ambiguity for image recognition. To address this problem, this paper proposes a novel Feature Enhancement Module (FE-Module). The module first extracts similar features as the pre-trained classification networks. Then it captures features across different depths to make use of all the hierarchical features. Finally, the module explores the patches with similar structures to remedy local feature smoothness for accurate low-resolution image classification. Extensive experiment results demonstrate that the proposed method can effectively enhance the feature discrimination ability and improve recognition performance.

Keywords: Low-resolution image classification · Feature enhancement · Long-range dependency

1 Introduction

The image classification task [7,8,13] has made great break-throughs benefited from the emergence of large scale image datasets such as ImageNet [3]. These datasets contain enormous images with manual annotations, which provide sufficient data with semantic supervision. However, a problem that cannot be ignored is that the images in these datasets are almost high-quality ones. While in practice, the input image for the classification model is likely to be a low-resolution one. Given a low-resolution image, the performance of classification models pre-trained on the ImageNet dataset will drop greatly. For example, when evaluating the pre-trained VGG16 [19] on 4× downsampled images, the accuracy will drop from 70% to 41%. The main reason why low-resolution affects image classification is that the loss of details leads to the image smoothness and the structural proprieties within local regions obstructed.

B. Þór Jónsson et al. (Eds.): MMM 2022, LNCS 13142, pp. 3–14, 2022.
https://doi.org/10.1007/978-3-030-98355-0_1

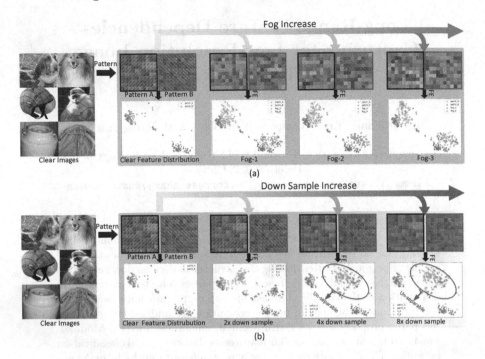

Fig. 1. The feature distribution visualization of foggy and low-resolution patches. As the degradation degree increases, the characteristic responses of the two foggy image patches are always separable. As a contrast, as the resolution decreases, the image smoothness gradually increases, resulting in the feature distribution of two low-resolution image blocks becoming inseparable. The features are extracted by conv2_2 in VGG16.

A straightforward method to address the low-resolution image classification problem is to first recover the structure information with Super Resolution (SR) methods and then perform image classification. However, the SR methods [2,4,5,10,14,15,17,26,27] are mainly devised for achieving a visually pleasing effect for human eyes and cannot guarantee that the structural similar regions can be enhanced consistently [25], leading to negligible improvement or even negative effect as shown in Table 1. Another feasible solution for this problem is to perform enhancement operations in the deep presentation space. For example, TAN *et al.* [21] proposed a GAN-based feature super-resolution method that improves the recognition accuracy of low-resolution images by enhancing the features of MLP layers. But this method requires the semantic labels for supervision and enormous images for retraining, which is time-consuming and the original training data is not available anymore in many cases. To get rid of the limitations of semantic labels, Wang *et al.* [25] proposed the Deep Degraded Prior (DDP) for low-contrast image (*e.g.* Fog) classification. They found that the distributions of corresponding structure-similar patches in low- and high-quality images have uniform margins under the same degradation condition, as shown in

Fig. 1 (a). However, the DDP cannot directly be extended to degradation conditions with structural loss, such as low resolution. For example, the classification accuracy drops from 52.54% to 50.54% on 3× downsampled ImageNet validation set when test DDP model trained on the synthesized low-resolution training set.

The reason is that foggy images mainly change the pixel intensity distribution, but discriminative gradient information still exists. Therefore, in the deep representation space, the image patches with different structures still have different marginal distributions after feature drifting as shown in Fig. 1 (a), and it is possible to learn a feature de-drifting mapping by using statistical properties of local patches. However, in low-resolution images, degraded cues will cause the loss of structure and gradient information, resulting in image smoothing. This will cause the different structural patches to have uniform feature distribution in deep representation space, as shown in Fig. 1 (b). In this situation, it is almost impossible to learn correct mappings for different patches by only using the local statistical properties.

To effectively restore structural details, a transformer-based Feature Enhancement Module which consists of three sub modules and progressively enhances the degraded features for low-resolution image classification is proposed. This method is based on the observations that low-resolution will result in ambiguous local features. Specifically, we propose Shallow Feature Extraction (SFE) which has a similar structure with the classification network to extract degraded features for further enhancement. The extracted feature are sent to Global Feature Fusion (GFF) module, which has a dense connection structure, to make use of all the hierarchical features by extracting features across different depths. Finally, a vanilla Transformer Layer (TL) is used to capture long-range feature dependencies for remedying local feature smoothness. Evaluations on the benchmark dataset demonstrate the performance of our proposed method on low-resolution image classification. The proposed method can improve the classification accuracy of ResNet50 [8] from 51% to 65%.

The contributions of this paper are mainly in the following three aspects:

- This paper finds that low-resolution will cause the different structural patches to have uniform feature distribution in deep representation space, which will introduce ambiguity for feature representation, leading to a decrease of image classification performance.
- This paper proposes a transformer-based feature enhancement network, which uses transformer layers to capture long-range feature dependencies to eliminate the ambiguity of local degraded features.
- Evaluations on the synthesized low-resolution dataset demonstrate the effectiveness of our proposed method under various downsample scales. The classification accuracy on ResNet50 improved from 51% to 65% after using our method.

2 Related Work

2.1 Image Super-Resolution

One alternative method of the low-resolution image classification is classification after super-resolution. We review some famous super-resolution methods as follows. Lim *et al.* [15] achieved better super-resolution results by using the new residual structure and the stacking of residual blocks. Ledig *et al.* [11] used GAN [6] and proposed a perceptual loss, which greatly improved low-resolution image visual performance. Zhang *et al.* [27] designed a residual in residual structure so that sufficient low-frequency information can pass through the multi-layer skip connection, and also used the channel attention mechanism to rescale the channel-wise feature. Li *et al.* [14] used the hidden states in a constrained RNN to realize a feedback super-resolution network so that the network can gradually produce high-resolution images. Dai *et al.* [2] proposed SAN, which strengthened the extraction of information between channels and used non-local networks [24] to achieve global information extraction. Zhang *et al.* [26] proposed an unfolding network that uses both learning-based methods and model-based methods, which decomposes the MAP (maximum a posteriori) problem into two subproblems and proposed an end to end training method to solve the subproblems.

2.2 Feature Enhancement

However, classification after super-resolution is not robust, so some feature enhancement methods were proposed to directly solve this problem. Li *et al.* [12] first proposed a GAN-based method to enhance features for small object detection. Tan *et al.* [21] proposed a GAN-based feature super-resolution method to minimize Euclid distance in feature shape. Noh *et al.* [18] proposed a feature enhancement network. They used atrous convolution to match the receptive fields of low-resolution images and high-resolution images, used GAN [6] to generate clean features, and achieved good results in small object detection. Son *et al.* [20] proposed a universal and recognition-friendly image enhancement network to avoid the problem of retraining on larger data sets by enhancing the input image. Wang *et al.* [25] proposed a feature de-drifting module to learn the mapping relationship between low- and high-quality image features. The most related work to ours is DDP [25]. However, their works are mainly designed to recover the statistical properties consistent for linear pixel-wise degradation conditions and cannot directly be extended to degradation conditions with structural loss, such as low-resolution.

3 Motivation

To illustrate the feature ambiguity caused by low-resolution images, we conduct a statistical experiment between low-contrast and low-resolution images by taking foggy images as an example of low-contrast images. Following the method in

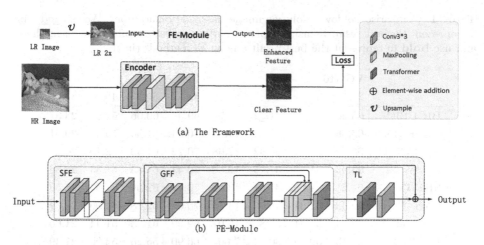

(a) The Framework

(b) FE-Module

Fig. 2. The framework of our module and the details of Feature Enhancement Module (FE-Module). As shown in (a), FE-Module is used to extract and enhance the degraded features of the low-resolution image. The details of the FE-Module are shown in (b), which consists of Shallow Feature Extraction (SFE), Global Feature Fusion (GFF), and Transformer Layer (TL).

ImageNet-C [9], the foggy images are synthesized on the ImageNet validation dataset. Referring to the patch selection method in DDP [25], two kinds of patches are selected. Each kind of patch contains 100 structural similar patches, as shown in Fig. 1. The corresponding foggy patches are sampled from the same position. In this experiment, we test three kinds of foggy conditions (Fog-1, Fog-2, Fog-3). The features of each patch are extracted by conv2_2 of pre-trained VGG16 and visualized by t-SNE [16]. We can observe that the fog degradation model changes the brightness distribution of images, therefore the feature drifted. However, the fog degradation will not change structural details for the images, which means that the degraded features remain independent and separable as shown in Fig. 1 (a). As degradation level increases, degraded feature drifting also increases but remain separable.

We perform the same statistical experiment on low-resolution images as shown in Fig. 1 (b). We can observe that low-resolution will also cause feature drifting. But different from foggy features, low-resolution features from different patches overlapped. And as the downsample scale increases, this overlap effect will be further aggravated and make the features more difficult to distinguish. This is because the loss of structural information will lead to the image smoothness that makes two different degraded patches looks similar, so as their features. So it is hard to learn a helpful feature enhancement that can map the degraded features to high-quality features with only local features. Because the transformer [22] can directly capture long-range dependencies between any two positions in a feature map by applying self-attention, we propose a transformer-based feature enhancement method to enhance the lost structural details by capturing long-range feature dependencies.

Table 1. Comparison of low-resolution image classification accuracy. We use <u>underline</u> to represent the best result by using super-resolution or feature enhancement methods, and use **bold** to represent the best result among all methods (in %).

	VGG16				ResNet50			
	2×	3×	4×	8×	2×	3×	4×	8×
BICUBIC	63.20	<u>52.54</u>	<u>41.32</u>	<u>14.77</u>	69.53	60.06	51.33	23.37
EDSR [15]	63.56	50.87	35.42	11.13	70.24	61.55	50.41	20.51
SRGAN [11]	63.42	51.14	38.82	12.68	70.22	61.59	52.10	20.88
RCAN [27]	63.93	51.59	37.15	12.50	70.43	61.85	51.33	22.36
SRFBN [14]	63.51	51.62	37.68	13.68	<u>70.44</u>	62.04	51.54	22.52
SAN [2]	62.48	52.31	40.69	14.15	70.03	<u>62.88</u>	<u>54.00</u>	<u>23.61</u>
USRNet [26]	62.94	51.41	37.85	12.07	69.59	61.23	51.44	21.60
DDP[25]	<u>67.13</u>	50.54	30.43	7.66	66.90	55.25	53.96	21.49
Ours	**68.50**	**59.95**	**50.95**	**19.55**	**72.92**	**69.85**	**65.51**	**40.48**

4   Feature Enhancement Module (FE-Module)

4.1   Overview

Given a high-resolution dataset without the semantic labels, our goal is to improve classification accuracy under the low-resolution condition without fine-tuning the classification model on semantic data. To this end, we propose an effective method that can extract and enhance the features from low-resolution images under the supervision of a simple Least Absolute Deviations loss (L1 loss).

The backbone network is split into two parts, with the shallow layers serving as the Backbone Encoder and the deep layers serving as the classifier. The Backbone Encoder is used to extract clear features from high-resolution images, which will be used as supervision for low-resolution image feature enhancement. The classifier is used to classify enhanced features during the test stage.

As shown in Fig. 2 (a), during the training stage, a low-resolution image is upsampled to half size of the high-resolution image. Then the enhanced features are estimated under the supervision of clear features by the FE-Module, which is composed of Shallow Feature Extraction, Global Feature Fusion, and Transformer Layer as shown in Fig. 2 (b). During the test stage, the enhanced features are sent to the classifier to get the correct label.

4.2   Shallow Feature Extraction (SFE)

Because our FE-Module needs to extract features as close as possible to clear features with no semantic labels available for training, the first part of FE-Module, which is named Shallow Feature Extraction (SFE), is designed to have the same structure as the Backbone Encoder. However, if we directly send the low-resolution image to SFE, it can not extract correct features because of the mismatch of the receptive field. So the image should be upsampled before being sent to the network.

In addition, we remove the first max-pool layer in SFE and the low-resolution images can be upsampled to half size compared to the high-resolution images. By this optimization, we can speed up training and testing while the receptive field and the resolution in feature space stay the same. We will demonstrate the superiority of this operation in the ablation study.

4.3   Global Feature Fusion (GFF)

After SFE serving as basic feature extraction, Global Feature Fusion is proposed to further extract features across different depth to make use of all the hierarchical features. It is composed of a convolution layer, C convolution blocks and a feature fusing block. GFF extracts global features F_{GF} by fusing features from all convolution blocks

$$F_{GF} = D([F_1, F_2, ..., F_C]) \tag{1}$$

Where F_i denotes the output of the ith convolution blocks, which is composed of two convolution layers and D is a fusing layer that concatenates all the output features and adaptively fuses them by a 1×1 convolution layer. Each F_i takes the output features of F_{i-1} as input.

4.4   Transformer Layer (TL)

As discussed in Sect. 3, the local features are not sufficient to restore structures under serious degradation, so a transformer [22] layer, which can capture long-range dependencies easily, is used to enhance the lost structural details by capturing long-range features dependencies. The output features of GFF are sent to Transformer Layer to get globally similar features to restore local features. The vanilla transformer encoder layer described in [22] is used to compose our Transformer Layer. The transformer takes 1D sequence as input but the output features are 2D. Therefore we reshape the features $\mathbf{x} \in \mathbb{R}^{C \times H \times W}$ into flattened 1D sequence $\mathbf{x_f} \in \mathbb{R}^{C \times (H \cdot W)}$. The features are reshaped backed to 2D features after the transformer layer. Finally, a skip connection is used to connect the start of GFF and the end of the TL to mitigate the vanishing gradient problem.

5   Experiment

5.1   Settings

Training Settings. We set the batch size to 128 and update the model with the Adam optimizer. The network has been trained for 300k iterations. The learning rate is 1×10^{-4} at the beginning and gradually rises to 1×10^{-3} within 20k iterations, and keeps stable for training until the last 30k times, when the cosine function is used to gradually decrease the learning rate to 1×10^{-5}. High-resolution

Table 2. Different enhance depth and corresponding accuracy

Network	D1	D2	D3	D4	D5
VGG16	38.78	50.82	49.19	**52.38**	44.88
ResNet50	58.50	56.50	59.41	**65.02**	61.84

Table 3. Accuracy of keep or remove the first max-pool layer in SFE. The image is 4× downsampled.

	Maxpool	No maxpool
VGG16	50.75	**50.95**
ResNet50	64.43	**65.51**

image patches are randomly cropped to 224 × 224 during training, applied the random horizontal and vertical flip and the corresponding low-resolution patches are generated using bicubic interpolation.

Datasets. The ImageNet-C [9] dataset was proposed to test the robustness of neural networks on low-quality images under different situations. However, the original ImageNet-C dataset doesn't contain low-resolution images. By referring to the low-quality generation process in ImageNet-C, we synthesize our test dataset at 2×, 3×, 4×, 8× downsampling scales on the ImageNet [3] validation dataset. Our training dataset is synthesized on CUB [23] dataset at the corresponding downsample scale.

5.2 Ablation Study

The Depth of Backbone Encoder. We analyze the influence of the Backbone Encoder depth on feature enhancement performance. For VGG16, we leverage the conv1_2, conv2_2, conv3_3, conv4_3, and conv5_3 with previous layers as Backbone Encoder and denote them as D1-D5, respectively. For ResNet50, we leverage the max pool, layer1, layer2, layer3 and layer4 with the previous layers as Backbone Encoder and denote them as D1-D5, respectively. The results are shown in Table 2. We can observe that better performance is achieved when the depth of the Backbone Encoder is neither shallow nor deep. This is because shallow Backbone Encoder's receptive field is too small to extract necessary structural information on low-resolution images, and deep Backbone Encoder contains too much semantic information, which will harm the performance when no semantic labels are available in the training set. We choose D2 as the backbone encoder for VGG16 for a trade-off between accuracy and training speed and D4 for ResNet50 because its performance is obviously beyond others.

Size of the Low-Resolution Image. We upsampled the low-resolution image to half size and remove the first max-pool layer in SFE to speed up training and match the receptive field. In comparison, we can resize the image to the same

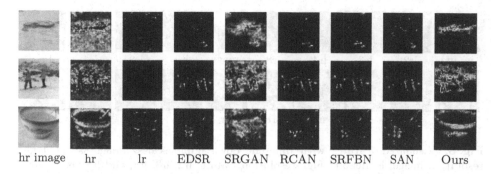

hr image   hr   lr   EDSR   SRGAN   RCAN   SRFBN   SAN   Ours

Fig. 3. Visualization of the feature maps of low-resolution images and SR results. The images are from ImageNet validation dataset [3]. The feature maps are extracted from Backbone Encoder of VGG16. The discrimination of the features of low-resolution images drop significantly, while the features extracted by our method successfully restores structural details.

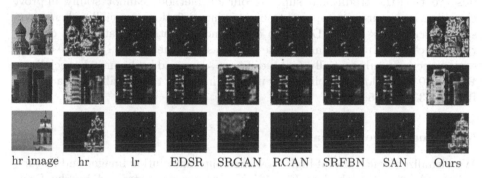

hr image   hr   lr   EDSR   SRGAN   RCAN   SRFBN   SAN   Ours

Fig. 4. Visualized features with different methods on CameraSR. The feature maps are extracted from Backbone Encoder of VGG16. All the methods are tested on models which are trained on 3× downsampled images.

size as high-resolution images and retain the original SFE structure. The result is shown in Table 3. We can find that in both backbones, SFE without maxpool performs better than the original version. This is reasonable because that resize operation will not introduce more information to the low-resolution images and the resized images will be more blurry.

5.3 Quantitative Comparisons

The performance with super-resolution methods like EDSR [15], SRGAN [11], RCAN [27], SRFBN [14], SAN [2] and USRNet [26] on low-resolution classification task is obtained by the following procedure: first retrain the model on the synthesized low-resolution images with different downsample scales, then generate super-resolution images using the trained model, finally calculate the classification accuracy with pre-trained VGG16 and ResNet50. We also reproduce the feature enhancement method DDP[25] and compare it with our methods.

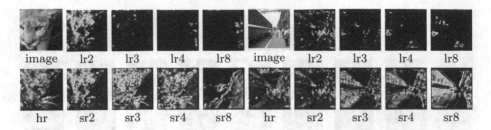

Fig. 5. Visualized features with different downsample scales. Image is the high-resolution image; hr denotes high-resolution feature; lr2, lr3, lr4, and lr8 denote low-resolution features with different downsample scales; sr2, sr3, sr4, and sr8 denote enhanced features by our method respectively.

The results of the quantitative experiments are shown in Table 1. We can observe that the traditional super-resolution methods cannot stably improve classification accuracy compared to bicubic interpolation, especially when downsample scale is 4× or 8×. DDP can only handle slight degradation but deteriorates quickly when downsample scale increases. Our method can improve classification accuracy substantially across different scales and backbones. Especially on ResNet50 at 4× downsampling, our method improves the classification accuracy from 51.33% to 65.02%.

5.4 Qualitative Comparison

We visualize the features of high-, low- and super-resolution images and features enhanced by our method in Fig. 3. The features are extracted by the Backbone Encoder of ResNet50. The images are 4× downsampled, which is a severe degradation. We can observe that super-resolution methods can only restore a few feature structures. Although the result of SRGAN is better than other super-resolution methods, the edges of the feature map are blurry and lack discrimination information. In comparison, FE-Module can successfully recover the structures.

We conduct a qualitative experiment on real low-resolution images proposed in CameraSR [1]. All the models are trained on 3× downsampled images because the resolution scale in CameraSR is 2.9× between high- and low-resolution images. The features extracted by the Backbone Encoder of VGG16 are visualized in Fig. 4. We can observe that all the super-resolution methods failed to restore the structure of features while FE-Module successfully restores structural details of real low-resolution images.

We also visualized our results on different downsample scales. As shown in Fig. 5, our model can restore structural details on different downsample scales consistently. Even at 8× downsample, our methods can still restore the main structure of the image.

6 The Conclusion

In this paper, we focus on improving image classification accuracy on low-resolution images. By extracting small image patches and visualize their features, we find that a low-resolution degradation model will cause the loss of structural details. To solve this problem, we propose a transformer-based feature enhancement module which exploits long-range feature dependencies for compensating local structural details loss. Our method can be trained without semantic labels and improves the classification result greatly.

Acknowledgements. This work was supported by the National Key R&D Program of China under Grand 2020AAA0105702, National Natural Science Foundation of China (NSFC) under Grants U19B2038, the University Synergy Innovation Program of Anhui Province under Grants GXXT-2019-025 and the key scientific technological innovation research project by Ministry of Education.

References

1. Chen, C., Xiong, Z., Tian, X., Zha, Z.J., Wu, F.: Camera lens super-resolution. In: Proceedings of the IEEE/CVF Conference on Computer Vision and Pattern Recognition, pp. 1652–1660 (2019)
2. Dai, T., Cai, J., Zhang, Y., Xia, S.T., Zhang, L.: Second-order attention network for single image super-resolution. In: Proceedings of the IEEE/CVF Conference on Computer Vision and Pattern Recognition, pp. 11065–11074 (2019)
3. Deng, J., Dong, W., Socher, R., Li, L.J., Li, K., Fei-Fei, L.: Imagenet: a large-scale hierarchical image database. In: 2009 IEEE Conference on Computer Vision and Pattern Recognition, pp. 248–255. IEEE (2009)
4. Dong, C., Loy, C.C., He, K., Tang, X.: Image super-resolution using deep convolutional networks. IEEE Trans. Pattern Anal. Mach. Intell. **38**(2), 295–307 (2015)
5. Fu, X., Zha, Z.J., Wu, F., Ding, X., Paisley, J.: JPEG artifacts reduction via deep convolutional sparse coding. In: Proceedings of the IEEE/CVF International Conference on Computer Vision, pp. 2501–2510 (2019)
6. Goodfellow, I.J., et al.: Generative adversarial networks. arXiv preprint arXiv:1406.2661 (2014)
7. Haralick, R.M., Shanmugam, K., Dinstein, I.H.: Textural features for image classification. IEEE Trans. Syst. Man Cybern. **6**, 610–621 (1973)
8. He, K., Zhang, X., Ren, S., Sun, J.: Deep residual learning for image recognition. In: Proceedings of the IEEE Conference on Computer Vision and Pattern Recognition, pp. 770–778 (2016)
9. Hendrycks, D., Dietterich, T.: Benchmarking neural network robustness to common corruptions and perturbations. arXiv preprint arXiv:1903.12261 (2019)
10. Huang, Y., Zha, Z.J., Fu, X., Hong, R., Li, L.: Real-world person re-identification via degradation invariance learning. In: Proceedings of the IEEE/CVF Conference on Computer Vision and Pattern Recognition, pp. 14084–14094 (2020)
11. Ledig, C., et al.: Photo-realistic single image super-resolution using a generative adversarial network. In: Proceedings of the IEEE Conference on Computer Vision and Pattern Recognition, pp. 4681–4690 (2017)

12. Li, J., Liang, X., Wei, Y., Xu, T., Feng, J., Yan, S.: Perceptual generative adversarial networks for small object detection. In: Proceedings of the IEEE Conference on Computer Vision and Pattern Recognition, pp. 1222–1230 (2017)
13. Li, L., Jiang, S., Zha, Z.J., Wu, Z., Huang, Q.: Partial-duplicate image retrieval via saliency-guided visual matching. IEEE Multimedia **20**(3), 13–23 (2013)
14. Li, Z., Yang, J., Liu, Z., Yang, X., Jeon, G., Wu, W.: Feedback network for image super-resolution. In: Proceedings of the IEEE/CVF Conference on Computer Vision and Pattern Recognition, pp. 3867–3876 (2019)
15. Lim, B., Son, S., Kim, H., Nah, S., Mu Lee, K.: Enhanced deep residual networks for single image super-resolution. In: Proceedings of the IEEE Conference on Computer Vision and Pattern Recognition Workshops, pp. 136–144 (2017)
16. Van der Maaten, L., Hinton, G.: Visualizing data using t-SNE. J. Mach. Learn. Res. **9**(11) (2008)
17. Min, S., Yao, H., Xie, H., Wang, C., Zha, Z.J., Zhang, Y.: Domain-aware visual bias eliminating for generalized zero-shot learning. In: Proceedings of the IEEE/CVF Conference on Computer Vision and Pattern Recognition, pp. 12664–12673 (2020)
18. Noh, J., Bae, W., Lee, W., Seo, J., Kim, G.: Better to follow, follow to be better: towards precise supervision of feature super-resolution for small object detection. In: Proceedings of the IEEE/CVF International Conference on Computer Vision, pp. 9725–9734 (2019)
19. Simonyan, K., Zisserman, A.: Very deep convolutional networks for large-scale image recognition. arXiv preprint arXiv:1409.1556 (2014)
20. Son, T., Kang, J., Kim, N., Cho, S., Kwak, S.: URIE: universal image enhancement for visual recognition in the wild. In: Vedaldi, A., Bischof, H., Brox, T., Frahm, J.-M. (eds.) ECCV 2020. LNCS, vol. 12354, pp. 749–765. Springer, Cham (2020). https://doi.org/10.1007/978-3-030-58545-7_43
21. Tan, W., Yan, B., Bare, B.: Feature super-resolution: make machine see more clearly. In: Proceedings of the IEEE Conference on Computer Vision and Pattern Recognition, pp. 3994–4002 (2018)
22. Vaswani, A., et al.: Attention is all you need. In: Advances in Neural Information Processing Systems, pp. 5998–6008 (2017)
23. Wah, C., Branson, S., Welinder, P., Perona, P., Belongie, S.: The Caltech-UCSD Birds-200-2011 Dataset. Technical report, CNS-TR-2011-001, California Institute of Technology (2011)
24. Wang, X., Girshick, R., Gupta, A., He, K.: Non-local neural networks. In: Proceedings of the IEEE Conference on Computer Vision and Pattern Recognition, pp. 7794–7803 (2018)
25. Wang, Y., Cao, Y., Zha, Z.J., Zhang, J., Xiong, Z.: Deep degradation prior for low-quality image classification. In: Proceedings of the IEEE/CVF Conference on Computer Vision and Pattern Recognition, pp. 11049–11058 (2020)
26. Zhang, K., Gool, L.V., Timofte, R.: Deep unfolding network for image super-resolution. In: Proceedings of the IEEE/CVF Conference on Computer Vision and Pattern Recognition, pp. 3217–3226 (2020)
27. Zhang, Y., Li, K., Li, K., Wang, L., Zhong, B., Fu, Y.: Image super-resolution using very deep residual channel attention networks. In: Proceedings of the European Conference on Computer Vision (ECCV), pp. 286–301 (2018)

An IBC Reference Block Enhancement Model Based on GAN for Screen Content Video Coding

Pengjian Yang[1], Jun Wang[2(✉)], Guangyu Zhong[1], Pengyuan Zhang[3],
Lai Zhang[1], Fan Liang[1], and Jianxin Yang[2]

[1] Electronics and Information Technology, Sun Yat-sen University,
Guangzhou, China
{yangpj5,zhonggy5,zhanglai3}@mail2.sysu.edu.cn, isslf@mail.sysu.edu.cn
[2] Zhuhai Jieli Technology Co., Ltd., Zhuhai, China
wangj387@mail.sysu.edu.cn, yangjianxin@zh-jieli.com
[3] Wuhan Research Institute of Posts and Telecommunications, Wuhan, China

Abstract. As a special kind of video coding, screen content coding (SCC) has received widespread attention because of the popularity of online classes and conferences. However, few people use neural networks to improve the compression efficiency of SCC. Intra block copy (IBC) is one of the most important coding tools in SCC, which can save half of the bitrate. Due to the need to copy the content of the reference block, the performance of IBC mode largely depends on the quality of the reference block. In the standard encoding process of Versatile Video Coding (VVC), the IBC reference block is not filtered, and there are still serious compression artifacts. This will result in a decrease in IBC search accuracy and SCC compression efficiency. Inspired by in-loop filtering, we propose an IBC reference blocks enhancement network based on GAN (IREGAN) to filter the reference blocks before IBC estimation, which can improve the quality of IBC reference block and the accuracy of IBC matching. In addition to the generator used for image enhancement, our model also includes a variance-based classifier and a discriminator obtained from adversarial training. The classifier can effectively improve the efficiency of the model and the discriminator can improve the robustness of the entire system. Experimental results demonstrate the performance gains of IREGAN with VTM10.0, offering about 6.98% BDBR reduction, 0.71dB BDPSNR gains in average (luminance). SSIM increased by 0.0113 and the number of blocks using IBC mode is increased by 1.42%.

Keywords: Generative Adversarial Network (GAN) · Versatile Video Coding (VVC) · Intra block copy (IBC) · Screen content coding (SCC)

This work was supported by Key-Area R&D Program of Guangdong Province under Grant 2019B010135002, and Innovative & Enterprising Team of Zhuhai under Grant 2019ZHCDGY07.

© Springer Nature Switzerland AG 2022
B. Þór Jónsson et al. (Eds.): MMM 2022, LNCS 13142, pp. 15–26, 2022.
https://doi.org/10.1007/978-3-030-98355-0_2

1   Introduction

In 2020, due to the spread of the COVID-19 disease, more and more people use video for online classes and conferences, screen content videos are widely used in these video applications. As a result, the networks have been profoundly impacted by excessive traffic. Because of the large amount of raw video data, to transmit or store the video, it must be compressed to reduce bitrate and storage requirements. Versatile Video Coding (VVC) is the latest generation of video coding standards, compared with other coding standards, the performance is improved by about 30% [1]. Even so, it is difficult to meet diverse needs.

Most of the online classes and conferences transmit screen content videos, which are derived from screens, and mainly contain texts, tables, and charts, coding this type of video is called screen content coding (SCC). For SCC, VVC has a dedicated coding tool called Intra block copy (IBC), which is shown in Fig. 1 left. IBC is a very efficient tool that can bring about 50% BD-rate gain for SCC [2,3]. When encoding the current block, the Block Vector (BV) search is performed, if a reference block is found to be similar to the current block, the BV will be used to point from the current block to the reference block. In this way, only BV and residuals need to be transmitted to complete the encoding of the current block, which can save a lot of bandwidth. Therefore, the more similarity between the reference block and the current block, the higher the probability of an IBC hit, and the smaller the residual data that needs to be transmitted.

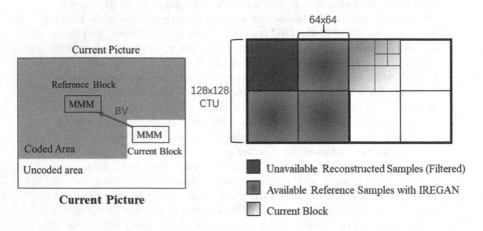

Fig. 1. Schematic diagram of IBC mode & IBC search range

However, from the flow chart of VVC (Fig. 2), the in-loop filtering is performed after one frame is reconstructed, which means that the IBC reference area has not been filtered, image distortion and compression artifacts greatly affect the performance of IBC mode. Not only that, the reconstructed block may be referenced by subsequent blocks, which may cause accumulation of distortion.

But few researchers have conducted relevant research so far, therefore, it is necessary to filter the IBC reference block before IBC search. In VVC, the search range of IBC is limited to the three neighboring 64 * 64 blocks (Fig. 1 right), but according to our statistics, even with the limitation of the search range, there are still 30%–60% CUs using IBC mode in SCC. Therefore, improving the performance of IBC mode is of great significance to improve the compression efficiency.

In this work, an IBC reference block enhanced Network based on GAN (IREGAN) is proposed to enhance the performance of IBC. Through adversarial training, the proposed IREGAN can effectively improve the quality of images and remove compression artifacts. Overall, the main contributions of our paper are summarized as follows.

1. We design a model to effectively improve the coding efficiency of SCC, which uses GAN to filter IBC reference blocks and improve video quality
2. We use a variety of evaluations to evaluate the performance of our model and propose a new evaluation: IBC-hitrate to assess the impact of the model on the IBC mode. Experimental results show that IREGAN is able to improve the overall quality better than the generic networks.

To the best of our knowledge, we are the first to propose improving compression efficiency by enhancing the IBC reference block. It provides a new idea for subsequent researchers to combine neural networks with video coding. Not only that, our work may be combined with other traditional IBC methods [4–7] to further improve the performance of the IBC mode.

2   Related Works

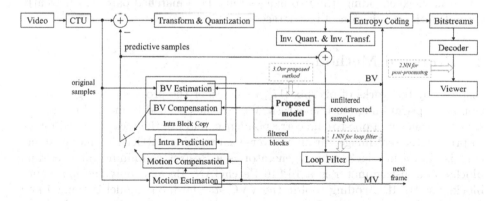

Fig. 2. The flowchart of VVC & Related works

The flow chart of VVC (black part) and the location of related work (dotted border) is shown in Fig. 2. We can see that common method to enhance the video quality by using Neural Networks (NN) are generally divided into two categories. Some researchers replace the traditional in-loop filters with NN to enhance the quality of reconstructed frames. Pan et al. [8] proposed Enhanced Deep Convolutional Neural Networks (EDCNN) to replace traditional loop-filter. Zhang et al. [9] proposed Residual Highway Convolutional Neural Networks (RHCNN) to enhance the quality of reconstructed frames. Dai et al. [10] proposed a Variable filter size Residue learning CNN (VRCNN) to predict the residual image of a frame, and then add the residual image and the reconstructed image to obtain an enhanced image.

Other researchers use NN as a post-processing module to enhance the overall quality of the images. Lu et al. [11] proposed an image restoration network as the post-processing module for emerging VVC Intra Profile to process the images output by the decoder. Xue et al. [12] proposed an attention-based convolutional neural network for low bitrate compression to post-process the output of the traditional image compression decoder. Cho et al. [13] proposed a groped residual dense network to enhance the quality of video in low bitrate. The advantage of the post-processing module is that it is more flexible and can be easily added or replaced. However, since post-processing is not related to the encoding process, the video encoding efficiency cannot be improved. Therefore, when the bandwidth is limited, post-processing cannot solve the problem.

According to our investigation, using GAN to process IBC reference blocks may have better performance. With the development of theory and the propose of frameworks, GAN has made significant progress in image inpainting [14], super-resolution [15], and deblurring [16]. Inspired by these classic models, we consider the enhancement of IBC reference blocks as a special image-to-image task. We input the reconstructed images into the network and hope to get the results closer to real images. A big problem with GAN is that it is difficult to find paired images, however, since there is an original image and a reconstructed image in video encoding, the two images must be a matched pair, which greatly simplifies the acquisition of the datasets.

3   Proposed Method

Inspired by the works of pix2pix [17], we consider the process of image restoration as a special image-to-image task. We cut the encoded frame and the reconstructed frame in a one-to-one correspondence, and use the reconstructed image to predict the real image through adversarial training. IREGAN's model structure is shown in Fig. 3, which generator is a ResNet containing nine residual blocks, and discriminator is a 16*16 PatchGAN. Because only the luminance blocks use the IBC coding tool in the VVC standard, our model is trained and tested for luminance only. Even so, due to the relationship between the luma blocks and the chroma blocks, the image quality of the chroma blocks will also be improved.

We implement and verify the model in the reference software VTM10.0 [24]. The flow chart of our model is shown in Fig. 4 left. The input of the model is

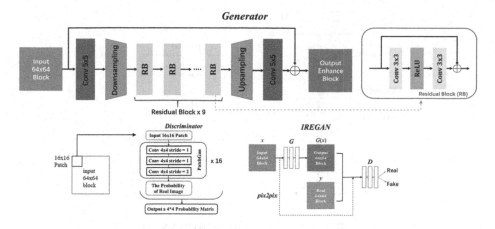

Fig. 3. Model structure

a 64 * 64 reconstructed block, the input image will first go through a classifier, and the classifier decides whether it needs to be filtered. The classifier classifies the images to be processed into two categories: "background" areas with simple textures and "content" areas with more complex textures. When an image block is classified as background, it means that the texture of the image is simpler and no further processing is needed. We skip the processing of these images directly, which can effectively reduce the time complexity.

After getting an enhanced image, input both reconstructed image and enhanced image into the discriminator, compare their probability of being a true image, and retain the image with a higher probability value as the final output. Higher probability means that the image is closer to the real image and has less distortion. Our model does not need to transmit additional flags, just load the same model on the encoder and decoder to ensure the consistency of the codec.

Classification Algorithm. The first module of our model is a classifier to decide whether the reference block should be filtered by the generator. Inspired by the works of Tsang [6] and Galteri [18], we think that when people watch SCC video, there are bound to be areas of interest and disinterest, so we can enhance the quality for the "content" and ignore the "background", which can reduce the coding time without compromising the subjective video quality. We try the classifier based on NN, image gradient and variance, and find that a simple algorithm is enough. We proposed a classification algorithm based on sub-block pixel variance (SVC), which can be seen in Fig. 4 right. The input 64 * 64 blocks will be divided into four 32 * 32 sub-blocks and calculated the variances separately. When there is more than one sub-block with zero variance, skip the processing of this 64 * 64 block. Although this algorithm is not complicated, it workes well, experimental results show that this method can save about 30% of NN forward time, and the PSNR of video can be slightly improved. According

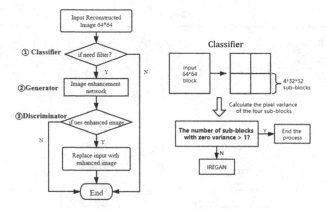

Fig. 4. The flowchart of IREGAN

to our analysis, there are a large number of simple blocks (with a single color) in SCC, encoding these regions does not produce distortion, so NN should not process them further.

Generator. We used a residual network containing nine residual blocks as the generator of IREGAN. A 5 * 5 convolutional kernel is used to the first layer of the generator, which is able to extract high-level and abstract features in the image. Then we apply the convolution layer with stride equal to 2 to implement the down-sampling of the feature. The image features can be more focused through down-sampling, and the generator across different scales can fuse coarse and fine information to enhance the representation capability. The middle layers consist of nine residual blocks, and the skip connection is adopted between the start and the end positions of the residual blocks for better performance and convergence results. After residual blocks, the image is up-sampling by transpose convolution to restore the image to its original size. Through up-sampling and residual connection, feature information of different scales can be extracted and fused to achieve a good image restoration effect. We use a structure like U-net, adding a shortcut between the input and output image, which can effectively recover clean image details and tackle the gradient vanishing problem.

Discriminator. The discriminator of our IREGAN is a fully convolutional network called PatchGAN [17]. Unlike generic discriminators that return a probability value between 0 and 1, PatchGAN maps the input to a N*N matrix X, each value in the matrix represents a perceptual field in the input image, corresponding to the probability that a patch of the input image is a true sample and the average value of each element in the matrix is the final output. PatchGAN is more suitable for generating high-resolution, clear-textured images because it refers to the influence of different parts of the image, and only penalizes structure at the scale of patches. In IREGAN, we use a PatchGAN consisting of a three-layer fully convolutional network, which means that each node of the output corresponds to a patch of 16 * 16 in the input image. According to our experiments, using this size of patch gives the best results for the output image.

In general, the discriminator is only used in training against the generator, where people are more interested in the quality of the generated images than in the truth or falsity. After our special design, the discriminator in our model is also used as the judgment of the final image output. We input the reconstructed and the enhanced blocks into the discriminator and output the one with high probability, a higher probability means that this image is closer to the real image. Using the discriminator of GAN to determine the image quality is an innovative attempt to improve system robustness, and we think it has great potential.

Loss Function. To restore the distortion while keeping the original image structure, we use the pix2pix loss and conditional GAN loss [19]. The loss of GAN is that the generator (G) tries to minimize the loss while the discriminator (D) tries to maximize the loss, the two fight against each other. Based on it, both generator and discriminator should follow the constraints of the input image to ensure the relevance between the input image and generated image. The formulas are shown in Eq. 1 and Eq. 2, where x is the input image and y is the real image.

$$\mathcal{L}_{pix2pix}(G, D) = E_{x,y}[\log D(\mathrm{x}, \mathrm{y})] + E_x[\log(1 - D(x, G(x)))] \tag{1}$$

$$\mathcal{L}_{GAN} = \arg\min_G \max_D \mathcal{L}_{pix2pix}(G, D) \tag{2}$$

The L1 loss is very useful for improving the low-frequency characteristics of the image, which is defined as Eq. 3. In addition, referring to the research of Zhu et al. [20], the identity loss (Eq. 4) is used in the loss function to avoid over-filtering of high-quality images. By inputting the real image (without distortion) into the generator, we hope that the generated image should also be the same.

$$\mathcal{L}_1(G) = E_{x,y}[\|y - G(x)\|_1] \tag{3}$$

$$\mathcal{L}_{idt}(G) = E_y[\|y - G(y)\|_1] \tag{4}$$

The final loss function of the generator is defined as Eq. 4, where $\lambda_1 = 100$ and $\lambda_2 = 50$ are the weights of GAN loss and identity loss.

$$LOSS_G = \mathcal{L}_{GAN} + \lambda_1 \mathcal{L}_1(G) + \lambda_2 \mathcal{L}_{idt}(G) \tag{5}$$

Relying on L1 loss to ensure low-frequency correctness, the high-frequency information is maintained by discriminator (PatchGAN). The loss function of the discriminator is Least Squares GANs (LSGAN) [21], which can make the training process more stable and produce higher quality images.

$$LOSS_D = \mathcal{L}_{LSGAN} = \frac{1}{n} E_{x,y}[\|y - G(x)\|_2] \tag{6}$$

4 Experimental Result

4.1 Model Training

The datasets we used in our experiment are cropped from the SCC video sequence. The corresponding train sets and test sets are given in Table 1. All video sequences in the table are coded with all intra and classSCC configuration, and the level is 6.2. We match the reconstructed image to the original image in pairs and randomly crop and de-duplicate it into $64 * 64$ blocks. In addition, the blocks classified by SVC as background have been removed from the datasets. We finally acquired about 100,000 pairs of images as the training set.

Table 1. Datasets

Datasets	Sequence	
	Basketball Screen	MissionControlClip2
	BitstreamAnalyzer	Program
Training Sets	ChineseDocumentEditing	Programming
	Console	SlideEditing
	FlyingGraphics	Web_browsing
Validation Sets	MissionControlClip3	SlideShow
	ChineseEditing	Spreadsheet
Testing Sets	Desktop	Web_en
	EnglishDocumentEditing	word_excel

Our model is implemented based on Pytorch framework with NVIDIA Titan Xp GPU, i7-8700k CPU. We use reference software VTM10.0 [24] and the QPs are set to 37,40,43,46. The model is trained using the Adam optimizer with $\beta_1 = 0.9$, $\beta_2 = 0.999$, and $\varepsilon = 10^{-8}$, dropout $= 0.5$.

4.2 Experimental Result

Since no researchers have done similar work compared with us before, to further validate the effectiveness of our model, we retrain two in-loop filter networks including EDCNN [8] and RHCNN [9]. To make the comparison results convincing, the other variables of the experiment are the same except for the models.

The experimental images with QP $= 40$ are shown in Fig. 5. We can see that there are obvious compression artifacts in the reconstructed image encoded by VTM10.0 (which can be seen around the text and numbers in the last two images), which cannot be completely removed by EDCNN or RHCNN, but our model can remove it more effectively. In addition, the textures of the first two images are somewhat distorted, and our model can also restore the images to a certain extent, which is difficult to achieve with traditional methods.

In video coding, two objective evaluation metrics: Bjontegaard delta bitrate (BDBR) and Bjontegaard delta peak signal-to-noise rate (BDPSNR) [22] are

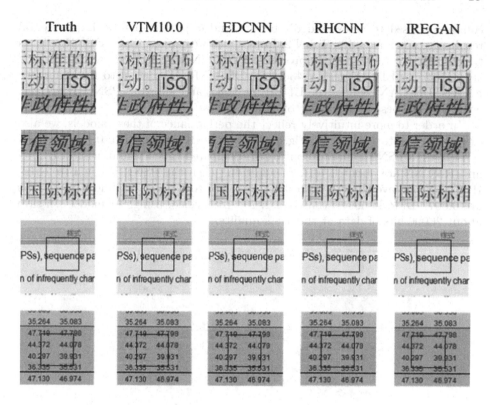

Fig. 5. Experimental images with QP = 40

Table 2. Coding performance comparison for all-intra coding structure

Sequence	EDCNN[8] vs. VTM10.0		RHCNN[9] vs. VTM10.0		IREGAN vs. VTM10.0	
	BDBR (%)	BDPSNR (dB)	BDBR (%)	BDPSNR (dB)	BDBR (%)	BDPSNR (dB)
ChineseEditing	-4.91	0.28	-5.71	0.36	-7.43	0.57
Desktop	-3.89	0.39	-4.14	0.43	-3.91	0.53
EnglishDocumentEditing	-2.98	0.29	-3.52	0.33	-10.45	1.08
Spreadsheet	-4.06	0.42	-4.04	0.41	-7.46	0.93
web-en	-4.30	0.37	-5.19	0.56	-4.86	0.43
word-excel	-4.87	0.39	-5.61	0.47	-7.76	0.70
average	-4.17	0.36	-4.70	0.43	-6.98	0.71

Table 3. SSIM & IBC-hitrate comparison for all-intra coding structure

Sequence	VTM10.0		EDCNN[8]		RHCNN[9]		IREGAN	
	SSIM	IBC-hitrate	SSIM	IBC-hitrate/%	SSIM	IBC-hitrate/%	SSIM	IBC-hitrate/%
ChineseEditing	0.9389	24.88	0.9472	25.91	0.9478	25.79	0.9518	27.00
			0.0082	1.03	0.0089	0.91	0.0129	2.12
Desktop	0.9785	41.76	0.9819	41.70	0.9815	41.44	0.9834	42.69
			0.0033	-0.06	0.0030	-0.32	0.0049	0.93
EnglishDocumentEditing	0.9376	51.83	0.9326	52.48	0.9358	52.29	0.9633	53.27
			-0.0051	0.66	-0.0018	0.46	0.0257	1.44
Spreadsheet	0.9704	62.05	0.9763	61.93	0.9750	62.36	0.9825	63.47
			0.0060	-0.13	0.0046	0.31	0.0121	1.41
web-en	0.9832	38.96	0.9870	40.04	0.9871	40.15	0.9872	40.28
			0.0037	1.07	0.0039	1.19	0.0039	1.32
word-excel	0.9777	46.83	0.9811	47.24	0.9810	47.49	0.9864	48.08
			0.0034	0.40	0.0033	0.66	0.0087	1.25
Average	0.9644	44.38	0.9677	44.88	0.9680	44.92	0.9757	45.80
			0.0033	0.50	0.0036	0.54	0.0113	1.42

commonly used to assess video's bitrate and objective quality. Experimental results are summarized in Tabel 2, from which we can see that EDCNN reduces the BDBR by 4.17% and improves the BDPSNR by 0.36dB, while RHCNN is −4.70% for BDBR and +0.43dB for BDPSNR. Compared to the other two models, IREGAN reduces the BDBR by 6.98% and improves PSNR by 0.71dB, achieving the best performance of these models.

In order to more intuitively reflect the performance of these models, we also draw a rate-distortion curve (Fig. 6). When the BPP is equal to 0.15, IREGAN can obtain a PSNR gain of about 0.7dB compared to VTM10.0, while EDCNN and RNCNN are about 0.4dB. In addition, when the PSNR is equal to 31dB, IREGAN can save about 0.0126 BPP compared to VTM10.0, while other models are 0.0072 BPP. It means that in a 1920 * 1080 video, using our model can save about 26000 bits of data at the same quality.

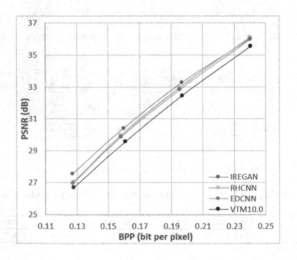

Fig. 6. R-D curve comparison of the three models

Compared with PSNR, SSIM is closer to human subjective evaluation [23], not only that, we introduce additional evaluation metrics called IBC-hitrate (Eq. 7) to assess the performance of the models. The IBC-hitrate clearly reflects the impact of the model on IBC, where n is the number of CU using IBC mode and N is the total number of CU in one frame.

$$IBC\_hitrate = \frac{n}{N} \times 100\% \tag{7}$$

Experimental results are shown in Table 3. Compared with the other two CNN-based models, IREGAN obtains a gain with 0.0113 SSIM and 1.41% IBC-hitrate improvement, achieving better results in both metrics, which indicates that our model can effectively restoration the image distortion and improve the accuracy of IBC estimation. In addition, the other two models get negative gains in part of the test sequence (Table 3 red part), which shows that our model is more robust and reliable.

5 Conclusion

In this paper, we propose an IBC reference block enhancement model for screen content coding, which can effectively improve the video quality and the compression efficiency of SCC. The model includes a classifier based on sub-block variance, a generator based on ResNet, and a full convolution of discriminator. After a 64 * 64 block is reconstructed, our model will immediately filter it for IBC search. To the best of our knowledge, we are the first to propose to improve the quality of SCC by filtering the IBC reference blocks, which provides a new idea for subsequent researchers. Compared with the standard reference software VTM10.0, our proposed model result in a significant improvement in video coding efficiency (both bitrate and video quality). In addition, we propose a new evaluation IBC-hitrate to reflect the impact of different models on IBC mode (increasing by 1.41%), which means that our model can effectively increase the number of CUs using IBC mode. A variety of evaluation indicators show that our model is better than reference software and generic filtering models.

References

1. Zhao, X., Liu, S., Zhao, L., Xu, X., Zhu, B., Li, X.: A comparative study of HEVC, VVC, VP9, AV1 and AVS3 video codecs. In: Applications of Digital Image Processing XLIII, vol. 11510, p. 1151011. International Society for Optics and Photonics (2020)
2. Xu, X., et al.: Intra block copy in HEVC screen content coding extensions. IEEE J. Emerg. Sel. Top. Circuits Syst. **6**(4), 409–419 (2016)
3. Hu, Y., Li, Y., Chen, Z., Xu, X., Liu, S.: Performance analysis of intra block copy for screen content coding in AVS3. In: 2020 IEEE Conference on Multimedia Information Processing and Retrieval (MIPR), pp. 123–126. IEEE (2020)
4. Xu, X., Liu, S.: Screen content coding in recently developed video coding standards. In: 2020 IEEE International Conference on Visual Communications and Image Processing (VCIP), pp. 1–2. IEEE (2020)
5. Cao, J., Li, Z., Liang, F., Wang, J.: An intra-affine current picture referencing mode for screen content coding in VVC. In: 2019 Picture Coding Symposium (PCS), pp. 1–5. IEEE (2019)
6. Tsang, S.H., Kwong, N.W., Chan, Y.L.: Fastsccnet: fast mode decision in VVC screen content coding via fully convolutional network. In: 2020 IEEE International Conference on Visual Communications and Image Processing (VCIP), pp. 177–180. IEEE (2020)
7. Xu, X., Li, X., Liu, S.: Intra block copy in versatile video coding with reference sample memory reuse. In: 2019 Picture Coding Symposium (PCS), pp. 1–5. IEEE (2019)
8. Pan, Z., Yi, X., Zhang, Y., Jeon, B., Kwong, S.: Efficient in-loop filtering based on enhanced deep convolutional neural networks for HEVC. IEEE Trans. Image Process. **29**, 5352–5366 (2020)

9. Zhang, Y., Shen, T., Ji, X., Zhang, Y., Xiong, R., Dai, Q.: Residual highway convolutional neural networks for in-loop filtering in HEVC. IEEE Trans. Image Process. **27**(8), 3827–3841 (2018)
10. Dai, Y., Liu, D., Wu, F.: A convolutional neural network approach for post-processing in HEVC intra coding. In: Amsaleg, L., Guðmundsson, G.Þ, Gurrin, C., Jónsson, B.Þ, Satoh, S. (eds.) MMM 2017. LNCS, vol. 10132, pp. 28–39. Springer, Cham (2017). https://doi.org/10.1007/978-3-319-51811-4_3
11. Lu, M., Chen, T., Liu, H., Ma, Z.: Learned image restoration for VVC intra coding. In: CVPR Workshops (2019)
12. Xue, Y., Su, J.: Attention based image compression post-processing convlutional neural network. In: CVPR Workshops (2019)
13. Cho, S., et al.: Low bit-rate image compression based on post-processing with grouped residual dense network. In: CVPR Workshops (2019)
14. Pathak, D., Krahenbuhl, P., Donahue, J., Darrell, T., Efros, A.A.: Context encoders: feature learning by inpainting. In: Proceedings of the IEEE Conference on Computer Vision and Pattern Recognition, pp. 2536–2544 (2016)
15. Ledig, C., et al.: Photo-realistic single image super-resolution using a generative adversarial network. In: Proceedings of the IEEE Conference on Computer Vision and Pattern Recognition, pp. 4681–4690 (2017)
16. Kupyn, O., Budzan, V., Mykhailych, M., Mishkin, D., Matas, J.: Deblurgan: blind motion deblurring using conditional adversarial networks. In: Proceedings of the IEEE Conference on Computer Vision and Pattern Recognition, pp. 8183–8192 (2018)
17. Isola, P., Zhu, J.Y., Zhou, T., Efros, A.A.: Image-to-image translation with conditional adversarial networks. In: Proceedings of the IEEE Conference on Computer Vision and Pattern Recognition, pp. 1125–1134 (2017)
18. Galteri, L., Bertini, M., Seidenari, L., Uricchio, T., Del Bimbo, A.: Increasing video perceptual quality with GANs and semantic coding. In: Proceedings of the 28th ACM International Conference on Multimedia, pp. 862–870 (2020)
19. Mirza, M., Osindero, S.: Conditional generative adversarial nets. arXiv preprint arXiv:1411.1784 (2014)
20. Zhu, J.Y., Park, T., Isola, P., Efros, A.A.: Unpaired image-to-image translation using cycle-consistent adversarial networks. In: Proceedings of the IEEE International Conference on Computer Vision, pp. 2223–2232 (2017)
21. Mao, X., Li, Q., Xie, H., Lau, R.Y., Wang, Z., Paul Smolley, S.: Least squares generative adversarial networks. In: Proceedings of the IEEE International Conference on Computer Vision, pp. 2794–2802 (2017)
22. Bjontegaard, G.: Calculation of average PSNR differences between RD-curves. VCEG-M33 (2001)
23. Hore, A., Ziou, D.: Image quality metrics: PSNR vs. SSIM. In: 2010 20th International Conference on Pattern Recognition, pp. 2366–2369. IEEE (2010)
24. The VTM reference software for VVC development, version 10.0. https://vcgit.hhi.fraunhofer.de/jvet/VVCSoftware_VTM/-/tree/VTM-10.0

AS-Net: Class-Aware Assistance and Suppression Network for Few-Shot Learning

Ruijing Zhao, Kai Zhu, Yang Cao$^{(\boxtimes)}$, and Zheng-Jun Zha

School of Information Science and Technology, University of Science and Technology of China, Hefei, China

{zrj1997,zkzy}@mail.ustc.edu.cn, {forrest,zhazj}@ustc.edu.cn

Abstract. Few-shot learning targets to recognize objects while only limited data is provided for each class. Existing methods tend to solve this problem by mapping the raw inputs into a shared embedding space and averaging them at the class level to form the corresponding prototypes. However, the prototypes are vulnerable to outliers, as they can contribute significantly to the class description when there is little data. In this paper, a class-aware assistance and suppression framework (AS-Net) is proposed to identify the informative patches and outliers as well as to further facilitate the rectification of prototypes. Specifically, we firstly introduce local features commonly shared across the whole set while distinguishable to other classes. These additional features can enhance the image embeddings and narrow the distance between the outliers and the majority of the class. We then attenuate the effect of outliers on the prototype by assigning lower weights to them. During these two stages, each labeled sample assists the rest samples of the same class to recognize their commonality, which provides positive attention for the intra-class consistency, *i.e.*, which area or sample to focus on. At the same time, it suppresses the samples of other classes with similar features, which provides negative attention for the inter-class distinction, *i.e.*, which area or sample not to focus on. Extensive experiments on several benchmark datasets demonstrate the superiority of our proposed method over the state-of-the-art approaches in the few-shot learning task.

Keywords: Few-shot learning · Attention · Metric learning

1 Introduction

Deep learning has made remarkable breakthroughs in various tasks like classification and detection with the help of sufficient data [13]. However, annotating adequate data is expensive, time-consuming, and laborious. It's necessary to develop deep learning under data scarcity. Therefore, few-shot learning task [3,6,15,16] attracts much attention in the multimedia and computer vision community, which aims at learning to generalize new categories with a few labeled samples from unseen classes. Given an unlabeled query sample, a few-shot model

© Springer Nature Switzerland AG 2022
B. Þór Jónsson et al. (Eds.): MMM 2022, LNCS 13142, pp. 27–39, 2022.
https://doi.org/10.1007/978-3-030-98355-0_3

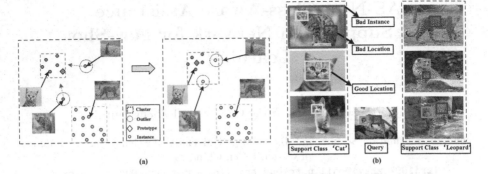

Fig. 1. The motivation of class-aware assistance and suppression network. (a) Left: Prototype affected by outliers. Right: Prototype affected by improved outliers. Light green represents that the contribution of these data points to the prototype is reduced. (b) The green, red and yellow boxes each highlight a kind of feature. The brown square represents that the quality of the image is low in this specific task. (Color figure online)

aims to classify it into a set of new categories with just a small number of labeled instances in each class.

Metric-based approaches [7,15,20] have been widely regarded as a dominant technique in few-shot learning, which can be divided into two stages: 1) generating an embedding for each image through a backbone network named instance-level embedding and 2) combining all features in a class to make a good description of the category named class-level prototype [15]. The query image is assigned to the class which has the closest prototype.

With limited support data, a prototype is extremely tricky to calculate accurately, which is of vital importance in few-shot learning. As shown in the circled samples of Fig. 1(a), there exist outliers usually present away from the corresponding clusters, but contribute to the closest prototype in the same way as high-quality images. Many methods that work at different stages have been proposed to alleviate this problem. For example, a typical approach is to introduce cross attention [4] to enhance the embedding of each image or to produce an attentive prototype with the support-query pair-wise relationship [18]. The performance will be greatly improved if the embeddings of outliers can be pulled towards the majority of the class, and less attention can be paid to them during the prototype generation as shown in the right of Fig. 1(a). But lots of these methods face a vital problem: importance identification. Concretely, distinguishing informative features or samples accurately is important for the construction of a suitable embedding space in metric-based methods.

Instead, we humans can easily identify an outlier by capturing the relevance among the objects from all the same and different categories. A simple 2-way 3-shot example is presented to illustrate the process in Fig. 1(b). We can see that the image in the upper left corner is an outlier because of its similarity of the fur to the other class *"leopard"*. However, we can also notice that it still shares some commonality with the other images of category *"cat"* (*e.g.* the face).

These findings inspire us that the few-shot models can also achieve importance identification through the explicit interaction between all classes.

In this paper, we propose that the images from the same class can provide positive attention while the images from the different classes are utilized to compute negative attention to measure importance. Further, we present AS-Net, a class-aware assistance and suppression network which introduces an AS-LWA module to produce local features and an AS-IWA module to compute an attentive prototype respectively. Concretely, for the first stage, our proposed Assistance and Suppression Location Weight Assignment (AS-LWA) module assigns weights to different locations in the feature map, with the goal to search for features that are commonly shared within the same category but excluded by other categories. The highlighted locations of the image are then re-examined by the backbone network to formalize information-supplementary local features. For the second phase, an Assistance and Suppression Instance Weight Assignment (AS-IWA) module is introduced to measure the importance of each sample in the context of all the support classes and conduct the attentive prototypes by aggregating corresponding instances adaptively [9].

Our contributions are summarized as follows:

- An assistance and suppression network (AS-Net) is proposed for few-shot classification, in which the distribution of outliers are pulled towards the class cluster, reducing the negative effect on the class descriptions.
- A location weight assignment module (AS-LWA) is introduced, which searches the informative local regions among an image, enhancing the rectification of representative embeddings.
- A sample weight assignment module (AS-IWA) is introduced, which selects the distinguishable embeddings among the whole class, promoting the generation of preferable prototypes.
- Extensive experiments on several datasets show the superiority of our framework. Besides, a thorough ablation study validates the effectiveness of each component of our algorithm.

2   Related Work

Many approaches [2,3,7,10,19] have been proposed to explore the few-shot classification problem in recent works. In general, they can be divided into three categories: optimization-based methods, data augmentation-based methods and metric-based methods.

Optimization-Based Methods. These approaches which belong to the mainstream topic called meta-learning [3,11] aim to modify the gradient-based optimization, where the parameters of the model can adapt to new tasks quickly. An additional fine-tuning is required for each new few-shot task during testing. The initial model is optimized according to the support set of each task. Some works like MAML [3] propose to learn good initialization for all meta tasks while [11] attempt to learn update optimization algorithms through LSTMs.

Data Augmentation-Based Methods. Another kind of methods target to enhance the support set to improve the few-shot models. They try to produce more instances with known labels for each class with deep generative models [2,8]. Some works [2] synthesize new samples with the help of intra-class deformations directly. Further, noise is used to produce more variants in [8] during the augmentation. However, it's not easy to generate synthetic data with high diversity.

Metric-Based Methods. These approaches target to construct a learned embedding space to better adapt to the pre-specified distance metric functions, e.g., cosine similarity or Euclidean distance [7,15,16,20,22]. Some works directly measure the similarity between all the image pairs [16]. Further, there are other methods producing a prototype for each class in the support set to reduce the impact of noise [15].

3   Problem Description

A well organized few-shot learning task $\mathcal{T}$ also called *episode* is composed of two sets, the labeled support set $\mathcal{S} = \{(x_i^s, y_i^s)\}_{i=1}^{N_S}$ and the unlabeled query set $\mathcal{Q} = \{x_i^q\}_{i=1}^{N_Q}$. Given the training data $\mathcal{D}_{train}$, we sample N classes and K instances from each class as the support set $\mathcal{S}$. Q images per class that are disjoint from $\mathcal{S}$ are sampled as the query set $\mathcal{Q}$. Therefore, a few-shot learning task is usually represented as a N-way K-shot Q-query problem. The labels are provided for both support and query set during training. A model f which is trained through multiple tasks aims to minimize the averaged error over the training data.

$$f^* = \arg\min_f E_{\mathcal{T}}[\frac{1}{Q \times N} \sum_{x_i \in \mathcal{Q}} (f(x_i; \mathcal{S}), y_i)], \tag{1}$$

where y_i is the true label of sample x_i and the refers to the loss that measures the discrepancy between the prediction and the true label. For the testing data $\mathcal{D}_{test}$, only the labels of support set are provided. The model f tries to assign the correct labels to the query set.

4   Method

Firstly, we present the overall of our framework in Sect. 4.1. Then we will introduce the two proposed modules in Sect. 4.2 and Sect. 4.3, respectively. The classification loss is described in Sect. 4.4. The framework of our model is shown in the Fig. 2.

4.1   Overall

For the support images, they are firstly fed into a backbone network. Given the feature maps produced by the last block, on the one hand, they are processed

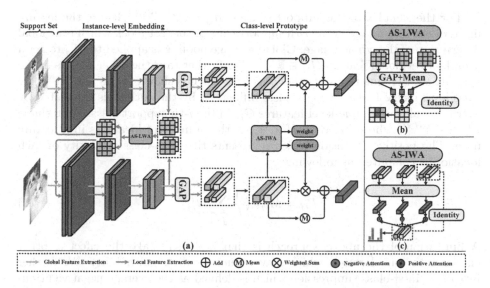

Fig. 2. (a) The overall framework of our AS-Net. For the support images, the backbone network is firstly applied to extract global features. Then the output of the last block is refined by the AS-LWA module to produce the attention map and tell the input where the model concerns most. These regions will be processed by the model once again to produce a local feature. But for the query images, a simplified AS-LWA module is applied to produce the local feature. Then our AS-IWA module assigns the corresponding weights to the instances in each support class to conduct an attentive prototype. (b) The structure of the complete AS-LWA module. (c) The structure of the AS-IWA module. Best viewed in color.

by the GAP (global average pooling) to generate a global feature. On the other hand, the AS-LWA module is applied to them to search the activated informative locations. Then the regions corresponding to the locations are cut from the input images and fed into the backbone again to produce the local feature which is combined with the global feature to generate an embedding for each image. The AS-IWA module is applied to the embedding set of each support class to formulate an attentive prototype per category.

For each image in the query set, we can get the global feature in a similar way to the support images. A simplified AS-LWA module is applied to produce the local features and the final embeddings because we have no access to the labels of the query samples which prevent the complete module from working. Finally, the category with a closest prototype to the query is chosen as the classification result.

4.2 AS-LWA Module for Instance Embedding

Given a feature map, the proposed AS-LWA module can assign different weights to all the locations and output a refined attention map.

For the samples of the support set, let $M_{ij} \in \mathbb{R}^{H \times W \times C}$ denote the feature maps of the j-th image in the i-th support class of the last block which is a global description of the whole image. Global average pooling is applied to M_{ij} to get a sample-level global feature $G_{ij} \in \mathbb{R}^{1 \times C}$. We further take the other images of the support set to refine the process of selection which is shown in the Fig. 2(b). The class-level global feature which is less influenced by the outliers is calculated by averaging all the sample-level features G_{ij} in the i-th support class. We reshape M_{ij} to $\mathbb{R}^{M \times C}$ where $M(M = H \times W)$ is the number of locations in a feature map. The positive attention which represents the intra-class similarity of each location is computed as following:

$$P_{ij} = M_{ij} \cdot (\frac{1}{K} \sum_{j=1}^{K} G_{ij}^T), \qquad (2)$$

A limitation of the above approach is that it doesn't take the effect of other classes into consideration which may reduce its distinguishability. We further introduce inter-class suppression which is defined as the average negative attention value between the feature maps M_{ij} and the global features of other classes. The total suppression strength of each location is computed as:

$$N_{ij} = -\frac{1}{N-1} \sum_{t=1, t \neq i}^{N} M_{ij} \cdot (\frac{1}{K} \sum_{j=1}^{K} G_{tj}^T), \qquad (3)$$

Finally, the weight map A_{ij} of the support images can be calculated by:

$$A_{ij} = P_{ij} + N_{ij}, \qquad (4)$$

For the q-th image in the query set, the difference is that we apply a simplified module to search the informative locations. Concretely, we directly compute the dot product between the feature map $M_q \in \mathbb{R}^{M \times C}$ and its sample-level global feature $G_q \in \mathbb{R}^{1 \times C}$ to produce the corresponding weight map $A_q = M_q \cdot G_q^T$.

Given the weight map A_{ij} of the support images and A_q of the query images, we reshape them to $\mathbb{R}^{H \times W}$ and apply *softmax* to it across all locations. The initial feature map is weighted by $(1 + A_{ij})$ for the support set and $(1 + A_q)$ for the query set to produce the refined attention map. Then the refined attention map and the input image are both upsampled to a pre-defined size. And the location with the largest value in the attention map is chosen as the center of the regions to be selected. Next, a patch of fixed size is cut from the input image which is then fed into the backbone network again. The output of its last block after global average pooling is taken as a local feature.

Finally, we can get a global feature described in Sect. 4.1 and a local feature after above process. They are concatenated to form the instance-level embedding referred to as $e_{ij} \in \mathbb{R}^{1 \times 2C}$ for the j-th image in the i-th support class and $e_q \in \mathbb{R}^{1 \times 2C}$ for the q-th image in the query set.

4.3   AS-IWA Module for Class Prototype

Given all the K instance embeddings of the i-th support class, a naïve method to produce the prototype is to assign the same weights to all instances. It's independent of the task context while a more comprehensive weight generation approach is introduced in our paper. The introduced AS-IWA module is detailed below and also visualized in the Fig. 2(c).

The embedding e_{ij} is referred as the output to the AS-LWA module of j-th image in the i-th support class. $E_i = (e_{i1}, e_{i2}, ...e_{iK}) \in \mathbb{R}^{K \times 2C}$ is the set of the K embeddings of i-th class and $mean(E_i) \in \mathbb{R}^{1 \times 2C}$ is the mean of E_i. The positive attention p_i and negative attention n_i are computed as the dot products of different class descriptions with the input features.

$$p_i = mean(E_i) \cdot E_i^T,$$

$$n_i = -\frac{1}{N-1} \sum_{t=1, t \neq i}^{N} mean(E_t) \cdot E_i^T, \tag{5}$$

The module will appreciate the feature that bears a larger similarity with the description of the same class and a lower similarity with the other classes' descriptions according to the above formula.

After acquiring the attention value, a weighted sum is applied to combine all the embeddings of each support category and a residual connection which is the mean of K support features is also added for easy learning,$i.e.$

$$e_i = mean(E_i) + exp(\gamma) \cdot softmax(p_i + n_i) \cdot E_i, \tag{6}$$

where γ is a parameter learned during training. For the setting of N-way 1-shot classification, we apply $sigmoid$ to replace the $softmax$ and prevent the weight from simplified to 1.

4.4   Classification Loss

We target to classify query as one of the support categories. Euclidean distance is applied to compute the distance between the prototypes and the query embeddings. The final score which indicates the probability of the query-prototype pair belonging to the same class is computed as follows:

$$p(y = i) = \frac{exp(-E(e_i, e_q))}{\sum_{j=1}^{N} exp(-E(e_j, e_q))}, \tag{7}$$

where e_i is the attentive prototype of the i-th class, e_q is the embedding of the query sample described in Sect. 4.2, and $E(e_i, e_q)$ is the Euclidean distance between the e_i and e_q. Cross entropy loss is applied during model training. During testing phase, the class with the highest similarity between the prototype and the query is chosen as the classification result.

Table 1. Comparison with state-of-the-art approaches on MiniImageNet and Tiered-ImageNet datasets. The average accuracy and 95% confidence interval of 5-way 1-shot and 5-way 5-shot settings tested on 600 meta tasks are reported.

Method	MiniImageNet		TieredImageNet	
	1-shot	5-shot	1-shot	5-shot
MAML [3]	48.70 ± 1.84	63.15 ± 0.91	–	–
MetaOptNet [6]	62.64 ± 0.61	78.63 ± 0.46	65.99 ± 0.72	81.56 ± 0.53
IDeMe-Net [2]	59.14 ± 0.86	74.63 ± 0.74	–	–
AFHN [8]	62.38 ± 0.72	78.16 ± 0.56	–	–
Prototypical Net [15]	49.42 ± 0.78	68.20 ± 0.66	65.65 ± 0.92	83.40 ± 0.65
MatchingNet [16]	63.08 ± 0.80	75.99 ± 0.60	68.50 ± 0.92	80.60 ± 0.71
CAM [4]	63.85 ± 0.48	79.44 ± 0.34	69.89 ± 0.51	84.23 ± 0.37
CTM [7]	64.12 ± 0.82	80.51 ± 0.13	68.41 ± 0.39	84.28 ± 1.73
DeepEMD [21]	65.91 ± 0.82	82.41 ± 0.56	71.16 ± 0.87	86.03 ± 0.58
FEAT [20]	66.78	82.05	70.80 ± 0.23	84.79 ± 0.16
FRN [17]	66.45 ± 0.19	82.83 ± 0.13	71.16 ± 0.22	86.01 ± 0.15
AS-Net	**68.37 ± 0.80**	**83.85 ± 0.52**	**71.72 ± 0.91**	**86.43 ± 0.63**

5   Experiment

5.1   Datasets

*Mini*ImageNet. The *Mini*ImageNet [16] is a subset of the ILSVRC-12 dataset [13]. It contains 100 classes in total and each class has 600 images. We follow the split in [11] and use 64 categories for training, 16 categories for validation, and 20 categories for testing. *Tiered*Imagenet. The *Tiered*ImageNet [12] is also a subset of the ILSVRC-12 dataset [13]. It contains 779,165 images in total. The total number of classes is 608 and the dataset is derived from 34 high-level categories. All of the high-level categories are divided into 20 training (351 classes), 6 validation (97 classes), and 8 test (160 classes) categories. **CIFAR-FS.** The CIFAR-FS [1] dataset is derived from CIFAR-100 [5]. It contains 100 categories with 600 images in each class. It is divided into 64, 16, and 20 classes for training, validation, and testing, respectively.

5.2   Experimental Setting

Evaluation Metric. Following the protocol in [7], the mean accuracy of 600 randomly generated episodes, as well as the 95% confidence intervals, is reported in our paper. We conduct 5-way 5-shot and 5-way 1-shot experiments. In every meta task, we sample 15 images per category as the query set $\mathcal{Q}$.

Implementation Details. For a fair comparison with the state-of-the-art methods, we utilize a 12-layer residual network as the backbone in all of our experiments following [20]. The width per block is 64, 160, 320, 640, respectively. The input size of the backbone is 84 × 84. An additional pre-training stage suggested in [20] for the backbone over the training set is applied. The details can be found in [20]. Then the whole model is optimized through episodes-based protocols. We apply Adam optimizer with an initial learning rate of 0.002. The model is trained for 200 epochs and there are 100 episodes in each epoch. The learning rate is halved every 40 epochs for the 5-way 5-shot setting and every 20 epochs for the 5-way 1-shot setting. The weight decay is set 0.0005. The refined attention map and the input image are firstly resized to 128×128, and a 84×84 patch is selected and cropped to produce the local feature. Random horizontal flipping and color distortion are applied as the image augmentations.

Table 2. Comparison with state-of-the-art approaches on CIFAR-FS dataset. The average accuracy and 95% confidence interval of 5-way 1-shot and 5-way 5-shot settings tested on 600 meta tasks are reported.

Method	CIFAR-FS	
	1-shot	5-shot
Prototypical Net [15]	72.2 ± 0.7	83.5 ± 0.5
MetaOpt-RR [6]	72.6 ± 0.7	84.3 ± 0.5
MetaOpt-SVM [6]	72.0 ± 0.7	84.2 ± 0.5
DSN [14]	72.3 ± 0.8	85.1 ± 0.6
AS-Net	$\mathbf{73.99 \pm 0.85}$	$\mathbf{86.83 \pm 0.58}$

5.3   Comparison to State-of-the-Art Approaches

We conduct two experiment settings, *i.e.* 5-way 5-shot and 5-way 1-shot on three baseline datasets and compare our approach to several state-of-the-art methods of few-shot classification in Table 1 and Table 2. The comparative methods are categorized into three groups, *i.e.* optimization-based methods, data augmentation-based methods and metric-based methods. Compared to other metric-based methods which only take the pair-wise similarity [16,21] or treat the support set as a whole [7], our model explicitly introduces the relations between the same and different classes. It can be seen that our method outperforms all of the listed three groups of baselines and state-of-the-art algorithms. The presumable reason is that a more representative set of features derived from the feature maps describes the images more accurately and produces a more concentrated data distribution. What's more, the AS-IWA module reduces the impact of outliers and improves the contrast of all categories of prototypes because it prevents the different classes from owning similar features.

5.4   Ablation Study

These experiments are all conducted on the *Mini*ImageNet dataset.

Effectiveness of Each Module. We build two experimental settings, each with one module removed to investigate the individual effect of these two improvements. It can be seen from Table 3 that the performance drops regardless of which module misses. Therefore, these two modules both promote the accuracy of concept learning.

Table 3. Negative impact when removing either module from our method. AS-Net is our complete algorithm. AS-LWA and AS-IWA mean that the other module is removed from the algorithm, respectively.

Method	Operation	1-shot
AS-Net	–	**68.37 ± 0.80**
AS-LWA	without IWA	65.63 ± 0.87
AS-IWA	without LWA	67.61 ± 0.82

Analysis of the AS-LWA Module. We will show the difference of our attentive method with the random and central selection from a quantification perspective. For the baseline of random selection, the model extracts the feature of a randomly selected area to produce a local feature. Similarly, the model takes the feature of the central area as a local feature in the central selection approach. Then attentive method is to apply the AS-LWA module to select the informative regions. The produced local feature is concatenated with the global one to form the final image embedding. The prototype is generated simply by averaging the K embeddings from the same category. From Table 4, we can see that a better result can be obtained when selecting with the refined attention maps rather than random or central operation. It means that the generated attention maps are exactly a great guide to the selection of the areas. We further target to visualize the rectification effect of the module on the feature maps. Given an image of a dog, the value of the feature map directly generated by the last block is visualized in the top of the Fig. 3(a). Then the feature map is processed by the AS-LWA module to produce a refined attention map which is present in the bottom of the Fig. 3(a). We can see that the bench is also focused on in the directly generated feature map. But the attention map refined by our AS-LWA module can highlight the dog correctly which means that the commonly shared features can be searched through our attention module.

Table 4. Attentive selection compared to random selection and central selection

Selection method	1-shot
Random	63.47 ± 0.84
Central	65.10 ± 0.87
Attentive	**65.63 ± 0.87**

Analysis of the AS-IWA Module. The proposed AS-IWA module targets to assign weights according to their similarity to the other support images. We visualize the two types of attention value *i.e.* positive attention value and negative attention value in Fig. 3(b). The first line is the images of arctic foxes, and the values in red are the positive attention values computed among the three images according to the first in formula 5 which measure the intra-class commonality. The head in the first image is hard to recognize, therefore results in a low positive value. The second line is another category of samples, and the absolute negative attention value of each image in green is calculated according to the second in formula 5 which represents the similarity of itself to the samples in the class arctic foxes. Specifically, the more similar the picture in the second row is to the first row, the larger its value should be. We can see that the last one with a large similarity in color and posture is assigned the largest value.

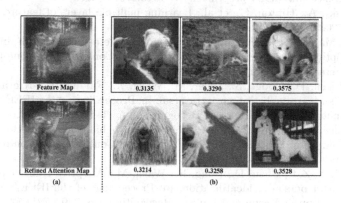

Fig. 3. (a) Visualization of the feature map and the refined attention map by AS-LWA module. (b) Visualization of positive and negative attention. The images in the first and second rows are from different categories. The values in red are positive attention computed among the images in the first row. The values in green are negative attention of the second row computed to the images in the first row. (Color figure online)

6 Conclusion

We believe that the assistance and suppression network which fully exploit the interaction within the support set is an avenue to improve the performance of few-shot classification. We further introduce class-aware local features and attentive prototypes in the context of all the support categories in the algorithm. They can promote the few-shot models by pulling the outliers close to the center of the class and weaken their effect on the final concept. Our algorithm achieves superior performance compared with existing state-of-the-art methods on benchmark datasets.

Acknowledgement. This work was supported by the National Key R&D Program of China under Grand 2020AAA0105702, National Natural Science Foundation of China (NSFC) under Grants U19B2038, the University Synergy Innovation Program of Anhui Province under Grants GXXT-2019-025 and the key scientific technological innovation research project by Ministry of Education.

References

1. Bertinetto, L., Henriques, J.F., Torr, P.H., Vedaldi, A.: Meta-learning with differentiable closed-form solvers. arXiv preprint arXiv:1805.08136 (2018)
2. Chen, Z., Fu, Y., Wang, Y.X., Ma, L., Liu, W., Hebert, M.: Image deformation meta-networks for one-shot learning. In: Proceedings of the IEEE/CVF Conference on Computer Vision and Pattern Recognition, pp. 8680–8689 (2019)
3. Finn, C., Abbeel, P., Levine, S.: Model-agnostic meta-learning for fast adaptation of deep networks. In: Proceedings of the 34th International Conference on Machine Learning, vol. 70, pp. 1126–1135 (2017)
4. Hou, R., Chang, H., Ma, B., Shan, S., Chen, X.: Cross attention network for few-shot classification. arXiv preprint arXiv:1910.07677 (2019)
5. Krizhevsky, A., Hinton, G., et al.: Learning multiple layers of features from tiny images (2009)
6. Lee, K., Maji, S., Ravichandran, A., Soatto, S.: Meta-learning with differentiable convex optimization. In: Proceedings of the IEEE Conference on Computer Vision and Pattern Recognition, pp. 10657–10665 (2019)
7. Li, H., Eigen, D., Dodge, S., Zeiler, M., Wang, X.: Finding task-relevant features for few-shot learning by category traversal. In: Proceedings of the IEEE Conference on Computer Vision and Pattern Recognition, pp. 1–10 (2019)
8. Li, K., Zhang, Y., Li, K., Fu, Y.: Adversarial feature hallucination networks for few-shot learning. In: Proceedings of the IEEE/CVF Conference on Computer Vision and Pattern Recognition, pp. 13470–13479 (2020)
9. Liu, J., Zha, Z.J., Chen, D., Hong, R., Wang, M.: Adaptive transfer network for cross-domain person re-identification. In: Proceedings of the IEEE/CVF Conference on Computer Vision and Pattern Recognition, pp. 7202–7211 (2019)
10. Min, S., Yao, H., Xie, H., Wang, C., Zha, Z.J., Zhang, Y.: Domain-aware visual bias eliminating for generalized zero-shot learning. In: Proceedings of the IEEE/CVF Conference on Computer Vision and Pattern Recognition, pp. 12664–12673 (2020)
11. Ravi, S., Larochelle, H.: Optimization as a model for few-shot learning (2016)
12. Ren, M., et al.: Meta-learning for semi-supervised few-shot classification. arXiv preprint arXiv:1803.00676 (2018)
13. Russakovsky, O., et al.: Imagenet large scale visual recognition challenge. Int. J. Comput. Vision **115**(3), 211–252 (2015)
14. Simon, C., Koniusz, P., Nock, R., Harandi, M.: Adaptive subspaces for few-shot learning. In: Proceedings of the IEEE/CVF Conference on Computer Vision and Pattern Recognition, pp. 4136–4145 (2020)
15. Snell, J., Swersky, K., Zemel, R.: Prototypical networks for few-shot learning. In: Advances in Neural Information Processing Systems, pp. 4077–4087 (2017)
16. Vinyals, O., Blundell, C., Lillicrap, T., Wierstra, D., et al.: Matching networks for one shot learning. In: Advances in Neural Information Processing Systems, pp. 3630–3638 (2016)
17. Wertheimer, D., Tang, L., Hariharan, B.: Few-shot classification with feature map reconstruction networks. In: Proceedings of the IEEE/CVF Conference on Computer Vision and Pattern Recognition, pp. 8012–8021 (2021)
18. Wu, F., Smith, J.S., Lu, W., Pang, C., Zhang, B.: Attentive prototype few-shot learning with capsule network-based embedding. In: Vedaldi, A., Bischof, H., Brox, T., Frahm, J.-M. (eds.) ECCV 2020. LNCS, vol. 12373, pp. 237–253. Springer, Cham (2020). https://doi.org/10.1007/978-3-030-58604-1_15

19. Wu, J., Zhang, T., Zha, Z.J., Luo, J., Zhang, Y., Wu, F.: Self-supervised domain-aware generative network for generalized zero-shot learning. In: Proceedings of the IEEE/CVF Conference on Computer Vision and Pattern Recognition, pp. 12767–12776 (2020)

20. Ye, H.J., Hu, H., Zhan, D.C., Sha, F.: Few-shot learning via embedding adaptation with set-to-set functions. In: Proceedings of the IEEE/CVF Conference on Computer Vision and Pattern Recognition, pp. 8808–8817 (2020)

21. Zhang, C., Cai, Y., Lin, G., Shen, C.: Deepemd: few-shot image classification with differentiable earth mover's distance and structured classifiers. In: Proceedings of the IEEE/CVF Conference on Computer Vision and Pattern Recognition, pp. 12203–12213 (2020)

22. Zhu, K., Zhai, W., Zha, Z.J., Cao, Y.: One-shot texture retrieval with global context metric. arXiv preprint arXiv:1905.06656 (2019)

DIG: A Data-Driven Impact-Based Grouping Method for Video Rebuffering Optimization

Shengbin Meng[1,2(✉)], Chunyu Qiao[1], Junlin Li[1], Yue Wang[1],
and Zongming Guo[2]

[1] Video Architecture Team, ByteDance Inc., Beijing, China
{mengshengbin,qiaochunyu,lijunlin.li,wangyue.v}@bytedance.com
[2] Wangxuan Institute of Computer Technology, Peking University, Beijing, China
guozongming@pku.edu.cn

Abstract. Rebuffering is known to be the dominant metric that affects the user experience of video streaming applications. In this paper, we propose a data-driven impact-based grouping (DIG) method for video rebuffering optimization. By analyzing data of 74.5 million video sessions collected in a real video streaming system, several key features with most significant and temporally persistent impact on video rebuffering are identified. Based on the values of these features, similar video sessions are grouped together. Within each group, we forecast future rebuffering events via a simple and efficient model, exploiting the insight that all video sessions in the same group face a similar risk of rebuffering. If rebuffering is predicted to happen in a coming session, we try to avoid it by selecting a better content distribution network (CDN) for this video. Experimental results show that our method can successfully predict 46% of the rebuffering sessions, and reduce the average rebuffering rate by 18.4%.

Keywords: Video rebuffering · Feature ranking · CDN selection

1 Introduction

Video streaming has become one of the most popular applications in recent years. Nowadays, there are many platforms (e.g., Netflix [1], YouTube [2]) that allow people to watch videos on the Internet. These streaming service providers generally have business models based on subscription and advertising, where video quality and user engagement play a critical role. If the quality is not sufficient, users will quickly become unsatisfied and abandon video sessions, leading to significant losses in revenue [6]. Therefore, streaming service providers strive to deliver high quality-of-experience (QoE).

Among the quality metrics that affect user QoE, video rebuffering (i.e., the client player waiting for empty data buffer to refill again) is known to be the dominant one. It is reported in a study that user viewing time will decrease

© Springer Nature Switzerland AG 2022
B. Þór Jónsson et al. (Eds.): MMM 2022, LNCS 13142, pp. 40–51, 2022.
https://doi.org/10.1007/978-3-030-98355-0_4

3 min with 1% increase on rebuffering ratio [6]. Rebuffering can be caused by different factors, including the video bitrate, the client's network conditions, the player buffer strategy, the content distribution network (CDN) currently-used for video data delivery, etc. Due to this complexity, as well as its importance, video rebuffering has attracted many research efforts to understand and optimize it (see related work in Sect. 2).

One effective scheme to reduce video rebuffering is to forecast it beforehand and then avoid it by adjusting some system variables (e.g., the video bitrate, CDN). Being able to accurately forecast whether or when video rebuffering will happen is the key point of this scheme. It is also a challenging problem, given the fact that rebuffering events are relatively rare and happen quite sparsely among the large amount of video sessions. Taking our own data for example, the proportion of video sessions with rebuffering is only about 1.1%. Under this unbalanced sampling condition, it is difficult to achieve high forecasting performance using general predictive models. In addition, a complex model usually requires tens of minutes to update when the number of video sessions is large, and thus suffers from data staleness in the system [9].

To better forecast and avoid video rebuffering, we propose a data-driven impact-based grouping (DIG) method in this paper. By analyzing the data of 74.5 million video sessions from a real-world mobile streaming application, several key features with most significant and temporally persistent impact on video rebuffering are identified. Instead of forecasting in a global way, we divide the video sessions into different groups based on the values of those features. Then video rebuffering is forecast separately in each group, exploiting the insight that all video sessions in the same group face a similar risk of rebuffering.

Once a new video session is predicted to have rebuffering, the rebuffering might be avoided by either switching to a lower bitrate or choosing a better CDN. Since a lower bitrate also brings video quality degradation, in this work we try to avoid the rebuffering through CDN reassignment. We traverse other available CDN providers and carefully select one with higher potential quality for this session. Assigning one specific CDN during a short time might bring huge overload for it, therefore we randomly choose from the top-half better performing ones instead of always picking the best one. This makes the algorithm more deployment-friendly, though a little performance is sacrificed. In our evaluation, the proposed DIG method can successfully forecast 46% of the rebuffering sessions and reduce the average rebuffering rate (in this paper, "rebuffering rate" of a video session is defined as the rebuffering count per 100 s of watching time) by 18.4%, outperforming several baseline methods.

The rest of this paper is organized as follows. Section 2 summarizes related work on understanding and optimizing Internet video QoE. Section 3 introduces two insights from our real data, identifying the key features that impact video rebuffering. Section 4 presents the group-based rebuffering forecasting and avoiding method in detail. Section 5 provides experimental results to evaluate the performance of our proposed method. And finally, Sect. 6 gives concluding remarks.

2   Related Work

Internet Video Quality. Quality metrics of Internet videos have been widely investigated. In a qualitative way, subjective studies [5,7] reveal that video rebuffering and average bitrate have significant influence on the user-perceived quality. To be more quantitative, Dobrian et al. [6] and Shafiq et al. [12] take measurement-driven studies to understand the impacts of video quality metrics and network dynamics on user engagement. Through these and other works, rebuffering is currently known to be a dominant factor of Internet video quality. That is also the motivation for us to focus on video rebuffering optimization in this paper.

Video Quality Prediction. One important part of optimizing the video quality is being able to predict it. Video quality prediction can be regarded as two classes: 1) Intra-session prediction, which predicts certain quality metrics during the progress of video playback. For example, some adaptive bitrate (ABR) algorithms predict the available bandwidth and rebuffering time of the next video chunks to aid bitrate decision [3,11,17], where the accuracy of video quality prediction determines the performance of those algorithms. 2) Inter-session prediction, which predicts the overall potential quality before the video begins to play. These methods [8,13] can help to choose an appropriate startup configuration (e.g., the initial bitrate, CDN), and are especially useful for the scenario where ABR is not implemented yet or not applicable (e.g., for short videos). Our work focuses on inter-session video quality prediction, from which better CDN selection is achieved.

CDN-Centric Video Streaming Optimization. CDN plays an important role distributing video content to client players, and draws much attention for optimization. Most CDN-centric video streaming optimization involves resource allocation and scheduling. Alabbasi et al. [4] optimize stall duration tail probability by considering the limited caching spaces for CDN sites. Yang et al. [16] try to maximize the profit of video service providers with a viewer engagement oriented stream distribution algorithm. Others propose to speed up multi-CDN content delivery (a.k.a. content multihoming) [15] or dynamically switch from a CDN server to another during one video session [14]. In this paper, we deal with CDN assignment before each video begins to play, aiming to minimize the average rebuffering rate for all video sessions.

3   Data-Driven Insights on Video Rebuffering

In order to optimize video rebuffering, we first try to better understand it. In this section, data of real video streaming sessions are analyzed, and two valuable questions on rebuffering are answered.

Table 1. Video session features in our dataset.

Feature	Description
ISP	The internet service provider for the client
CDN	CDN chosen for this video session
Network type	Network type when the video begins to play (e.g., Wi-Fi, 4G)
Province	Province where the client is located
City	City where the client is located
OS type	Type of operating system (e.g., iOS, Android)
Resolution	The resolution of the played video (e.g., 480p, 720p)
Cold start	Whether or not the application starts first time since booting

3.1 What are the Most Significant Features that Impact Video Rebuffering?

In real video systems, the factors impacting video rebuffering are usually complex. To find out features that impact video rebuffering most significantly, we take a data-driven approach. We collect data of real video sessions from Xigua Video (https://en.wikipedia.org/wiki/Xigua_Video), a YouTube-like video streaming mobile application owned by the company ByteDance. As a data cleaning procedure, we filter out abnormal records and discard video sessions with viewing time less than 1 s. A total of 74.5 million video sessions are sampled and used for analysis. Each session has several features that might correlate to video rebuffering, as listed in Table 1.

To rank all these features and select the ones that impact video rebuffering most significantly, we use a hybrid feature ranking method. For each feature, we calculate an Impact Score, which is defined as the sum of a Correlation-based score and a CFA-based score. Correlation-based scores are simply the normalized Kendall correlation coefficient [10] between those features and the rebuffering rate. The CFA-based score, inspired by the Critial Feature Analysis (CFA) method [8], is calculated as follows.

Given a specific video session, its "critical features" are obtained by the following equation:

$$argmin_{F \subseteq 2^{F_{ALL}}} |R(S(F, \Delta)) - R(S(F_{ALL}, \Delta))|, \tag{1}$$

where $S(F, \Delta)$ is the set of video sessions matching on features F and occurring within the last Δ time interval, and R denotes the distribution of rebuffering rate of a set of sessions. The critical features F are chosen such that the quality distribution of sessions matching on F is most similar to that of sessions matching on all features F_{ALL}. We set $\Delta = 2$ min and obtain the critical features for all video sessions. Then we count each feature's total number of occurrences in all those critical features. The counts are normalized to become the CFA-based scores.

Table 2. Video session features and their impact scores on video rebuffering.

Feature	Correlation-based score	CFA-based score	Impact score
ISP	0.06	0.16	**0.22**
CDN	0.13	0.09	**0.22**
Network type	0.32	0.20	**0.52**
Province	0.08	0.10	0.18
City	0.01	0.02	0.03
OS type	0.04	0.01	0.05
Resolution	0.26	0.20	**0.46**
Cold start	0.10	0.22	**0.32**

The results of our hybrid feature ranking method are shown in Table 2. It can be seen that, while Correlation-based score and CFA-based score may have different favors for some borderline features (such as ISP, CDN and Province), Impact Score determines the final ranks more clearly. Sorting by Impact Score, we find the five most significant key features to be: *Network type*, *Resolution*, *Cold start*, *CDN*, and *ISP*.

3.2 Are Their Impacts Large Enough and Temporally Persistent?

To examine the impacts of the high-ranking features on video rebuffering, we perform a quantitative analysis using *Network type*, *Resolution*, and *Cold start* as examples. We calculate average rebuffering rate of video sessions in the following groups, for each hour in a day:

1. **Global**, the group contains all video sessions;
2. **(Wi-Fi)**, the group with *Network type* Wi-Fi;
3. **(4G)**, the group with *Network type* 4G;
4. **(Wi-Fi, 540p, No cold start)**, the group with *Network type* Wi-Fi, *Resolution* 540p, and *Cold start* No;
5. **(4G, 720p, Cold start)**, the group with *Network type* 4G, *Resolution* 720p, and *Cold start* Yes.

The results are shown in Fig. 1. It can be seen that, with specific feature values, the rebuffering rate is distinguished from Global. For example, video sessions of 4G have a higher average rebuffering rate compared to Global, while the other feature value Wi-Fi corresponds to a lower average rebuffering rate than Global. When new high-ranking features, i.e., *Resolution* and *Cold start*, are added, the difference is more obvious. Most noticeably, for combination of "negative" (or "rebuffering-prone") feature values such as the (4G, 720p, Cold start) group, the rebuffering rate can be several times higher than that of Global. Furthermore, we can see that the average rebuffering rate and the difference between each group is relatively stable during the hours of a day. Therefore, it

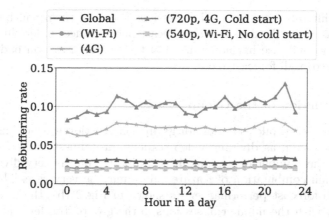

Fig. 1. Average rebuffering rate for different groups in each hour.

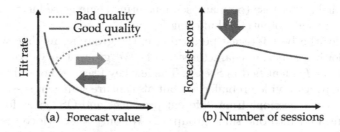

Fig. 2. Trends diagram of forecasting performance. In (a), hit rates on good and bad quality change with the forecast value. In (b), the forecast score changes with the number of video sessions in a group.

can be concluded that the impacts of high-ranking features on video rebuffering are both large enough and temporally persistent.

In summary, our insights are twofold: 1) Learned by a hybrid feature ranking method, the key features that have most significant impact on video rebuffering are *Network type, Resolution, Cold start, CDN*, and *ISP*; and 2) The impacts of the key features are large enough to be notable and also persistent over time. These insights motivate us to use the key features for grouping, and forecast video rebuffering in each group separately.

4   Group-Based Rebuffering Forecast and Avoidance

For any forecasting method, the hit rates on bad quality (video session with rebuffering) and good quality (video session without rebuffering) are of the opposite trends, as shown in Fig. 2 (a). On one hand, if we tend to give small values of rebuffering as forecast, we may predict all good quality video sessions accurately, but bad quality sessions will not be easily identified. On the other hand, giving larger forecast values will forecast more bad quality sessions, but we may sacrifice the hit rate on good quality sessions (more of them will be predicted as bad mistakenly). To measure the forecast performance under this trade-off, in this work we will use harmonic mean of the two hit rates on bad and good quality as the overall forecast score.

4.1   Construction of the Group

One straight-forward pilot solution for group construction is grouping by all the features, also known as dividing video sessions into "finest groups". However, we find that the number of sessions in each finest group is very diverse in our data, as certain combination of feature values may be very rare. This leads to unpredictable forecast performance. As shown in Fig. 2 (b), the forecast score varies largely with the number of sessions in the group. Too few video sessions provide insufficient information and thus cannot guarantee a reliable forecast. Too many video sessions, however, also result in a slightly lower forecasting score, presumably because too many sessions bring some noise factors and make it difficult to reveal potential rebuffering.

Aiming for the best forecast performance, the grouping method we propose has the following superior characteristics: 1) We group the video sessions by the key features F identified in Sect. 3. The few key features not only have most significant impact on video rebuffering, but also ensure sufficient sessions in each group (since video sessions from different provinces and OS types, for example, will be aggregated into one same group). 2) We only select video sessions that are within a small time interval Δ before the current session. This prevents data staleness. 3) Motivated by the observation that too many sessions will also decrease forecast performance, we incorporate a constrained number n_{cons} when constructing the final group used for forecasting. In another word, we only pick the most recent n_{cons} video sessions when there are more sessions in that small time interval.

4.2   Rebuffering Forecast and Avoidance

We use $G(F, \Delta, n_{cons})$ to denote the current session's forecasting group, which contains the n_{cons} video sessions in last Δ time inteval matching the key features F. Then this session's rebuffering expectation is calculated as:

$$exp_{rebuf} = rebufRatio * rebufValue, \tag{2}$$

$$rebufRatio = \frac{\sum_{ss \in G(F, \Delta, n_{cons})} I(rebufRate(ss))}{|G(F, \Delta, n_{cons})|}, \tag{3}$$

$$rebufValue = \frac{\sum_{ss \in G(F, \Delta, n_{cons})} rebufRate(ss)}{|G(F, \Delta, n_{cons})|}, \tag{4}$$

where $rebufRate(ss)$ is the rebuffering rate of session ss, and $I(x) = 1$ if $x > 0$ else 0. Basically, the rebuffering expectation exp_{rebuf} is the product of the proportion of rebuffering sessions ($rebufRatio$) and the average rebuffering rate of

---

Algorithm 1. Rebuffering forecast and avoidance.

Input: Current session under forecasting s; Time interval Δ; Key feature set F; Threshold for rebuffering forecasting r_{thr}; Constrained number of video sessions for forecasting n_{cons}; All available CDNs.

Output: CDN;

1: Construct group $group_s$ using the n_{cons} most recent sessions matching s on F and within time interval Δ;
2: $rebufRatio$ = ratio of rebuffering sessions in $group_s$;
3: $rebufValue$ = average rebuffering rate of sessions in $group_s$;
4: **if** $rebufRatio * rebufValue \leq r_{thr}$ **then**
5:     **return** CDN of s;   ▷ No rebuffering will occur, keep current CDN
6: **else**   ▷ Assign a new CDN for s
7:     $Candidates = \emptyset$;   ▷ Candidate groups
8:     **for** cdn in all other available CDNs **do**
9:         $features_{cdn}$ = feature values of s with CDN replaced by cdn;
10:         $group_{cdn}$ = group of the n_{cons} most recent sessions matching $features_{cdn}$ and within time interval Δ;
11:         Calculate exp_{rebuf} of $group_{cdn}$;
12:         Add $(group_{cdn}, exp_{rebuf})$ pair in $Candidates$;
13:     **end for**
14:     $Group_{half}$ = half of groups in $Candidates$ with smaller exp_{rebuf};
15:     $group_{rand}$ = randomly select one group from $Group_{half}$;
16:     **return** CDN of $group_{rand}$;
17: **end if**

---

sessions ($rebufValue$) in the forecasting group. Given the rebuffering expectation of a session, we set a threshold r_{thr} to forecast whether rebuffering events will happen in it. More specifically, a video session is forecast to have rebuffering when $exp_{rebuf} > r_{thr}$.

Once video rebuffering is forecast to happen in a coming session, we try to avoid it by reassigning a better CDN. A natural idea is to traverse all groups matching on other key features except the CDN, and choose the CDN from the group that has the lowest rebuffering rate. However, selecting the best group does not mean we can get the best quality for this specific session. Besides, always assigning one specific CDN (with best performance in past minutes) during a short time might bring huge overload for it, and result in performance degradation [9]. With these considerations, we introduce a random yet effective CDN selection strategy. Specifically, we first explore all groups and find half of them with lower average rebuffering rates as candidates. Then we randomly select one from those candidates and use its CDN as the final choice for reassignment.

The procedure of our method is shown in Algorithm 1, including both the rebuffering forecasting and avoiding steps.

4.3 Algorithm Complexity

We now analyze the algorithm's time and space complexity. In the algorithm, we need to maintain the n_{cons} recent video sessions for all groups. So the space complexity is $N_{groups} * V(n_{cons})$, where N_{groups} is the number of groups. N_{groups} depends on the key features and their value counts. In our data it is $2 \times 9 \times 4 \times 8 \times 2$ ($N_{Network\ type} \times N_{CDN} \times N_{Resolution} \times N_{ISP} \times N_{Cold\ start}$) $= 1152$. When searching groups of all optional CDNs to avoid rebuffering, we need to calculate the ratio of rebuffering sessions and the average rebuffering rate in each group. This calculation's time complexity is $N_{CDN} * O(n_{cons})$. On the whole, our algorithm's complexity is linearly in the order of n_{cons} (the constrained number of video sessions in a group), so it is efficient for online deployment.

5   Evaluation

In this section, the performance of the proposed DIG method is evaluated through extensive experiments.

5.1   Experiment Settings

Parameter Setup. We first clarify the parameter settings in our experiments. The experiments are conducted with simulation on the dataset of our company's real video streaming application (see Sect. 3.1). In this dataset, the proportion of rebuffering video sessions is 1.1%, and the average rebuffering rate is 0.030. We set $\Delta = 2$ min, i.e., using video sessions in the last 2 min for group construction. The constrained number of recent video sessions for forecasting n_{cons} is set as 200. As for the threshold r_{thr}, we set it as 0.004 for network type Wi-Fi, while 0.022 for 4G, since the average rebuffering rate of 4G is higher as shown in Fig. 1. To simplify the simulation, we separate the video sessions by intervals of 2 min. In each 2-min session set, we use the most recent 10% sessions as test sessions for rebuffering forecasting and avoidance, and the other 90% video sessions as history data for grouping.

Evaluating CDN Reassignment. When another CDN is assigned to avoid rebuffering, how to evaluate the result of this reassignment is an issue in simulation, because we don't have the ground-truth quality after this reassignment. To tackle this issue, we use similar video sessions in future 2 min to estimate the result of reassignment and the potential rebuffering reduction. Specifically, we select video sessions that match all features including the newly assigned CDN, and calculate their average rebuffering rate as the result of the reassignment for current session. Lacking ground-truth, we believe that this is a fair and good enough alternative, under the assumption that video sessions matches on all feature values in the near future generally share the same quality.

5.2   Performance Comparison

With the above experimental configuration, we compare the performance of the proposed DIG method with the following baseline methods:

1. **Global**: Forecast is performed globally using all video sessions in the last 2 min, i.e., without grouping;

Table 3. Performance of different methods, including the hit rates on good and bad quality sessions, forecast score, and the average rebuffering reduction.

Method	Good quality hit rate	Bad quality hit rate	Forecast score	Rebuffering reduction
Global	0.85	0.12	0.21	2.6%
G-CDN	0.63	0.38	0.48	9.6%
G-Network	**0.92**	0.25	0.39	12.8%
G-Province	0.76	0.20	0.31	4.2%
Finest	0.83	0.30	0.44	12.5%
CFA	0.84	0.26	0.40	12.3%
DIG-NC	0.84	0.42	0.56	17.3%
DIG	0.75	**0.46**	**0.57**	18.4%
DIG-Best	0.75	0.46	0.57	**22.6%**

2. **G-CDN**: Video sessions are grouped by CDN;
3. **G-Network**: Video sessions are grouped by Network type;
4. **G-Province**: Video sessions are grouped by Province.
5. **Finest**: Video sessions are grouped by matching all features listed in Table 1;
6. **CFA**: Video sessions are grouped by features learned with the "critical feature analysis" (CFA) method [8].

And to better demonstrate the design highlights of DIG, its two variants are also compared:

1. **DIG-NC**: DIG without the constrained number n_{cons} when grouping;
2. **DIG-Best**: DIG that doesn't consider the overload of CDN when reassigning: always select the best (with the lowest average rebuffering rate) instead of randomly choosing one from the top half ones.

The results are shown in Table 3. It can be seen that, DIG achieves a forecast score of 0.57, outperforming all other methods, including CFA proposed in [8]. The performance of Global method, as expected, is the worst. Note that it is much easier to achieve high hit rates for good quality sessions (without rebuffering) than bad quality sessions (with rebuffering), due to the fact that bad quality sessions are rare and only account for a small proportion (1.1%) of the real data. Though other methods may achieve higher good quality hit rates (e.g., 0.92 for G-Network), DIG is superior in bad quality hit rate (0.46), resulting in the highest forecast score. Without constraining on session number, the method DIG-NC performs a little worse than DIG, but still much better than other baseline methods.

By reassigning a better CDN to avoid rebuffering, all the methods can reduce the average rebuffering rate to some degree, as shown in the last column of Table 3. Based on its forecasting performance, DIG achieves 18.4% rebuffering

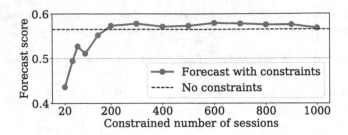

Fig. 3. Performance of DIG with different constrained number of sessions in a group.

reduction on average, more than other methods except DIG-Best. Although DIG-Best achieves the largest rebuffering reduction (22.6%), its "always-selecting-the-best" strategy will bring huge overload for one specific CDN during a short time, which is a concern already mentioned above. All things considered, DIG is the most promising method for deployment in the real video streaming system.

In the design of our method, an appropriate constrained number (n_{cons}) of sessions in a group is set to achieve best-possible forecasting performance. The final value is chosen by evaluating the performance across different constrained numbers, ranging from 10 to 1000. As shown in Fig. 3, the forecasting score is low when the number of video sessions is small. It goes higher as the session number increases to around 200. After that, the performance becomes stable, though it is still a bit higher than DIG-NC (No constraints).

6   Conclusion

To reduce video rebuffering, DIG, a data-driven impact-based grouping method is proposed in this paper. First, several key features with most significant and temporally persistent impact on video rebuffering are identified through analysis of real data. Then based on the values of these features, similar video sessions are grouped together to forecast whether rebuffering will occur in future video sessions. If rebuffering is predicted to happen in a coming session, we try to avoid it by reassigning a better CDN for this video. Evaluated under simulation of real-world video session data, the proposed DIG method can successfully predict 46% of the rebuffering sessions, and reduce the average rebuffering rate by 18.4%. The method will be deployed and validated online in our future work.

Acknowledgment. We would like to thank some other engineers of ByteDance Inc., especially Yuelong Huang, Honglei Gao, Darui Wang and Luna Mi, for their valuable discussion and helpful work on deployment of the proposed algorithm.

References

1. Netflix. https://www.netflix.com/
2. Youtube. https://www.youtube.com/

3. Akhtar, Z., et al.: Oboe: auto-tuning video ABR algorithms to network conditions. In: Proceedings of the 2018 Conference of the ACM Special Interest Group on Data Communication, pp. 44–58 (2018)
4. Al-Abbasi, A., Aggarwal, V., Lan, T., Xiang, Y., Ra, M.R., Chen, Y.F.: Fast-Track: minimizing stalls for CDN-based over-the-top video streaming systems. IEEE Trans. Cloud Comput. **9**(4), 1453–1466 (2019)
5. Ceaparu, I., Lazar, J., Bessiere, K., Robinson, J., Shneiderman, B.: Determining causes and severity of end-user frustration. Int. J. Hum.-Comput. Interact. **17**(3), 333–356 (2004)
6. Dobrian, F., et al.: Understanding the impact of video quality on user engagement. ACM SIGCOMM Comput. Commun. Rev. **41**(4), 362–373 (2011)
7. Gulliver, S.R., Ghinea, G.: Defining user perception of distributed multimedia quality. ACM Trans. Multimed. Comput. Commun. Appl. **2**(4), 241–257 (2006)
8. Jiang, J., Sekar, V., Milner, H., Shepherd, D., Stoica, I., Zhang, H.: CFA: a practical prediction system for video QoE optimization. In: 13th USENIX Symposium on Networked Systems Design and Implementation, pp. 137–150 (2016)
9. Jiang, J., Sun, S., Sekar, V., Zhang, H.: Pytheas: enabling data-driven quality of experience optimization using group-based exploration-exploitation. In: 14th USENIX Symposium on Networked Systems Design and Implementation, pp. 393–406 (2017)
10. Kendall, M.G.: Rank correlation methods (1948)
11. Mao, H., Netravali, R., Alizadeh, M.: Neural adaptive video streaming with pensieve. In: Proceedings of the 2017 Conference of the ACM Special Interest Group on Data Communication, pp. 197–210 (2017)
12. Shafiq, M.Z., Erman, J., Ji, L., Liu, A.X., Pang, J., Wang, J.: Understanding the impact of network dynamics on mobile video user engagement. ACM SIGMETRICS Perform. Eval. Rev. **42**(1), 367–379 (2014)
13. Sun, Y., et al.: CS2P: improving video bitrate selection and adaptation with data-driven throughput prediction. In: Proceedings of the 2018 Conference of the ACM Special Interest Group on Data Communication, pp. 272–285 (2016)
14. Viola, R., et al.: Predictive CDN selection for video delivery based on LSTM network performance forecasts and cost-effective trade-offs. IEEE Trans. Broadcast. **67**(1), 145–158 (2020)
15. Wang, H., Tang, G., Wu, K., Fan, J.: Speeding up multi-CDN content delivery via traffic demand reshaping. In: 2018 IEEE 38th International Conference on Distributed Computing Systems, pp. 422–433. IEEE (2018)
16. Yang, W., Hu, Y., Ding, L., Tian, Y.: Viewer-oriented CDN scheduling on crowd-sourced live video stream. In: 2019 IEEE 2nd International Conference on Electronics and Communication Engineering, pp. 112–117. IEEE (2019)
17. Yin, X., Jindal, A., Sekar, V., Sinopoli, B.: A control-theoretic approach for dynamic adaptive video streaming over HTTP. In: Proceedings of the 2015 Conference of the ACM Special Interest Group on Data Communication, pp. 325–338 (2015)

Indie Games Popularity Prediction by Considering Multimodal Features

Yu-Heng Huang and Wei-Ta Chu[✉][iD]

National Cheng Kung University, Tainan City, Taiwan
wtchu@gs.ncku.edu.tw

Abstract. We present a popularity prediction system for independent computer games (indie games), by jointly considering visual, text, and metadata information. An indie game dataset is first collected and labeled. According to the number of sales, we label an indie game as popular or not. Different types of information is extracted by specific feature extractors, and then is fused to construct a neural network-based classifier. We demonstrate that jointly considering multimodal information yields promising performance. In addition, we show that, with helps of state-of-the-art feature embeddings, the proposed method outperforms the only existing SVM-based method.

Keywords: Popularity prediction · Indie games · Information fusion

1 Introduction

The video games market has been growing since the 1970s. Recently, more and more digital platforms emerge and enable game developers to sell their own products. For instance, GooglePlay and APP Store are two most popular platforms for distributing mobile game APPs. For PC games, the Steam platform[1] owned by Valve is the largest platform.

On these platforms, any game developer can sell their products, no matter they are big corporations, like Nintendo, Ubisoft, SEGA, or small game developing studios. When games are onboard, developers provide text-based description and choose some screenshots to describe and advertise games. Customers can pick the games of their attraction by surfing on these platforms. However, there have been millions of games on the platforms, and how to attract users becomes a key challenge for game developers.

In this work, we would like to study game information provided on the Steam platform and predict whether a game will be popular after it is released. Better popularity prediction can be made if we can model multimodal game information more appropriately. If we can discover how this multimodal information influences popularity, it could be important clues for game developers to decide

---

[1] https://store.steampowered.com.

© Springer Nature Switzerland AG 2022
B. Þór Jónsson et al. (Eds.): MMM 2022, LNCS 13142, pp. 52–61, 2022.
https://doi.org/10.1007/978-3-030-98355-0_5

how to present information on the Steam platform to attract more attention. This is the main potential value of this work.

Usually large game corporations have more resources to advertise their products via ads or online events. Users may buy games developed by these corporations due to the brand effect or the reputation of other games developed by the same corporations. On the other hand, small game studios only can rely on solid game design and visual/textual description. To avoid the influence of advertisement outside the information available on the online platform, we focus on independent games (indie games). Notice that, in this work, the definition of indie games is the games designed and released by small game studios. They don't necessarily target at the audience different from mainstream games developed by famous companies. Design features of indie games may also be similar to mainstream games. Specific for indie games, we more focus on the effect of visual and text information on popularity prediction for video games.

Popularity prediction has been studied for years. In [3], Ding et al. developed a deep neural network based on popularity-discriminable image pairs to predict the potential of a social image to go viral. Only visual content is considered, and the rank consistency in image pairs are utilized to optimize the proposed network. Zhang and Jatowt [8] focused on predicting popularity for tweet posts with images. Text and images in a post are jointly considered by a convolutional neural network (CNN) to predict popularity. The definition of popularity is based on the number of re-tweets and likes. Also focusing on images posted on a social platform, Abousaleh et al. [1] proposed to jointly consider visual content and social features in a visual-social convolutional neural network, which is actually constituted by two CNNs. Popularity of images posted on Flickr is estimated. Although we just briefly review most recent popularity prediction here, we observe that most works focus on social images. This may be mostly because popularity of social images can be easily defined based on number of likes or similar concepts. In this work, we target at popularity prediction for independent games.

Although many reports were made regularly to predict sales of video games from the business perspective, very few studies have been conducted to predict popularity of video games from the technical perspective or in the way of machine learning. Trneny [7] developed several machine learning methods like random forest and support vector machines to predict success of video games. The success is defined as the number of concurrent players active in playing games, or the number of users who own the game. The features to build the machine learning methods were mainly metadata, such as tags, genres, price, and so on. Inspired by the recent success of deep neural networks, we propose a network that jointly considers information of game's screenshots, text-based description, tags, and other metadata, in predicting popularity of a game.

Comparing with previous works, the main contribution of this work include:

- The topic of popularity prediction for indie games is unique and was rarely studied before. This work shows that this is a doable research topic, which may bring commercial benefits.

– We demonstrate that integrating information from multiple modalities yields good popularity prediction results. The state-of-the-art techniques are utilized to extract visual and text features, which are then seamlessly integrated to achieve good performance.

The rest of this paper is organized as follows. Data collection and processing are described in Sect. 2. Section 3 provides details of the proposed method. Section 4 describes experimental results, followed by concluding remarks in Sect. 5.

Fig. 1. A sample web page from the game Terraria.

2   Data Collection and Processing

We take an open dataset named Steam Store Games (Clean dataset) published on Kaggle[2] for evaluation. It contains most games on the Steam platform released prior to May 2019. We pick 4,036 games which were released from May 2018 to May 2019 and have "Indie" in its tag set. We pick the games released in the most recent one year since the game market is mercurial and changes quickly. Old games are less influential than recent games in predicting future market taste.

The dataset contains the following game's information: ID in steam platform, game name, price, release date, tags, first five screenshots, and short text description. Figure 1 shows a web page of a game "Terraria" released on Steam. Four different types of information are extracted to build the popularity prediction model. Taking Terraria as the example, the information includes:

– Screenshots: The game's visual content, which the largest block on the website customers can see at the first glance. The screenshots show information of the game's visual content and art style.

---

[2] http://www.kaggle.com.

- Description: Text description shortly describes the game's content, story, and special features. Here is the example of Terraria's description: "Dig, fight, explore, build! Nothing is impossible in this action-packed adventure game. Four Pack also available!"
- Tags: Information about games genre, number of players it supports (single player, multiple players), and special features defined by player community. Here are some examples of Terraria's tags: "Sandbox", "Survival", "Adventure", "Multiplayer", "RPG", "Co-op", and "Crafting".
- Other metadata: Basic metadata of the game, like game's price and release time.

Based on this dataset, we define the measure of popularity for Indie games. By inspecting information available in this dataset, an indie game is defined "popular" if this game was sold more than 20,000 copies. We thus turn popularity prediction into a binary classification problem. The output of the developed model is how likely the sale of a given game is more than 20,000 copies.

Another reason why we take popularity prediction for indie games as a binary classification problem is that this dataset suffers from the data imbalance problem. Only around 10% of games' sales are over 20,000 copies and are labeled as positive. This reflects the situation in the real world, i.e., most games are not popular. This imbalance significantly impedes us to model popularity prediction as a regression problem. Accurately predicting "popularity values" that spread quite sparsely is not feasible based on the current dataset.

Particularly working on popularity classification, we split the dataset into the training set and the validation set, where the training set contains 3,252 games, and the validation set contains 501 games. In the training set, only 314 games are positive. To diminish the problem of data imbalance, we oversample positive samples to balance negative and positive simples. There are totally 3,140 positive samples and 3,221 negative samples after oversampling. The validation set contains 45 positive samples and 456 negative samples. The validation set was not oversampled in order to reflect the real world scenario.

3   Method

We extract features from the aforementioned four types of data. Because their modalities and meanings are diverse, different feature extractors are designed, and then different types of features are fused later.

3.1   Features Extracted from Screenshots

The ResNet18 model [4] pre-trained on ImageNet is used as the image feature extractor. Five 256×256 screenshot images are input to the model, and a 5×512 feature map is output. This feature map is then passed into a maximum pooling layer, which outputs the maximum value of each dimension and finally gives rise to a 1×512 feature vector. This 512-dimensional vector holistically represents information from five screenshots.

The adopted ResNet18 model was pre-trained on the ImageNet dataset. However, this dataset is mainly composed of daily object images like animals, vehicles, and plants. We think that these images have a different distribution to game's screenshots, since game's screenshots are usually artificially generated rather than natural photos, as shown in Fig. 1.

To tackle this problems, we fine-tune the pre-trained ResNet18 based on a game genre classification task. According to tag information, a game can be labeled with one or more genres. There are eight different genres in total, including action, adventure, casual, RPG, racing, simulation, sports, and strategy. The last layer of the ResNet18 model is modified to be a fully-connected layer with eight neurons, associated with the sigmoid function. The last layer outputs a 8-dimensional confidence vector showing how likely the input game belongs to these genres. If the confidence value of the ith dimension is larger than a predefined threshold, say 0.5, we say that this game can be labeled with the ith genre. To fine-tune the ResNet18 model, the soft-F1 loss [5] is calculated between the predicted confidence vector and the ground truth vector. After this fine-tuning, the ResNet18 model can better describe game's screenshot images.

3.2 Features Extracted from Description

Game's description is usually a short paragraph presenting brief introduction of a game. To get a compact embedding from this sequential text, we adopt BERT [2] pre-trained based on the Wikipedia and BookCorpus datasets to extract features from description. The reason to adopt BERT is that game description is a complete paragraph. Context information between words is important. BERT is a state-of-the-art model widely adopted to describe natural language.

In particular, the adopted BERT model is constituted by four self-attention (SA) modules. In each SA module, four attention heads are adopted, and the dimension of embedding is 256. Given a game's text description, we utilize the pre-trained BERT model to process and embed text information, and get the 256-dimensional embedding output by the last SA module as the representation of game description.

3.3 Features Extracted from Tags

Different from game's description, tags associated with each game are isolated and have no contextual relationship between neighboring tags. Given N tags associated with a game, they are concatenated as a string, separated by blanks. This string is then input to the Word2Vec model [6], and is embedded as a 250-dimensional vector after processing. Different games may have different numbers of tags. In this way, we can represent each game's tags information as a 250-dimensional vector. The Word2Vec model is pre-trained on the Wiki-Words-250 dataset, and characterizes similarity between words, i.e., it projects words/tags of similar semantics into a locality in the feature vector space.

3.4 Features from Metadata

Most games are sold from 0 to 50 US dollars. We encode a game's price into a 52-dimensional one-hot vector according to its price. The last dimension is set as 1 if a game costs more than 51 dollars.

Game's release time is encoded as a 12-dimensional one-hot vector. In the evaluation dataset, we only take the data from May 2018 to April 2019 for training and testing. If a game was released in May 2018, its date information is encoded as $100\cdots00$. If a game was released in June 2018, its date information is encoded as $010\cdots00$, and so on.

3.5 Popularity Prediction Framework

Figure 2 shows the whole framework. Different types of features are extracted separately by specific models, and are finally concatenated into a 1082-dimensional vector. This integrated vector is input to a classifier consisting of four fully-connected layers. The last layer with the sigmoid activation function outputs a value ranging 0 to 1, showing how likely the input test game is popular. In this work, the game with a predicted confidence value higher than 0.5 is classified as popular, and is classified as non-popular otherwise.

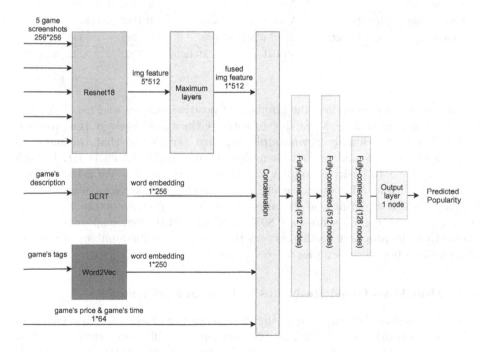

Fig. 2. Illustration of the proposed framework.

4   Experiments

As mentioned earlier, we take 3,140 positive samples and 3,221 negative samples for training. The validation set contains 45 positive samples and 456 negative samples (most games are not popular, i.e., less than 20,000 sales).

4.1   Overall Performance

Table 1 shows performance variations in terms of precision, recall, and F1 score when different types of information is considered. Comparing visual+metadata with text+metadata, we see that text-based description is more effective than visual content to predict popularity. This seems reasonable because whether a game is popular more depends on the design of game scenarios. By integrating visual, text, and metadata, even better performance (0.6607 of F1 score) can be obtained. This shows visual and text content provides complementary information, and better performance can be obtained when we jointly consider them.

Table 1. Performance variations when different types of information is considered.

Information	Note	Precision	Recall	F1
Screenshots + Metadata	Visual + Metadata	0.4107	0.5111	0.4554
Description + Tags + Metadata	Text + Metadata	0.5789	0.7333	0.6470
All	Visual + Text + Metadata	0.5522	0.8222	0.6607

As we mentioned earlier, the numbers of positive samples and negative samples are quite imbalance. To further investigate the effectiveness of the proposed method, we intentionally downsample negative samples so that the numbers of positive samples and negative samples in each testing batch is 1:1. In each batch, we have 45 positive samples and 45 negative samples. We calculate precision, recall, and F1 score for each patch, and report average values over 10 batches. In this experimental scenario, we finally get average precision, average recall, and average F1 score as 0.8975, 0.8866, and 0.8888, respectively. This shows that the proposed method is very promising when the numbers of positive samples and negatives samples are balanced.

4.2   How Fine-Tuned ResNet18 Influences Performance

Here we also show how fine-tuning the ResNet18 model to extract visual features influences performance. Table 2 shows performance difference when the visual features are extracted by the fine-tuned ResNet18 or the pre-trained ResNet18. As can be seen, by fine-tuning the ResNet18 through the genre classification task, the F1 score can be boosted around 0.04.

Table 2. Performance variations when the ResNet18 model is fine-tuned or not.

Fine-tuned or Not	Precision	Recall	F1
All (with pre-trained ResNet18)	0.5410	0.7333	0.6226
All (with fine-tuned ResNet18)	0.5522	0.8222	0.6607

4.3 Performance Comparison

Very few works have been done for popularity prediction for games. The most relevant work would be [7]. Because their dataset and code are not released, we implement their method and evaluate on our dataset for fair comparison. In [7], they jointly considered information like number of players in a game, language support, GPU requirements, tags, genres, and descriptions, and showed that the best popularity prediction can be obtained when a support vector machine (SVM) classifier is constructed based on these features. Our dataset doesn't contain all these features. We thus only can consider the features described in Sect. 3 and implement their SVM approach.

Table 3 shows results of comparison. As can be seen, the SVM approach only achieves 0.5067 F1 score, while our proposed method achieves 0.6111 F1 score. We think the main performance gain comes from the state-of-the-art feature embeddings like BERT and ResNet18, as well as the deep learning-based classifier.

Table 3. Performance comparison with one existing method.

Methods	Precision	Recall	F1
SVM [7]	0.3619	0.8444	0.5067
Our	0.5522	0.8222	0.6607

4.4 Sample Results

Table 4 shows a sample of the game "BLOCKPOST". It is a free-to-play multiplayer shooting game. The short description states that this game consists of most popular and functional gaming solutions. We see that screenshots appropriately show the shooting game scenario, and visual quality looks good. It is labeled as a popular indie game because it was sold over 20,000 copies. The last row of Table 4 shows that the value predicted by our method is 0.974, which is much higher than the popularity threshold 0.5. We thus correctly classify this game as a popular one.

Table 5 shows another sample of the game "Space Engineers". It is a simulation, strategy, and sandbox game where we can act as a space engineer. We see that high-quality screenshots faithfully show the simulation scenario. It is also a popular indie game. However, the last row of Table 5 shows that the value predicted by our method is just 0.169. We observe that when the content of game's screenshots focus more on game's scene or movie-like screenshots rather than game's control panel, game's UI, or game's playability, the proposed model may perform poorly.

Table 4. The first sample of game popularity prediction.

Game name	BLOCKPOST
Release date	2019-04-25
Price	0 USD
Tags	action, free to play, indie, fps, online multiplayer
Description	Procedural cubic 3D-shooter in the best traditions of the genre. The game is a rich cocktail consisting of the most popular and functional gaming solutions. Customization of characters, opening cases and improving the existing arsenal – all this is available in the game now.
Ground truth: 1; Predicted: 0.974	

Table 5. The second sample of game popularity prediction.

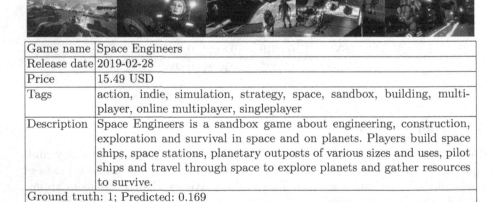

Game name	Space Engineers
Release date	2019-02-28
Price	15.49 USD
Tags	action, indie, simulation, strategy, space, sandbox, building, multiplayer, online multiplayer, singleplayer
Description	Space Engineers is a sandbox game about engineering, construction, exploration and survival in space and on planets. Players build space ships, space stations, planetary outposts of various sizes and uses, pilot ships and travel through space to explore planets and gather resources to survive.
Ground truth: 1; Predicted: 0.169	

5   Conclusion

We have presented a multi-modal popularity prediction method for indie games. Visual (screenshot images), text (game description, tags), and metadata information is extracted by specific models, and is then fused to input to a classifier. The classifier determines whether a given game is popular or not. We have demonstrated that jointly considering multiple modalities yields better performance. By comparing with the only relevant work, we show that the state-of-the-art feature extractors really bring benefits in popularity prediction.

Currently we use the number of sales as the indicator showing whether an indie game is popular or not. This obviously is not the only index for popularity. Data collection and label definition are thus still challenging and ongoing issues. In addition, we currently only work on "popularity classification", rather than predict popularity values in a regression way. This can be studied further in the future.

Acknowledgement. This work was funded in part by Qualcomm through a Taiwan University Research Collaboration Project and in part by the Ministry of Science and Technology, Taiwan, under grants 110-2221-E-006-127-MY3, 108-2221-E-006-227-MY3, 107-2923-E-006-009-MY3, and 109-2218-E-002-015.

References

1. Abousaleh, F.S., Cheng, W.H., Yu, N.H., Tsao, Y.: Multimodal deep learning framework for image popularity prediction on social media. IEEE Trans. Cogn. Develop. Syst. **13**(3), 679–692 (2020)
2. Devlin, J., Chang, M.W., Lee, K., Toutanova, K.: Bert: pre-training of deep bidirectional transformers for language understanding. In: Proceedings of The North American Chapter of the Association for Computational Linguistics (2019)
3. Ding, K., Ma, K., Wang, S.: Intrinsic image popularity assessment. In: Proceedings of ACM International Conference on Multimedia, pp. 1979–1987 (2019)
4. He, K., Zhang, X., Ren, S., Sun, J.: Deep residual learning for image recognition. In: Proceedings of IEEE Conference on Computer Vision and Pattern Recognition (2016)
5. Maiza, A.: The Unknown Benefits of using a Soft-F1 Loss in Classification Systems (2019). https://towardsdatascience.com/the-unknown-benefits-of-using-a-soft-f1-loss-in-classification-systems-753902c0105d
6. Mikolov, T., Chen, K., Corrado, G., Dean, J.: Efficient estimation of word representations in vector space. In: Proceedings of ICLR Workshop (2013)
7. Trneny, M.: Machine learning for predicting success of video games. Master thesis, Masaryk University (2017)
8. Zhang, Y., Jatowt, A.: Image tweet popularity prediction with convolutional neural network. In: Proceedings of European Conference on Information Retrieval, pp. 803–809 (2019)

An Iterative Correction Phase of Light Field for Novel View Reconstruction

Changjian Zhu[1] , Hong Zhang[2] ([✉]), Ying Wei[1], Nan He[2], and Qiuming Liu[3]

[1] School of Electronic Engineering, Guangxi Normal University, Guilin, China
changjianzhu@alumni.hust.edu.cn
[2] Department of Mathematics and Computer Science, Guilin Normal College, Guilin 541000, China
henan@mail.glnc.edu.cn
[3] School of Software Engineering, Jiangxi University of Science and Technology, Nanchang, China
liuqiuming@jxust.edu.cn

Abstract. We present an iterative correction phase algorithm (ICPA) for light field reconstruction. We study novel views of light field that satisfy certain conditions can be reconstructed from the phase spectrum. The ICPA includes phase corrections in both time domain and frequency domain of discrete light filed. Furthermore, the phase corrections are "light field truncation" in the time domain and "phase replacement" in the frequency domain. Thus, the estimation of the reconstructed light field improves with each iteration. Our ICPA predicts the characteristics of light field such as phase and amplitude. Predictions on the frequency content can then be used to improve the rendering quality of novel views. Finally, to verify the claimed performance, we also compare the ICPA with the most advanced light field reconstruction algorithms. The experimental results show that the proposed ICPA outperforms other known reconstruction schemes.

Keywords: Light field reconstruction · Phase spectrum · Rendering quality

1 Introduction

Light field rendering (LFR) [1,2] is a powerful technique to reconstruct novel views of a scene from a set of captured images for 3D computational imaging. The advantage of LFR is to use a set of real images without the need for detailed scene geometric information, so as to obtain a realistic stereo effect [3–6] as shown in Fig. 1. Nonetheless, whether light field sampling [7–12] or reconstruction [14], the solutions described previous still have some limitations. For instance, the reconstruction methods are difficult to generate good enough 3D geometry for the foreground with complex objects shapes or sharp objects with discontinuous depth [15].

Currently, existing techniques for light field reconstruction have studied mathematical model [16,17]. Such as, reference [18] provided a reconstruction

© Springer Nature Switzerland AG 2022
B. Þór Jónsson et al. (Eds.): MMM 2022, LNCS 13142, pp. 62–72, 2022.
https://doi.org/10.1007/978-3-030-98355-0_6

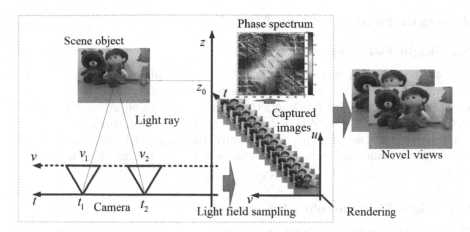

Fig. 1. Conceptual illustration of light field. A camera capture scene object along the camera plane (t, s) in different positions. The captured images can be denoted using image plane (u, v), and then the novel views are rendered by these captured images.

filter from a set of captured images. This reconstruction filter was a linear, spatially invariant reconstruction filter for reconstructing light field. Similarly, Hoshino *et al.* [19] also presented an appropriate prefilter to limit the aliasing of reconstituted images. In [20,21] Wu *et al.* applied convolutional neural network (CNN) to analyze the texture structure of Epipolar-plane image (EPI) [22] in the light field data and modeled the problematic light field reconstruction from a sparse set of views. Reference [23] also provided a light field reconstruction using shearlet transform theory. Vagharshakyan *et al.* used a sparsely represented EPI in a directionally sensitive transform domain obtained from an adapted discrete shearlet transform. In [24], Shi *et al.* presented a light field reconstruction method using sparsity in the continuous Fourier domain. Additionally, Jung *et al.* proposed a flexible connection scheme for multiple-light field systems that takes advantage of the constant radiance of rays [6]. In [25], Farrugia *et al.* presented a learning-based spatial light field superresolution method using a deep CNN. This algorithm allows for the restoration of the entire light field with consistency across all angular views. Recently, Pendu *et al.* provided a fourier disparity layer representation for light fields to study the light field reconstruction [26]. The solutions described above mainly use the amplitude spectrum of the light field signal to design the reconstruction filter, or use the learning method to iteratively optimize the reconstruction quality. However, for complex foreground objects reconstruction often does not improve, while leading to more redundant captured images.

We present an iterative correction phase algorithm (ICPA) to compensate for incorrect or incomplete geometric information of light field reconstruction by phase spectrum of light filed. Our ICPA predicts the characteristics of light field such as phase and amplitude. Predictions on the frequency content can then be used to improve the rendering quality.

2 Light Field Sampling Model

2.1 Light Field Representation

The 4D light field is represented using two parallel planes: camera plane (t, s) and image plane (u, v), which is written as $p(t, s, v, u)$ and follow the method in [8]. The 4D light filed function $p(t, s, v, u)$ can be simplified to 2D light filed $p(t, v)$ as show in Fig. 1. When the result of (t, v) is obtained, it can be easily extended to the case of (s, u). Additionally, the mapping between scene object and camera plane and image plane can be quantified using the conception of EPI [22].

2.2 Light Field Sampling Requirements

To reduce the number of redundant captured images, it is necessary to determine a reasonable acquisition image based on the light field sampling theory [7–12]. Given a scene, the spacing between two captured cameras is determined by the scene texture distribution, the resolution of the sampling camera (Δv), the resolution of the rendering camera, and the scene attribute $\psi(t, v)$ that affects the light field sampling, such as occlusion, non-Lambertian reflection, texture color change, geometric shape, and whether it is smooth [7–12]. Generally, the spacing between two cameras is represented as

$$\Delta t_{\max} = \frac{(v_2 - v_v) \cdot z_{opt} \cdot \psi(t, v)}{f} = \frac{\Delta v \cdot z_{opt} \cdot \psi(t, v)}{f}, \tag{1}$$

where $\psi(t, v)$ is written as

$$\psi(t, v) = \begin{cases} o(x, v) \\ \rho(x, v) \\ \tau(x, v) \\ g(x, v), \end{cases} \tag{2}$$

where $o(x, v)$ is occlusion function, $\rho(x, v)$ is non-Lambertian reflection function, $\tau(x, v)$ is texture function, and $g(x, v)$ is geometric information function. Using (1), we can determine the minimum sampling rate for LFR, and then capturing a set of multi-views images. Based on the sampling theory, we mathematically derive a light field reconstruction by phase spectrum of light filed in the next section.

3 Reconstruction Model Using Light Field Phase Spectrum

3.1 Light Field Phase Spectrum

To analyze the phase of light field, the 2D light field $p(t, v)$ may be written in terms of their magnitude and phase as

$$p(t, v) = |p(t, v)| \exp[j(\phi_t(t) + \phi_v(v))], \tag{3}$$

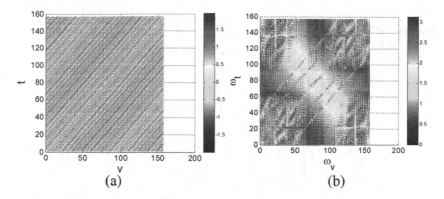

Fig. 2. Diagram (a) shows a EPI for a sine function of a texture signal; diagram (b) shows the phase light field spectrum.

where $\phi_t(t)$ and $\phi_v(v)$ are phases. The Fourier transform result of light field is

$$P(\omega_t, \omega_v) = |P(\omega_t, \omega_v)| \exp\left[j\left(\Phi_t(\omega_t) + \Phi_t(\omega_v)\right)\right]. \tag{4}$$

When continuous light field is sampled by (n_t, m_v) to obtain discrete light field, and will be denoted by $p(n_t, m_v)$. The z-transform of $p(n_t, m_v)$, denoted by $P(z_t, z_v)$, is defined by

$$P(z_t, z_v) = \sum_{n_t}\sum_{m_v} p(n_t, m_v) z^{-n_t} z^{-m_v}. \tag{5}$$

In this case, the Fourier transform exists and is given by

$$\begin{aligned} P(\omega_t, \omega_v) &= P(z_t, z_v)|_{z_t=\exp(j\omega_t), z_v=\exp(j\omega_v)} \\ &= \sum_{n_t}\sum_{m_v} p(n_t, m_v) \exp\left(-j\left(n_t\omega_t + m_v\omega_v\right)\right). \end{aligned} \tag{6}$$

Since $P(\omega_t, \omega_v)$ is, in general, a complex-valued function of light field, it may be expressed in terms of its real and imaginary parts as

$$P(\omega_t, \omega_v) = P_R(\omega_t, \omega_v) + j \cdot P_I(\omega_t, \omega_v), \tag{7}$$

where

$$|P(\omega_t, \omega_v)|^2 = [P_R(\omega_t, \omega_v)]^2 + [P_I(\omega_t, \omega_v)]^2, \tag{8}$$

and

$$\tan\left[\Phi_t(\omega_t)\right] = \frac{P_I(\omega_t, \cdot)}{P_R(\omega_t, \cdot)}, \tan\left[\Phi_v(\omega_v)\right] = \frac{P_I(\cdot, \omega_v)}{P_R(\cdot, \omega_v)}. \tag{9}$$

By (9), we can calculate the phase spectrum of light field. We use a sine function to construct a light field with the texture information as shown in Fig. 2(a), and the corresponding phase spectrum of light field is presented in Fig. 2(b). It can see that the phase spectrum consists of six parallel oblique lines. These six parallel phase spectra are important information for constructing the light field.

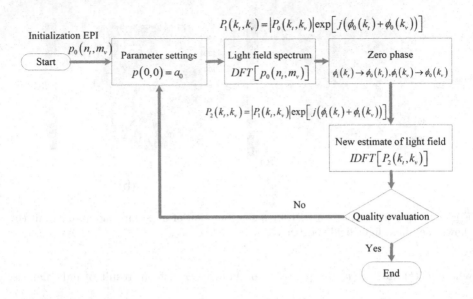

Fig. 3. Framework of the deep probability model with the position and direction of the camera.

3.2   Reconstruction Model

Based on the above phase spectrum of light field, we derive a reconstruction model. It is always possible to find another discrete light field which has a Fourier transform with the same phase by simply convolving $p(n_t, m_v)$ with a zero phase sequence $g(n_t, m_v)$,

$$p_2(n_t, m_v) = p(n_t, m_v) * g(n_t, m_v). \tag{10}$$

where $*$ denotes convolution operation. In the frequency domain, this is the form of multiplying two functions as

$$
\begin{aligned}
P_2(\omega_t, \omega_v) &= P(\omega_t, \omega_v)\,[P_2(\omega_t, \omega_v)/P(\omega_t, \omega_v)] \\
&= P(\omega_t, \omega_v) \cdot G(\omega_t, \omega_v).
\end{aligned}
\tag{11}
$$

Thus,

$$\phi_2(\omega_t) = \phi_p(\omega_t) + \phi_g(\omega_t), \phi_2(\omega_v) = \phi_p(\omega_v) + \phi_g(\omega_v). \tag{12}$$

If $\phi_2(\omega_t) = \phi_p(\omega_t)$, then $\phi_g(\omega_t) = 0$. If $\phi_2(\omega_v) = \phi_p(\omega_v)$, then $\phi_g(\omega_v) = 0$. For zero phase function, estimation of phase function is

$$n_0 = \frac{1}{\pi}\left[\hat{\phi}_t(\pi) - \hat{\phi}_t(0)\right], n_1 = \frac{1}{\pi}\left[\hat{\phi}_v(\pi) - \hat{\phi}_v(0)\right]. \tag{13}$$

$$\psi(\omega_t) = \hat{\phi}_t(\omega_t) - n_0\omega_t - \hat{\phi}_t(0). \tag{14}$$

$$\psi(\omega_v) = \hat{\phi}_v(\omega_v) - n_0\omega_v - \hat{\phi}_v(0). \tag{15}$$

Fig. 4. The phase spectrum of light field for two actual scenes: ragdoll and orchid. (a) The ragdoll scene and its phase spectrum; (b) the orchid scene and its phase spectrum.

The ICPA is presented for reconstructing a discrete light field from samples of the phase of its Fourier transform. Therefore, a heuristic approach for reconstructing $p_0(n_t, m_v)$ is an iterative algorithm. This algorithm is characterized by the repeated transformation between the time and frequency domains where, in each domain, the known information about the desired sequence is imposed on the current estimate light field. Additionally, the iteration may be described as:

- **Step 1:** Beginning with $|P_0(k_t, k_v)|$, an initial guess of the unknown DFT magnitude, the first estimate, $P_1(k_t, k_v)$, of $P_0(k_t, k_v)$ is formed by combining $|P_0(k_t, k_v)|$ with the known phase, i.e.,

$$P_1(k_t, k_v) = |P_0(k_t, k_v)| \exp\left[j\left(\phi(k_t) + \phi(k_v)\right)\right]. \tag{16}$$

Computing the inverse DFT of $P_1(k_t, k_v)$ provides the first estimate light field , $p_1(n_t, m_v)$, of $p_0(n_t, m_v)$. Because the light field signal has zero phase in the frequency domain, then $p_1(n_t, m_v)$ is equal to $p_0(n_t, m_v)$ to within a scale factor.

- **Step 2:** From $p_0\,(n_t, m_v)$, another discrete light field, $p_1\,(n_t, m_v)$, is formed as follows:

$$p_1\,(n_t, m_v) = \begin{cases} p_0\,(n_t, m_v)\,, \text{for} n_t < N, m_v < M \text{and} n \neq 0 \\ A, \text{for}, n = 0 \\ 0, \text{otherwise} \end{cases} \tag{17}$$

- **Step 3:** The magnitude $|P_1\,(k_t, k_v)|$ of the DFT of $p_1\,(n_t, m_v)$ is then used as the new estimate light field of $|P_2\,(k_t, k_v)|$ and the next estimate light field of $P_2\,(k_t, k_v)$ is formed by

$$P_2\,(k_t, k_v) = |P_1\,(k_t, k_v)| \exp\left[j\,(\phi\,(k_t) + \phi\,(k_v))\right]. \tag{18}$$

A new estimate light field, $p_2\,(n_t, m_v)$, is then obtained by taking the inverse DFT of $P_2\,(k_t, k_v)$. Repeated application of steps two and three defines the iteration.

$$p_2\,(n_t, m_v) = IDFT\left[P_2\,(k_t, k_v)\right]. \tag{19}$$

The flowchart of the above light field reconstruction steps also is shown in Fig. 3.

4   Experimental Results and Analysis

4.1   Light Field Phase Spectrum Analysis

We have tested our light field phase spectrum algorithm on two real datasets: ragdoll and orchid, where scenes are shown on the top of Fig. 4. Each scene captures 200 images uniformly at different positions, with each image having a pixel of 320 * 240. Then, the 200 captured images compose EPI, and then perform 2D Fourier transform on EPI to obtain phase spectrum presented in Figs. 4(a) and (b). It can be find that the series of parallel phase lines are not visible in the ω_t, ω_v-plane. The reason for this phenomenon is the complexity of the scene, making the light field signal not just a periodic signal. There are other noise and interference signals that make the phase parallel lines inconspicuous. The more complicated the scene, the more cluttered the phase spectrum, such as the difference between Figs. 4(a) and (b). Therefore, we can use the phase spectrum to iteratively modify the phase of the light field to obtain the light field information and improve the quality of the rendering quality.

4.2   Comparison of Light Field Reconstruction

To evaluate the performance of the ICPA in improving the quality of LFR, we use synthetic scenes and actual scenes to reconstruct the light field. Each scene captures a set of images (sampling rate calculated by [10]) uniformly at different positions, and then these captured images are used for rendering novel views. Additionally, 200 novel multiviews are reconstructed for each scene. The reconstruction method considers three models: ICPA, Wu *et al.* light field reconstruction using a convolutional network on EPI (CNNE) [21] and Shi *et al.* light field reconstruction using sparsity in the continuous Fourier domain (SCFD) [24].

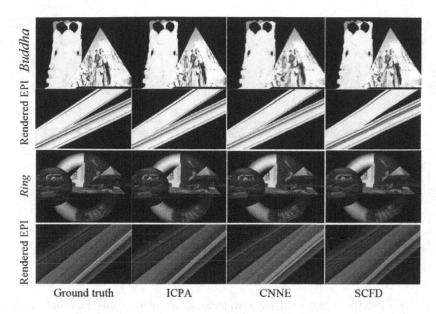

Fig. 5. The rendered novel views and corresponding rendered EPI for two synthetic scenes.

Synthetic Scenes. To verify that our ICPA can improve the rendering quality of the light field, we capture images from data sets and reconstruct views using two synthetic scenes (buddha and ring by 3ds Max) depicted in Fig. 5. The light field reconstruction results in Fig. 5 show that the novel views reconstructed using the ICPA, SCFD and CNNE methods have similar effects. The results of reconstruction have not obvious distortion. For example, for the Buddha scene, the results reconstructed do not show distortion. A similar phenomenon can be seen from either the reconstructed EPI or a single rendered view. The quality of the rendered views is measured by the peak signal-to-noise ratios (PSNRs) against the ground truth image as show in Fig. 6. Furthermore, similar phenomena can be seen from the reconstructed EPI and novel views of the ring scene. From these experimental results, we find that the ICPA has good light field reconstruction.

Actual Scenes. We evaluate the proposed approach using two actual scenes of ragdoll and orchid, as depicted in Fig. 4. For the rendering results, Fig. 7 shows that the reconstructed views have some obvious ghosting and aliasing in either the ragdoll scene and orchid scene. Apparently, the rendering quality of the ICAP is better than that of the CNNE and SCFD in the ragdoll scene. Ghosting occurs because scene complexities, such as the leafage and irregular shape, are challenging to reconstruct accurately. However, when using the ICAP, ghosting and aliasing in the rendered views decrease. There are identical phenomena that occur the orchid scene. These results also suggest that the ICAP can be applied to analyze complex scenes for light field reconstruction.

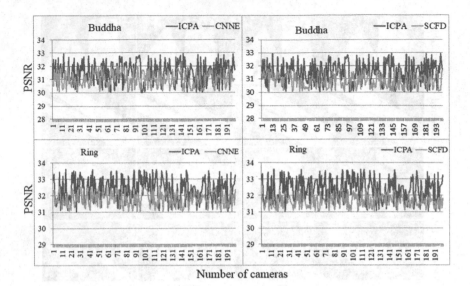

Number of cameras

Fig. 6. The PSNRs of 200 rendered novel views for different methods and synthetic scenes.

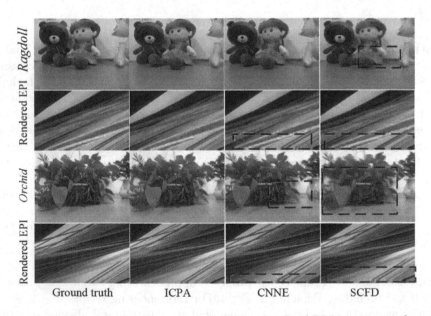

Fig. 7. The rendered novel views and corresponding rendered EPI for two actual scenes.

5   Conclusion

In this paper, we have proposed an ICAP model of LFR using the phase spectrum theory. This reconstruction model has been studied, and its spectrum is presented. We present a light field reconstruction algorithm based on phase iterative correction. Based on the phase spectrum correction, the novel views of light field can be reconstructed. Furthermore, the rendering quality of light field can be improved for the complex scenes.

Acknowledgments. This work was supported in part by National Natural Science Foundation of China under Grant 61961005 and 61871437, and in part by the Guangxi Natural Science Foundation Project 2019AC20121 (AD19245085) and 2018GXNS-FAA281195, and in part by the Natural Science Foundation of Jiangxi Province under Grant YG2018042 and Grant 20202BAB212003.

References

1. Gortler, S., Grzeszczuk, R., Szeliski, R., Cohen, M.: The lumigraph. In: Proceedings of SIGGRAPH, pp. 43–54 (1996)
2. Levoy, M., Hanrahan, P.: Light field rendering. In: Proceedings of SIGGRAPH, New Orleans, USA, pp. 31–40 (1996)
3. Levoy, M.: Light fields and computational imaging. IEEE Comput. **8**, 46–55 (2006)
4. Berent, J., Dragotti, P.L.: Plenoptic manifolds. IEEE Signal Process. Mag. **24**(6), 34–44 (2007)
5. Koniaris, C., Kosek, M., Sinclair, D., Mitchell, K.: Compressed animated light fields with real-time view-dependent reconstruction. IEEE Trans. Vis. Comput. Graph. **25**(4), 1666–1680 (2019)
6. Jung, H., Lee, H.J., Rhee, C.E.: Flexibly connectable light field system for free view exploration. IEEE Trans. Multimedia **22**(4), 980–991 (2019)
7. Chai, J.-X., Tong, X., Chan, S.-C., Shum, H.-Y.: Plenoptic sampling. In: Proceedings of SIGGRAPH, New York, NY, USA, pp. 307–318 (2000)
8. Zhang, C., Chen, T.: Spectral analysis for sampling image-based rendering data. IEEE Trans. Circuits Syst. Video Technol. **13**(11), 1038–1050 (2003)
9. Do, M.N., Marchand-Maillet, D., Vetterli, M.: On the bandwidth of the plenoptic function. IEEE Trans. Image Process. **21**(2), 708–717 (2012)
10. Gilliam, C., Dragotti, P., Brookes, M.: On the spectrum of the plenoptic function. IEEE Trans. Image Process. **23**(2), 502–516 (2014)
11. Zhu, C.-J., Yu, L.: Spectral analysis of image-based rendering data with scene geometry. Multimedia Syst. **23**(5), 627–644 (2016). https://doi.org/10.1007/s00530-016-0515-8
12. Zhu, C., Yu, L., Yan, Z., Xiang, S.: Frequency estimation of the plenoptic function using the autocorrelation theorem. IEEE Trans. Comput. Imaging **3**(4), 966–981 (2017)
13. Durand, F., Holzschuch, N., Soler, C., Chan, E., Sillion, F.X.: A frequency analysis of light transport. ACM Trans. Graph. **24**(3), 1115–1126 (2005)
14. Buehler, C., Bosse, M., McMillan, L., Gortler, S.J., Cohen, M.F.: Unstructured lumigraph rendering. In: Proceedings of SIGGRAPH, pp. 425–432 (2001)
15. Chaurasia, G., Sorkine-Hornung, O., Drettakis, G.: Silhouette-aware warping for image-based rendering. Proc. Comput. Graph. Forum **30**(4), 1223–1232 (2011)

16. Jin, J., Hou, J., Chen, J., Zeng, H., Kwong, S., Yu, J.: Deep coarse-to-fine dense light field reconstruction with flexible sampling and geometry-aware fusion. IEEE Trans. Pattern Anal. Mach. Intell. (2020). https://doi.org/10.1109/TPAMI.2020.3026039

17. Meng, N., So, H.K.-H., Sun, X., Lam, E.Y.: High-dimensional dense residual convolutional neural network for light field reconstruction. IEEE Trans. Pattern Anal. Mach. Intell. **43**(3), 873–886 (2021)

18. Stewart, J., Yu, J., Gortler, S.J., McMillan, L.: A new reconstruction filter for undersampled light fields. In: ACM International Conference Proceeding Series, pp. 150–156, June 2003

19. Hoshino, H., Okano, F., Yuyama, I.: A study on resolution and aliasing for multi-viewpoint image acquisition. IEEE Trans. Circuits Syst. Video Technol. **10**(3), 366–375 (2000)

20. Wu, G., Zhao, M., Wang, L., Dai, Q., Chai, T., Liu, Y.: Light field reconstruction using deep convolutional network on EPI. In: 2017 IEEE Conference on Computer Vision and Pattern Recognition (CVPR), pp. 1638–1646 (2017)

21. Wu, G., Liu, Y., Fang, L., Dai, Q., Chai, T.: Light field reconstruction using convolutional network on EPI and extended applications. IEEE Trans. Pattern Anal. Mach. Intell. **41**(7), 1681–1694 (2018)

22. Bolles, R., Baker, H., Marimont, D.: Epipolar-plane image analysis: an approach to determining structure from motion. Int. J. Comput. Vis. **1**(1), 7–55 (1987)

23. Vagharshakyan, S., Bregovic, R., Gotchev, A.: Light field reconstruction using Shearlet transform. IEEE Trans. Pattern Anal. Mach. Intell. **40**(1), 133–147 (2018)

24. Shi, L., Hassanieh, H., Davis, A., Katabi, D., Durand, F.: Light field reconstruction using sparsity in the continuous fourier domain. ACM Trans. Graph. (TOG) **34**(1), 12 (2014)

25. Farrugia, R., Guillemot, C.: Light field super-resolution using a low-rank prior and deep convolutional neural networks. IEEE Trans. Pattern Anal. Mach. Intell. **42**(5), 1162–1175 (2019)

26. Le Pendu, M., Guillemot, C., Smolic, A.: A fourier disparity layer representation for light fields. IEEE Trans. Image Process. **28**(11), 5740–5753 (2019)

Multi-object Tracking with a Hierarchical Single-Branch Network

Fan Wang, Lei Luo, En Zhu$^{(\boxtimes)}$, and SiWei Wang

School of Computer, National University of Defense Technology, Changsha, China
{wangfan10,l.luo,enzhu,wangsiwei13}@nudt.edu.cn

Abstract. Recent Multiple Object Tracking (MOT) methods have gradually attempted to integrate object detection and instance re-identification (Re-ID) into a united network to form a one-stage solution. Typically, these methods use two separated branches within a single network to accomplish detection and Re-ID respectively without studying the inter-relationship between them, which inevitably impedes the tracking performance. In this paper, we propose an online multi-object tracking framework based on a hierarchical single-branch network to solve this problem. Specifically, the proposed single-branch network utilizes an improved Hierarchical Online Instance Matching (iHOIM) loss to explicitly model the inter-relationship between object detection and Re-ID. Our novel iHOIM loss function unifies the objectives of the two sub-tasks and encourages better detection performance and feature learning even in extremely crowded scenes. Moreover, we propose to introduce the object positions, predicted by a motion model, as region proposals for subsequent object detection, where the intuition is that detection results and motion predictions can complement each other in different scenarios. Experimental results on MOT16 and MOT20 datasets show that we can achieve state-of-the-art tracking performance, and the ablation study verifies the effectiveness of each proposed component.

Keywords: Multi-object tracking · Hierarchical network · Joint detection and tracking

1 Introduction

Multi-object tracking (MOT) is the basis of high-level scene understanding from video, which underpins significance application from video surveillance to autonomous driving. Recently, a few works have been proposed since the release of MOTChallenge which is the most commonly used benchmark for MOT. Generally, these works can be clustered into two categories: 1) *two-stage* methods, namely *tracking-by-detection* methods, that solve the problem of tracking

F. Wang and L. Luo—Equal contribution.
This work was supported by the Natural Science Foundation of China under contracts 61872377.

© Springer Nature Switzerland AG 2022
B. Þór Jónsson et al. (Eds.): MMM 2022, LNCS 13142, pp. 73–83, 2022.
https://doi.org/10.1007/978-3-030-98355-0_7

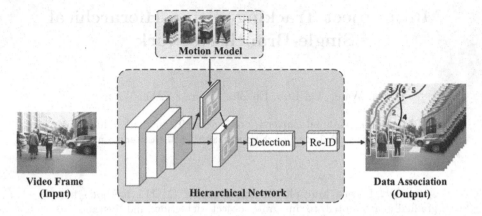

Fig. 1. Overview of our online multi-object tracking framework. The input video frames are fed into a hierarchical network to get object detection results and Re-ID features simultaneouly, in which motion information is integrated to complement the detection proposal process. Then, a data association operation is applied to get final object trajectories.

multiple objects as two separate steps: object detection and data association; and 2) *one-stage* methods that try to solve object detection, instance re-identification (Re-ID) and even data association in an end-to-end model. Commonly, two-stage methods [3,13,21,23,25] utilize a trained model to localize all instances in each video frame in the object detection step, and then, link detection results together to form object trajectories in the data association step. It means the MOT system requires at least two compute-intensive components: an object detector and a Re-ID model, which is intolerable for time-critical applications. One-stage methods [1,19,22,26,28,30] view MOT as a multi-task learning problem which avoid re-computation by sharing low-level features among different subtasks. In other words, how to effectively integrate different subtasks, such as object detection and Re-ID, into a single network is the key to ensure MOT performance.

As another important task in computer vision, person search aims to retrieve a person's image and corresponding position from an image dataset. Therefore, when the tracking object is a person, the tasks of MOT and person search share many similarities. The only difference is that MOT localizes and tracks objects on time-series video frames, while person search is based on a cluttered image dataset. In recent years, the research on person search has also undergone a progress from two-stage methods to one-stage methods. One-stage methods [6,7,24] greatly improve the speed of network inference while ensuring accuracy, but they suffer from contradictory objectives of detection and Re-ID. As discussed in [6], simple concatenation of a detector and a linear embedding layer without harmonizing the two subtasks only leads to conflicting focusing points. In order to solve this problem, [5] proposes a hierarchical structure which explicitly models the relationship between pedestrian detection and Re-ID, and further exploits it as a prior to guide the one-stage model learning. The state-of-the-art performance in [5] shows that such a structure effectively integrates the commonness and uniqueness of pedestrian features and alleviates the contradictory objectives of detection and re-ID.

Inspired by the work above, we propose a hierarchical network combining motion information for multi-object tracking. As shown in Fig. 1, each frame of a video is fed into a hierarchical network to get object detection results and Re-ID features simultaneouly. Then, data association utilizing spatial information and Re-ID features is applied to get final object trajectories. Specifically, the proposed single-branch deep network contains a hierarchical structure with two special layers, which are designed for detection and Re-ID respectively. The first layer captures the human *commonness* and distinguish person from background, the second layer aims to classify persons' identities according to their *uniqueness*. We improve the Hierarchical Online Instance Matching (HOIM) loss from [5] to explicitly formulate the inter-relationship between pedestrian detection and Re-ID. Moreover, we fuse the object motion predictions and region proposed network (RPN) outputs together as object region proposals. In this way, the hierarchical network not only uses the object appearance features, but also integrates the time-series information.

In summary, our contribution is three-fold. First, a hierarchical single-branch network is proposed to explicitly model the inter-relationship between pedestrian detection and Re-ID. Second, we introduce object time-series information (object motion model) into the hierarchical single-branch network to better localize objects. Third, we propose a one-shot framework for multi-object tracking and achieve state-of-the-art performance.

2 Related Work

2.1 Joint Detection and Tracking

A recent trend in multi-object tracking is to combine detection and tracking into a single framework, namely one-stage methods. Specifically, there are two ways: one is to combine detection and Re-ID into a single network to localize objects and extract appearance features simultaneouly; the other is to convert a object detector into a tracker directly.

One-Stage Methods with Re-ID. Wang et al. [22] formulate MOT as a multi-task learning problem with multiple objectives, such as anchor classification, bounding box regression and embedding learning, and reports the first near real-time MOT system. Zhang et al. [28] study the essential reasons of the degraded results when attempting to accomplish detection and Re-ID in a single network, and presents a simple baseline to addresses this problem. Shuai et al. [19] propose a detect-and-track framework, namely Siamese Track-RCNN, which consists of three functional branches: the detection branch, the Siamese-based track branch and the object re-identification branch. Peng et al. [20] propose a simple online model named Chained-Tracker, which naturally integrates object detection, object embedding and data association into an end-to-end solution.

Although these methods try to use a single-shot deep network to accomplish detection and Re-ID, they do not essentially study the conflict between the two tasks. Instead, our proposed hierarchical structure explicitly formulates the relationship between detection and Re-ID, which is simple and efficient.

One-Stage Methods Without Re-ID. Bergmann et al. [1] directly propagate identities of region proposals using bounding box regression to realize data association. Zhou et al. [30] propose a simple online model named CenterTrack which only associates objects in adjacent frames, without reinitializing lost long-range tracks. Zhang et al. [26] design an end-to-end DNN tracking approach with two efficient trackers: FlowTracker and FuseTracker. The FlowTracker explores complex object-wise motion patterns and the FuseTracker refines and fuses objects from FlowTracker and detectors. These methods achieve a compromise between tracking speed and accuracy without using Re-ID features.

2.2 Fusion of Detection and Motion Prediction Results

How to effectively fuse results from motion model and detectors is also the key to improving the tracking accuracy. Zhang et al. [29] integrate the detection and tracking more tightly by conditioning the object detection in the current frame on tracklets computed in prior frames. In this way, the object detection results not only have high detection response, but also benefit a lot from existing tracklets. Feichtenhofer et al. [11] link the frame level detections based on the across-frame tracklets to produce high accuracy detections at the video level. Chen et al. [13] present a novel scoring function based on a fully convolutional neural network to select a considerable amount of candidates from detection and motion model results. The major motivation for this is that detection and tracks can complement each other in different scenarios. Shuai et al. [19] integrate a Siamese-based single object tracker into their proposed Track-RCNN which is robust to appearance changes and fast motion. Although these methods can fuse detections and tracks to a certain extent, they are usually complex and high computation. In our MOT framework, the motion model produces another kind of object region proposals which can be naturally merged into the proposed hierarchical network.

3 Proposed Method

In this work, we propose an online multi-object tracking framework with a hierarchical single-branch network which is shown in Fig. 1. When a video frame is fed into the hierarchical single-branch network, we can get all object detection results and corresponding Re-ID features. Then, we obtain the object trajectories using a DeepSort [23] framework. In this section, we first present an overview of the novel hierarchical single-branch network in Sect. 3.1. Then, we describe the improved Hierarchical Online Instance Matching (iHOIM) loss in Sect. 3.2 which explicitly formulates the relationship between detection and Re-ID.

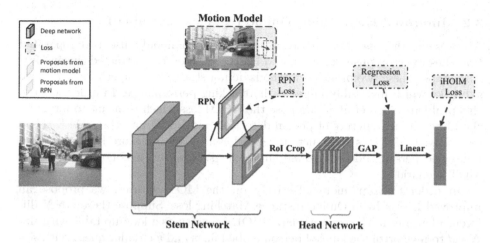

Fig. 2. Overview of our hierarchical single-branch network. Our network is based on Faster R-CNN [17] with a ResNet-50 [12] backbone. In order to further improve the accuracy of object detection, we put the predictions of motion model as prior knowledge into the hierarchical network during inference, and fuse the PRN outputs and predictions together as object region proposals for subsequent box regression and feature extraction.

3.1 Hierarchical Single-Branch Network

As shown in Fig. 2, the proposed hierarchical single-branch network is based on Faster R-CNN [17] with a ResNet-50 [12] backbone which is composed of a stem network for sharing feature learning, a region proposal network (RPN) for generating object proposals, a motion model for object position prediction, and a head network (R-CNN) for box regression. At the end of the network, an extra L_2-normalized linear layer is added upon the top of the head network to extract object Re-ID feature.

During training, we remove the motion model from the hierarchical single-branch network. Following the configurations in [5], we train the whole network jointly using Stochastic Gradient Descent (SGD) together with RPN loss (including proposal classification and regression loss), R-CNN box regression loss and the proposed iHOIM loss.

During inference, we firstly feed the input video frame denoted as $\mathbf{I}_t \in \mathbb{R}^{3 \times w \times h}$ into the hierarchical single-branch network, a series of regions of interest $\mathbf{R}_t = \{r_t^1, r_t^2, ..., r_t^l\}$ can be obtained at RPN layer. Simultaneously, a motion model is applied to predict object positions $\mathbf{M}_t = \{m_t^1, m_t^2, ..., m_t^s\}$ in current frame based on the existing trajectories $\mathbf{T}_t$. Secondly, we fuse the boxes $\mathbf{R}_t$ and $\mathbf{M}_t$ as object region proposals $\mathbf{P}_t = \{r_t^1, ..., r_t^l, m_t^1, ..., m_t^s\}$ which will be fed into the head network. Finally, we can get object detection results $\mathbf{B}_t = \{b_t^1, b_t^2, ..., b_t^n\}$ and Re-ID features $\mathbf{F}_t = \{f_t^1, f_t^2, ..., f_t^n\}$ corresponding to the input video frame $\mathbf{I}_t$ at the last two layers of the network.

3.2   Improved Hierarchical Online Instance Matching Loss

At present, the one-stage networks [19,20,22] commonly use two separated branches to accomplish detection and Re-ID based on the extracted sharing feature maps. These two branches methods do not study the competition of the two subtasks which inevitably impedes the tracking performance. In order to solve this problem, Chen et al. [5] propose the HOIM loss which is meant to integrate the hierarchical structure of person detection and Re-ID into the OIM [24] loss explicitly. HOIM loss constructs three different queues to store labeled person, unlabeled person and background embeddings. However, it is not applicable in MOT scenario.

In order to train more effectively on the MOT dataset, we propose an improved Hierarchical Online Instance Matching loss. Suppose there are N different identities in the training data, iHOIM constructs a look-up table with size $N \times d$ to memorize the labeled person embeddings and a circular quene with size $B \times d$ to store a number of background embeddings. Together the look-up table and circular queue forms a projection matrix $\mathbf{W} \in \mathbb{R}^{(N+B) \times d}$. Given a proposal embedding $\mathbf{x} \in \mathbb{R}^d$, we can get the cosine distance between $\mathbf{x}$ and the stored embeddings by calculating a linear projection as follows:

$$\mathbf{s} = \mathbf{W}\mathbf{x} \in \mathbb{R}^{N+B},$$
$$\text{where } \mathbf{s} = [s_1, s_2, \ldots, s_N, s_{N+1}, \ldots, s_{N+B}], \tag{1}$$

then the probability of $\mathbf{x}$ belonging to an arbitrary person or background can be calculated by a softmax function:

$$p_i = \frac{e^{s_i/\tau}}{\sum_{j=1}^{N+B} e^{s_j/\tau}}, \tag{2}$$

where τ is the temperature factor to control the softness of the probability distribution. Then the hierarchical structure that describes the inter-relationship between object detection and Re-ID can be formulated on the law of total probability, which is shown in Fig. 3.

For the first level of iHOIM loss for detection, we firstly consider the probability of an arbitrary embedding $\mathbf{x}$ that represents a person (denoted as Λ):

$$p(\Lambda) = \sum_{i=1}^{N} p_i. \tag{3}$$

Then, the probability of $\mathbf{x}$ represents background (denoted as Φ) could be formulated in the same manner:

$$p(\Phi) = \sum_{i=N+1}^{N+B} p_i. \tag{4}$$

Combining these two probabilities, we formulate the object detection loss as a binary cross entropy loss:

$$\mathcal{L}_{\text{det}} = -y \log(p(\Lambda)) - (1-y) \log(p(\Phi)), \tag{5}$$

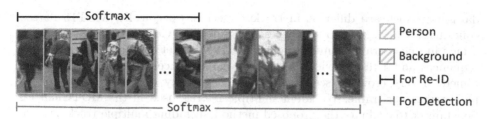

Fig. 3. The hierarchical structure that describes the inter-relationship between object detection and Re-ID. All the training losses are formulated on the law of total softmax probability (black for detection loss and blue for Re-ID loss).

where y is a binary label which equals 1 if $\mathbf{x}$ is a person, otherwise equals 0.

For the second level, we follow [24] to formulate the OIM loss for Re-ID. Given an embedding $\mathbf{x}$, the probability of $\mathbf{x}$ being a person and belonging to identity k (denoted as id $= k$) can be produced by a softmax function:

$$p(\text{id} = k, \varLambda) = \frac{e^{s_k/\tau}}{\sum_{j=1}^{N} e^{s_j/\tau}}. \qquad (6)$$

Then, the objective of instance re-identification is to maximize the expected log-likelihood:

$$\mathcal{L}_{\text{OIM}} = \mathbb{E}_{\mathbf{x}}[\log p(\text{id} = k, \varLambda)], \quad k = 1, 2, \ldots, N. \qquad (7)$$

Finally, our proposed iHOIM loss is the linear combination of the two-level losses:

$$\mathcal{L}_{\text{iHOIM}} = \mathcal{L}_{\text{det}} + \lambda \mathcal{L}_{\text{OIM}}, \quad \text{where } \lambda = 2p(\varLambda)^2, \qquad (8)$$

where λ is the loss weight for $\mathcal{L}_{\text{OIM}}$. It dynamically weighs the importance of the two tasks based on detection confidence $p(\varLambda)$. The model focuses on identifying the detected person when the detection score is high, or focuses on detection task. By removing the circular quene for unlabeled person in HOIM [5] loss, our iHOIM loss is simpler and occupies less memory. It is not only able to identify different persons, but also classifies person from cluttered background. Thus, the embeddings are more robust and the detections are more accurate.

During training, the look-up table is update with a momentum of η:

$$\mathbf{w}_k \leftarrow \eta \mathbf{w}_k + (1 - \eta)\mathbf{x}, \quad \text{if } \mathbf{x} \text{ belongs to identity } k, \qquad (9)$$

and the circular quene replaces old embeddings with the new ones to preserve a fixed size.

4   Experiments

4.1   Experiment Setup

Datasets and Metrics. To evaluate the performance of our proposed tracking method, we conduct sufficient experiments on MOT16 [16] and MOT20 [9] datasets, which are different in tracking scenes. Specifically, MOT16 dataset contains 7 training video sequences and 7 testing video sequences which are filmed in unconstrained environments. MOT20 dataset contains 4 training video sequences and 4 testing video sequences. All sequences in MOT20 dataset are filmed in very crowded scenes in which the density can reach values of 246 pedestrians per frame. We adopt multiple metrics used in the MOTChallenge benchmark to evaluate the proposed method, including multiple tracking accuracy (MOTA) [2], identification F1 score (IDF1) [18], identity switches (IDSw), false positives (FP) and false negatives (FN).

Implementation Details. During training, we use Stochastic Gradient Descent (SGD) optimizer with the target learning rate of 0.003 which is gradually warmed-up at the first epoch and decayed by a factor of 0.1 at the 16 epoch, to train our hierarchical network on the training set of MOT16 and MOT20 respectively. The whole training process converges at epoch 22 with the batch size of 3 when we train it on a single GeForce TITAN Xp GPU. The momentum η and softmax temperature τ of iHOIM are set to 0.5 and 1/30. Sizes of the embedding buffers, *i.e.* N and B, are set individually according to the trajectories in different training datasets. For MOT16, they are 517, 500; for MOT20, N is set to 2332, and B is set to 2000 to balance the probability distribution. Also, we employ the Selective Memory Refreshment (SMR) method from [5] to update the look up table for labeled person embeddings and circular quene for background embeddings.

During inference and tracking, we introduce the DeepSORT [23] framework to tracking multiple objects based on the extracted detection results and corresponding embeddings. We choose the Kalman Filter as motion model to predict object positions based on the existing trajectories, which will be fed into the hierarchical network and work as region proposals for subsequent object detection.

4.2   Experimental Results and Analysis

Evaluation on Test Set. Experimental results in Table 1 show that our proposed method achieves state-of-the-art performance compared with other advanced two-stage methods. Even in an extremely crowded scene like MOT20 dataset, our method still performs excellent. It shows that the proposed hierarchical structure effectively unifies the two tasks of object detection and Re-ID. We beat the previous best tracker by 1.6%/2.6% MOTA on MOT16/MOT20 respectively, which owes to the efficacy of our hierarchical network. Moreover, our one-stage MOT framework have much lower computational complexity and is about 5 times faster than the listed two-stage methods. The reason for the high IDSw and FP is that our model focuses on improving the quality of detection and Re-ID, while pays less attention to optimize tracking. It may be a future research direction of this work.

Ablation Studies. In order to demonstrate the effectiveness of different components of our tracking framework, we ablate the two main components: iHOIM loss and motion model on the MOT20 test set. We first realize a OIM [24] loss based

Table 1. Results on the MOT Challenge test set benchmark. Up/down arrows indicate higher/lower is better.

Mode	Method	One-stage	MOTA(%)↑	IDF1(%)↑	IDSw↓	FP↓	FN↓
MOT16							
Batch	GCRA [14]	✗	48.2	48.6	821	**5104**	88586
	LMP [21]	✗	48.8	51.3	481	6654	86245
	HCC [15]	✗	49.3	50.7	**391**	5333	86795
	MPN [4]	✗	**55.9**	**59.9**	431	7086	**72902**
Online	RAR16 [10]	✗	45.9	48.8	**648**	**6871**	91173
	MOTDT [13]	✗	47.6	50.9	792	9253	85431
	STRN [25]	✗	48.5	**53.9**	747	9083	84178
	KCF [8]	✗	48.8	47.2	906	5875	86567
	Ours	✓	**50.4**	47.5	1826	18730	**69800**
MOT20							
Online	SORT [3]	✗	42.7	45.1	4470	**27521**	264694
	MLT [27]	✗	48.9	**54.6**	**2187**	45660	216803
	Ours	✓	**51.5**	44.5	4055	38223	**208616**

Table 2. Ablation study results on MOT20 test set. **MM:** Motion Model, **Δ:** Value Increment.

Method	MOTA(%)↑	IDF1(%)↑	Δ
OIM-MM	49.2	41.4	
iHOIM-MM	51.2	43.0	(+2.0, +1.6)
iHOIM+MM	51.5	44.5	(+0.3, +1.5)

tracking framework without using motion model. It shares the same network structure with our proposed model except that it separates detection and Re-ID supervisions into two independent losses, namely R-CNN classification loss and OIM loss. Then we add the proposed iHOIM loss into the hierarchical network without using motion model as well. As shown in Table 2, the iHOIM loss helps to improve MOTA/IDF1 by 2.0%/1.6%. After adding motion model into the whole framework, we can get another 0.3%/1.5% increment on MOTA/IDF1. The exceptional performance substantially verifies the effectiveness of all the components.

5 Conclusion

In this paper, we propose an online multi-object tracking framework based on a hierarchical single-branch network. Concretely, we introduce an improved Hierarchical Online Instance Matching loss which explicitly models the inter-relationship between object detection and Re-ID. Moreover, a motion model is integrated into the proposed hierarchical single-branch network to complement the detection proposal process which improves tracking performance a lot. Compared with the two-stage methods on MOT16 and MOT20 datasets, our model achieves a new state-of-the-art performance even in crowded tracking scenes.

References

1. Bergmann, P., Meinhardt, T., Leal-Taixe, L.: Tracking without bells and whistles. In: Proceedings of the IEEE International Conference on Computer Vision, pp. 941–951 (2019)
2. Bernardin, K., Stiefelhagen, R.: Evaluating multiple object tracking performance: the CLEAR MOT metrics. EURASIP J. Image Video Process. 1–10 (2008). https://doi.org/10.1155/2008/246309
3. Bewley, A., Ge, Z., Ott, L., Ramos, F., Upcroft, B.: Simple online and realtime tracking. In: 2016 IEEE International Conference on Image Processing (ICIP), pp. 3464–3468. IEEE (2016)
4. Brasó, G., Leal-Taixé, L.: Learning a neural solver for multiple object tracking. In: Proceedings of the IEEE/CVF Conference on Computer Vision and Pattern Recognition, pp. 6247–6257 (2020)
5. Chen, D., Zhang, S., Ouyang, W., Yang, J., Schiele, B.: Hierarchical online instance matching for person search (2020)
6. Chen, D., Zhang, S., Ouyang, W., Yang, J., Tai, Y.: Person search via a mask-guided two-stream CNN model. In: Proceedings of the European Conference on Computer Vision (ECCV), pp. 734–750 (2018)
7. Chen, D., Zhang, S., Yang, J., Schiele, B.: Norm-aware embedding for efficient person search. In: Proceedings of the IEEE/CVF Conference on Computer Vision and Pattern Recognition, pp. 12615–12624 (2020)
8. Chu, P., Fan, H., Tan, C.C., Ling, H.: Online multi-object tracking with instance-aware tracker and dynamic model refreshment. In: 2019 IEEE Winter Conference on Applications of Computer Vision (WACV), pp. 161–170. IEEE (2019)
9. Dendorfer, P., et al.: Mot20: a benchmark for multi object tracking in crowded scenes. arXiv preprint arXiv:2003.09003 (2020)
10. Fang, K., Xiang, Y., Li, X., Savarese, S.: Recurrent autoregressive networks for online multi-object tracking. In: 2018 IEEE Winter Conference on Applications of Computer Vision (WACV), pp. 466–475. IEEE (2018)
11. Feichtenhofer, C., Pinz, A., Zisserman, A.: Detect to track and track to detect. In: Proceedings of the IEEE International Conference on Computer Vision, pp. 3038–3046 (2017)
12. He, K., Zhang, X., Ren, S., Sun, J.: Deep residual learning for image recognition. In: Proceedings of the IEEE Conference on Computer Vision and Pattern Recognition, pp. 770–778 (2016)
13. Long, C., Haizhou, A., Zijie, Z., Chong, S.: Real-time multiple people tracking with deeply learned candidate selection and person re-identification. In: ICME (2018)
14. Ma, C., et al.: Trajectory factory: tracklet cleaving and re-connection by deep siamese Bi-GRU for multiple object tracking. In: 2018 IEEE International Conference on Multimedia and Expo (ICME), pp. 1–6. IEEE (2018)
15. Ma, L., Tang, S., Black, M.J., Van Gool, L.: Customized multi-person tracker. In: Jawahar, C.V., Li, H., Mori, G., Schindler, K. (eds.) ACCV 2018. LNCS, vol. 11362, pp. 612–628. Springer, Cham (2019). https://doi.org/10.1007/978-3-030-20890-5_39

16. Milan, A., Leal-Taixé, L., Reid, I., Roth, S., Schindler, K.: Mot16: a benchmark for multi-object tracking. arXiv preprint arXiv:1603.00831 (2016)
17. Ren, S., He, K., Girshick, R., Sun, J.: Faster R-CNN: towards real-time object detection with region proposal networks. In: Advances in Neural Information Processing Systems, pp. 91–99 (2015)
18. Ristani, E., Solera, F., Zou, R., Cucchiara, R., Tomasi, C.: Performance measures and a data set for multi-target, multi-camera tracking. In: Hua, G., Jégou, H. (eds.) ECCV 2016. LNCS, vol. 9914, pp. 17–35. Springer, Cham (2016). https://doi.org/10.1007/978-3-319-48881-3_2
19. Shuai, B., Berneshawi, A.G., Modolo, D., Tighe, J.: Multi-object tracking with siamese track-RCNN. arXiv preprint arXiv:2004.07786 (2020)
20. Tai, Y., Wang, C., Li, J., Huang, F., Fu, Y.: Chained-tracker: chaining paired attentive regression results for end-to-end joint multiple-object detection and tracking (2020)
21. Tang, S., Andriluka, M., Andres, B., Schiele, B.: Multiple people tracking by lifted multicut and person re-identification. In: Proceedings of the IEEE Conference on Computer Vision and Pattern Recognition, pp. 3539–3548 (2017)
22. Wang, Z., Zheng, L., Liu, Y., Wang, S.: Towards real-time multi-object tracking. arXiv preprint arXiv:1909.12605 (2019)
23. Wojke, N., Bewley, A., Paulus, D.: Simple online and realtime tracking with a deep association metric. In: 2017 IEEE International Conference on Image Processing (ICIP), pp. 3645–3649. IEEE (2017)
24. Xiao, T., Li, S., Wang, B., Lin, L., Wang, X.: Joint detection and identification feature learning for person search. In: Proceedings of the IEEE Conference on Computer Vision and Pattern Recognition, pp. 3415–3424 (2017)
25. Xu, J., Cao, Y., Zhang, Z., Hu, H.: Spatial-temporal relation networks for multi-object tracking. In: Proceedings of the IEEE International Conference on Computer Vision, pp. 3988–3998 (2019)
26. Zhang, J., et al.: Multiple object tracking by flowing and fusing. arXiv preprint arXiv:2001.11180 (2020)
27. Zhang, Y., Sheng, H., Wu, Y., Wang, S., Ke, W., Xiong, Z.: Multiplex labeling graph for near-online tracking in crowded scenes. IEEE Internet Things J. 7(9), 7892–7902 (2020)
28. Zhang, Y., Wang, C., Wang, X., Zeng, W., Liu, W.: A simple baseline for multi-object tracking. arXiv preprint arXiv:2004.01888 (2020)
29. Zhang, Z., Cheng, D., Zhu, X., Lin, S., Dai, J.: Integrated object detection and tracking with tracklet-conditioned detection. arXiv preprint arXiv:1811.11167 (2018)
30. Zhou, X., Koltun, V., Krähenbühl, P.: Tracking objects as points. arXiv:2004.01177 (2020)

ILMICA - Interactive Learning Model of Image Collage Assessment: A Transfer Learning Approach for Aesthetic Principles

Ani Withöft[1(✉)], Larbi Abdenebaoui[1], and Susanne Boll[2]

[1] OFFIS - Institute for Information Technology, Oldenburg, Germany
{ani.withoeft,larbi.abdenebaoui}@offis.de
[2] Carl von Ossietzky University, Oldenburg, Germany
susanne.boll@uni-oldenburg.de

Abstract. The beauty of moments can be expressed in many ways. One of them is the image collage which captures events and expresses emotions. Nowadays there is a large number of digital images. Aesthetic analyses of image collages are rarely performed due to their complexity and time-consuming nature. For this reason, this is an important issue that has to be addressed. In this paper, we propose an interactive learning model for image collage assessment. It consists of two components: A pre-trained convolutional neural network with built-in knowledge about aesthetics obtained from single image analysis, and an "Interactive Transfer Learning" component specialized in collage aesthetics which is adaptable via Active Learning. We present a mixed method study in which rules for software-based collage generation are identified and a dataset of automatically generated collages representative of the rules is created. ILMICA's performance is analyzed by a user survey. It is found that the knowledge transfer from single image assessment to collage assessment works: ILMICA can assess collage aesthetics based on predefined rules, thereby demonstrating the system's ability to learn. Thus, this process can alleviate the end user and simplify aesthetic collage evaluations.

Keywords: Multimedia · Aesthetic collage evaluation · User-centered design · Convolutional neural networks · Transfer and active learning

1 Introduction

Pictures have the power of documentation. They embrace moments and visualize memories of our life. One way to capture meaningful events using photos are picture collages. These can be described as a visual summary, where the input images can be placed on a canvas, allowing for several design arrangements [16]. These arrangements and layout configurations relate to image aesthetics, depend on various (subjective) factors, and are hence very complex [5,6,15,18]. In this paper we define *collage* as a compilation of different single images on

© Springer Nature Switzerland AG 2022
B. Þór Jónsson et al. (Eds.): MMM 2022, LNCS 13142, pp. 84–96, 2022.
https://doi.org/10.1007/978-3-030-98355-0_8

a background. Collages can be represented by various products, e.g. posters or a page of a photo book. The aesthetic quality of collages is a major factor in creating photo collections. However, people often fail to know what aesthetic collages look like. Even if such knowledge were available, this assessment would be extremely time-consuming. In a photo book, for example, every single page could be a collage, increasing the effort immensely. Thus, particularly in the context of photo books, this process should be alleviated. Therefore, we focus on collages that represent one photo book page. We believe that our proposed system can be generalized with little effort and can be useful to many end users.

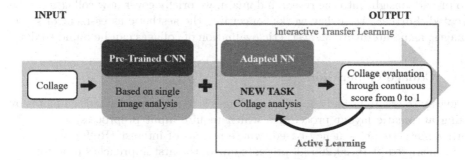

Fig. 1. Conceptual idea of ILMICA.

The goal of this work is to develop a model called *ILMICA*, an acronym for *Interactive Learning Model of Image Collage Assessment*, which is a feedback tool for aesthetic features of collages. Up to now, the aesthetic assessment of collages using state-of-the-art technologies, in particular Deep Learning (DL), has not been well researched. The aesthetic assessment of single images is a well studied problem, which we thus use as a basis for this work. In this field the development of Machine Learning (ML) based solutions is pursued [1,15,18]. Our work integrates Artificial Intelligence (AI) into collage evaluation, as AI systems have recently become powerful and promising for integration into diverse application domains [11]. Yet, numerous of the AI approaches are designed without adequate involvement of end users [11]. To avoid associated difficulties, we employ a user-centered design. Also, we employ interactivity through Active Learning (AL). The presented topic is a relevant issue that has not yet been addressed w.r.t. the technological DL developments of the last decade [8,21,26]. Thus, this paper could fill a research gap by addressing how aesthetic guidelines already well known from single image analyses can be transferred to collages.

To achieve this research objective, we design the system shown in Fig. 1. ILMICA consists of two main components: A pre-trained convolutional neural network (CNN) with embedded knowledge about aesthetics obtained from the analysis of single images, and an "Interactive Transfer Learning (TL)" component specialized in the aesthetics of collages, which can be adapted through AL. The model takes a collage as input and returns a value from 0 to 1 as an output. The main contributions of this paper can be listed as follows:

- We demonstrate that a domain knowledge transfer from single image assessment to collage assessment by TL is feasible and functional.
- We define rules for aesthetic collage assessment through an explicit user-centered design and create a new dataset of collages.
- We propose an interactive architecture based on the integration of an AL component.

2 Related Work

To provide insight into the research domain, we briefly cover how collages can be created. Further, we review works concerning the aesthetic assessment of single images, as no literature on aesthetic evaluation of collages can be found to date.

2.1 Collage Generation

One way to create visually appealing collages is to apply predefined templates by using automatic layout procedures which require input preprocessing [7,8,25]. Other methods are saliency-based, where regions of interest (ROIs) of pictures are considered [9,16,20,26]. [9] presents one of the first approaches to automatically create collages from a set of images, including faces as ROIs in photos. The model of [20] creates photo collections by seamlessly arranging images, producing summaries of the input image key topics. Saliency-based approaches are functional but tedious and inherently uncertain if all of the user's ROIs are covered [25]. Content-preserving methods avoid the aforementioned aspects by keeping the images' visual information [2,24]. Thereby, the aspect ratio and the image orientation is maintained. [2] presents an example method for automatic layout generation. The proposed algorithm arranges an arbitrary number of images on a rectangular area without overlaps [2]. Another approach of generating collages can be employed by integrating multimedia contents. [21] chooses aesthetic principles as a starting point, defines three aesthetic features and combines photos with text as a further media type on two pages of a photo book [21].

2.2 Aesthetic Assessment of Single Images

Aesthetic assessment deals with the judgement of image beauty and is a highly complex task [1]. This difficulty relates to principles of beauty and also to personal beliefs that are strongly influenced by culture and society [1,5]. In general, image analysis can be achieved through algorithms that evaluate pictures based on predefined rules by e.g. professional designers [21]. Further, optimization algorithms or algorithms with pipeline sequences including automatic selection procedures can be utilized [4,20]. However, algorithms are static closed systems with no interactivity. Recently, image analyses can also be performed by means of DL concepts [6,18], representing a more appropriate way.

ML Methods Application. Several papers use CNNs for single image analyses [1,17,18,23]. [17] is one of the first to apply deep CNNs to aesthetic assessment prediction. A two-column deep CNN is utilized to unify the automatic feature learning and classifier training [17]. [18] constructs a multitask deep CNN that simultaneously learns multiple aesthetic features together with an overall aesthetic evaluation. Based on discussions with professional photographers, eight aesthetic attributes are defined: *Rule of thirds, balancing elements, color harmony, content, depth of field, light, object emphasis, vivid color* [18]. Moreover, TL and Interactive Machine Learning (IML) need to be mentioned. [1] uses the former method in which a deep CNN model is designed that integrates knowledge from different datasets. For a given image, three types of aesthetic information (technical/semantic quality, photographic rule description) are predicted based on sequential adaptation. Thereby, the system analyzes the same eight aesthetic features as in [18]. IML is employed in [19] focusing on individual image aesthetics. A deep CNN is trained to predict a continuous generic aesthetic score formulated as a regression problem [19]. Apart from the already described aesthetic features, *Symmetry* and *Repetition* are evaluated as well. IML is implemented via an AL algorithm that optimizes the personalized aesthetics prediction.

User-Centered Design Inclusion. In [15] a deep CNN is proposed that learns rankings of photo aesthetics. A sampling strategy using mixed image pairs within and across raters is employed to compute pairwise ranking losses of the training images [15]. All of the previously stated aesthetic features plus *Motion Blur* are used. For training and analysis of the model, the *Aesthetics and Attributes Database* (AADB) is created, which contains aesthetic scores and the above named attributes [15]. The AADB integrates evaluations given by the same users for different photos. The dataset provides a balanced amount of professional and private images and various image qualities [15]. A recently published study [14] deals with the question as to why an image is perceived as beautiful by a human viewer. The *Explainable Visual Aesthetics* (EVA) dataset is proposed, which explores four attribute clusters: *Composition and Depth, Light and Color, Quality,* and *Semantics* [14]. An explicit user-centered approach is followed and a qualitative experiment is conducted. Four questions are designed to assess the overall image aesthetic quality, the difficulty of judging, the liking of the clusters, and the importance of different aesthetic features [14].

It is evident that the topic at hand is complex. We deduct that the main emphasis of research contributions in the domain are either on modern ML methods (TL, AL) or on user-centered design with dataset generation. But neither focus is associated and applied to collages. The last two studies mentioned are most relevant for our model. We base ILMICA's network design on [15] and our attribute clusters (introduced in Sect. 4.1) are inspired by [14].

3 Proposed Approach

We use methods from three areas that, to our knowledge, are applied to collage assessment for the first time. Humans are systematically involved in system development through Human-Centered Design (HCD) in combination with TL and AL approaches. Hence, DL and HCD are joined with the field of aesthetics.

3.1 Human-Centered Design

In our work, we utilize an approach to interactive system development. It aims to make systems usable by focusing on user needs, applying human factors and usability techniques [12]. We employ four HCD process steps during development: (1) Understand context of use, (2) Specify requirements, (3) Produce design solutions, (4) Evaluate designs. This way, we intend to increase efficiency and provide the best possible user satisfaction. Steps (1) and (2) applied to the underlying problem are shown in Sect. 4.1. Step (3) is outlined in Sect. 4.2 and step (4) complies to Sect. 4.3. Figure 2 displays our development procedure steps (marked in italic) which follow the HCD process from [13].

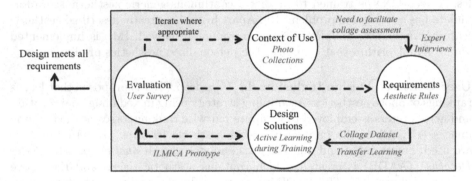

Fig. 2. Our workflow in the development of ILMICA using the HCD process.

3.2 Transfer Learning

TL refers to the knowledge transfer situation where what has been learned in one domain is used to improve generalization in another domain [1,10]. We decide to use the regression model by [15] as a basis since it contains learned knowledge about significant photographic attributes and image content information. It incorporates eleven aesthetic features and an overall aesthetic score. Thus, ILMICA's core is an adapted ResNet50 from [15]. Following the TL idea, the first 150 layers are frozen, i.e. no gradient calculation is performed. This way, the knowledge about single image analysis is kept. We adjust the last convolution block in order to fit our requirements. ILMICA's output is one continuous overall aesthetic score ranging from 0 to 1 (1 represents "beautiful" and 0 "not beautiful") based on knowledge from single image analyses.

3.3 Active Learning

The idea of AL is to achieve higher accuracy with less labeled training instances by a ML model [22]. In AL, queries in form of unlabeled instances can be posed by an active learner to be labeled by an oracle (e.g. a human annotator) through which the cost of obtaining labeled data is minimized [22]. We use a pool-based AL approach, in which queries are selected from a pool of unlabeled instances. To that end, we employ an uncertainty sampling strategy. Therefore, we incorporate the externally added Loss-Prediction Module (LPM) from [27] in our training process which is learned together with ILMICA. The LPM helps to identify collages with high labeling uncertainty. During the AL training, ILMICA (backbone model) and the LPM (module) are connected via a feature transmission after the 3rd, 7th, 13th and 16th layer from the backbone model to the module. This conjunction, which is implemented based on [27], enables the overall loss calculation (addition of both losses) which is used to update the gradients.

4 Experiments

This section describes the results of our experiments. Since we follow a user-centered design, our experiments report not only on the training of the developed model, but also on the design and results of our studies with end users.

4.1 Rules Determination

We conduct a requirements analysis through semi-structured interviews (SSI). Criteria relevant for the aesthetic assessment of collages are identified, from which rules for software-based implementation are derived.

Design. All interviews were carried out in a semi-structured one-on-one format. Due to the COVID-19 pandemic, the SSI were performed remotely in a private online room. A total of twelve different manually created collages were presented (each consisting of 4, 6, 8 or 10 single images from the PEC dataset [3]). After an introduction, a discussion and analysis of the collages followed. Therefore, we used the questions from [14] which were modified to the theme of collages.

Participants. Subjects for the SSI were recruited with the help of friends and colleagues. Properties such as overall interest in photography or general work with photos were relevant. In total, $N = 13$ (4 female) completed the SSI. The participants' age ranged from 21 to 42 years ($\emptyset = 28.62$, $SD = 5.60$). Five of the 13 subjects were experts: three were professional photographers and two worked in the field of photo book design. The remaining participants were non-experts.

Procedure. Participants received general information and a consent form via email. Then, the subjects were interviewed individually for one hour. Active participation and critical reflection on aesthetic features by the participants was encouraged. Subjects were asked to share feedback and comments in any form.

Attribute Clusters. We consider five aesthetic attribute clusters in the study, which we adapted from [14]. This modification is necessary, in our view, in order to assess the aesthetics of collages as accurately as possible. We define and focus on the clusters *Composition, Content, Brightness, Color* and *Visual Quality.*

Qualitative Analysis Results. We analyze the results of the SSI qualitatively through a thematic analysis which identifies three main terminologies: *Preconditions*, *Likes* and *Dislikes*. The term *Preconditions* refers to elements that must be specified in advance, such as photo book scale, one matching theme, clear visibility and illumination. *Likes* specify preferences about visually pleasant collages, such as balancing elements, variety of colors and calm atmosphere. The term *Dislikes* refers to aspects that should be avoided in aesthetically pleasing collages. These include the usage of dark colors, mixing black and white (b&w) images with colored images, and an overload of information or displayed people. Note that based on the analysis of SSI, all of the above aspects could be translated into rules for ILMICA. In the scope of this work, we focus specifically on the *Dislikes*. We believe that these are most likely to yield promising results for implementation and testing. The three rules are the following:

1. Rule: Mixed collages (consisting out of colored and gray single images) shall be rated worse than colored collages and fully gray collages.
2. Rule: Dark collages shall be rated worse than bright collages or collages with good illumination.
3. Rule: Collages that show many people shall be rated worse than collages that display only a few people.

4.2 Dataset and Training

Dataset. Since, to the best of our knowledge, there is no openly available collage dataset to date, we construct a novel dataset consisting of 1191 collages representing the defined rules (using single images from the PEC dataset [3]). We employ an automatic labeling process of collages by the adapted pre-trained CNN. Note that the aesthetic score calculation is adjusted w.r.t. the three rules described above. For this, we performed a subtraction from the originally calculated aesthetic score. The subtracted values were determined experimentally and ranged from 0.1 to 0.2. This way, we label 950 collages. Figures 3, 4, 5 and 6 show anonymized examples created for each rule.

Training. In this work, 90% of the labeled data is used for training purposes and 10% is utilized for validation. We modified several parameters during training, such as the number of AL cycles and the corresponding number of iterations (epochs) in one AL cycle, the batch size, the learning rate, the amount of collages added to the training process after each cycle and the initial number of labeled collages displayed to the model at the beginning. On the basis of several iterations and monitoring model performance we employ a learning rate of 0.00001, 6 AL cycles, 150 epochs per cycle (resulting in 900 epochs), 70 initial collages, and add 20 collages after each cycle. These parameters are kept for the training, which is performed five times each with uncertainty sampling.

After comparing two different sampling strategies, we report our best findings here. Figure 7 shows our training results with an uncertainty sampling strategy.

Fig. 3. Mixed collage used for 1. rule.   **Fig. 4.** Gray collage used for 1. rule.

Fig. 5. Dark collage used for 2. rule.   **Fig. 6.** Crowded collage used for 3. rule.

In all five training runs, learning occurs mainly within the first and second AL cycle (cf. the slope during 150 and 300 epochs). The graph corresponds to a classical convergence curve, indicating the learning effect of the underlying model which shows the feasibility of the chosen approach. To improve results, we will consider several opportunities in the near future. These include performance comparisons with other models, techniques and AL strategies, training with new collages that contain more variety, and considering a more interactive and viable AL, where the end user manually labels the presented collages.

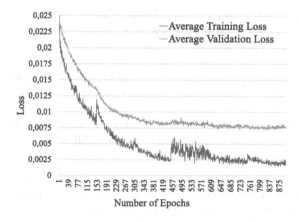

Fig. 7. Uncertainty sampling strategy training results.

4.3   Evaluation

To investigate our models performance, we conduct a user survey which is needed to validate the rules and analyze ILMICA's collage rankings.

Design. The online user survey was designed as a between-subject study. The dependent variable is defined as the *Assessment of Collage Aesthetics* performed by ILMICA. The influencing factor *Collage Rankings* is determined as the independent variable, which is observed and is represented in two forms.

In the first condition, the three rules on which ILMICA is trained are presented to the subjects. Participants are asked to rank the collages according to their personal aesthetic assessment and, in addition, to consider the three rules. Predefined rankings determined by ILMICA's software-based calculations are presented (1st, 2nd or 3rd place) and subjects are asked to indicate their agreement or disagreement. The aim of the first condition is to examine the collage rankings calculated by ILMICA. In the second condition, subjects are asked to give their personal aesthetic rating of the collages presented while not being shown the three rules. They must indicate which of the collages shown they find the most beautiful, average or least beautiful, in the form of a ranking (1st, 2nd or 3rd place). This second condition is generated to obtain human ratings regarding collage aesthetics in form of rankings. Please note that the resulting numerical rankings of both conditions are used as data for the (statistical) calculations below. The following hypotheses are investigated:

- H1: There is a significant relationship indicated by a high correlation between the software-based collage rankings defined by ILMICA and the collage rankings defined by humans in the 1st condition (for every rule).
- H2: There is a significant relationship indicated by a moderate or low correlation between the software-based collage rankings defined by ILMICA and the collage rankings defined by humans in the 2nd condition (for every rule).

Participants. The same recruitment channels were employed as for the SSI. No specified target group characteristics were considered, since ILMICA can be utilized by the general population. $N = 19$ (13 female) participated the online user survey. Participants were 18 to 37 years old ($\varnothing = 27.79$, $SD = 4.12$), including one pupil, ten university students, and eight professionals. Ten subjects were randomly allocated to the first condition and nine people to the second one.

Procedure. Participants received the consent form in advance by e-mail. After accepting it, they clicked on the provided link and filled out the user survey.

Quantitative Analysis Results. To examine our formulated hypotheses, we calculate Spearman correlations, since the data obtained is non-parametric (i.e., not normally distributed). Table 1 reports our results.

The results as per the first hypothesis H1 reveal high, positive and significant correlations, overall and for each rule. The findings of the second hypothesis H2

Table 1. Results of the correlation from the hypotheses.

Hypothesis	Overall	Rule1	Rule2	Rule3	Significance
H1	.76 **	.57 **	.86 **	.56 **	** $= p < .01$
H2	.37 **	.09	.46 *	.19	* $= p < .05$

overall and for the second rule show positive, moderate and significant correlations. The results as per the first and third rule from the second hypothesis depict low, positive and non-significant (R1: $p = .54$, R3: $p = .38$) correlations.

In summary, the correlations indicate that if the rules are presented in the first condition, the participants do comply with rules and rank collages in terms of their aesthetics similarly to ILMICA. In comparison, if the rules are not shown in the second condition, the ratings by the subjects differ from those of ILMICA.

Qualitative Analysis Results. According to the qualitative analysis of the user survey, the most frequently mentioned features are *Color, Content* and *Composition*. *Color* was mentioned first by almost all participants, with emphasis on avoiding dark colors and mixing colored images with b&w images. Further, *Content* is a highly relevant feature for collages in terms of consistent theme, coherence of single images, diversity and an appropriate ratio between people, nature or landscapes. Lastly, *Composition* is a complex feature. Users note that the arrangement and size of collages and excerpts, formats and transitions of single images are important. However, replies were diverse.

Overall Results and Discussion. During the collage labeling procedure the defined rules are not followed to the full extent by ILMICA. The aesthetic assessment of collages w.r.t. three rules yet functions mainly which emphasizes that ILMICA has the capability to learn and comply to pre-defined rules. This also shows that the TL approach works, since the aesthetics of novel collages have been assessed by the learning model. Please note, that three aesthetic rules are not sufficient to represent a generalized human aesthetic perception. But ILMICA has a high potential to easily integrate additional rules due to its interactivity. Therefore, further iterations and training with enhanced collage labels are promising. We also plan to explore the feature *Composition*, including effects of background colors, relative positioning, and overlaps of single images. Since the number of participants in this paper is relatively low, future studies will include a larger and more balanced number of subjects to ensure generalization.

5   Conclusion

In this paper, we proposed ILMICA, an interactive learning model of image collage assessment, which evaluates collage aesthetics based on specific rules by displaying a continuous score from 0 to 1. We have modified a CNN so that it is capable to learn and adapt to aesthetic rules on the basis of which it has been trained. We portray a functional domain knowledge transfer from single image assessment to collage assessment by TL. The training results show a classical convergence curve indicating a learning effect. This also shows the feasibility of our three interconnected approaches. Future steps include implementing more aesthetic rules based on end-user feedback. Also, additional data representative of the rules will be created including the collection of more ground-truth labels. We plan to design a graphical user interface, integrate system personalization, and implement more detailed content-based analyses. We believe that our work is a first step towards facilitating the complex issue of aesthetic collage assessment.

Acknowledgements. We thank the reviewers for their valuable suggestions and comments. We appreciate the time and effort they invested in the review.

References

1. Abdenebaoui, L., Meyer, B., Bruns, A., Boll, S.: UNNA: a unified neural network for aesthetic assessment. In: 2018 International Conference on Content-Based Multimedia Indexing (CBMI), La Rochelle, pp. 1–6. IEEE (2018). https://doi.org/10.1109/CBMI.2018.8516273
2. Atkins, C.B.: Blocked recursive image composition. In: Proceeding of the 16th ACM International Conference on Multimedia - MM 2008, Vancouver, British Columbia, Canada, pp. 821–824. ACM Press (2008). https://doi.org/10.1145/1459359.1459496
3. Bossard, L., Guillaumin, M., Van Gool, L.: Event recognition in photo collections with a stopwatch HMM. In: 2013 IEEE International Conference on Computer Vision, Sydney, Australia, pp. 1193–1200. IEEE (2013). https://doi.org/10.1109/ICCV.2013.151
4. Ceroni, A., Solachidis, V., Niederée, C., Papadopoulou, O., Kanhabua, N., Mezaris, V.: To keep or not to keep: an expectation-oriented photo selection method for personal photo collections. In: Proceedings of the 5th ACM on International Conference on Multimedia Retrieval, Shanghai, China, pp. 187–194. ACM Press (2015). https://doi.org/10.1145/2671188.2749372
5. Datta, R., Joshi, D., Li, J., Wang, J.Z.: Studying aesthetics in photographic images using a computational approach. In: Leonardis, A., Bischof, H., Pinz, A. (eds.) ECCV 2006. LNCS, vol. 3953, pp. 288–301. Springer, Heidelberg (2006). https://doi.org/10.1007/11744078_23
6. Deng, Y., Loy, C.C., Tang, X.: Image aesthetic assessment: an experimental survey. IEEE Signal Process. Mag. **34**(4), 80–106 (2017). https://doi.org/10.1109/MSP.2017.2696576
7. Diakopoulos, N., Essa, I.: Mediating photo collage authoring. In: Proceedings of the 18th Annual ACM Symposium on User Interface Software and Technology, Seattle, WA, USA, pp. 183–186. ACM Press (2005)
8. Fogarty, J., Forlizzi, J., Hudson, S.E.: Aesthetic information collages: generating decorative displays that contain information. In: Proceedings of the 14th Annual ACM Symposium on User Interface Software and Technology, Orlando, Florida, pp. 141–150. ACM Press (2001). https://doi.org/10.1145/502348.502369

9. Girgensohn, A., Chiu, P.: Stained glass photo collages. In: IEEE International Conference on Image Processing, vol. 2, pp. 871–874 (2004)
10. Goodfellow, I., Bengio, Y., Courville, A.: Deep Learning. MIT Press, Cambridge (2016)
11. Inkpen, K., Chancellor, S., De Choudhury, M., Veale, M., Baumer, E.P.S.: Where is the human?: bridging the gap between AI and HCI. In: Extended Abstracts of the 2019 CHI Conference on Human Factors in Computing Systems, Glasgow, Scotland, UK, pp. 1–9, May 2019. https://doi.org/10.1145/3290607.3299002
12. ISO9241: Ergonomics of human-system interaction - Part 210: Human-centred design for interactive systems (ISO 9241-210:2019) (2019)
13. Jendryschik, M.: DIN EN ISO 9241-210 konkretisiert user experience - Gesamtbetrachtung. iX Magazin für Professionelle Informationstechnik **7**, 108–111 (2020)
14. Kang, C., Valenzise, G., Dufaux, F.: EVA: an explainable visual aesthetics dataset. In: Joint Workshop on Aesthetic and Technical Quality Assessment of Multimedia and Media Analytics for Societal Trends, Seattle, WA, USA, pp. 5–13, October 2020. https://doi.org/10.1145/3423268.3423590
15. Kong, S., Shen, X., Lin, Z., Mech, R., Fowlkes, C.: Photo aesthetics ranking network with attributes and content adaptation. arXiv:1606.01621, pp. 662–679, July 2016
16. Liu, T., Wang, J., Sun, J., Zheng, N., Tang, X., Shum, H.Y.: Picture collage. IEEE Trans. Multimedia **11**(7), 1225–1239 (2009). https://doi.org/10.1109/TMM.2009.2030741
17. Lu, X., Lin, Z., Jin, H., Yang, J., Wang, J.Z.: RAPID: rating pictorial aesthetics using deep learning. In: Proceedings of the ACM International Conference on Multimedia - MM 2014, Orlando, Florida, USA, pp. 457–466. ACM Press (2014). https://doi.org/10.1145/2647868.2654927
18. Malu, G., Bapi, R.S., Indurkhya, B.: Learning photography aesthetics with deep CNNs. arXiv preprint arXiv:1707.03981, July 2017
19. Ren, J., Shen, X., Lin, Z., Mech, R., Foran, D.J.: Personalized image aesthetics. In: 2017 IEEE International Conference on Computer Vision (ICCV), Venice, pp. 638–647. IEEE, October 2017. https://doi.org/10.1109/ICCV.2017.76
20. Rother, C., Bordeaux, L., Hamadi, Y., Blake, A.: Autocollage. ACM Trans. Graph. **25**(3), 847–852 (2006). https://doi.org/10.1145/1141911.1141965
21. Sandhaus, P., Rabbath, M., Boll, S.: Employing aesthetic principles for automatic photo book layout. In: Lee, K.-T., Tsai, W.-H., Liao, H.-Y.M., Chen, T., Hsieh, J.-W., Tseng, C.-C. (eds.) MMM 2011. LNCS, vol. 6523, pp. 84–95. Springer, Heidelberg (2011). https://doi.org/10.1007/978-3-642-17832-0_9
22. Settles, B.: Active learning. Synth. Lect. Artif. Intell. Mach. Learn. **6**(1), 1–114 (2012)
23. Wang, W., Zhao, M., Wang, L., Huang, J., Cai, C., Xu, X.: A multi-scene deep learning model for image aesthetic evaluation. Signal Process. Image Commun. **47**, 511–518 (2016). https://doi.org/10.1016/j.image.2016.05.009
24. Wu, Z., Aizawa, K.: PicWall: photo collage on-the-fly. In: Asia-Pacific Signal and Information Processing Association Annual Summit and Conference, Kaohsiung, Taiwan, pp. 1–10. IEEE, October 2013. https://doi.org/10.1109/APSIPA.2013.6694305
25. Wu, Z., Aizawa, K.: Very fast generation of content-preserved photo collage under canvas size constraint. Multimedia Tools Appl. **75**(4), 1813–1841 (2014). https://doi.org/10.1007/s11042-014-2375-6

26. Xiao, J., Zhang, X., Cheatle, P., Gao, Y., Atkins, C.B.: Mixed-initiative photo collage authoring. In: Proceeding of the 16th ACM International Conference on Multimedia, Vancouver, British Columbia, Canada, pp. 509–518. ACM Press (2008). https://doi.org/10.1145/1459359.1459427
27. Yoo, D., Kweon, I.S.: Learning loss for active learning. In: 2019 IEEE/CVF Conference on Computer Vision and Pattern Recognition, Long Beach, CA, USA, pp. 93–102. IEEE, June 2019. https://doi.org/10.1109/CVPR.2019.00018

Exploring Implicit and Explicit Relations with the Dual Relation-Aware Network for Image Captioning

Zhiwei Zha[1], Pengfei Zhou[1,2], and Cong Bai[1(✉)]

[1] College of Computer Science and Technology, Zhejiang University of Technology, Hangzhou, China
congbai@zjut.edu.cn
[2] Institute of Computing Technology, Chinese Academy of Sciences, Beijing, China

Abstract. Recently, Transformer based architectures using object region features and graph convolutional networks using scene graphs have made significant progress in the image captioning task. However, previous works paid little attention to discovering the high-level semantic relations in visual space. Specifically, they typically neglected the problem of relation mismatching between sentences and images, which may result in generating a pale list of image objects. From the perspective of alignment, there are elements such as objects, attributes, and relations in a sentence, but in visual space, there are only objects and their attributes that can be directly detected. Previous works merely focused on aligning objects and attributes between sentences and images while ignoring the relations that just appeared in sentences but cannot be visually observed in images. In this paper, we introduce a novel dual relation-aware network (DRAN) for image captioning which composes of a dual-path relation encoder and an adaptive context relation decoder to alleviate this problem. Concretely, the dual-path relation encoder in DRAN learns to encode implicit relations and explicit relations between objects into relation-aware features. Then the contextual gated fusion module in the decoder fuses adaptively two types of relation-aware features to help the decoder generate semantically richer captions. Experimental results on the MSCOCO dataset demonstrate the superiority of DRAN in relation encoding and learning, which indicates that the proposed DRAN can capture more semantic relations and details. These conclusions are reflected by the best performance of SPICE score and also by the visual examples illustrated qualitatively.

Keywords: Image captioning · Implicit and explicit relations · Dual relation-aware network · Transformer · Scene graph

1 Introduction

As one of the core tasks in vision and language fields, image captioning is gaining increasing attention in recent years. It requires recognizing salient objects in

B. Þór Jónsson et al. (Eds.): MMM 2022, LNCS 13142, pp. 97–108, 2022.
https://doi.org/10.1007/978-3-030-98355-0_9

an image, identifying the appearance attributes of objects, understanding their interactions, and finally verbalizing them with natural language, thus making it a challenging task.

To solve the problem of vision and language tasks like image captioning, the key point is to find a way to bridge the giant semantic gap between visual modality and language modality. Firstly, we need to extract high-quality low-level appearance features in visual space, which can be done with object detection networks. Then we need to explore the high-level semantic information between objects and align them with the lingual words in semantic space.

Remarkable progress [2–4,20] has been made in recent years with the help of deep learning based encoder-decoder architecture. Attention and self-attention mechanism show great competitiveness in the latest image captioning framework. Anderson et al. [2] use visual region features detected with object detection networks to replace the features extracted by CNNs, which greatly improves the quality of visual appearance representation. Scene graph based [13,21,22,24] image captioning and Transformer based [5,7,18] image captioning have explored the structured semantic information in visual space and the interactions between objects, respectively. However, most previous works paid little attention to discovering high-level semantic relations in visual space. Specifically, they typically neglected the problem of relation mismatching between sentences and images. Take the image sentence pair in Fig. 1 as an example, "people and city street and snow and cars" can be visually observed from the image, but "skiing" and "clean snow off cars" are high-level semantic relations between objects which need to be discovered or inferred from the image content. This problem of relation mismatching hinders the precise alignment of visual and language semantics, ignoring which may result in generating a pale list of detected objects. Therefore, discovering and describing the relations between the objects correctly is of great importance to generate high-quality, semantically rich, and vivid captions. In this research, we pay more attention to discovering high-level semantic relations between objects, including implicit relations and explicit relations, with the proposed DRAN model which composes of a dual-path relation encoder and an adaptive contextual relation decoder to alleviate this problem.

Specifically, we use a Transformer-based encoder to learn implicit relations and use a GCN-based encoder to learn explicit relations. These two types of relations are softly encoded in the relation-aware features which are the output of relation encoders. To make better use of these encoded features, we devise a contextual gated fusion module in our decoder to fuse the implicit and explicit relation-aware visual features. We evaluate our model on the MSCOCO [12] dataset and the results show that our method achieves the best performance in terms of BLEU@4, METEOR, ROUGE-L, and SPICE compared with other methods. In addition, we conduct ablation studies on different variants of our model and demonstrate that our method captures more semantic relations and details, which are reflected in the SPICE score quantitatively and also reflected by the visual examples qualitatively.

Overall, the major contributions of this paper are summarized as follows:

- We propose a dual-path relation encoder to learn relations between objects and thus two types of relation-aware visual features are produced. Specifically, we introduce a Transformer-based encoder to learn implicit relations and introduce a GCN-based encoder to learn explicit relations.
- We design an adaptive context relation decoder to decode sentences from the encoded relation-aware features, in which a contextual gated fusion module is devised to fuse implicit and explicit relation-aware visual features.
- Experimental results on the MSCOCO dataset show that our method outperforms previous state-of-the-art models in most metrics. Results and examples indicate that our approach captures more semantic relations than other methods.

2   DRAN

In this section, we introduce a novel dual relation-aware network (DRAN) for image captioning, which composes of a dual-path relation encoder and an adaptive context relation decoder. It takes advantage of the high-level semantic features for modeling implicit and explicit relations between objects. The overall structure of our model is illustrated in Fig. 1.

2.1   Problem Formulation

We claim that the image captioning problem can be viewed as a weakly supervised multi-classification task while iterating through time. In time step t, the objective of classification can be formulated as:

$$w_0 = <S>,$$
$$w_t = F(I, w_0, w_1, ..., w_{t-1}), \tag{1}$$

where I is the representation of the image, w_i is the word embedding of the i-th word, and $<S>$ is the starting token. F is the learned model whose function is to map from image representation and partially complete sentences to the next word.

To solve this problem with our proposed DRAN, we first use the object detector of Faster-RCNN with a backbone of ResNet-101 [6] to extract a set of object region features and use the scene graph detector of Motif-Net to extract an image scene graph. Then the extracted features are fed to our dual-path relation encoder to learn the implicit relation-aware and explicit relation-aware attended features. In the next step, the embedding of the partially complete sentence serves as the context to help our adaptive context relation decoder to fuse two types of relation-aware features adaptively. Based on the fused visual features, our decoder takes into account implicit relations and explicit relations in this way to generate the remaining tokens. We will introduce more details of the components of the DRAN in the following sections.

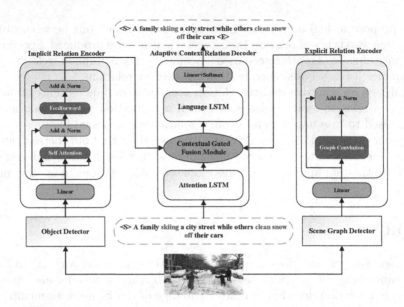

Fig. 1. Overview of the proposed DRAN which composes of a dual-path relation encoder and an adaptive context relation decoder. The input of the implicit relation encoder (left) is the output of the object detector. The input of the explicit relation encoder (right) is the output of the scene graph detector. The word embedding of the partially complete sentence is fed to the Attention LSTM in the decoder to get a sentence representation. The outputs of the dual-path relation encoder and the sentence representation are then fed to the contextual gated fusion module in the adaptive context relation decoder (middle) to help the decoder to generate the next token.

2.2   Dual Path Relation Encoder

The dual-path relation encoder consists of an implicit relation encoder and an explicit relation encoder. We consider two types of relations for our model to learn, namely, implicit relations and explicit relations. Implicit relations are such kinds of relations that can be inferred from the appearance features of objects in images. For example, "next to" is a kind of positional relation that can be inferred from a close distance between two objects. And we believe that there are more implicit relations beyond positional relations that can be inferred from the appearance features of objects in images, such as actions or interactions of two objects. While explicit relations are relations detected by our scene graph detector and then directly encoded in word embedding of relation labels. To promote the diversity of relations, the explicit relation encoder is a complementary method to discover relations between objects.

Implicit Relation Encoder. Self-attention operation in Transformer can learn implicit relations and finally reflect in the attended version of object features, which makes Transformer a good implicit relation encoder. Since objects that are more similar in appearance tend to have stronger connections, we introduce the Transformer as our implicit encoder to discover the implicit relations between objects. We modify the Transformer encoder by applying a layer-wise residual connection between Transformer blocks, which makes our encoder network deeper, thus increasing the possibility of more abstract relations being learned. Specifically, we denote the extracted object features as X_{obj}, then the implicit encoder is given formally by:

$$X_Q = X_K = X_V = X_{obj},$$
$$\hat{X}_V = Attention(W^Q X_Q, W^K X_K, W^V X_V)$$
$$V_{imp} = X_{obj} + \hat{X}_V, \tag{2}$$

where

$$Attention(Q, K, V) = softmax(\frac{QK^T}{\sqrt{d_k}})V,$$

and X_Q, X_K, X_V, W^Q, W^K, W^V, d_k are standard Transformer components. Multi-head self-attention, layer normalization, point-wise feed-forward layer, and another layer normalization operation in a Transformer block are omitted for the simplicity of description. Details about Transformer can be found in [18]. The output of the implicit relation encoder is the attended version of object features, in which the implicit relations are softly encoded.

Explicit Relation Encoder. Due to the ability to aggregate information from neighboring nodes, we introduce the graph convolutional operation in our explicit relation encoder to learn explicit relations between objects. The aggregated information from the neighborhood help refines the explicit relations. In this research, we extend the graph convolution so that it can perform convolution operations on graphs with edge features. Specifically, a node feature is updated with the sum of incoming edge features when the node is a subject and with the sum of outgoing edge features when a node is an object and its own feature. Correspondingly, an edge feature is updated with the sum of the features of its connected nodes and its own feature. Firstly, We denote the node feature matrix as $X_n^f = [x_n^f] \in \mathbb{R}^{d_f \times |N|}$ and the edge feature matrix as $X_e^f = [x_e^f] \in \mathbb{R}^{d_f \times |E|}$. Then aggregation and update operation is given formally by:

$$X_{e\_nbr}^f = ReLU(W_{rs} X_e^f A_{rs}) + ReLU(W_{ro} X_e^f A_{ro}),$$
$$\hat{X}_n^f = X_n^f + X_{e\_nbr}^f,$$
$$X_{n\_nbr}^f = ReLU(W_{sr} X_n^f A_{sr}) + ReLU(W_{or} X_n^f A_{or}),$$
$$\hat{X}_e^f = X_e^f + X_{n\_nbr}^f, \tag{3}$$

where $W_{rs}, W_{ro}, W_{sr}, W_{or} \in \mathbb{R}^{d^f \times d^f}$ are learnable parameters that connect relation features with object or subject features and X_{e_nbr}, X_{n_nbr} are the aggregated neighboring features from edges and nodes, respectively. $A_{rs}, A_{ro} \in$

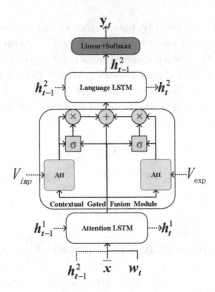

Fig. 2. Overview of the adaptive context relation decoder which composes of an attention LSTM a contextual gated fusion module and a language LSTM. The input of attention operation in contextual gated fusion module are the two types of relation-aware features from the dual-path relation encoder and the output of the attention LSTM.

$\mathbb{R}^{|E| \times |N|}, A_{sr}, A_{or} \in \mathbb{R}^{|N| \times |E|}$ are the normalized adjacency matrix between relations and subjects, between relations and objects, between subjects and relations and between objects and relations, respectively. $\hat{X}_n^f, \hat{X}_e^f$ are the updated node features and edge features, respectively. Then, a stack of graph convolution layers makes up our explicit relation encoder. The output of the explicit relation encoder is the updated and explicit relation-aware node features, which would be further used in our decoder.

2.3   Adaptive Context Relation Decoder

Based on the top-down attention LSTM [2], we design an adaptive context relation decoder which is composed of an attention-based LSTM, a contextual gated fusion module, and a language LSTM. The overall structure of our adaptive context relation decoder and the details of the contextual gated fusion module are shown in Fig. 2. We claim that our decoder has an adaptive functionality because, during the training process, our decoder learns to determine the fusion ratio of the implicit relation-aware features and the explicit relation-aware features to help the model understand and predict more reasonable relations between objects. When decoding the next word, the inputs of our decoder are the representation of the partially complete sentences and two types of aforementioned relation-aware features which are the outputs of the implicit encoder and explicit encoder, respectively.

Attention-Based LSTM. We denote the outputs of implicit relation encoder and explicit relation encoder as V_{imp}, V_{exp}, respectively. At time step t, the input of the Attention LSTM which is denoted as $LSTM_A$ is composed of the following four parts: the previous hidden state of the Attention LSTM, the previous output of the Language LSTM, the mean-pooled visual features $\bar{x} = \frac{1}{N}\sum_{i=1}^{N} X_i$, which is a global representation of input image and the word embedding of the input token at time step t. Formally, the attention-based LSTM is given by:

$$h_t^1 = LSTM_A([h_{t-1}^1, h_{t-1}^2, \bar{x}, w_t]),$$
$$\alpha_t^1 = softmax(W_{a1}^T tanh(W_{vi}V_{imp} + W_{hi}h_t^1)),$$
$$\alpha_t^2 = softmax(W_{a2}^T tanh(W_{ve}V_{exp} + W_{he}h_t^1)),$$
$$\hat{V}_{imp} = \alpha_t^1 V_{imp},$$
$$\hat{V}_{exp} = \alpha_t^2 V_{exp}, \qquad (4)$$

where $h_{t-1}^1, h_{t-1}^2, \bar{x}, w_t$ are the previously mentioned four parts of the input of the top LSTM and $W_{a1}^T, W_{a2}^T, W_{vi}, W_{ve}, W_{hi}, W_{he}$ are all learned parameters.

Contextual Gated Fusion Module. We design a contextual gated fusion module for the decoder to adaptively fuse two types of learned relation-aware features. When predicting the next word, this kind of gating control allows the decoder to adaptively attend to more implicit relations or more explicit relations based on the contextual information. Formally, the contextual gated fusion module is given by:

$$\alpha_1 = \sigma(W_h^1 h_t^1 + W_v^1 \hat{V}_{imp}),$$
$$\alpha_2 = \sigma(W_h^2 h_t^1 + W_v^2 \hat{V}_{exp}),$$
$$\hat{V}_f = \frac{\alpha_1 \times \hat{V}_{imp} + \alpha_2 \times \hat{V}_{exp}}{\sqrt{2}} \qquad (5)$$

where h_t^1 are the output of the Attention LSTM and $W_h^1, W_h^2, W_v^1, W_v^2$ are learned parameters. $\hat{V}_f$ is the fused visual features.

Language LSTM and Objective. The language LSTM and a generator layer which consists of a linear layer and a softmax activation generate a distribution of words. Then the distribution of the entire sentence is generated as the product of a series of conditional distributions at all time steps. Given a ground truth sequence $Y_{1:T}^*$ and an image captioning model with parameter θ, we optimize the cross-entropy loss:

$$Loss_{XE}(\theta) = -\sum_{t=1}^{T} log(p_\theta(Y_t^* | Y_{1:t-1}^*)). \qquad (6)$$

3   Experiments

3.1   Datasets

All our experiments are conducted on the benchmark dataset of image caption-ing, MSCOCO [12], which contains 123,287 images. Each image has 5 different artificially labeled captions. We adopt the Karpathy splits [8] as [2,21,22,24] used for our offline testing. Specifically, 113,287 images are used for training, and 5,000 images are used for validation and testing respectively. For pre-processing, we convert all sentences to lower case, tokenize and discard words that occur less than 5 times, and trim each caption to a maximum of 16 words, resulting in the final vocabulary of 9,487 words.

3.2   Metrics

Standard automatic evaluation metrics including BLEU@N [14], METEOR [17], ROUGE-L [11], CIDEr [19], and SPICE [1] are used to evaluate the quality of generated captions. A higher value suggests a better performance for all those above-mentioned metrics.

3.3   Settings

To extract object features, we use the pre-trained Faster-RCNN [16] with ResNet-101 from [2]. To extract image scene graphs, we follow previous work [24], in which a Motif-Net [23] is trained on Visual Genome [10] with 1600/200 object/relation classes. We apply the detector for each image and 36/64 objects/triplets are kept in the scene graph. 2048D visual features and 300D GloVe [15] word embedding for labels of nodes and edges are projected into 1024D before feeding to encoders. For the Transformer encoder, we set the num-ber of heads to 8 and d_{model} to 1024. The number of encoder layers is set to 4. For the GCN encoder, we set GCN_{dim} to 1024 and the number of layers to 4. For training, we use Adam [9] optimizer with an initial learning rate of 0.0005 and a mini-batch of 100 images. Beam search is adopted in the decoding phase with beam size 3. Testing results are reported on Karpathy split of the MSCOCO [12] dataset using cross-entropy loss optimization and without using reinforcement learning optimization.

3.4   Performance Comparison

Table 1 shows the performance comparison between the proposed DRAN and state-of-the-art methods in recent three years. The models we compared include Up-Down [2], GCN-LSTM [22], SGAE [21], Sub-GC [24], among which the last three also take advantage of image scene graphs like us. We present the results of our model with the concatenation fusion method and with the gated fusion method for fusing two types of relation-aware features.

Table 1. Comparison results on MSCOCO caption dataset using Karpathy split. B@1, B@4, M, R, C, and S represent BLEU-1, BLEU-4, METEOR, ROUGE-L, CIDEr, and SPICE scores respectively. The same below.

Method	B@1	B@4	M	R	C	S
Up-Down [2]	77.2	36.2	27.0	56.4	113.5	20.3
GCN-LSTM [22]	77.3	36.8	27.9	57.0	116.3	20.9
SGAE [21]	**77.6**	36.9	27.7	**57.2**	**116.7**	20.9
Sub-GC [24]	76.8	36.2	27.7	56.6	115.3	20.7
DRAN (w/concat)	76.8	36.6	28.0	57.1	115.5	21.0
DRAN (w/gated fusion)	76.9	**37.1**	**28.1**	**57.2**	116.1	**21.1**

As shown in Table 1, our DRAN model surpasses all other approaches in terms of BLEU@4, METEOR, and SPICE, and shares the best with [21] on ROUGE-L while achieving comparable performance on BLEU@1 and CIDEr compared to others. Note that two different fusion methods of our model achieve the first and second place in performance on SPICE respectively, which is a metric measuring how well caption models recover objects, attributes, and relations. It proves that our model captures more semantic relation information than other methods.

Table 2. Ablation study on different variants of our model

Model	B@1	B@4	M	R	C	S
Implicit relation encoder	76.4	36.3	27.8	56.7	114.6	20.9
Explicit relation encoder	76.2	36.4	27.7	56.6	114.0	20.8
DRAN (Concatenation)	76.8	36.6	28.0	57.1	115.5	21.0
DRAN (Gated fusion)	**76.9**	**37.1**	**28.1**	**57.2**	**116.1**	**21.1**

3.5 Ablation Study

We conduct several ablation studies to further verify the effectiveness of each component of our method. Following the previous finding, we set the layer number of the encoder to 4 and conduct the ablation study on different variants of the model, as follows:

- **Implicit Relation Encoder:** It only uses the implicit relation encoder, i.e., the Transformer-based encoder and the decoder of LSTM.
- **Explicit Relation Encoder:** It only uses the explicit relation encoder, i.e., the GCN-based encoder and the decoder of LSTM.

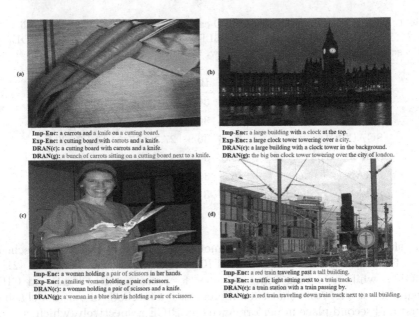

Imp-Enc: a carrots and a knife on a cutting board.
Exp-Enc: a cutting board with carrots and a knife.
DRAN(c): a cutting board with carrots and a knife.
DRAN(g): a bunch of carrots sitting on a cutting board next to a knife.

Imp-Enc: a large building with a clock at the top.
Exp-Enc: a large clock tower towering over a city.
DRAN(c): a large building with a clock tower in the background.
DRAN(g): the big ben clock tower towering over the city of london.

Imp-Enc: a woman holding a pair of scissors in her hands.
Exp-Enc: a smiling woman holding a pair of scissors.
DRAN(c): a woman holding a pair of scissors and a knife.
DRAN(g): a woman in a blue shirt is holding a pair of scissors.

Imp-Enc: a red train traveling past a tall building.
Exp-Enc: a traffic light sitting next to a train track.
DRAN(c): a train station with a train passing by.
DRAN(g): a red train traveling down train track next to a tall building.

Fig. 3. Examples of image captioning results generate by different variants of our model. The captured implicit and explicit relations are marked in red and the captured details from the two encoders are marked in blue. (Color figure online)

– **DRAN + Concatenation:** It uses simultaneously the dual-path relation encoder and the adaptive context relation decoder, with the concatenation fusion method to fuse two types of relation-aware visual features.
– **DRAN + Gated Fusion:** It uses simultaneously the dual-path relation encoder and the adaptive context relation decoder, but with the contextual gated fusion method to fuse two types of relation-aware visual features.

As shown in Table 2, simultaneous using dual-path relation encoders achieve better performance than using one of them alone on all the metrics, regardless of whether the fusion method is concatenation or contextual gated fusion. When comparing two different fusion methods, the contextual gated fusion is a better one to fuse the implicit and explicit relation-aware features, which proves that our gated fusion method can adaptively fuse more accurate semantic relation information to generate the better captions.

Several visual examples are illustrated in Fig. 3. We present the captioning results of the Implicit Relation Encoder model, the Explicit Relation Encoder model, the DRAN(concatenation) model, and the DRAN(gated fusion) model respectively under each image of examples. We denote these four models as **Imp-Enc, Exp-Enc, DRAN(c), DRAN(g)**, respectively. As suggested by these examples, the proposed DRAN can generally capture more high-level semantic relation information and generate more accurate and semantically rich descriptions. For example, in Fig. 3, the single encoder model typically captures a list of detected objects while the dual-path encoder model capture semantic relations like "sitting on" and "next to" in (a), "towering over" in (b), "traveling down" and "next to" in (d). We infer that relations related to position or direction like "next to", "on top of" are typically learned by the implicit relation encoder while relations composed of verbs are typically learned by the explicit relation encoder, both of which may occur in the process of dynamically fusing visual features for decoding sentences. In addition, we find that the dual-path encoder model with the gated fusion method can also capture and fuse richer and more precise details like attributes of an object from the two encoders respectively. For example, "a bunch of" in (a), "the big ben clock" and "london" in (b), "a red train" and "train track" in (d), "a blue shirt" in (c) and so on. The captured implicit and explicit relations are marked in red and the captured details from the two encoders are marked in blue in Fig. 3.

4   Conclusion

In this paper, we propose a novel image captioning model named DRAN which composes of a dual-path relation encoder and an adaptive context relation decoder. The problem of relation mismatching between sentences and images is alleviated by our relation-aware encoder-decoder framework. Specifically, the dual-path encoder learns to encode implicit relations and explicit relations into relation-aware features. Then the contextual gated fusion module we devised adaptively fuse these two types of features to help the decoder generate semantically richer captions. Experimental results on the MSCOCO dataset and visual examples we illustrated indicate that our method captures more semantic relations and details quantitatively and qualitatively.

Acknowledgement. This work is partially supported by Zhejiang Provincial Natural Science Foundation of China under Grant No. LR21F020002 and Natural Science Foundation of China under Grant No. U20A20196, 61976192. The source code of this work will be released on https://github.com/Zjut-MultimediaPlus.

References

1. Anderson, P., Fernando, B., Johnson, M., Gould, S.: SPICE: semantic propositional image caption evaluation. Adapt. Behav. **11**(4), 382–398 (2016)
2. Anderson, P., et al.: Bottom-up and top-down attention for image captioning and visual question answering (2017)
3. Bai, C., Huang, L., Chen, J.N., Pan, X., Chen, S.Y.: Optimization of deep convolutional neural network for large scale image classification. J. Softw. **29**, 1029–1038 (2018)
4. Bai, C., Zheng, A., Huang, Y., Pan, X., Chen, N.: Boosting convolutional image captioning with semantic content and visual relationship. Displays **70**, 102069 (2021)
5. Cornia, M., Stefanini, M., Baraldi, L., Cucchiara, R.: Meshed-memory transformer for image captioning. In: 2020 IEEE/CVF Conference on Computer Vision and Pattern Recognition (CVPR) (2020)

6. He, K., Zhang, X., Ren, S., Sun, J.: Deep residual learning for image recognition. IEEE (2016)
7. He, S., Liao, W., Tavakoli, H.R., Yang, M., Rosenhahn, B., Pugeault, N.: Image captioning through image transformer. arXiv (2020)
8. Karpathy, A., Fei-Fei, L.: Deep visual-semantic alignments for generating image descriptions. IEEE Trans. Pattern Anal. Mach. Intell. **39**(4), 664–676 (2016)
9. Kingma, D.P., Ba, J.: Adam: a method for stochastic optimization. arXiv e-prints (2014)
10. Krishna, R., Zhu, Y., Groth, O., Johnson, J., Li, F.F.: Visual genome: connecting language and vision using crowdsourced dense image annotations. Int. J. Comput. Vis. **123**(1), 32–73 (2017)
11. Lin, C.Y.: ROUGE: a package for automatic evaluation of summaries. In: Text Summarization Branches Out, Barcelona, Spain, pp. 74–81. Association for Computational Linguistics, July 2004
12. Lin, T.-Y., et al.: Microsoft COCO: common objects in context. In: Fleet, D., Pajdla, T., Schiele, B., Tuytelaars, T. (eds.) ECCV 2014. LNCS, vol. 8693, pp. 740–755. Springer, Cham (2014). https://doi.org/10.1007/978-3-319-10602-1_48
13. Liu, F., Liu, Y., Ren, X., He, X., Sun, X.: Aligning visual regions and textual concepts for semantic-grounded image representations. In: 33rd Conference on Neural Information Processing Systems (NeurIPS 2019) (2019)
14. Papineni, K.: BLEU: a method for automatic evaluation of MT. Research Report, Computer Science RC22176 (W0109–022) (2001)
15. Pennington, J., Socher, R., Manning, C.: Glove: global vectors for word representation. In: Conference on Empirical Methods in Natural Language Processing (2014)
16. Ren, S., He, K., Girshick, R., Sun, J.: Faster R-CNN: towards real-time object detection with region proposal networks (2017)
17. Satanjeev, B.: METEOR: an automatic metric for MT evaluation with improved correlation with human judgments. In: ACL-2005, pp. 228–231 (2005)
18. Vaswani, A., et al.: Attention is all you need. arXiv (2017)
19. Vedantam, R., Zitnick, C.L., Parikh, D.: CIDEr: consensus-based image description evaluation. In: 2015 IEEE Conference on Computer Vision and Pattern Recognition (CVPR) (2015)
20. Vinyals, O., Toshev, A., Bengio, S., Erhan, D.: Show and tell: lessons learned from the 2015 MSCOCO image captioning challenge. IEEE Trans. Pattern Anal. Mach. Intell. **39**(4), 652–663 (2016)
21. Yang, X., Tang, K., Zhang, H., Cai, J.: Auto-encoding scene graphs for image captioning (2018)
22. Yao, T., Pan, Y., Li, Y., Mei, T.: Exploring visual relationship for image captioning. In: Ferrari, V., Hebert, M., Sminchisescu, C., Weiss, Y. (eds.) Computer Vision – ECCV 2018. LNCS, vol. 11218, pp. 711–727. Springer, Cham (2018). https://doi.org/10.1007/978-3-030-01264-9_42
23. Zellers, R., Yatskar, M., Thomson, S., Choi, Y.: Neural motifs: Scene graph parsing with global context (2017)
24. Zhong, Y., Wang, L., Chen, J., Yu, D., Li, Y.: Comprehensive image captioning via scene graph decomposition. In: Vedaldi, A., Bischof, H., Brox, T., Frahm, J.-M. (eds.) ECCV 2020. LNCS, vol. 12359, pp. 211–229. Springer, Cham (2020). https://doi.org/10.1007/978-3-030-58568-6_13

Generative Landmarks Guided Eyeglasses Removal 3D Face Reconstruction

Dapeng Zhao[1] and Yue Qi[1,2,3(✉)]

[1] State Key Laboratory of Virtual Reality Technology and Systems,
School of Computer Science and Engineering, Beihang University, Beijing, China
qy@buaa.edu.cn
[2] Peng Cheng Laboratory, Shenzhen, China
[3] Qingdao Research Institute of Beihang University, Qingdao, China

Abstract. Single-view 3D face reconstruction is a fundamental Computer Vision problem of extraordinary difficulty. Current systems often assume the input is unobstructed faces which makes their method not suitable for in-the-wild conditions. We present a method for performing a 3D face that removes eyeglasses from a single image. Existing facial reconstruction methods fail to remove eyeglasses automatically for generating a photo-realistic 3D face "in-the-wild". The innovation of our method lies in a process for identifying the eyeglasses area robustly and remove it intelligently. In this work, we estimate the 2D face structure of the reasonable position of the eyeglasses area, which is used for the construction of 3D texture. An excellent anti-eyeglasses face reconstruction method should ensure the authenticity of the output, including the topological structure between the eyes, nose, and mouth. We achieve this via a deep learning architecture that performs direct regression of a 3DMM representation of the 3D facial geometry from a single 2D image. We also demonstrate how the related face parsing task can be incorporated into the proposed framework and help improve reconstruction quality. We conduct extensive experiments on existing 3D face reconstruction tasks as concrete examples to demonstrate the method's superior regulation ability over existing methods often break down.

Keywords: 3D face reconstruction · Eyeglasses · Occluded scenes · Face parsing

1 Introduction

3D face reconstruction is an important and popular research field of computer vision [4,12,33]. It is widely used in face recognition, video editing, film avatars and so on. Face occlusions (such as eyeglasses, respirators, eyebrow pendants and so on.) can degrade the performance of face recognition and face animation evidently. We cannot use artificial intelligence to robustly predict the 3D texture of the occluded area of the face. How to remove occlusions on face image robustly and automatically becomes one crucial problem in 3D face reconstruction processing.

© Springer Nature Switzerland AG 2022
B. Þór Jónsson et al. (Eds.): MMM 2022, LNCS 13142, pp. 109–120, 2022.
https://doi.org/10.1007/978-3-030-98355-0_10

As the human face is one kind of particular image (the face area is not large, but there are many features, and humans are very familiar and sensitive to it), common image inpainting techniques cannot be used to remove face occlusions. The traditional image inpainting methods reconstruct the damaged image region by its same surrounding pixels, which does not consider the structure of the face. For example, if an eye of a human is occluded, the conventional inpainted face cannot reconstruct the eye image, and the output 2D face will have only one eye [36]. However, things have changed in recent years. Due to the rapid development of deep learning and face parsing methods, face inpainting approaches have developed rapidly. Some common extreme scenarios (*i.e.*, with eyeglasses) become easy to handle.

3D morphable models 3DMM was proposed in 1999, which was a widely influential template reconstruction method [3,4,7,25,38,40]. Since the facial features are distributed very regularly, the application of the template method has continued until now. On the other hand, due to the limitation of the template's space, the expressiveness of the model is very lacking, especially the geometric details.

In this paper, we proposed a robust and fast face eyeglasses removal reconstruction algorithm based on face parsing and the deep learning method. **The main contributions are summarized as follows:**

- We propose a novel algorithm that combines feature points and face parsing map to generate face which removes eyeglasses.
- In order to solve the problem of the invisible face area under eyeglasses occluded scenes, we propose synthesizing input face image based on Generative Adversarial Network rather than reconstructing 3D face directly.
- We have improved the loss function of our 3D reconstruction framework for eyeglasses occluded scenes. Our method obtains state-of-the-art qualitative performance in real-world images.

2   Related Work

2.1   Generic Face Reconstruction

Blanz *et al.* [3,35] proposed the 3D Morphable Model (3DMM) for modeling the 3D face from a single face photo. 3DMM is a statistical model which transforms the shape and texture into a vector space representation. Though a relatively robust face model result can be achieved, the expressive power of the 3D model is limited. In addition, this method suffers from high computational costs. Rara *et al.* [28] proposed a regression model between the 2D face landmarks and the corresponding 3DMM coefficient. They employed principal component regression for face model coefficient prediction. Since large facial pose changes may reduce the performance of 2D facial landmark detection, Dou *et al.* [9] proposed a dictionary-based representation of 3D face shape; They then adopted sparse coding to predict model coefficients. The related comparative experiment shows that their method achieved better robustness to the previous facial landmark detection method. Following this work, Zhou *et al.* [41] also utilize a dictionary-based model; they introduced a convex formulation to estimate model parameters.

With the development of deep learning, 3D face reconstruction has witnessed remarkable progress in both quality and efficiency by Convolution Neural Network (CNN). In 2017, Anh *et al.* [33] utilized ResNet to estimate the 3D Morphable Model parameters. However, the performance of the methods is restricted due to the limitation of the 3D space defined by the face model basis or the 3DMM templates.

2.2   Face Parsing

The unique structure pattern of human face contains rich semantic representation, such as eyes, mouth, nose and so on. The low and intermediate visual features of the known region are not enough to infer the missing effective semantic features, so it is impossible to model the face geometry [2,16]. Generate Face Completion [21] introduces face parsing to form regular semantic constraints. As shown in Fig. 1, the adoption of face parsing map can assist the face inpainting task.

2.3   Deep Face Synthesis Methods

In the existing depth learning based face inpainting methods, due to the adoption of standard convolution layer, the synthetic pixels of the area to be inpainting comes from two parts: the valid value of the unobstructed area and the substitute value of the occluded area. This approach usually leads to color artifacts and visual blur. Deep learning has been widely used in face synthesis tasks. Li *et al.* [21] introduced the face parsing map into the face synthesis task in order to guide GAN to generate a reasonable more brilliant face structure.

3   Our Method

3.1   Landmark Estimation Network

In the landmark estimation task, we built the sufficiently effective landmark estimation network (Fig. 2) based on the MobileNet-V3 model [15]. In our method, accurate facial landmark $\mathbf{L_{face}} \in \mathbb{R}^{2 \times 68}$ generation is a crucial part. The network $\mathcal{N}_L$ aims to generate $\mathbf{L_{face}}$ from a face image $\mathbf{I_{in}}$: $\mathbf{L_{face}} = \mathcal{N}_L(\mathbf{I_{in}}; \theta_{lmk})$, where θ_{lmk} denotes the model parameters. $\mathcal{N}_L$ is designed to extract facial features instead of face recognition, which is different from traditional detectors [19,37]. We set the loss function as follows:

$$\mathcal{L}_{lmk} = \|\mathbf{L_{face}} - \mathbf{L_{gt}}\|_2^2 \tag{1}$$

where $\mathbf{L_{gt}}$ denotes the ground truth face landmarks and $\|\cdot\|_2$ denotes the L_2 norm.

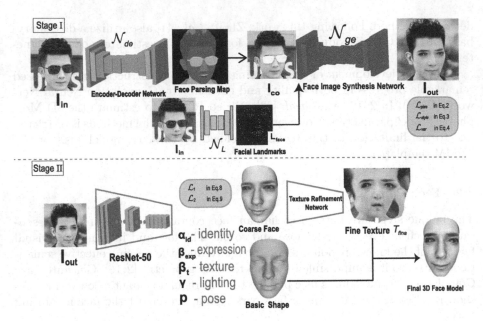

Fig. 1. Our method overview. See related sections for details.

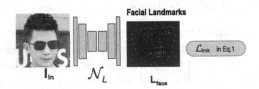

Fig. 2. Landmark prediction network of our method.

3.2 Face Synthesis Module

Overall, We design the synthesis module $\mathcal{N}_s$ to synthesize a 2D image of a human face without eyeglasses. The module $\mathcal{N}_s$ consists of three parts: *deleter, generator* and *discriminator*.

Deleter. Normally, the task of the deleter is to delete the occluded eyeglasses areas $\mathbf{I_m}$ of the facial features in the input image $\mathbf{I_{in}}$ (Fig. 3). Overall, the deleter $\mathcal{N}_{de}$ is based on the U-Net structure [30]. Inspired by the annotated face dataset CelebAMask-HQ [20], we used the encoder-decoder architecture $\mathcal{N}_{de}$ to estimate pixel-level label classes. Given the input face image $\mathbf{I_{in}} \in \mathbb{R}^{H \times W \times 3}$, we applied the trained model $\mathcal{N}_{de}$ to obtain the face parsing map $\mathbf{M} \in \mathbb{R}^{H \times W \times 1}$. According to the map $\mathbf{M}$, we identify and delete the eyeglasses area $\mathbf{I_m}$ to obtain the corrupted image $\mathbf{I_{co}}$.

Fig. 3. Face parsing module of our method.

Generator. The generator $\mathcal{N}_{ge}$ is also based on the U-Net structure, which desires to synthesize the full face by taking corrupted images $\mathbf{I_{co}}$ and landmarks $\mathbf{L}$ ($\mathbf{L_{face}}$ or $\mathbf{L_{gt}}$). The generator can be formulated as $\mathbf{I_{out}} = \mathcal{N}_{ge}(\mathbf{I_{co}}, L; \theta_{ge})$, with θ_{ge} the trainable parameters.

Discriminator. The purpose of the discriminator is to judge whether the data distribution meets our requirements. The ambition of face synthesis is achieved when the generated results are not distinguishable from the real ones.

Loss of Discriminator. We use a combination of an adversarial loss, a per-pixel loss, a perceptual loss, a style loss, a total variation loss and an adversarial loss, for training the face synthesis network.

The per-pixel loss is formulated as follows:

$$\mathcal{L}_{pixe} = \frac{1}{S} \|\mathbf{I_{out}} - \mathbf{I_{in}}\| \tag{2}$$

where S denotes the mask size and $\|\cdot\|$ denotes the L_1 norm. Here, S is the denominator and its role is to adjust the penalty. A straightforward objective of per-pixel loss is to minimize the differences between the input face images and the synthetic images. It should be pointed out that our input image will not contain occlusion, so we don't need to consider this.

The style loss computes the style distance between two images as follows:

$$\mathcal{L}_{style} = \sum_{n} \frac{1}{O_n \times O_n} \left\| \frac{G_n(\mathbf{I_{out}} \odot \mathbf{I_m}) - G_n(\mathbf{I_{in}} \odot \mathbf{I_m})}{O_n \times H_n \times W_n} \right\| \tag{3}$$

where $G_n(\mathbf{x}) = \varphi_n(x)^T \varphi_n(x)$ denotes the Gram Matrix corresponding to $\varphi_n(x)$, $\varphi_n(\cdot)$ denotes the O_n feature maps with the size $H_n \times W_n$ of the n-th layer.

Due to the use of the normalization tool, the synthesized face may have artifacts, checkerboards, or water droplets. We define the total variation loss as:

$$\mathcal{L}_{var} = \frac{1}{P_{\mathbf{I_{in}}}} \|\nabla \mathbf{I_{out}}\| \tag{4}$$

where $P_{\mathbf{I_{in}}}$ is the pixel number of $\mathbf{I_{in}}$ and ∇ is the first order derivative, containing ∇_h (horizontal) and ∇_v (vertical).

The total loss with respect to the face synthesis module:

$$\mathcal{L}_{fsm} = \lambda_{pixe} \mathcal{L}_{pixe} + \lambda_{style} \mathcal{L}_{style} + \lambda_{var} \mathcal{L}_{var} \tag{5}$$

Here, we use $\lambda_{pixe} = 1$, $\lambda_{style} = 250$ and $\lambda_{var} = 0.1$ in our experiments.

3.3   3D Face Reconstruction

The classic single-view 3D face reconstruction methods utilize a 3D template model (*e.g.*, 3DMM)) to fit the input face image [3,25]. This type of method usually consists of two steps: face alignment and regressing the 3DMM coefficients. The seminal work [4,8,11] describe the 3D face space with PCA:

$$\mathbf{S} = \overline{\mathbf{S}} + \mathbf{A_{id}}\alpha_{id} + \mathbf{B_{exp}}\beta_{exp}, \mathbf{T} = \overline{\mathbf{T}} + \mathbf{B_t}\beta_t \tag{6}$$

where $\overline{\mathbf{S}}$ and $\overline{\mathbf{T}}$ denote the mean shape and texture, $\mathbf{A_{id}}$, $\mathbf{B_{exp}}$ and $\mathbf{B_t}$ denote the PCA bases of identity, expression and texture. $\alpha_{id} \in \mathbb{R}^{80}$ and $\beta_{exp} \in \mathbb{R}^{64}$, and $\beta_t \in \mathbb{R}^{80}$ are the corresponding 3DMM coefficient vectors.

After the 3D face is reconstructed, it can be projected onto the image plane with the perspective projection:

$$\mathbf{V_{2d}}\left(\mathbf{P}\right) = f * \mathbf{P_r} * \mathbf{R} * \mathbf{S_{mod}} + \mathbf{t_{2d}} \tag{7}$$

where $V_{2d}\left(\mathbf{P}\right)$ denotes the projection function that turned the 3D model into 2D face positions, f denotes the scale factor, $\mathbf{P_r}$ denotes the projection matrix, $\mathbf{R} \in SO(3)$ denotes the rotation matrix and $\mathbf{t_{2d}} \in \mathbb{R}^3$ denotes the translation vector.

Therefore, we approximated the scene illumination with Spherical Harmonics (SH) [6,23,26,27] parameterized by coefficient vector $\gamma \in \mathbb{R}^9$. In summary, the unknown parameters to be learned can be denoted by a vector $y = (\alpha_{id}, \beta_{exp}, \beta_t, \gamma, \mathbf{p}) \in \mathbb{R}^{239}$, where $\mathbf{p} \in \mathbb{R}^6 = \{\mathbf{pitch}, \mathbf{yaw}, \mathbf{roll}, f, \mathbf{t_{2D}}\}$ denotes face poses. In this work, we used a fixed ResNet-50 [14] network to regress these coefficients.

The corresponding loss function consists of two parts: pixel-wise loss and face feature loss.

Pixel-Wise Loss. The purpose of this loss function is very simple, which is to minimize the difference between the input image $\mathbf{I}_{out}^{(i)}$ and the rendered image $\mathbf{I}_y^{(i)}$. The rendering layer renders back an image $\mathbf{I}_y^{(i)}$ to compare with the image $\mathbf{I}_{out}^{(i)}$. The pixel-wise loss is formulated as:

$$\mathcal{L}_1 = \left\| \mathbf{I}_{out}^{(i)} - \mathbf{I}_y^{(i)} \right\|_2 \tag{8}$$

where i denotes pixel index and $\|\cdot\|_2$ denotes the L_2 norm.

Face Features Loss. We introduce a loss function at the face recognition level to reduce the difference between the 3D model of the face and the 2D image. The loss function computes the feature difference between the input image $\mathbf{I}_{out}$ and rendered image $\mathbf{I}_y$. We define the loss as a cosine distance:

$$\mathcal{L}_2 = 1 - \frac{<G(\mathbf{I}_{out}), G(\mathbf{I}_y)>}{\|G(\mathbf{I}_{out})\| \cdot \|G(\mathbf{I}_y)\|} \tag{9}$$

where $G(\cdot)$ denotes the feature extraction function by FaceNet [31], $<\cdot, \cdot>$ denotes the inner product.

In summary, we used the loss function $\mathcal{L}_{3D}$ to reconstruct the basic shape of the face. We set $\mathcal{L}_{3D} = \lambda_1\mathcal{L}_1 + \lambda_2\mathcal{L}_2$, where $\lambda_1 = 1.4$ and $\lambda_2 = 0.25$ respectively in all our experiments. We then used a coarse-to-fine graph convolutional network based on the frameworks of Lin *et al.* [22] for producing the fine texture T_{fina}.

4 Experimental Details and Results

4.1 Implementation Details

In consideration of the module of $\mathcal{N}_{cont}$, we used the ground truth of CelebA-HQ datasets [18] as the reference. Considering the generator $\mathcal{N}_{ge}$, it consists of three gradually down-sampled encoding blocks, followed by seven residual blocks with dilated convolutions and a long-short term attention block. Then, the decoder processes the feature maps gradually up-sampled to the same size as input.

4.2 Qualitative Comparisons with Recent Arts

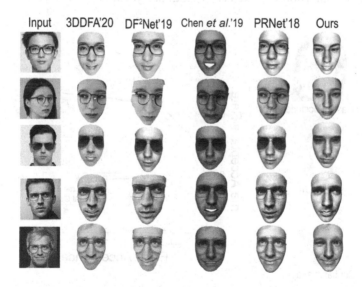

Fig. 4. Comparison of qualitative results. Baseline methods from left to right: 3DDFA, DF2Net, Chen *et al.*, PRNet, and our method.

Figure 4 shows our experimental results compared with the others [5,10,13,39]. The result shows that our method is far superior to other frameworks. Our 3D reconstruction method can handle eyeglasses occluded scenes, such as transparent glasses and sunglasses. Other frameworks can not handle eyeglasses well; they are more focused on the generation of high-definition textures.

4.3 Quantitative Comparison

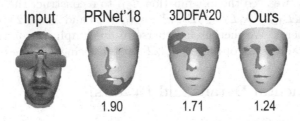

Fig. 5. Comparison of error heat maps on the MICC Florence datasets. Digits denote 90% error (mm).

Comparison Result on the MICC Florence Datasets. MICC Florence dataset [1] is a 3D face dataset that contains 53 faces with their ground truth models. We artificially added eyeglasses as input. We calculated the average 90% largest error between the generative model and the ground truth model. Figure 5 shows that our method can effectively handle eyeglasses.

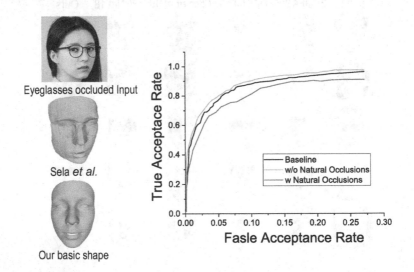

Fig. 6. Reconstructions with eyeglasses. Left: qualitative results of Sela *et al.* [17] and our shape. Right: LFW verification ROC for the shapes, with and without eyeglasses.

Eyeglasses Invariance of the Foundation Shape. Our choice of using the ResNet-50 to regress the shape coefficients is motivated by the unique robustness to extreme viewing conditions in the paper of Deng *et al.* [29]. To fully support the application of our method to occluded face images, we test our system on the Labeled Faces in the Wild datasets (LFW) [24]. We used the same face test system from Anh *et al.* [34], and we refer to that paper for more details.

Figure 6 (left) shows the sensitivity of the method of Sela *et al.* [32]. Their result clearly shows the outline of a finger. Their failure may be due to more focus on local details, which weakly regularizes the global shape. However, our method recognizes and regenerates the occluded area. Our method much robust provides a natural face shape under eyeglasses scenes. Though 3DMM also limits the details of shape, we use it only as a foundation and add refined texture separately.

Table 1. Quantitative evaluations on LFW.

Method	100%-EER	Accuracy	nAUC
Tran *et al.* [33]	89.40 ± 1.52	89.36 ± 1.25	95.90 ± 0.95
Ours (w/Gla)	84.77 ± 1.23	87.05 ± 0.89	92.77 ± 1.26
Ours (w/o Gla)	89.33 ± 1.15	89.80 ± 0.89	96.09 ± 0.61

We further quantitatively verify the robustness of our method to eyeglasses. Table 1 (top) reports verification results on the LFW benchmark with and without cyeglasses (see also ROC in Fig. 6-right). Though eyeglasses clearly impact recognition, this drop of the curve is limited, demonstrating the robustness of our method.

5   Conclusions

We propose a novel method to reconstruct a 3D face model from an eyeglass occluded RGB face photo. Given the input image and a pre-trained Rc3Net, we fit the face model to a template model (3DMM). In order to robustly reconstruct RGB face without glasses, we design a deep learning network, which remakes reasonable texture intelligently. Comprehensive experiments have shown that our method outperforms previous arts by a large margin in terms of both accuracy and robustness.

Acknowledgment. This paper is supported by National Natural Science Foundation of China (No. 62072020), National Key Research and Development Program of China (No. 2017YFB1002602), Key-Area Research and Development Program of Guangdong Province (No. 2019B010150001) and the Leading Talents in Innovation and Entrepreneurship of Qingdao (19-3-2-21-zhc).

References

1. Bagdanov, A.D., Del Bimbo, A., Masi, I.: The florence 2D/3D hybrid face dataset. In: Proceedings of the 2011 Joint ACM workshop on Human Gesture and Behavior Understanding, pp. 79–80 (2011)

2. Bertalmio, M., Sapiro, G., Caselles, V., Ballester, C.: Image inpainting. In: Proceedings of the 27th Annual Conference on Computer Graphics and Interactive Techniques, pp. 417–424 (2000)
3. Blanz, V., Vetter, T.: A morphable model for the synthesis of 3D faces. In: Siggraph, vol. 99, pp. 187–194 (1999)
4. Blanz, V., Vetter, T.: Face recognition based on fitting a 3D morphable model. IEEE Trans. Pattern Anal. Mach. Intell. **25**(9), 1063–1074 (2003)
5. Chen, A., Chen, Z., Zhang, G., Mitchell, K., Yu, J.: Photo-realistic facial details synthesis from single image. In: Proceedings of the IEEE International Conference on Computer Vision, pp. 9429–9439 (2019)
6. Dapeng, Z., Yue, Q.: Generative landmarks guided eyeglasses removal 3D face reconstruction. In: Pór Jónsson, B., et al. (eds.) MMM 2022. LNCS, vol. 13142. pp. 109–120. Springer, Heidelberg (2022)
7. Dapeng, Z., Yue, Q.: Generative contour guided occlusions removal 3D face reconstruction. In: 2021 International Conference on Virtual Reality and Visualization (ICVRV), pp. 74–79. IEEE (2021)
8. Dapeng, Z., Yue, Q.: Learning detailed face reconstruction under occluded scenes. In: 2021 International Conference on Virtual Reality and Visualization (ICVRV), pp. 80–84. IEEE (2021)
9. Dou, P., Wu, Y., Shah, S.K., Kakadiaris, I.A.: Robust 3D face shape reconstruction from single images via two-fold coupled structure learning. In: Proceedings of the British Machine Vision Conference. pp. 1–13 (2014)
10. Feng, Y., Wu, F., Shao, X., Wang, Y., Zhou, X.: Joint 3D face reconstruction and dense alignment with position map regression network. In: Ferrari, V., Hebert, M., Sminchisescu, C., Weiss, Y. (eds.) Computer Vision – ECCV 2018. LNCS, vol. 11218, pp. 557–574. Springer, Cham (2018). https://doi.org/10.1007/978-3-030-01264-9_33
11. Gerig, T., et al.: Morphable face models-an open framework. In: 2018 13th IEEE International Conference on Automatic Face & Gesture Recognition (FG 2018), pp. 75–82. IEEE (2018)
12. Gilani, S.Z., Mian, A.: Learning from millions of 3D scans for large-scale 3D face recognition. In: Proceedings of the IEEE Conference on Computer Vision and Pattern Recognition, pp. 1896–1905 (2018)
13. Guo, J., Zhu, X., Yang, Y., Yang, F., Lei, Z., Li, S.Z.: Towards fast, accurate and stable 3D dense face alignment. arXiv preprint arXiv:2009.09960 (2020)
14. He, K., Zhang, X., Ren, S., Sun, J.: Deep residual learning for image recognition. In: Proceedings of the IEEE Conference on Computer Vision and Pattern Recognition, pp. 770–778 (2016)
15. Howard, A., et al.: Searching for MobileNetV3. In: Proceedings of the IEEE/CVF International Conference on Computer Vision, pp. 1314–1324 (2019)
16. Huang, J.B., Kang, S.B., Ahuja, N., Kopf, J.: Image completion using planar structure guidance. ACM Trans. Graph. (TOG) **33**(4), 1–10 (2014)
17. Isola, P., Zhu, J.Y., Zhou, T., Efros, A.A.: Image-to-image translation with conditional adversarial networks. In: Proceedings of the IEEE Conference on Computer Vision and Pattern Recognition, pp. 1125–1134 (2017)
18. Karras, T., Aila, T., Laine, S., Lehtinen, J.: Progressive growing of GANs for improved quality, stability, and variation. arXiv preprint arXiv:1710.10196 (2017)
19. Kumar, A., Chellappa, R.: Disentangling 3D pose in a dendritic CNN for unconstrained 2D face alignment. In: Proceedings of the IEEE Conference on Computer Vision and Pattern Recognition, pp. 430–439 (2018)

20. Lee, C.H., Liu, Z., Wu, L., Luo, P.: MaskGAN: towards diverse and interactive facial image manipulation. In: Proceedings of the IEEE/CVF Conference on Computer Vision and Pattern Recognition, pp. 5549–5558 (2020)

21. Li, Y., Liu, S., Yang, J., Yang, M.H.: Generative face completion. In: Proceedings of the IEEE Conference on Computer Vision and Pattern Recognition, pp. 3911–3919 (2017)

22. Lin, J., Yuan, Y., Shao, T., Zhou, K.: Towards high-fidelity 3D face reconstruction from in-the-wild images using graph convolutional networks. arXiv preprint arXiv:2003.05653 (2020)

23. Müller, C.: Spherical Harmonics, vol. 17. Springer, Heidelberg (2006)

24. Pan, J., et al.: Video generation from single semantic label map. In: Proceedings of the IEEE/CVF Conference on Computer Vision and Pattern Recognition, pp. 3733–3742 (2019)

25. Paysan, P., Knothe, R., Amberg, B., Romdhani, S., Vetter, T.: A 3D face model for pose and illumination invariant face recognition. In: 2009 Sixth IEEE International Conference on Advanced Video and Signal Based Surveillance, pp. 296–301. IEEE (2009)

26. Ramamoorthi, R., Hanrahan, P.: An efficient representation for irradiance environment maps. In: Proceedings of the 28th Annual Conference on Computer Graphics and Interactive Techniques, pp. 497–500 (2001)

27. Ramamoorthi, R., Hanrahan, P.: A signal-processing framework for inverse rendering. In: Proceedings of the 28th Annual Conference on Computer Graphics and Interactive Techniques, pp. 117–128 (2001)

28. Rara, H.M., Farag, A.A., Davis, T.: Model-based 3D shape recovery from single images of unknown pose and illumination using a small number of feature points. In: 2011 International Joint Conference on Biometrics (IJCB), pp. 1–7. IEEE (2011)

29. Richardson, E., Sela, M., Kimmel, R.: 3D face reconstruction by learning from synthetic data. In: 2016 Fourth International Conference on 3D Vision (3DV), pp. 460–469. IEEE (2016)

30. Ronneberger, O., Fischer, P., Brox, T.: U-Net: convolutional networks for biomedical image segmentation. In: Navab, N., Hornegger, J., Wells, W.M., Frangi, A.F. (eds.) MICCAI 2015. LNCS, vol. 9351, pp. 234–241. Springer, Cham (2015). https://doi.org/10.1007/978-3-319-24574-4_28

31. Schroff, F., Kalenichenko, D., Philbin, J.: FaceNet: a unified embedding for face recognition and clustering. In: Proceedings of the IEEE Conference on Computer Vision and Pattern Recognition, pp. 815–823 (2015)

32. Sela, M., Richardson, E., Kimmel, R.: Unrestricted facial geometry reconstruction using image-to-image translation. In: Proceedings of the IEEE International Conference on Computer Vision, pp. 1576–1585 (2017)

33. Tuan Tran, A., Hassner, T., Masi, I., Medioni, G.: Regressing robust and discriminative 3D morphable models with a very deep neural network. In: Proceedings of the IEEE Conference on Computer Vision and Pattern Recognition, pp. 5163–5172 (2017)

34. Tun Trn, A., Hassner, T., Masi, I., Paz, E., Nirkin, Y., Medioni, G.: Extreme 3D face reconstruction: seeing through occlusions. In: Proceedings of the IEEE Conference on Computer Vision and Pattern Recognition, pp. 3935–3944 (2018)

35. Wang, S., Cheng, Z., Deng, X., Chang, L., Duan, F., Lu, K.: Leveraging 3D blendshape for facial expression recognition using CNN. Sci. China Inf. Sci **63**(120114), 1–120114 (2020)

36. Wang, Z.M., Tao, J.H.: Reconstruction of partially occluded face by fast recursive PCA. In: 2007 International Conference on Computational Intelligence and Security Workshops (CISW 2007), pp. 304–307. IEEE (2007)
37. Wu, W., Qian, C., Yang, S., Wang, Q., Cai, Y., Zhou, Q.: Look at boundary: a boundary-aware face alignment algorithm. In: Proceedings of the IEEE Conference on Computer Vision and Pattern Recognition, pp. 2129–2138 (2018)
38. Yongkang, Z., Jun, L., Zhiping, S., Na, j., Zhilei, L.: Tssn: temporal self-attention and self-supervision network for efficient action recognition. In: 2021 International Conference on Virtual Reality and Visualization (ICVRV), pp. 87–92. IEEE (2021)
39. Zeng, X., Peng, X., Qiao, Y.: DF2Net: a dense-fine-finer network for detailed 3D face reconstruction. In: Proceedings of the IEEE International Conference on Computer Vision, pp. 2315–2324 (2019)
40. Zhao, D., Qi, Y.: Generative face parsing map guided 3D face reconstruction under occluded scenes. In: Magnenat-Thalmann, N., et al. (eds.) CGI 2021. LNCS, vol. 13002, pp. 252–263. Springer, Cham (2021). https://doi.org/10.1007/978-3-030-89029-2_20
41. Zhou, X., Leonardos, S., Hu, X., Daniilidis, K.: 3D shape reconstruction from 2D landmarks: a convex formulation. In: Proceedings of the IEEE Conference on Computer Vision and Pattern Recognition, pp. 4447–4455. Citeseer (2015)

Patching Your Clothes: Semantic-Aware Learning for Cloth-Changed Person Re-Identification

Xuemei Jia[1], Xian Zhong[1,2]([✉]), Mang Ye[3], Wenxuan Liu[1], Wenxin Huang[4], and Shilei Zhao[1]

[1] School of Computer and Artificial Intelligence, Wuhan University of Technology, Wuhan, China
zhongx@whut.edu.cn
[2] School of Electronics Engineering and Computer Science, Peking University, Beijing, China
[3] School of Computer Science, Wuhan University, Wuhan, China
[4] School of Computer Science and Information Engineering, Hubei University, Wuhan, China

Abstract. Great advances have been observed in conventional person re-identification (Re-ID), which heavily relies on the assumption that the cloth remains unchanged. However, this dramatically limits their applicability in practical cloth-changed scenarios, leading to dramatic performance drop. Existing cloth-changed methods mainly exploit the body shape information, ignoring the relation between different clothes of the same identity. In this paper, we present a powerful semantic-aware patching strategy for clothes augmentation. It greatly enriches the cloth styles by randomly assembling the semantic cloth patches, simulating the appearances of the same person under different clothes. This augmentation strategy has two primary advantages: 1) It significantly reinforces the robustness against clothes variations without additional cloth collection. 2) It does not damage semantic structure, fitting well with cloth-unchanged scenarios. To further address the uncertainty in cloth changed, a Semantic Part-aware Feature Learning scheme is incorporated to mine fine-grained granularities, addressing the misalignment issue under changed clothes. Extensive experiments conducted on both clothing-changed and cloth-unchanged tasks demonstrate our proposed method's superiority, consistently improving the performance over various baselines.

Keywords: Person re-identification · Cloth-changed · Semantic-aware Patching Augmentation · Semantic Part-aware Feature Learning

1 Introduction

Given a target person image, person Re-ID aims to search for images of the same person from non-overlapping viewpoints. Conventionally, we assume pedestrians keep clothes unchanged in a short time under various cameras. Many deep

© Springer Nature Switzerland AG 2022
B. Þór Jónsson et al. (Eds.): MMM 2022, LNCS 13142, pp. 121–133, 2022.
https://doi.org/10.1007/978-3-030-98355-0_11

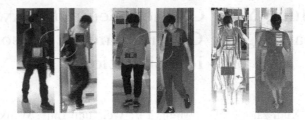

Fig. 1. Example pairs patched by Semantic-aware Patching Augmentation (SPA). The red boxes indicate semantic-aware patches we locate, and the green boxes denote the position where the patches are pasted. There are apparent appearance changes after patching the clothes, while it does not damage the semantic structure. (Color figure online)

learning [25,27] methods cope with difficulties in person Re-ID, such as occlusion, pose, and viewpoint variation. Moreover, these conventional Re-ID models are based on the assumption of unchanged clothes.

In practical long-term surveillance scenarios, a target person may consciously change the clothes for camouflage, *e.g.* a criminal probably disguises himself by changing the clothes when he escapes from the crime scene. This results in a challenging cloth-changed person Re-ID problem, where the same person might have different visual appearances with changing clothes across the multiple-camera network. In addition to the traditional difficulties, *e.g.* pose variations, misalignments, *etc.*, the cloth-changed person Re-ID suffers from two major challenges: 1) Simply using visual appearance information leads to easy filtration of the same identity with changing clothes. Meanwhile, different identities with similar clothes are likely to be misidentified. 2) There exists considerable uncertainty in cloth-changed patterns for different identities, *e.g.* suspects might completely change their clothes, partially replace the accessories or keep their clothes unchanged in some cameras. These properties significantly limit the applicability of existing Re-ID methods for cloth-changed scenarios.

Presciently, some researchers have noticed that issue and reported their approaches. Zheng *et al.* [26] proposed a joint learning framework to learn appearance and structure features, respectively. However, the use of appearance to perform re-ID is dominated by clothing color information. Then Li *et al.* [12] proposed to leverage gray-scale images to derive visual features of the same distribution across clothing color variations. However, they conducted experiments on conventional cloth-unchanged or synthesized cloth-changed datasets far from real situations. Recently, a few cloth-changed datasets have been released [8,14,20,22]. Among them, Huang *et al.* [8] introduced a two-step strategy by mining global and local features, incorporating with a conventional Re-ID method to handle clothes variation. [22] and [14] proposed similar ideas that disentangle identity-relevant and identity-unrelated features. These methods are built upon combining different visual cues, but their performance is limited by the dataset size and the variety of clothes changes. Compared to cloth-unchanged Re-ID, the data collection and annotation costs are greatly increased, involving an astonishing amount of laborious work. As a result, a corpus of cloth-changed Re-ID training data is costly to collect and typically limited in scale and variety. This motivates us to investigate a cost-efficient solution to enrich cloth-changed training data as shown in Fig. 1, promoting the advancement under wild scenarios.

This paper proposes a low-cost yet effective semantic-aware patching strategy for clothes augmentation (SPA), significantly enriching the training dataset without additional laborious annotation cost. It simulates appearances of the same identity wearing different outfits by generating semantic cloth patches, alleviating the discrepancies caused by various clothes. Meanwhile, the enriched diverse samples help improve robustness against clothes variations without extra clothes collection. This semantic patching does not undermine the semantic structures, making it fit well in cloth-unchanged scenarios. In addition, considering the misalignment caused by various clothes styles, we also further develop Semantic Part-aware Feature Learning (SPFL) module for global-local aggregation. It learns part-aware features via mining fine-grained parts, where the first branch extracts global features and the others exploit corresponding body parts information. Based on these, we propose a Semantic-aware Patching Augmentation Network (SPANet) to address the challenging cloth-changed Re-ID problem.

The main contributions of this work are threefold:

- We propose an effective data augmentation named SPA, which efficiently enriches cloth styles and enlarges the training set without introducing severe artifacts. This greatly enhances the robustness against clothes variations in Re-ID, seamlessly improving the accuracy of Re-ID without modifying the structure. Importantly, this operation works well with other data augmentations under various settings.
- We devise an adaptive SPFL strategy to aggregate the global and local features, capturing fine-grained parts. It effectively handles misalignments caused by varying clothes and poses.
- We demonstrate the consistent improvement of our method on various baseline methods, achieving state-of-the-art performance on both cloth-changed and cloth-unchanged Re-ID tasks. To the best of our knowledge, this is the first work to achieve this goal. It shows significance for practical model deployment under wild settings, providing essential guidance for future developments.

2   Related Work

2.1   Conventional Cloth-Unchanged Re-ID

Conventional person Re-ID without clothes variation has been widely researched. To obtain global and local cues, Wang et al. [18] design MGN to mine different granularities. Zhou et al. [29] propose OSNet to facilitate variable homogeneous and heterogeneous scales feature learning. Zheng et al. [26] adopt generative adversarial networks to generate new images by exchanged extracted person features, distilling id-related attributes.

Cloth-unchanged models mainly depend on different visual cues for identification that is sensitive to cloth changes. We enrich cloth styles and increase data diversity in this work, improving the robustness against clothes variations.

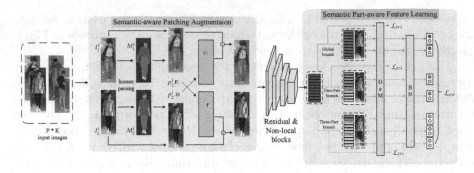

Fig. 2. Overview of SPANet, which mainly consists of SPA module and SPFL module. SPA utilizes human parsing models to generate segmentation maps M_1^i, M_2^i of images I_1^i, I_2^i. In the constraint of semantic segmentation, we randomly generate patches p_1^i, p_2^i from the same cloth semantic area. Then p_2^i is patched to I_1^i the same cloth semantic area to generate new patched image I_1^{i*}, and I_2^{i*} is similar. The patched images are transferred to subsequent feature extraction. The backbone of feature extraction is residual blocks inserted with non-local blocks. Furthermore, after residual blocks, SPFL is split into Global branch, Two-Part branch, and Three-Part branch. Global branch keeps the complete feature maps while Two-Part and Three-Part branches adopt semantic part-aware split operation according to the semantic segmentation of SPA.

2.2   Cloth-Changed Re-ID

Nowadays, researchers have paid more attention to clothing changed issues because of its broad practicality. Huang *et al.* [8] release a cloth-changed dataset Celebrities-reID and propose to mine both full images and body parts features. Yu *et al.* [22] introduce BC-Net to obtain biometric characteristics and clothes features, respectively. Additionally, they introduce a COCAS dataset aiming at pedestrian clothing changes. A polar transformation network is used in [20] to learn more fine-grained contour sketch features. [14] aims to eliminate clothing appearance features and focus on the body shape information. Hong *et al.* [7] propose to learn appearance and body shape knowledge by mutual learning.

To assist Re-ID under clothes variation, existing cloth-changed models leverage body shape and other biometric cues. In this work, we present SPA to alleviate the discrepancy among different outfits, retaining the semantic structure.

2.3   Data Augmentation

Data augmentation is a commonly used technique in deep learning, which enriches the training sets and enhances the robustness against variations. Fang *et al.* [1] paste objects in the neighboring of its original position, with additional jittering on scale and rotation. CutMix [23] augmentation cuts and pastes patches among training images where the labels are also mixed proportionally. Additionally, [28] presents to simulate occlusion by adding some random noises to promote model robustness and reduce data overfitting.

Differently, our Semantic-aware Augmentation is designed to simulating appearance changes of the person under different clothes based on semantic patching, which keeps semantic structure while enriching cloth styles. Besides, SPA also works well with other augmentation to further improve model performance.

3 Proposed Method

3.1 Overview

The architecture is shown in Fig. 2. Before feature extraction, Semantic-aware Patching Augmentation (SPA) module enriches cloth styles to promote robustness against clothes variations. As SPA module could be integrated with the most current Re-ID models, e.g. AGW [21], the backbone can be selected according to different requirements of accuracy and speed. After residual blocks, the subsequent network consists of three streams. The Global branch extracts the global feature from the whole image. The other two branches focus on semantic part-aware features. Semantic Part-aware Feature Learning (SPFL) strategy is designed to handle misalignments among clothes and pose variations and exploit fine-grained granularities. The details are shown in the following subsections.

3.2 Semantic-aware Patching Augmentation

The SPA we design enriches cloth styles and enlarges the training set without additional artifacts. Like common data augmentation, the SPA module preprocesses the images in the mini-batches before they are transferred to the following feature extraction network.

Different from randomly erasing patches in [28], we consider the constraint of human semantics. This not only enriches cloth styles but also avoids cloth structure damage. Given a person image, clothes occupy a large proportion, causing the importance of clothes information in identity representation. To alleviate the discrepancy clothes variation brings, we propose to patch clothing areas, generating more cloth styles of the same person. Thus, the patched images keep their body shape structure with their labels unchanged. Specifically, given two images I_1^i, I_2^i within the same identity i, we obtain semantic segmentation via off-the-shelf models. Then we randomly choose one clothing semantic that exists in both the two images I_1^i, I_2^i, e.g. coats and pants. Under the constraint of the two semantic regions, we distill two patches p_1^i, p_2^i. We also choose adaptive heights and widths of the semantic regions by the constraint of segmentation to avoid the patches being out of bounds to undermine the body contour. And then, we paste the patches on the other image, which is represented as: $(I_1^i)^* = f(\Theta(I_2^i), I_1^i)$ and $(I_2^i)^* = f(\Theta(I_1^i), I_1^i)$, where $\Theta(\cdot)$ denotes the operation of cutting patches, $f(\cdot, \cdot)$ represents to paste corresponding patches to the other image.

SPA could be conveniently integrated with the most current Re-ID models. Implementing with SPA reinforces the robustness of these models against clothes variations, retaining complete body shape information.

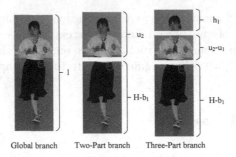

Global branch   Two-Part branch   Three-Part branch

Fig. 3. Illustration of the semantic-aware part segmentation. For Global branch, we do not adopt split operations. For Two-Parts branch, the body is stripped into upper body and bottom body in horizontal orientation. For Three-Parts branch, the body is striped into head, middle body, and bottom body. For Two-Parts and Three-Parts branches, there is some overlap of the feature map to keeping complete part features.

3.3 Semantic Part-aware Feature Learning

To handle misalignments caused by various clothes and poses, we design SPFL to aggregate global and local features. The semantic segmentation in SPA is utilized for more proper horizontal stripes.

For the mutual backbone, we adopt non-local attention blocks to capture long-range dependencies. We apply the default setting from [19] to insert the non-local attention blocks. We divide the next part after *res_conv4_1* block into three independent branches, which share the architecture based on ResNet-50 [5]. The first global branch applies no partition operation. Following ResNet-50, we employ down-sampling with a stride-2 convolution layer in *res_conv5_1* block, but following a generalized-mean (GeM) pooling [15] on the corresponding output feature map, which captures the discriminative features. After that, a 1×1 convolution layer with batch normalization (BN) [10] and rectified linear unit (ReLU) to reduce the 2048-dim features to 256-dim.

We abandon the stiff operation to split the body into equal horizontal strips. SPFL is designed to obtain more adaptive part features. As shown in Fig. 3, given a image with size of (H, W), we inference the relative complete two split body parts where the proportion $u_2 : H - b_1$ is operating on the corresponding feature maps. Similarly, the Three-Part branch utilizes the proportion $h_1 : u_2 - u_1 : H - b_1$ to split the feature maps. We adopt the eight 256-dim features, consisting of three global features from each branch and five local features from two part branches, to concatenate during the testing phases to form the final identity representation.

In line with semantic segmentation in SPA, SPFL exploits part-aware features of multiple granularities, thus retaining the completeness of main body parts.

3.4 Loss Function

Referring to typical person Re-ID models, we adopt triplet and cross-entropy loss. We employ cross-entropy losses to three global features before 1×1

convolution reduction and five-part features after reduction. Triplet loss is utilized for training three global features after reduction to enhance ranking performances. Referring to [18], we employ triplet loss on the three non-reduced 2048-dim global features.

4 Experimental Results

4.1 Datasets and Evaluation Metrics

The experiments to evaluate our proposal are conducted on two cloth-changed Re-ID datasets and mainstream cloth-unchanged Re-ID datasets.

LTCC-reID [14] is consisting of 17,138 person images of 152 identities. Specifically, 91 persons appear with 417 different sets of outfits in 14,756 images, and the others keep cloth-unchanged without outfit changes in 2,382 images.

PRCC-reID [20] contains 33,698 images from 221 people, which are captured by 3 cameras. Each person in Cameras A and B is wearing the same clothes. The person under Camera C wears different clothes from A and B.

Market-1501 [25] includes images of 1,501 persons captured from 6 different cameras. The dataset consists of 12,936 images of 751 identities for training and 19,732 images of 750 identities for testing. Only a single query setting is utilized.

DukeMTMC-reID [16] is collected from 8 cameras and contains 36,411 images that belong to 1,404 identities. It contains 16,522 training images from 702 identities, 2,228 query and 17,661 gallery images from the other 702 identities.

We employ mean average precision (mAP) [25], cumulative matching characteristics (CMC) [3], and mINP [21], which uses inverse negative penalty to measure the cost to find the hardest correct match.

4.2 Experiments Setup

We refer to [17] and resize input images to 384 × 128. We adopt PSPNet [24] pre-trained on look into person (LIP) dataset [2] to obtain human parts segmentation. Each mini-batch is sampled with randomly selected P identities and randomly sampled K images for each identity from the training set. Here we adopt recommendation[1] of P = 4 and K = 16 to train our proposed model. Among each mini-batch, we randomly generate K/2 patched images within the same identities. Thus, we replace the original training batch with the generated K/2 patched images and half the original images. We choose AGW [21] as our backbone. We employ concatenated reduced features from all branches during testing as the final feature representation of a pedestrian image.

For **LTCC-reID**, we follow the settings in [14], 1) *Standard Setting*: Images in testing set with the same identity and the same camera view are discarded when computing evaluation scores. 2) *Cloth-changed Setting*: Differently, not only the images with the same identity and camera view are discarded, but also the images with the same identity and clothes are discarded during testing phases.

---

[1] https://github.com/JDAI-CV/fast-reid.

Table 1. Comparison of rank-r accuracy (%) and mAP (%) performances with the state-of-the-arts on **LTCC-reID** and **PRCC-reID**. Bold and blue numbers are the best and second-best results.

Approach	Venue	LTCC-reID				PRCC-reID			
		Standard		Cloth-changed		Cloth-changed		Cloth-mixing	
		rank-1	mAP	rank-1	mAP	rank-1	mAP	rank-1	mAP
ResNet-50 [5]	CVPR '16	58.82	25.98	20.08	9.02	–	–	–	–
PCB [17]	ECCV '18	65.11	30.60	23.52	10.03	22.86	–	–	–
MGN [18]	ACM MM '18	70.59	35.01	29.85	13.87	49.31	60.16	75.59	79.66
OSNet [29]	ICCV '19	66.07	31.18	23.43	10.56	–	–	–	–
BOT [13]	CVPR '19	72.21	34.75	28.83	12.67	45.99	56.05	73.26	77.69
CESD [14]	ACCV '20	71.39	34.31	26.15	12.40	–	–	–	–
SBS [6]	arXiv '20	66.73	31.66	30.10	12.44	46.34	55.28	74.87	79.30
GI-ReID [11]	arXiv '21	73.59	36.07	28.11	13.17	–	–	–	–
FSAM [7]	CVPR '21	73.20	35.40	38.50	16.20	54.50	–	–	–
AGW [21]	TPAMI '21	71.81	34.91	32.40	14.23	49.59	59.79	74.27	78.68
SPANet (ours)		**74.65**	**37.90**	**38.78**	**18.22**	**54.76**	**65.54**	**76.42**	**81.81**

For **PRCC-reID**, similar to its original settings, we randomly choose one image of each identity in Camera A to form the gallery set for single-shot matching. Images in Camera C form the probe set for cloth-changed matching, images in Camera B and C form the probe set to perform cloth-mixing matching. Specially, we perform mixing matching using Camera B and C to compose the probe, which means both cloth-changed and cloth-unchanged identities are utilized in testing.

4.3 Experiments on Cloth-Changed Re-ID

To evaluate performance of our proposal, we compare our method with competitive Re-ID models on cloth-changed datasets **LTCC-reID** and **PRCC-reID**. The results are listed in Table 1. We select state-of-the-art models to demonstrate the effectiveness of our proposed network.

As shown in Table 1, on **LTCC-reID**, SPANet achieves the best performance, 74.65% and 37.90% of rank-1 accuracy and mAP, over all the listed state-of-the-arts. For standard setting, GI-ReID achieves the second-best results of 73.59% and 36.07% on rank-1 accuracy and mAP because of their insights of gait recognition. For cloth-changed setting, SPANet gives 6.38% 3.99% and 0.83% higher in rank-1, mAP, and mINP than AGW. Figure 4 shows the retrieval results of SPANet. SPANet easily finds images of changing clothes or accessories partially or totally. Images wearing different appear in the results, which proves the ability of our proposal to retrieve the cloth-changed images.

On **PRCC-ReID**, the performance of proposed SPANet is far beyond others. For cloth-changed setting, our SPANet performs excellently for the comparison of the released and evaluated results. Especially, our SPANet obtains 54.76% and 65.54% on rank-1 accuracy and mAP, which is 5.17% and 5.76% higher than AGW.

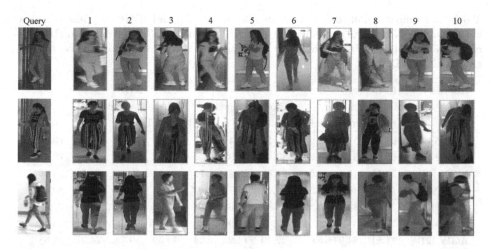

Fig. 4. Top-10 retrieved results of some example queries with the proposed method on **LTCC-reID** datasets by SPANet. The retrieved images are all from the gallery set but not from the same camera shot. The images with green borders belong to the same identity as the given query, and those with red borders do not. (Color figure online)

For the cloth-mixing setting, the proposed SPANet also achieves the best over all comparison models, showing the ability of SPANet for discriminative features.

4.4   Ablation Study

To verify effectiveness of each component in SPANet, we conduct extensive ablation studies on **LTCC-reID** and **PRCC-reID** based on the baseline.

As shown in Table 2 shows the results of some fashion Re-ID models complemented with SPA. On **LTCC-reID**, SPA promotes the performances under both settings. Especially for the cloth-changed, SPA gives significant performance gains of 2.30%, 3.57%, 5.61%, and 4.33% on rank-1 accuracy for SBS, MGN, BOT, and AGW, respectively. Moreover, SPA promotes mINP significantly, demonstrating that our SPA reinforces retrieving the hardest correct match. The outstanding performance gains on the two cloth-changed datasets prove that SPA significantly enhances the robustness against clothes variation.

Existing part-based methods have proved the significance of part-aware detailed information. However, our experiment results provide robust evidence that SPFL has excellent effects on cloth-changed issue, as shown in Table 3. Complementing SPFL on the baseline, the model achieves 0.80% and 3.04% performance gains of rank-1 for standard and cloth-changed setting on **LTCC-reID**. And the performance on **PRCC-reID** proves the effectiveness of SPFL as well.

4.5   Experiments on Cloth-Unchanged Re-ID

The results in Table 4 on two conventional datasets confirm that SPANet fits well with cloth-unchanged scenarios, outperforming the existing cloth-changed

Table 2. Comparison of rank-r accuracy (%), mAP (%), and mINP (%) performances with the state-of-the-arts implemented with SPA module on **LTCC-reID** and **PRCC-reID**. Note that mINP owns the same meaning as mAP because of the special setting on **PRCC-reID**.

| Approach | LTCC-reID | | | | | | PRCC-reID | | | |
| | Standard | | | Cloth-changed | | | Cloth-changed | | Cloth-mixing | |
	rank-1	mAP	mINP	rank-1	mAP	mINP	rank-1	mAP	rank-1	mAP
SBS [6]	66.73	31.66	4.93	30.10	12.44	2.24	46.34	55.28	74.87	79.30
SBS w SPA	67.53	31.44	5.22	32.40	12.82	2.54	46.93	56.18	73.52	79.13
MGN [18]	70.59	35.01	6.01	29.85	13.87	2.71	49.31	60.16	74.59	79.66
MGN w SPA	70.79	36.11	**6.85**	33.42	14.78	**2.87**	50.01	59.58	75.10	80.36
BOT [13]	72.21	34.75	5.39	28.83	12.67	2.19	45.99	56.05	73.26	77.69
BOT w SPA	72.41	34.89	6.04	34.44	14.90	2.27	**54.25**	**63.97**	74.21	78.87
AGW [21]	71.81	34.91	5.91	32.40	14.23	2.24	49.59	59.78	74.27	78.68
AGW w SPA	**75.66**	**37.00**	6.21	**36.73**	**17.65**	2.50	52.36	62.29	**78.11**	**82.69**

Table 3. Performance comparison of rank-r accuracy (%), mAP (%), and mINP (%) with different variants of our method on **LTCC-reID** and **PRCC-reID**. We denote AGW w SPA, AGW w SPFL by implementing baseline with SPA, SPFL. Note that mINP owns the same meaning as mAP because of the special setting on **PRCC-reID**.

| Approach | LTCC-reID | | | | | | PRCC-reID | | | |
| | Standard | | | Cloth-changed | | | Cloth-changed | | Cloth-mixing | |
	rank-1	mAP	mINP	rank-1	mAP	mINP	rank-1	mAP	rank-1	mAP
AGW [21]	71.81	34.91	5.91	32.40	14.23	2.24	49.59	59.78	74.27	78.68
AGW w SPA	**75.66**	37.00	6.21	36.73	17.65	2.50	52.36	62.29	**78.11**	**82.69**
AGW w SPFL	72.41	35.09	6.15	35.46	15.09	2.97	49.68	61.51	74.87	80.24
SPANet (ours)	74.65	**37.90**	**6.97**	**38.78**	**18.22**	**3.07**	**54.76**	**65.54**	76.42	81.81

and cloth-unchanged competitors. We list the state-of-the-arts to two types, cloth-changed models and conventional cloth-unchanged models.

On **Market-1501**, SPANet achieves 96.1% and 90.5% in rank-1 and mAP, which is 1.5% and 4.8% higher than the second-best CASE-Net [12]. Even for comparison with cloth-unchanged models, SPANet achieves the best, which proves its practical model deployment under wild setting. As well, SPANet gives the best results on **DukeMTMC-reID**. SPANet achieves 92.0% and 83.2% in rank-1 and mAP, which outperforms all cloth-changed and -unchanged models. The experiments conducted on these two cloth-unchanged datasets provide solid proof that our proposal is also a feasible solution for cloth-unchanged scenarios.

Table 4. Comparison of rank-r accuracy (%) and mAP (%) performances with the state-of-the-arts on **Market-1501** and **DukeMTMC-reID**. † denotes the methods conducted on cloth-changed task.

Approach	Venue	Market-1501			DukeMTMC-reID		
		rank-1	mAP	mINP	rank-1	mAP	mINP
2SF-BPart [8] †	IJCNN '19	91.2	77.2	–	–	–	–
ReIDCaps [9] †	TCSVT '20	92.8	78.0	–	83.8	67.8	–
CASE-Net [12] †	WACV '20	94.6	85.7	–	86.4	75.4	–
FSAM [7] †	CVPR '21	94.6	85.6	–	86.4	75.7	–
PCB [17]	ECCV '18	92.3	77.4	–	81.8	66.1	–
MGN [18]	ACM MM '18	95.7	86.9	64.6	88.7	78.4	45.4
DG-Net [26]	CVPR '19	94.4	85.2	–	86.3	75.1	
BOT [13]	CVPR '19	94.9	87.6	64.1	89.3	79.6	45.2
ISP [30]	ECCV '20	95.3	88.6	–	89.6	80.0	–
SBS [6]	arXiv '20	95.7	89.3	67.5	90.8	81.2	47.0
CDNet [4]	CVPR '21	95.1	86.0	–	88.6	76.8	–
AGW [21]	TPAMI '21	95.1	88.7	67.1	90.5	80.8	47.6
SPANet (ours)		**96.1**	**90.5**	**69.2**	**92.0**	**83.2**	**49.6**

5 Conclusion

We have proposed an effective data augmentation name SPA, which enriches cloth styles without additional data collection. SPA significantly reinforces the robustness against clothes variation, improving the performance with no semantic structure damage. Additionally, we design an adaptive SPFL strategy to capture fine-grained granularities by aggregating global and local features. The adaptive strategy properly handles the misalignments among various clothes. Extensive experiments conducted on cloth-changed and cloth-unchanged datasets prove our improvements on various baselines. Our work provides essential guidance for practical model deployment under wild settings.

Acknowledgement. This work was supported in part by the Department of Science and Technology, Hubei Provincial People's Government under Grant 2021CFB513, in part by the Hubei Key Laboratory of Transportation Internet of Things under Grant 2020III026GX, and in part by the Fundamental Research Funds for the Central Universities under Grant 191010001.

References

1. Fang, H., Sun, J., Wang, R., Gou, M., Li, Y., Lu, C.: Instaboost: boosting instance segmentation via probability map guided copy-pasting. In: ICCV (2019)

2. Gong, K., Liang, X., Zhang, D., Shen, X., Lin, L.: Look into person: self-supervised structure-sensitive learning and a new benchmark for human parsing. In: CVPR (2017)
3. Gray, D., Brennan, S., Tao, H.: Evaluating appearance models for recognition, reacquisition, and tracking. In: PETS (2007)
4. Hanjun Li, Gaojie Wu, W.S.Z.: Combined depth space based architecture search for person re-identification. In: CVPR (2021)
5. He, K., Zhang, X., Ren, S., Sun, J.: Deep residual learning for image recognition. In: CVPR (2016)
6. He, L., Liao, X., Liu, W., Liu, X., Cheng, P., Mei, T.: FastReID: a pytorch toolbox for general instance re-identification. arXiv:2006.02631 (2020)
7. Hong, P., Wu, T., Wu, A., Han, X., Zheng, W.S.: Fine-grained shape-appearance mutual learning for cloth-changing person re-identification. In: CVPR (2021)
8. Huang, Y., Wu, Q., Xu, J., Zhong, Y.: Celebrities-ReID: a benchmark for clothes variation in long-term person re-identification. In: IJCNN (2019)
9. Huang, Y., Xu, J., Wu, Q., Zhong, Y., Zhang, P., Zhang, Z.: Beyond scalar neuron: adopting vector-neuron capsules for long-term person re-identification. TCSVT **30**(10), 3459–3471 (2020)
10. Ioffe, S., Szegedy, C.: Batch normalization: Accelerating deep network training by reducing internal covariate shift. In: ICLR (2015)
11. Jin, X., et al.: Cloth-changing person re-identification from a single image with gait prediction and regularization. arXiv:2103.15537 (2021)
12. Li, Y., Luo, Z., Weng, X., Kitani, K.M.: Learning shape representations for clothing variations in person re-identification. In: WACV (2020)
13. Luo, H., Gu, Y., Liao, X., Lai, S., Jiang, W.: Bag of tricks and a strong baseline for deep person re-identification. In: CVPR Workshops (2019)
14. Qian, X., et al.: Long-term cloth-changing person re-identification. In: ACCV (2020)
15. Radenovic, F., Tolias, G., Chum, O.: Fine-tuning CNN image retrieval with no human annotation. TPAMI **41**(7), 1655–1668 (2019)
16. Ristani, E., Solera, F., Zou, R., Cucchiara, R., Tomasi, C.: Performance measures and a data set for multi-target, multi-camera tracking. In: Hua, G., Jégou, H. (eds.) ECCV 2016. LNCS, vol. 9914, pp. 17–35. Springer, Cham (2016). https://doi.org/10.1007/978-3-319-48881-3_2
17. Sun, Y., Zheng, L., Yang, Y., Tian, Q., Wang, S.: Beyond part models: person retrieval with refined part pooling (and a strong convolutional baseline). In: Ferrari, V., Hebert, M., Sminchisescu, C., Weiss, Y. (eds.) ECCV 2018. LNCS, vol. 11208, pp. 501–518. Springer, Cham (2018). https://doi.org/10.1007/978-3-030-01225-0_30
18. Wang, G., Yuan, Y., Chen, X., Li, J., Zhou, X.: Learning discriminative features with multiple granularities for person re-identification. In: ACM MM (2018)
19. Wang, X., Girshick, R.B., Gupta, A., He, K.: Non-local neural networks. In: CVPR (2018)
20. Yang, Q., Wu, A., Zheng, W.: Person re-identification by contour sketch under moderate clothing change. TPAMI **43**(6), 2029–2046 (2020)
21. Ye, M., Shen, J., Lin, G., Xiang, T., Shao, L., Hoi, S.C.H.: Deep learning for person re-identification: a survey and outlook. TPAMI (2021, early access). https://doi.org/10.1109/TPAMI.2021.3054775
22. Yu, S., Li, S., Chen, D., Zhao, R., Yan, J., Qiao, Y.: COCAS: a large-scale clothes changing person dataset for re-identification. In: CVPR (2020)

23. Yun, S., Han, D., Chun, S., Oh, S.J., Yoo, Y., Choe, J.: CutMix: regularization strategy to train strong classifiers with localizable features. In: ICCV (2019)
24. Zhao, H., Shi, J., Qi, X., Wang, X., Jia, J.: Pyramid scene parsing network. In: CVPR (2017)
25. Zheng, L., Shen, L., Tian, L., Wang, S., Wang, J., Tian, Q.: Scalable person re-identification: a benchmark. In: ICCV (2015)
26. Zheng, Z., Yang, X., Yu, Z., Zheng, L., Yang, Y., Kautz, J.: Joint discriminative and generative learning for person re-identification. In: CVPR (2019)
27. Zhong, X., Lu, T., Huang, W., Ye, M., Jia, X., Lin, C.: Grayscale enhancement colorization network for visible-infrared person re-identification. TCSVT (2021, early access). https://doi.org/10.1109/TCSVT.2021.3072171
28. Zhong, Z., Zheng, L., Kang, G., Li, S., Yang, Y.: Random erasing data augmentation. In: AAAI (2020)
29. Zhou, K., Yang, Y., Cavallaro, A., Xiang, T.: Omni-scale feature learning for person re-identification. In: ICCV (2019)
30. Zhu, K., Guo, H., Liu, Z., Tang, M., Wang, J.: Identity-guided human semantic parsing for person re-identification. In: Vedaldi, A., Bischof, H., Brox, T., Frahm, J.-M. (eds.) ECCV 2020. LNCS, vol. 12348, pp. 346–363. Springer, Cham (2020). https://doi.org/10.1007/978-3-030-58580-8_21

Lightweight Wavelet-Based Network for JPEG Artifacts Removal

Yuejin Sun, Yang Wang, Yang Cao$^{(\boxtimes)}$, and Zheng-Jun Zha

Department of Automation, University of Science and Technology of China,
Hefei 230027, China
yjsun97@mail.ustc.edu.cn, {ywang120,forrest,zhazj}@ustc.edu.cn

Abstract. In recent years, deep learning-based methods have made remarkable progress in removing blocking artifacts caused by JPEG compression. However, most of these methods directly learn the mapping between compressed images and corresponding clear versions in pixel domain by designing complex network structures and consuming huge computing power, which limits the application on mobile devices. To address this issue, we propose a lightweight wavelet-based network for JPEG compression artifact removal. Specifically, we observe that the signal removal operation in JPEG will introduce diverse distortion for different sub-frequency spectrums. Based on this, we propose a divide-and-conquer strategy to learn the mapping on each sub-frequency spectrum with a lightweight sub-network to reduce network parameters and save computation power. Furthermore, we speed up the inference time by integrating reparameterization technology. The comparison results with the state-of-the-art methods on mobile device demonstrate that our method achieves comparable deblocking performance with ×100 less computationally complex and ×50 faster inference time.

Keywords: Lightweight · Wavelet · JPEG artifacts removal

1 Introduction

The lossy image compression standards, *e.g.* JPEG, have been widely embedded in mobile devices for bandwidth and storage saving. However, the signal removal operation in JPEG will inevitably introduce blocking artifacts, which will degrade both perceptual quality and downstream high-level vision tasks, such as image classification [7]. Therefore, removing blocking artifacts and improving the quality of compression images is urgently needed and has drawn great attention in recent years [3,5,13,15,18,20].

Given a high-quality image, the JPEG compression scheme first translates the RGB image into YCbCr color space and divides the image into non-overlap 8 × 8 blocks. Then, discrete cosine transform (DCT) is performed on each block. After that, the DCT coefficients are quantized to remove high-frequency parts using the pre-defined quantification matrix. Finally, the compressed image is

© Springer Nature Switzerland AG 2022
B. Þór Jónsson et al. (Eds.): MMM 2022, LNCS 13142, pp. 134–145, 2022.
https://doi.org/10.1007/978-3-030-98355-0_12

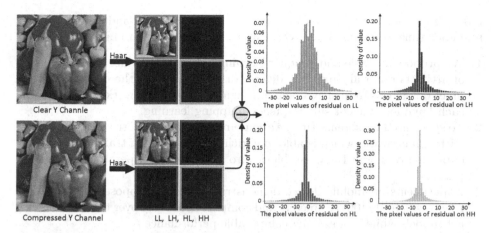

Fig. 1. The statistical histograms of residual pixel values between compressed image and corresponding clean version in each sub-band. The red, green, blue, yellow histograms denote the residual pixel values distribution of LL, LH, HL, HH channel, respectively. The distortion distribution in different sub-bands is greatly different, especially between low frequency and high frequency sub-bands. (Color figure online)

obtained by applying an inverse DCT to the quantized coefficients. However, the different quantification steps on frequency components will introduce diverse distortions on different frequency spectrums, which leads to the complex artifacts (*e.g.* blocking, banding effects, and blurring).

Recently, various learning-based methods have been proposed for JPEG artifacts removal [3,5,13,18,20]. However, most of these methods directly learn the mapping relationship between compressed images and corresponding clear versions in pixel domain. For example, ARCNN [3] first proposes a deep neural network to learn the nonlinear mapping in pixel domain. DnCNN [18] presents a residual network to achieve better performance on deblocking. Besides, considering the complexities of artifacts (*e.g.* blocking, banding effects, and blurring), learning mapping in pixel domain is extremely difficult, as shown in Fig. 1. To this end, diverse strategies are proposed to improve the performance of artifact removal. For instance, DCSC [5] utilizes dilated convolution to enrich feature space, which enables a single model to handle multiple compression ratios. RNAN [20] adopts non-local operations to enlarge the receptive field for more robust feature representation. However, these strategies inevitably introduce more parameters and computation power, which limits the applications on mobile devices.

To address the issue, we propose a **L**ightweight **W**avelet-**B**ased network (LWBNet) for removing the artifacts efficiently. Observing that distortion varies in different sub-frequency intervals, we decompose the compressed images in wavelet domain. In this way, a lightweight sub-network can be utilized in the special frequency domain to recover sub-frequency information efficiently. Besides, the reparameterization technology is utilized in multi-scale feature extracted block, which enriches the feature space in training phase and speeds up the inference time in testing phase. Overall, our contributions are mainly threefold:

1. We propose a divide-and-conquer learning strategy to reduce the complexity of artifacts removal caused by diverse distortions. After the conversion from pixel domain to frequency domain, a lightweight sub-network is employed in each band for efficient sub-frequency mapping learning.
2. To speed up the inference time, we combine the reparameterization technology with sub-network, which is able to enrich feature space in training phase and equivalently merge RepConv block into a single conv operator in inference phase.
3. Experiments on mobile device demonstrate that our proposed method only requires 1/10–1/100 parameters and computational cost over the state-of-the-art models while maintaining comparable performance.

2 Related Work

2.1 Frequency Decomposition

Frequency-based methods have been explored in various low-level tasks, including Super Resolution, Denoising, Derain, and Deblocking. Liu et al. [10] utilized a Haar wavelet decomposition to extract the multi-scale feature details in the frequency domain. Fu et al. [4] proposed a pyramid network to convert rainy images to Laplace pyramid domain, which transforms one hard problem into serval easier sub-problems. Liu et al. [9] adopted wavelet transform in demoiréing tasks and attained promising results on moire artifacts removal. Frequency domain knowledge is also explored in JPEG artifacts removal, Wang et al. [16] proposed a dual-domain framework to obtain better deblocking performance. Zhang et al. [19] presented dual-domain multi-scale CNN to take full advantage of redundancies on both the pixel and DCT domains. However, the existing frequency-related deblocking methods utilize frequency knowledge as an auxiliary term. The computational complexity of hybrid models will increase because of dual-domain learning, while our proposed method can reduce that through a divide-and-conquer way.

2.2 Multi-scale Feature Extraction

Multi-branch topology existing in Inception-style block is proved an effective method to improve the performance of CNN networks. Previous deblocking models adopted various methods to extract multi-scale features. For example, DCSC [5] utilizes multi-branch dilated convolutions to obtain a larger receptive field, which enables a single model to handle different multiple JPEG compression qualities. RNAN [20] designs non-local attention blocks in network to obtain correspondence information across the whole image. However, the above methods introduce more computational complexity and parameters, which increase the inference time on efficiency-sensitive devices.

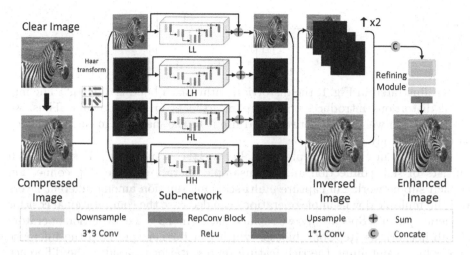

Fig. 2. The architecture of our proposed LWBNet. Compressed image is first converted to frequency domain through Haar transform. Each sub-network consists of a UNet style lightweight network with residual learning. The inversed image is concated with upsampled sub enhanced results, then feed to the refining module for better deblocking performance.

3 Proposed LWBNet

In this section, we first introduce the architecture of proposed LWBNet. Subsequently, we present the detailed descriptions of the different transformation processes for convolutional combinations of different branches (e.g. 1×1 following aftr 3×3 and 3×3 following after 1×1). At last, we describe the adopted loss function in detail. Figure 2 shows our networks architecture.

3.1 The Architecture

As shown in Fig. 2, The compressed image is first decomposed into four sub-frequency spectrums (LL, LH, HL, HH) with Haar transform. Then, a lightweight UNet [11] like network is devised and utilized on each sub-band to learn the mapping between compressed frequency component and corresponding clear version. After that, the inversed image is obtained by applying an inverse Haar transform to enhanced frequency components. Finally, the enhanced frequency components are upsampled ($\times 2$) and concated with the inversed image and feed to the refining module for better deblocking results.

We utilize Haar transform to convert the image from pixel domain to frequency domain efficiently. The Haar wavelet consists of four orthogonal filters, which are defined as:

$$F_{LL} = \begin{bmatrix} 1 & 1 \\ 1 & 1 \end{bmatrix}, F_{LH} = \begin{bmatrix} -1 & -1 \\ 1 & 1 \end{bmatrix},$$
$$F_{HL} = \begin{bmatrix} -1 & 1 \\ -1 & 1 \end{bmatrix}, F_{HH} = \begin{bmatrix} 1 & -1 \\ -1 & 1 \end{bmatrix}. \tag{1}$$

As illustrated in Fig. 1, the distortion within each band is different. The mix of all distortions introduces the complex artifacts in pixel domain. Thus, we propose a lightweight sub-network and use it to the mapping in each frequency band respectively.

As shown in Fig. 2, the proposed lightweight is in UNet [11] style, which consists of skip connection and downsample operations. The skip connection in each sub-network can capture multi-scale information among different layers and the multiple downsample operations can decrease the computational cost for efficiency pursuit. Specifically, we replace the normal 3 × 3 convolution operators in sub-network as RepConv blocks, which can further speed up the inference time while maintaining the rich feature representations. Besides, the difference between the compressed image and clean version usually is tiny, which is known to be the situation where residual learning excels. Thus, we combine the residual learning [6] with sub-network in each band for better performance.

After sub-frequency mapping learning in each band, we apply 2D IDWT to obtain the inversed image from wavelet domain to pixel domain. To further relieve the artifacts, we concatenate the enhanced frequency components and the inversed image, and feed them to the refining module. Note that the sub enhanced results are upsampled (×2). The refining module is composed of four simple Conv-Relu layers, which counts a small part of the overall computation.

3.2 RepCov Block

To further decrease the computational complexity, we employ the reparameterize technology [1,2] to build the RepConv block, which has the same performance while only requiring the inference time of a single conv block. As shown in Fig. 3, The key point of reparameterize conv block is to convert the multi-branch weight to a single conv before inference. The details of reparameterizing conv block are as follows:

Multi-branch in Training. Considering the computation limitation in mobile devices, low computation conv operators, e.g. 1 × 1 and 3 × 3, are suitable for deployment [2]. As shown in Fig. 3, the cascade of 1 × 1 and 3 × 3 can enrich multi-scale feature space during the training process. We adopt a sum operation for fusing multi-branch information at the end of the block.

Merge Between Convolutions. As explained in [1,2], a cascade of two convolution operations can be merged into a single conv. For a cascade of 1 × 1 and 3 × 3, the merge process can be written as:

$$W' \otimes X_{in} = W^{3\times3} \otimes \left(W^{1\times1} \otimes X_{in} \right), \tag{2}$$

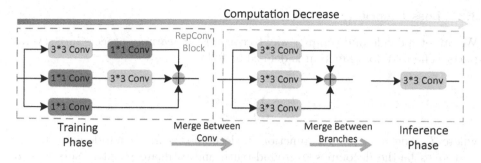

Fig. 3. Different modes of RepConv block in training and inference phase. The multi-branch conv block can capture multi-scale feature in training phase. The RepConv block can be merged into a single 3 × 3 conv operator to speed up the inference time.

where X_{in}, $\otimes$ denote input tensor and convolution operator, respectively. $W^{1\times1} \in \mathbb{R}^{B\times A\times1\times1}$ and $W^{3\times3} \in \mathbb{R}^{C\times B\times3\times3}$ mean the weights of 1×1, 3×3 conv. The merge process can be written as:

$$W' = W^{3\times3} \otimes Trans\left(W^{1\times1}\right). \tag{3}$$

where $Trans$ and $W' \in \mathbb{R}^{C\times A\times3\times3}$ represent the transposed operations and converted weight.

Similarly, the cascade of 3×3 and 1×1 can be merged as:

$$W'_i = \sum_{j=1}^{B} W_{ij}^{1\times1} * W_j^{3\times3}, 1 \leq i \leq C. \tag{4}$$

where $W^{3\times3} \in \mathbb{R}^{B\times A\times3\times3}$ and $W^{1\times1} \in \mathbb{R}^{C\times B\times1\times1}$ mean the weights of $3\times3, 1\times1$ conv, and the $W' \in \mathbb{R}^{C\times A\times3\times3}$ is the converted weight.

Merge Between Branches. Due to the linearity of convolutions, different branches can be easily added to a single conv [2]. The merger process among different branches can be formulated as:

$$W' \otimes X_{in} = W^1 \otimes X_{in} + W^2 \otimes X_{in} + ... + W^i \otimes X_{in}, \tag{5}$$

where the final merged conv weight W' can be calculated as:

$$W' = \sum_{k=1}^{i} W^k. \tag{6}$$

3.3 Loss Function

We adopt a divide-and-conquer way to convert the learning process into several parts. The total loss function is defined as follow:

$$L = \sum_{i=1}^{4} L_{w_i} + L_p, \tag{7}$$

where L_{w_i} denotes the loss function in decomposed frequency domain. Let s_i and $\hat{s}_i$ to be the decomposed ground-truth and estimate result of sub-band i. The L_{w_i} can be written as:

$$L_{w_i} = \|\hat{s}_i - s_i\|_2, \tag{8}$$

We further feed the enhanced results to refining module for better performance. The pixel loss can be written as:

$$L_p = \alpha \|\hat{y} - y\|_2 + (1 - \alpha) \|\hat{y} - y\|_1. \tag{9}$$

where $\hat{y}$ is the ground-truth and y is the final refine output. Since the MSE loss may cause the over-smooth effects, we add α for better balance. The weight parameter α is set to 0.5 in this work.

4 Experiments

4.1 Datasets and Settings

Datasets. Four datasets are used in our experiments, one for training and the others for testing. We randomly crop 18000 patches with the size 128×128 from DIV2K dataset (800 images) [14] for training. Following the previous setting, only the Y channel of YCbCr space is utilized. We conduct comparisons on two synthetic datasets, *i.e.* Classic5 (5 images) [17] and LIVE1 (29 images) [12]. To further evaluate the generalization ability, we test our method on *Twitter* dataset (10 images) [3], which consists of images having unknown complex artifacts caused by the uploading process.

Metrics. Same as [3], we employ peak signal-tonoise ratio (PSNR) and structural similarity (SSIM) for quantitative assessment. For efficiency evaluations, we report the inference time on a real mobile device with Snapdragon 865. We use ncnn, a high-performance inference computing framework optimized for mobile platforms, to get the CPU and GPU running time. We calculate the average running time for 10 loops for each model.

Table 1. The model inference time on Snapdragon 865 devices with input size of 224 × 224. Compared with state-of-the-art methods, our method has the lowest computation (around ×100 less) and faster running time (×50 fewer).

Methods	Param (M)	Flops (G)	CPU (ms)	GPU (ms)
ARCNN [3]	**0.12**	5.9	101	98
DnCNN [18]	0.59	28.1	643	575
MemNet [13]	2.91	146.3	1214	1220
DCSC [5]	6.07	304.1	2820	3070
RNAN [20]	8.90	312.9	NaN	NaN
Ours w/o reparameter	2.42	8.4	192	187
Ours	0.67	**3.6**	**28**	**60**

Implementation Details. Following previous works, We use the Matlab JPEG encoder to generate JPEG compressed images by setting the quality factor (QF) to 10, 20, and 30. Similar to [5], we train a single model with mixed training data to handle all these three JPEG qualities. Our model is training on a single 1080ti GPU with a batch size of 128. The learning rate is set to 0.0001 and the input image is randomly cropped to 128 × 128. We utilize the Adam [8] optimizer to optimize the model.

4.2 Experimental Results

We make a comprehensive comparison with ARCNN [3], DnCNN [18], Mem-Net [13], DCSC [5] and RNAN [20], both in quantitation and qualitation. Specially, we evaluate the running performance of all models on mobile device for efficiency comparison, as well as PSNR and SSIM.

Inference Time Evaluation. We conduct inference time experiments on mobile devices (Snapdragon 865) to explore the deployment potential among deblocking methods. Note that the CPU is usually better optimized on mobile devices, which may cause the situation that inference on CPU is faster than on GPU. The results are presented in Table 1. Among all the experimental methods, RNAN [20] and DCSC [5] achieve better performance at the cost of huge computational complexity. The Flops of RNAN and DCSC with input size of 224 × 224 are much larger than that in others. RNAN even fails to run due to the large memory cost in non-local operations. Although the computational complexity of DnCNN [18] and MemNet [13] is smaller than that in RNAN, it is still far from the real-time requirement on mobile devices. Compared with the above methods, our method requires much less computation, which is essential for deployment on mobile devices. Besides, the reparameterize technology can efficiently reduce the number of parameters (×5) and computation (×3) after branch merging.

Quantitative Evaluation. The quantitative results on PSNR, SSIM are represented in Fig. 4. Compared with ARCNN [3], our method gains 0.4 dB

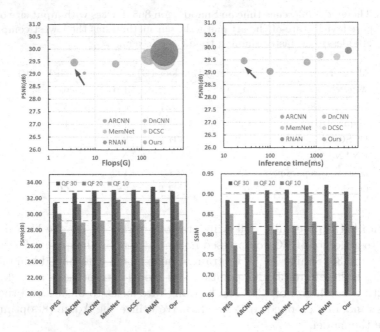

Fig. 4. Top left: the evaluation of PSNR and Flops on Classic 5 of QF 10, larger bubble represents more parameters. Top right: the evaluation of inference time and PSNR on Classic 5. Bottom left: the quantitative evaluation on LIVE1 dataset on PSNR metrics. Bottom right: the quantitative evaluation on LIVE1 dataset on SSIM metrics.

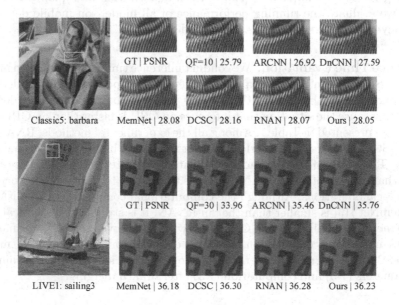

Fig. 5. Visual comparison on JPEG compressed images from synthesis datasets.

GT | PSNR   JPEG | 24.79   ARCNN | 25.09   DnCNN | 25.13

MemNet | 25.54   DCSC | 25.74   RNAN | 25.68   Ours | 25.59

GT | PSNR   JPEG | 25.17   ARCNN | 25.32   DnCNN | 25.19

MemNet | 27.54   DCSC | 25.20   RNAN | 27.16   Ours | 26.74

Fig. 6. Visual comparison on unknown compressed images from *Twitter* datasets.

Table 2. The comparison results with UNet trained in pixel domain. Our method achieves better performance on PSNR and SSIM.

Methods	Param (M)	Flops (G)	PSNR	SSIM
UNet [11]	0.61	3.54	29.23	0.799
Ours	0.67	3.60	**29.46**	**0.808**

improvement in Classic5 when QF is 10. Besides, our single model achieves comparable performance on LIVE1 dataset, compared with DnCNN [18] and MemNet [13].

Qualitative Evaluation. As shown in Fig. 5, our method can remove the artifacts and restore the details in *barbara*, *i.e.,* ours recovered stripe is clear and similar to that of state-of-the-art methods. We also experiment on the Y channel of unknown compression type dataset. As can be seen in Fig. 6, the ringing effects that existing around characters are reduced to a certain extend, which indicates that our method generalizes well in real-world situations.

4.3 Ablation Study

We conduct a series of ablation studies to verify the effectiveness of our method. All the models are tested on Classic 5 with JPEG qualities of 10. To verify the advantage of frequency-decomposed methods, we train an UNet [11] model in pixel domain whose params and flops are closed to ours for fair comparison. As shown in Table 2, the wavelet-based method outperforms the UNet in 0.20 dB on the PSNR metric, which demonstrates the effectiveness of wavelet-decomposition in deblocking.

We also perform the ablation studies on the components of loss function and modules. We use L_w to ensure the sub-frequency learning, and use L_p and

Table 3. Ablation on different loss functions and modules. The best results are highlighted in bold.

L_w	L_p	RepConv	Refine	PSNR	SSIM
with	w/o	w/o	w/o	29.02	0.796
w/o	with	w/o	w/o	29.17	0.797
with	with	w/o	w/o	29.28	0.800
with	with	with	w/o	29.38	0.803
with	with	with	with	**29.46**	**0.808**

refining module for better results. As shown in Table 3, both loss components, repconv block, and refining module contribute better performance.

5 Conclusion

In this work, we propose a divide-and-conquer strategy for designing lightweight deblocking models. Utilizing the observation that distortions vary in wavelet sub-bands, we employ Haar wavelet transform to convert the image to the wavelet domain. A lightweight sub-network is adopted in each sub for sub-frequency mapping learning. Furthermore, we utilize the reparameterization technology to speed up the running time in inference phase. Specially, we test the model on mobile devices to get actual running stats on computing-sensitive devices, rather than evaluating on a PC server. Compared with the state-of-the-art deblocking methods, our method achieves comparable performance with much faster inference time.

Acknowledgments. This work was supported by National Key R&D Program of China under Grant 2020AAA0105701, National Natural Science Foundation of China (NSFC) under Grants 61872327 and Major Special Science and Technology Project of Anhui (No. 012223665049).

References

1. Ding, X., Zhang, X., Han, J., Ding, G.: Diverse branch block: building a convolution as an inception-like unit. In: Proceedings of the IEEE/CVF Conference on Computer Vision and Pattern Recognition, pp. 10886–10895 (2021)
2. Ding, X., Zhang, X., Ma, N., Han, J., Ding, G., Sun, J.: RepVGG: making VGG-style convnets great again. In: Proceedings of the IEEE/CVF Conference on Computer Vision and Pattern Recognition, pp. 13733–13742 (2021)
3. Dong, C., Deng, Y., Loy, C.C., Tang, X.: Compression artifacts reduction by a deep convolutional network. In: Proceedings of the IEEE International Conference on Computer Vision, pp. 576–584 (2015)
4. Fu, X., Liang, B., Huang, Y., Ding, X., Paisley, J.: Lightweight pyramid networks for image deraining. IEEE Trans. Neural Netw. Learn. Syst. **31**(6), 1794–1807 (2019)

5. Fu, X., Zha, Z.J., Wu, F., Ding, X., Paisley, J.: JPEG artifacts reduction via deep convolutional sparse coding. In: Proceedings of the IEEE/CVF International Conference on Computer Vision, pp. 2501–2510 (2019)
6. He, K., Zhang, X., Ren, S., Sun, J.: Deep residual learning for image recognition. In: Proceedings of the IEEE Conference on Computer Vision and Pattern Recognition, pp. 770–778 (2016)
7. Hendrycks, D., Dietterich, T.: Benchmarking neural network robustness to common corruptions and perturbations. In: International Conference on Learning Representations (2018)
8. Kingma, D.P., Ba, J.: Adam: a method for stochastic optimization. arXiv preprint arXiv:1412.6980 (2014)
9. Liu, L., et al.: Wavelet-based dual-branch network for image Demoiréing. In: Vedaldi, A., Bischof, H., Brox, T., Frahm, J.-M. (eds.) ECCV 2020. LNCS, vol. 12358, pp. 86–102. Springer, Cham (2020). https://doi.org/10.1007/978-3-030-58601-0_6
10. Liu, P., Zhang, H., Lian, W., Zuo, W.: Multi-level wavelet convolutional neural networks. IEEE Access **7**, 74973–74985 (2019)
11. Ronneberger, O., Fischer, P., Brox, T.: U-Net: convolutional networks for biomedical image segmentation. In: Navab, N., Hornegger, J., Wells, W.M., Frangi, A.F. (eds.) MICCAI 2015. LNCS, vol. 9351, pp. 234–241. Springer, Cham (2015). https://doi.org/10.1007/978-3-319-24574-4_28
12. Sheikh, H.: Live image quality assessment database release 2 (2005). http://live.ece.utexas.edu/research/quality
13. Tai, Y., Yang, J., Liu, X., Xu, C.: MemNet: a persistent memory network for image restoration. In: Proceedings of the IEEE International Conference on Computer Vision, pp. 4539–4547 (2017)
14. Timofte, R., Agustsson, E., Van Gool, L., Yang, M.H., Zhang, L.: NTIRE 2017 challenge on single image super-resolution: methods and results. In: Proceedings of the IEEE Conference on Computer Vision and Pattern Recognition Workshops, pp. 114–125 (2017)
15. Wang, M., Fu, X., Sun, Z., Zha, Z.J.: JPEG artifacts removal via compression quality ranker-guided networks. In: IJCAI, pp. 566–572 (2020)
16. Wang, Z., Liu, D., Chang, S., Ling, Q., Yang, Y., Huang, T.S.: D3: deep dual-domain based fast restoration of JPEG-compressed images. In: Proceedings of the IEEE Conference on Computer Vision and Pattern Recognition, pp. 2764–2772 (2016)
17. Zeyde, R., Elad, M., Protter, M.: On single image scale-up using sparse-representations. In: Boissonnat, J.-D., et al. (eds.) Curves and Surfaces 2010. LNCS, vol. 6920, pp. 711–730. Springer, Heidelberg (2012). https://doi.org/10.1007/978-3-642-27413-8_47
18. Zhang, K., Zuo, W., Chen, Y., Meng, D., Zhang, L.: Beyond a Gaussian denoiser: residual learning of deep CNN for image denoising. IEEE Trans. Image Process. **26**(7), 3142–3155 (2017)
19. Zhang, X., Yang, W., Hu, Y., Liu, J.: DMCNN: dual-domain multi-scale convolutional neural network for compression artifacts removal. In: 2018 25th IEEE International Conference on Image Processing (ICIP), pp. 390–394. IEEE (2018)
20. Zhang, Y., Li, K., Li, K., Zhong, B., Fu, Y.: Residual non-local attention networks for image restoration. In: International Conference on Learning Representations (2019)

Shared Latent Space of Font Shapes and Their Noisy Impressions

Jihun Kang[1]([✉]), Daichi Haraguchi[1], Seiya Matsuda[1], Akisato Kimura[2], and Seiichi Uchida[1][ID]

[1] Kyushu University, Fukuoka, Japan
jihun.kang@human.ait.kyushu-u.ac.jp
[2] NTT Communication Science Laboratories, NTT Corporation, Atsugi, Kanagawa, Japan

Abstract. Styles of typefaces or fonts are often associated with specific impressions, such as heavy, contemporary, or elegant. This indicates that there are certain correlations between font shapes and their impressions. To understand the correlations, this paper constructs a shared latent space where a font and its impressions are embedded nearby. The difficulty is that the impression words attached to a font are often very noisy. This is because impression words are very subjective and diverse. More importantly, some impression words have no direct relevance to the font shapes and will disturb the construction of the shared latent space. We, therefore, use DeepSets for enhancing shape-relevant words and suppressing shape irrelevant words automatically while training the shared latent space. Quantitative and qualitative experimental results with a large-scale font-impression dataset demonstrate that the shared latent space by the proposed method describes the correlation appropriately, especially for the shape-relevant impression words.

Keywords: Font shape · Font impression · Shared latent space

1 Introduction

Font is multi-modal. This is because a font is comprised of not only a set of visible letter shapes (from 'A' to 'z') but also a set of impressions. Figure 1 shows several examples of fonts and their impressions from MyFonts dataset [1]. For example, the font 4-square is tagged with a set of impression words {heavy, headline, display, logo, square}. This is an interesting phenomenon in that a shape gives a specific impression; however, the correlation between shape and impression is not well studied in a reliable and objective data-driven analysis.

Our research aims to construct a *shared latent space* of the two modalities in order to understand their correlation. Figure 2 illustrates the shared latent space. Let $\mathbf{X}_i$ denote the i-th font (i.e., a set of images from 'A' to 'Z' of the i-th font) and assume a set of J_i impression words $\mathbf{W}_i = \{w_{i,1}, \ldots, w_{i,j}, \ldots, w_{i,J_i}\}$ are attached to the font $\mathbf{X}_i$. In the d-dimensional shared latent space, we expect

© Springer Nature Switzerland AG 2022
B. Þór Jónsson et al. (Eds.): MMM 2022, LNCS 13142, pp. 146–157, 2022.
https://doi.org/10.1007/978-3-030-98355-0_13

Fig. 1. Examples of font images with their impression words (from [1].)

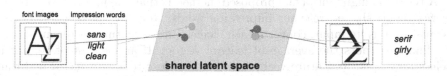

Fig. 2. The shared latent space of font shapes and their impressions. The set of font images $\mathbf{X}_i$ and the set of impression words $\mathbf{W}_i$ of the ith font are embedded in the space by the embedding functions f and g, respectively.

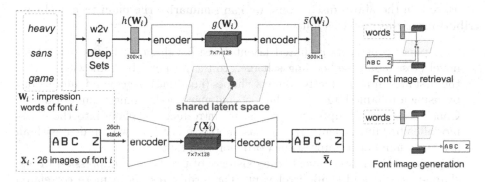

Fig. 3. Left: an overview of the proposed method. Right: examples of applications.

that $f(\mathbf{X}_i) \sim g(\mathbf{W}_i)$ for all i, where the embedding functions f and g give d-dimensional representations of $\mathbf{X}_i$ and $\mathbf{W}_i$, respectively. Therefore, the construction of the latent space is the task of getting the representation functions f and g that satisfy this proximity condition.

For constructing the shared latent space, we need to deal with the *noisiness* of the impression words. The noisiness comes from two reasons. First, the impression of a font is subjective and will be variable with its observers. The second and more serious reason is that impression words are often irrelevant to font shape. In Fig. 1, an impression *soccer* is attached to the font international. This impression might be attached because the font is used for the uniform of a soccer team. As revealed by this example, there are two types of impression words, *shape-relevant* and *shape-irrelevant*. The former type (such as *sans-serif* and *heavy*) is our target; however, the latter will disturb the construction of the shared latent space and its effect should be weakened.

This paper proposes a novel method for constructing the shared latent space while weakening the effect of noisy (i.e., shape-irrelevant) impression words. Figure 3 shows the overall structure of the proposed method. It is a cross-modal embedding scheme and comprised of two autoencoders for word and image modalities. These autoencoders are co-trained so that $f(\mathbf{X}_i) \sim g(\mathbf{W}_i)$, while guaranteeing accurate reconstruction at each modality. Once we construct the shared latent space, it can be used for several applications, such as font image retrieval and font image generation, as shown in Fig. 3; given a set of impression words, we can retrieve several existing font images or generate new font images.

A technical highlight of the proposed method is that it employs DeepSets [2] for weakening shape-irrelevant impression words. Roughly speaking, DeepSets accepts a set as its input, converts each element into a feature vector internally, and finally outputs the average of feature vectors. If an element of the set is useless for a task, its feature vector will become close to a zero vector and thus its effect on the final output is minimized. In our case, this set corresponds to a set of impression words, and the effect of the impression word that disturbs our task will be minimized. Note that DeepSets is also suitable to deal with the arbitrary number of impression words.

Based on the above discussions, we can summarize the main technical contributions of this paper as follows:

- This paper constructs a shared latent space for shape and impression by a novel cross-modal embedding scheme. To the authors' best knowledge, it is the first attempt to directly connect shapes (i.e., font images) and impressions by using a reliable large-scale dataset and machine-learning framework.
- Considering noisy impression words, we introduce DeepSets into the cross-modal embedding scheme. It also has another merit that we can deal with an arbitrary number of impression words for each font.
- Experimental analysis reveals the existence of two-type of impression words, shape-relevant, and shape-irrelevant. The former results in more correlated embedding in the shared latent space than the latter.
- Experimental results show that it is possible to retrieve and generate font images by specifying shape-relevant impression words.

2 Related Work

2.1 Font Shape and Impression

In the fields of psychology and marketing, the relationship between fonts and their impressions has been analyzed experimentally for many years [3–7]. These trials often use a small number of fonts. In fact, only 12 fonts are used in the rather recent trial [7]. Nowadays, analysis with larger font image datasets [1,8–10] has been conducted. Among them, the font-impression dataset by O'Donovan et al. [9] realizes impression-based font recommendation systems [11,12]. MyFonts dataset by Chen et al. [1] is a far more large dataset and used for impression-based font retrieval [1] and impression-specific font image generation [13].

The recent attempts are rather application-oriented and thus do not focus on the essential correlation between font styles and the impressions. To the authors' best knowledge, this is the first attempt to understand the correlation between the shape (, or image) $\mathbf{X}_i$ and the impression words $\mathbf{W}_i$ of the ith font by embedding them into the same d-dimensional vector space to satisfy $f(\mathbf{X}_i) \sim g(\mathbf{W}_i)$ as possible, while weakening the effect of shape-irrelevant noisy impression words.

2.2 Latent Space Embedding

In multi-modal modeling of images and words (or texts), many attempts have been made for shared latent space embedding of the images and words. Socher et al. [14] have proposed a model that segments and annotates images by mapping images associated with the words to a latent semantic space. The same group extended this idea [15] by incorporating a neural network-based representation learning scheme of the image modality. In this work, the word modality is encoded by a hand-crafted feature, and then the image modality is mapped to the fixed word modality. In the works focusing on neural language caption generation [16–18], images and texts are not embedded into the same latent space explicitly, but image features by Convolutional Neural Networks (CNNs) are used as an input of Recurrent Neural Networks (RNNs) that generate textual information.

In the document analysis research field, Almazán et al. [19] have published a pioneering work that a word image and its textual information are embedded into the same space for word spotting and recognition even in a zero-shot manner. Such an embedding strategy is nowadays extended to deal with a tough multi-modal task, called Text VQA [20]. Sumi et al. [21] constructed a shared latent space between online and offline handwriting sample pairs and proved that a stroke order recovery is possible via the shared latent space.

2.3 Representation Learning for a Set

When each training sample comprises a different number of elements without any specific order, some machine learning architecture that accepts a set as its input sample is necessary. DeepSets [2] has been proposed as a simple but powerful framework to deal with sets as samples. In recent years, Saito et al. [22] have proposed the architecture to use sets by capturing the properties from the basis of set matching mathematically and have tried novel fashion item matching using sets.

In this paper, we treat the impression words $\mathbf{W}_i$ attached to the ith font as a set. The number of the attached words is different among fonts, as shown in Fig. 1. In addition, the words have no specific order. We, therefore, use DeepSets to treat $\mathbf{W}_i$ as a set. Note that the other modality $\mathbf{X}_i$ is represented as a stack of images instead of a set because $\mathbf{X}_i$ always contains a fixed number of elements from 'A' to 'Z.'

3   MyFonts Dataset [1]

As the font dataset with impression words, we employ the dataset published by Chen et al., [1]. This dataset, hereafter called the MyFonts dataset, comprises

18,815 fonts collected at MyFonts.com. As shown in Fig. 1, each font is tagged with $0 \sim 184$ impression words attached by crowd-sourcing. This means that the impression words have a large variability according to the crowd-sourcing workers' subjective bias. The vocabulary size of the impression words is 1,824. As noted in Sect. 1, impression words are often shape-relevant (such as *heavy* in Fig. 1) but sometimes rather shape-irrelevant (such as *soccer*).

Since we need to train several networks as a function $g(\cdot)$ with sufficient samples, we removed non-frequent impression words attached to less than 100 fonts. Consequently, we used 451 impression words in our experiments[1]. In addition, we removed the dingbat (pictorial symbols) fonts and the circled fonts from the MyFonts dataset by manual inspections by three persons. We also removed fonts without any impression words (after the above non-frequent word removal). Consequently, we used 9,980, 2,992, and 1,223 fonts for training, validating, and testing, respectively. Hereafter Ω_{train}, Ω_{val} and Ω_{test} denote the training, validation, and test font sets, respectively. We used 26 capital letter images of 'A' to 'Z' in each font in the later experiment since we found several fonts where small letter images are collapsed.

4   Shared Latent Space of Font Shape and Impression

This section provides the method to train our model of Fig. 3. The training is organized in a two-step manner for faster and more accurate convergence. We first perform two independent training pipelines as an initialization of the cross-modal embedding scheme. More specifically, we independently train two different autoencoders for font shapes (the bottom pipeline of Fig. 3) and impression words (the upper pipeline). The latent vectors of those autoencoders correspond to $f(\mathbf{X}_i)$ and $g(\mathbf{W}_i)$, respectively. Second, the end-to-end co-training will be performed to embed those latent vectors into the shared space to satisfy the condition $f(\mathbf{X}_i) \sim g(\mathbf{W}_i)$, while keeping the autoencoders' outputs accurate enough.

4.1   Font Shape Encoding by Autoencoder

An autoencoder is used for generating the latent vector $f(\mathbf{X}_i)$ of the image modality, i.e., font shapes. As shown at the bottom of Fig. 3, the autoencoder accepts $\mathbf{X}_i$ as its input and generate $\bar{\mathbf{X}}_i$ via an intermediate compressed representation $f(\mathbf{X}_i)$. Both of $\mathbf{X}_i$ and $\bar{\mathbf{X}}_i$ are 26 images (stacked as 26 channels) and expected to be similar with each other, i.e., $\mathbf{X}_i \sim \bar{\mathbf{X}}_i$, in order to guarantee that $f(\mathbf{X}_i)$ carries the original shape information of $\mathbf{X}_i$ sufficiently. Note that $f(\mathbf{X}_i)$ is emitted from the autoencoder as a tensor of $7 \times 7 \times 128$, whereas it is flattened as a $d = 7 \times 7 \times 128 = 6,272$-dimensional vector in the shared latent space. In the following, these two representations are not distinguished unless otherwise mentioned ($g(\mathbf{W}_i)$ also).

---

[1] It does not guarantee that each of the training and test sets contains more than 100 fonts for each of the 451 impression words.

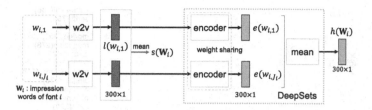

Fig. 4. Word vector by aggregating the word vectors of multiple impression words by word2vec (w2v) and DeepSets.

The encoder ($\mathbf{X}_i \mapsto f(\mathbf{X}_i)$) is based on ResNet18 (pre-trained with ImageNet) and the decoder ($f(\mathbf{X}_i) \mapsto \bar{\mathbf{X}}_i$) is comprised of several deconvolutional layers. (See Sect. 5.1 for the detail.) They are trained to minimize the reconstruction loss function $L_{\text{shape}} = \sum_{i=1}^{N} \|\mathbf{X}_i - \bar{\mathbf{X}}_i\|$, where N is the number of fonts used for training.

4.2 Noise-Tolerant Impression Word Encoding by DeepSets

Like the image modality, an autoencoder is used for generating the impression word vectors $g(\mathbf{W}_i)$. However, the word modality requires extra modules to accept an arbitrary number of impression words $\mathbf{W}_i = \{w_{i,1}, \ldots, w_{i,j}, \ldots, w_{i,J_i}\}$ as its input. Moreover, each impression word $w_{i,j}$ should be converted to a semantic vector so that similar impression words give similar effects to the system. Therefore, as shown in Fig. 4, the impression word $w_{i,j}$ is converted to a semantic vector $l(w_{i,j})$ by Word2vec [23] (pretrained by Google News dataset), and then all the semantic vectors are aggregated to a single fixed-dimensional vector $h(\mathbf{W}_i)$ by DeepSets [2].

Figure 4 shows how DeepSets converts the J_i semantic vectors $\{l(w_{i,j})|j = 1, \ldots, J_i\}$ into a single vector $h(\mathbf{W}_i)$. DeepSets has two functions: a trainable encoding scheme, or representation learning, and an aggregation scheme. The former is a deep neural network and gives a new representation $e(w_{i,j})$ for the word2vec vector $l(w_{i,j})$. The latter is the simple averaging process $h(\mathbf{W}_i) = \sum_j e(w_{i,j})/J_i$. This simple aggregation scheme allows accepting any number of impression words.

The most promising property of DeepSets for our task is that it can automatically learn the feasibility of impression words for constructing the shared latent space. Therefore, if an impression word $w_{i,j}$ is shape-irrelevant and disturbs the construction, its effect will be weakened. As the result, even though the relationship $f(\mathbf{X}_i) \sim g(w_{i,j})$ will not hold for the shape-irrelevant word $w_{i,j}$, the relationship will still hold for most shape-relevant words.

As shown at the top of Fig. 3, the autoencoder for the impression word modality accepts $h(\mathbf{W}_i)$ as its input and derives the latent representation $g(\mathbf{W}_i)$. Note that if we train the autoencoder and DeepSets in an end-to-end manner to minimize the reconstruction loss of $h(\mathbf{W}_i)$, it results in the trivial solution that $h(\mathbf{W}_i) = \bar{h}(\mathbf{W}_i) = 0$. We, therefore, train them to minimize the loss function

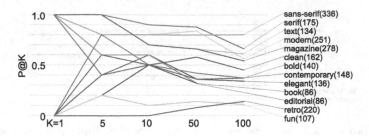

Fig. 5. P@K(↑) for several impression words. The parenthesized number is the number of test fonts having the impression word.

$L_{\text{impression}} = \sum_{i=1}^{N} \|s(\mathbf{W}_i) - \bar{s}(\mathbf{W}_i)\|$, where $s(\mathbf{W}_i) = \sum_j l(w_{i,j})/J_i$ (as shown in Fig. 4) and $\bar{s}(\mathbf{W}_i)$ is the decoder output.

4.3 Co-Training for the Shared Latent Space

After the pre-training of the autoencoder for both modalities, all the modules of both modalities are co-trained to construct the shared latent space. From its purpose to have $f(\mathbf{X}_i) \sim g(\mathbf{W}_i)$, we have the loss function $L_{\text{share}} = \sum_{i=1}^{N} \|f(\mathbf{X}_i) - g(\mathbf{W}_i)\|$. Consequently, the overall loss function of the proposed method becomes $L = L_{\text{shape}} + L_{\text{impression}} + L_{\text{share}}$. In the process of minimizing the loss function L, the weights of all autoencoders and DeepSets are trained simultaneously. During this, we expect that the effect of the shape-irrelevant impression words that have no clear correlation with font shapes will be minimized in DeepSets.

5 Experimental Results

5.1 Implementation Details

For the image modality, the encoder $(\mathbf{X}_i \mapsto f(\mathbf{X}_i))$ is ResNet18 (pre-trained by ImageNet) that have additional convolution layer at the last whose kernel size is 1×1 and number of channel is 128. The decoder $(f(\mathbf{X}_i) \mapsto \bar{\mathbf{X}}_i)$ is $D_{(512,1,0)}^{1 \times 1}$–R–$D_{(256,2,1)}^{4 \times 4}$–R–$D_{(128,2,1)}^{4 \times 4}$–R–$D_{(64,2,1)}^{4 \times 4}$–R–$D_{(32,2,1)}^{4 \times 4}$–R–$D_{(26,2,1)}^{4 \times 4}$ where D and R show a deconvolution layer and a ReLU function respectively. The parenthesized description shows (channels, stride, padding) and the superscript shows the kernel size. For the impression word modality, the encoder $(h(\mathbf{W}_i) \mapsto g(\mathbf{W}_i))$ is $F_{(1024)}$–R–$F_{(2048)}$–R–$F_{(6272)}$, and the decoder $(g(\mathbf{W}_i) \mapsto \bar{s}(\mathbf{W}_i))$ is $F_{(2048)}$–R–$F_{(1024)}$–R–$F_{(300)}$ where F shows a fully-connected layer. Note that the parenthesized description shows hidden units.

The entire network is trained by the training font set Ω_{train} (9,980 fonts) and tested by the test set Ω_{test} (1,223 fonts). The hyper-parameters and the training epochs are optimized by Ω_{val} (2,992 fonts).

Table 1. Average retrieval rank, where (*) indicates a similar setup to [15].

Method	$R_{\text{image}\rightarrow\text{word}}$	$R_{\text{word}\rightarrow\text{image}}$
Independent	608.7	612.5
Image $\mapsto$ Word(*)	608.1	612.2
Word $\mapsto$ Image(*)	516.9	553.0
Proposed	**172.6**	**356.6**

5.2 Quantitative Analysis

We have conducted font image retrieval from a given set of impression words, which is an application task shown in Fig. 3. If a font shape $\mathbf{X}_i$ and its corresponding impression words $\mathbf{W}_i$ are embedded appropriately while satisfying $f(\mathbf{X}_i) \sim g(\mathbf{W}_i)$, we can retrieve the font $\mathbf{X}_i$ from $\mathbf{W}_i$ by a simple nearest neighbor search in the shared latent space. In the following, we use a simpler setup that uses only a single impression word as the query for the retrieval. This setup allows us to understand how individual impression words are more shape-relevant or irrelevant.

Figure 5 shows the quantitative retrieval performance on the test set $\mathbf{\Omega}_{\text{test}}$. The performance is measured by precision at K (P@K) at different K. P@K indicates the ratio of the correct fonts among K retrieved fonts. More specifically, we first retrieve the K nearest fonts for the specified impression word w by the nearest neighbor search in the latent space. Therefore, each retrieved font X will satisfy $f(\mathbf{X}) \sim g(w)$. Then, if a font X has the impression word w in its tag set, it is a correctly retrieved font. If P@K is 1, all the K-neighboring font shapes have the impression word w in their ground-truth.

Figure 5 shows P@K for 13 impression words which are 11 words with the highest P@10 and two words, *retro* and *fun*, with rather lower P@10 values (0 and 0.1, respectively). Most of the 11 words with higher P@10 are obviously shape-relevant words, such as *serif*, *sans-serif*, and *bold*. This proves that our framework can successfully learn the representation describing the relationship between font shapes and their impressions. It is also noteworthy that more subjective impression words such as *modern* and *elegant*, have a high P@10 value. Although the "elegant"ness of a font may vary among people, this result indicates there are common shape-relevant characteristics about it.

Table 1 shows a more overall evaluation result of font image retrieval performance. By giving an impression word set $\mathbf{W}_i$ of the i-th test font as a query, all the images $\mathbf{X} \in \mathbf{\Omega}_{\text{test}}$ are then ranked by the distance $\|f(\mathbf{X}) - g(\mathbf{W}_i)\|$. Then, the rank r_i of the correct image $\mathbf{X}_i$ among $|\mathbf{\Omega}_{\text{test}}|$ images is determined. Finally, the average retrieval rank $R_{\text{word}\rightarrow\text{image}} = \sum r_i/|\mathbf{\Omega}_{\text{test}}|$ is the evaluation metric in this evaluation. In a similar manner, we can obtain the average rank $R_{\text{image}\rightarrow\text{word}}$ for the task of word retrieval with a given font image.

To our best knowledge, this is the first attempt at the cross-modal embedding of font impression and font shape into the shared latent space; therefore, there is no appropriate comparative baseline for this study. We, therefore, consider the following ablation cases to confirm the advantage of the proposed method.

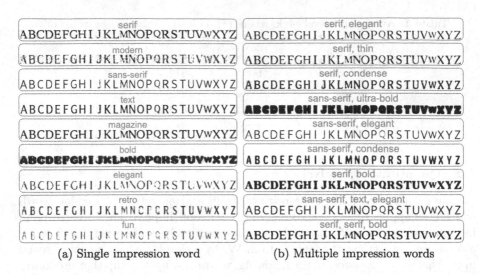

(a) Single impression word   (b) Multiple impression words

Fig. 6. Generating images from a single impression word and multiple impression words. Note that *retro* and *fun* are shape-irrelevant words with lower P@K, whereas the others are shape-relevant.

- Proposed: $f(\mathbf{X}_i)$ and $g(\mathbf{W}_i)$ are embedded by the co-trained encoder (Sect. 4.3).
- Independent: $f(\mathbf{X}_i)$ and $g(\mathbf{W}_i)$ are embedded by the encoders by the initial training steps (Sects. 4.1 and 4.2). No co-training has been made.
- Image $\mapsto$ Word: After initializing the encoders, the encoder for the word modality is fixed. The encoder and decoder of the image modality are then trained so that $f(\mathbf{X}_i) \sim g(\mathbf{W}_i)$. This setup is very similar to a well-known previous research named cross-modal transfer [15].
- Word $\mapsto$ Image: The opposite of the Image $\mapsto$ word setting. After initializing the encoder for the image modality, the encoder for the image modality is fixed. The encoder and decoder of the word modality are then trained so that $f(\mathbf{X}_i) \sim g(\mathbf{W}_i)$.

Table 1 indicates that the proposed method greatly outperformed the others. It also indicates that both Image $\mapsto$ Word and Word $\mapsto$ Image settings did not work well, which implies that our proposal with joint optimization of cross-modal autoencoders was a key for obtaining meaningful representations.

5.3 Font Image Generation with Specific Impressions

As shown in Fig. 3, we can use the shared latent space for generating font images with specific impressions. Feeding $g(\mathbf{W}_i)$ to the decoder of the image modality, we can generate the alphabet images from 'A' to 'Z' in a stacked manner. This is not only an interesting application but also a test to understand how the cross modal embedding is successful for each impression word. If a generated font

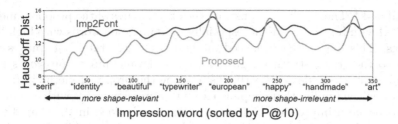

Fig. 7. Quality of the generated font image for each impression word. The quality is measured by Hausdorff distance ($\downarrow$). The words are sorted by the P@10 ranking, i.e., shape-relevance.

image for a word w is not appropriate, it indicates that w is a shape-irrelevant word and thus $f(\mathbf{X}) \not\sim g(w)$.

Figure 6(a) shows the results when generating font images with a single impression word. For the shape-relevant words such as *serif* to *sans-serif*, legible font images with the specified impression are generated successfully, thanks to the property $f(\mathbf{X}) \sim g(w)$. We obtained the expected results also for shape-irrelevant words such as *fun* and *retro*. Since there is no specific trend in the shapes for shape-irrelevant words, the generated font images are in a neutral style. Figure 6(b) shows the results when generating font images with multiple impression words. The font images generated by specifying two shape-relevant words such as (*serif, thin*) and (*sans-serif* and *bold*) become a mixed style successfully. The last example shows the case that the same word is specified twice; according to the nature of DeepSets, we can strengthen an impression by this strategy.

We evaluated the quality of generated font images quantitatively by Hausdorff distance. We compared the proposed method with the Impressions2Font [13], which is a GAN-based method for generating font images from impression words. In this experiment, we generate font images from each impression word w of a test font $\mathbf{X}$ by using the proposed method and Impression2Font, respectively[2], and then compare the generated image with $\mathbf{X}$. For the comparison by Hausdorff distance, the generated images are binarized by the Otsu method and then converted to edge images by the Canny method. The Hausdorff distance is calculated at each of 26 alphabets and then median over them[3].

Figure 7 shows the experimental results, where the horizontal axis corresponds to the impression word w sorted by the P@10 ranking for the image

---

[2] Precisely speaking, 34 compounded impression words, such as *caps-only* and *t-shirt*, are not acceptable by Impression2Font and thus omitted in the evaluation. Moreover, since we use P@10 in the evaluation of Fig. 7, we also remove the impression words attached only to less than 10 test fonts. Consequently, we used 350 impression words in this experiment.

[3] Impression2Font is GAN and thus can generate different images with different random value inputs. Therefore, we used 10 random value inputs sampled from a standard normal distribution and generate 10×26 images. Consequently, we use the median of all 260 Hausdorff distance values.

retrieval task[4]. The results demonstrate the effectiveness of the proposed method compared with Impression2Font, especially for impression words with high P@10 rankings. This means the proposed method could generate font images more similar to the ground-truth images for shape-relevant impression words w. As the ranking of P@K decreases, the distance by the proposed method gradually increases, which implies that shape-irrelevant impression words with a weak relationship between impression and shape are not embedded in the shared space. In other words, this result simply reflects the fact that it is difficult to estimate the font shape from shape-irrelevant words.

6 Conclusion

This paper showed that it is possible to construct a shared latent space where a font shape image and its multiple impression words are embedded as similar vectors. Through the shared latent space, we can handle font shapes and their impressions in a unified manner, which can lead us to generate and retrieve font images with specific fonts. Technically, we need to deal with shape-irrelevant impression words because they might disturb the unification; for this purpose, we incorporate DeepSets that can automatically weaken their effect. Experimental results revealed the existence of shape-relevant and shape-irrelevant impression words. The shape-relevant words give a higher correlation with their corresponding font shapes. The experimental results also show the possibility of impression-specific font retrieval and font generation by specifying shape-relevant impressions.

Future work will focus on additional experiments of font impression evaluation by translating font images to impression words via the shared latent space. We are also planning to standardize the impression words based on their degree of shape-relevance.

References

1. Chen, T., Wang, Z., Xu, N., Jin, H., Luo, J.: Large-scale tag-based font retrieval with generative feature learning. In: ICCV, pp. 9116–9125 (2019)
2. Zaheer, M., Kottur, S., Ravanbakhsh, S., Poczos, B., Salakhutdinov, R.R., Smola, A.J.: Deep sets. In: NIPS, pp. 3394–3404 (2017)
3. Childers, T.L., Jass, J.: All dressed up with something to say: effects of typeface semantic associations on brand perceptions and consumer memory. J. Consumer Psychol. **12**(2), 93–106 (2002)
4. Doyle, J.R., Bottomley, P.A.: Mixed messages in brand names: separating the impacts of letter shape from sound symbolism. Psychol. Market. **28**(7), 749–762 (2011)
5. Lewis, C., Walker, P.: Typographic influences on reading. British J. Psychol. **80**(2), 241–257 (1989)

---

[4] Since the original transitions of the Hausdorff distance values show more jaggedness that hides their general trends, we applied a smoothing filter to the original transitions for getting the curves of Fig. 7.

6. Shaikh, D., Chaparro, B.: Perception of fonts: perceived personality traits and appropriate uses. In: Digital Fonts and Reading, chapter 13, pp. 226–247. World Scientific (2016)
7. Velasco, C., Woods, A.T., Hyndman, S., Spence, C.: The taste of typeface. i-Perception 6(4), 1–10 (2015)
8. Shinahara, Y., Karamatsu, T., Harada, D., Yamaguchi, K., Uchida, S.: Serif or sans: Visual font analytics on book covers and online advertisements. In: ICDAR, pp. 1041–1046 (2019)
9. O'Donovan, P., Lībeks, J., Agarwala, A., Hertzmann, A.: Exploratory font selection using crowdsourced attributes. ACM Trans. Graph. 33(4), 1–9 (2014)
10. Ikoma, M., Iwana, B.K., Uchida, S.: Effect of text color on word embeddings. In: DAS, pp. 341–355 (2020)
11. Choi, S., Aizawa, K., Sebe, N: Fontmatcher: font image paring for harmonious digital graphic design. In: IUI, pp. 37–41 (2018)
12. Shirani, A., Dernoncourt, F., Echevarria, J., Asente, P., Lipka, N., Solorio, T.: Let me choose: from verbal context to font selection. In: ACL, pp. 8607–8613 (2020)
13. Matsuda, S., Kimura, A., Uchida, S.: Impressions2font: generating fonts by specifying impressions. In: ICDAR (2021)
14. Socher, R., Fei-Fei, L.: Connecting modalities: semi-supervised segmentation and annotation of images using unaligned text corpora. In: CVPR, pp. 966–973 (2010)
15. Socher, R., Ganjoo, M., Manning, C.D., Ng, A.: Zero-shot learning through cross-modal transfer. In: NIPS, pp. 935–943 (2013)
16. Fang, H., et al.: From captions to visual concepts and back. In: CVPR, pp. 1473–1482 (2015)
17. Karpathy, A., Fei-Fei, L.: Deep visual-semantic alignments for generating image descriptions. In: CVPR, pp. 3128–3137 (2015)
18. Vinyals, O., Toshev, A., Bengio, S., Erhan, D.: Show and tell: a neural image caption generator. In: CVPR, pp. 3156–3164 (2015)
19. Almazán, J., Gordo, A., Fornés, A., Valveny, E.: Word spotting and recognition with embedded attributes. IEEE Trans. Patt. Anal. Mach. Intell. 36(12), 2552–2566 (2014)
20. Biten, A.F., et al.: Scene text visual question answering. In: ICCV, pp. 4291–4301 (2019)
21. Sumi, T., Iwana, B.K., Hayashi, H., Uchida, S.: Modality conversion of handwritten patterns by cross variational autoencoders. In: ICDAR, pp. 407–412 (2019)
22. Saito, Y., Nakamura, T., Hachiya, H.: Exchangeable deep neural networks for set-to-set matching and learning. In: ECCV, pp. 626–646 (2020)
23. Mikolov, T., Sutskever, I., Chen, K., Corrado, G.S., Dean, J.: Distributed representations of words and phrases and their compositionality. In: NIPS, pp. 3111–3119 (2013)

Reconstructing 3D Contour Models of General Scenes from RGB-D Sequences

Weiran Wang, Huijun Di$^{(\boxtimes)}$, and Lingxiao Song

Beijing Laboratory of Intelligent Information Technology, School of Computer Science and Technology, Beijing Institute of Technology, Beijing 100081, China
{verawang,ajon,3120191041}@bit.edu.cn

Abstract. General 3D reconstruction methods use voxels, surfels, or meshes to represent the 3D model of a given scene. These surface-based methods are vulnerable to the loss of boundary details, which affects the completeness of the reconstructed model. In this paper, we focus on the boundary information of the scene and propose a novel method to reconstruct 3D models by using 3D contours extracted from input image sequences. We design a robust frame-to-model contour matching algorithm to solve the problem of finding many-to-many contour correspondences between different frames, and use contour-enhanced optimization to obtain more accurate camera poses. In order to make the reconstructed model more expressive of structural information, we propose a contour fusion algorithm that considers the connections between 3D contours. Compared with other methods which use straight lines or curve segments to reconstruct the scene model, our method can generate a more complete and regular 3D contour model with topological relationship. Experiments on several public datasets demonstrate the effectiveness of our method for both modeling and pose estimation.

Keywords: 3D Reconstruction · Topological relationship · 3D contour model

1 Introduction

3D reconstruction is a computer vision task which aims to recover 3D information from image sequences. It has been widely applied in the fields of augmented reality (AR), virtual reality (VR), robot navigation and automatic driving. General approaches represent the scene with voxels [3], surfels [27,29] or meshes [11,21], which can achieve high-quality surface reconstruction. However, their equal treatment of surfaces and boundaries easily leads to the loss of boundary details, affecting the completeness of the reconstructed model. The boundary, as a structural representation, can provide geometric constraints for the internal surface.

A few works have been proposed to represent the scene with edge features extracted from boundaries, which are generally parameterized by straight lines [7,8,18] or curves [1,4,12,17,24,26]. Since curves can parameterize scene

© Springer Nature Switzerland AG 2022
B. Þór Jónsson et al. (Eds.): MMM 2022, LNCS 13142, pp. 158–170, 2022.
https://doi.org/10.1007/978-3-030-98355-0_14

boundaries of various shapes, they are more attractive than straight lines to represent the structural information. According to different targets and techniques, the curve-based methods can be further categorized into: edge-based SLAM (Simultaneous Localization and Mapping) methods, the reconstruction of general scenes (e.g., indoor scenes) and the reconstruction of thin structures.

Edge-based SLAM methods [9,19,20,25,33] use edge features to achieve more robust localization. However, SLAM pays more attention to the accuracy of real-time localization than general 3D reconstruction methods, and weakens the mapping process. Therefore, these methods usually do not produce a complete edge map output. **The methods of reconstructing general scenes** [1,4, 12,17,24,26] correlate and reconstruct image curves across views to generate 3D curve structure models. Though the resulting curves are visually attractive, they are always discrete and lack inter-curve organization [26], which cannot be regarded as a complete framework of the internal surface. **The approaches for reconstructing thin structures**, such as [13–15,23,28], can construct complete skeletons of thin structures with curves meeting at junctions. Though the generated 3D models are exquisite, these methods lack generality, e.g.,they are not suitable for general scenes. Therefore, a robust edge-based reconstruction method is required to achieve accurate on-line localization and provide a more complete representation of scene boundaries.

In this paper, we propose a novel contour-based 3D reconstruction method to generate a complete and regular 3D contour model of a general scene represented by topologically connected contours. Firstly, we extract 3D contours from input RGB-D images. Then, the contour correspondences between different frames are obtained through a robust matching step, which provides constraints for contour-enhanced camera pose optimization. In the next step, we perform contour fusion and generate junctions between 3D contours to represent their topological relationship. Finally, by fusing all 3D contours, we can produce a global 3D contour model of the scene with topological connections.

The main contributions of this paper are as follows: a) We propose a robust frame-to-model curve matching algorithm to solve the problem of finding many-to-many contour correspondences between different frames, and a contour-enhanced optimization objective function to obtain more accurate camera poses. b) We present a contour fusion algorithm considering the topological relationship between contours, which can generate more complete 3D contours that meet at junctions. c) We generate a regular contour framework of the scene, which can distinguish the boundary from the internal region and make advantages to guide surface reconstruction.

2 Related Work

This section discusses related work in the area of edge-based SLAM and edge-based 3D reconstruction, which can be grouped into three categories: mapping with SLAM methods, reconstruction of general scenes and reconstruction of thin structures.

Mapping with SLAM Methods. Edge features are commonly-used in many computer vision tasks [30–32]. For SLAM methods, they make use of edge features to overcome the problem of easily losing point features in low-texture areas, and further improve the robustness of localization. Despite some of them [9,25] proposed effective pose optimization strategies enhanced by edge features, there were no mapping output shown in the results. Since other works like CannyVO [33] and RESLAM [20] treated edge points as discrete feature points for matching and tracking, the constructed maps were represented by discrete points rather than complete edges. Although CurveSLAM [19] could generate maps with curves, the curves were constrained to planar curves on the ground, thus losing the generality.

Reconstruction of General Scenes. Compared with SLAM methods, 3D reconstruction methods pay more attention to the quality of modeling and can produce better visual outputs. Fabbri et al. [4] developed the 3D Curve Sketch, a framework for multi-view reconstruction and calibration based on image curve features, which could generate a set of unorganized 3D curve fragments as a result. Bignoli et al. [1] matched image edges by epipolar and spatial constraints to recover 3D edges from an unordered image set. While the above methods used discrete curve segments as features, Usmezbas et al. [26] considered the topological relationship between curve segments and generated the 3D curve drawing into a graph of 3D curve segments intersecting at junctions. Their motivation is probably the most similar with ours, though, we have great differences: their system is off-line while ours is on-line. Their reconstructed model of a general scene is represented by discrete and redundant curve segments, while ours is represented by topologically connected 3D contours.

Reconstruction of Thin Structures. These methods are designed to reconstruct the common fine structures in real scenes, such as fences, wire frame sculptures and tree branches. Liu et al. [14] reconstructed wire-made objects with smoothness and simplicity priors. They were limited by the assumption that the images had relatively clean background, and could not handle objects with many complex junctions, which were overcome by CurveFusion [13]. Vid2Curve [28] applied the iterative optimization method to curve matching and better solved the problem of curve missing and topology's incorrect, which could reconstruct high-quality structure model of the thin structure. Though these methods can generate structure models with topologically connected curves, their targets are limited to single thin structures and are not suitable for general scenes.

3   Proposed Method

We use RGB-D image sequences as our input to reconstruct the 3D contour model of the scene. A general overview of our system is shown in Fig. 1, which consists of five main steps: 3D contour extraction, contour matching, camera

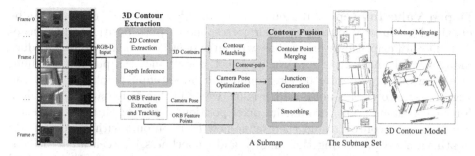

Fig. 1. The overview of our contour-based 3D reconstruction method. It consists of five key steps, while the steps shown in the green rectangle are implemented on the submap. The process is described as follows: (a) 3D contour extraction to obtain robust 3D contours from the RGB-D input. (b) Robust frame-to-model contour matching to find correspondences between 3D contours. (c) Contour-enhanced camera pose optimization for more accurate camera poses. (d) Efficient contour fusion to update the submap iteratively. (e) Submap merging to generate the complete 3D contour model.

pose optimization, contour fusion and submap merging. Note that we group the input frames into submaps for better computing efficiency and more robust modeling. A submap is composed of multiple consecutive frames, initialized by its first frame, and overlapping frames are set between two adjacent submaps to better align them in the merging step. On each submap, we perform iterative frame-to-model contour matching and contour fusion to construct a sub model as part of the global contour model.

The whole processes of the system are described as follows: First, we extract 2D contours from RGB images and **extract 3D contours** by accessing the depth information of the 2D contour pixels via a inference method. Then, we perform robust frame-to-model **contour matching** using the initial pose provided by our baseline ORB-SLAM2 [16] (*ORB2*), and utilize the resulting contour-pairs for contour-enhanced **camera pose optimization**. In the **contour fusion** step, we merge the matched contour segments to eliminate redundancy, and generate junctions to connect the unmatched parts. A smoothing step is then performed to eliminate the serrated connections. After all input frames have completed the above steps, we perform **submap merging** to construct the global contour model of the scene, which is represented by topologically connected 3D contours. In the following sections we will describe all these steps in more detail.

3.1   3D Contour Extraction

2D Contour Extraction. To obtain rich and accurate 2D contours, we detect Canny [2] edges on the RGB image and concatenate the discrete edges to generate 2D contours via a contour-tracer method, as shown in Fig. 2(a). A contour is parameterized by a set of points originating from pixels in the RGB image and can therefore be regarded as a polyline connected by multiple points with one-pixel width.

Depth Value Inference. It seems that the depth values of 2D contours can be obtained by directly looking up their corresponding pixel positions in the associated depth map. However, regions with large depth discrepancy often produce many invalid (marked as zero) or incorrect values since the points on boundaries are often a mixture of foreground and background points, as shown in Fig. 2(b). To solve this noise-ridden issue, we add some candidate depth values for each contour point (around its pixel position in the depth map) to generate some *wide* contours, and then refine new *thin* contours with more accurate depth values. Considering the validity and smoothness between adjacent contour points, we build a one-dimensional MRF (Markov Random Field) model for each *wide* contour and use BP (Belief Propagation) algorithm to solve this probability inference problem. The result shown in Fig. 2(c) confirms that the proposed algorithm is effective for robust 3D contour extraction.

(a)   (b)   (c)

Fig. 2. Illustration of the efficacy of depth inference. From left to right: (a) Extracted 2D contours. (b) Before depth inference. (c) After depth inference.

3.2   Contour Matching and Pose Optimization

Due to the variability of contours between different frames, contour matching is regarded as a many-to-many correspondence issue, which increases the complexity of implementation. In this section, we use the initial camera pose estimated by *ORB2* to perform contour matching, and provide a joint optimization objective function for a more accurate camera pose.

Contour Matching. The frame-to-model contour matching is carried out in the 2D coordinate system. We name the contour of model and of current frame as MC (Model Contour) and FC (Frame Contour) respectively. We specify that the initial model is composed of 3D contours extracted from the first frame of the model, and define the frame's pose (i.e., current camera pose) as the model's pose. Note that 3D MCs are defined in the model's coordinate system.

We use $\mathbf{T}_{wm}$ to represent the transformation matrix from the model's coordinate system to the world coordinate system. When a new frame comes, we first obtain the initial camera pose of current frame $\mathbf{T}_{fw}$ by tracking ORB features, and then compute the relative transformation $\mathbf{T}_{fm} = \mathbf{T}_{fw} \cdot \mathbf{T}_{wm}$ that transfers

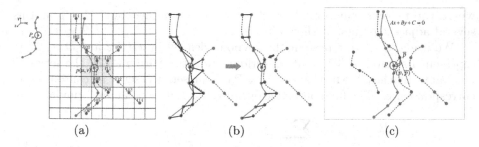

Fig. 3. The diagram of contour matching and contour-enhanced pose optimization algorithms. (a) A MC point $P_m \in \mathbb{R}^3$ is projected onto the lookup table generated by current frame as $p \in \mathbb{R}^2$ (circled in red). We visit a local path of p where we can find several candidate matched points (with sequence number $104, 105, 110$, and 111). (b) We select the FC point that has the minimum 3D distance with P_m and drop it if the distance exceeds a threshold (set to be $5\,\mathrm{cm}$ in our experiments). (c) The error term $d(p, \bar{p})$ is calculated by the distance between the projection position p and the tangent $Ax + By + C = 0$ generated by its matched FC point $\bar{p}$ via the equation (3).

the 3D contours from the model's coordinate system to the current frame's coordinate system. For newly arrived FCs, we generate a lookup table to mark 2D FC points at their corresponding pixels. We then project each 3D MC point $P_m \in \mathbb{R}^3$ onto the lookup table by:

$$p = \pi(P_f) = (f_x X_f / Z_f + c_u, f_y Y_f / Z_f + c_v), \tag{1}$$

where (f_x, f_y) is the focal length and (c_u, c_v) is the principal point. π denotes the projection function that maps $P_f \in \mathbb{R}^3$ in the frame's coordinate system to $p \in \mathbb{R}^2$ in the 2D coordinate plane. And P_f is calculated by:

$$P_f = \mathbf{T}_{fm} P_m = \mathbf{R}_{fm} P_m + \mathbf{t}_{fm}, \tag{2}$$

where $\mathbf{R}_{fm} \in SO(3)$ denotes the orientation matrix and $\mathbf{t}_{fm} \in \mathbb{R}^3$ denotes the translation vector.

We then scan a local patch of p to get several candidate matched points, as shown in Fig. 3(a). We select the FC point that has the minimum 3D distance with P_m and drop it if the distance exceeds a threshold, as depicted in Fig. 3(b). Through these point-to-point correspondences, we can get several FCs matched with current MC. For each contour-pair, we perform a post-processing step to eliminate outliers and add it to the result set only when the length of matched segment reaches a certain threshold.

Camera Pose Optimization. We enhance the motion-only BA (Bundle Adjustment) proposed in $ORB2$ by additional contour information to optimize the camera orientation $\mathbf{R}_{fw} \in SO(3)$ and translation $\mathbf{t}_{fw} \in \mathbb{R}^3$ of each frame. We define the distance between $p = (u, v)$ and its matched point $\bar{p}$ as:

$$d(p, \bar{p}) = |Au + Bv + C| \, / \, \sqrt{A + B}, \tag{3}$$

where the tangent equation $Ax + By + C = 0$ is obtained by fitting $\bar{p}$ and its several adjacent points, as shown in Fig. 3(c).

We use $o_j \in \mathbb{R}^2$ to represent the keypoint defined by $ORB2$ and $O_j \in \mathbb{R}^3$ to represent its matched 3D point in world coordinates, with $j \in \mathcal{OP}$ the set of all keypoints matches. We further use $i \in \mathcal{CP}$ to represent the set of all contour point correspondences. The final objective optimization function can be formulated as:

$$E_{pose}(\mathbf{R}_{fw}, \mathbf{t}_{fw}) = \sum_{i \in \mathcal{CP}} \omega\rho \left\| d(p_i, \bar{p}_i) \right\|^2$$
$$+ \sum_{j \in \mathcal{OP}} (1-\omega)\rho \left\| o_j - \pi(\mathbf{R}_{fw}O_j + \mathbf{t}_{fw}) \right\|^2, \quad (4)$$

where the second term denotes the reprojection error of ORB features, ρ is the robust *Huber* cost function and $\omega \in [0, 1]$ is a weight that balances the two terms.

We use the Levenberg-Marquardt method implemented in g^2o [10] to solve this optimization problem. The results show our contour-enhanced pose estimation algorithm can improve the localization accuracy, as detailed in Sect. 4.

3.3 Contour Fusion

Our goal is to obtain the contour model of the submap by fusing MCs and FCs in an iterative way, which is divided into three sub-tasks: contour point merging, junction generation and smoothing.

Contour Point Merging. We merge the matched segment of a contour-pair by weighted averaging, with the weight $i/(i+1)$ for MC points and $1/(i+1)$ for FC points (on the i-th frame of the submap), while keep the original contour segments for the unmatched areas.

Junction Generation. We use junctions to represent the topological relationship between 3D contours. When a contour-pair merge along a certain direction and deviate at one point, we generate a junction to connect the unmatched segment. We use two fusion primitives that are systematically worked out to cover

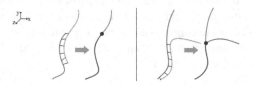

Fig. 4. We use two fusion primitives that are systematically worked out to cover all possible connections between a contour-pair. We use blue curve to represent the MC and yellow curve to represent the FC before fusion. Left: When the unmatched segment is an extend segment of the MC, we generate a junction at the endpoint of MC. Right: When the unmatched segment is related to a middle point of the MC, we split MC and generate a junction at the corresponding position.

all possible connections between a contour-pair, as shown in Fig. 4. We use blue curve to represent the *MC* and yellow one to represent the *FC* before fusion. The left case indicates when the unmatched segment is an extend segment of the *MC*, we generate a junction at the endpoint of *MC*. The right case indicates when the unmatched segment is related to a middle point of the *MC*, we split *MC* and generate a junction at the corresponding position.

Smoothing. To remove the serrated connection caused by the weighted averaging of matched contour segments, we perform smoothing via an optimization-based curve fitting method described in [13]. We compute the new point position $P'_t \in \mathbb{R}^3$ $(t = 0, 1, \ldots, T)$ by minimizing the following objective function:

$$E_{smooth} = \sum_{t=0}^{T} \left\| P'_t - P_t \right\|^2 + \lambda \sum_{t=0}^{T} \left\| P'_{t-1} - 2P'_t + P'_{t+1} \right\|^2, \tag{5}$$

where $P_t \in \mathbb{R}^3$ denotes the position before smoothing. The first term is a data fitting term, which maintains the original point positions, the second term ensures smoothness with adjacent points, and λ denotes the relative weight between two terms ($\lambda = 2$ in our tests).

3.4 Submap Merging

Considering that the pose estimation errors between close frames are negligible (i.e., a frame and its relative submaps), which can provide constraints for long-term accumulated errors, we use pose graph optimization to align the submaps.

In the iterative process, we store the poses of frames as $\bar{\mathbf{T}}_f$ and the poses of submaps as $\tilde{\mathbf{T}}_{submap}$. And we further define $\mathbf{T}_{rel}$ as the relative poses between each frame and its related submaps. We still use g^2o framework to implement this optimization step, where $\tilde{\mathbf{T}}_{submap}$ and $\bar{\mathbf{T}}_f$ are defined as vertices and $\mathbf{T}_{rel}$ are defined as edges between them. Because it is a lightweight optimization procedure without using landmarks like ORB features or our 3D contours, we can achieve it without losing computational efficiency. We use the optimized poses of the submaps to transform the 3D contours on each submap to the world coordinate system, and then match and fuse them in the similar way as described in Sect. 3.2 and Sect. 3.3. By fusing all submaps, we can eventually generate a global contour model of the scene.

4 Experiments

We evaluate the performance of the proposed method on ICL-NUIM [6] dataset and TUM RGB-D [22] dataset. All experiments are performed on a standard desktop with an Intel(R) Core(TM) i7-9700 CPU @ 3.00 GHz (16GB RAM).

4.1   Datasets

ICL-NUIM is a synthetic dataset with both surface and trajectory ground truth for evaluating RGB-D SLAM or 3D reconstruction systems. The living room scene of ICL-NUIM includes sofas, doors, lamps, curtains and other common objects in real environment. We choose the sequence *lr kt3* to evaluate our system, which contains 1241 images recorded 30 Hz frame rate and satisfies the loop closure condition.

The TUM RGB-D benchmark provides multiple real indoor sequences from RGB-D sensors to evaluate SLAM or VO (Visual Odometry) methods. The images were taken by a Microsoft Kinect sensor along the ground-truth trajectory of the sensor at full frame rate (30 Hz) and sensor resolution (640 × 480). We select six sequences, i.e., *fr1/desk*, *fr1/desk2*, *fr1/room*, *fr2/desk*, *fr2/xyz*, *fr3/office*, which were taken from three sensors with different camera intrinsic parameters to evaluate the localization accuracy of the proposed method.

4.2   Reconstruction Comparison

We compare our reconstruction results with BundleFusion [3], which is one of the most advanced surface-based reconstruction methods. For a more intuitive comparison, we extract points (from the dense point cloud generated by Bundle-Fusion) whose 2D and 3D distances are close to the contour points (generated by our method) to build the *edge point model* of BundleFusion. Figure 5 depicts the comparison of the two methods on the sequence *lr kt3* of ICL-NUIM. The partial scene shown in Fig. 5(a) includes a sofa, a floor lamp, a plant, a picture and a door, all with boundary structures. We can see that for objects with thin structures like the plant and the lamp-post, BundleFusion fails to capture their boundary structures while our method performs better. And for those edges at the intersection of foreground and background, our method can present the boundary information more completely, such as the cushions and the sofa arms. It also can be seen that due to the change of picture shooting angles, the extracted contours in different frames are changeable (e.g., one contour is probably divided into two in another frame, and vice versa), while our algorithm is able to deal with this issue and generate complete and regular contours across views that intersect at junctions.

The surface ground truth of the living room scene is shown in Fig. 6(a). Note that we remove the ceilings and some walls for better visualizing the ground truth model. Figure 6(b) depicts the global contour model generated by our method on sequence *lr kt3*, where we can see that except for some objects that are not photographed in this sequence, most of other objects or wall structures can be reconstructed well. We use an open-source tool called *CloudCompare*[1] to assess the accuracy of the reconstructed model. We align the contour model with the dense point cloud sampled from the surface ground truth, and then compute the absolute cloud-to-cloud (*C2C*) distances, which are visualized as

---

[1] http://www.danielgm.net/cc/.

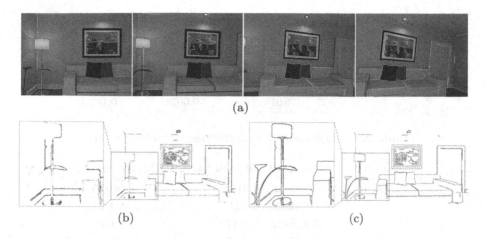

Fig. 5. The comparison of reconstruction results between BundleFusion and our method. (a) The *lr kt3* sequence and extracted 2D contours. (b) Edge points projected from the point cloud generated by BundleFusion. (c) 2D contours projected from the contour model generated by our method.

a heat map, as depicted in Fig. 6(c). We treat the *edge point model* the same way and calculate three error statistics, namely mean, median and standard deviation of the two models against the ground truth. The comparison results shown in Table 1 indicate that the contour model reconstructed by our method is more accurate than the *edge point model* generated by BundleFusion, with more complete boundary information.

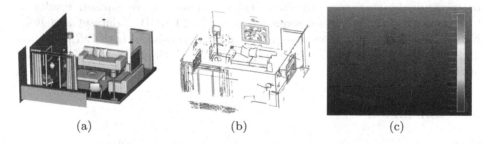

Fig. 6. The evaluation of modeling results of our method. (a) The surface ground truth of the living room scene. (b) The global contour model constructed by our method. (c) The heat map generated by aligning the contour model with the point cloud sampled from the surface ground truth. *(Please zoom in to examine closely.)*

Table 1. Comparison of Reconstruction Accuracy of Mean, Median and Std (m).

Dataset	Sequence	Error Statistics	BundleFusion	Ours
ICL-NUIM	lr kt3	Mean	0.0112	**0.0078**
		Median	0.0090	**0.0067**
		Std	0.0074	**0.0055**

Table 2. Comparison of Trajectory Translation RMSE (m).

Dataset	Sequence	ORB-SLAM2 (RGB-D)	Ours
TUM RGB-D	fr1/desk	0.016	**0.015**
	fr1/desk2	0.022	**0.021**
	fr1/room	**0.047**	0.053
	fr2/desk	**0.009**	0.010
	fr2/xyz	0.004	**0.003**
	fr3/office	**0.010**	0.018
ICL-NUIM	lr kt3	0.014	**0.010**

4.3   Localization Comparison

Expect for good modeling results, the proposed method can also improve the localization accuracy of the SLAM system. We compare the localization results with the baseline *ORB2* to demonstrate the effectiveness of the contour-enhanced pose optimization algorithm.

We use *evo* [5], a Python package for the evaluation of VO and SLAM, to measure the trajectory accuracy. Table 2 shows the comparison results of translation RMSE on several sequences from TUM RGB-D dataset and ICL-NUIM dataset. In most sequences, our results are consistent with *ORB2*. While in a few sequences, there is a slight improvement, which proves the effectiveness of the proposed method.

5   Conclusion

In this paper, we propose a novel approach for contour-based 3D reconstruction, which can perform accurate pose estimation and generate a contour model of the scene represented by topologically connected 3D contours. As a representation of boundary structure information, the resulting contour model can be viewed as a framework for the internal region, which is helpful to guide the surface reconstruction. Compared with previous edge-based SLAM methods, ours has more attractive modeling results. Compared with other edge-based 3D reconstruction systems, our approach can perform on-line reconstruction for general scenes to generate complete and regular contour models with topological relationships.

In future work, we plan to expand our work to monocular and binocular sensors for more applicability. In addition, we would like to combine the proposed method with surface-based 3D reconstruction algorithms to generate scene models with more semantic information.

References

1. Bignoli, A., Romanoni, A., Matteucci, M., di Milano, P.: Multi-view stereo 3D edge reconstruction. In: WACV, pp. 867–875 (2018)
2. Canny, J.: A computational approach to edge detection. IEEE TPAMI **8**(6), 679–698 (1986)
3. Dai, A., Nießner, M., Zollhöfer, M., Izadi, S., Theobalt, C.: BundleFusion: Realtime globally consistent 3D reconstruction using on-the-fly surface reintegration. ACM TOG **36**(4), 1 (2017)
4. Fabbri, R., Kimia, B.: 3D curve sketch: flexible curve-based stereo reconstruction and calibration. In: CVPR, pp. 1538–1545 (2010)
5. Grupp, M.: evo: Python package for the evaluation of odometry and SLAM (2017). https://github.com/MichaelGrupp/evo
6. Handa, A., Whelan, T., McDonald, J., Davison, A.: A benchmark for RGB-D visual odometry, 3D reconstruction and SLAM. In: ICRA, pp. 1524–1531 (2014)
7. Hofer, M., Maurer, M., Bischof, H.: Improving sparse 3D models for man-made environments using line-based 3D reconstruction. In: 3DV, vol. 1, pp. 535–542 (2014)
8. Hofer, M., Maurer, M., Bischof, H.: Efficient 3D scene abstraction using line segments. Comput. Vis. Image Underst. **157**, 167–178 (2017)
9. Kim, C., Kim, P., Lee, S., Kim, H.J.: Edge-based robust RGB-D visual odometry using 2D edge divergence minimization. In: IROS, pp. 1–9 (2018)
10. Kümmerle, R., Grisetti, G., Strasdat, H., Konolige, K., Burgard, W.: g2o: a general framework for graph optimization. In: ICRA, pp. 3607–3613 (2011)
11. Ladicky, L., Saurer, O., Jeong, S., Maninchedda, F., Pollefeys, M.: From point clouds to mesh using regression. In: ICCV, pp. 3893–3902 (2017)
12. Li, S., Yao, Y., Fang, T., Quan, L.: Reconstructing thin structures of manifold surfaces by integrating spatial curves. In: CVPR, pp. 2887–2896 (2018)
13. Liu, L., Chen, N., Ceylan, D., Theobalt, C., Wang, W., Mitra, N.: CurveFusion: reconstructing thin structures from RGB-D sequences. ACM TOG **37**(6) (2018)
14. Liu, L., Ceylan, D., Lin, C., Wang, W., Mitra, N.J.: Image-based reconstruction of wire art. ACM TOG **36**(4), 1–11 (2017)
15. Martin, T., Montes, J., Bazin, J.C., Popa, T.: Topology-aware reconstruction of thin tubular structures. In: ACM SIGGRAPH, vol. 12 (2014)
16. Mur-Artal, R., Tardós, J.D.: ORB-SLAM2: an open-source SLAM system for monocular, stereo, and RGB-D cameras. IEEE TRO **33**(5), 1255–1262 (2017)
17. Nurutdinova, I., Fitzgibbon, A.: Towards pointless structure from motion: 3D reconstruction and camera parameters from general 3D curves. In: ICCV, pp. 2363–2371 (2015)
18. Ramalingam, S., Antunes, M., Snow, D., Lee, G.H., Pillai, S.: Line-sweep: cross-ratio for wide-baseline matching and 3D reconstruction. In: CVPR, pp. 1238–1246 (2015)
19. Rao, D., Chung, S.J., Hutchinson, S.: CurveSLAM: an approach for vision-based navigation without point features. In: IROS, pp. 4198–4204 (2012)

20. Schenk, F., Fraundorfer, F.: RESLAM: a real-time robust edge-based SLAM system. In: ICRA, pp. 154–160 (2019)
21. Schöps, T., Sattler, T., Pollefeys, M.: Surfelmeshing: online surfel-based mesh reconstruction. IEEE TPAMI **42**(10), 2494–2507 (2019)
22. Sturm, J., Engelhard, N., Endres, F., Burgard, W., Cremers, D.: A benchmark for the evaluation of RGB-D slam systems. In: IROS, pp. 573–580 (2012)
23. Tabb, A.: Shape from silhouette probability maps: reconstruction of thin objects in the presence of silhouette extraction and calibration error. In: CVPR, pp. 161–168 (2013)
24. Takeyama, K.: 3D reconstruction of edge line by ICP-based matching with geometric constraints. In: 2020 Digital Image Computing: Techniques and Applications (DICTA), pp. 1–8 (2020)
25. Tarrio, J.J., Pedre, S.: Realtime edge-based visual odometry for a monocular camera. In: ICCV, pp. 702–710 (2015)
26. Usumezbas, A., Fabbri, R., Kimia, B.B.: From multiview image curves to 3D drawings. In: ECCV, pp. 70–87 (2016)
27. Wang, K., Gao, F., Shen, S.: Real-time scalable dense Surfel mapping. In: ICRA, pp. 6919–6925 (2019)
28. Wang, P., Liu, L., Chen, N., Chu, H.K., Theobalt, C., Wang, W.: Vid2Curve: simultaneous camera motion estimation and thin structure reconstruction from an RGB video. ACM TOG **39**(4), 1–132 (2020)
29. Whelan, T., Salas-Moreno, R.F., Glocker, B., Davison, A.J., Leutenegger, S.: ElasticFusion: real-time dense SLAM and light source estimation. IJRR **35**(14), 1697–1716 (2016)
30. Zhou, T., Li, J., Wang, S., Tao, R., Shen, J.: Matnet: motion-attentive transition network for zero-shot video object segmentation. IEEE TIP **29**, 8326–8338 (2020)
31. Zhou, T., Wang, S., Zhou, Y., Yao, Y., Li, J., Shao, L.: Motion-attentive transition for zero-shot video object segmentation. In: AAAI, pp. 13066–13073 (2020)
32. Zhou, T., Wang, W., Qi, S., Ling, H., Shen, J.: Cascaded human-object interaction recognition. In: CVPR, pp. 4263–4272 (2020)
33. Zhou, Y., Li, H., Kneip, L.: Canny-VO: visual odometry with RGB-D cameras based on geometric 3D–2D edge alignment. IEEE TRO **35**(1), 184–199 (2018)

SUnet++:Joint Demosaicing and Denoising of Extreme Low-Light Raw Image

Jingzhong Qi[1] , Na Qi[1,2] , and Qing Zhu[1,2]([⊠])

[1] Faculty of Information Technology, Beijing University of Technology, Beijing, China
qijingzhong@emails.bjut.edu.cn, {qina,ccgszq}@bjut.edu.cn
[2] Beijing Institute of Artificial Intelligence, Beijing, China

(a)Input   (b)Traditional pipeline   (c)SID   (d)Ours   (e)Ground truth   (f)SID−ground truth

Fig. 1. Illustration of extremely low-light images in our network model. (a) the input raw image in extremely low-light condition, (b) the results of traditional camera processing pipeline, (c) Image generated by SID method applied to the raw image (a), (d)Image generated by our SUnet++ applied to the raw image (a), (e) the ground truth, and (f) the difference between (b) and (c), respectively. As shown in this figure, our results is very close to the ground truth.

Abstract. Despite the rapid development of photography equipment, shooting high-definition RAW images in extreme low-light environments has always been a difficult problem to solve. Existing methods use neural networks to automatically learn the mapping from extreme low-light noise RAW images to long-exposure RGB images for jointly denoising and demosaicing of extreme low-light images, but the performance on other datasets is unpleasant. In order to address this problem, we present a separable Unet++ (SUnet++) network structure to improve the generalization ability of the joint denoising and demosaicing method for extreme low-light images. We introduce Unet++ to adapt the model to other datasets, and then replace the conventional convolutions of Unet++ with M sets of depthwise separable convolutions, which greatly reduced the number of parameters without losing performance. Experimental results on SID and ELD dataset demonstrate our proposed SUnet++ outperform the state-of-the-arts methods in term of subjective and objective results, which further validates the robust generalization of our proposed method.

Keywords: Joint denoising and demosaicing · Extreme low-light image · Raw image · Unet · Unet++

© Springer Nature Switzerland AG 2022
B. Þór Jónsson et al. (Eds.): MMM 2022, LNCS 13142, pp. 171–181, 2022.
https://doi.org/10.1007/978-3-030-98355-0_15

1   Introduction

With the rapid development of photography, storage, and display equipment, people begin to pursue high-quality images. As a common format in the real world, RGB images have good convenience in storage and display. The denoising research based on RGB images is gradually unable to satisfy the needs for high quality. RAW images have a higher resolution and store more information than RGB images, each RAW image with high resolution is about 30M-60M. Many denoising studies [9,13,16] based on RAW images have obtained higher-quality denoising results. The mapping relationship from RAW images to RGB images is studied for joint demosaicing and denoising. Moreover, the joint demosaicing and denoising problem of RAW images has received attention from researchers.

Previous joint demosaicing and denoising methods are usually designed independently and implemented sequentially in the ISP [7]. After obtaining the raw data from an imaging sensor, the traditional image processing pipeline applies a sequence of modules such as white balance, demosaicing, denoising, sharpening, color space conversion, gamma correction, and others. Figure 1(b) is the result of the image processing pipeline applied to the raw image (a). But, because the noise of the RAW image is more in line with our commonly used statistical model [18], the error generated by the demosaicing process will complicate the denoising process [6]. At present, the joint demosaicing and denoising research implemented by different technologies has achieved remarkable results [5,10,11], but their effectiveness is limited in extreme conditions. Recently, some methods have made breakthroughs in the joint demosaicing and denoising of RAW images in extreme low-light environments [2,3,15], Fig. 1(c) shows a result of SID [3] method. These methods are mostly data-driven learning methods, where deep convolutional neural networks are trained on pairwise datasets with RAW noisy mosaicked images and their clean RGB ground truths. However, these studies still face three major challenges in terms of color accuracy, high-quality denoising, and robust generalization.

The color cast problem exists in the raw image processing under extreme low-light condition, especially the magenta noise, shown in Fig. 1(f). The magenta noise in extreme low-light images will result in the blue-greenish in the denoising results, as shown in Fig. 1(c). Moreover, the noise is still obvious after magnifying several times due to the high resolution of the raw image. In addition, the serious shortage of training data and the expensive cost of computation hinder the performance of the raw denoising via deep learning methods. The latest methods [2,15] from the perspective of immersive data alleviate the lack of training data and reduce the time cost. These joint demosaicing and denoising methods [2,15] have good performance under specific datasets but do not work well for other ones, which will influence the robust generalization of the raw denoising method.

The Unet++ [19] has been successfully applied in the image segmentation by exploiting multiscale features from different layers of Unet [14] networks with the redesigned skip connections of Unet. However, it will take large computation costs. In this paper, we integrate depthwise separable convolution [4] to the Unet++ to propose a novel neural network named SUnet++ to realize the joint demosaicing and denoising of RAW images by automatically learning the mapping from extreme low-light noise RAW images to long-exposure RGB images. Our SUnet++ can reduce the parameter number of the Unet++ by using the depthwise separable convolutions without losing the performance. Experimental results on SID and ELD dataset demonstrate our proposed SUnett++ outperforms the state-of-art-methods and obtain the reconstructed results with more accurate colors, clearer details, and better peak signal-to-noise ratio (PSNR) and structural similarity (SSIM). In addition, our SUnet++ can reduce 22% parameters in comparison with Unet++.

2   Related Work

In this section, we briefly review the related work on the extreme low-light RAW image denoising method and some deep-learning networks.

As we all know, RGB images are converted from RAW images through image signal processing(ISP). Considering this transformation process, many studies have achieved remarkable results. Brooks T et al. proposed a UPI method to address the shot and read noise in the RAW image by inversely inferring the ISP and adding the residual error back to the input image to obtain more accurate noise image [2]. Zamir SW et al. proposed the CycleISP to improve the denoising performance by CNN fitting the changes in the process of data conversion, where the process of cyclic RAW image conversion into RGB image is used and the noise changes generated are focused [18]. Based on the understanding of the ISP principle, Wei et al. presented an effective noise generation model (ELD) by estimating the noise parameters one by one [15]. These studies have made in-depth discussions on data generation and preprocessing, but few of these studies focus on this problem for targeted network model improvement.

The Unet as a popular neural network has been successfully applied in image segmentation [14] and image computer vision tasks [17]. There are some researches to refine the structure of the Unet. Oktay O et al. introduce a plug-and-play module for Attention Gate to Unet to improve the accuracy of the image segmentation by selectively learning the interrelated areas and suppressing the saliency of irrelevant regions [12]. Zhou Z et al. redesigned skip connection to aggregate features of different semantic scales on the decoder sub-network to propose the Unet ++) [19], and thus the generalization ability of Unet is greatly improved through the effective integration of multiscale features from different layers. However, additional large number of parameters are brought even though the improvement of the image segmentation by Unet++. Fortunately, Chllet F et al. propose a depthwise separable convolution to greatly reduce the parameter numbers, where the separable convolution includes the plane convolution performed channel by channel and the 1×1 convolution between channels performed pixel by pixel [4]. We will utilize the depthwise separable convolution and the Unet++ to propose our dedicated network for joint demosaicing and denoising of extreme low-light raw image.

3 Method

3.1 Demosaicing and Denoising Method Based on SUnet++

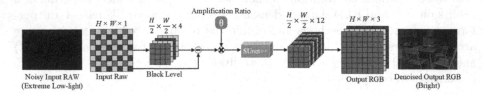

Fig. 2. The joint demosaicing and denoising pipeline with our proposed SUnet++ framework. The noise-free RGB image with normal light can be reconstructed from a noisy RAW image captured by a real camera under extreme low light condition.

This paper presents a new end-to-end learning method to train the mapping from the noisy RAW image captured by a real camera under extreme low light condition to output noise-free RGB image with normal light, as shown in Fig. 2. The separable Unet++ is utilized for jointly demosaicing and denoising of extreme low light images. The input data of the system is a Bayer mode RAW image of size $H \times W \times 1$, where H and W are the height and width of the image and the channel is 1. Then, the RGBG format denoted as a 4-channel tensor of size $\frac{H}{2} \times \frac{W}{2} \times 4$ are generated where the spatial resolution is halved. The desired amplification ratio θ is used to amplify the RGBG data for eliminating black pixels, where θ can be $\times 100$ or $\times 300$. Then these data are fed into our proposed SUnet++ to generate the tensor of size $\frac{H}{2} \times \frac{W}{2} \times 12$, which is reorganized to the tensor of size $H \times W \times 3$. The size of the reorganized tensor is the same as the resolution of the RGB image.

3.2 SUnet++ Network Structure

We take advantage of the good performance by the Unet++ and introduce the depthwise separable convolution operation to the Unet++ to present a new SUnet++ to alleviate the problem of multiple parameters taken by Unet++.

The structure of the SUnet++ is shown in Fig. 3. The node $N_{i,j}$ represents the j-th node of the i-th layer, and $F_{i,j}$ represents the set of operations to obtain node $N_{i,j}$ from other nodes, where the positive integers i and j satisfy $i+j \leq 6$, and take a value in the range of ($1 \leq i \leq 5, 1 \leq j \leq 5$). When $j = 1$, $N_{i,j}$ is obtained from $N_{i-1,j}$ through the operation α and γ; when $j > 1$, $N_{i,j}$ is obtained from $N_{i,j-1}$ and $N_{i+1,j-1}$ through the operation α and β. Finally, the packed and amplified data $N_{1,5}$ is fed into a fully-convolutional network G [3]. The output is a 12-channel image with half the spatial resolution. The operation $F_{i,j}$ is expressed as:

$$F_{i,j} = \begin{cases} \gamma(\alpha(\cdot)) & (j = 1) \\ \alpha(\beta(\cdot)) & (j > 1) \end{cases}. \tag{1}$$

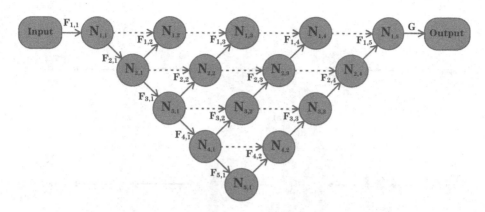

Fig. 3. The topological structure diagram of our proposed SUnet++. Each node in the graph represents a multi-channel feature map, downward arrows indicate the operation $\gamma(\alpha(\cdot))$ mentioned in Eq. (1) and Eq. (2), upward arrows and dot arrows indicate the operation $\alpha(\beta(\cdot))$ mentioned in Eq. (1) and Eq. (2).

The $N_{i,j}$ obtained from $F_{i,j}$ is expressed as:

$$N_{i,j} = \begin{cases} \gamma(\alpha(N_{i-1,j})) & (j=1) \\ \alpha(\beta(N_{i+1,j-1}, N_{i,j-1})) & (j>1) \end{cases}, \tag{2}$$

where α represents a operation composed of a conventional convolution and m depthwise separable convolutions, γ represents a max-pooling operation. When $j=1$, $N_{i,1}$ is obtained from $N_{i-1,1}$ after the operation $F_{i,1}$, as shown in Fig. 4(b). β represents the set of operations including a deconvolution, upsampling and fusion operation. The node $N_{i+1,j-1}$ after the deconvolution and upsampling is fused with the $N_{i,j-1}$ to perform the α operation to obtain the node $N_{i,j}$, as shown in Fig. 4(c).

The input of our joint demosaicing and denoising scheme is a tensor of size $\frac{H}{2} \times \frac{W}{2} \times 4$, and $N_{i,j}$ is a tensor of size $\frac{H}{2^i} \times \frac{W}{2^i} \times 2^{i+4}$ after a series of operations $\{F_{i,j}\}_{i=1}^{m}{}_{j=1}^{n}$. Therefore, $N_{1,5}$ is a tensor of size $\frac{H}{2} \times \frac{W}{2} \times 32$, which passes through a conventional convolution with a convolution kernel of size 12 to obtain a tensor of size $\frac{H}{2} \times \frac{W}{2} \times 12$ as the output of the network.

3.3 Depthwise Separate Convolution Part Parameters

As shown in Fig. 5, we take a tensor whose input channel is 4 as an example to illustrate the change of the parameter numbers after the α operation. Assuming that the input channels of the tensor fed into the convolution operation of $F_{i,j}$ is $c_{in}^{i,j}$, the output channels of the corresponding tensor is $c_{out}^{i,j}$, the size of the convolution kernel is $k \times k$, the number of parameters of a set of conventional convolution operations of $\{F_{i,j}\}_{i=1}^{m}{}_{j=1}^{n}$ is $C_{args}^{i,j}$, and the number of parameters of a set of depthwise separable convolution operations of $\{F_{i,j}\}_{i=1}^{m}{}_{j=1}^{n}$ is $S_{args}^{i,j}$. The parameter calculation formula is as follow,

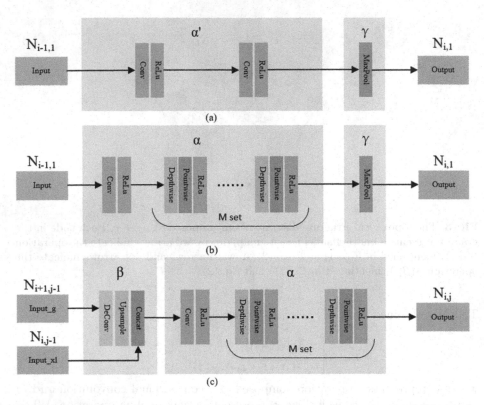

Fig. 4. Flowcharts of the operations utilized in Unet++ and our proposed SUnet++, where the conventional convolution is utilized in Unet++ rather than the depthwise separable convolution operation. (a) α' composes of ReLu and two conventional convolutions. (b) α composes of a conventional convolution, ReLu, and m depthwise separable convolutions. (b) The operation β includes the deconvolution, the upsample operation and the concatenation operation.

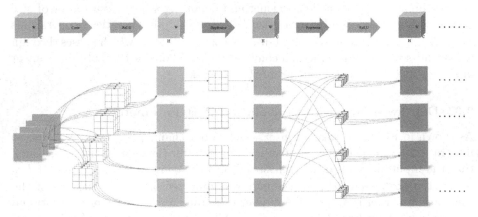

Fig. 5. Illustration of the change of the parameter numbers after the conventional convolution and the depthwise separable convolutions of the α operation.

$$C_{\text{args}}^{i,j} = \sum_{i=1}^{m} \sum_{j=1}^{n} c_{\text{in}}^{i,j} \times k^2 \times c_{\text{out}}^{i,j}, \tag{3}$$

$$S_{\text{args}}^{i,j} = \sum_{i=1}^{m} \sum_{j=1}^{n} m \times c_{\text{in}}^{i,j} \times (k^2 + c_{\text{out}}^{i,j}). \tag{4}$$

As shown in Fig. 4(a), the number of parameters in the α' operation of Unet++* method is $2C_{\text{args}}^{i,j}$. As shown in Fig. 4(b), the number of parameters in the α operation of SUnet++ method is $C_{\text{args}}^{i,j} + S_{\text{args}}^{i,j}$.

4 Experiments

4.1 Experimental Setting

Dataset. We evaluate our proposed SUnet++ on the SID dataset [3] and the ELD dataset [15], which are taken by Sony A7S2 cameras. The SID dataset contains 2697 short-exposure RAW images, and 231 corresponding long-exposure reference RAW images. Those images with different shutter speeds which means different brightness are utilized to form multiple pairs, shown in Fig. 6. Moreover, 1865, 598 and 234 data pairs are utilized as training, test and validation set, respectively. The ELD dataset contains 49 short-exposure RAW images and 10 long-exposure counterpart RAW images, which is only used as a test set. In each pair, the amplification ratio of long and short exposure time is between 100 and 300.

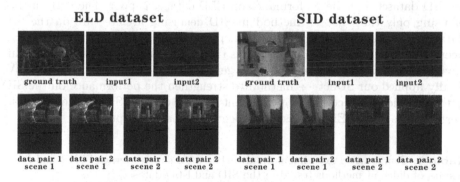

Fig. 6. Examples of images in the SID and ELD dataset. Each dataset includes the ground truth and different inputs which are captured with different shutter speeds, leading to different brightness. Each data pair is combined by the ground truth and an input with a certain brightness.

Competing Methods. We compare our method with the traditional pipeline [3], BM3D [1] and SID [3] on the SID as well as the ELD dataset. On the basis of the SID method, we propose a joint demosaicing and denoising method with the SUnet++, which improves the efficiency by modifying the network of conventional convolution. We replace the Unet++ of the conventional CNN in SID method, and further utilize the SUnet++ as our scheme by using the depthwise seperable convolutions. These methods are denoted as SID+Unet++ and our SUnet++.

Training Configuration. We train the networks from scratch using the L1 loss and the Adam optimizer [8]. The parameter m before the depthwise separable convolution operation is 2, that is, two depthwise separable convolutions are used to replace one conventional convolution. During training, the input to the network is the raw data of the short-exposed image and the ground truth is the corresponding long-exposure image in sRGB space (processed by libraw, a raw image processing library). The amplification ratio is set to be the exposure difference between the input and reference images (e.g., ×100, ×250, or ×300) for both training and testing. In each iteration, we randomly crop a 512×512 patch for training and apply random flipping and rotation for data augmentation. The learning rate is initially set to 10^{-4} and is reduced to 10^{-5} after 2000 epochs. Training proceeds for 6000 epochs.

4.2   Experimental Results

To verify the efficacy of the proposed network, we compare our method with other methods on the SID and ELD dataset. Table 1 shows the quantitative results (PSNR/SSIM) of all competing methods on the SID and ELD dataset. It can be seen that the latest methods represented by SID have shown good results on SID dataset, but the performance on ELD dataset is poor. The performance of using only the Unet++ method in SID denoising architecture on the SID dataset has slightly decreased, but the performance on the ELD dataset has been significantly improved. It indicates that the application of Unet++ in this environment does indeed improve the generalization ability of the model. We finally applied our SUnet++ method to strengthen the performance on the SID dataset, which has a certain improvement over the original SID method, and the performance on the ELD dataset has been significantly improved.

Table 1. Comparative experiment results. The table shows average PSNR and SSIM results of different methods tested in the SID and ELD dataset.

Method	SID dataset		ELD dataset	
	PSNR	SSIM	PSNR	SSIM
Traditional pipeline	14.98	0.14	18.08	0.19
BM3D	16.75	0.32	18.64	0.38
SID	28.96	0.89	20.60	0.69
SID+Unet++	28.93	0.89	20.73	0.71
Ours	28.99	0.89	20.77	0.72

Fig. 7. Color comparison in different network models. The results of different methods, including (a) traditional camera processing pipeline [3], (b) the SID method [3], (c) our SID+Unet++ and (d) SUnet++. (e) The ground truth. As shown in figure, the color of our results is closer to the ground truth than others.

From Fig. 7, we can see that our results have more accurate colors. From the thumbnails of Fig. 8, we can observe that the SID method has achieved good results. However, when focused on extreme small details, it still has plenty of shortcomings. From the detailed comparison chart, we can see that our method has been greatly improved.

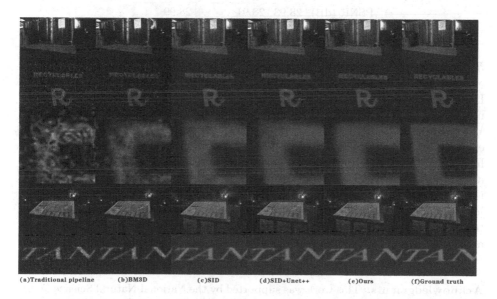

Fig. 8. Visual quality comparison with different joint demosaicing and denoising methods. The results of (a) traditional camera processing pipeline [3], (b) BM3D method [1], (c) the SID method [3], (d) our SID+Unet++ and (e) Our SUnet++. (f) The ground truth. As shown in figure, the detail of our results is closer to the ground truth.

4.3 Parameter Analysis

We use m sets of depthwise separable convolutions in our SUnet++ instead of a set of conventional convolutions in Unet++, as shown in Fig. 4(a) and (b). For simplicity, we only consider the parameters of the changed area, that is, only the parameter changes in operation α and α'.

Substituting the number of channels described in 3.2 into the formula in 3.3, we calculate that the parameters used a set of conventional convolution operations are 4.2M, and the parameters used 2 sets of depthwise separable convolution operations are 0.96M. The parameters are reduced to 22.9% of the original. If only a set of depthwise separable convolution operations are used, this number can even drop to 11.5% while the result is similar to a set of conventional convolution operations. But we use double depthwise separable convolution operations for better results (see Table 2).

Table 2. Comparison of the parameter numbers with different convolutions, including the conventional convolution (CC) in the operation α' as well as the depthwise separable convolution (DSC) of different numbers in the operation α, and the PSNR (dB) performance.

	CC	DSC(m=1)	DSC(m=2)
Parameters	4.2M	0.48M	0.96M
PSNR (dB)	28.93	28.91	28.99

5 Conclusion

In this paper, we present a SUnet++ network structure by utilizing the performance of Unet++ and the effectiveness of the depthwise separable convolutions. We utilize the SUnet++ network for the joint demosaicing and denoising of extreme low-light noisy RAW images by learning the mapping from extreme low-light noisy RAW images to long-exposure RGB images. The parameter numbers are greatly reduced while the performance is improved. Experimental results on the SID and ELD dataset demonstrate that the effectiveness and efficiency of our joint demosaicing and denoising pipeline can be taken by the SUnet++. In the future, we will apply our framework for the extreme low-light video enhancement and other image enhancement. In addition, we will establish the interpretable network for the extreme low-light noisy RAW image enhancement.

Acknowledgments. This work was supported by the National Natural Science Foundation of China under Grant 61906009, the Scientific Research Common Program of Beijing Municipal Commission of Education KM202010005018, and the International Research Cooperation Seed Fund of Beijing University of Technology (Project No. 2021B06).

References

1. Image denoising by sparse 3-D transform-domain collaborative filtering. IEEE Trans. Image Process. **16**(8), 2080–2095 (2007)

2. Brooks, T., Mildenhall, B., Xue, T., Chen, J., Sharlet, D., Barron, J.T.: Unprocessing images for learned raw denoising. In: Proceedings of the IEEE/CVF Conference on Computer Vision and Pattern Recognition, pp. 11036–11045 (2019)
3. Chen, C., Chen, Q., Xu, J., Koltun, V.: Learning to see in the dark. In: Proceedings of the IEEE Conference on Computer Vision and Pattern Recognition, pp. 3291–3300 (2018)
4. Chollet, F.: Xception: deep learning with depthwise separable convolutions. In: Proceedings of the IEEE Conference on Computer Vision and Pattern Recognition, pp. 1251–1258 (2017)
5. Ehret, T., Davy, A., Arias, P., Facciolo, G.: Joint demosaicking and denoising by fine-tuning of bursts of raw images. In: Proceedings of the IEEE/CVF International Conference on Computer Vision, pp. 8868–8877 (2019)
6. Guo, S., Liang, Z., Zhang, L.: Joint denoising and demosaicking with green channel prior for real-world burst images. arXiv preprint arXiv:2101.09870 (2021)
7. Jin, Q., Facciolo, G., Morel, J.M.: A review of an old dilemma: demosaicking first, or denoising first? In: Proceedings of the IEEE/CVF Conference on Computer Vision and Pattern Recognition Workshops, pp. 514–515 (2020)
8. Kingma, D.P., Ba, J.: Adam: a method for stochastic optimization. arXiv preprint arXiv:1412.6980 (2014)
9. Koskinen, S., Yang, D., Kämäräinen, J.K.: Reverse imaging pipeline for raw RGB image augmentation. In: 2019 IEEE International Conference on Image Processing (ICIP), pp. 2896–2900. IEEE (2019)
10. Liu, L., Jia, X., Liu, J., Tian, Q.: Joint demosaicing and denoising with self guidance. In: Proceedings of the IEEE/CVF Conference on Computer Vision and Pattern Recognition, pp. 2240–2249 (2020)
11. Liu, S., Chen, J., Xun, Y., Zhao, X., Chang, C.H.: A new polarization image demosaicking algorithm by exploiting inter-channel correlations with guided filtering. IEEE Trans. Image Process. 29, 7076–7089 (2020)
12. Oktay, O., et al.: Attention u-net: learning where to look for the pancreas. arXiv preprint arXiv:1804.03999 (2018)
13. Pan, Z., Li, B., Cheng, H., Bao, Y.: Deep residual network for MSFA raw image denoising. In: ICASSP 2020–2020 IEEE International Conference on Acoustics, Speech and Signal Processing (ICASSP), pp. 2413–2417. IEEE (2020)
14. Ronneberger, O., Fischer, P., Brox, T.: U-Net: convolutional networks for biomedical image segmentation. In: Navab, N., Hornegger, J., Wells, W.M., Frangi, A.F. (eds.) MICCAI 2015. LNCS, vol. 9351, pp. 234–241. Springer, Cham (2015). https://doi.org/10.1007/978-3-319-24574-4_28
15. Wei, K., Fu, Y., Yang, J., Huang, H.: A physics-based noise formation model for extreme low-light raw denoising. In: Proceedings of the IEEE/CVF Conference on Computer Vision and Pattern Recognition, pp. 2758–2767 (2020)
16. Yang, C.C., Guo, S.M., Tsai, J.S.H.: Evolutionary fuzzy block-matching-based camera raw image denoising. IEEE Trans. Cybern. 47(9), 2862–2871 (2016)
17. Man, Y., Huang, Y., Feng, J., Li, X., Wu, F.: Deep Q learning driven CT pancreas segmentation with geometry-aware u-net. IEEE Trans. Med. Imaging (2019)
18. Zamir, S.W., et al.: Cycleisp: real image restoration via improved data synthesis. In: Proceedings of the IEEE/CVF Conference on Computer Vision and Pattern Recognition, pp. 2696–2705 (2020)
19. Zhou, Z., Siddiquee, M.M.R., Tajbakhsh, N., Liang, J.: Unet++: redesigning skip connections to exploit multiscale features in image segmentation. IEEE Trans. Med. Imaging 39(6), 1856–1867 (2019)

HyText – A Scene-Text Extraction Method for Video Retrieval

Alexander Theus[ID], Luca Rossetto[✉][ID], and Abraham Bernstein[ID]

Department of Informatics, University of Zurich, Zurich, Switzerland
{rossetto,bernstein}@ifi.uzh.ch

Abstract. Scene-text has been shown to be an effective query target for video retrieval applications in a known-item search context. While much progress has been made in scene-text extraction from individual pictures, the special case of video has so far received less attention. This paper introduces HyText, a scene-text extraction method for video with a focus on retrieval applications. HyText uses intermittent scene-text detection in combination with bi-directional tracking in order to increase throughput without reducing detection accuracy.

Keywords: Scene-text extraction · Video text extraction · Video retrieval

1 Introduction

As multimedia collections grow larger in terms of size, heterogeneity, and variety of media types, the quest for accessing the knowledge contained within them becomes more onerous. The traditional approach of manually annotating media objects, and retrieving them at a later point based on this metadata has various deficiencies. Firstly, the sheer size of media collections and their progressive growth renders prior annotation unfeasible. Secondly, textual descriptions tend to be subjective due to language, culture, expertise, and personal experience. While several means of querying for video have been proposed, querying for text, which is visible in a video sequence, enables effective and lossless query expression, particularly in a known-item search scenario [15]. This not only works for artificial text overlays but also for text which is an inherent part of the scene.

This type of naturally occurring text is termed *scene-text*. Due to the abundance of textual content in natural scenes and especially in urban settings [13] the task of scene-text extraction (STE) has received a lot of interest from the computer vision community, and has been propelled by advances in deep learning. While STE in still images remains a problem, several approaches have emerged which show a sufficiently high performance to be useful for general purpose applications. STE in videos, however, is still an under-explored field, even though it is of similar importance.

In this paper, we introduce HyText, a scene-text extraction method for video. Rather than applying a costly scene-text detection step on every frame, HyText

B. Þór Jónsson et al. (Eds.): MMM 2022, LNCS 13142, pp. 182–193, 2022.
https://doi.org/10.1007/978-3-030-98355-0_16

uses intermittent detection combined with bi-directional tracking to localize and transcribe text instances in video. This not only substantially reduces end-to-end inference time, it also ensures that reoccurring text instances do not lead to duplicated transcriptions.

The remainder of this paper is structured as follows: Sect. 2 provides an overview of related scene-text detection, recognition and extraction methods. The proposed method is detailed in Sect. 3 and its effectiveness is evaluated in Sect. 4. Section 5 then offers some concluding remarks.

2   Related Work

Current approaches for scene-text extraction primarily focus on individual images. Those methods can be roughly divided into two groups: two-stage methods and end-to-end methods. Two-stage methods use two independent components for scene-text detection and subsequent scene-text recognition, while end-to-end methods have no such clear component division.

One of the more popular methods for scene-text detection is the 'Efficient and Accurate Scene Text Detector' (EAST) [22], which uses a convolutional neural network to predict the position of words in natural scenes. Other methods such as 'Character Region Awareness For Text detection' (CRAFT) [1] even perform such predictions for individual characters.

State-of-the-art methods for scene-text recognition can be divided into segmentation-based and segmentation-free methods. Segmentation-based methods are architecturally suitable for two-dimensional prediction problems. Taking advantage of this, Liao et al. [11] introduce a segmentation-based scene-text recognizer that regards scene-text as a two-dimensional spatial distribution of features. The 'Convolutional Recurrent Neural Network' (CRNN) [19] was one of the early adopters of the segmentation-free method. Even though this method is rather old, it is still widely used as a basis for various methods such as [5,10,12]. However, this method has its limitations when it comes to irregular text.

Comparatively less work has been done on methods, which explicitly focus on video. A method introduced by Wang et al. [20] approached STE in video by first detecting and recognizing text in each frame via a jointly-trained STE method. After extracting text in each individual frame, the method uses a similarity function comprised of the position of the text instance, the recognized text as well as the frame offset to match equivalent text instances. The method then uses majority voting to determine the most likely text for the text stream. Unfortunately, the paper does not mention how they deal with scenarios in which there is no singular majority string.

The aforementioned method has been criticized by Cheng et al. [3]. They argue that reading text in every frame is excessively computationally costly and thus operationally unsuitable. Moreover, recognizing text in every frame also introduces erroneous results due to the abundance of *low quality* (e.g., due to blurring, rotation, perspective distortion, poor illumination, etc.) text regions. To circumvent these problems, Cheng et al. introduce a method called 'You Only

Recognize Once' (YORO), which, as the name already suggests, only recognizes text in one region from a text stream by selecting the most *high quality* one. YORO, like the previously introduced method, follows the tracking-by-detection framework by detecting text in every frame. The detection module is based on the EAST text detector, and its score output map is temporally enhanced via a spatial-temporal aggregation strategy that optimizes the output in the current frame by referring to the output in adjacent frames. Then, a module they call 'Text Recommender' is responsible for three tasks: text quality scoring, text tracking, and text recognition. All of these tasks depend on the same feature map produced by a ResNet-based feature extractor. The text quality scoring is performed on each detected text region and computes scores between 0 and 1, where 1 denotes the highest quality achievable. The text tracking is achieved by comparing the L2 normalized feature maps, and optimal matches are determined via the use of the Hungarian Algorithm [8]. At this point, text streams have been generated, and each text region within the stream has a quality score. The region with the highest quality is selected and an attention-based recognition module produces the final string.

3   HyText

Similar to Cheng et al. [3], we argue that recognizing text in each frame is too computationally expensive and might introduce erroneous recognitions. However, in contrast to Cheng et al. we argue that the computational cost of STE in video is mainly driven by the detection module. This is confirmed by the results presented in Sect. 4. Thus, unless the video has an unusually high amount of text instances per frame, the detection module is the main driver in computational cost. Moreover, recognized text is a very salient component of a text stream. It is therefore well suited to validate the internal consistency of a text stream, and for associations to other streams. To take advantage of this observation, we introduce the **Hy**brid Bidirectional **T**ext **Ex**tractor (HyText), which can reliably extract scene-text from videos by only detecting text in a subset of frames. Moreover, it can utilize recognized text to validate streams for inter-frame association, without having to rely on per-frame recognition. The following details the three primary components of HyText: text stream formation, text stream recognition, and text stream aggregation.

3.1   Text Stream Formation

A text stream consists of a single text instance which is tracked across a series of consecutive frames. While conventional single-object tracking with a Bayesian framework or template matching cannot handle re-initialization in a multi-object scene, it has a few important advantages over tracking-by-detection. For one, since the relative region of the text in the previous frame is known, these methods seem to be substantially faster than object detection. Moreover, they can handle occlusion a lot better since they are able to estimate the probable region

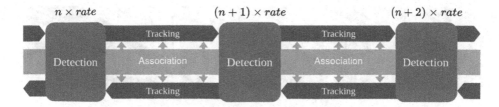

$n \times rate$ $(n + 1) \times rate$ $(n + 2) \times rate$

Fig. 1. Abstract illustration of a snippet of the text stream formation procedure of HyText. The labels above the detection box describe the index of the frame at which it was performed.

of the text. Thus, HyText aims to take advantage of the speed and superior occlusion treatment, while still being able to take into account newly appearing text instances. HyText accomplishes this by allowing the user to define a rate at which the detections should occur. For example, if the user of the method specifies the rate to be two, then a detection will be done at every second frame. In order to not miss text occurrences between the frames at which detections were done, HyText uses the discriminative correlation filter method named CSR-DCF [16] to track text instances in the frames at which no detection was performed.

Figure 1 provides an abstract illustration of the text stream formation procedure. First, text is detected in frame $n \times rate$, where $n \in \mathbb{N}$ and $rate$ is the rate at which detection should occur. Then, the detected text instances are tracked via CSR-DCF just before frame $(n + 1) \times rate$ is reached. Subsequently, text is detected in frame $(n + 1) \times rate$, and tracked backwards until frame $n \times rate$. These tracked text instances are likely going to describe the same text instance. Since bi-directional tracking allows for intra-frame rather than inter-frame association – which is conventional for multi-object tracking – the temporal aspect of association is removed, which radically simplifies the similarity function. In order to find out which text streams describe the same text instance, the average Intersection over Union (IoU) is computed, and the Hungarian Algorithm is applied to find optimal matches. If the average IoU of the optimal match is below a threshold (empirically set to 0.6) the tracked text instances between frame $n \times rate$ and $(n + 1) \times rate$ are removed, and the text streams are regarded as separate. If the average IoU is above the threshold, then the text streams are merged, and the average bounding boxes of the tracked text is used. This procedure is then continued for $n \in \{0, 1, 2, \ldots, m \mid m = \lceil \frac{V}{rate} \rceil - 1\}$, where V is the total number of frames in a video. Thus, instead of performing detections on all frames, HyText only applies detection on $\lceil \frac{V}{rate} \rceil$ frames, and applies the much faster CSR-DCF tracker for the remaining ones, which account for $V - \lceil \frac{V}{rate} \rceil$ frames.

3.2   Text Stream Recognition

Once the previously described procedure is complete, we will have a list of text streams describing individual text instances. The next step is to extract the

Fig. 2. Example of the disappearing text phenomenon where quality scoring and unfiltered majority polling produce incorrect results. Image taken from Text in Videos dataset.

correct string from the streams. In order to do this, we introduce a hybrid approach that does neither entirely depend on majority voting, nor on text selection such as in YORO [3]. We argue that unfiltered majority voting may introduce flawed text recognitions, which can be easily filtered out. Moreover, the text scoring system in YORO may reliably select the highest quality bounding box for recognition. However, it neglects the most radical deteriorating factor: disappearing text. Cut text is a particularly abundant characteristic in video, since a text instance may be in the center of the image in one frame, but then, as the camera moves, progressively disappear. In the process, the text gets cut increasingly, and if that text is used for recognition, the recognition will necessarily be incorrect (or incomplete). This phenomenon is exemplified in Fig. 2.

In order to address this, we calculate the aspect ratio of each bounding box within a stream and prune those whose aspect ratio is below the median. With this procedure, we effectively mitigate the problem of disappearing text and simultaneously reduce computational cost. For the remaining bounding boxes, the recognition is performed, and the final string is obtained via majority voting. However, there may be cases in which two or more strings appear equally often in the stream. As a means to address this, we prune streams that cannot agree on one or two strings, as they may be indicative of unreliability. If two strings remain after the majority voting procedure, we apply a global pairwise sequence alignment algorithm called *Needleman-Wunsch* [18]. The Needleman-Wunsch algorithm is typically used in bioinformatics to align protein or nucleotide sequences. In our case, we use the algorithm to extract a common substring from the two recognitions. While this may not result in a completely accurate final recognition, it is still of value in a retrieval application, since scene-text search will commonly not look for complete matches, but for relative matches using a string edit distance.

3.3 Text Stream Aggregation

With the aforementioned steps completed, the STE task for video could be regarded as concluded. However, the procedure so far can still be improved to handle text instances that disappear and reappear again. If a text instance disappears at a time at which a detection is performed, and then reappears later, two text streams will be formed for the same text instance, which results in unwanted duplicity. This can also occur in the case that the detector module simply does not detect a text instance in a certain frame, e.g. due to high motion blur. As a means to overcome this problem, we introduce an additional step that is heavily inspired by the method introduced by Wang et al. [20]. We start with text streams that have the minimal distance between them, which in all cases would be the rate that the user specified. The distance between two text streams is regarded as the difference between the tail and the head of a stream (see Eq. 5). To check whether or not they actually describe the same text instance, the following similarity measure is applied:

$$S_{ab} = k_1 \times S_{dis}^{spatial} + k_2 \times S_{op}^{area} + k_3 \times S_{winkler}^{jaro} + k_4 \times S_{offset}^{frame} \qquad (1)$$

where the S_y^x are defined as below and k_1, k_2, k_3, k_4, are weights, empirically set to 1, 1, 10, and 0.2, respectively. S_{ab} stands for the cost of merging two streams a and b, where stream b appears after stream a.

$S_{dis}^{spatial}$ refers to the spatial distance between the bounding boxes and is calculated like the following:

$$S_{dis}^{spatial} = \frac{mean(x_i^a - x_i^b)}{max(W_a, W_b)} + \frac{mean(y_i^a - y_i^b)}{max(H_a, H_b)} \qquad (2)$$

Where $(x_i, y_i), i \in \{1, 2, 3, 4\}$ are the coordinates of the quadrilateral bounding box. W and H refer to the width and the height of the boxes, respectively.

S_{op}^{area} refers to the inverse IoU to capture the overlap between the two boxes:

$$S_{op}^{area} = 1 - \frac{Area(a \cap b)}{Area(a \cup b)} \qquad (3)$$

$S_{winkler}^{jaro}$ is the inverse Jaro Winkler Distance [21] between the two strings. This metric is particularly informative, hence it is given the highest weight of 10.

$$S_{winkler}^{jaro} = 1 - JW(str_a, str_b) \qquad (4)$$

Finally, the distance between the two frames, or in other words the frame offset S_{offset}^{frame}, is also an important characteristic to consider. To include it, we simply take the difference between the head and the tail of the two streams.

$$S_{offset}^{frame} = head_b - tail_a \qquad (5)$$

The optimal match between the streams is calculated via the Hungarian Algorithm. If the final score S_{ab} is below the empirically determined threshold of 8, then the streams will be combined and regarded as one. The recognition of the stream which spans the most frames, will be regarded as the recognition for the new combined stream. This procedure will be continued to be done for $distance \in \{rate, 2 \times rate, 3 \times rate, \ldots, n \times rate \mid (n+1) \times rate \geq \frac{threshold}{k_4}\}$. Finally, HyText prunes very short text streams that appeared for fewer than 10 consecutive frames. This is done to remove unreliable text streams, and to prune those, which appeared for only a small amount of time. In such cases, the user would probably not have been able read them, which makes such stream uninteresting for a retrieval application.

4   Evaluation

The following shows comparative evaluations of isolated scene-text detection
(STD) and recognition (STR) methods as well as the complete HyText pipeline
in different configurations. All runtime measurements were performed using an
Intel core i7-10700KF and 32 GB DDR4-3600 memory. To minimize implemen-
tation-specific effects, no GPU acceleration was used, since it was not supported
by all available implementations.

4.1   Scene-Text Detection

First, we evaluate several state-of-the-art scene-text detection methods to be
able to compare their accuracy and runtime performance on the same data.
EAST[1] [22], PixelLink[2] [4], CRAFT[3] [1], and the detection module of EasyOCR[4]
are evaluated according to two datasets that carry distinct characteristics. The
novel tightness-aware intersection-over-union metric [14] will be used to calculate
the correspondence between ground truth bounding boxes and the detected ones.
Furthermore, the inference time is captured to put the computed accuracy in
perspective.

Two distinct datasets called ICDAR2015 [7] and Text in Videos[5] were chosen
to evaluate the STD methods. ICDAR2015 is a dataset based on still images. In
contrast to other mainstream detection datasets, ICDAR2015 is characterized
by its particular presence of blurred and low-resolution text. Text in Videos is,
as the name already suggests, a dataset based on video footage. It contains 15
videos which all in all make up almost 10 000 frames. In order to adapt the
dataset to something more manageable for frame-by-frame detection, random
frames from each video were selected to create a new and more manageable
dataset which is comprised of 538 images. These two datasets were specifically
chosen to simulate the detection of scene-text in visual multimedia. Moreover,
the groundtruth of both datasets are quadrilateral bounding boxes, which is
particularly important in this case since the output of the chosen STD methods
are also quadrilateral bounding boxes. If the ground-truth were rectangular boxes
or rotated rectangular boxes, the increased tightness of quadrilateral bounding
boxes could not be captured. Last but not least, the dataset Text in Videos also
serves the function of capturing the generalizability of the STD methods since
all of them were trained on ICDAR2015.

Table 1 shows the results with respect to both accuracy and inference time.
CRAFT is the most accurate of the compared methods but also the slowest.
EAST however, while being by far the fastest of the compared methods still
demonstrates only slightly worse accuracy. PixelLink shows comparable accuracy to EAST but with substantially higher inference times while the detection

---

[1] https://github.com/argman/EAST.
[2] https://github.com/ZJULearning/pixel_link.
[3] https://github.com/clovaai/CRAFT-pytorch.
[4] https://github.com/JaidedAI/EasyOCR.
[5] https://rrc.cvc.uab.es/.

module of EasyOCR shows the worst accuracy of all compared methods. For other STE methods for video, such as YORO, which apply detection to every frame, the trade-off between accuracy and inference time would probably lead them to use EAST in most circumstances, due to its high frame rate, despite some loss in accuracy. HyText will however be less affected in this case, since it only needs to perform detection on a subset of frames. For this reason, HyText will not only be evaluated with EAST, but also with CRAFT to see whether or not increasing the rate can allow for computationally extensive detectors such as CRAFT to be used for STE in videos.

Table 1. Overview of weighted average STD results. The results on ICDAR2015 have the weight of 0.75, and results on Text in Videos of 0.25. This is done because ICDAR2015 is a more reliable and commonly used dataset for text detection.

Name	FPS (Rank)	TIoU mean (Rank)	IoU mean (Rank)
EAST	2.84 (**1**)	52.7% (2)	76.0% (3)
EasyOCR	1.88 (2)	23.6% (4)	36.73% (4)
PixelLink	1.14 (3)	52.6% (3)	76.2% (2)
CRAFT	0.58 (4)	56.6% (**1**)	79.3% (**1**)

4.2 Scene-Text Recognition

In order to find a suitable STR component for our pipeline, we compare the performance of several methods proposed over the last few years. Specifically, we compare CRNN [19], TPS-ResNet-BiLSTM-CTC (TRBC), TPS-ResNet-BiLSTM-Attn (TRBA), SARN [9], CSTR [2] and the recognition module of EasyOCR (based on CRNN). All these methods except for the EasyOCR recognition module are trained on Synthtext [6] to allow for a fair comparison. Easy-OCR does unfortunately not share how and with which dataset their recognition module was trained on, nor does it give the possibility to train the module oneself.

In order to evaluate the performance of STR methods, the widely used word recognition accuracy (WRA) is used which is defined as:

$$WRA = \frac{W_r}{W} \tag{6}$$

where W_r is the number of correctly recognized words and W the number of total words. Inspired by how Liu et al. [14] view the correspondence between detection and ground-truth not as a binary matter (*matching* or *not-matching*), but as a spectrum which can range from *matching* to *not-matching*, we extend the mainstream WRA metric to be tightness-aware. Consequently, instead of classifying a recognition as being "correct" or "incorrect", the Jaro-Winkler Distance [21] will be used to measure the correspondence between the predicted and the ground-truth string. This new metric will be termed Tightness-aware Word Recognition Accuracy ($TWRA$) and is defined as

$$TWRA = \frac{1}{N} \sum_{i=1}^{N} JW(s_{target_i}, s_{pred_i}) \tag{7}$$

where s_{target} is the ground-truth string and s_{pred} the predicted string. JW is short for Jaro-Winkler Distance, which captures the normalized similarity between strings where 1 describes the case in which s_{target} and s_{pred} are the same and 0 the case in which they are not matching at all. Furthermore, the inference time will be captured.

The datasets used to evaluate the STR methods are ICDAR2015 [7], IIIT5K [17], and Text in Videos. They were specifically chosen because each of them carries distinct characteristics that can affect the performance of STR in visual multimedia. Namely, the images in ICDAR2015 and Text in Videos are often heavily blurred, which is a particular characteristic of natural images and especially frames in videos. IIIT5K is a dataset with more regular text. However, even though the images are rarely blurred, the fonts are often very peculiar, which is also a characteristic of natural images. For example brand names often appear in natural images, and brands often do not choose regular fonts. The company symbol for "Coca Cola" is a primary example of that. Text in Videos also distinguishes itself from the other two datasets by being based on videos.

Table 2. Overview of the weighted average STR results. Results on ICDAR2015 and IIIT5K have weights two times as high as Text in Videos, because the former two are more commonly used and reliable datasets for STR.

Method	FPS (Rank)	WRA (Rank)	TWRA (Rank)
CRNN[a]	158.3 (**1**)	54.4% (5)	81.3% (5)
EasyOCR[b]	93.79 (2)	30.4% (6)	65.0% (6)
TRBC[a]	35.56 (3)	60.7% (4)	84.1% (4)
TRBA[c]	26.25 (4)	66.6% (2)	85.8% (3)
SARN[c]	10.32 (5)	67.9% (**1**)	87.3% (**1**)
CSTR[c]	5.6 (6)	65.9% (3)	86.7% (2)

[a]https://github.com/clovaai/deep-text-recognition-benchmark
[b]https://github.com/JaidedAI/EasyOCR
[c]https://github.com/Media-Smart/vedastr

Table 2 again shows the results of the compared methods for both accuracy and frame rate. CRNN is by far the fastest method, its accuracy is however comparatively low. In contrast, the most accurate of the compared methods SARN has a roughly 15 times lower frame rate. TRBA, while being almost as accurate as SARN is more than twice as fast. Because the inference time of STR is not a primary concern, as most methods have a frame rate which is an order of magnitude higher than any STR method, we select TRBA for the evaluation of the HyText pipeline, since it provides results comparable with the most accurate method in a reasonable time.

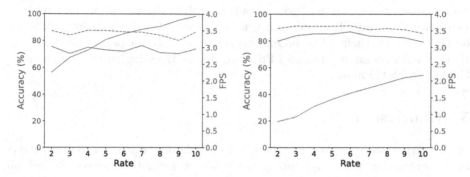

Fig. 3. Accuracy and frame rate for the full HyText pipeline with a detection rate from 2 to 10. The left plot shows results for EAST-TRBA, the right plot shows results for CRAFT-TRBA. The solid line shows WRA, the dotted line shows TWRA.

4.3 HyText

We evaluate the full HyText pipeline, sweeping the detection rate from 2 to 10 for both EAST and CRAFT for STD and TRBA for STR. Accuracy is measured using the F-Score for both WRA and TWRA. For WRA, precision (WRA_p) and recall (WRA_r) are calculated as follows:

$$WRA_p(G, D) = \frac{\sum_{j=1}^{|D|} match_D(D_j)}{|D|} \tag{8}$$

$$WRA_r(G, D) = \frac{\sum_{i=1}^{|G|} match_G(G_i)}{|G|} \tag{9}$$

where G and D represent the ground-truth and prediction set respectively. The *match* operation refers to a complete match between ground-truth and prediction. In contrast, TWRA uses the following definitions:

$$TWRA_p(G, D) = \frac{\sum_{j=1}^{|D|} match_D^*(D_j)}{|D|} \tag{10}$$

$$TWRA_r(G, D) = \frac{\sum_{i=1}^{|G|} match_G^*(G_i)}{|G|} \tag{11}$$

where *match** refers to the optimal similarity matches between two sets of strings, the Jaro-Winkler Distance is used to capture the normalized similarity between two strings, and the Hungarian Algorithm to find optimal matches.

The resulting values for WRA and TWRA as well as the frame rate of the full pipeline are shown in Fig. 3.

It can be seen that the accuracy remains consistently high throughout the entire range for the tested detection rate. Decreasing the detection rate from one in 2 frames to one in 10 frames leads to an increase in end-to-end frame rate of 174.3% when using EAST and 278.6% when using CRAFT for STD. This demonstrates that HyText can substantially increase throughput without sacrificing accuracy. The inference time for other STE methods for videos are bottlenecked by their STD module because they rely on per-frame detection. HyText achieves an end-to-end FPS score that is 375% higher than when using CRAFT for STD alone.

5   Conclusion

In this paper, we introduced HyText, a hybrid bi-directional scene-text extraction method for video. Its intermittent use of scene-text detection and bi-directional tracking can substantially increase throughput without reducing result accuracy. HyText is especially efficient in videos with a low text density, since the time requirements for the tracking component scale with the number of detected text instances. This is in contrast to other methods which apply scene-text detection regularly, since the time required for the detection process does not directly scale with the amount of text present. HyText is agnostic towards the components used for STD and STR and can therefore be easily tailored to a wide range of use cases. The evaluation showed that inference rate can be more than doubled by adjusting the rate of scene-text detection without a noticeable decrease in accuracy.

References

1. Baek, Y., Lee, B., Han, D., Yun, S., Lee, H.: Character region awareness for text detection. In: 2019 IEEE/CVF Conference on Computer Vision and Pattern Recognition (CVPR), pp. 9357–9366 (2019). https://doi.org/10.1109/CVPR.2019.00959
2. Cai, H., Sun, J., Xiong, Y.: Revisiting classification perspective on scene text recognition. arXiv preprint arXiv:2102.10884 (2021)
3. Cheng, Z., Lu, J., Xie, J., Niu, Y., Pu, S., Wu, F.: Efficient video scene text spotting: Unifying detection, tracking, and recognition. CoRR abs/1903.03299 (2019). http://arxiv.org/abs/1903.03299
4. Deng, D., Liu, H., Li, X., Cai, D.: Pixellink: detecting scene text via instance segmentation. CoRR (2018)
5. Du, Y., et al.: Pp-OCR: a practical ultra lightweight OCR system. ArXiv (2020)
6. Gupta, A., Vedaldi, A., Zisserman, A.: Synthetic data for text localisation in natural images. In: 2016 IEEE Conference on Computer Vision and Pattern Recognition (CVPR), pp. 2315–2324 (2016). https://doi.org/10.1109/CVPR.2016.254
7. Karatzas, D.: ICDAR 2015 competition on robust reading. In: 2015 13th International Conference on Document Analysis and Recognition (ICDAR), pp. 1156–1160 (2015). https://doi.org/10.1109/ICDAR.2015.7333942

8. Kuhn, H.W.: The Hungarian method for the assignment problem. Naval Res. Logist. Quart. **2**(1–2), 83–97 (1955)
9. Lee, J., Park, S., Baek, J., Oh, S.J., Kim, S., Lee, H.: On recognizing texts of arbitrary shapes with 2D self-attention. In: 2020 IEEE/CVF Conference on Computer Vision and Pattern Recognition Workshops (CVPRW), pp. 2326–2335 (2019). https://doi.org/10.1109/CVPRW50498.2020.00281
10. Liao, M., Shi, B., Bai, X.: Textboxes++: a single-shot oriented scene text detector. IEEE Trans. Image Process. **27**(8), 3676–3690 (2018). https://doi.org/10.1109/TIP.2018.2825107
11. Liao, M., et al.: Scene text recognition from two-dimensional perspective. In: Proceedings of the AAAI Conference on Artificial Intelligence, vol. 33, pp. 8714–8721 (2019). https://doi.org/10.1609/aaai.v33i01.33018714
12. Liao, M., Shi, B., Bai, X., Wang, X., Liu, W.: Textboxes: a fast text detector with a single deep neural network (2016)
13. Lin, T., et al.: Microsoft COCO: common objects in context. CoRR abs/1405.0312 (2014). http://arxiv.org/abs/1405.0312
14. Liu, Y., Jin, L., Xie, Z., Luo, C., Zhang, S., Xie, L.: Tightness-aware evaluation protocol for scene text detection. CoRR (2019)
15. Lokoč, J., et al.: Is the reign of interactive search eternal? Findings from the video browser showdown 2020. In: ACM Transactions on Multimedia Computing, Communications, and Applications, vol. 17, no. 3, July 2021. https://doi.org/10.1145/3445031
16. Lukezic, A., Vojír, T., Cehovin, L., Matas, J., Kristan, M.: Discriminative correlation filter with channel and spatial reliability. CoRR abs/1611.08461 (2016). http://arxiv.org/abs/1611.08461
17. Mishra, A., Alahari, K., Jawahar, C.V.: Scene text recognition using higher order language priors. In: BMVC (2012)
18. Needleman, S.B., Wunsch, C.D.: A general method applicable to the search for similarities in the amino acid sequence of two proteins. J. Molecular Biol. **48**(3), 443–453 (1970). https://doi.org/10.1016/0022-2836(70)90057-4
19. Shi, B., Bai, X., Yao, C.: An end-to-end trainable neural network for image-based sequence recognition and its application to scene text recognition. IEEE Trans. Pattern Anal. Mach. Intell. (2015). https://doi.org/10.1109/TPAMI.2016.2646371
20. Wang, X., et al.: End-to-end scene text recognition in videos based on multi frame tracking. In: 2017 14th IAPR International Conference on Document Analysis and Recognition (ICDAR), vol. 01, pp. 1255–1260 (2017). https://doi.org/10.1109/ICDAR.2017.207
21. Winkler, W.E.: String comparator metrics and enhanced decision rules in the Fellegi-sunter model of record linkage (1990)
22. Zhou, X., et al.: East: an efficient and accurate scene text detector. In: 2017 IEEE Conference on Computer Vision and Pattern Recognition (CVPR), pp. 2642–2651 (2017). https://doi.org/10.1109/CVPR.2017.283

Depthwise-Separable Residual Capsule
for Robust Keyword Spotting

Xianghong Huang$^{(\boxtimes)}$, Qun Yang, and Shaohan Liu

College of Computer Science and Technology, Nanjing University of Aeronautics and
Astronautics, Nanjing 210016, Jiangsu, China
xianghonghuang@nuaa.edu.cn

Abstract. Keyword spotting is widely used in device wake-up and user interaction
of smart devices. However, the resources in smart devices are limited. In order to
ensure that the keyword spotting system can always run efficiently and accurately
in smart devices, the size of the model must be compressed to realize a small and
compact model. In addition, in actual application scenarios, noise, speech rate,
and overlapped speech pose great challenges to the robustness of the model. In
order to solve the above problems, we propose a depthwise-separable residual
capsule neural network, which uses depthwise-separable convolution to achieve
a more compact design, and also uses a multi-scale capsule classifier to improve
the model's robustness in the above complex scenarios. We have achieved the best
accuracy on the Google Command dataset, and have fewer calculations and fewer
parameters than the previous methods.

Keywords: Keyword spotting · Residual neural network · Capsule neural
network

1 Introduction

The definition of keyword spotting (KWS) is to detect predefined keywords from input
audio. Recently, the market sales of smart devices such as smartphones and speakers
have gradually increased, making KWS receive more and more attention, because KWS
can wake up smart devices through spoken keywords and thus help to save energy of
the smart devices. Due to the special position of KWS in the system, if the performance
of KWS is not good, it will have a strong negative impact on user experience. Besides,
KWS must be kept running at all times to ensure that smart devices can respond to user
needs at any time, which will put a lot of restrictions on the performance of KWS. In
addition, mobile devices are often in complex environments, which brings additional
robustness challenges to KWS.

Traditional KWS systems usually use keyword/filling models. These models are
built through some traditional time series models, such as using Hidden Markov Models
(HMM) to characterize keywords and filling [1, 2], and then decode the input audio
on the above trained model to make a decision. Now, deep neural network (DNN) has
been used in KWS and achieved promising performance. In [3], DNN is used as a word

© Springer Nature Switzerland AG 2022
B. Þór Jónsson et al. (Eds.): MMM 2022, LNCS 13142, pp. 194–204, 2022.
https://doi.org/10.1007/978-3-030-98355-0_17

classifier to output posterior probabilities on a predefined set of keywords. [4] uses convolutional neural network (CNN) instead of DNN. [5] and [6] used residual connection and depthwise-separable convolution on the basis of CNN structure to improve the performance of the model. [7] proposes a joint end-to-end model of CNN and recurrent neural network (RNN). [8] and [9] use 1-D convolution instead of 2-D convolution in CNN. In order to effectively capture global features, [8] added an attention mechanism to the model, and [10] used graph convolution instead of the original model architecture. In addition, [10] uses 1x1 convolution to obtain a small-footprint model. In order to make full use of the feature information in the temporal feature space, [11] composed multiple temporal convolution filters into a CNN group, and the kernel sizes of these filters are different. [12] Define a region in advance, and then use microarchitecture technology to search for operators and corresponding connections in this region. Actually, many recent studies have carried out compact model design for equipment scenarios.

Overlapping speech processing is also an important problem in KWS application. The current solution for overlapping speech is to first separate the speech from each other, and then use algorithms trained on non-overlapping speech [13] to process the separated speech. Initial attempts to solve the problem of speech separation focused on traditional signal processing methods [14–17], but the improvements obtained are limited. In the field of deep learning, speech separation is defined as a supervised learning problem, that is, to find the distinguishing pattern of speech, speaker and background noise from training data [18]. Methods based on deep learning [19–21] have greatly improved compared to traditional methods. However, although progresses have been made the state-of-the-art result is not satisfied yet.

Existing overlapping keyword spotting systems rely on source separation. So far, there are some achievements on speech separation for multi-channel. For instance, [22] first uses the separation method to separate speech, and then recognizes the separated speech. [23] proposed a unmixing transducer. The unmixing transducer has many output channels, which can convert the input multi-channel voice into a time-synchronized voice stream. The voice of each speaker is separated and emitted from an output channel. Nevertheless, although these methods are promising in multi-channel situations, they are not suitable for single-channel scenarios. The speech detected by the keyword spotting system in most of the existing mobile devices is a single-channel speech, and the method of separating multi-channel speech cannot work in this environment. Besides, if the speech separation is performed first and then the detection is performed, the effect of the speech separation is not good, which will have a bad influence on the subsequent keyword spotting. Recently, the capsule network connects the capsule layer through dynamic routing, and has shown superior performance in overlapping digit recognition [24] and overlapping target segmentation in computer vision [25, 26]. Capsule network can achieve accurate classification of overlapping objects. In view of its advantage, we consider detecting single-channel overlapping speech through the capsule network.

In this paper, we aim at solving the robust problem of KWS for a smart device with single-channel overlapping speech. We propose a KWS architecture based on a depthwise-separable residual capsule neural network (DRCN). Our contributions in this work can be summarized into two folds: First, we reduce the network size by 4 to 20 times by applying the depthwise-separable convolution [6, 10] to the state-of-the-art keyword spotting model ResNet. Secondly, in order to ensure that our architecture can always run smoothly in smart devices, adopting the idea of multi-scale classification, we design a classifier that gathers features of multiple scales [27, 28], and use it to capture features of different time scales and depths. In the meantime, the capsule network is used as a classifier for accurate classification, which improves the robustness of KWS against noise, speech speed and overlapping speech. We also compared the previous best model on the Google Command dataset [29]. Based on the original Google Command dataset, we made a data set for a variety of environments, including a test set with noise, a test set with changes in speech rate, and a data set with overlapping speech. All experiments show that the performance of our DRCN network is better than the previous network architecture in various environments, and the overall size is smaller than the previous architecture.

This paper is organized as follows: Section 2 describes the details of our proposed method. Section 3 presents our experimental setup, results and analysis. Conclusions and future work will be discussed in Sect. 4.

2 Depthwise-Separable Residual Capsule Neural Network

2.1 Speech Preprocessing

We use a 1-s window to extract fixed-length speech segments from the speech stream at 0.5-s intervals. Each segment passes through a 20 Hz/4 kHz bandpass filter, and then uses voice activity detection (VAD) to detect the presence of voice in the audio segment and filter the silent segment. After VAD, all voice frames are divided into 30-ms frames with a frame shift of 10 ms. We calculate the 40-dimensional MFCC features of all frames and stack them into a two-dimensional feature matrix. We then use these features matrices as the input of DRCN.

2.2 System Overview

Our KWS system is shown in Fig. 1. The middle structure is a depthwise-separable residual capsule neural network (DRCN). It takes the two-dimensional feature matrix from the front-end preprocessing as input, and calculates multiple sets of probability distributions. These probability distributions include all keywords and silence items and filling items. Specifically, the input voice is the probability of each keyword in the keyword set, silence item and the filling item. Post-processing summarizes all probability distributions to make the final decision.

The DRCN structure is shown in Fig. 2. The DRCN is composed of multiple DR blocks and multi-scale capsule classifiers. After many experiments, we found that 13 DR blocks and multi-scale capsule classifiers have the best performance. The structure of the DR block is shown in Fig. 3. The depthwise-separable convolution technology is applied in the DR block to greatly compress the model size, and add a residual structure to prevent the model from generating gradient disappearance problems during the training process. The output of each DR block is converted into capsules and classified, so that the model can focus more on the keyword part of the input speech, and the capsule vector can distinguish between overlapping speech features to improve the model's robustness to noise, voice speed and overlapping speech.

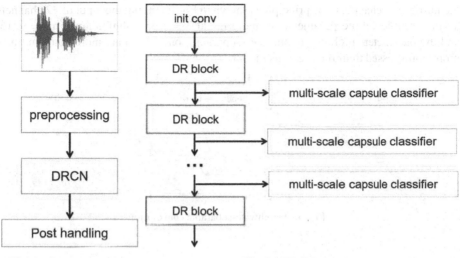

Fig. 1. System overview   **Fig. 2.** DRCN structure

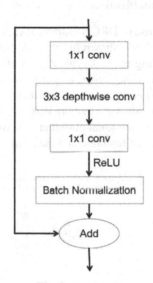

Fig. 3. DR block

2.3 Depthwise-Separable Convolution

Depthwise-separable convolution [30] has become the main method of compressing the size of the convolutional layer. Its main idea is to replace cross-channel convolution by using small cross-channel convolution and single-channel convolution. The number of parameters of the model can be greatly reduced through the reduction of channels and the use of single-channel convolution. In this article, we use 1×1 cross-channel convolution to compress the input feature map, then combine 3×3 single-channel convolution to transform the feature map, and finally use 1×1 cross-channel convolution to restore the number of channels, the principle is shown in Fig. 4. Taking the input of 32 channels as an example, all the parameters of the original 3×3 convolution are $3^2 n^2 = 9216$, and the parameters included in our deep separable convolution are more than ten times more compressed than the previous model.

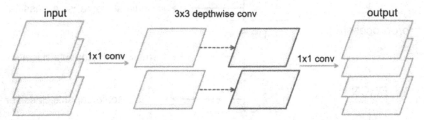

Fig. 4. Depthwise-separable convolution

2.4 Multi-scale Capsule Classification

In this article, we consider the use of DRCN outputs of various depths and time to jointly predict keywords. Our motivation is shown in Fig. 5. Although the DRCN input is a 1-s segment, the time corresponding to the keyword content may be shorter in the actual process. Therefore, we envision the model to put more attention on the keywords in the input speech. Our proposed multi-scale classification is shown in Fig. 6. Multi-scale classifiers can reduce the impact of non-keyword parts on the model. We also use a class capsule structure to replace the traditional classifier structure. The capsule network can contain multiple characteristics of features, and then can accurately identify and detect objects.

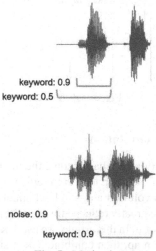

Fig. 5. Motivation

In the capsule network, the primary and class capsules process the output of the convolutional layer in an iterative manner. The primary capsule vector is converted from the output feature map. The 12 class capsules represent 12 keyword classes respectively. The information flow between the primary and class capsules is completed by a dynamic routing algorithm [24]. Each primary capsule contains multiple capsule units, and the capsule units represent the input characteristics. Each capsule unit has a weight value, which is similar to the neuron unit in a neural network, except that the neuron unit is a scalar and the capsule unit is a vector. The dynamic routing algorithm can dynamically adjust the weight value of each capsule unit during the inference process. A large weight value means that the capsule unit contributes more to the class capsule. In the end, the main capsule transmits the information of all capsule units to the class capsule through the dynamic routing algorithm. We determine the final classification by comparing the module length of the class capsule. Since the cost of using the dynamic routing algorithm is relatively large, we set the number of iterations of the dynamic routing algorithm to 3 in advance. Refer to [24], the dimension of the capsule unit is set to 16 dimensions.

The structure of our proposed multi-scale capsule classifier is shown in Fig. 6. We first use average pooling to process the features, and then convert the average pooled features into capsule vectors, and route all capsule vectors to the class through a dynamic routing algorithm. In capsules, all classes of capsules share weights to ensure the compactness of the model. The entire model can be trained in an end-to-end manner. We refer to [24] and use the cross-entropy objective function to train the entire model. Equation (1) describes the loss L_k of class k:

$$L_k = T_k max(0, m^+ - ||v_k||)^2 + \lambda(1 - T_k)max(0, ||v_k|| - m^-)^2 \qquad (1)$$

Where V_k is the length of the class capsule k, if class k exists $T_k = 1, m^- = 0.1$ and $m^+ = 0.9, \lambda$ are the descending weights of the missing class, $\lambda = 0.5$.

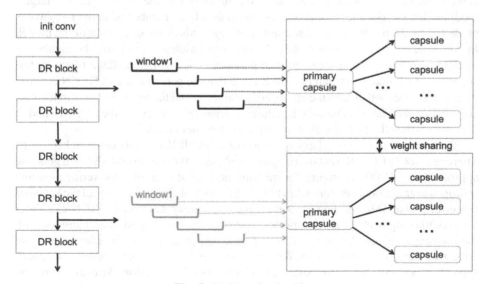

Fig. 6. Multi-scale classifier

3 Experiment

3.1 Experimental Setup

We use keywords in the Google Command dataset to evaluate the DRCN, which was released under the Creative Commons License in August 2017. The dataset contains 65,000 composed of 30 short words from thousands of different people. A one-second long speech, and background noise samples. Refer to the experiment in the paper [5], we selected the following ten types of commands: "backward", "bed", "follow", "forward", "marvin", "nine", "sheila", "six", "visual", "wow" as keyword class and all other 20 as filler class, background noise is the silence class. We divide the dataset into three parts: training set, verification machine, and test set, the ratio of which is 8:1:1. This will generate approximately 19,000 examples for training, and 2,200 examples for verification and testing. The speakers in the training set, validation set and test set have no overlapping parts. Our baseline model is similar to [5], with trad-fpool3, tpool2, one-stride1 and two variants of ResNet, Res8 and Res15.

We use cross-entropy loss with stochastic gradient descent, momentum is 0.9, and initial learning rate is 0.1. We use the Adam optimizer described in [24] to train the DRCN network. We use a batch size of 64 and train the network for 40 epochs. We use PyTorch 1.4.1 framework on Linux Ubuntu. The machine is configured as Xeon(R) W-2123 @3.6GHz, 32GB RAM and a Nvidia GeForce GTX TITAN Xp 11GB.

3.2 Experiment and Evaluation

In this experiment, we use ten classes of keywords to evaluate the performance of DRCN and compare it with the state-of-the-art baseline model. The traditional neural network determines the final classification based on the largest probability value, while the DRCN determines the final classification based on the class capsule vector with the largest modulus length. For the metric, we use the ratio of the number of correct keywords predicted by the model to the total number of keywords as the evaluation of the model. In addition, compare the size of DRCN and each baseline model, use the number of model multiplications and the number of parameters as evaluation. Table 1 lists the test accuracy of all models. In Table 1, we can see that the performance of DRCN is better than all baseline models, and the number of parameters and the number of multiplications are much lower than other models, and the performance is far beyond the previous model. This shows the effectiveness of our compression model method.

We build a dataset of overlapping keywords using all 10 chosen classes of keywords. There are a total of 45 different overlapping combinations of keywords. This will generate approximately 81,000 examples for training, and 9,900 examples for verification and testing. The traditional network takes the two largest probabilities among all the keyword posterior probabilities as the decision for the final output keywords. DRCN calculates the module length of all class capsules, and uses the two largest class capsules with the module length as the decision for the final output keywords. In order to compare with the method of separation and detection, we use TasNet, which has the best speech separation performance, as the baseline model for speech separation. We use overlapping keyword datasets to train TasNet for speech separation. Next, we use the Res15 model

Table 1. The size and accuracy results of each model

Model	#param	#mul	Accuracy
trad-fpool3	1.73M	125M	90.5%
tpool2	1.09M	103M	91.7%
one-stride1	954K	5.76M	77.9%
res15	238K	894M	95.8%
res8	110K	30M	94.1%
DRCN	**64.5K**	**9.67M**	**96.02%**

trained in the previous experiment as the detection model. In the test phase, TasNet takes overlapping keywords as input and outputs separated keyword voices, and then uses Res15 to recognize the separated keyword voices. We make an noise test set and an quick speech test set. The noise test set is based on the original pure speech test set, adding 3 kinds of noise (flowing water sound, office sound, car sound), and the random signal-to-noise ratio is between 5 dB–15 dB. The quick speech test set is constructed through a 1.2 times time stretch.

The results in Table 2 show that for the test set with noise, fast speech interference and overlapping keywords, multi-scale capsule classification helps to improve the accuracy of all variables in all test sets. The improvement in the fast speech test set shows that multi-scale classification can resist the influence of time stretch on keyword content. For the test set with overlapping keywords, both Res15 and DRCN have higher accuracy than the separation + recognition method realized by TasNet + Res15. Although the samples separated by TasNet are understandable to humans, there are also some human factors that will negatively affect subsequent keyword detection algorithms.

Table 2. Keyword spotting robustness experimental results

Model	Accuracy (noise)	Accuracy (fast)	Accuracy (overlapped)
TasNet + Res15			73.08%
Res15	89.2%	91.7%	88.75%
DRCN	**91.75%**	**94.2%**	**90.01%**

3.3 Feature Visualization

Figure 7 visualizes the feature maps of two noisy speech at specific layers. It can be observed from Fig. 7 that the noise features are more obvious in the shallow layer (left figure), and the keyword features are relatively fuzzy, but in the deep layer (right figure), the opposite is true, and the areas of the keyword parts contained in the feature maps of different layers are not the same. Using proper interval for pooling can avoid the interference of non-overlapping noise features in the time dimension, thereby having better noise robustness.

Figure 8 shows the feature maps of fast-speaking keywords on different layers collected by multi-scale capsule classification: The left picture shows the shallow features, and the right picture shows the deep features. As expected, The features of the shallow layer are more compact, and the features of the deep layer are more divergent. Therefore, the shallow pool can provide more meaningful keyword features to help the model detect.

As shown in Fig. 9, we used the reconstruction network [24] to reconstruct the spectrograms of the overlapping words "cat" and "dog" and compare them with their original spectrograms. The figure on the left is the reconstructed spectrogram, and the picture on the right is the original spectrogram. We can see that the two pictures are very similar, which proves that the capsule network in DRCN can fully tap the unique features in overlapping speech. The capsule layer uses multi-dimensional vectors to encode features to enable the network to make more accurate decisions. Traditional convolutional neural networks use pooling operations to make feature detection decisions. However, pooling operations will cause many features to be filtered out, such as location, size, and direction. Therefore, although the pooling operation can detect general voices well, the performance of the pooling operation is not ideal when there are overlapping voices.

Fig. 7. Input feature map for noisy speech

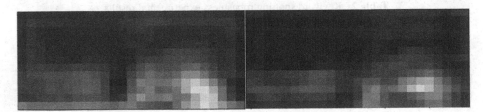

Fig. 8. Input feature map for fast-speaking speech

Fig. 9. The spectrogram restored by the capsule classifier and the original spectrogram

4 Conclusion

This paper proposes a keyword spotting model that combines depthwise-separable residual blocks and multi-scale capsule classifiers. This model is more compact than previous models and achieves promising performance in complex scenes such as noise, overlapping speech and fast speech scenes. In future work, we plan deeper research to explain the robustness of the multi-scale method to the noise that the model does not train, and continue to explore the architecture of a more suitable DRCN model, as well as the DRCN in more overlapping speech environments. Exploring these mechanisms will help design a more principled but still compact KWS architecture and training method.

References

1. Wu, M., Panchapagesan, S., Sun, M., et al.: Monophone-based background modeling for two-stage on-device wake word detection. In: 2018 IEEE International Conference on Acoustics, Speech and Signal Processing (ICASSP), pp. 5494–5498. IEEE (2018)
2. Ge, F., Yan, Y.: Deep neural network based wake-up-word speech recognition with two-stage detection. In: 2017 IEEE International Conference on Acoustics, Speech and Signal Processing (ICASSP), pp. 2761–2765. IEEE (2017)
3. Chen, G., Parada, C., Heigold, G.: Small-footprint keyword spotting using deep neural networks. In: 2014 IEEE International Conference on Acoustics, Speech and Signal Processing (ICASSP), pp. 4087–4091. IEEE (2014)
4. Sainath, T.N., Parada, C.: Convolutional neural networks for small-footprint keyword spotting. In: Sixteenth Annual Conference of the International Speech Communication Association (2015)
5. Tang, R., Lin, J.: Deep residual learning for small-footprint keyword spotting. In: 2018 IEEE International Conference on Acoustics, Speech and Signal Processing (ICASSP), pp. 5484–5488. IEEE (2018)
6. Zhang, Y., Suda, N., Lai, L., et al.: Hello edge: keyword spotting on microcontrollers. arXiv preprint arXiv:1711.07128 (2017)
7. Arik, S.O., Kliegl, M., Child, R., et al.: Convolutional recurrent neural networks for small-footprint keyword spotting. arXiv preprint arXiv:1703.05390 (2017)
8. Bai, Y., Yi, J., Tao, J., et al.: A time delay neural network with shared weight self-attention for small-footprint keyword spotting. In: INTERSPEECH 2019, pp. 2190–2194 (2019)
9. Choi, S., Seo, S., Shin, B., et al.: Temporal convolution for real-time keyword spotting on mobile devices. arXiv preprint arXiv:1904.03814 (2019)
10. Chen, X., Yin, S., Song, D., et al.: Small-footprint keyword spotting with graph convolutional network. In: 2019 IEEE Automatic Speech Recognition and Understanding Workshop (ASRU), pp. 539–546. IEEE (2019)

11. Li, X., Wei, X., Qin, X.: Small-Footprint Keyword Spotting with Multi-Scale Temporal Convolution. arXiv preprint arXiv:2010.09960 (2020)
12. Mo, T., Yu, Y., Salameh, M., et al.: Neural architecture search for keyword spotting. arXiv preprint arXiv:2009.00165 (2020)
13. Chen, Z., Xiao, X., Yoshioka, T., et al.: Multi-channel overlapped speech recognition with location guided speech extraction network. In: 2018 IEEE Spoken Language Technology Workshop (SLT), pp. 558–565. IEEE (2018)
14. Boll, S.: Suppression of acoustic noise in speech using spectral subtraction. IEEE Trans. Acoust. Speech Signal Process. **27**(2), 113–120 (1979)
15. Ephraim, Y., Malah, D.: Speech enhancement using a minimum-mean square error short-time spectral amplitude estimator. IEEE Trans. Acoust. Speech Signal Process. **32**(6), 1109–1121 (1984)
16. Bregman, A.S.: Auditory Scene Analysis: The Perceptual Organization of Sound. MIT Press, Cambridge (1994)
17. Hu, G., Wang, D.L.: A tandem algorithm for pitch estimation and voiced speech segregation. IEEE Trans. Audio Speech Lang. Process. **18**(8), 2067–2079 (2010)
18. Wang, D.L., Chen, J.: Supervised speech separation based on deep learning: an overview. IEEE/ACM Trans. Audio Speech Lang. Process. **26**(10), 1702–1726 (2018)
19. Huang, P.S., Kim, M., Hasegawa-Johnson, M., et al.: Deep learning for monaural speech separation. In: 2014 IEEE International Conference on Acoustics, Speech and Signal Processing (ICASSP), pp. 1562–1566. IEEE (2014)
20. Luo, Y., Mesgarani, N.: TasNet: time-domain audio separation network for real-time, single-channel speech separation. In: 2018 IEEE International Conference on Acoustics, Speech and Signal Processing (ICASSP), pp. 696–700. IEEE (2018)
21. Yu, D., Kolbæk, M., Tan, Z.H., et al.: Permutation invariant training of deep models for speaker-independent multi-talker speech separation. In: 2017 IEEE International Conference on Acoustics, Speech and Signal Processing (ICASSP), pp. 241–245. IEEE (2017)
22. Boakye, K., Trueba-Hornero, B., Vinyals, O., et al.: Overlapped speech detection for improved speaker diarization in multiparty meetings. In: 2008 IEEE International Conference on Acoustics, Speech and Signal Processing, pp. 4353–4356. IEEE (2008)
23. Yoshioka, T., Erdogan, H., Chen, Z., et al.: Recognizing overlapped speech in meetings: a multichannel separation approach using neural networks. arXiv preprint arXiv:1810.03655 (2018)
24. Sabour, S., Frosst, N., Hinton, G.E.: Dynamic routing between capsules. arXiv preprint arXiv: 1710.09829 (2017)
25. LaLonde, R., Bagci, U.: Capsules for object segmentation. arXiv preprint arXiv:1804.04241 (2018)
26. Afshar, P., Mohammadi, A., Plataniotis, K.N.: Brain tumor type classification via capsule networks. In: 2018 25th IEEE International Conference on Image Processing (ICIP), pp. 3129–3133. IEEE (2018)
27. Ren, S., He, K., Girshick, R., et al.: Faster R-CNN: towards real-time object detection with region proposal networks. Adv. Neural. Inf. Process. Syst. **2015**(28), 91–99 (2015)
28. Liu, W., et al.: SSD: single shot multibox detector. In: Leibe, B., Matas, J., Sebe, N., Welling, M. (eds.) ECCV 2016. LNCS, vol. 9905, pp. 21–37. Springer, Cham (2016). https://doi.org/10.1007/978-3-319-46448-0_2
29. Warden, P.: Speech commands: a dataset for limited-vocabulary speech recognition. arXiv preprint arXiv:1804.03209 (2018)
30. Chollet, F.: Xception: deep learning with depthwise separable convolutions. In: Proceedings of the IEEE Conference on Computer Vision and Pattern Recognition, pp. 1251–1258 (2017)

Adaptive Speech Intelligibility Enhancement for Far-and-Near-end Noise Environments Based on Self-attention StarGAN

Dengshi Li[1](✉), Lanxin Zhao[1], Jing Xiao[2], Jiaqi Liu[2], Duanzheng Guan[1], and Qianrui Wang[1]

[1] School of Artificial Intelligence, Jianghan University, Wuhan 430056, China
reallds@jhun.edu.cn
[2] National Engineering Research Center for Multimedia Software,
School of Computer, Wuhan University, Wuhan 430072, China

Abstract. When exposed to adverse noisy environments, it is difficult for listeners to obtain information even if the device outputs clear speech. Using Lombard effect, previous studies introduced the conversion from normal speech without noise to Lombard speech at the near-end. However, these method ignored the noise at the far-end and were very poorly effective in strong noise at the near-end interference with very low signal-to-noise ratios (SNRs). In this paper, Adaptive Self-Attention StarGAN (AdaSAStarGAN) is proposed to designe an adaptive Speech Style Conversion (SSC) scheme for near-and-far-end ambient noise. The generator of StarGAN combined the self-attention mechanism and AdaIN with convolutional neural networks (CNNs). In addition, the model was trained on corpus recorded in different noise conditions. Subjective and objective evaluation results show that this method has better intelligibility and naturalness in different far-and-near-end noise environments, especially in low SNRs environments. It enables flexible conversion between normal speech and multi-level Lombard speech, thus making speech intelligibility enhancement more widely used in practice.

Keywords: Speech intelligibility enhancement · Lombard effect · StarGAN · Self-attention mechanism · AdaIN

1 Introduction

In recent years, how to enhance the intelligibility of speech in noisy environments has gathered increasing interest. This topic is known as speech intelligibility enhancement [1] or near-end listening enhancement, which is a perceptual

Supported by Natural Science Foundation of China (No. 61701194), Nature Science Foundation of Hubei Province (2017CFB756), Application Foundation Frontier Special Project of Wuhan Science and Technology Plan Project (No. 2020010601012288) and Doctoral Research Foundation of Jianghan University (2019029).

© Springer Nature Switzerland AG 2022
B. Þór Jónsson et al. (Eds.): MMM 2022, LNCS 13142, pp. 205–217, 2022.
https://doi.org/10.1007/978-3-030-98355-0_18

enhancement technique for clean (non-noisy) speech reproduced in noisy environments. It is typically used in the listening stage of multimedia communications, such as listening to telephones or other multimedia interactive devices.

In early studies, speech intelligibility enhancement was mainly accomplished by energy redistribution over frequency-domain based on acoustic masking principles and digital signal processing (DSP) algorithms [2]. However, this approach was very crude and caused a serious decline in the naturalness of speech [3]. For maintaining the naturalness, a new data-driven approach is drawing increasing attention, which was inspired by a human vocal mechanism named Lombard effect [4]. The Lombard effect shows that the speaking style of the speaker involuntarily changes due to noise levels. Loud noise leads to a more pronounced Lombard effect, which results in improving speech intelligibility with a major acoustical and linguistic change. This approach utilizes the data to learn and model these changes, similar to the popular visual signal enhancement tasks [5–8]. Specifically, it uses normal style speech (i.e., speaking in quiet environments) and Lombard style speech (i.e., speaking in noisy environments) to train a normal-to-Lombard style conversion system, which is also called as speaking style conversion (SSC). SSC methods enhance speech intelligibility while better maintaining speech naturalness.

Many previous studies (e.g., [3,9]) are parallel SSC, which relies on the availability of parallel utterance pairs of the source (normal) and target (Lombard) speech. However the speaker usually has a slower speech rate under the Lombard reflex. Parallel SSC needs time-alignment operations to preprocess training data, which is conducted by lossy algorithms (e.g., dynamic time warping) resulted in some feature distortions. It encourages the use of non-parallel SSC to avoid time-alignment operations. Some recent studies [10,11] have incorporated cycle-consistent generative adversarial networks (CycleGANs) [12] and StarGAN [13] show promising results. This makes it possible to learn a sequence-based mapping function without relying on parallel data. Compared with parallel SSC they have better intelligibility and naturalness. Moreover, StarGAN addresses multi-domain SSC more effectively than CycleGAN and learns mappings between multiple domains (e.g., multiple levels of Lombard language).

However, in practical applications, there are limitations in simply converting from normal to Lombard speech, as the speaker needs to be in a completely noise-free environment in order to speak normal speech. In some voice calls, the speaker (for the far-end) and the receiver (for the near-end) are in different noisy environments, making the speaker use Lombard speech. In this scenario, the implementation of normal-to-Lombard speech style conversion is not as effective as expected. The non-parallel SSC framework of the latest baseline methods is given as Fig. 1 (a). Furthermore, even using StarGAN, there is still an insurmountable gap between real and converted speech. SSC only with the Lombard effect still does not work well in strong noise interference with very low signal-to-noise ratios (SNRs). StarGAN-VC2 [14] uses conditional instance normalization (CIN) [15] to improve the speaker adaptation ability of the model. However, the parameters in CIN are learned during training, which may reduce the efficiency of training.

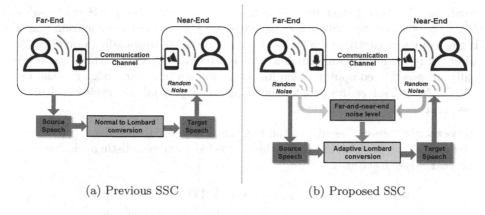

(a) Previous SSC

(b) Proposed SSC

Fig. 1. Non-parallel SSC.

To overcome the first limitation, we designed a non-parallel SSC framework for adaptive speech enhancement for far-end and near-end noise environments for the need of converting the Lombard speech from the far-end environment to the near-end environment. As seen in Fig. 1 (b), in the application scenario where noise is present at both the far-and-near-ends, the far-end noise level and the near-end noise level are used as conversion conditions to achieve conversion between different Lombard speeches and normal speech.

To overcome the second limitation, we proposed the use of Adaptive Instance Normalization (AdaIN) [16] and Self-Attention mechanism [17], which combine with Convolutional Neural Networks (CNNs) as a generator for StarGAN named AdaSAStarGAN. We examined the performance of the proposed methods on the multi-level SSC task using the Lombard speech database for German Language [18]. An objective evaluation demonstrates that the proposed methods has better results in terms of evaluation indicators.

In Sect. 2, we review the baseline StarGAN-VC2. In Sect. 3, we describe the proposed AdaSAStarGAN. In Sect. 4, we report the experimental results. We conclude in Sect. 5 with a brief summary.

2   Baseline: StarGAN-VC2

StarGAN can effectively solve multi-domain SSC. StarGAN-VC2 [14] is the latest approach to multi-domain SCC using StarGAN, which addresses the problem of multi-person identity voice conversion (VC). VC studies different human tone styles, and conversion between Lombard speech and Normal speech studies the style of different Lombard levels. Therefore, StarGAN-VC2 is chosen as the baseline for this paper.

The goal of training StarGAN-VC2 is to get a single generator G and learn mappings between multiple domains. More precisely, StarGAN-VC2 learns a generator G that converts an input acoustic feature x into an output feature y'

conditioned on the target domain code n', i.e., $G(\boldsymbol{x}, n') \rightarrow \boldsymbol{y}'$. Here, let $\boldsymbol{y}' \in \mathbb{R}^{Q \times T}$ be an acoustic feature sequence where Q is the feature dimension and T is the sequence length, and let $n \in \{1, ..., N\}$ be the corresponding domain code where N is the number of domains. Inspired by StarGAN [13], which was originally proposed in computer vision for multi-domain image-to-image translation, StarGAN-VC2 solves this problem by using an adversarial loss, cycle-consistency loss, and identity-mapping loss.

Adversarial Loss: The adversarial loss full name source-and-target conditional adversarial loss is used to render the converted feature indistinguishable from the real target feature:

$$
\begin{aligned}
\mathcal{L}_{st-adv} = \mathbb{E}_{(\boldsymbol{x},n) \sim P(\boldsymbol{x},n), n' \sim P(n')} \left[\log D\left(\boldsymbol{x}, n', n\right) \right] \\
+ \mathbb{E}_{(\boldsymbol{x},n) \sim P(\boldsymbol{x},n), n' \sim P(n')} \left[\log D\left(G\left(\boldsymbol{x}, n, n'\right), n, n'\right) \right]
\end{aligned}
\tag{1}
$$

where $n' \sim P(n')$ is randomly sampled independently of real data. Where D is a target conditional discriminator. By maximizing this loss, D attempts to learn the best decision boundary between the converted and real acoustic features conditioned on the target domain codes (n and n'). In contrast, G attempts to render the converted feature indistinguishable from real acoustic features conditioned on n' by minimizing this loss.

Cycle-Consistency Loss: Although the adversarial loss and classification loss encourage a converted acoustic feature to become realistic and classifiable, respectively, they do not guarantee that the converted feature will preserve the input composition. To mitigate this problem, the cycle-consistency loss is used:

$$
\mathcal{L}_{cyc} = \mathbb{E}_{(\boldsymbol{x},n) \sim P(\boldsymbol{x},n), n' \sim P(n')} \left[\|\boldsymbol{x} - G\left(G\left(\boldsymbol{x}, n'\right), n\right)\|_1 \right]
\tag{2}
$$

This cyclic constraint encourages G to find out an optimal source and target pair that does not compromise the composition.

Identity-Mapping Loss: To impose a further constraint on the input preservation, the identity-mapping loss is used:

$$
\mathcal{L}_{id} = \mathbb{E}_{(\boldsymbol{x},n) \sim P(\boldsymbol{x},n)} [\|G(\boldsymbol{x}, n) - \boldsymbol{x}\|]
\tag{3}
$$

where D and G are optimized by minimizing $\mathcal{L}_{st-adv}$, $\mathcal{L}_{cyc}$, and $\mathcal{L}_{id}$, respectively.

3   Method

3.1   Adaptive for Far-and-Near-end Noise Environments

In this section, we will introduce our proposed Noise Adaptive Self-Attention StarGAN (AdaSASTarGAN). The structure of the framework is shown in Fig. 2.
    The input to this framework is far-end ambient noise mixed with the speaker's speech. The following operations include speech separation stage, preprocessing stage, feature mapping stage and target speech synthesis stage. In the speech separation stage, the far-end speech is separated into the far-end noise and the

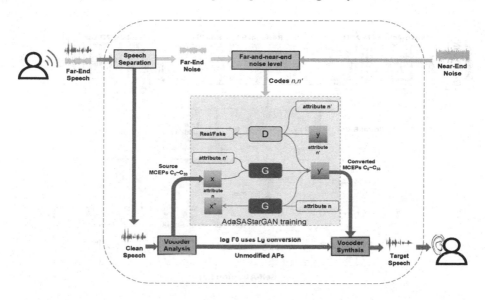

Fig. 2. The overall framework of our proposed method. The input to this frame is the far-end speaker's speech mixed with ambient noise. After speech separation, considering the necessity of noise adaptation, we add the near-and-far-end noise levels as the mapping condition.

clean speech as the source speech. In the preprocessing stage, WORLD [19] vocoder is used to extract features Mel-cepstral coefficients (MCEPs), logarithmic fundamental frequency (log F0) and aperiodicities (APs) from the source speech. Then, we obtain the far-end noise level and the near-end noise level simultaneously. In feature mapping stage, the far-and-near-end noise levels are used as conditions for mapping source speech features to target speech features. In target speech synthesis stage, the WORLD vocoder synthesizes the target enhanced speech. Finally, the target enhancement speech is obtained.

Under this framework, multi-level SSC between multi-level Lombard speeches and normal speech can be realized according to different near-and-far-end noise levels. It can better ensure the intelligibility and naturalness of the converted speech.

3.2 Self-attention Layer: SA

In this section, we introduce self-attention layer [20] into the generator of the StarGAN framework, enabling the generator and discriminator to model the relationships between widely separated spatial regions effectively. The self-attention layer can increase the number of model parameters and improve the fitting ability of the model. Since it contains self-attention module, we call this method AdaSAStarGAN. Figure 3 shows the generator's structure, where we add the self-attention layer in the residual block and show the proposed self-attention module.

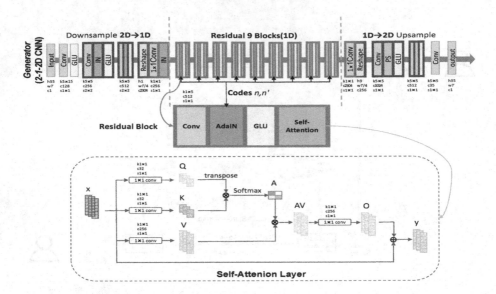

Fig. 3. Generator network structure, residual block structure and self-attention module. Source domain code n and target domain code n' input AdaIN. In input, output, and reshape layers, h, w, and c represent height, width, and number of channels, respectively. In each convolution layer, k, c, and s denote kernel size, number of channels, and stride, respectively.

The proposed self-attention laye given the feature map $\boldsymbol{x} \in \mathbb{R}^{L \times C}$ output by a convolutional layer, where L is the time dimension, C is the number of channels. Note that the feature dimension is one since we are using 1D convolution to deal with raw speech input in this case. The query matrix $\boldsymbol{Q}$, the key matrix $\boldsymbol{K}$, and the value matrix $\boldsymbol{V}$ are obtained via transformations:

$$\mathbf{Q} = \boldsymbol{x}\mathbf{W}_Q, \mathbf{K} = \boldsymbol{x}\mathbf{W}_K, \mathbf{V} = \boldsymbol{x}\mathbf{W}_V \tag{4}$$

where $\mathbf{W}_Q \in \mathbb{R}^{C \times \frac{C}{k}}, \mathbf{W}_K \in \mathbb{R}^{C \times \frac{C}{k}}$, and $\mathbf{W}_V \in \mathbb{R}^{C \times \frac{C}{k}}$ denote the weight matrices which are implemented by a 1×1 convolution layer of $\frac{C}{k}$ filters. That is, in the new feature spaces, the channel dimension is reduced by the factor k mainly for memory reduction. Furthermore, given the $O\left(n^2\right)$ memory complexity, we also reduce the number of keys and values (i.e. the time dimension of $\mathbf{K}$ and $\mathbf{V}$) by a factor of p for memory efficiency. This is accomplished by a max pooling layer with filter width and stride size of p. We use $k = 8$ and $p = 4$ here. The size of the matrices are, therefore, $\mathbf{Q} \in \mathbb{R}^{L \times \frac{C}{k}}, \mathbf{K} \in \mathbb{R}^{\frac{L}{p} \times \frac{C}{k}}$, and $\mathbf{V} \in \mathbb{R}^{\frac{L}{p} \times \frac{C}{k}}$. The attention map $\mathbf{A}$ and the attentive output $\mathbf{O}$ are then computed as

$$\mathbf{A} = \text{softmax}\left(\mathbf{Q}\overline{\mathbf{K}}^{\top}\right), \quad \mathbf{A} \in \mathbb{R}^{L \times \frac{L}{p}} \tag{5}$$

$$\mathbf{O} = (\mathbf{AV})\mathbf{W}_O, \quad \mathbf{W}_O \in \mathbb{R}^{\frac{C}{k} \times C} \tag{6}$$

Each element $a_{ij} \in \mathbf{A}$ indicates the extent to which the model attends to the jth column $\mathbf{v}_j$ of $\mathbf{V}$ when producing the ith output $\mathbf{O}_i$ of O. In addition, a transformation with weight $\mathbf{W}_O$ realized by a 1×1 convolution layer of C filters is applied to $\mathbf{AV}$ to restore the shape of O to the original shape $L \times C$.

Finally, we make use of a shortcut connection to facilitate information propagation, where β is a learnable parameter, with the final output given as:

$$y = \beta \mathbf{O} + x \tag{7}$$

3.3 Adaptive Instance Normalization: AdaIN

Adaptive instance normalization [16] (AdaIN) was initially proposed for image style transfer tasks. It enables real-time arbitrary style conversion compared to CIN, which requires a slower iterative optimization process. AdaIN changes the data distribution at the level of feature map and aligns the mean value and variance of content features with style features. Figure 3 shows AdaIN in the residual layer, which receives data with source and target domain codes n and n' in addition to speech features.

Given the source feature x and target feature y, their domain codes are n and n'. AdaIN conducts the following procedure:

$$\text{AdaIN}(x, y) = \sigma(y) \left(\frac{x - \mu(x)}{\sigma(x)} \right) + \mu(y) \tag{8}$$

where μ and σ are the mean and the standard deviation of the feature.

4 Experiments

4.1 Experimental Setup

Dataset: We evaluated our method on the multi-level lombard SSC task using Lombard speech database for German Language [18]. The dataset contains and normal speech recorded in a noiseless environment and two levels of Lombard speech recorded in a low or high noise environment. Each of these has 96 and 24 sentences for training and evaluation, respectively. The recordings were downsampled to 16 kHz for this challenge.

Environmental Noise: Two types of noise were involved in the experiments from NOISEX-92 database [21], referring to relevant studies. They were Factory1 (non-stationary) and Babble (stationary).

SSC Implementation. We designed the network architectures on the basis of StarGAN-VC2 [14], i.e., we used a 2-1-2D CNN in G and a 2D CNN in D. For a GAN objective, we used a least squares GAN. IN, GLU and PS indicate instance normalization, gated linear unit, pixel shuffler, and global sum pooling, respectively. The generator is fully convolutional. We trained the networks using the Adam optimizer with a batch size of 8, in which we used a randomly cropped segment (128 frames) as one instance. The number of iterations was set to 2×10^4, learning rates for G and D were set to 0.0002 and 0.0001, respectively, and the momentum term was set to 0.5. We set $\lambda_{cyc} = 10$, $\lambda_{id} = 5$, and $\lambda_{cls} = 1$.

4.2   Experiment Content

Table 1 shows whether the methods can be used in different near-and-far-end noise environments, and Table 2 shows the contents of three objective and subjective experiments. Two comparison methods are the latest non-parallel SSC method based on CycleGAN(CGAN) [10] and Stargan-VC2 (SGAN) [14] respectively. Where CGAN is a one-to-one mapping, a model is trained for each case in this paper.

Table 1. Methods that can be used in different near-and-far-end environments.

Methods	Noise level (Far-end - Near-end)					
	Zero-Low	Zero-High	Low-Zero	Low-High	High-zero	High-low
CGAN	√	√	×	×	×	×
SGAN	√	√	√	√	√	√
AdaSAStarGAN	√	√	√	√	√	√

Table 2. Objective and subjective experiment content.

Experiment		Comparison method	Far-end noise level	Near-end noise level
Objective	1	CGAN & SGAN	Zero	Low & High
	2	SGAN	Low	High
	3	CGAN & SGAN	All conversion	
Subjective		CGAN & SGAN	Zero & Low & High	Changing ambient noise

In the table, Zero, low and high represent the environmental noise level. The level mark in the front indicates the far-end noise level, and the level mark in the back indicates the near-end noise level. (e.g., Zero-Low means that far-end has no noise and the noise level at near-end is low.). "All conversion" in Table 2 indicates that objective experiment 3 will consider 6 conversion scenarios.

We set up three objective experiments: 1) the far-end has no noise and the near-end has noise of different levels and types; 2) the far-end has low noise and the near-end has high noise with different types; 3) All far-and-near-end noise cases with noise type are factory1. Experiment 1 was a conventional test in the field of speech intelligibility enhancement, but the far-end no-noise setting was often inconsistent with practical application. Therefore, we set up experiments 2 and 3 to show the objective experimental results under different conditions.

We designed three scenarios in the subjective experiment. The far-end was set to three noise levels, thus the source speech was normal speech, Low Lombard speech and high lombard speech respectively. We produced the 20 s of audio to simulate the changing near-end environment, in which each noise was 4 s, in the order of high-babble, low-babble, zero, low-factory1, and high-factory1. The current speech intelligibility enhancement method does not have the noise adaptive mechanism and does not convert different levels of Lombard speech, so we only used the model of normal speech converted to high Lombard speech for the comparison method.

4.3 Objective Evaluation

Two objective intelligibility metrics were used for objective evaluation: 1) speech intelligibility in bits with the information capacity of a Gaussian channel ($SIIB^{Gauss}$) [22] is used to estimate the amount of information shared between the speaker and listener in bits/s. 2) short-time objective intelligibility (STOI) [23] to predict human perception and intelligibility of an utterance from 0 (0%) to 1 (100%).

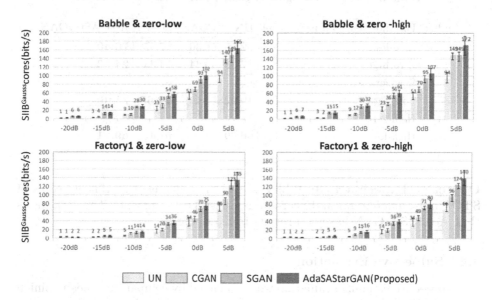

Fig. 4. No noise at the far-end. Objective $SIIB^{Gauss}$ scores with 95% confidence intervals at different SNRs, near-end noise types and different target Lombard levels of conversion.

Objective Experiment 1: Figure 4 gives objective evaluation scores of $SIIB^{Gauss}$. UN means unprocessed speech. Compared to UN, AdaSAStarGAN improves intelligibility significantly and $SIIB^{Gauss}$ scores increase 110%. Compared to CGAN and SGAN, AdaSAStarGAN improves $SIIB^{Gauss}$ scores by approximately 30% and 11% respectively.

Objective Experiment 2: Figure 5 shows the objective experiment scores of $SIIB^{Gauss}$. In this case, the source speech (UN) was low Lombard speech. $SIIB^{Gauss}$ scores are two times and one times higher than UN and SGAN at low SNRs, respectively. This shows that AdaSastrgan can keep good intelligibility at very low SNRs.

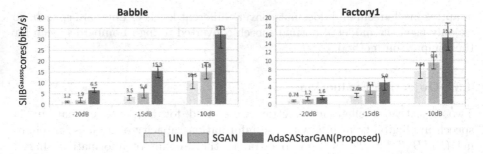

Fig. 5. Low level noise at the far-end. Objective $SIIB^{Gauss}$ scores with 95% confidence intervals at different SNRs and near-end noise types.

Table 3. Average intelligibility score STOI under Factory noise.

Index	Far-and-Near-end noise level	UN	CGAN	SGAN	AdaSAStarGAN
STOI	Zero-low	62.55	66.30	67.57	**70.40**
	Zero-high	17.36	19.44	24.33	**24.82**
	Low-zero	–	–	–	–
	Low-high	19.92	–	**22.60**	22.16
	High-zero	–	–	–	–
	High-low	66.99	–	61.41	**69.21**

Objective Experiment 3: Table 3 shows the objective experiment scores of STOI under different far-and-near-end noise level environments. The data shows that AdaSAStarGAN has good results in most cases.

4.4   Subjective Evaluation

The subjective listening evaluation was conducted by comparative mean opinion score (CMOS) standard [24]. The listeners were asked to give a relative score of two methods on the same utterance from −3 to 3 rating: −3) much worse; −2) worse; −1) slightly worse; 0) about the same; 1) slightly better; 2) better; 3) much better. The ratings were based on intelligibility and naturalness, respectively. Twenty participants tested in an anechoic chamber with the Audio-Technica ATH-M50x headphones, where the speech had been processed and mixed with noise. They were aged 20 to 40. Each listener evaluated 64 records: 4 methods per utterance × (2 females + 2 males) × 4 groups of comparisons.

Figure 6 shows the results for CMOS, there is no score below 0, which means AdaSAStarGAN has stable improvements over reference methods. Compared to UN, AdaSAStarGAN gets about 1.6 to 2 scores with an average of 1.8, which denotes significant intelligibility improvements. Compared to CGAN, SGAN and AdaSAStarGAN with a single conversion, AdaSAStarGAN gets about 0.5 to 1 scores with an average of 0.8. It is a relatively effective improvement. When noise

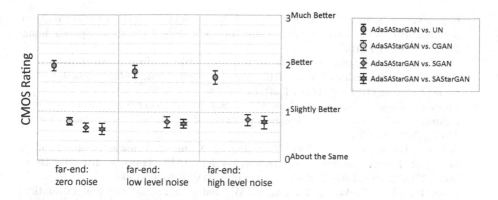

Fig. 6. CMOS for naturalness with 95% confidence intervals.

appears at the far-end, AdaSAStarGAN has better intelligibility and naturalness. Overall, the results of subjective experiments are basically consistent with the performance of objective experiments.

5 Conclusion

In this paper, we propose an adaptive speech intelligibility enhancement method based on Adaptive Self-Attention StarGAN in far-and-near-end noise environments, named AdaSAStarGAN. Compared with previous methods, it has two main advantages. One is that we applied the self-attention layer and Adaptive Instance Normalization (AdaIN) in the convolution layer of CNNs as the generator of AdaSAStarGAN. Another point is that AdaSAStarGAN has the flexibility to convert between normal speech and different levels of Lombard speech depending on the far-and-near-end noise environments. In objective evaluation, AdaSAStarGAN is better than reference methods with significant improvement in different indexes. Our method maintaining both intelligibility and naturalness in low SNRs environments, making the application of speech intelligibility enhancement more widespread.

References

1. Kleijn, W.B., Crespo, J.B., Hendriks, R.C., Petkov, P., Sauert, B., Vary, P.: Optimizing speech intelligibility in a noisy environment: a unified view. IEEE Signal Process. Mag. **32**(2), 43–54 (2015)
2. Zorila, T.C., Kandia, V., Stylianou, Y.: Speech-in-noise intelligibility improvement based on spectral shaping and dynamic range compression. In: Thirteenth Annual Conference of the International Speech Communication Association (2012)
3. Jokinen, E., Remes, U., Takanen, M., Palomäki, K., Kurimo, M., Alku, P.: Spectral tilt modelling with extrapolated GMMs for intelligibility enhancement of narrowband telephone speech. In: 2014 14th International Workshop on Acoustic Signal Enhancement (IWAENC), pp. 164–168. IEEE (2014)

4. Garnier, M., Henrich, N.: Speaking in noise: how does the lombard effect improve acoustic contrasts between speech and ambient noise? Comput. Speech Lang. **28**(2), 580–597 (2014)
5. Hu, M., et al.: Capturing small, fast-moving objects: Frame interpolation via recurrent motion enhancement. IEEE Trans. Circuits Syst. Video Technol. (2021). https://doi.org/10.1109/TCSVT.2021.3110796
6. Liao, L., Xiao, J., Wang, Z., Lin, C.W., Satoh, S.: Uncertainty-aware semantic guidance and estimation for image inpainting. IEEE J. Sel. Top. Signal Process. **15**(2), 310–323 (2021)
7. Xiao, J., Hu, R., Liao, L., Chen, Y., Wang, Z., Xiong, Z.: Knowledge-based coding of objects for multisource surveillance video data. IEEE Trans. Multimedia **18**(9), 1691–1706 (2016). https://doi.org/10.1109/TMM.2016.2581590
8. Liao, L., Xiao, J., Wang, Z., Lin, C.-W., Satoh, S.: Guidance and evaluation: semantic-aware image inpainting for mixed scenes. In: Vedaldi, A., Bischof, H., Brox, T., Frahm, J.-M. (eds.) ECCV 2020. LNCS, vol. 12372, pp. 683–700. Springer, Cham (2020). https://doi.org/10.1007/978-3-030-58583-9_41
9. Li, G., Wang, X., Hu, R., Zhang, H., Ke, S.: Normal-to-lombard speech conversion by LSTM network and BGMM for intelligibility enhancement of telephone speech. In: 2020 IEEE International Conference on Multimedia and Expo (ICME), pp. 1–6. IEEE (2020)
10. Seshadri, S., Juvela, L., Yamagishi, J., Räsänen, O., Alku, P.: Cycle-consistent adversarial networks for non-parallel vocal effort based speaking style conversion. In: ICASSP 2019–2019 IEEE International Conference on Acoustics, Speech and Signal Processing (ICASSP), pp. 6835–6839. IEEE (2019)
11. Li, G., Hu, R., Ke, S., Zhang, R., Wang, X., Gao, L.: Speech intelligibility enhancement using non-parallel speaking style conversion with stargan and dynamic range compression. In: 2020 IEEE International Conference on Multimedia and Expo (ICME), pp. 1–6. IEEE (2020)
12. Zhu, J.Y., Park, T., Isola, P., Efros, A.A.: Unpaired image-to-image translation using cycle-consistent adversarial networks. In: Proceedings of the IEEE International Conference on Computer Vision, pp. 2223–2232 (2017)
13. Choi, Y., Choi, M., Kim, M., Ha, J.W., Kim, S., Choo, J.: Stargan: unified generative adversarial networks for multi-domain image-to-image translation. In: Proceedings of the IEEE Conference on Computer Vision and Pattern Recognition, pp. 8789–8797 (2018)
14. Kaneko, T., Kameoka, H., Tanaka, K., Hojo, N.: StarGAN-VC2: rethinking conditional methods for StarGAN-based voice conversion. arXiv preprint arXiv:1907.12279 (2019)
15. Dumoulin, V., Shlens, J., Kudlur, M.: A learned representation for artistic style. arXiv preprint arXiv:1610.07629 (2016)
16. Huang, X., Belongie, S.: Arbitrary style transfer in real-time with adaptive instance normalization. In: Proceedings of the IEEE International Conference on Computer Vision, pp. 1501–1510 (2017)
17. Vaswani, A., et al.: Attention is all you need. In: Advances in Neural Information Processing Systems, pp. 5998–6008 (2017)
18. Soloducha, M., Raake, A., Kettler, F., Voigt, P.: Lombard speech database for German language. In: Proceedings of DAGA 42nd Annual Conference on Acoustics (2016)
19. Morise, M., Yokomori, F., Ozawa, K.: World: a vocoder-based high-quality speech synthesis system for real-time applications. IEICE Trans. Inf. Syst. **99**(7), 1877–1884 (2016)

20. Phan, H., et al.: Self-attention generative adversarial network for speech enhancement. In: ICASSP 2021–2021 IEEE International Conference on Acoustics, Speech and Signal Processing (ICASSP), pp. 7103–7107. IEEE (2021)
21. Varga, A., Steeneken, H.J.: Assessment for automatic speech recognition: II. NOISEX-92: a database and an experiment to study the effect of additive noise on speech recognition systems. Speech Commun. **12**(3), 247–251 (1993)
22. Van Kuyk, S., Kleijn, W.B., Hendriks, R.C.: An evaluation of intrusive instrumental intelligibility metrics. IEEE/ACM Trans. Audio Speech Lang. Process. **26**(11), 2153–2166 (2018)
23. Taal, C.H., Hendriks, R.C., Heusdens, R., Jensen, J.: An algorithm for intelligibility prediction of time-frequency weighted noisy speech. IEEE Trans. Audio Speech Lang. Process. **19**(7), 2125–2136 (2011)
24. ITU-T Recommendation P.800: Methods for subjective determination of transmission quality, June 1996

Personalized Fashion Recommendation Using Pairwise Attention

Donnaphat Trakulwaranont[1,2]($\boxtimes$) (iD), Marc A. Kastner[1] (iD),
and Shin'ichi Satoh[1,2] (iD)

[1] National Institute of Informatics, Tokyo, Japan
{mkastner,satoh}@nii.ac.jp
[2] The University of Tokyo, Tokyo, Japan
d.trakulwaranont@gmail.com

Abstract. The e-commerce fashion industry is booming and comes with the need for proper search and recommendation. However, sufficient user personalization is still a challenging task. In this paper, we introduce a personalized fashion recommendation system based on high-dimensional input of user- and environment information. The proposed framework is used to estimate suitable categories and style of clothing depending on customized settings such as body type, age, occasion, or season. The goal is to recommend a full fitting outfit from the estimated suggestions. However, various personal attributes add up to a high dimensionality, and datasets are often very unbalanced or biased, making it difficult to do a proper recommendation. To solve this, we propose a pairwise-attention module to improve the performance of our framework. Our model can improve the performance up to 53.29% over the comparison method on MSE, mAP, and Recall. Moreover, in a subjective evaluation with human participants, the recommendations of the proposed method are preferred over the comparison method.

Keywords: Recommendation systems · Personalized recommendation · Fashion media

1 Introduction

Clothing is one of the first impressions that people get from one another. Fashion tells a story about what we are and what we want to be. This is reflected in the fashion industry, which reported a growth of revenue from 1.3 trillion U.S. dollars (in 2012) to 1.8 trillion U.S. dollars (in 2019)[1]. More recently, fashion trends were further influenced by digital disruption and cross-border challenges. A major fashion trend is to get more personalized [3], resulting in online fashion retailers to invest and use more recent machine learning-based technology. Further, it is becoming more global and digital [2], accelerated through the global pandemic [1]. However, online fashion shopping leads to obstacles, such as the

---

[1] https://www.oberlo.com/statistics/apparel-industry-statistics.

© Springer Nature Switzerland AG 2022
B. Þór Jónsson et al. (Eds.): MMM 2022, LNCS 13142, pp. 218–229, 2022.
https://doi.org/10.1007/978-3-030-98355-0_19

difficulty of judging whether a certain piece of clothing looks good on oneself or which kind of clothing item is more suitable.

To help customers to make a decision in their fashion shopping, traditional methods use the purchase history and examples of clothing items to make better suggestions. However, this cannot suit clothing recommendations to specific users or scenarios, especially for rare occasions or lesser-known users. Some work [9,10] started to introduce body measurements or 3D body shape as an input to suggest suitable clothing. Others [21] proposed to use more personal information such as event and gender information, and also use preferred outfit images to query the outfit from the database based on similarity. Although these works can achieve some of their objectives, there still are some limitations and drawbacks such as missing important personal information, a low variety of clothing types, and limitations in suggested clothing category and style.

To conquer these limitations, our objective is to improve personalization in fashion recommendation systems by including a high number of personal attributes (such as age, ethnicity, and body shape) as well as environmental information (such as occasion or season) at the same time. Media datasets are commonly unbalanced and often contain only sufficient data for a part of users (e.g., a common bias is towards white males, young age groups, and so on). Due to this, a high dimensionality of user inputs becomes an issue. To solve this, we propose a pairwise attention module to combine each attribute and improve the training performance for lesser-known combinations of queries. With this, we can receive a more personalized recommendation system for suggesting types and styles of clothing. The proposed method is evaluated and compared to a comparison method [10], showing promising performance. We further employed a subjective evaluation with a user study, where a majority of participants preferred the recommendations of our system compared to the comparison method.

The main contribution of this paper can be summarized as follows:

- We propose a multi-attribute recommendation-query framework to suggest the outfit most appropriate to a specific person on a specific occasion/season.
- To solve issues with data imbalance for lesser-known input combinations, we propose a novel pairwise attention module, which is able used to better understand the connection of existing data samples.
- We evaluate the framework both in comparison with an existing method on quantitative measures, as well as a subjective evaluation with human participants.

2 Related Work

In the following, we discuss existing related work on recommendation systems, both general-purpose as well as those targeting fashion media.

General-Purpose Recommendation. Zheng et al. [22] introduce a recommendation system called DeepCoNN, which works with text-based user reviews. They used a pre-trained word embedding to embed text information for input to CNN layers, to extract multiple levels of features from text input. Finally, they use a Factorization Machine [17] (FM) as a rating estimator. Rawat et al. [16] propose ConTagNet for recommending tags based on input image and user-context using the YFCC100M [20] dataset. They use AlexNet [12] to extract features from input images and a custom neural network to extract features from tag information. After that, they concatenate both features to perform a multi-label classification to predict tag scores. He et al. [8] use a CNN to learn the interaction between user and item information using Yelp reviews and Gowalla check-in data. They embed user and item information to each feature vector, and generate an interaction map using outer product operation. Then, using ConvNCF which is a stack of six convolutional layers to learn the correlations between user and item on interaction map, they predict the item recommendation.

Personalized Fashion Recommendation. Compared to the general-purpose recommendation, personalized fashion recommendation is usually more closely tight to user information as not only age, and body type, but also the target occasion play a very crucial role in deciding the right outfit. "What dress fit me best" [9] proposes fashion item recommendation based on a correlation between body shape and clothing style. They construct a celebrity dataset "Style4BodyShape", featuring body measurement, stylist information, and related fashion outfits. They propose a method that calculates body shape into seven types and do a personalized style suggestion on top of that. Hsiao et al. [10] propose ViBE, recommending clothing based on the relation between body shape, clothing, and clothing attribute. However, instead of using only body measurement, they also include 3D body shape images in the proposed method to predict more close recommendations. Most recently, Fashionist [21] do personalization by including more user information such as gender and occasion. They also use a user's preference based on the preferred outfit image, then use the visual preference modeling to extract the semantic information from the preferred outfit image.

In this work, we are inspired by this variety of work introducing additional attributes into the personalized fashion recommendation. However, we also note dataset imbalance and insufficient data for lesser observed input combinations, especially if introducing a high number of customizable personal attributes. Thus, the target of this research is to solve these remaining issues and propose a more robust personalized recommendation system.

3   Proposed Framework

Our goal is to create a recommendation system to suggest an outfit based on personal- and environmental information. Our proposed method can be divided into three stages: First, we augment the data of existing fashion datasets by extraction. Second, in the recommendation stage, clothing categories and attributes are suggested based on the high-dimensional input of personal attributes, wearing occasion, and wearing season. Third, in the query stage, an

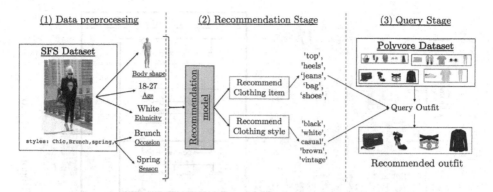

Fig. 1. Overview of proposed framework. The proposed framework consists of three stages: (1) Dataset preprocessing, extracting visual information from existing fashion datasets to augment the usable data, (2) Recommendation stage, that uses a recommendation model to predict the clothing item and attribute, (3) Query stage that uses output from recommendation stage to query outfit as overall system output.

adequate outfit that matches the recommended output from the recommendation stage is selected from a large outfit dataset. The overall structure is shown in Fig. 1.

3.1 Dataset Preprocessing

Browsing existing fashion datasets [5,6] quickly reveals some limitations for personalized recommendation. There often is a dataset imbalance, with some occasions or gender/age combinations being highly available while there are almost no samples for other combinations. Further, by its nature fashion attributes are long-tailed, making them hard to train and recommend. This makes the data noisy, often also resulting in inconsistent or incomplete annotations.

To solve these limitations, we extract additional data from all available images to augment the existing dataset. Using existing methods [18,19], we estimate personal attributes from user images. We generate estimates for ethnicity, age, and body shape type.

3.2 Recommendation Stage

The architecture of the recommendation stage is designed with a stack of convolution layers followed by a BatchNorm layer, a ReLU layer, and Residual layers [7] to form feature extractor Fe. To deal with the high number of inputs, we form a feature extractor for each type of input and then combine it after feature extraction as shown in the left part of Fig. 2.

For the pairwise attention module, the main objective is to generate a weight attention score for each type of input, such as different user- or environment information. Therefore, when the model encounters each combination of input,

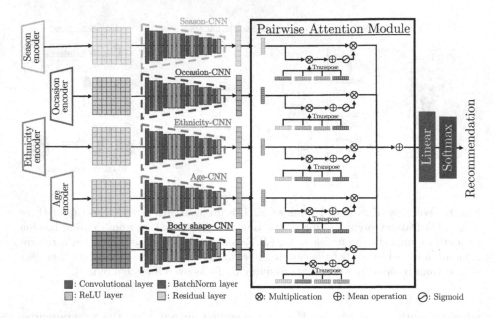

Fig. 2. Recommendation model architecture which consists of two part: (1) feature extraction part that uses convolution layers with BatchNorm, ReLU and Residual layers to extract features, and (2) feature combination part is a pairwise attention module which is used for generate weight attention score for each type of input data.

it can properly weigh each input feature, being able to give better recommendations for lesser-known combinations. A weight attention score is generated using multiplication between feature vectors and using the Sigmoid function to map the value to 0 to 1. The structure of the pairwise attention module is shown in the right-side box in Fig. 2. The module can be described as Eq. 1:

$$F = \left\{ f_{occasion}, f_{season}, f_{age}, f_{ethnicity}, f_{body} \right\},$$

$$W_f = Sigmoid \left(\frac{1}{|F| - 1} \sum_{x \in F - f} f \otimes x^T \right),$$

$$F_{fusion} = \frac{1}{|F|} \sum_{f \in F} W_f \otimes f, \tag{1}$$

where f_x refers to the features of data x, $Sigmoid$ refers to the Sigmoid activation function, $\otimes$ is a multiplication operator, and F_{fusion} is an output from the pairwise attention module.

Finally, the F_{fusion} is passed to the fully connected layer and Softmax Layer to predict the probability of each class (i.e., 24 categories for clothing items and 65 types for clothing attributes).

3.3 Query Stage

For this stage, the output from the recommendation stage is used to query the best fitting outfits from an outfit dataset. For this, a GloVe embedding [15] is used to embed the output of the recommendation stage into a textual feature vector. After that, we use the cosine similarity to measure the similarity between recommended output and all available outfits in the query dataset. Finally, the chosen outfit will be the result of the query stage, a set of clothing items, that best matches the output from the recommendation stage. We employ:

$$Similarity(A,B) = \frac{A \cdot B}{\|A\| \times \|B\|} = \frac{\sum_{i=1}^{N} A_i \times B_i}{\sqrt{\sum_{i=1}^{N} A_i^2} \times \sqrt{\sum_{i=1}^{N} B_i^2}}, \tag{2}$$

where A and B are different feature vectors with the same size and dimension, and N is the dimensionality of features. Moreover, a two-step filtering step is used for the refinement of the results. For this, we choose to filter for attribute information first, then for clothing items second, to query the final outfit.

4 Evaluations

In this section, we evaluate the performance of the proposed method in comparison to existing methods.

4.1 Environment

Datasets. For the recommendation stage, we employ the Street-Fashion-Style [5] (SFS) dataset, which is a collection of street photos. It provides difficult to collect annotations such as suitable outfits for specific events. In each data sample, a user image is connected with an outfit, including relevant information such as appropriate occasion, current season, and details of each clothing item (e.g. category, color, or material). As discussed in Sect. 3.1, we perform a pre-processing step to augment the data for more detailed user information. For this, we use the LightFace Library [19] which is built upon VGG-Face [13] to extract age and ethnicity information. Next, the user's body shape is predicted by FrankMocap [18] which includes SMPL-X [14]. Finally, after removing incomplete or missing data, our pre-processed dataset results in 85,353 data samples. The dataset is split into 70% for training, 15% for testing, and 15% for validation. Examples of the pre-processed data are shown in Fig. 3.

For the query stage, we employ the Polyvore [6] dataset. It contains 164,000 clothing items which group into 21,889 outfits. Each clothing item is further annotated with category, style, and details (e.g. brand, color, or material).

Ground-Truth. After the dataset is processed, we define a *ground-truth* used for evaluation. For each combination of inputs, we collect all data samples fitting this scenario. Next, we determine the likelihood distribution of which clothing types and styles are the most fitting, essentially summarizing the outfit choices of exiting users. With this, we gain 2,545 scenarios across the 85,353 data samples with a likelihood distribution across 24 types and 65 styles of clothing.

USER_NAME	PIC_NAME	IMAGE	OCCASION	SEASON	AGE	ETHNICITY	BODY SHAPE IMAGE
29Skirts	91006.jpg		Vacation	Spring	18-27	White	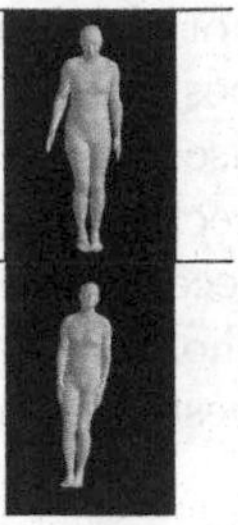
fashionophile	123139.jpg		Everyday	Fall	28-37	Asian	

Fig. 3. Example of preprocessed dataset. It is based on the Street-Fashion-Style [5] dataset, but includes extra data extracted through our preprocessing step.

Comparison Methods. To evaluate our framework we use two comparison methods. First, we implemented a naïve baseline model. It is just convolution layers with an Attentional Feature Fusion (AFF) [4] to fuse all input features at the same time. Second, we use ViBE [10] as an existing comparison method.

Proposed Method. We implemented the proposed method as introduced in this paper. For the recommendation stage, we embed each input into a 64-dim feature vector. Next, the feature extractor will transform it into a 1024-dim feature vector. The pairwise attention module combines the 5×1024-dim features into a 1024-dim feature vector. Lastly, it is passed into the fully connected layer and softmax layer to map into a 24-dim output for clothing items and 65-dim output for clothing attributes. It is trained using Adam optimizer [11] with an initial learning rate of 0.005, decay learning rate with gamma(γ) = 0.1 every 7 steps, and trained for 20 epoches. For the query stage, we create a 300-dim GloVe [15] vector to embed the clothing items and attribute from the recommendation model as well as the information of outfits in the Polyvore dataset. For top-k query, k is set to 5 and similarity threshold = 0.5.

4.2 Experiments

Quantitative Evaluation. For this experiment, we analyze the quantitative metrics MSE, mAP@k, and mAR@k and compare our proposed method to the two comparison methods. We predict the recommended output of 24 clothing types and 65 clothing styles using each method. Then, we compare the output from each method with our previously defined ground-truth likelihood. To better understand the performance for different choices of user inputs, we also evaluate sub-models using only a subset of personal attributes for the recommendation.

Subjective Evaluation. To evaluate the human perception of recommended outfits, we do a subjective evaluation by a user study. In a questionnaire, we asked participants to decide between the two outfits for a given query. Each question shows attributes such as body shape, occasion, season, age, and ethnicity,

Fig. 4. Example of question in user study. Each participant is asked to decide the better outfit for a certain input query, as shown in the top right. The selectable outfits 1 and 2 are recommendations generated by the comparison and proposed method, respectively.

and then two outfit choices. The two outfits are generated by ViBE [10] and the proposed method, making it possible to evaluate which method's outputs is preferred by each participant. An example of the survey is shown in Fig. 4. We gathered 43 outfit pairs made from a random season, occasion, and age. The survey had 34 participants of Asian ethnicity, which can be divided into two genders, 24 female and 10 male. As all participants were of Asian ethnicity, all queries were done with Asian ethnicity.

4.3   Results

Quantitative Evaluation. First, we evaluate the performance of the proposed method, as shown in Table 1 (item recommendation) and Table 2 (attribute recommendation). For item recommendation, the proposed method with all inputs achieves the highest performance in MSE metric, mAP, and mAR at k = 5, 20. The proposed method improves 53.29% over the ViBE comparison method, and there is a significant improvement for mAP and mAR at k = 5. Note, that the approach proposed by ViBE is mostly targeting body-type recommendations, unlike ours which covers a full range of user- and environmental attributes. For attribute recommendation, the ViBE model does not recommend clothing attributes. Because of this, we cannot compare to ViBE, but only to the naïve baseline as our proposed method with several different input settings. The proposed method with all input information has an average performance better than every other model.

Ablation Study on Fusion Method. When preparing the dataset, we noticed an imbalance of annotations as well as a long-tailed distribution which would yield issues with a high-dimensional input recommendation. To test this, we also evaluated the naïve baseline method, as it uses no comprehensive pairwise attention to solve this dataset issue. As expected, the results shown in Table 3 prove this intuition, by showing a decreasing performance in $mAP@5$ and $mAP@10$ when adding extra input features. To further ablate this, we compared the performance of attention fusion, shown in Table 4. It can be seen that by adding the

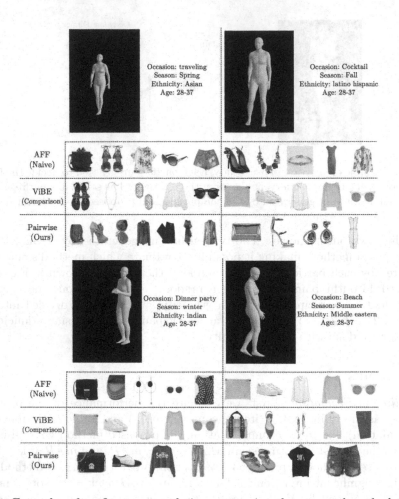

Fig. 5. Examples of outfit recommendation, comparing the proposed method to the comparison methods on four different queries.

Table 1. Quantitative results on clothing item recommendation comparisons of the proposed method with comparison method. The input for our method is abbreviated as **(O)**ccasion, **(S)**eason, **(A)**ge, **(E)**thnicity, and **(B)**ody shape.

Model input	MSE	mAP@5	mAR@5	mAP@20	mAR@20
Comp. method (ViBE [10])	0.00676	0.4859	0.4865	0.7103	0.6108
Naïve (AFF, All)	0.30336	0.5708	0.5714	0.8165	0.8676
Ours (O+S)	0.00032	0.8023	0.8029	0.8781	0.8814
Ours (O+S+A)	0.00032	0.8039	0.8045	0.8773	0.8822
Ours (O+S+A+E)	**0.00030**	0.8279	0.8286	0.8893	0.8900
Ours-proposed (All)	**0.00030**	**0.8311**	**0.8316**	**0.8907**	**0.8905**

Table 2. Quantitative results on clothing attribute recommendation comparisons of the proposed method with comparison method. The input for our method is abbreviated as **(O)**ccasion, **(S)**eason, **(A)**ge, **(E)**thnicity, and **(B)**ody shape.

Model input	MSE	mAP@5	mAR@5	mAP@20	mAR@20
Naïve (AFF, All)	0.00513	0.7427	0.5701	0.7810	0.4356
Ours (O+S)	0.00016	0.8234	0.8240	0.8057	0.8113
Ours (O+S+A)	0.00027	0.7849	0.7854	0.7991	0.7789
Ours (O+S+A+E)	0.00592	**0.8842**	0.6263	**0.9459**	0.2871
Ours-proposed (All)	**0.00015**	0.8377	**0.8382**	0.8188	**0.8203**

Table 3. Quantitative results of naïve method. The input dimension is abbreviated as **(O)**ccasion, **(S)**eason, **(A)**ge, **(E)**thnicity, and **(B)**ody shape.

Model input	mAP@5	mAP@10	mAP@15	mAP@20
Naïve (O+S)	**0.7137**	**0.7850**	0.8052	0.8136
Naïve (O+S+A)	0.6490	0.7568	0.7939	0.8113
Naïve (O+S+A+E)	0.5597	0.7235	0.7961	0.8311
Naïve (All)	0.5706	0.7331	**0.8063**	**0.8419**

Table 4. Ablation study on the attention fusion model, comparing the naïve method and the proposed method.

Fusion method	mAP@5	mAP@10	mAP@15	mAP@20
Naïve (AFF)	0.5708	0.5714	0.8165	0.8676
Ours (Pairwise)	**0.8311**	**0.8316**	**0.8907**	**0.8905**

Table 5. Subjective evaluation. Questionnaire result comparisons of the proposed method with comparison method.

Preferred recommendation	Female	Male	All
From ViBE [10]	**19** (44.19%)	15 (34.88%)	20 (46.51%)
From Proposed model	**19** (44.19%)	**21** (48.84%)	**22** (51.16%)
Tied between both	5 (11.63%)	7 (16.28%)	1 (2.33%)

pairwise attention, the performance increases around 45.6% over the naïve baseline method at $mAP@5$ and $mAP@10$.

Subjective Evaluation. The results of the subjective evaluation method are shown in Table 5. Out of 43 outfits, the proposed model gave the better recommendation for 22 outfits, giving slightly better recommendations than the comparison method. While these results are close, a tendency towards the proposed model can be seen. It is larger for male participants, where a majority of users preferred our recommendation. For female participants, the results are tied.

Qualitative Evaluation. Figure 5 shows examples of outfit recommendations for each tested model with all input information. Each example shows the subject's estimated body shape and personal attributes as an input for each model, and each row shows the output for the corresponding model. The proposed method can generally recommend outfits based on some specific information such as season and occasion. For example, in the first column, the proposed method suggests a comfortable outfit with a colorful long sleeve t-shirt and jeans for dinner parties in the winter season. In the second column, the proposed method recommends a t-shirt, short jeans, and sandals for going to the beach in summer which might be more suitable than the recommended outfit from the comparison method that suggests a blouse, shirt, and heels.

5 Conclusion

In this work, we proposed a novel method for recommending clothing items and styles with high-dimensional personalization, including personal attributes (age, ethnicity, body shape) and environment information (occasion and season). To solve data imbalance issues with existing datasets, we introduce a pairwise attention module to improve the performance of the recommendation. This module can weigh the importance between each input data type, better understanding the data in case of lesser-known input combinations. We evaluate our proposed method and compare it to an existing method. We can show an average improvement in 53.29% and 38.24% on recommending clothing items and styles respectively over the comparison method. The ablation study on attention methods confirms dataset imbalance issues. Moreover, in a subjective evaluation with human participants, we can show a tendency towards preferring our recommendations over the comparison method.

References

1. Amed, I., Balchandani, A., Berg, A., Hedrich, S., Jensen, J.E., Rölkens, F.: The State of Fashion 2021. McKinsey & Company (2021)
2. Amed, I., et al.: The State of Fashion 2020. Business of Fashion and McKinsey & Company (2020)
3. Amed, I., et al.: The State of Fashion 2019; Business of Fashion Mckinsey & Company (2018)
4. Dai, Y., Gieseke, F., Oehmcke, S., Wu, Y., Barnard, K.: Attentional feature fusion. In: IEEE Winter Conference on Applications Computer Vision, WACV, pp. 3559–3568 (2021). https://doi.org/10.1109/WACV48630.2021.00360
5. Gu, X., Wong, Y., Peng, P., Shou, L., Chen, G., Kankanhalli, M.S.: Understanding fashion trends from street photos via neighbor-constrained embedding learning. In: Proceedings of the 2017 ACM Multimedia Conference, pp. 190–198 (2017). https://doi.org/10.1145/3123266.3123441
6. Han, X., Wu, Z., Jiang, Y., Davis, L.S.: Learning fashion compatibility with bidirectional LSTMs. In: Proceedings of the 2017 ACM Multimedia Conference, pp. 1078–1086 (2017). https://doi.org/10.1145/3123266.3123394

7. He, K., Zhang, X., Ren, S., Sun, J.: Deep residual learning for image recognition. In: 2016 IEEE Conference on Computer Vision and Pattern Recognition, CVPR, pp. 770–778 (2016). https://doi.org/10.1109/CVPR.2016.90
8. He, X., Du, X., Wang, X., Tian, F., Tang, J., Chua, T.: Outer product-based neural collaborative filtering. In: Lang, J. (ed.) Proceedings of the Twenty-Seventh International Joint Conference on Artificial Intelligence, IJCAI, pp. 2227–2233. ijcai.org (2018)
9. Hidayati, S.C., Hsu, C., Chang, Y., Hua, K., Fu, J., Cheng, W.: What dress fits me best?: fashion recommendation on the clothing style for personal body shape. In: 2018 ACM Multimedia Conference, pp. 438–446 (2018). https://doi.org/10.1145/3240508.3240546
10. Hsiao, W., Grauman, K.: Vibe: dressing for diverse body shapes. In: 2020 IEEE/CVF Conference on Computer Vision and Pattern Recognition, CVPR 2020, Seattle, WA, USA, 13–19 June 2020, pp. 11056–11066 (2020). https://doi.org/10.1109/CVPR42600.2020.01107
11. Kingma, D.P., Ba, J.: Adam: a method for stochastic optimization. In: 3rd International Conference on Learning Representations, ICLR (2015)
12. Krizhevsky, A., Sutskever, I., Hinton, G.E.: ImageNet classification with deep convolutional neural networks. In: 26th Annual Conference on Neural Information Processing Systems (NIPS), pp. 1106–1114 (2012)
13. Parkhi, O.M., Vedaldi, A., Zisserman, A.: Deep face recognition. In: Proceedings of the British Machine Vision Conference BMVC, pp. 41.1–41.12 (2015). https://doi.org/10.5244/C.29.41
14. Pavlakos, G., et al.: Expressive body capture: 3D hands, face, and body from a single image. In: IEEE Conference on Computer Vision and Pattern Recognition, CVPR, pp. 10975–10985 (2019). Computer Vision Foundation/IEEE. https://doi.org/10.1109/CVPR.2019.01123
15. Pennington, J., Socher, R., Manning, C.D.: Glove: global vectors for word representation. In: Proceedings of the 2014 Conference on Empirical Methods in Natural Language Processing, EMNLP, pp. 1532–1543 (2014). https://doi.org/10.3115/v1/d14-1162
16. Rawat, Y.S., Kankanhalli, M.S.: ConTagNet: exploiting user context for image tag recommendation. In: Proceedings of the 2016 ACM Conference on Multimedia, pp. 1102–1106. ACM (2016)
17. Rendle, S.: Factorization machines with libFM. ACM Trans. Intell. Syst. Technol. 3(3), 57:1–57:22 (2012)
18. Rong, Y., Shiratori, T., Joo, H.: FrankMocap: fast monocular 3D hand and body motion capture by regression and integration. CoRR arXiv:2008.08324 (2020)
19. Serengil, S.I., Ozpinar, A.: LightFace: a hybrid deep face recognition framework. In: 2020 Innovations in Intelligent Systems and Applications Conference (ASYU), pp. 1–5 (2020)
20. Thomee, B., et al.: Yfcc100m: the new data in multimedia research. Commun. ACM 59(2), 64–73 (2016)
21. Verma, D., Gulati, K., Goel, V., Shah, R.R.: Fashionist: personalising outfit recommendation for cold-start scenarios. In: 28th ACM International Conference on Multimedia, pp. 4527–4529 (2020). https://doi.org/10.1145/3394171.3414446
22. Zheng, L., Noroozi, V., Yu, P.S.: Joint deep modeling of users and items using reviews for recommendation. In: Proceedings of the Tenth ACM International Conference on Web Search and Data Mining, WSDM, pp. 425–434 (2017)

Graph Neural Networks Based Multi-granularity Feature Representation Learning for Fine-Grained Visual Categorization

Hongyan Wu[1], Haiyun Guo[2], Qinghai Miao[1], Min Huang[1(✉)], and Jinqiao Wang[1,2]

[1] School of Artificial Intelligence, University of Chinese Academy of Sciences, Beijing, China
`wuhongyan19@mails.ucas.ac.cn`, {`miaoqh,huangm`}`@ucas.ac.cn`
[2] Institution of Automation, Chinese Academy of Sciences, Beijing, China
{`haiyun.guo,jqwang`}`@nlpr.ia.ac.cn`

Abstract. There inherently exists a hierarchy with different levels of classification granularity for object categories. This hierarchy involves rich semantic relationships among categories, which can benefit fine-grained visual categorization (FGVC) but is overlooked by most of previous works. In this paper, a novel graph neural networks based multi-granularity feature representation learning framework is presented for FGVC, which boosts feature learning of different grain levels simultaneously and enhances multiple granularity categorization. Under this framework, we propose two kinds of correlation graphs, i.e., Abstract Graph (AG) and Detailed Graph (DG). AG assigns one node for each grain level while DG regards different categories at each grain level as different nodes. With AG and DG, two graph neural networks based multiple grain feature learning methods are proposed. With AG, graph gate neural network is utilized to explore the interactions between features from different grain levels and help learn more discriminative and comprehensive feature representation for each grain level. Based on DG, we employ graph convolutional network to model the category hierarchical semantic relationships and enhance the feature by regularizing the semantic space division. To facilitate the research, we construct a large-scale car dataset, i.e., Car-FG3K (Available at http://www.nlpr.ia.ac.cn/iva/homepage/jqwang/Car-FG3K.htm), which covers three-level categories and is more challenging than the existing car datasets in terms of category count and view variation. We conduct experiments on this new dataset and two other datasets, i.e., CUB-200-2011 and FGVC-Aircraft, and our methods achieve comparable results to state-of-the-art methods.

Keywords: Multi-granularity feature learning · Graph neural networks · Fine-grained visual categorization

B. Þór Jónsson et al. (Eds.): MMM 2022, LNCS 13142, pp. 230–242, 2022.
https://doi.org/10.1007/978-3-030-98355-0_20

1   Introduction

Fine-grained visual categorization (FGVC), refers to distinguish sub-ordinate categories of some general classes like birds [25], flowers [23], cars [19,28,30] and aircrafts [22], has attracted much research attention due to plenty of applications. It's more challenging than general classification problem because it needs to discern more subtle difference between the fine-grained categories. Accordingly, it's of vital importance to learn discriminative feature representation for FGVC. Recent research efforts are mostly devoted to capture discriminative local parts [10,13,32]. However, this paper focuses on exploiting the class hierarchy to learn more discriminative features for FGVC, which is overlooked by most of previous works.

There inherently exists a hierarchy with different levels of classification granularity for object categories. The higher level refers to coarser-grained category while the lower level refers to finer-grained category. The category hierarchy contains rich semantic relationships among categories across different levels, which can benefit FGVC by providing effective regularization on semantic space division and helping focus on more subtle regions to discriminate fine-grained categories.

According to [1], some works focus on leveraging class hierarchy to make better mistakes for image classification, which are categorized into three kinds, i.e., embedding the class hierarchy into the label representation, classification loss function and classifier architecture. While this paper aims to embed the class hierarchy into the feature learning network to promote accuracy for FGVC. And [5] firstly integrates the structured correlation information into the deep neural network for FGVC. However, it only utilizes the learnt semantics in the higher level to improve the feature learning and categorization in the lower level. And [3] disentangles coarse-level features with fine-grained ones and uses finer-grained features to help the coarser-level classification. We believe that the learning of multi-granularity features can boost each other, thus [3] and [5] are suboptimal.

In this paper, we propose to model the hierarchical semantic correlation relationship via the Graph Neural Networks (GNNs) [24] and build the GNN-based multi-granularity feature learning framework. Our framework builds a mutual boost mechanism among feature learning across different levels, which promotes the categorization performance at multiple granularity levels. To be specific, we firstly construct two kinds of hierarchical correlation graphs, i.e., abstract graph (AG) and detailed graph (DG). AG assigns one node for all categories in each grain level while DG takes the whole category hierarchy into consideration and regards different categories at one grain level as different nodes. Based on AG and DG, we propose two different GNN-based multi-granularity feature learning methods.

The first approach, denoted by GGNN-AG, exploits the Gate Graph Neural Network (GGNN) [20] to model the AG and explores the interactions between image features of different grain levels via a graph propagation mechanism. Specifically, GGNN-AG captures the related regions of interest between features of different grain levels, and highlights these regions by reinforcing the activation intensity of them and their neighborhoods, resulting in more discriminative and comprehensive multi-granularity representations.

The second approach, denoted by GCN-DG, employs Graph Convolutional Network (GCN) [18] to model the DG and integrates semantic correlation in the category hierarchy into the multi-granularity feature learning network. We initialize each node of the DG with one sparse vector, in which only one specific dimension is non-zero and set to the corresponding label prediction logit. By regarding logits of one grain level as feature, GCN-DG regularizes the feature space and guides multi-granularity feature learning from two aspects. On the one hand, when category confusion occurs in one specific level, the features from other grain level can provide distinguishing information to correct this false prediction. On the other hand, for the finer-grained recognition which may suffer from overfitting due to insufficient training data, the prior knowledge from coarser-grained level will help finer-grained feature fixate on more subtle but discriminative patterns.

Furthermore, we collect a large-scale car dataset, Car-FG3K, which is more challenging than the existing car datasets such as Stanford car [19], Comp-Cars [30] and Car333 [28] in terms of category count and viewpoint variation. Thus it is of great practical value. It covers three-level hierarchy, eight viewpoints and consists of 21,351 images, which belong to 191 brands, 1,895 models and 3,269 categories concerning manufacture year.

In summary, this paper contributes in following aspects:

– We formulate a novel GNN-based multi-granularity feature learning framework for FGVC, which establishes a mutual boost mechanism for features from different levels. To the best of our knowledge, we are the first to learn the semantic correlation of category hierarchy based on GNNs in FGVC.
– We design two specific methods, GGNN-AG and GCN-DG, to embed the semantic correlation information of category hierarchy into the feature learning network and both of them achieve comparable performance to the state-of-the-art methods on CUB-200-2011 [25], FGVC-Aircraft [22] and Car-FG3K.
– We build a large-scale car recognition dataset, Car-FG3K, which poses more challenges for FGVC to facilitate the research.

2   Related Work

2.1   Fine-Grained Recognition

The existing fine-grained recognition methods [10,13,32] mostly focus on localizing and describing discriminative object parts to capture the subtle difference between sub-ordinate categories. Recently, some researchers explore the category hierarchy in FGVC, and propose several methods to incorporate this structured semantic relationship into feature learning. Zhou *et al.* [34] exploit the rich relationships to construct class bipartite graphs, which are embedded into the objective function. Different from [34], this paper is devoted to embed the class hierarchy into the network, thus are compatible with and complementary to them. [3] leverages finer-grained features to participate in coarser-grained label predictions. [5] uses score prediction of higher level as prior knowledge to learn finer-grained representation for the lower level. Comparing with [3] and [5], this

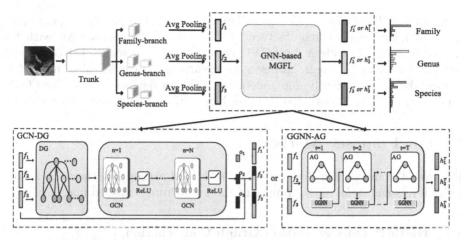

Fig. 1. The proposed GNN-based multi-granularity feature learning (denoted by MGFL) framework (take the three-level category hierarchy as example). f_1, f_2, f_3 denote the primitive features for each grain level. h_1, h_2, h_3 and f_1', f_2', f_3' denote the learnt multi-granularity feature for each grain level with the method GGNN-AG and GCN-DG respectively. f_1', f_2', f_3' are obtained separately by concatenating f_1, f_2, f_3 with the output of GCN, i.e., o_1, o_2, o_3. t and n are iteration number of GGNN and layer number of GCN.

paper takes a further step by building a mutual boost mechanism between features from different grain levels. Additionally, Bertinetto *et al.* [1] leverage the class hierarchy to make better mistakes. Our work differs from them in two ways. First, we focus on embedding the class hierarchy into feature learning network. Second, the target of our methods is to promote the top-1 accuracy of FGVC, not to reduce the mistake severity.

2.2 Graph Neural Networks

GNN is widely applied for relationship modeling in computer vision [16,26,31]. For category hierarchical correlation modeling, it can learn the interaction among hierarchical representations by aggregating information from neighborhood and updating nodes state based on history as well as the message received from neighborhood. In FGVC, Chen *et al.* [4] organize the labels and visual concepts in the form of knowledge graph, and employ GGNN to generate knowledge embedding representation. [27] explores and exploits region correlations based on graph propagation. While both of them neglect the hierarchical semantic correlation of multiple grain, and our methods embed it with GGNN and GCN.

2.3 Car Category Recognition Datasets

As the first car category recognition dataset, Stanford car [19] only has 196 categories, and doesn't offer class hierarchy. Car333 [28] enlarges the category count to 333. The following CompCar [30] consists of three layers, i.e., car make, car model, and year of manufacture. Additionally, it labels each car with five viewpoints, and the subset for FGVC constitutes 75 car make, 431 car model, and 1,342 manufacture year. However, as the arising of deep learning, more challenging dataset is urgently demanded. We collect a dataset named Car-FG3K, which contains much more categories in hierarchy and more diverse viewpoints.

3   The Proposed Method

The overall framework is illustrated in Fig. 1. And we suppose there are L hierarchy levels and $l_1, l_2, \cdots, l_L$ represent the levels from coarse to fine.

3.1   Hierarchical Correlation Graph Construction

We construct two graphs, AG and DG, to describe the semantic correlation of the category hierarchy. And they are denoted by AG and DG in Fig. 1.

AG. The graph is defined as $\mathcal{G}_\mathcal{R} = \{\mathcal{V}, \mathcal{E}\}$, where $\mathcal{V}$ is the node set referring to hierarchy levels and $\mathcal{E}$ is the edge set representing the correlation between two corresponding hierarchy levels. Specifically, we define $\mathcal{V} = \{v_1, v_2, \cdots, v_L\}$, where v_k corresponds to hierarchy level l_k, and $\mathcal{E} = \{e_{v_i, v_j} : i \neq j\}$ is composed of undirected edges between every two hierarchy levels. So we can capture the semantic correlation between different grain levels to the full extent.

DG. We define the DG as $\mathcal{G}_\mathcal{L} = \{\mathcal{U}, \mathcal{B}\}$. The node set $\mathcal{U}$ refers to categories of all grains, and the edge set $\mathcal{B}$ indicates the correlation between two category from different levels. Concretely, assuming that l_k hierarchy level owns c_k category and u_i corresponds to one specific category of them, $\mathcal{U}$ is represented as $\{u_1, u_2, \cdots, u_{c_1+c_2+\cdots+c_L}\}$. As a subset of $\mathcal{U}$, $\mathcal{U}_k$ consists of nodes in grain level l_k. And $\mathcal{B}$ is denoted by $\{b_{u_i, u_j} : u_i \in \mathcal{U}_k \ \& \ u_j \notin \mathcal{U}_k\}$, suggesting that there are only undirected edges between two categories from different grain levels.

3.2   Multi-granularity Feature Learning Based on GNNs

GGNN-AG. For a given image, we feed it into the network and attain the primitive features $f_1, f_2, \cdots, f_L$ for multiple grain levels. We initialize the hidden state of node h_v^0 by f_k, where v is the node corresponding to level l_k. For each node $v \in \mathcal{V}$, at time step t, the propagation consists of aggregation and combination. The node v aggregates information from its neighbors v':

$$a_v^t = \sum_{v' \in \mathcal{N}_v \cup \{v\}} W^{t-1} h_{v'}^{t-1} \tag{1}$$

where $h_{v'}^{t-1}$ denotes the feature of node v' at $t-1$ and $\mathcal{N}_v = \{v' : e_{v', v} \in \mathcal{E}\}$ means the neighbors of v. $W^{t-1} \in \mathbb{R}^{d_r \times d_r}$ are weights of a linear layer shared across all nodes at $t-1$. d_r is the feature dimension of the node hidden state.

The combination updates the state of v with the aggregation feature, a_v^t, in a gating mechanism, similar to Gate Recurrent Unit (GRU) [7]. And it can be formulated as

$$\begin{cases} z_v^t = \sigma(W_z a_v^t + U_z h_v^{t-1} + b_z) \\ r_v^t = \sigma(W_r a_v^t + U_r h_v^{t-1} + b_r) \\ \tilde{h}_v^t = tanh(W_h a_v^t + U_h(r_v^t \odot h_v^{t-1}) + b_h) \\ h_v^t = (1 - z_v^t) \odot h_v^{t-1} + z_v^t \odot \tilde{h}_v^t \end{cases} \tag{2}$$

where σ is the logistic sigmoid function, $\odot$ is element-wise multiplication, and $W_z, U_z, b_z, W_r, U_r, b_r, W_h, U_h$ and b_h are learnable weights and biases shared across nodes and steps.

At each time step t, each level aggregates features from the others, and transfers them through AG meanwhile. When it recurs T steps, we obtain the output features of nodes, $\{h_v^T : v \in \mathcal{V}\}$, containing the specific semantic information of its grain and other grains. Features in each level are refined by the information of multiple granularity, becoming more comprehensive and discriminative.

Finally, we utilize the hidden states of all nodes to predict categories of all levels in hierarchy. For each level, we employ a softmax classifier to predict the category: $s_v = \text{Softmax}(W_v h_v^T + b_v)$. W_v and b_v are weights and biases of the fully connected layer, and s_v is a probability distribution of input image belonging to categories in grain level v.

Alternative of GGNN. In terms of modeling hierarchical correlation of different grain levels, Bidirectional Recurrent Neural Network (Bi-RNN) [35] is one of the alternative options, which is widely used in computer vision [9,11,13] to code the contextual relationship. Regarding the multi-granularity features extracted by the network as a sequence, which is sorted from coarse to fine, we can utilize Bi-RNN to model the contextual correlation between multiple granularity. And we demonstrate the superiority of GGNN to it in multi-granularity categorization in Sect. 5.2. Note that for a fair comparison to our GGNN, we utilize GRU to update the hidden state in Bi-RNN.

GCN-DG. To make more consistent predictions across hierarchy levels, we use classification logit for each category to initialize the node in the DG. Specifically, $u_i \in \mathcal{U}_k$ is initialized by corresponding class logit in level l_k. We use features f_k extracted by our network to estimate the logits of all categories in level l_k, which can be formulated by $Z_k = W_k f_k + b_k$. $Z_k \in \mathbb{R}^{c_k}$ is a logits vector for level l_k, and z_i is the logit corresponding to u_i in vector Z_k. W_k and b_k are the weights and bias of a fully connected layer. Then, we can formulate the initialization feature of u_i as: $x_i = [\mathbf{0}_{i-1} \quad z_i \quad \mathbf{0}_{c_1+c_2+\cdots+c_L-i}]$, where $\mathbf{0}_*$ represents a zero vector. In other words, x_i is a vector with a dimension of $c_1 + c_2 + \cdots + c_L$, where all elements are 0 except the element at dimension i.

Referring to [29], it's concluded that as long as the node features are diverse and rarely repeat, GCN can capture structure information in graph effectively. Due to the great diversity of our node features, GCN is competent in encoding the rich information of label hierarchical structure.

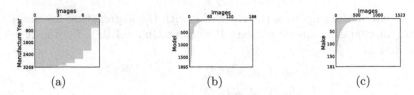

Fig. 2. Images distribution of Car-FG3K at make, model and manufacture year level.

We stack N linear convolution layers and each layer is followed by a non-linearity layer. We feed the initialization features x_i to u_i, and GCN learns label structure layer by layer, which means that layer n regards nodes features of previous convolutional layer $n-1$ as input and outputs new nodes representations M^n. The operation in layer n conducts aggregation and combination as follows:

$$M^n = \text{ReLU}(\tilde{D}^{-\frac{1}{2}}\tilde{A}\tilde{D}^{-\frac{1}{2}}M^{n-1}\Theta^{n-1}) \tag{3}$$

where $M^{n-1} \in \mathbb{R}^{|\mathcal{U}| \times d_s^{n-1}}$ is composed of $|\mathcal{U}|$ nodes and each of them is a d_s^{n-1}-dimensional feature vector. $\Theta^{n-1} \in \mathbb{R}^{d_s^{n-1} \times d_s^n}$ is a matrix of d_s^n filter parameters, and $M^n \in \mathbb{R}^{|\mathcal{U}| \times d_s^n}$ is the convolved signal matrix, comprised by d_s^n-dimensional feature vectors of $|\mathcal{U}|$ nodes. $\tilde{A}$ and $\tilde{D}$ are the renormalization versions: $\tilde{A} = A + I_N$ and $\tilde{D}_{ii} = \sum_j \tilde{A}_{ij}$, and A is the adjacent matrix obtained from $\mathcal{B}$.

Then, output of GCN, M^N, is separated into $|\mathcal{U}|$ vectors to attain the individual node output features m_u^N, and these individual features which belong to grain level l_k are concatenated to get o_k. To enhance the descriptive and discriminative ability of the feature, o_k is concatenated with f_k to generate the final feature f_k'. The prediction of level l_k can be represented by: $p_k = \text{Softmax}(W_k'f_k' + b_k')$, where W_k' and b_k' are weights and biases of the fully connected layer in level l_k.

3.3 Network Architecture

As most objects in FGVC tasks at least comprise three levels in hierarchy, here our network is designed for 3 hierarchy levels, as shown in Fig. 1. To extract multi-granularity features simultaneously, we design a network structure based on ResNet50 [15], which consists of a shared trunk and three individual branches. Moreover, considering that object categorization in coarser level is generally easier than that in finer-grained level, we design different network depth for each grain level and assign deeper network branch to the finer-grained categorization. More specifically, the trunk is constituted by conv1, conv2_x and conv3_x of ResNet50. The family branch is formed by conv4_x, the genus branch consists of conv4_x and conv5_x, and the species branch is similar to genus branch, which is illustrated in Fig. 1. Note that the trunk is shared across different levels while each branch differs. For each branch, the output feature maps will be fed into a average pooling layer to generate the final representation for this grain level.

4 Car-FG3K

Car-FG3K is collected from the web, i.e., the car forums, online stores and search engines. Similar to [30], the category is organized into a three-level hierarchy structure, incorporating makes, models and manufacture years. There are a total of 21,351 images covering 191 makes, 1,895 car models and 3,269 manufacture years. Overall, the difficulty of our dataset is compounded by viewpoint variation and category quantity. Each car is captured with one specific view of eight viewpoints, including front, rear, left-side, right-side, left-front-side, right-front-side, left-rear-side, and right-rear-side. In each subordinate category, every camera viewpoint only corresponds to one image, yielding large intra-class variance. Compared with existing car model recognition datasets presented in Table 1, we incorporate more subordinate categories, resulting in subtler appearance difference. And the distribution of images at each grain level is illustrated in Fig. 2. For the experiment, we extract 10,676 images for training and 10,661 images for testing, covering 191 makes, 1,892 models and 3,255 manufacture years.

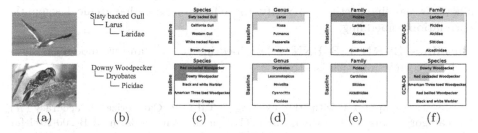

Fig. 3. Comparison between Baseline and GCN-DG method. (a) Two examples of testing images. (b) The ground truth of two examples from species to family. (c) (d) (e) The top-5 predictions attained by Baseline method in species, genus and family level, respectively. (f) The top-5 predictions generated by GCN-DG method in family (top) and species (bottom) level. And GCN-DG also predicts the right categories in other grain levels. Pink and green means false and right predictions. Best viewed in color. (Color figure online)

5 Experiment

5.1 Experiment Setting

Datasets. Our experiments are conducted on CUB-200-2011, FGVC-aircraft, and the proposed Car-FG3K. Specifically, the hierarchical organization of CUB-200-2011 is built according to [5], with 3 layers, i.e., family, genus and species. CUB-200-2011 contains 5,994 images for training and 5,794 images for testing, and FGVC-aircraft consists of 6,667 images for training and 3,333 images for testing. In details, there are 37, 122 and 200 categories in 3 layers of CUB-200-2011. And FGVC-aircraft is composed of 30, 70, 100 classes in 3 levels.

Implementation Details. The trunk network along with 3 branch networks are pretrained on the FGVC datasets firstly. Both of the GGNN-AG and GCN-DG use cross-entropy loss. For data augmentation, we firstly resize the input image into 512×512, then randomly crop it into 448×448 patches, which are randomly horizontally flipped before fed into the network. We adopt SGD algorithm with a batch size of 8, a momentum of 0.9 and a base learning rate set as 0.0001, which decays by 0.1 when confronted with error plateaus. The dimensions of f_1, f_2 and f_3 are 1,024, 2,048 and 2,048. For GGNN, we set the dimension of the hidden state, d_r, as 2048, and the iteration number T as 1. For GCN, we stack 3 convolution layers with d_s^0, d_s^1, d_s^2 and d_s^3 as $|\mathcal{U}|$, $|\mathcal{U}|$, $|\mathcal{U}|$ and 10, respectively. For Car-FG3K, we use 1 convolution layer with d_s^0, d_s^1 set as $|\mathcal{U}|$, 5.

5.2   Ablation Study

We conduct ablation studies on CUB-200-2011 and verify the effectiveness of our approaches.

Baseline. we train the ResNet50 based network simply with three softmax classifiers as baseline method to verify the effectiveness of hierarchical semantic correlation embedding.

Baseline+Bi-RNN. Bi-RNN is described in Sect. 3.2, and we model the hierarchical correlation with Bi-RNN.

Table 1. Comparison with the existing car category datasets. The CompCar (FG) means the subset of CompCar for FGVC. Stanford Car and Car333 only have one label level without viewpoint annotation.

Dataset	Images	Make	Model	Year	Viewpoint
Stanford car	16,185	–	–	196	–
Car333	157,023	–	–	333	–
CompCar (FG)	30,955	75	431	1,342	5
Car-FG3K	21,351	191	1,895	3,269	8

Table 2. Categorization accuracy (%) in different levels on CUB-200-2011 for ablation studies.

Methods	Family	Genus	Species
Baseline	90.5	91.5	85.4
Baseline + Bi-RNN	94.3	92.3	86.7
Ours (GGNN-AG)	**95.2**	**92.5**	87.2
Ours (GCN-DG)	93.8	92.4	**87.4**

It has been validated by [5] that compared with training a set of classifiers separately and training a classifier for the finest grain level then backtracking through the hierarchy to obtain the categorization results of the other levels, hierarchical semantic correlation embedding method can improve the performance of multiple grain classification, so we skip it here.

The Superiority of GGNN to Bi-RNN in AG Embedded Representation Learning and Recognition. In Table 2, compared with the 'Baseline' method, both 'Baseline+Bi-RNN' and our GGNN-AG improve the accuracy by 1.3% and 1.8% in species level, indicating the effectiveness of hierarchical semantic correlation embedding. However, our GGNN-AG consistently surpasses 'Baseline+Bi-RNN' by 0.9%, 0.2% and 0.5% in family, genus and species level. It validates the superiority of GGNN to Bi-RNN in multi-granularity feature learning. Moreover, the better performance improvement of family level verifies that the fine-grained semantic features can provide extra guidance for even the coarsest category classification. Contrastly, the finer-grained levels have already captured many discriminative features, restricting the improvement partly.

The Effectiveness of GCN-DG. In Table 2, GCN-DG brings an overall boost of 3.3%, 0.9% and 2.0% in three-level over 'Baseline', which may be attributed to that GCN-DG can effectively regularize the feature space and correct the inconsistent false prediction of the minority to make it accord with the majority. Figure 3 compares 'Baseline' and GCN-DG. In top row, the 'Baseline' method confuses 'Laridae' with 'Picidae' in family level, while GCN-DG can correct the false predictions by incorporating the information from other levels. And GCN-DG also predicts accurately when 'Baseline' makes mistake with 'Red cocka ded Woodpecker' and 'Downy Woodpecker' for the bottom row. And more accuracy promotion is suggested in the family level, owing to the fact that one family level class usually has several sub-categories in finer levels and these sub-categories all can help rectify the prediction in family level. Nevertheless, species level categorization obtains more improvement than the genus. Such phenomenon just verifies that apart from rectifying false prediction, semantic space regularization can also prevent overfitting occurring in finest-grain level.

5.3 Comparison with State-of-the-Art Methods

We also implement our methods with LIP-ResNet50 [12]. Irrespective of the backbone networks, the proposed GGNN-AG and GCN-DG achieve best performance on FGVC-aircraft and Car-FG3K, and obtain competitive results with the state-of-the-art methods on CUB-200-2011, as shown in Table 3.

CUB-200-2011. Compared with methods employing the ResNet50 as backbone, our methods show competitive performance. GCL and WPS-CPM first localize object parts on input images, then extract their features for classification. The computational burden of them is much heavier than ours, especially WPS-CPM, which uses Mask-RCNN [14] and CRF to offer complementary object parts. And PMG needs four sub-iterations within one iteration, which leads to a time-consuming training phase. HSE is the most relevant work. It builds a four-level category hierarchy by a network with 126.1M parameters, while our GGNN-AG employs merely three-level category hierarchy and a network of 78.9M parameters. Considering more category hierarchy level and larger number of model parameters can benefit the multiple granularity categorization, our GGNN-AG achieves a competitive result with nearly half parameters. Besides,

Table 3. FGVC accuracy (%) comparisons on CUB-200-2011, FGVC-aircraft and Car-FG3K.

Method	Base model	CUB-200	Aircraft	Car-FG3K
GN-BGL [34]	GoogLeNet	76.9	–	–
ResNet50 [15]	ResNet50	84.5	90.3	82.1
FGN [3]	ResNet50	86.8	92.8	–
KERL [4]	CB-CNN	87.0	-	–
RG [17]	ResNet101	87.3	–	–
SEF [21]	ResNet50	87.3	92.1	–
MC-Loss [2]	ResNet50	87.3	92.6	–
DCL [6]	ResNet50	87.8	93.0	83.3
HSE [5]	ResNet50	88.1	–	–
GCL [27]	ResNet50	88.3	93.2	–
PMG [8]	ResNet50	88.9	92.8	85.2
WPS-CPM [13]	ResNet50	**90.4**	–	–
GCN-DG	ResNet50	87.4	93.2	87.1
GGNN-AG	ResNet50	87.2	93.3	**87.5**
GCN-DG	LIP-ResNet50	87.7	**93.4**	86.4
GGNN-AG	LIP-ResNet50	88.2	**93.4**	86.6

Fig. 4. The visualization of CAMs of ground truth categories. At the 1st row is the CAM of baseline method, and those of our GGNN-AG are shown at 2nd row. Specifically, the columns are input images, CAMs of family, those of genus and those of species level.

though DCL obtains higher accuracy on CUB-200-2011, ours achieve better performance on other two datasets.

FGVC-Aircraft. Our approaches exhibit superiority over all the comparison methods based on ResNet50.

Car-FG3K. As Car-FG3K is newly presented, the results and the newly proposed methods can serve as baselines for further exploration. Compared with the results on other datasets, the accuracy on Car-FG3K is much lower, which demonstrates the difficulty of the proposed dataset Car-FG3K.

5.4   Feature Visualization

We conduct the feature visualization experiments to validate that GGNN-AG can learn more discriminative and comprehensive feature for categorization in multiple levels. At each level, we remove the average pooling layer and feed the feature at each spatial location of output of "conv4_x" (family level) or "conv5_x" (genus and species level) into GGNN to get enhanced feature maps output by GGNN, which is further put into the fully connected layer to get class activation map (CAM) [33] of its ground truth category. For fair comparison, the corresponding CAM of baseline method is visualized similarly. In Fig. 4, GGNN-AG emphasizes the leg for family level, which is critical for classification. And in other levels, the response region on the pattern of wing, which is slight in baseline method, is intensely highlighted by our GGNN-AG. Besides, GGNN-AG enlarges its response region, covering the surrounding of the wing pattern, i.e. the whole wing and leg, which is less-discriminative. Overall, we tend to magnify the responses of discriminative regions, and discover more less-discriminative regions, which provides some insights for the better performance of GGNN-AG.

6   Conclusion

In this paper, we propose a GNN-based feature learning framework by exploiting the hierarchical semantic correlations among multiple grain categories. Extensive experiments exhibit the superiority of our methods on various FGVC tasks. And we collect a more challenging car dataset for FGVC with more category count in all levels and more viewpoint variations. Nevertheless, we will explore the performance of our methods on larger scale dataset for further investigation.

Acknowledgements. This work was supported by National Natural Science Foundation of China (No. 61772527, 62002356, 62076235, 61976210, 62176254, 62002357 and 62006230), Ministry of Education industry-University Cooperative Education Program (Wei Qiao Venture Group, No. E1425201) and Open Research Projects of Zhejiang Lab (No. 2021KH0AB07).

References

1. Bertinetto, L., Müller, R., Tertikas, K., Samangooei, S., Lord, N.A.: Making better mistakes: leveraging class hierarchies with deep networks. In: CVPR (2020)
2. Chang, D., et al.: The devil is in the channels: mutual-channel loss for fine-grained image classification. IEEE Trans. Image Process. **29**, 4683–4695 (2020)
3. Chang, D., Pang, K., Zheng, Y., Ma, Z., Song, Y.Z., Guo, J.: Your "flamingo" is my "bird": fine-grained, or not. In: CVPR (2021)
4. Chen, T., Lin, L., Chen, R., Wu, Y., Luo, X.: Knowledge-embedded representation learning for fine-grained image recognition. In: IJCAI (2018)
5. Chen, T., Wu, W., Gao, Y., Dong, L., Luo, X., Lin, L.: Fine-grained representation learning and recognition by exploiting hierarchical semantic embedding. In: MM (2018)
6. Chen, Y., Bai, Y., Zhang, W., Mei, T.: Destruction and construction learning for fine-grained image recognition. In: CVPR (2019)
7. Cho, K., van Merrienboer, B., Gulcehre, C., Bougares, F., Schwenk, H., Bengio, Y.: Learning phrase representations using RNN encoder-decoder for statistical machine translation. In: EMNLP (2014)
8. Du, R., et al.: Fine-grained visual classification via progressive multi-granularity training of jigsaw patches. In: Vedaldi, A., Bischof, H., Brox, T., Frahm, J.-M. (eds.) ECCV 2020. LNCS, vol. 12365, pp. 153–168. Springer, Cham (2020). https://doi.org/10.1007/978-3-030-58565-5_10
9. Fang, H., Xu, Y., Wang, W., Liu, X., Zhu, S.: Learning knowledge-guided pose grammar machine for 3D human pose estimation. In: AAAI (2018)
10. Fu, J., Zheng, H., Mei, T.: Look closer to see better: recurrent attention convolutional neural network for fine-grained image recognition. In: CVPR (2017)
11. Gao, Y., Chen, Y., Wang, J., Lu, H.: Progressive rectification network for irregular text recognition. Sci. China Inf. Sci. **63**(2), 1–14 (2020). https://doi.org/10.1007/s11432-019-2710-7
12. Gao, Z., Wang, L., Wu, G.: Lip: local importance-based pooling. In: ICCV (2019)
13. Ge, W., Lin, X., Yu, Y.: Weakly supervised complementary parts models for fine-grained image classification from the bottom up. In: CVPR (2019)
14. He, K., Gkioxari, G., Dollár, P., Girshick, R.B.: Mask R-CNN. In: ICCV (2017)

15. He, K., Zhang, X., Ren, S., Sun, J.: Deep residual learning for image recognition. In: CVPR (2016)
16. Huang, L., Huang, Y., Ouyang, W., Wang, L.: Part-level graph convolutional network for skeleton-based action recognition. In: AAAI (2020)
17. Huang, Z., Li, Y.: Interpretable and accurate fine-grained recognition via region grouping. In: CVPR (2020)
18. Kipf, T., Welling, M.: Semi-supervised classification with graph convolutional networks. ArXiv (2017)
19. Krause, J., Stark, M., Deng, J., Fei-Fei, L.: 3D object representations for fine-grained categorization. In: 3dRR-13 (2013)
20. Li, Y., Tarlow, D., Brockschmidt, M., Zemel, R.S.: Gated graph sequence neural networks. CoRR (2016)
21. Luo, W., Zhang, H., Li, J., Wei, X.: Learning semantically enhanced feature for fine-grained image classification. IEEE Signal Process. Lett. **27**, 1545–1549(2020)
22. Maji, S., Kannala, J., Rahtu, E., Blaschko, M., Vedaldi, A.: Fine-grained visual classification of aircraft. Technical report (2013)
23. Nilsback, M.E., Zisserman, A.: Automated flower classification over a large number of classes. In: ICVGIP (2008)
24. Scarselli, F., Gori, M., Tsoi, A.C., Hagenbuchner, M., Monfardini, G.: The graph neural network model. IEEE Trans. Neural Netw. **20**(1), 61–80 (2009). https://doi.org/10.1109/TNN.2008.2005605
25. Wah, C., Branson, S., Welinder, P., Perona, P., Belongie, S.: The caltech-UCSD birds-200-2011 dataset. Technical report (2011)
26. Wang, Y., et al.: Multi-label classification with label graph superimposing. In: AAAI (2020)
27. Wang, Z., Wang, S., Li, H., Dou, Z., Li, J.: Graph-propagation based correlation learning for weakly supervised fine-grained image classification. In: AAAI (2020)
28. Xie, S., Yang, T., Wang, X., Lin, Y.: Hyper-class augmented and regularized deep learning for fine-grained image classification. In: CVPR (2015)
29. Xu, K., Hu, W., Leskovec, J., Jegelka, S.: How powerful are graph neural networks? In: ICLR (2019)
30. Yang, L., Luo, P., Loy, C.C., Tang, X.: A large-scale car dataset for fine-grained categorization and verification. In: CVPR (2015)
31. Yang, L., Zhan, X., Chen, D., Yan, J., Loy, C.C., Lin, D.: Learning to cluster faces on an affinity graph. In: CVPR (2019)
32. Zheng, H., Fu, J., Zha, Z., Luo, J.: Looking for the devil in the details: learning trilinear attention sampling network for fine-grained image recognition. In: CVPR (2019)
33. Zhou, B., Khosla, A., Lapedriza, À., Oliva, A., Torralba, A.: Learning deep features for discriminative localization. In: CVPR (2016)
34. Zhou, F., Lin, Y.: Fine-grained image classification by exploring bipartite-graph labels. In: CVPR (2015)
35. Zhou, P., et al.: Attention-based bidirectional long short-term memory networks for relation classification. In: ACL (2016)

Skeletonization Based on K-Nearest-Neighbors on Binary Image

Yi Ren(iD), Min Zhang(✉)(iD), Hongyu Zhou, and Ji Liu(iD)

College of Computer Science, Chongqing University,
No. 174, Shapingba Main Street, Chongqing, China
zm@cqu.edu.cn

Abstract. Skeletonization on binary image is a process for reducing foreground regions to a skeletal remnant, which largely preserves the original region's connectivity. An algorithm for skeletonization based on k-nearest-neighbors is proposed in this paper. Instead of the fixed 8-neighborhood approach, which is the most common in the thinning field, our algorithm implements skeletonization based on k-nearest-neighbors. The method mainly consists of two stages: raw skeleton extraction and a novel thinning for post-processing. Extensive experiments are conducted and results show that the skeleton extracted by our method is precise, clean, and much smoother than the previous works.

Keywords: Skeletonization · Thinning · K-nearest-neighbors

1 Introduction

Skeletonization provides a practical and compact representation of an image object by reducing its dimensionality to a *medial axis* or *skeleton* defined by [5] while preserving the topologic and geometric properties of the original object. The skeleton extracted can be used as a useful tool for shape description and is also a well-known pre-processing of image analysis and shape recognition.

Many algorithms for obtaining skeletons in 2-D space have been encountered in the literature. We can classify them as follows:

- *skeletonization methods based on thinning*: In an intuitive manner, it consists of "peeling" the shape for the purpose of obtaining a set of connected points with a single pixel width, which preserves the topology of the shape [15]. In other words, thinning is an operation that aims to remove non-terminal simple points in a parallel or sequential manner. The main advantage of these algorithms is the preservation of the shape topology [3,13].

Supported by the Chongqing Research Program of Basic Research and Frontier Technology (Grant No. cstc2019jcyj-msxmX0033), National Key R&D Program of China (Grant No. 2019YFD1100501) and National Natural Science Foundation of China (Grant No. 61701051).

© Springer Nature Switzerland AG 2022
B. Þór Jónsson et al. (Eds.): MMM 2022, LNCS 13142, pp. 243–254, 2022.
https://doi.org/10.1007/978-3-030-98355-0_21

(a) Original object

(b) Raw skeleton

(c) Final skeleton

Fig. 1. Skeletonization.

- *skeletonization methods based on a distance map*: The objective is to identify the key points on the distance map, where each pixel is labeled with the value of its distance to the nearest background pixel [1,8,11]. Different distance maps approximate or compute exactly the Euclidean distance. For example, squared Euclidean distance [12], signed Euclidean distance [16] and honeycomb [7].

The k-nearest neighbor search algorithm is used to collect the local information of neighborhood and has been widely implemented in data science, such as classification [6,14] and clustering [10]. Inspired by [18], we propose a skeletonization based on k-nearest-neighbors which preserves more neighbors and local information for each sample pixel, resulting in a cleaner and smoother skeleton. We first compute the sum of the vectors of each foreground pixel in its search field to get an initial direction of its movement, and then perform principal component analysis to optimize the previously computed vector. Next, we move each pixel along the optimized displacement vector and redraw image based on the set of moved points. Steps above are repeated until the termination conditions are met, and then a post-processing is performed to obtain the final skeleton.

2 Proposed Method

In this section, we present an iterative skeletonization algorithm based on k-nearest-neighbors on binary image. Note that all the distances we mention in the paper are Euclidean.

2.1 K-Nearest-Neighbors Based Extraction

A binary image S is represented by a matrix P, of size $m \times n$, where $P(i,j)$ represents the binary value of the pixel at the position (i,j). Given a set of foreground pixels, by computing the sum of vectors around each sample pixel, we will have the following displacement vector:

$$u_i = \frac{1}{k_i} \sum_{j \in N_{i,k}} (x_j - x_i) \tag{1}$$

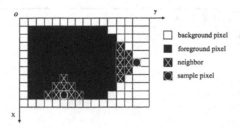

Fig. 2. Sample pixels with their neighbors.

where $N_{i,k}$ is the set of k-nearest-neighbors of sample pixel x_i. The displacement vector u_i determines the primary direction of movement. However, when faced with a pixel with special local information, it does not work as what we expect, such as the sample pixel on the right in Fig. 2, which also acts as an extremity. It should not be moved, but its u_i calculated is $(0, -1)$ after rasterization. Thus, we perform a principal component analysis (PCA) for each foreground pixel on its $N_{i,k}$ before moving it. Then, we obtain a symmetric 2×2 positive semi-definite matrix:

$$M = \sum_{x_j \in N_{i,k}} (x_j - x_i) \otimes (x_j - x_i) \tag{2}$$

where $\otimes$ is the outer product vector operator. Then we compute its σ_i as below to measure linearity of the neighborhood:

$$\sigma_i = \frac{\lambda_i^p}{\lambda_i^1 + \lambda_i^2} \tag{3}$$

where λ_i^1 and λ_i^2 denote the eigenvalue of eigenvector v_i^1 and v_i^2 respectively. The principal eigenvalue λ_i^p would be defined as $max(\lambda_i^1, \lambda_i^2)$ with v_i^p denoting principal direction. Furthermore, v_i^p and $cos\,(v_i^p, u_i)$ would both become the opposite if $cos\,(v_i^p, u_i) < 0$. One key point is that when $cos\,(v_i^p, u_i)$ is small, the sample pixel

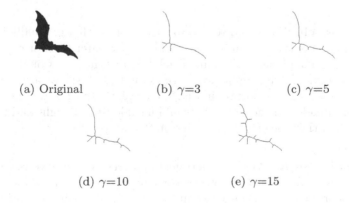

(a) Original   (b) γ=3   (c) γ=5

(d) γ=10   (e) γ=15

Fig. 3. Extraction with gradually increasing γ on object bat.

Algorithm 1. Skeleton Extraction

Require: The original image S
 1: $k \leftarrow 22$
 2: **repeat**
 3:     Generate sample pixel set $X = \{x_i\}_{i \in I}$ from S
 4:     **for** $\forall x_i \in X$ **do**
 5:         Compute Δx_i
 6:         $x_i \leftarrow x_i + \lfloor \Delta x_i \rfloor$
 7:     **end for**
 8:     Redraw S based on moved X
 9: **until** $\bar{\sigma}$ remains same for 3 times

---

x_i should move further, whereas when $\cos(v_i^p, u_i)$ is large, it should move less or even remain stationary. In addition, we want to clearly distinguish which pixels should or should not be moved, so we add a Gaussian weight to adjust the final displacement vector. And we obtain the following optimized displacement vector:

$$\Delta x_i = u_i e^{-a\gamma \cos^2 (v_i^p, u_i)} \tag{4}$$

where the detail factor γ, which defaults to 5, stands for the level of detail of the extracted skeleton. The higher the γ, the more detail the skeleton would have, see Fig. 3. Symbol a is a scaling factor and defaults to 10.

The mean of all linearity measurements σ_i denoted as $\bar{\sigma}$, indicates the degree of linearity of skeleton. As extraction proceeds, $\bar{\sigma}$ will get closer to 1. And the extraction would be stopped when $\bar{\sigma}$ remains unchanged three times in a row. At the end of each iteration, there will be many duplicate points due to movement, which can be removed by simply redrawing by position. The extraction process is described in Algorithm 1. And this is followed by a post-processing to further thin the raw skeleton.

2.2   Calculation of the Number of Nearest Neighbors

Neighbor Search. We would search for neighbors with a gradually increasing Euclidean radius until the number of neighbors is greater than or equal to k. If there are additional pixels at the same Euclidean distance, we would also include it in the neighbors of that sample pixel. For example, let's say we are now working on the sample pixel at the bottom in Fig. 2. If k is 2, that means we are looking for the 2 nearest pixels. But actually we would include its left, right and top pixels, because each of them has the same effect on the sample pixel.

Determination of K. As the experiments progressed, we have tested various pixel objects with different k. However, some unexpected terminations occurred. To solve this problem, two typical examples are studied, as shown in Fig. 4. These two examples are horizontal and 45° of inclination. An experiment is conducted

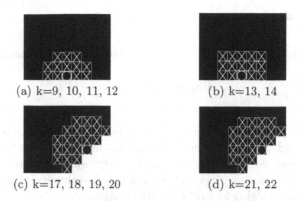

(a) k=9, 10, 11, 12   (b) k=13, 14

(c) k=17, 18, 19, 20   (d) k=21, 22

Fig. 4. Sample pixels with their different number of nearest neighbors.

Table 1. Pixels and u_i

Sample pixel	k	u_i
a	9, 10, 11, 12	$(0, -0.92)$
b	13, 14	$(0, -1.07)$
c	17, 18, 19, 20	$(0.95, -0.95)$
d	21, 22	$(1.04, -1.04)$

for them, the results of which are listed in Table 1. We see that the pixels that should be moved are not moved because of the too small k.

In addition, we noticed that the skeleton may break after a certain number of iterations. For example, when we are extracting a segment of arcs, too many neighbors are acquired, resulting in too much movement of pixels, which makes the skeleton break. One extreme case where a skeleton with a ninety degree bend in the width of a single pixel is studied, as shown in Fig. 5(a). When k equals to 23 or 24, a broken skeleton is generated, while when k equals to 21 or 22, the skeleton still maintains the connectivity, see Fig. 5(b) (c).

Therefore, according to the experimental results above, k should be restricted to a number greater than or equal to 21, less than or equal to 22. Considering the symmetry, we choose 22 as our final k value.

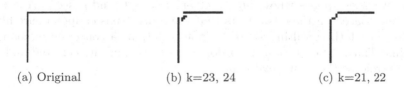

(a) Original   (b) k=23, 24   (c) k=21, 22

Fig. 5. Results of ninety degree skeleton.

(a) Two rectangles   (b) Erroneous Skeleton

Fig. 6. Perturbation.

Perturbation. When we search for neighbors, if we encounter the case in Fig. 6(a), it would result in pixels being perturbed to some extent. In extreme cases, such as two rectangles separated by only one pixel, this can lead to a large number of erroneous pixel movements because the pixels near the contour acquire the wrong local neighborhood information.

To solve this problem, if we find that the neighborhood of a sample pixel is not a unique but a series of discrete connected domains, we consider only the connected domain where the sample pixel is located. This avoids the perturbation caused by the close distance of pixels in two different parts.

2.3   Post-processing

After the aforementioned extraction, we would get a relatively thick but topologic-preserved raw skeleton, as the middle shown in Fig. 1. Obviously, the raw skeleton should be thinned furthermore.

The basic idea is that if a pixel is removed without changing the connectivity of the graph, then the pixel can actually be removed. But endpoints should be kept first, because if we keep removing along the endpoints, we can both maintain the graph's connectivity and cause the entire skeleton to disappear, which is not the result we expect. A novel thinning method based on both u_i and $\cos(v_i^p, u_i)$ is introduced in this part.

Endpoints Search. We can see that for a pixel at the end of the skeleton, its neighbors are always on one side and cannot be on both sides at the same time, just as the sample pixel on the right in Fig. 2. Therefore, the component length of the endpoint's u_i in at least one of the x and y directions must be greater than 1. In addition, the value of $\cos(v_i^p, u_i)$ will be higher at points close to the central axis of the skeleton because the more symmetrical and elongated the distribution of neighbors, the smaller the angle between v_i^p and u_i will be. Hence, we select pixels whose $|u_{i_x}| \geq 1$ or $|u_{i_y}| \geq 1$, and $\cos(v_i^p, u_i) \geq 0.8$ as endpoints. Based on these two facts that the central-axis endpoints are filtered out. Note that the resulting set of endpoints may be a collection of connected domains. Thus, for each connected domain, we compute its centroid and treat that centroid as the actual endpoint.

Thinning. Since the raw skeleton is not strictly smooth, as shown in Fig. 7(a). If we simply remove pixels from one direction, or from multiple directions, we would end up with an unevenly thinned skeleton, see Fig. 7(b). According to the

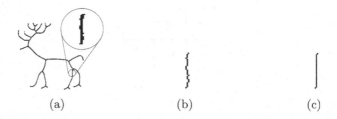

Fig. 7. (a) Detail of raw skeleton. (b) Result using simple thinning method. (c) Result using our thinning scheme.

properties of the length of u_i, i.e., $|u_i|$, we propose a novel thinning method for our post-processing.

We can see that for the foreground pixel, the closer it is to the contour, the larger its $|u_i|$ is. So we can first sort the pixels in descending order by the value of $|u_i|$ and then remove them consecutively. This will ensure that we always remove the outermost pixels first and the corresponding result is shown in Fig. 7(c). The entire algorithm for post-processing is described in Algorithm 2.

3   Comparisons and Results

In this section, we first introduce the performance measurements and some basic notions. Then, an extensive comparison of the proposed method with four classical methods, ZS [17], BB [4], Hybrid [2] and DM [9] is conducted.

The results show that our skeletonization can extract correct skeleton from various binary images. We also discuss the parameter setting strategy and the main limitation of our skeletonization algorithm in this section, and present two effective ways to optimize it.

Algorithm 2. Post-processing

Require: The raw skeleton image S

1: Generate sample pixel set $X = \{x_i\}_{i \in I}$ from S
2: Initialize endpoint set E
3: **for** $\forall x_i \in X$ **do**
4:    **if** $(|u_{i_x}| \geq 1$ or $|u_{i_y}| \geq 1)$ and $\cos(v_i^p, u_i) \geq 0.8$ **then**
5:        Add x_i to E
6:    **end if**
7: **end for**
8: Calculate centroids for each connected domain in E
9: $A \leftarrow$ Sort X in descending order by the value of $|u_i|$
10: **for** $i \leftarrow 0$ to $n - 1$ **do**
11:    **if** $A[i]$ is not centroid and doesn't affect the connectivity if removed **then**
12:        Remove $A[i]$ in S
13:    **end if**
14: **end for**

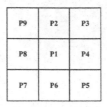

Fig. 8. 8-neighborhood configuration.

3.1   Basic Notions and Performance Measurements

It is assumed that the 8-neighborhood neighbors of the sample pixel (i, j) are $(i-1, j)$, $(i-1, j+1)$, $(i-1, j-1)$, $(i+1, j+1)$, $(i+1, j)$, $(i+1, j-1)$, $(i, j-1)$, and $(i, j+1)$. See Fig. 8.

- $A(p_1)$ calculates the number of "0–1" pairs in the clock-wise traversal of the 8-neighborhood of p_1.
- $B(p_1)$ produces the number of foreground pixels in 8-neighborhood.
- $C(p_1)$ represents the number of 8-foreground-pixel connected components in the neighborhood of "p_1" defined as follows:

$$C(p_1) = \neg p_2 \wedge (p_3 \vee p_4) + \neg p_4 \wedge (p_5 \vee p_6) \\ + \neg p_6 \wedge (p_7 \vee p_8) + \neg p_8 \wedge (p_9 \vee p_2) \tag{5}$$

- **Thinning Rate (TR)**: represents the degree of thinness of the image. This measure was proposed in [19].
  When $TR = 1$, it means that the image is perfectly thinned.
- **Redundant Pixels Percentage (RPP)**: is defined as the percentage of redundant pixels left in the skeleton. The RPP is computed using the following formula:

$$RPP = \frac{RP}{SP} * 100 \tag{6}$$

  where *Skeletal Pixels* (SP) is the total number of foreground pixels remaining after the process. *Redundant Pixels* (RP) are the skeletal boundary pixels p_1's whose deletion does not alter the local connectivity (i.e. verify $C(p_1) = 1$ and $2 \leq A(p_1) \leq 3$ and $B(p_1) \geq 1$)
- **Disconnected Points (DP)**. It evaluates the ability of the method to preserve the skeleton from disconnected problem. The number of connected components in the skeleton image and original image should be equal. Any connected component labeling method can be used in this measurement.
- **Execution Time (ET)**: is the real time cost by the algorithm. ET is calculated as the mean of 50 experiments on the same object.

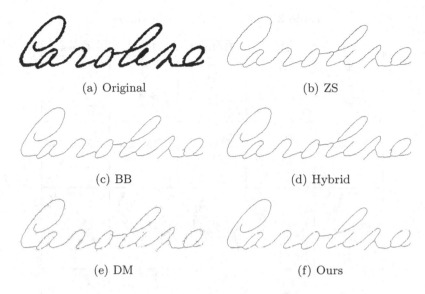

(a) Original   (b) ZS

(c) BB   (d) Hybrid

(e) DM   (f) Ours

Fig. 9. Results on hand-written characters.

3.2 Results and Discussions

Results. We implement the skeletonization algorithm under the environment of C++17 and run it on a desktop which has 16 GB memory and an AMD Ryzen 5 3600X 6-Core Processor running at 2.20 GHz. The operating system for the laptop is Ubuntu 20.04.1 LTS. For ZS, BB and Hybrid algorithms, codes are reproduced by reading the relevant papers. For the latest method DM, we download source code directly from the authors' Github repository and build it in our environment. For each presented result of all methods with parameters, we tried at least five sets of parameters and picked out the best skeleton for comparison. The databases for our experiment are MPEG7, Tetrapod120 and H_DIBCO2010_GT.

The visual evaluation aims to compare these five algorithms in terms of skeleton quality. As can be witnessed from Table 3 and Fig. 9, our method can extract correct, clean and well-centered skeleton from a variety of shapes, and the

Table 2. Results of statistical experiments

Method	TR	RPP	DP	ET
ZS	95.44	17.51	0	1.93
BB	99.84	0	0	**0.52**
Hybrid	99.80	0.20	0	0.73
DM	98.38	0.12	9.67	1.11
Ours	**99.97**	0	0	2.06

Table 3. Results of visual experiments

ZS	BB	Hybrid	DM	Ours

extracted skeletons are much smoother than the others'. And it can be seen that the skeleton generated by our method has fewer problem branches and incorrect connections than the other methods. It is noteworthy that skeleton generated by DM is not clean which can be seen in Fig. 9(e).

We also evaluate these algorithms statistically, as listed in Table 2. These are the average results of experiments on 20 different objects. The average TR accuracy rate of the proposed methods is 99.97% compared to 95.44%, 99.84%, 99.80% and 98.38% for ZS, BB, Hybrid and DM respectively. And the RPP of both our and BB's method is 0, compared to 17.51, 0.20 and 0.12 for each of ZS, Hybrid and DM. All methods do not have any disconnected points, except for DM where there are always some discrete points near the contour which can be seen on its visual results.

Our algorithm performs quite well on all the metrics except for ET. Because of the relatively large number of neighbors computed for each pixel, it leads to a larger calculation load and consumes more on execution time (ET).

All the results listed above show that our algorithm can extract extremely smooth and clean skeletons on objects of various shapes and score high on most statistical evaluations.

Discussions. There is only one single parameter γ we need to consider in our algorithm. For images with complex shapes, we may need to increase γ, for example, from 1 to 5, or even to 10 or 20, in order to get more detail in the final skeleton. In our experiments, the default value of γ works quite well for most objects.

The main limitation of our skeletonization algorithm is its relatively high computation complexity compared to previous methods, as the ET shown in Table 2. For this reason, we have also developed two methods to reduce the computation load. They are described in the following below.

First, when we find that the computed u_i is equal to 0, that is, the neighborhood of the sample pixel is a perfectly symmetric region, then the pixel must not have to be moved in this iteration. So we do not have to necessarily conduct the principal component analysis, and just set its Δx_i to (0,0).

$$N(r) = 1 + 4 \sum_{i=0}^{\infty} \left(\left\lfloor \frac{r^2}{4i+1} \right\rfloor - \left\lfloor \frac{r^2}{4i+3} \right\rfloor \right) \tag{7}$$

The second optimization is based on the Gauss circle problem. As Eq. (7) shows, new neighbors are possible only when the radius reaches certain thresholds. For example, when the radius is between 2 and 2.3, none of the new neighbors would appear, and only after the radius reaches 2.3 does it lead to a possible change in the number of neighbors. This reveals an acceleration strategy, where we do not need to increase the radius bit by bit to search for neighbors, but save in advance the relative positions of the possible neighbor points in the next iteration in an array, and in the next iteration, directly calculate the absolute position of the points based on the relative positions in the array. We implemented this acceleration strategy in our final program and it brought a 4x speedup.

4   Conclusion

In this paper, we propose an skeletonization algorithm based on k-nearest-neighbors, which collects more local information than the common 8-neighborhood. We first compute the displacement vector for each foreground pixel and optimize it through a PCA process. After several iterations, we would get the raw skeleton, and post-process it to obtain the final skeleton. It can handle a variety of shapes on binary images, and the skeletons extracted are smooth and clean. One direction for future work is to find a way to set the parameter γ to achieve adaptivity.

References

1. Baja, G., Thiel, E.: Skeletonization algorithm running on path-based distance maps. Image Vis. Comput. **14**(1), 47–57 (1996)
2. Ben Boudaoud, L., Solaiman, B., Tari, A.: A modified ZS thinning algorithm by a hybrid approach. Vis. Comput. **34**(5), 689–706 (2017). https://doi.org/10.1007/s00371-017-1407-4
3. Bertrand, G., Couprie, M.: Powerful parallel and symmetric 3D thinning schemes based on critical kernels. J. Math. Imaging Vis. **48**(1), 134–148 (2012). https://doi.org/10.1007/s10851-012-0402-7

4. Bilal, B.: An iterative thinning algorithm for binary images based on sequential and parallel approaches. Representation, Processing, Analysis, and Understanding of Image, pp. 34–43 (2018)
5. Blum, H.: A transformation for extracting new descriptors of shape. Models Percept. Speech Vis. **19**, 362–380 (1967)
6. Boiman, O., Shechtman, E.: In defense of nearest-neighbor image classification (2008)
7. Borgefors, G., Baja, G.: Skeletonizing the distance transform on the hexagonal grid. In: 9th International Conference on Pattern Recognition, 1988 (1988)
8. Choi, W.P., Lam, K.M., Siu, W.C.: Extraction of the Euclidean skeleton based on a connectivity criterion. Pattern Recognit. **36**(3), 721–729 (2003)
9. Durix, B., Morin, G., Chambon, S., Mari, J.L., Leonard, K.: One-step compact skeletonization. In: Cignoni, P., Miguel, E. (eds.) Eurographics 2019 - Short Papers. The Eurographics Association (2019). https://doi.org/10.2312/egs.20191005
10. Franti, P., Virmajoki, O., Hautamaki, V.: Fast agglomerative clustering using a k-nearest neighbor graph. IEEE Trans. Pattern Anal. Mach. Intell. **28**(11), 1875–1881 (2006)
11. Latecki, L.J., Li, Q., Xiang, B., Liu, W.: Skeletonization using SSM of the distance transform. IEEE (2007)
12. Meijster, A., Roerdink, J.B.T.M., Hesselink, W.H.: A general algorithm for computing distance transforms in linear time. in: Goutsias, J., Vincent, L., Bloomberg, D.S. (eds.) Mathematical Morphology and its Applications to Image and Signal Processing. CIV, vol. 18, pp. 331–340. Springer, Boston (2002). https://doi.org/10.1007/0-306-47025-X_36
13. Palágyi, K.: Equivalent 2D sequential and parallel thinning algorithms. In: International Workshop on Combinatorial Image Analysis (2014)
14. Piotrowska, M., Kostek, B., Ciszewski, T., Cyzewski, A.: Machine learning based analysis of English lateral allophones. Int. J. Appl. Math. Comput. Sci. **29**(2), 393–405 (2019)
15. Tabedzki, M., Saeed, K., Szczepański, A.: A modified K3M thinning algorithm. Int. J. Appl. Math. Comput. Sci. **26**(2), 439–450 (2016)
16. Ye, Q.Z.: The signed Euclidean distance transform and its applications. In: 9th International Conference on Pattern Recognition, 1988 (1988)
17. Zhang, T.Y., Suen, C.Y.: A fast parallel algorithm for thinning digital patterns. Commun. ACM **27**(3), 236–239 (1984)
18. Zhou, J., Liu, J., Zhang, M.: Curve skeleton extraction via k-nearest-neighbors based contraction. Int. J. Appl. Math. Comput. Sci. **30**, 123–132 (2020)
19. Zhou, R.W., Quek, C., Ng, G.S.: A novel single-pass thinning algorithm and an effective set of performance criteria. Pattern Recognt. Lett. **16**(12), 1267–1275 (1995). https://doi.org/10.1016/0167-8655(95)00078-X

Classroom Attention Estimation Method Based on Mining Facial Landmarks of Students

Liyan Chen[1,2], Haoran Yang[1], and Kunhong Liu[1,2]([✉])

[1] School of Informatics, Xiamen University, Xiamen 361001, China
lkhqz@xmu.edu.cn
[2] School of Film, Xiamen University, Xiamen 361001, China

Abstract. Classroom attention estimation aims to capture the multi-modal semantic information contained in the teaching situation and analyze the level of concentration and participation of students in the classroom. However, it is a challenge to mine different modal information in non-experimental real teaching scenes to construct a unified attention mode. In order to advance these researches, this paper proposes a new method of automatically estimating attention through facial feature points. This method uses face detection and face alignment algorithms to capture 68 landmarks on student faces in classroom videos, and introduces face reference information to constrain landmarks and extract feature sets. The purpose is to reduce the sensitivity of the attention model to differences in different face information. The automatic evaluation module uses machine learning algorithms to train the classifier to estimate the individual student's attention level. In a large number of experiments conducted on multiple real classroom video data, our three-level attention classifier achieves an accuracy of 82.5%, which can achieve better results than other studies in the field of student participation analysis. The results show that the method based on facial landmark mining can more accurately predict the individual student's classroom attention level, and can be used as a non-intrusive automatic analysis method for real classroom multimedia data analysis.

Keywords: Classroom attention estimation · Facial landmarks · Machine learning

1 Introduction

The focus of this article is on participation during classroom learning, called classroom attention. As an optional research material, classroom videos contain rich semantic information, which provides data support for the analysis of learning in traditional classrooms. Mining these semantic information to evaluate the concentration of classroom attention is helpful to construct an innovative conceptual model and improve the rules of teaching evaluation. After knowing the level of students' attention, teachers can optimize the curriculum design at the level of content difficulty and teaching interaction, and

---

L. Chen and H. Yang—These authors contributed equally to this work.

© Springer Nature Switzerland AG 2022
B. Þór Jónsson et al. (Eds.): MMM 2022, LNCS 13142, pp. 255–266, 2022.
https://doi.org/10.1007/978-3-030-98355-0_22

improve the scientific nature of teaching links and the quality of classroom teaching. Knowing the level of classroom attention is also helpful for students' self-reflection on classroom behaviors and attitudes, as well as for the adjustment of learning plans. Rivera et al. [1] surveyed the public's attitude towards the quantitative feedback system for lectures, courses, and conferences, indicating that this idea will be widely supported. Raca et al. [2] extracted features by manually observing classroom videos and questionnaires, and used statistical methods to study the correlation between attention and student movement. Zaletelj et al. [3] used Kinect sensors to obtain the gaze point and body posture of students to analyze the relationship between observable behavior and attention. Monkaresi et al. [4] used remote heart rate measurement and expression detection of Kinect sensors to extract features from classroom videos, and combined machine learning tools for supervised learning to analyze participation. Xu et al. [5] used the Euler angle constraint method to estimate the head posture of the students in the classroom, and scored the attention based on the face orientation. Zheng et al. [6] designed a student behavior analysis system, which mainly focused on automatically detecting classroom behaviors in videos. These studies show that classroom attention estimation can be achieved through external observable and detectable factors.

However, most studies use experimental instruments and frontal video to extract appearance features. Although the accuracy of the features extracted by this method is high, the application effect is limited because the error factors in the actual classroom are not considered. Some researches start with the detection of actions and postures, but students' postures and actions in class are usually affected by the occlusion of objects, destroying the integrity of the information and making it difficult to accurately identify them. Relatively speaking, the facial information of the students is relatively completely retained in the classroom videos. Making full use of the well-preserved facial information helps to analyze and recognize the attention of the students. Therefore, we propose a classroom attention analysis model based on facial features, which aims to use computer vision methods to extract feature sets from faces in real teaching environments and use these features to estimate attention levels. In the feature extraction process, we introduce the reference information of the face to constrain, and combine with the supervised machine learning algorithm to train the classifier. The purpose of introducing constraints is to improve the accuracy of feature extraction and minimize the impact of different face deflection angles and facial features that are common in classroom videos on the location of facial landmarks. Since there is no public classroom multimedia data set, the experiment uses the classroom video data collected by this research group to verify the proposed method, and the results show that the model can accurately analyze attention.

2   Related Work

2.1   Face Detection

Face detection is a widely discussed problem in the field of computer vision, and a large number of studies have proposed very diverse methods for this. Some face detection algorithms show relatively good results on public data sets. Multitask Cascaded Convolutional Networks (MTCNN) [7] uses a cascaded architecture with three stages of deep convolutional networks to predict face and landmark location in a coarse-to-fine manner. Faster R-CNN [8] introduces a Region Proposal Network (RPN) that shares full-image convolutional features with the detection network, thereby enabling nearly cost-free region proposals. Single Stage Headless Face Detector (SSH) [9] places multi-scale face detection modules on three convolutional layers with different network depths to improve performance and reduce time overhead. Face detection is the first step of our method. Since SSH [9] performs well in terms of speed and accuracy, and shows adaptability in face detection at different scales, we chose SSH [9] as the algorithm of the face detection module. It was found to show good results on our classroom data set.

2.2 Face Alignment

Face alignment aims at locating a sparse set of fiducial facial landmarks. Some classic face alignment algorithms are often used to compare performance. Xiong et al. [10] proposes a Supervised Descent Method (SDM) for minimizing a Non-linear Least Squares (NLS) function and its applications to facial feature detection. Kazemi et al. [11] presents a general framework based on gradient boosting for learning an ensemble of regression trees, achieving super-realtime performance with high quality predictions. CNN based methods have shown great potential and achieved even better performance on the task of face alignment. Zhang et al. [12] investigates the possibility of improving detection robustness through multi-task learning. Wang et al. [13] proposes a graph structure reasoning network for face alignment and reconstruction. Although the CNN-based method may achieve higher accuracy, we found that the performance of using ERT [11] on our data is good enough and has a faster processing speed. Therefore, the method of ERT [11] is selected as the algorithm of face alignment module. In addition, influenced by Shao et al. [14], we adopt a compression-based data enhancement strategy to adapt to the small faces that are ubiquitous in classroom videos and improve the robustness of the model.

2.3 Student Engagement Modeling

Grafsgaard et al. [15] used a variety of models including facial expressions, postures and gestures to predict student participation and frustration in the learning process. Zaletelj et al. [3] used Kinect sensors to capture students' gaze points and body postures to analyze observable behaviors for attention modeling. Whitehill et al. [16] used a laboratory camera to record the face video of each subject during the learning period to detect their facial expressions, and combined machine learning to estimate the degree of participation, indicating that machine learning methods can be used to develop real-time automatic participation detectors. The accuracy of the detector is even comparable to that of a human observer. However, these methods do not consider the problems of multiple faces, multiple angles, and differences in facial features in real classrooms, and are limited to laboratory scenes. Xu et al. [5] used the Euler angle constraint method to estimate the head posture of students in the classroom to solve the problem of changes in head posture in complex situations. Yang et al. [17] proposes a progressively refined imputation for multi-modalities by auto-Encoder (PRIME) for block wise missingness handling in classroom multimodal data. These two methods try to solve the objective problems in the classroom environment, and have more practical value in application and promotion. We combine these ideas and use classroom facial information and machine learning knowledge to build an attention model. Then, considering the possible individual sample deviations in the face information extracted from the real classroom, a face benchmark is introduced to reduce the impact of deviations on the model.

3 The Proposed Method

This paper uses the detection module to capture student faces and 68 facial landmarks. The face reference is introduced, and the feature is extracted by the difference between the landmark and the reference information. Then combined with machine learning algorithms, we analyze and estimate the level of student attention. We recorded real classroom videos and used it as experimental material to verify the proposed method. This section first introduces the face detection and face alignment algorithms used in this article, then proposes bias correction and feature extraction methods, and finally describes the attention analysis method combined with machine learning. The flow chart of attention estimation method is shown in Fig. 1.

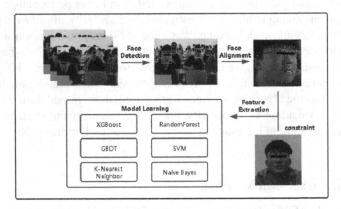

Fig. 1. Flow chart of attention estimation method.

3.1 Face Detection and Face Alignment

Face detection is the first step of our method. SSH [9] detects small, medium and large faces by placing detection modules with strides of 8, 16, and 32 on three different convolutional layers of the network. It shows good performance when detecting faces of different scales, especially small faces in the WIDER dataset [18]. In order to adapt to the multi-scale face in the classroom, we use SSH [9] as the algorithm of the face detection module. Then the detected face feature map is passed to the face alignment module as a parameter. In the face alignment module, we use the ERT [11] method to capture face landmarks. The core idea of the algorithm is to return the face shape from the current shape to the real shape step by step, by building a cascaded residual regression tree. ERT

[11] estimates the location of face landmarks from a sparse subset of pixel intensities (pixel gray values). This method is not suitable for low-resolution faces. Influenced by Shao et al. [14], we adopt a compression-based data enhancement strategy to adapt the face alignment module to small face images. Specifically, we compress the images used for training with JPEG quality of 50 and 25 respectively, and then input the face images of different qualities and the corresponding adjusted 68-point annotations into the model to learn the features at different resolutions, thus Improved robustness. This makes it possible to achieve the alignment of some low-resolution small faces.

3.2 Constraint Landmarks and Feature Extraction

The 68 facial landmarks obtained above represent the position of the pixel in the picture, which is affected by the distance and angle between the camera and the student's position. The first problem we have to overcome is the difference in facial features and angles. A benchmark state is set for each experimental subject, and the general state change of the face is reflected by the difference between all current landmarks and the corresponding benchmark, which can reduce the influence of facial feature differences. Inspired by [19], a landmark restoration method through geometric transformation is proposed to solve the problem of deviation angle. The method of [19] is to connect the feature points of the head in turn to form a large number of dense triangles, and reconstruct the three-dimensional face based on geometric transformation. Similarly, we use the Delaunay triangulation method [20]. However, it only needs to transform the landmark to the position at the corresponding angle, instead of restoring the fine lines of the entire face. We divide the face landmark into five triangular regions. (see Fig. 2). The principle that we select these points as the transformation vertices is that these points are only related to the angle of the face during the transformation process, and will not change position according to changes in facial expressions.

Fig. 2. Five triangular regions.

Each feature point has a barycentric coordinate in the triangle. For example, the point $p(x, y)$ has a geometric relationship in the triangle ABC, such as formula (1) (2) (3).

$$p = uA + vB + wC \tag{1}$$

$$1 = u + v + w \tag{2}$$

$$0 \leq u, v, w \leq 1 \tag{3}$$

The point (u, v, w) is the center of gravity of the triangle where p is located. Since it is known that the position of the center of gravity of a point will not change during the affine transformation process, we can obtain the new coordinates of the point p through the above formula. In the case of introducing a face benchmark for each experimental subject, we use the three vertices of the triangle as a reference for each region of the benchmark. Through the changes expressed by these three points, the points associated with each area are mapped to a new reference position. For example, the transformation of area 1 is illustrated in Fig. 3. The associated points include the landmarks of the right eye and the right eyebrow. These points are mapped to the new location using the same rules as the triangle of area 1. The frontal reference image is changed five times in total. Respectively extract the location points associated with the five regions to construct the corresponding reference map for angle adaptation. This is an approaching thought. Our task is to extract the approximate position of the reference landmark at the corresponding angle, so as to reduce the deviation caused by the face to the landmark when the angle changes. This does not make any requirement for the accurate restoration of the 3D face. In the fourth section, we verify the superiority of our method with actual experiments.

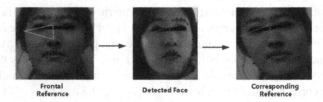

Frontal Reference   Detected Face   Corresponding Reference

Fig. 3. The transformation of area 1

After obtaining the benchmark of the corresponding angle, we further constrain the detected face landmarks. Since each point represents the pixel position in the image, it is not conducive to the comparison of the detected face with the corresponding reference. We use formula (4) to express all the points as relative positions. The brow center point represented by the 28th landmark. The face size is affected by the distance between the face and the camera. We use formula (5) to normalize the detected face and the reference face of different scales to a unified measurement.

$$(x_i, y_i) = (x_i, y_i) - (x_{28}, y_{28}) \tag{4}$$

$$(x_i, y_i) = (x_i, y_i)/d \tag{5}$$

d represents the distance from the center of the brow to the midpoint of the chin. Finally, we use the difference between the detected face landmarks and the corresponding points of the reference face to reflect general facial changes to extract a 136-dimensional feature set.

3.3 Attention Classification Modeling

Attention classification modeling is to input the extracted 136-dimensional features (consisting of the changes of the x and y coordinates of 68 landmarks relative to the reference) and the attention level of manual annotation into the classifier. The attention estimation model is built by supervised learning the characteristics of each class. This part uses Scikit-Learn to achieve modeling. We selected some commonly used classifiers for training and testing, and also selected appropriate parameters for each classifier to improve the effect. This process is carried out through grid search after a certain range is given to each parameter.

The ratio of our sample set on the three classes is about 2:10:3, and there is a phenomenon of data imbalance. It is widely acknowledged that a serious imbalance in the categories of the data set will have a bad impact on the performance and efficiency of the classifier. The research of [21] shows that balancing the data set by combining clustering and down-sampling methods is conducive to preserving the typicality of large classes of samples. It is also an effective means to improve the performance of the classifier. We use K-Means to divide the class 2 in the training set into 3 clusters, and then use down sampling to balance the data. In addition, in order to make full use of all samples, after clustering the major categories, we sequentially perform random sampling from each cluster without replacement to make the number of samples of the major and minor classes basically equal. Then, each group of samples from class 2 is mixed with all the other two classes of samples to train multiple classifiers. Finally, the voting strategy is used in the classification process (see Fig. 4).

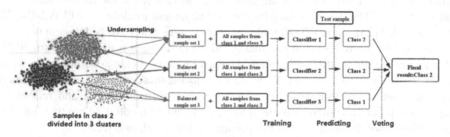

Fig. 4. Classifier training process using our data balancing strategy

We evaluate the performance of different classifiers to select the most suitable classifier for attention modeling and explore the best effect our model can achieve. The selected criteria are accuracy, macro F1-Score, macro recall and macro precision. The macro represents the average of multiple class standards, and the calculation method is as formula (6) (7) (8).

$$MacP = \frac{1}{n}\sum_{i=1}^{n} Pi \tag{6}$$

$$MacR = \frac{1}{n}\sum_{i=1}^{n} R_i \tag{7}$$

$$MacF1 = \frac{2 \times MacP \times MacR}{MacP + MacR} \tag{8}$$

4 Experiment

We use public data sets to train the face detection module and the face alignment module. Then the collected real classroom video was applied to the experiment to verify our aforementioned method. Finally, the performance of our model is comprehensively evaluated by four evaluation criteria.

4.1 Dataset

The classroom video used in the experiment was collected by a camera placed next to the classroom platform, and the data collection was all approved by the students. The video we collected comes from some engineering courses at Xiamen University in China, including a total of 36 engineering undergraduates, 23 males and 13 females. For the convenience of processing, we split the original video and obtained 91 videos in total, each of which lasted about 2 min. We use manual observation to mark the visual attention of each student visible in the video, in seconds. The evaluation criteria are divided into three levels, which respectively indicate high, medium, and low attention levels. In order to reduce the influence of individual subjective factors, we determine the final attention level by voting by multiple observers. The face detection module uses the WIDER FACE dataset [18] for training. The data contains 32,203 images and 393,703 annotated faces, of which 40% is the training set, and the rest is the cross-validation set and the test set. The data sets used by the face alignment module are AFLW2000 [22] and 300W-LP [23]. AFLW2000 contains 2000 images that have been annotated with image-level 68-point 3D facial landmarks. 300W-LP Dataset is expanded from 300W, which standardises multiple alignment databases with 68 landmarks, including AFW, LFPW, HELEN, IBUG and XM2VTS. We not only use these data for learning landmark detection, but also select some of them for compression processing and relabel the positioning points, and then input them into the alignment module for training together, in order to improve the accuracy of alignment on low-resolution faces.

4.2 Experimental Results

Face Detection and Face Alignment. Regarding the performance of the methods we cited on public data sets, their authors have carried out tests and comparisons, so this article won't repeat them. In our classroom data set, a total of 25 different faces and their facial landmarks were successfully obtained through the detection module, including 19 males and 6 females. The rest are not detected due to occlusion, low resolution, picture distortion, or other reasons. Since our classroom face data is not marked with landmarks, we adopted manual methods to filter the effective images with accurate landmarks. According to statistics, the accurately aligned faces accounted for 87.4% of the total.

Constraint Landmarks and Feature Extraction. For each subject, we obtained their frontal reference image. Combining the facial landmark data obtained by the detection module and applying our constraint and extraction method, a total of 4062 samples are obtained, which constitute a feature vector of 4062×136. These samples correspond to the manually-annotated attention labels according to time and person.

Attention Classification Modeling. We have compared several commonly used classifiers. In order to verify the robustness of the method and avoid the influence of the correlation between multiple samples from the same student, 23 students' feature samples were randomly selected from the data set as the training set, and the data of the remaining 2 students were used as the test. We repeat this process ten times and average the results, using accuracy, macro F1-Score, macro recall and macro precision as our evaluation criteria. The detailed classifier evaluation results are shown in Table 1. It can be seen that the best performance is the Gradient Boosting Decision Tree (GBDT), which achieves an accuracy of 82.5%, and other indicators are also the highest.

Table 1. The detailed classifier evaluation results.

Classifier	Accuracy	F1-score	Recall	Precision
XGBoost	0.810	0.742	0.713	0.804
RandomForest	0.796	0.686	0.646	0.770
GBDT	0.825	0.762	0.735	0.813
SVM	0.772	0.652	0.607	0.754
k-Nearest Neighbors	0.787	0.667	0.614	0.789
Native Bayes	0.756	0.674	0.654	0.716

We continue to use the GBDT classifier to carry out ablation experiments. The evaluation results of the ablation experiment are shown in Table 2. The classification performance of extracting features after using frontal references to constrain landmarks is better than extracting the relative positions of landmarks directly (using formulas 4 and 5 for the original landmarks). Further introducing the reference of adapting the angle transformation can make our model achieve the optimal effect, which verifies the effectiveness and robustness of our method.

Table 2. The evaluation results of the ablation experiment.

Method	Accuracy	F1-score	Recall	Precision
Original landmark +balanced data	0.677	0.572	0.593	0.596
Frontal reference +balanced data	0.751	0.606	0.643	0.648
Corresponding reference +unbalanced data	0.841	0.654	0.590	0.816
Corresponding reference +balanced data (ours)	0.825	0.762	0.735	0.813

Although the accuracy appears to be slightly higher when the data is unbalanced, the other three indicators are significantly lower. By observing the confusion matrix, we find that unbalanced data performs poorly on classes with a small number of samples, which is a failure for a classifier. After our data balance processing, the performance of the classifier in class 2 is slightly reduced, but the performance of the other two classes is significantly improved. The evaluation and comparison of the performance of unbalanced data and balanced data on the three classes is shown in Fig. 5. It is distinguished by two color marks, the test result of unbalanced data is on the left, and the test result of balanced data is on the right. This shows the superiority of our data balancing method.

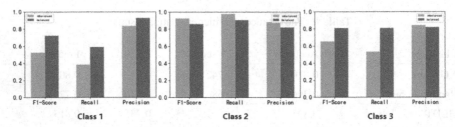

Fig. 5. The evaluation and comparison of the performance of unbalanced data and balanced data on the three classes

5   Conclusion

We proposes an attention estimation model. In our model, face landmarks are captured through face detection and face alignment modules, reference constraints are used to extract the features of facial landmark changes, and then a classifier is trained to estimate students' attention in class. In order to reduce the adverse effects from the deviation of position, angle and facial features in the real classroom, we introduced frontal reference information for processing, designed a landmark restoration method through geometric transformation to adapt to the angle transformation, and constrained landmarks to improve the accuracy of feature extraction. In the classifier training stage, we propose a data balancing scheme based on clustering and down sampling to improve classification performance. Applying our method to classroom data, better experimental results have been obtained, which proves that the method based on student facial landmarks mining is an effective means of estimating attention. It is worth noting that recording the performance of students in the classroom and using their faces to carry out experiments is related to personal privacy. Therefore, we have fully informed before recording and using the data, and have received the support of the students. The images used for display have also been blurred. In addition, all the data we collect comes from university classrooms, and the same methods and conclusions may not be applicable to other classroom environments. In the future, we will combine other features that can be captured in classroom multimedia to further explore their relationship with attention, so as to form a unified attention analysis model of multi-modal information fusion, which will help to develop a non-intrusive real-time classroom feedback system to benefit teachers and students. This work has great potential and significance.

Acknowledgments. This work is supported by the National Natural Science Foundation of China (No. 61772023), National Key Research and Development Program of China (No. 2019QY1803), Fujian Science and Technology Plan Industry-University-Research Cooperation Project (No.2021H6015), the National College Student Innovation and Entrepreneurship Training Program of China (202110384258) and The Social Science Program of Fujian Province (FJ2020B062).

References

1. Rivera-Pelayo, V., Munk, J., Zacharias, V., Braun, S.: Live interest meter – learning from quantified feedback in mass lectures. In: International Conference on Learning Analytics & Knowledge, pp. 23–27 (2013)
2. Raca, M., Tormey, R., Dillenbourg, P.: Sleepers' lag-study on motion and attention. In: Proceedings of the Fourth International Conference on Learning Analytics and Knowledge, pp. 36–43. ACM (2014)
3. Zaletelj, J., Košir, A.: Predicting students' attention in the classroom from Kinect facial and body features. J. Image Video Process. **2017**, 80 (2017). https://doi.org/10.1186/s13640-017-0228-8
4. Monkaresi, H., Bosch, N., Calvo, R.A., D'Mello, S.K.: Automated detection of engagement using video-based estimation of facial expressions and heart rate. IEEE Trans. Affect. Comput. **8**(1), 15–28 (2017). https://doi.org/10.1109/TAFFC.2016.2515084
5. Xu, X., Teng, X.: Classroom attention analysis based on multiple euler angles constraint and head pose estimation. In: Ro, Y.M., et al. (eds.) MMM 2020. LNCS, vol. 11961, pp. 329–340. Springer, Cham (2020). https://doi.org/10.1007/978-3-030-37731-1_27
6. Zheng, R., Jiang, F., Shen, R.: Intelligent student behavior analysis system for real classrooms. In: ICASSP 2020 - 2020 IEEE International Conference on Acoustics, Speech and Signal Processing (ICASSP), pp. 9244–9248 (2020). https://doi.org/10.1109/ICASSP40776.2020.9053457
7. Zhang, K., Zhang, Z., Li, Z., Qiao, Y.: Joint face detection and alignment using multitask cascaded convolutional networks. IEEE Signal Process. Lett. **23**(10), 1499–1503 (2016). https://doi.org/10.1109/LSP.2016.2603342
8. Ren, S., He, K., Girshick, R., Sun, J.: Faster R-CNN: towards real-time object detection with region proposal networks. IEEE Trans. Pattern Anal. Mach. Intell. **39**(6), 1137–1149 (2017). https://doi.org/10.1109/TPAMI.2016.2577031
9. Najibi, M., Samangouei, P., Chellappa, R., Davis, L.S.: SSH: single stage headless face detector. In: 2017 IEEE International Conference on Computer Vision (ICCV), pp. 4885–4894 (2017). https://doi.org/10.1109/ICCV.2017.522
10. Xiong, X., De la Torre, F.: Supervised descent method and its applications to face alignment. In: 2013 IEEE Conference on Computer Vision and Pattern Recognition, pp. 532–539 (2013). https://doi.org/10.1109/CVPR.2013.75
11. Kazemi, V., Sullivan, J.: One millisecond face alignment with an ensemble of regression trees. In: 2014 IEEE Conference on Computer Vision and Pattern Recognition, pp. 1867–1874 (2014). https://doi.org/10.1109/CVPR.2014.241
12. Zhang, Z., Luo, P., Loy, C.C., Tang, X.: Facial landmark detection by deep multi-task learning. In: Fleet, D., Pajdla, T., Schiele, B., Tuytelaars, T. (eds.) ECCV 2014. LNCS, vol. 8694, pp. 94–108. Springer, Cham (2014). https://doi.org/10.1007/978-3-319-10599-4_7
13. Wang, X., Li, X., Wu, S.: Graph structure reasoning network for face alignment and reconstruction. In: Lokoč, J., et al. (eds.) MMM 2021. LNCS, vol. 12572, pp. 493–505. Springer, Cham (2021). https://doi.org/10.1007/978-3-030-67832-6_40

14. Shao, Z., Ding, S., Zhu, H., Wang, C., Ma, L.: Face alignment by deep convolutional network with adaptive learning rate. In: 2016 IEEE International Conference on Acoustics, Speech and Signal Processing (ICASSP), pp. 1283–1287 (2016). https://doi.org/10.1109/ICASSP.2016. 7471883
15. Grafsgaard, J.F., et al.: The additive value of multimodal features for predicting engagement, frustration, and learning during tutoring. In: Proceedings of the 16th International Conference on Multimodal Interaction, pp. 42–49. ACM (2014)
16. Whitehill, J., Serpell, Z., Lin, Y., Foster, A., Movellan, J.R.: The faces of engagement: automatic recognition of student engagement from facial expressions. IEEE Trans. Affect. Comput. 5(1), 86–98 (2014). https://doi.org/10.1109/TAFFC.2014.2316163
17. Yang, X., Kim, Y.-J., Taub, M., Azevedo, R., Chi, M.: PRIME: block-wise missingness handling for multi-modalities in intelligent tutoring systems. In: Ro, Y.M., et al. (eds.) MMM 2020. LNCS, vol. 11962, pp. 63–75. Springer, Cham (2020). https://doi.org/10.1007/978-3-030-37734-2_6
18. Yang, S., Luo, P., Loy, C.C., Tang, X.: WIDER FACE: a face detection benchmark. In: 2016 IEEE Conference on Computer Vision and Pattern Recognition (CVPR), pp. 5525–5533 (2016). https://doi.org/10.1109/CVPR.2016.596
19. Zhu, J., Liu, Y., Zhang, L.: 3D face reconstruction based on geometric transformation. In: 2012 International Conference on Virtual Reality and Visualization, pp. 46–49 (2012). https://doi.org/10.1109/ICVRV.2012.10
20. Su, P., Drysdale, R.L.S.: A comparison of sequential delaunay triangulation algorithms. Comput. Geom. Theory Appl. 7, 361–358 (1997)
21. Li, X., Chen, Z., Yang, F.: Exploring of clustering algorithm on class-imbalanced data. In: 2013 8th International Conference on Computer Science & Education, pp. 89–93 (2013). https://doi.org/10.1109/ICCSE.2013.6553890
22. Zhu, X., Lei, Z., Liu, X., Shi, H., Li, S.Z.: Face alignment across large poses: a 3D solution. In: 2016 IEEE Conference on Computer Vision and Pattern Recognition (CVPR), pp. 146–155 (2016). https://doi.org/10.1109/CVPR.2016.23
23. Sagonas, C., Tzimiropoulos, G., Zafeiriou, S., Pantic, M.: 300 faces in-the-wild challenge: the first facial landmark localization challenge. In: 2013 IEEE International Conference on Computer Vision Workshops, pp. 397–403 (2013). https://doi.org/10.1109/ICCVW.2013.59

A Novel Chinese Sarcasm Detection Model Based on Retrospective Reader

Lei Zhang[1,2], Xiaoming Zhao[1], Xueqiang Song[1], Yuwei Fang[1], Dong Li[4], and Haizhou Wang[3(✉)]

[1] College of Computer Science, Sichuan University, Chengdu 610065, China
[2] Institute for Industrial Internet Research, Sichuan University, Chengdu 610065, China
[3] School of Cyber Science and Engineering, Sichuan University, Chengdu 610065, China
whzh.nc@scu.edu.cn
[4] Department of Computer Technology and Applications, Qinghai University, Xining 810016, Qinghai, China

Abstract. Sarcasm is a subtle form of language in which people express the opposite of what is implied. Existing research works for Chinese sarcasm detection focused on extracting features of target texts. However, there is a lot of contextual information on online social networks, which is insufficient to detect sarcasm based only on target texts. In this paper, we construct a large-scale Chinese sarcasm dataset with contextual information. Meanwhile, a sarcasm detection method based on deep learning is proposed. We used a retrospective reader in the detection process, which includes two parallel modules: Sketchy Reading and Intensive Reading. The Sketchy Reading module reads the target text and contextual information to get an initial impression. The Intensive Reading module uses a hierarchical method to get an intensive impression. Finally, we integrate the two parts to get the final prediction. Evaluation results on the dataset demonstrate the efficacy of our proposed model and the usefulness of contextual information for Chinese sarcasm detection. The research in this paper provides methods and ideas for future work in Chinese sarcasm detection on other social networking platforms.

Keywords: Sarcasm detection · Chinese · Contextual information · Retrospective reader · Online social network

1 Introduction

Merriam Webster defines sarcasm as "a mode of satirical wit depending for its effect on bitter, caustic, and often ironic language that is usually directed against an individual". It can not only disguise the hostility of the speaker but also enhance the effect of mockery or humor on the listener [2]. Because of these characteristics of sarcasm, people often use sarcasm to express their strong emotions on social media. Automatic sarcasm detection plays a significant role in various applications

© Springer Nature Switzerland AG 2022
B. Þór Jónsson et al. (Eds.): MMM 2022, LNCS 13142, pp. 267–278, 2022.
https://doi.org/10.1007/978-3-030-98355-0_23

that require the knowledge of people's sentiment or opinions [3], such as customer service, political stance detection and user intent recognition.

Existing research works for Chinese sarcasm detection mainly focused on extracting features of target texts and proposed some supervised algorithms [4,5]. However, the use of sarcasm also relies on context, which involves the presumption of commonsense and background knowledge of an event [6]. It is very difficult to determine the true intention of the speaker by only focusing on the target text. Therefore, contextual information is crucial for the task of sarcasm detection.

In this paper, inspired by the task of machine reading comprehension [1], we propose a deep learning model based on the retrospective method for sarcasm detection, that utilizes both target text and contextual information. Firstly, we take the target texts and contextual information as Input, and use the pre-trained Chinese word vector [7] for encoding. Secondly, we use two parallel modules to process the Input, namely Sketchy Reading module and Intensive Reading module. Sketchy Reading module uses the attention mechanism to simulate human behavior, and get the initial impression of the Input. Intensive Reading module uses a hierarchical method to process the Input. The Input is first passed through a recurrent layer to extract the temporal features of both target texts and contextual information, and we summarize the temporal features of contextual information. The summarized contextual information is then convoluted with the temporal features of target text to get the result. Finally, we concatenate the results of the two modules and send it to the fully connected layer to detect whether the target text is sarcastic or not. Our main contributions are summarized as follows:

Firstly, most existing sarcasm annotation corpus is in English but few in Chinese, which is a significant barrier to undertake sarcasm detection research on Chinese scenarios [25–27]. In this paper, we construct a large-scale Chinese sarcasm dataset with contextual information from 108,641 comments, which includes 2,814 manual annotated sarcastic texts and 764,231 non-sarcastic texts. Secondly, we propose a deep learning model based on the retrospective method for sarcasm detection, that utilizes both target text and contextual information. On the balanced dataset, our model achieved the highest F-score of 0.6942 and Accuracy of 0.6940. On the imbalanced dataset, our method also outperforms other baselines. Thirdly, in the component ablation test, we demonstrate the importance of the Sketchy Reading module and the Intensive Reading module, and we also show the influence of contextual information on Chinese sarcasm detection.

2   Related Work

The sarcasm detection task is a relatively new research area in natural language processing and it has become a popular research area in recent years. Sarcasm detection was initially performed using rule-based approaches. Bharti et al. [11] proposed two methods for detecting sarcastic tweets. The first is a dictionary generation algorithm based on parsing, and the second is to use exclamation points when detecting. Riloff et al. [8] presented rule-based classifiers that look for a positive verb and a negative situation phrase in a sentence. Statistical feature based approaches were used for sarcasm detection. Farias et al. [9] uses features from a variety of emotional vocabulary, and they also use features such as semantic similarity, emoticons, and counterfactuals. Reyes et al. [10] uses features such as ambiguity, unexpectedness, emotional scenario, and uses unexpectedness to measure semantic relatedness. Reyes et al. [12] uses skip-gram and character n-gram features to detect sarcasm. Machine learning algorithms were also used for sarcasm detection. The majority of work in sarcasm detection earlier relied on Support Vector Machine (SVM) [13] and Logistic Regression (LR) [14]. In recent years, people have begun to use deep learning methods for sarcasm detection. Amir et al. [15] applied convolution operation on user embedding and the utterance embedding for sarcasm detection. User embedding allowed them to learn user specific context, and auxiliary features to train the convNet. Ghosh et al. [16] uses several types of LSTM networks to model the conversation context and responses. Xu et al. [3] proposed a network to extract the differences and the semantic associations between the modalities. The importance of combining contextual information for sarcasm detection has also been realized.

For Chinese sarcasm detection, related research is still limited [17]. Liu et al. [18] constructed three unbalanced datasets based on sarcastic data from Sina Weibo, Tencent Weibo and Netease Forum, respectively. They also proposed a multi-strategy integrated learning method to solve the data imbalance problem in sarcasm detection. Tang et al. [4] constructed a traditional Chinese corpus for irony detection. In their work, some common ironic patterns were also mined. These works mainly focused on extracting features of target texts, and the use of contextual information is still lacking in Chinese sarcasm detection.

3   Dataset

In this section, we construct a large-scale Chinese sarcasm dataset with contextual information from 108,641 comments, which includes 2,814 manual annotated sarcastic texts and 764,231 non-sarcastic texts.

3.1   Data Collection

Currently, most existing sarcasm annotation corpus is in English but few in Chinese, which is a significant barrier to undertake sracasm detection research on Chinese scenario [25–27]. Previous Chinese sarcasm datasets were often constructed based on Sina Weibo [4,18,28]. However, datasets constructed based on Sina Weibo are often small in scale and only contain the target text. Moreover, the distribution of sarcastic data on Sina Weibo is relatively sparse and there is not enough contextual information. Bilibili is a video sharing website in China like YouTube but with enhanced social features [29]. Bilibili has 237 million monthly active users, which means it is one of the most popular platforms in

China. We found that there is a lot of sarcastic information in many specific topics of bilibili. Therefore, we chose to construct a data set from bilibili, and we collected a total of 108,641 target texts and related contextual information. The contextual information includes the title, introduction, reply, etc. We pre-process raw data similar to [30]. Specifically, we remove invalid strings such as web links, identifiers, and extra spaces in the text, and keep the exclamation mark. The raw data is divided into two parts: the target text and the contextual information. For the long text features in the contextual information, such as content introduction, we extract 10 words as keywords.

3.2 Manually Labeling

We have five annotators. All the annotators are postgraduate students, aged between 22 and 25, and all of them are Chinese native speakers. The annotation process follows the Irony Identification Procedure (IIP) [19]. Since the under-standing of sarcasm can be subjective, we defined three fine-grained classes for sarcastic ratings: 0 (sarcastic), 1 (not sarcastic), 2 (ambiguous). To ensure the annotation quality, we synthesize the opinions of five annotators for the ambiguous cases. Then we adopt the majority if more than 80% annotators vote for it, and drop the data otherwise.

4 Approach

Figure 1 shows our deep learning model based on retrospective method for sarcasm detection. Firstly, we use the Encoder to get the initial vector representation of Input, and then send Input representation to two parallel modules, i.e., Sketchy Reading module and Intensive Reading module. In the Sketchy Reading module, we use the attention mechanism and Multilayer Perceptron (MLP) to get the initial impression. In the Intensive Reading module, we use a hierarchical method to get the intensive impression. Finally, we concatenate the outputs of the two parts to get the final representation, and send it to the prediction layer to get the final result. In this section, we will introduce the various structures of our proposed model in detail.

4.1 Word Embedding

We take contextual information and target text as Input, $I = \{i_1, \ldots, i_m\}$ represents our input sequence, m is the number of input features. We use the Encoder to obtain the initial vector representation of Input. First, the Encoder divides each input feature i_j into a sequence of words $W_j = \{w_{j1}, \ldots, w_{jn}\}$, then it uses the dense Chinese word vector proposed by [7] to convert the word sequence $W_j = \{w_{j1}, \ldots, w_{jn}\}$ into a vector representation $V_j = \{v_{j1}, \ldots, v_{jn}\}$, and finally get the Input vector representation $V = \{V_1, \ldots, V_m\}$.

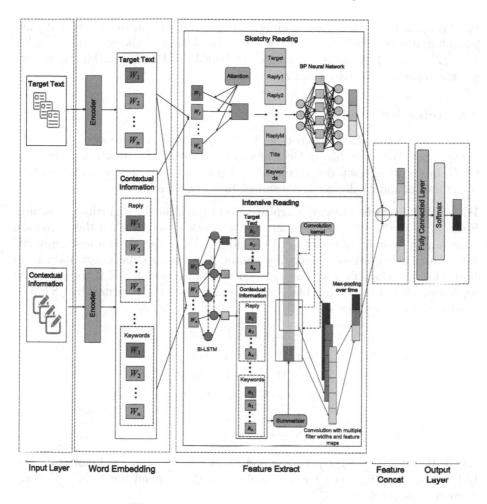

Fig. 1. Overview of our proposed model

4.2 Sketchy Reading

The purpose of the Sketchy Reading module is to get an initial impression of the Input. We use the attention mechanism to process the target text and contextual information. The vector representation V_j is passed through a two-layer neural network to obtain the attention weights α_i and construct the final feature vector representation R_j. The related equations are as follows:

$$\alpha_i = W_2 \cdot \tanh\left(W_1 \cdot v_{ji} + b_1\right) + b_2 \tag{1}$$

$$\alpha = \text{softmax}(\alpha) \tag{2}$$

$$R_j = \sum_{i=1}^{n} \alpha_i v_{ji} \tag{3}$$

272   L. Zhang et al.

Where v_{ji} is the ith word embedding of the jth Input feature; W_1 and W_2 are weight matrices; b_1 and b_2 are biases; n is the length of the sequence. Finally, $R = \{R_1, ..., R_m\}$ are passed through the Multilayer Perceptron(MLP), and we get the output of Sketchy Reading.

4.3 Intensive Reading

Unlike the Sketchy Reading module, in this part we pay more attention to the target text. We use a hierarchical method to process the Input, and then use CNN Layer to extract the relationship between the target text and context information, and finally get the result of Intensive Reading.

Bi-LSTM Encoder Layer. Each feature of the input is originally a sentence. Each word in the sentence is independent of other words, when the words are represented by making use of word embedding V. In this part, a new representation for each word is achieved by summarizing contextual information from both the directions in a sentence. We use a bidirectional LSTM to get a new representation of the Input. The equations of operations performed by LSTM at time step t are as follows:

$$i_t = \sigma\left(W_i \cdot x_t + U_i \cdot h_{t-1}\right) \tag{4}$$

$$f_t = \sigma\left(W_f \cdot x_t + U_f \cdot h_{t-1}\right) \tag{5}$$

$$o_t = \sigma\left(W_o \cdot x_t + U_o \cdot h_{t-1}\right) \tag{6}$$

$$\tilde{c}_t = \tanh\left(W_c \cdot x_t + U_c \cdot h_{t-1}\right) \tag{7}$$

$$c_t = f_t \odot c_{t-1} + i_t \odot \tilde{c}_t \tag{8}$$

$$h_t = o_t \odot \tanh\left(c_t\right) \tag{9}$$

where W_i, W_f, W_o, U_i, U_f, U_o are weight matrices; x_t, h_t are input state and hidden state at time step t respectively; σ is the sigmoid function; $\odot$ denotes element-wise product.

The bidirectional LSTM is a combination of forward LSTM $\vec{h}$, which reads the sentence from w_1 to w_n, and a backward LSTM $\overleftarrow{h}$, which reads the sentence from w_n to w_1:

$$\vec{h}_t = \overrightarrow{\mathrm{LSTM}}\left(w_t, \overrightarrow{h_{t-1}}\right) \tag{10}$$

$$\overleftarrow{h}_t = \overleftarrow{\mathrm{LSTM}}\left(w_t, \overleftarrow{h_{t+1}}\right) \tag{11}$$

After this operation, for each word, we have got the forward and backward hidden state. For example, for the word t, we get $h_t = \left[\vec{h}_t, \overleftarrow{h}_t\right]$. For the target text, we expect to get as much information as possible, so we save the hidden state of all words. Finally we get the representation of the target text $H_{target} = \{h_1, h_2, \ldots, h_n\}$, where $H_{target} \in \mathbb{R}^{n \times d_{lstm}}$.

Context Summarization Layer. The size of contextual information vector after the BiLSTM encoder layer may be too large to process. For example, we now have 10 replies, the number of BiLSTM units d_{lstm} is 300 and the maximum sentence length $d_{sentence}$ is 100, then the final representation will be of size $13 \times 100 \times 300$. In order to obtain a summarized context, we send the contextual information to Context Summarization Layer. In the Context Summarization Layer, we obtain the summarized context, i.e., $H_{context} = \{h_1, \ldots, h_{m-1}\}$, where $h_i = \{h_i^{\text{fl}}, h_i^{\text{bl}}\}$, h_i^{fl} is the last forward hidden state of the ith Input feature, h_i^{bl} is the last backward hidden state of the ith Input feature. In this way, we obtain the word embedding that summarizes the entire sentence information, and the final output dimension is $H_{context} \in \mathbb{R}^{(m-1) \times d_{lstm}}$.

CNN Layer. In [21], the author proposed a hybrid multi-channel CNN to capture the N-grams features in a text by varying the kernel size. We take $H_{context}$ and H_{target} as input $X \in \mathbb{R}^{(m-1+n) \times d_{lstm}}$, then use the 1D convolutional layer to capture the relationship between the contextual information and the target text.

$$c_i = f(\mathbf{w} \cdot \mathbf{x}_{i:i+h-1} + b) \tag{12}$$

Where $\mathbf{x}_{i:i+h-1}$ refers to the concatenation of $\mathbf{x}_i, \mathbf{x}_{i+1}, \ldots, \mathbf{x}_{i+h-1}$; filter is represented by $\mathbf{w} \in \mathbb{R}^{h \times d_{lstm}}$; h is the number of features of X used to generate new features; b is a bias term and f is a non-linear function. Filter is applied to the sequence X to produce a feature map $\mathbf{C} = \{c_1, c_2, \ldots, c_{m+n-h}\}$. In this section, we use filters with window sizes of 2, 3, and 4 to capture different N-gram features. Then the feature map $\mathbf{C}$ is sent to the MAXPOOL layer to get the most relevant feature $\hat{c}$ among the N-gram features. Finally, the most relevant features are concatenated together as the output of the Intensive Reading module.

4.4 Output Layer

We concatenate the outputs of the two parallel modules and send it to the Fully Connected Layer to get the final prediction.

$$\hat{y} = \text{softmax}(W_f \cdot O_{final} + b_f) \tag{13}$$

Where W_f is the weight matrix; b_f is the bias.

5 Experiments

In this section, we evaluate the performance of the proposed model for sarcasm detection. All experiments were undertook on a workstation with an Intel Core i9-10900 CPU and NVIDIA GeForce RTX 3070 GPU with 8 GB of RAM. We use Accuracy, Recall, Precision, and F-score to evaluate the performance of our detection method.

5.1 Performance Comparison with the Baseline Approaches

In this section, we constructed a balanced dataset, which includes 2,814 sarcastic data and 2,814 non-sarcastic data randomly selected. We divide the data into training set, development set and test set with a ratio of 80%:10%:10%. Meanwhile, we implemented the following baselines:

1. **Bi-LSTM.** Bi-LSTM is one of the most popular methods for solving text classification problems. It was used as a baseline model in sarcasm detection [3].
2. **Text CNN.** Text CNN is another great approach that has appreciable effects in detecting Chinese sarcastic texts [5].
3. **DPCNN.** It is difficult for Text CNN to obtain the long-distance relationship of the text through convolution, whereas DPCNN [22] can express the long-distance relationship in the text by increasing the network depth.
4. **ERNIE.** ERNIE [23] is a pre-training model proposed by Baidu. It implicitly learned the information about knowledge and longer semantic dependency. It has achieved good performance in many Chinese NLP fields.
5. **Hierarchical Attention Network.** HAN [24] uses the attention mechanism to classify documents. We form a document with contextual information and target text, and then use HAN for classification. HAN is an excellent baseline in sarcasm detection [31], which can utilize the contextual information.

Table 1 shows the performance of different deep learning models and R-net on the dataset. The Receiver Operating Characteristic(ROC) curve is shown in Fig. 2.

Table 1. The performance of different deep learning models and R-Net on the dataset.

Model	F-score	Precision	Recall	Accuracy
BiLSTM [20]	0.6141	0.6184	0.6175	0.6143
Text CNN [21]	0.5865	0.5966	0.5910	0.5938
DPCNN [22]	0.5840	0.5937	0.5907	0.5859
HAN [24]	0.6678	0.6797	0.6697	0.6743
ERNIE [23]	0.6411	0.6443	0.6415	0.6442
R-Net(our model)	**0.6942**	**0.6949**	**0.6940**	**0.6953**

From the Table 1, we can see that BiLSTM performs better than Text CNN and DPCNN, which indicates that BiLSTM have an advantage of extracting features, and that is why we use it in the Intensive Reading module. However, the methods that only focus on the target text (BiLSTM, Text CNN, DPCNN) do not perform well, and the HAN that uses the contextual information performs the best besides our method. The performance of our model is also better than the pre-trained model ERNIE. The ERNIE is likely to be affected by the pre-training data field, and cannot be perfectly applied to the field of Chinese sarcasm detection. In conclusion, our model achieved the best F-score and accuracy. In addition, the AUC score shown in Fig. 2 also proves that the performance of the method using contextual information is better than other methods that only focus on the target text, which shows that contextual information is very important for Chinese sarcasm detection.

5.2 Robustness Analysis with the Baseline Approaches

In the previous subsection, we used a balanced dataset to undertake model comparison experiment. However, in realistic scenarios, there may be only a small

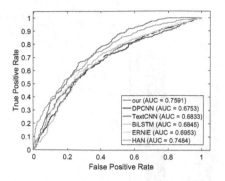

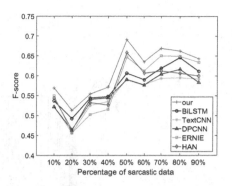

Fig. 2. The ROC curve.

Fig. 3. Comparison of the models trained on the datasets with different percentages of sarcastic texts. The total number of texts is 3,000.

proportion of sarcastic texts. To verify the robustness of the proposed model, we tested their performances on different proportions of sarcastic texts. We fixed the capacity of our dataset to 3,000 and varied the percentage of sarcastic texts from 10% to 90% at increments of 10%. As shown in Fig. 3, it can be seen that our method and HAN achieved the best performance when the sarcastic texts accounted for 50%. However, other models get the best performance when the percentage of sarcastic texts is relatively high. When the proportion of sarcastic texts exceeds 60%, our method is closer to the performance of ERNIE. Compared with other models, our model always has a better performance. Therefore, our method is more robust than other methods in realistic scenarios.

5.3 Component Analysis of Our Model

We further evaluate the influence of Sketchy Reading module, Intensive Reading module, as well as contextual information on the final performance. The subsets of the component set can be represented by the set difference function given as

$$F \backslash F' = \{x \mid x \in F \wedge x \notin F'\} \tag{14}$$

where F is the R-Net, F' is the component of R-Net. The components we used in component ablation test are as follows:

- F: All components of the proposed model will be used.
- $F \backslash SR$: Remove Sketchy Reading module from R-Net.
- $F \backslash IR$: Remove the Intensive Reading module from R-Net.
- $F \backslash CI$: Remove contextual information from R-Net.

The evaluation results are shown in Fig. 4. We can see that both the Sketchy Reading module and the Intensive Reading module improve the performance of the model. Moreover, the Intensive Reading module are more effective than the

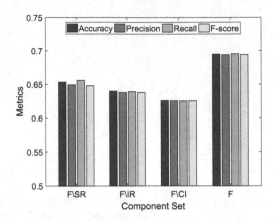

Fig. 4. The performance of different components in component ablation test.

Sketchy Reading module in the detection. This is because the intensive impression of sarcastic data is more important. In addition, when we remove the contextual information, the model performs the worst, which shows that contextual information is also very important in Chinese sarcasm detection.

6   Conclusion and Future Work

In this paper, we have contracted a Chinese sarcasm dataset with contextual information. Meanwhile, we propose a deep learning model based on retrospective method for sarcasm detection. The evaluation results demonstrate the effectiveness of our model and the usefulness of contextual information for Chinese sarcasm detection. In future work, we will incorporate auxiliary information (such as user information) in the dataset into the task of Chinese sarcasm detection, and we will also study how to use common sense knowledge in our method.

Acknowledgements. This work is supported by the National Natural Science Foundation of China (NSFC) under grant nos. 61802270, 61802271, 81602935, and 81773548. In addition, this work is also partially supported by Joint Research Fund of China Ministry of Education and China Mobile Company (No. CM20200409), the Key Research and Development Program of Science and Technology Department of Sichuan Province (No. 2020YFS0575), and the Sichuan University and Yibin Municipal People's Government University and City Strategic Cooperation Special Fund Project (Grant No. 2020CDYB-29).

References

1. Zhang, Z., Yang, J., Zhao, H.: Retrospective reader for machine reading comprehension. In: Proceedings of the 35th AAAI Conference on Artificial Intelligence, pp. 14506–14514 (2021)

2. Tay, Y., Luu, A.T., Hui, S.C., Su, J.: Reasoning with sarcasm by reading in-between. In: Proceedings of the 56th Annual Meeting of the Association for Computational Linguistics, pp. 1010–1020 (2018)
3. Xu, N., Zeng, Z., Mao, W.: Reasoning with multimodal sarcastic tweets via modeling cross-modality contrast and semantic association. In: Proceedings of the 58th Annual Meeting of the Association for Computational Linguistics, pp. 3777–3786 (2020)
4. Tang, Y.J., Chen, H.H.: Chinese irony corpus construction and ironic structure analysis. In: Proceedings of the 25th International Conference on Computational Linguistics, pp. 1269–1278 (2014)
5. Lin, S.K., Hsieh, S.K.: Sarcasm detection in Chinese using a crowdsourced corpus. In: Proceedings of the 28th Conference on Computational Linguistics and Speech Processing, pp. 299–310 (2016)
6. Hazarika, D., Poria, S., Gorantla, S., Cambria, E., Zimmermann, R., Mihalcea, R.: CASCADE: contextual sarcasm detection in online discussion forums. In: Proceedings of the 27th International Conference on Computational Linguistics, pp. 1837–1848 (2018)
7. Li, S., Zhao, Z., Hu, R., Li, W., Liu, T., Du, X.: Analogical reasoning on Chinese morphological and semantic relations. In: Proceedings of the 56th Annual Meeting of the Association for Computational Linguistics, pp. 138–143 (2018)
8. Riloff, E., Qadir, A., Surve, P., De Silva, L., Gilbert, N., Huang, R.: Sarcasm as contrast between a positive sentiment and negative situation. In: Proceedings of the 10th Conference on Empirical Methods in Natural Language Processing, pp. 704–714 (2013)
9. Farías, D.I.H., Patti, V., Rosso, P.: Irony detection in Twitter: the role of affective content. ACM Trans. Internet Technol. 16(3), 1–24 (2016)
10. Reyes, A., Rosso, P., Buscaldi, D.: From humor recognition to irony detection: the figurative language of social media. Data Knowl. Eng. 74, 1–12 (2012)
11. Bharti, S.K., Babu, K.S., Jena, S.K.: Parsing-based sarcasm sentiment recognition in Twitter data. In: Proceedings of the 7th IEEE/ACM International Conference on Advances in Social Networks Analysis and Mining, pp. 1373–1380 (2015)
12. Reyes, A., Rosso, P., Veale, T.: A multidimensional approach for detecting irony in twitter. In: Proceedings of the 8th International Conference on Language Resources and Evaluation, pp. 239–268 (2013)
13. Ghosh, A., et al.: SemEval-2015 task 11: sentiment analysis of figurative language in Twitter. In: Proceedings of the 9th International Workshop on Semantic Evaluation, pp. 470–478 (2015)
14. Bamman, D., Smith, N.A.: Contextualized sarcasm detection on Twitter. In: Proceedings of 9th International AAAI Conference on Web and Social Media, pp. 261–265 (2015)
15. Amir, S., Wallace, B.C., Lyu, H., Carvalho, P., Silva, M.J.: Modelling context with user embeddings for sarcasm detection in social media. In: Proceedings of the 20th SIGNLL Conference on Computational Natural Language Learning, pp. 167–177 (2016)
16. Ghosh, D., Fabbri, A.R., Muresan, S.: Sarcasm analysis using conversation context. In: Proceedings of the 26th International Conference on Computational Linguistics Computational Linguistics, pp. 755–792 (2018)
17. Van Hee, C., Lefever, E., Hoste, V.: SemEval-2018 task 3: Irony detection in English Tweets. In: Proceedings of the 12th International Workshop on Semantic Evaluation, pp. 39–50 (2018)

18. Liu, P., Chen, W., Ou, G., Wang, T., Yang, D., Lei, K.: Sarcasm detection in social media based on imbalanced classification. In: Proceedings of the 15th International Conference on Web-Age Information Management, pp. 459–471 (2014)

19. Li, A.R., Chersoni, E., Xiang, R., Huang, C.R., Lu, Q.: On the "easy" task of evaluating Chinese irony detection. In: Proceedings of the 33th Pacific Asia Conference on Language, Information and Computation, pp. 452–460 (2019)

20. Hochreiter, S., Schmidhuber, J.: Long short-term memory. Neural Comput. **9**(8), 1735–1780 (1997)

21. Kim, Y.: Convolutional neural networks for sentence classification. In: Proceedings of the 11th Conference on Empirical Methods in Natural Language Processing, pp. 1746–1751 (2014)

22. Johnson, R., Zhang, T.: Deep pyramid convolutional neural networks for text categorization. In: Proceedings of the 55th Annual Meeting of the Association for Computational Linguistics, pp. 562–570 (2017)

23. Zhang, Z., Han, X., Liu, Z., Jiang, X., Sun, M., Liu, Q.: ERNIE: enhanced language representation with informative entities. In: Proceedings of the 57th Annual Meeting of the Association for Computational Linguistics, pp. 1441–1451 (2019)

24. Yang, Z., Yang, D., Dyer, C., He, X., Smola, A., Hovy, E.: Hierarchical attention networks for document classification. In: Proceedings of the 14th Conference of The North American Chapter of The Association for Computational Linguistics: Human Language Technologies, pp. 1480–1489 (2016)

25. Joshi, A., Sharma, V., Bhattacharyya, P.: Harnessing context incongruity for sarcasm detection. In: Proceedings of the 53rd Annual Meeting of the Association for Computational Linguistics and the 7th International Joint Conference on Natural Language Processing, pp. 757–762 (2015)

26. Oraby, S., Harrison, V., Reed, L., Hernandez, E., Riloff, E., Walker, M.: Creating and characterizing a diverse corpus of sarcasm in dialogue. In: Proceedings of the 17th Annual Meeting of the Special Interest Group on Discourse and Dialogue, pp. 31–41 (2016)

27. Khodak, M., Saunshi, N., Vodrahalli, K.: A large self-annotated corpus for sarcasm. In: Proceedings of the 10th Language Resources and Evaluation Conference, pp. 641–646 (2018)

28. Xiang, R., et al.: Ciron: a new benchmark dataset for Chinese irony detection. In: Proceedings of the 12th Language Resources and Evaluation Conference, pp. 5714–5720 (2020)

29. Yan, L., Cha, N., Cho, H., Hwang, J.: Video diffusion in user-generated content website: an empirical analysis of Bilibili. In: Proceedings of the 21st International Conference on Advanced Communication Technology, pp. 81–84 (2019)

30. Gong, X., Zhao, Q., Zhang, J., Mao, R., Xu, R.: The design and construction of a Chinese sarcasm dataset. In: Proceedings of the 12th Language Resources and Evaluation Conference, pp. 5034–5039 (2020)

31. Srivastava, H., Varshney, V., Kumari, S., Srivastava, S.: A novel hierarchical BERT architecture for sarcasm detection. In: Proceedings of the 2nd Workshop on Figurative Language Processing, pp. 93–97 (2020)

Effects and Combination of Tailored Browser-Based and Mobile Cognitive Software Training

Mareike Gabele[1,3]([✉]), Andrea Thoms[2], Simon Schröer[1], Steffi Hußlein[3], and Christian Hansen[1]

[1] Faculty of Computer Science, University of Magdeburg, Magdeburg, Germany
{mareike,hansen}@isg.cs.uni-magdeburg.de
[2] HASOMED GmbH, Paul-Ecke-Straße 1, 39114 Magdeburg, Germany
[3] Institute Industrial Design, Magdeburg-Stendal University of Applied Sciences, Magdeburg, Germany

Abstract. Software-based training supports maintenance or recovery of cognitive abilities. However, regular use needs a high self-motivation. For this, the individual needs of users should be taken into account during the development process. Thus, in this work, two possibilities for tailoring in combination of application, and media devices in practice are investigated in an explorative between-subject design and hypothesis-generating study (N = 68). First, the effect of a browser-based training without gamification or with assignment of gamification appropriate to mean user characteristic on training duration is investigated. Second, the effect of this training and a subsequent serious game app on perception and possible combinations of different media is investigated. The results of behavior lead to the hypothesis that with tailored gamification in browsers, users may train longer in the middle range of training duration. The results of perception show a significant difference and higher perceived value/usefulness and overall rating, as well as the assumption of a higher effect in computer and mobile training in the group with tailored gamification. This could therefore provide a basis for combinations. A combination of both usage scenarios is perceived by users as most reasonable for a positive training effect. Nevertheless, there is a high variance for self-assessed usage. Thus, the results support developing multiple combinable scenarios, tailored to the user, in media devices and game integration to address intended effects, development and user needs to support the effect of cognitive software training in practice.

Keywords: Motivation · Combining multimedia · Cognitive training

1 Introduction and Related Work

Software-based cognitive training can help individuals to regain important cognitive skills, but the number of training sessions is a relevant factor [29]. However, in e-health, early dropping-out is a typical problem [7] and high self-motivation

© Springer Nature Switzerland AG 2022
B. Þór Jónsson et al. (Eds.): MMM 2022, LNCS 13142, pp. 279–291, 2022.
https://doi.org/10.1007/978-3-030-98355-0_24

is important to carry out training as required. This can be addressed via games or game-based extensions [13], which can be used and combined on different multimedia devices and ways of designing applications.

1.1 Tailored Gamification in Practical Implementation

Gamification refers to combining non game-content with game elements [4] and creating a valuable experience [12]. Its integration is challenging [19], but shows the potential to support motivation and behavior [1,8]. Relevant to the combination of therapy and gaming is that they are intertwined [30], and gamification elements should be tailored to the user [8]. Therefore it is important to know the user group, their characteristics and needs [19]. Based on characteristics and suitable for gamification the 'Player and User Types Hexad' [18,26] divides users into six types (motivations): Philanthropist (purpose/altruism), Free Spirit (autonomy), Achiever (mastery/competence), Socialiser (social relatedness), Player (rewards), and Disruptor (change). They can be used to integrate game elements, achieve a better understanding of target groups, or to make individual adjustments [26] to create positive and avoid negative effects [20]. For this, there are several methods for implementation: firstly, offer elements suitable to all users. Secondly, offer the most suitable element for each type. Thirdly, offer elements suitable for a combination/group of types. A challenge when assigning users to gamification elements is that they are often a mix of different characteristics [25]. Additionally, in practice, there is usually a short time frame and limited financial options for the development of gamified systems [19]. To achieve a positive effect of gamification using few resources for development and include all characteristics, we targeted the third option and have applied a possible grouping by summarizing groups of character traits in the mean. This leads to the following research question (RQ1): **What is the effect of grouping characteristics in the mean and assigning them to a rather appropriate gamification scenario in browser-based cognitive training on behavior in training duration?** For this we implemented three application scenarios (one without and two with grouped tailored gamification) and considered training behavior in the self-selected training duration as an indicator of motivation.

1.2 Training in Different Application and Multimedia Devices

In addition to behavior, tailoring may be reflected also in the perception of users. Furthermore, not only tailoring in a single application, but also in combinations of different multimedia devices, such as computers and mobiles is relevant. In everyday life, often multiple devices are used, whereby their tasks and the combination of the personal systems vary [14]. With the high usage [14] and increasing availability of mobile devices, apps also offer potential for use in the health sector [16]. Existing training systems offer flexible use as a download for computer, browser-based or app for mobile devices [10]. Mobile devices offer easy accessibility and partly positive results, partly just marginal or no differences to computer-based versions [13]. Despite an increased difficulty in mobile training games by changing the surrounding, they may support the practical training needed and the learning effect [5]. For users, apps do not replace playing on the computer [6], as they serve different requirements. A typical reason for playing games on mobile devices is to bridge time in waiting situations [6]. To support motivation, there is a wide variance of integrated gaming components from basic training tasks to serious brain training game apps. Serious game app concepts are also partly inspired by basic cognitive training approaches, as in a previous work by Endler et al. [5]. In contrast to gamification, 'serious games' not only use elements, but pursue a game with a serious goal beyond mere entertainment [24]. Depending on the way of combining both training applications and multimedia devices, there could be different effects. To address this, we have considered a possible usage scenario by a serious game app video prototype in addition to the browser-based training versions. It is based on the first implementation approach, using an element that is rather suitable for all users. Thus, we considered the following research question (RQ 2): **How are the application and combinations of a previous browser-based training A) without and B) with gamification, with a subsequent serious mobile game app, perceived?** For this we consider the perception and comparison of both applications and combinations by participants.

1.3   Overview

The main contributions of the work are the consideration of 1) the effect in training behavior by user grouping and assignment to (gamified) cognitive training and 2) the perception and potential in ways of combining different applications and media devices. To address this, we have considered two possible ways of combining different training scenarios in practice: a browser-based training without (one version) or with (two versions for tailored use) gamification and a subsequently mobile serious game video prototype addressed to all users were designed and evaluated as possible combinations. The goal of this work is to explore basics for developing and connecting cognitive training in different multimedia in practice. The results contribute to its development to support user motivation.

2   Concept and Implementation of the Prototypes

A mental calculation training was chosen as an application example close to everyday life. Based on a pilot study (N = 13, 10 calculation tasks) we identified a suitable difficulty level. In mean (standard deviation), individual calculation skills (5-point Likert scale: 1:poor, 5:good) were rated at 3.15 (0.95). 4.08 min (2.09) were needed, and 1.38 (1.39) errors were made. Using the NASA TLX (21-point Likert scale, 0:low, 20:high) most results were in the medium to rather low range: Mental Demand (8.62 (4.76)), Effort (8.54 (4.41)), Performance (7.77 (6.12)), Temporal Demand (7.15 (3.86)), and Frustration (5.62 (4.29)). Physical Demand was rated lower (1.62 (1.86)).

Regarding browser-based training, one basic version, inspired by an existing medical training [22], and two extensions for gamified versions were designed. The Unity based prototypically implementations were integrated for usage independently at home in an existing online training environment for cognitive rehabilitation [21]. After tasks for familiarization, the basic training (Fig. 1A) contains blocks of 10 tasks each according to the pre-study: exercises range between 1 and 1000, up to three decimal places. Then a hint appears to start the next block. The two additional gamified versions and elements were chosen based on the results of Tondello et al. [26] in a way that each type can be assigned to an element that is rather appropriate: for the category 'Immersion' (suitable for: Philanthropist, Free Spirit, Achiever, Disruptor) a story based on the popular leisure activities gardening, going shopping or out for a meal was added (Fig. 1B). It is wrapped around the basic training task blocks. For 9 or 10 correct answers, users receive a compliment and a story related picture, for less, a supportive remark. For 'Socialization' (suitable for: Socialiser, Player) a cooperative setting was integrated (Fig. 1C), which has shown a higher effect than competition in physical activity [3]. The player is assigned a computer generated teammate, who simulates a real player, but behaves the same way for each participant. Both calculate simultaneously individually received tasks. For 9 or 10 correct answers, both receive a green star, for less, a supportive remark.

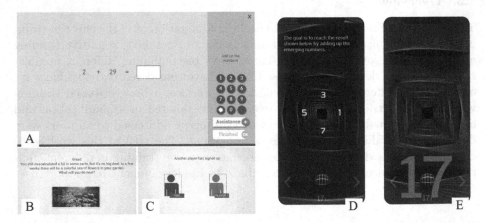

Fig. 1. Browser-based cognitive training software: A) Basic training and extension (zoomed in) by B) a Story and C) Cooperation; Serious game app: D) Selection of numbers, E) Successfully achieved result

Regarding the combination, a serious game app video prototype was designed (Fig. 1D, E). Based on the suitability for all users, its concept is based on 'Progress' as this is high requested in the cognitive training of patients [8]. Due to potential distractions in the environment, the difficulty may be lower than that of computer training. The game is intended to compete with other games on the mobile phone in terms of entertainment value [6]. Short exercises allow users to start and stop the app flexible. The goal is to calculate a target number (17 in this example) by collecting and adding numbers. To collect, a ball moves through a tunnel, which can be rotated by arrows. The numbers are created in a way that the target number can be reached.

3 Evaluation

3.1 Method

An explorative between-subject design study with two groups was conducted: without (Group A) and with tailored gamification elements (Group B) in browser-based training followed by a serious game app video prototype. The study was conducted in three steps (Table 1) and blinded for participants. They were given the opportunity to receive personal partial results and/or to take part in a draw for a gift. Participants over 18 years who showed interest in improving their mental calculation skills were recruited. Sufficient language skills, basics in addition, access to computer, internet, and e-mail were required.

Table 1. Procedure of the explorative study

Step 1		Step 2 (browser-based)		Step 3 (mobile app)	
Pre-survey and assignment	**Group A**	Calculation without gamification	Post survey A	Serious game	Post survey
(Between groups and in group B gamification)	**Group B**	Calculation with gamification (immersion or cooperation)	Post survey B	App video prototype	

In step 1, after informed consent, a pre-survey was conducted to collect demographic data, self-assessment, and player type (based on User Types Hexad [27]). To avoid bias, group A and B were balanced according to enjoyment and self-assessed abilities in calculation (7-point Likert Scale (1: Absolutely no/very bad, 7: Absolutely yes/very good)), age, and gender. For a possible way of assigning gamification (B), the mean values between the results for the types that are suitable for the two gamification versions as described above were used.

In step 2, participants received information and login data via email. The training had to be conducted once with a free choice of time, place and duration. To avoid overload, maximum duration was set to 90 min (including gamification) similar to a lecture. For the analysis of training duration (excluding gamification), the time considered was reduced: 1. Since different amounts of time for familiarization was needed, the longest required time (10.42 min) was considered as the starting point for all. Lower total times were set to 0. 2. Since gamification also requires additional time, in Group B of those who reached the total time (90 min) the minimum calculation time (without gamification) was considered (68.5 min). If the training was started more than once, only the first start up to stop via 'esc' was included. An unpaired t-test was used for significance in training duration between group A and B (two-tailed, threshold for significance: 0.05). In the post-survey, questions about the perception were asked: Personal Gratification based on questions of GUESS, Value/Usefulness, Enjoyment, Competence on parts of questions of IMI, workload on NASA TLX, possible (A) and used (B) gamification, presentation, effect, requests and reasons for stopping.

In step 3, the participants received the link to the serious game video prototype and post-survey via email. Questions were asked about the perception, effect, possible use, relevance of different aspects, and comparison between web-based training, app and combination. A Mann-Whitney U-test was used for significance in difference of perception between Group A and B and browser and app based prototype (two-tailed, threshold for significance: 0.05).

Exclusions in the analysis are based on technical, procedural or organizational problems, misunderstanding tasks or missing steps. For quantitative analysis of training times (RQ1), participants are included who completed the browser-based training. For perception (RQ2), to draw conclusions between the prototypes, participants who answered all questionnaires and did not independently conduct types of training that were not part of the study were included.

3.2   Results

In the following, the summarized results considered regarding RQ 1 and 2 in the explorative study are presented. The number of missing data is indicated by the number of asterisks in the corresponding parts. Significant p-values are printed in bold. 68 participants started, 49 were included in different parts of the analysis, without significant difference regarding assignment factors between Group A and B in both RQs. 17 were dropped out before, 2 during browser based training, and 10 at different points later. Reasons included technical, organizational and language problems, and dropping out without feedback.

Regarding the behavior (RQ 1), 42 participants were included in the analysis regarding training duration. 20 participants in group A (mean age: 44.05 years, age range: 20–83 years, female: 10, male: 10, enjoyment (4.40) and individual abilities (4.05) in calculation) and 22 participants in group B (mean age: 44.64 years, age range: 22–73 years, female: 10, male: 12, enjoyment (5.09) and individual abilities (4.68) in calculation). Deducting the reduced times the training duration results in a median of 7.49 min in group A and 28.30 min in group B (no significant difference (t = −1.1443, p = 0.2593)). The individual values are shown in Fig. 2.

Regarding the perception and comparison (RQ 2) of browser-based training and the serious game app, 34 participants are included. 15 participants were in group A (mean age: 39.33 years, age range: 20–70 years, female: 7, male: 8, enjoyment (4.53) and individual abilities (4.33) in calculation) and 19 in group B (mean age: 44.95, age range: 24–73 years, female: 9, male: 10, enjoyment (5.26) and individual abilities (4.74) in calculation). Results are presented in

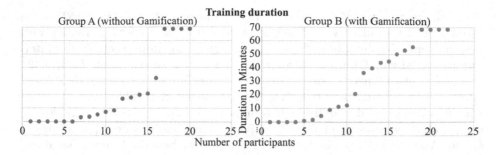

Fig. 2. Training duration of participants without and with gamified training (pure time of calculation, reduced and sorted by duration)

mean (SD). In the post-survey of step 2, a significant difference has emerged for (Group A, Group B, p-value): Value/Usefulness (5.13, 5.88, **0.02642**) and overall rating on a 7-point Likert scale (1: very poor - 7: very good) (4.73, 5.42, **0.0466**). No significant difference has emerged for: Personal Gratification (5.57, 5.87, 0.34212), Enjoyment (4.60, 5.28, 0.05), Competence (5.20, 5.37, 0.28014) and the scales of NASA TLX. In detail, in the ratings of the individual aspects of training and gamification and the request for integration, a wide variety was observed. Reasons why the training was stopped were, among others, in group A: lost interest, repetitive, same types of tasks, no progress/goal indicated; concentration waned; trained enough/end of training reached; and in Group B: no progress/goal indicated, concentration waned; same types of tasks, trained enough/end of training reached.

Table 2. Presumed effect and individual training behavior in browser-based training and serious game app (7-point Likert Scale (1: Absolutely not true, 7: Absolutely true))

Effect and usage	Browser-based Train.			Serious game app		
	A	B	p val	A	B	p val
With regular use, the training has a positive effect on my calculation skills.	5.14* (0.83)	6.21 (0.77)	**0.00318**	4.79* (1.21)	5.47 (1.19)	0.08726
I should do training like this, adapted to my abilities, more often	5.07 (1.18)	5.47 (1.39)	0.34212	4.36* (1.34)	4.89 (1.48)	0.29834
I would like to do training like this, adapted to my abilities, more often.	4.40 (1.14)	4.58 (1.57)	0.75656	4.21* (1.86)	4.44* (1.67)	0.78716
I will do training like this, adapted to my abilities, more often.	3.40 (1.25)	4.28* (1.66)	0.15854	3.31** (1.54)	4.05 (1.70)	0.25848

The number of asterisks represents the number of missing data

In the post-survey of step 3, the serious game app (4.73, 5.33*, 0.15272) was rated overall also rather well. The relevance of different aspects in training were assessed on a 7-point Likert Scale (1: absolutely not important, 7: absolutely important) (Item (Group A, Group B)): train at a time I want (5.93, 6.42), train at a place where I want (5.6, 5.95), have fun with training (5.8, 6.26), effectiveness of the training (5.86*, 6.05). Assessment of possible effect and usage within browser-based training and serious game app are shown in Table 2. A comparative assessment of the effect for different multimedia applications in Group A and B is shown in Table 3. Figure 3 shows how the browser-based and app-based training was perceived in comparison. Figure 4 shows which way of combination is perceived as most effective and most likely to be used.

Table 3. Presumed effect for training in different ways and multimedia (7-point Likert Scale (1: Absolutely do not agree, 7: Absolutely agree))

Presumed effect	Group A	Group B	p value
Training on the computer results in a high training effect	5.00 (1.10)	5.89* (0.81)	**0.0226**
Training on the mobile phone results in a high training effect	4.71* (1.03)	5.72* (0.93)	**0.03**
A game on the computer results in a high training effect	5.33 (0.70)	5.47** (1.19)	0.40654
A game on the mobile phone results in a high training effect	4.92** (1.07)	5.47** (1.14)	0.22628
I would like to use the training from the computer as it is as an app for mobile phone/tablet (instead of the app as in the video).	4.47 (1.86)	4.65** (1.57)	0.89656

The number of asterisks represents the number of missing data

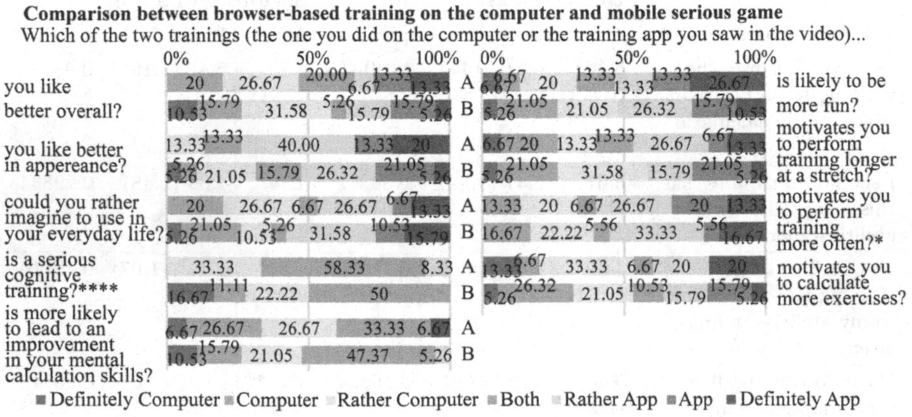

Fig. 3. Comparison between browser-based (gamified) training and serious game app

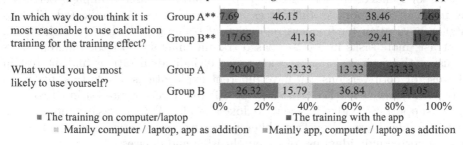

Fig. 4. User report on most reasonable and preferred method

4   Discussion

4.1   RQ 1: Behavior in Tailored Browser-Based Training

Although there are significant differences in behavior in other domains [1], in line with other work [8], there was no significant difference between training duration with and without gamification in browser-based cognitive training. However, the median with use of gamification is noticeably higher. Without, in line with Knop [15], the large proportion of participants showed rather low usage, also some high performers and few users in the middle range of training duration. In the middle range participants with gamification achieve partly higher training durations. However, the hypothesis that tailored gamification in cognitive training may support increasing the training duration in the middle range should be evaluated in further studies, which include a classification of the basic behavior. Also, it should be considered why this occurs only in some participants. For development of tailored gamified applications in practice a compromise is integrated between a few elements to be used, considering the mix of user characteristics and assignment of users to the solution that may be most appropriate for them.

4.2   RQ 2: Perception and Combination

The higher perception of value/usefulness of gamified browser-based training in group B shows an effect on emotions. However, the users missed a presentation of a goal or progress, what is highly requested in cognitive training [8]. Feedback on progress is relevant for users in training [11] and to repeat the behavior [23]. Its integration may further support emotions, for example in enjoyment, where the results are on the verge of significance. Especially with increasing age, the focus shifts from competence to enjoyment [2]. The significantly higher assumed effect in gamified training and training on computers and mobiles in Group B is particularly relevant. The belief in the effectiveness of cognitive training is a relevant predictive factor for the willingness of users to carry out training [9]. This indicates that the integration of gamification can be a supporting factor in training behavior in different media devices. Although this difference is not shown for games or the serious game app and browser-based training is perceived as more skill-supportive, differences in the way of use are indicated. Slightly higher motivation for frequent repetition of training with the app and, and in contrast, more tasks in browser-based training may support the different ways of using the devices [14]. The wide range of individual ratings and interest in the use of both versions can have different explanations beside this: firstly, in line with Lessel et al. [17], there may be different levels of interest in integrating game support. Secondly, in line with Jokela et al. [14] device usage and needs in everyday life differs. Altogether, differences can be seen between assumed effects and preferred individual use of the application and devices.

4.3   General Discussion and Limitations

In the combination of applications and media devices, the suitability for the users, the training goals as well as the feasibility in development should be considered. The results indicate that tailoring gamification and grouping in mean characteristics could increase motivation and may partly influence training behavior, while integrating different user characteristics and lower complexity of development. This supports the suitability of this approach for practical development. The results, the level of potential effects on behavior and motivation and influence in training effect should be evaluated in further studies and directly compared with other ways of assigning gamification. To address the different needs shown in comparisons, based on adaptive game elements [28] and combining media devices, different usage possibilities can be developed. Thus, training can be individualized and adjusted to required training factors corresponding to the abilities, such as planned duration of use, distraction stimuli, etc. In this way, the relevance to consider users' needs [19] and learning therapy aspects can be included. However, it is relevant that all systems simply work with each other [14]. Altogether, the results indicate for practice, it seems useful to tailor the way of design applications and the combination of different multimedia products.

Some limitations should be considered. The browser-based prototype was used once and the serious game app watched as a video prototype. The presumed use is based on participants' assumptions. Using both (longer), a different implementation or gamification, or another study design can influence the results. The sample size of participants is rather small. A transfer of the results to other countries or cultural groups cannot be guaranteed. Although the non-gamified browser-based training is inspired by an existing clinical training [21], there is no direct comparison of the prototypes to state-of-the-art training. This should be considered further for comparison of behavior. Also, we considered only two combinations. In practice possibilities go beyond and should be analyzed further.

5   Conclusion

In this work, we considered 1) the effect of grouped mean characteristics and assignment to an appropriate gamification scenario in comparison between a stationary browser-based training with or without tailored gamification on behavior and 2) its effect on perception and the combination of different media devices by a subsequent serious game app for cognitive training. In the behavior in browser-based training, indicators were found for the hypothesis that users with gamification show a higher training duration in middle range than without. Regarding perception, after a higher perceived overall rating and value/usefulness with the use of gamification, a higher presumed effect in browser-based training, computer and mobile training is shown. This may support the conduction of training. Although the combined use of browser-based training and serious game app is assumed in both groups to have the highest effect, there is a wide variation in the demand for individual use. Based on the results, grouping characteristics in mean could be suitable for use in practice. For combinations, we recommend integrating a gamified training version, but also offering multiple combinable options in gamification or game integration and multimedia device combinations, adapted to the everyday life, intended usage behavior and users' needs. Thus, positive effects in combinations can be addressed, also for users for whom only one system is suitable. The overall results support the tailoring of game integration and multimedia devices to support behavior, perception and motivation in cognitive software training in practice.

Acknowledgments. This work was funded by the European Regional Development Fund, operation number ZS/2016/04/78123 and ZS/2017/01/83843 as part of the initiative 'Sachsen-Anhalt WISSENSCHAFT Schwerpunkte' and the European Social Fund (ESF) of Saxony-Anhalt, operation number CCI 2014DE05SFOP013 as part of the initiative 'Sachsen-Anhalt WISSENSCHAFT Chancengleichheit' with the program title 'FEMPower'. Thanks to Tom Heidel and Annika Endler for their contribution to the creation of the video prototype.

References

1. Altmeyer, M., Schubhan, M., Krüger, A., Lessel, P.: A long-term investigation on the effects of (personalized) gamification on course participation in a gym. In: Proceedings of the 5th International GamiFIN Conference, Levi (2021)
2. Birk, M.V., Friehs, M.A., Mandryk, R.L.: Age-based preferences and player experience: a crowdsourced cross-sectional study. In: Proceedings of the Annual Symposium on Computer-Human Interaction in Play (CHI Play), pp. 157–170 (2017)
3. Chen, Y., Pu, P.: HealthyTogether: exploring social incentives for mobile fitness applications. In: Proceedings of the Second International Symposium of Chinese CHI, pp. 25–34, Toronto (2014)
4. Deterding, S., Khaled, R., Nacke, L.E., Dixon, D.: Gamification: toward a definition. In: CHI 2011 Gamification Workshop Proceedings, pp. 12–15 (2011)
5. Endler, A., Gabele, M., Heidel, T., Husslein, S., Hansen, C.: To go: gameful extension for cognitive rehabilitation software. In: Proceedings of IEEE EMB ISC, p. 43, Magdeburg (2019)
6. Engl, S.: Mobile gaming - Eine empirische Studie zum Spielverhalten und Nutzungserlebnis in mobilen Kontexten. Magister thesis (2010)
7. Eysenbach, G.: The law of attrition. J. Med. Internet Res. **7**(1), e11 (2005)

8. Gabele, M., Weicker, J., Wagner, S., Thoms, A., Husslein, S., Hansen, C.: Effects and Ways of Tailored Gamification in Software-Based Training in Cognitive Rehabilitation. In: Proceedings of the 29th ACM Conference on User Modeling, Adaptation and Personalization (UMAP), pp. 158–168 (2021)
9. Harrell, E.R., Kmetz, B., Boot, W.R.: Is cognitive training worth it? Exploring individuals' willingness to engage in cognitive training. J. Cogn. Enhancement **3**(4), 405–415 (2019)
10. HeadApp. https://www.headapp.com/en/computer-based-cognitive-rehabilitation -therapy/. Accessed 24 Aug 2021
11. Hung, Y.X., Huang, P.C., Chen, K.T., Chu, W.C.: What do stroke patients look for in game-based rehabilitation: a survey study. Medicine **95**(11), e3032 (2016)
12. Huotari, K., Hamari, J.: A definition for gamification: anchoring gamification in the service marketing literature. Electron. Mark. **27**(1), 21–31 (2016). https://doi.org/10.1007/s12525-015-0212-z
13. Johnson, D., Deterding, S., Kuhn, K.A., Staneva, A., Stoyanov, S., Hides, L.: Gamification for health and wellbeing: a systematic review of the literature. Internet Interv. **6**, 89–106 (2016)
14. Jokela, T., Ojala, J., Olsson, T.: A diary study on combining multiple information devices in everyday activities and tasks. In: Proceedings of the 33rd annual ACM Conference on Human Factors in Computing Systems, pp. 3903–3912, Seoul (2015)
15. Knop, A.: Hometraining kognitiver Störungen mit Rehacom - Anwendungsbeobachtung, Presentation at GNP Tagung. (2014). https://hasomed.de/wp-content/uploads/2019/12/RehaCom-Hometraining-Anwendungsbeobachtung 2014.pdf/. Accessed 25 Aug 2021
16. Kumar, S., et al.: Mobile health technology evaluation: the mHealth evidence workshop. Am. J. Prev. Med. **45**(2), 228–236 (2013)
17. Lessel, P., Altmeyer, M., Schmeer, L.V., Krüger, A.: "Enable or Disable Gamification?" Analyzing the impact of choice in a gamified image tagging task. In: Proceedings of the 2019 Conference on Human Factors in Computing Systems (CHI), pp. 1–12, Glasgow (2019)
18. Marczewski, A.: Even Ninja Monkeys Like to Play. Blurb Inc. (2015)
19. Morschheuser, B., Hassan, L., Werder, K., Hamari, J.: How to design gamification? A method for engineering gamified software. Inf. Softw. Technol. **95**, 219–237 (2018)
20. Orji, R., Mandryk, R.L., Vassileva, J., Gerling, K.M.: Tailoring persuasive health games to gamer type. In: Proceedings of the SIGCHI Conference on Human Factors in Computing Systems (CHI), pp. 2467–2476, Paris (2013)
21. RehaCom. https://hasomed.de/produkte/rehacom/. Accessed 24 Aug 2021
22. RehaCom. https://hasomed.de/calc/. Accessed 10 Nov 2021
23. Robson, K., Plangger, K., Kietzmann, J.H., McCarthy, I., Pitt, L.: Is it all a game? Understanding the principles of gamification. Bus. Horiz. **58**(4), 411–420 (2015)
24. Susi, T., Johannesson, M., Backlund, P.: Serious games: an overview. Elearning **73**(10) (2007)
25. Tondello, G.F., Arrambide, K., Ribeiro, G., Cen, A.J.L., Nacke, L.E.: "I don't fit into a single type": a trait model and scale of game playing preferences. In: IFIP Conference on Human-Computer Interaction, pp. 375–395, Paphos (2019)
26. Tondello, G.F., Mora, A., Nacke, L.E. : Elements of gameful design emerging from user preferences. In: Proceedings of the Annual Symposium on Computer-Human Interaction in Play (CHI Play), pp. 129–142, Amsterdam (2017)

27. Tondello, G.F., Wehbe, R.R., Diamond, L., Busch, M., Marczewski, A., Nacke, L.E.: The gamification user types hexad scale. In: Proceedings of the Annual Symposium on Computer-Human Interaction in Play, pp. 229–243, Austin (2016)
28. Volkmar, G., Pfau, J., Teise, R., Malaka, R.: Player types and achievements-using adaptive game design to foster intrinsic motivation. In: Extended Abstracts of the Annual Symposium on Computer-Human Interaction in Play Companion Extended Abstracts (CHI Play), pp. 747–754, Barcelona (2019)
29. Weicker, J., Villringer, A., Thöne-Otto, A.: Can impaired working memory functioning be improved by training? A meta-analysis with a special focus on brain injured patients. Neuropsychology **30**(2), 190 (2016)
30. Wiemeyer, J.: Serious Games in der Neurorehabilitation-Ziele, Anforderungen und Perspektiven. neuroreha **9**(01), 19–23 (2017)

Progressive GAN-Based Transfer Network for Low-Light Image Enhancement

Shuang Jin[1] ⓘ, Na Qi[1,2(✉)] ⓘ, Qing Zhu[1,2] ⓘ, and Haoran Ouyang[1]

[1] Faculty of Information Technology, Beijing University of Technology, Beijing, China
JinS@emails.bjut.edu.cn, {qina,ccgszq}@bjut.edu.cn
[2] Beijing Institute of Artificial Intelligence, Beijing, China

Abstract. Images captured in low-light conditions usually suffer from very low contrast and underexpose, which cannot be directly utilized in the subsequent computer vision tasks, such as object recognition, detection, identification and tracking. Existing methods include HE based method, Retinex theory based method and deep learning method which may generate undesirable enhanced results including amplified noise, biased colors and extreme boundary. To address this problem, we utilize prior knowledge of Retinex theory and GAN based on data statistic to propose a progressive GAN-based Transfer network to realize the low-light enhancement. In this paper, the image is decomposed by JieP method based on the Retinex model to obtain the reflection and light components, and learn the relationship between the reflection component of the low-light image and normal light image via a reflection decomposition on network (RefDecN), and then generate the reflection component of the low-light image. Then, another illumination transfering network (IllumTransN) is utilized to transfer the light of normal light image to the reflection component to realize low-light enhancement. Experimental results of low-light image enhancement on RAISE, LOL and MEF datasets demonstrate our ProGAN can outperform state-of-the-art methods in terms of objective and subjective quality.

Keywords: Low-light enhancement · Reflection component · Illumination component · Retinex model · Generative adversarial network

1 Introduction

Images captured in low-light conditions are degraded within low visibility, low contrast, and some noises, which will increase difficulty of computer vision tasks [23, 24]. Low-light image enhancement approaches aim to increase the brightness or amplify the illumination to achieve normal visibility and visual quality. They can be roughly classified in three categories, including Histogram equalization (HE) based methods, Retinex theory based methods and deep learning method.

Histogram equalization makes dark images visible by stretching dynamic range of image [25, 26] and enhancing the contrast [1, 2]. In order to consider the various intensity distribution of regions rather than only considering global histogram of the image, some

B. Þór Jónsson et al. (Eds.): MMM 2022, LNCS 13142, pp. 292–304, 2022.
https://doi.org/10.1007/978-3-030-98355-0_25

variants of HE are proposed to mitigate the problem. AHE [1] adjusts image contrast and brightness of image by calculating local histogram and contrast limited adaptive histogram equalization (CLAHE) [2] is utilized in each divided block with contrast limiting. In [27], Wu et al. propose a method which can adaptively control contrast gain by finding best exposure ratio and visual importance. An exposure fusion framework using weight matrix of image fusion and camera response model is proposed to address the well-exposed problem in [32]. However, the results may result in over-enhancement and influenced by intensive noise [20].

Retinex theory assumes that images can be divided into reflection components and illumination components. Single-scale Retinex (SSR) [3] implements Gaussian filter on the surrounding of the Retinex center and Mutli-scale Retinex (MSR) [4] combines several SSR outputs to achieve the balance between color/lightness rendition and dynamic range compression. Besides, the Multi-scale retinex with color restoration (MSRCR) combines the dynamic range compression of small-scale retinex and the tonal rendition of large scale retinex with a universally applied color restoration [5]. Retinex based methods get achievements with some effective priors [6, 7, 21]. LIME [6] estimates illumination of each pixel individually by finding the maximal value in R, G, and B channels and adds structural priors to acquire enhanced image. JED [7] presents a joint low-light enhancement and denoising method based on noise-suppressed sequential decomposition to obtain the well-enhanced low-light images. The latest method LR3M first injects low-rank prior into a Retinex decomposition process to suppress noise in the reflectance map to achieve pleasant visual quality of the enhanced image [21]. Although Retinex theory based methods can get better results than HE based methods, it is still difficult to handle the low-light image enhancement with serious and amplified noise and extremely low light.

In the recent years, deep learning methods have become a mainstream due to its distinguished performance and flexibility. LLnet [8] is an earlier algorithm using deep learning network, which proves that the variant of stacked-sparse denoising autoencoder can achieve low light image enhancement and denoising. HDR-Net [9] proposes a neural network architecture with bilateral grid processing and local affine color transformation to learn parameters of the bilateral filters using pairs of input/output images. MBLLEN [10] utilizes multi-branch CNNs to produce enhanced images. EEMEFN [22] proposes an edge-enhanced multi-exposure fusion network to generate high quality enhance images with rich texture and clear edge. Retinex is also used in deep learning methods. MSR-net [11] first combines CNNs and Retinex to enhance images. The image decomposition and illumination mapping are integrated to propose a data-driven Retinex decomposition method named RetinexNet [12] to enhance low-light images with noise reduction in the reflection component. Three subnetworks for layer decomposition, illumination adjustment and reflection restoration are established in the KinD [13]. In addition, EnlightenGAN [14] achieves great success via using unpaired training set with a local-global discriminator. However, the detail and contrast distribution are not well handled.

In order to utilize the priors and data statistics, we propose a progressive GAN-based low-light enhancement method with Retinex theory and data-driven style transfer network. We utilize JieP model to decompose image to reflection and illumination components. Then, we use style transfer network to establish the mapping between reflection component of low-light image and normal light image. The content loss, color loss, light loss and adversarial loss are used to train the parameter of network to acquire the reflection image with complete content and the enhanced image with uniform lighting. Experimental results demonstrate that our proposed ProGAN can generate the images with more clearly texture details and closer illumination to normal-light images than those of state-of-the-arts methods.

2 Methodology

2.1 The ProGAN Framework

Fig. 1. Our proposed low-light image enhancement framework. '*LL*' represents low-light images, '*G(LL)*' represents the reflection component generated by the generator G, and '*F(G(LL))*' represents the enhanced image generated by by the generator F.

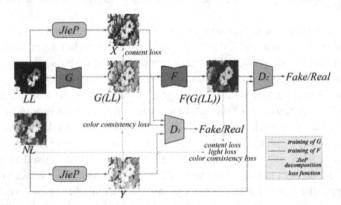

Fig. 2. Our proposed ProGAN low-light image enhancement framework. '*LL*' and '*NL*' represent low-light images and normal-light images, respectively. '*X*' and '*Y*' represent the reflection components of the low-light image and the normal-light image, respectively. '*G(LL)*' represents the reflection component generated by the generator G, and '*F(G(LL))*' represents enhanced images generated by the generator F.

As shown in Fig. 1, given training samples $S_{data}(l) = \{l_i | i = 1, \cdots, M\} \subset LL$, $S_{data}(h) = \{h_i | i = 1, \cdots, M\} \subset NL$, we aim to learn mapping functions between two domains LL and NL progressively, where LL and NL denote the sets of the low-light images and normal-light images, respectively. As shown in Fig. 2, our model includes two mappings: $G : LL \rightarrow X$ and $F : X \rightarrow NL$, where $S_{data}(x) = \{x_i|i = 1, \cdots , M\} \subset X$ are the reflection components of the training data LL. Then, given any low-light image l, we can obtain the enhanced image via $F(G(l))$. In addition, we introduce two adversarial discriminators D_1 and D_2, where D_1 aims to distinguish among images x, y and generated image $G(l)$, where y is the reflection component of the corresponding image h and $S_{data}(y) = \{y_i|i = 1, \cdots , M\} \subset Y$ are the reflection components of the training data NL; in the same way, D_2 aims to discriminate between the image h and the generated image $F(G(l))$. Thus, our objective function is formulated as:

$$(G^*, F^*) = arg \min_{G,F} \max_{D_1,D_2} L(G, F, D_1, D_2) \qquad (1)$$

Actually, the generator G is used to generate the reflection component of the given low-light image and the generator F is utilized to transfer the illumination from the normal image to the generated reflection component. The generators $\{G, F\}$ and the discriminators $\{D_1, D_2\}$ are iteratively trained via the GAN using the training datasets including the images comes from the real target manifold or the synthetic images. In order to obtain the generator $\{G, F\}$, we should efficiently estimate the reflection and illumination of the low-light and normal-light images. Thus, we integrate the joint intrinsic extrinsic prior (JieP) [18] into our ProGAN shown in Fig. 2 to learn the mapping function from the low-light image and normal-light image. Based on the JieP model, the illumination I and the reflection R of each low-light image or normal-light image S satisfy the following objective function,

$$E(I, R) = \|I \cdot R - S\|_2^2 + \alpha E_s(I) + \beta E_t(R) + \lambda E_l(I) \qquad (2)$$

where the first term is L_2 data fidelity term, the second term is structure prior with the local variation deviation to preserve the structure, the third term is texture prior to enforce the piece-wise continuous on reflection R, and the fourth term is illumination prior to constrain the color appearance change. α, β and λ are three parameters to balance these terms.

We decompose the low-light images $S_{data}(l) \subset LL$ and the normal-light images $S_{data}(h) \subset NL$ by the JieP model (2) to obtain the corresponding reflection components $S_{data}(x) \subset X$ and $S_{data}(y) \subset Y$, respectively. As shown in Fig. 3, the reflection component of low-light image is close to that of normal-light image. Thus, the difference between low-light image and normal-light image is on the illumination component. Moreover, we can observe that the detail of reflection of normal-light image is lost and there exists color loses and some noise. In order to train G via the GAN to generate appropriate reflection with structure, texture, content and color appearance of the object itself, we make use of reflection components of low-light image and normal-light image as different constraints on the loss function.

2.2 Reflection Component Decomposition and Illumination Transferring

The architecture of ProGAN is shown in Fig. 4. We use the same symmetrical encoder-decoder network in AnimeGAN [15] as the generator of our ProGAN, where the network includes standard Conv-Block, DSConv, the inverted residual block (IRB) and downsampling and upsampling modules. The IRBs are used to reduce the number of parameters. We take different discriminators in our ProGAN. In order to ensure the accuracy of illumination transferring, the layer of D_2 is deeper than that of D_1. All convolutional layers in the discriminators are the standard convolutions.

Fig. 3. Reflection comparison. From left to right: The low-light image, the normal-light image, the reflections of low-light and normal-light images, respectively.

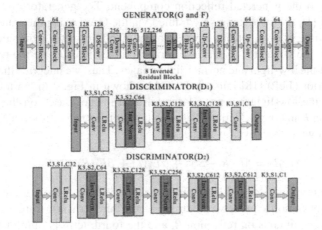

Fig. 4. The architecture of the generator and discriminator in our ProGAN. The numbers on the boxes in generator represent the number of channels and SUM means the element-wise sum. In the discriminator, 'K' is the kernel size, 'S' is the stride in each convolutional layer and 'C' is the number of feature maps. Inst_Norm indicates the instance normalization layer.

2.3 Loss Function

According to [16, 17], the appearance of object is influenced by internal and external properties. The intrinsic properties including shape and texture are independent of illumination. Our ProGAN include Reflection Decomposition network (RefDecN) and illumination transfer network (IllumTransN). The RefDecN is used to decompose low-light image to generate reflection component with the content and texture of low-light image and the color of normal-light images via GAN and JieP. The IllumTransN essentially uses GAN to preserve the structure of low-light image and reconstruct the illumination of normal-light image. $L_R(G, D_1)$ and $L_I(F, D_2)$ respectively represent the loss function of RefDecN and IllumTransN. Thus, the objective function in Sect. 2.1 is formulated as minimizing the following objection function:

$$\min_{G,F} \max_{D_1,D_2} L(G, F, D_1, D_2) = \min_{G,F}(L_R(G, D_1) + L_I(F, D_2)) \tag{3}$$

Loss Function in Reflection Decomposition Network. The loss function of RefDecN consists of the reflection adversarial loss $L_{adv}(G, D_1)$, the color consistency loss $L_{col}(G, D_1)$ and the content loss $L_{con}(G, D_1)$. Thus, $L_R(G, D_1)$ can be expressed as:

$$L_R(G, D_1) = \omega_{adv}L_{adv}(G, D_1) + \omega_{col}L_{col}(G, D_1) + \omega_{con}L_{con}(G, D_1) \tag{4}$$

where ω_{adv}, ω_{col} and ω_{con} are the weights to balance different losses in RefDecN. $L_{adv}(G, D_1)$ is adversarial loss to affects reflection decomposing process in generator G. $L_{col}(G, D_1)$ is used as color consistency loss to make the generated images have the right color of normal-light images, and $L_{con}(G, D_1)$ is content loss which helps to make the generated images retain the content of low-light image with details.

We introduce the perceptual loss in [27] as the content loss to calculate differences between high-level feature maps extracted by 19-layer VGG networks pretrained on ImageNet dataset. The perceptual loss is able to maintain the image content and the overall spatial structure. The content loss $L_{con}(G, D_1)$ is formulated as:

$$L_{con}(G, D_1) = \begin{cases} E_{l_i \sim S_{data}(l)}\big[\|VGG_k(l_i) - VGG_k(G(l_i))\|_1\big] & 0 \le t \le 5 \\ E_{x_i \sim S_{data}(x)}, E_{l_i \sim S_{data}(l)}\big[\|VGG_k(x_i) - VGG_k(G(l_i))\|_1\big] & t > 5 \end{cases} \tag{5}$$

where t is the training epoch. In the initial stage ($t = 0, ..., 5$), we first enforce the perceptual loss for the low-light image $S_{data}(l)$, and we impose the perceptual loss for the reflection components of low-light image to calculate differences between the reflection components of low-light image and the generated ones in the other training stages. $VGG_k(\cdot)$ is the feature map of the kth layer in VGG. The ℓ_1 sparse regularization is used to calculate $L_{con}(G, D_1)$.

The color consistency loss is utilized to constrain the color information of the reflection of the normal-light image and the generated reflection. We convert the RGB format image into YUV format to establish the color consistency loss to make sure the color of the generated reflection is as close as to that of the reflection of the normal image. We apply the ℓ_1 sparse constraint to the Y channel and Huber Loss to both the U and V channels. The color consistency loss can be defined as

$$L_{col}(G, D_1) = E_{l_i \sim S_{data}(l)}, E_{y_i \sim S_{data}(y)}\big[\|Y(G(l_i)) - Y(y_i)\|_1 + \|U(G(l_i)) - U(y_i)\|_H$$
$$+\|V(G(l_i)) - V(y_i)\|_H\big] \tag{6}$$

where $Y(\cdot)$, $U(\cdot)$ and $V(\cdot)$ represent three channels of the images in YUV format.

When considering the adversarial loss $L_{adv}(G, D_1)$, we introduce the least square Loss in least square generative network [28]. Finally, the generator G tries to generate an image $G(l_i)$, whose appearance and texture should be consistent with the reflection component of the low-light image and the loss function of G can be expressed as:

$$L(G) = \omega_{adv}E_{l_i \sim S_{data}(l)}\Big[(D_1(G(l_i)) - 1)^2\Big] + \omega_{col}L_{col}(G, D_1) + \omega_{con}L_{con}(G, D_1) \tag{7}$$

Edge-promoting adversarial loss $E_{x_i \sim S_{data}(x)}[(D_1(x_i))^2]$ [30] is utilized to make the images generated by RefDecN can clearly reproduce edges for discriminator. The discriminator D_1 aims to distinguish the synthesized image $G(l_i)$ from the reflection component x_i. The loss function of discriminator D_1 is expressed as:

$$L(D_1) = \omega_{adv}\left[E_{y_i \sim S_{data}(y)}\left[(D_1(y_i) - 1)^2\right] + E_{l_i \sim S_{data}(l)}\left[(D(G(l_i)))^2\right]\right. \\ \left. + E_{x_i \sim S_{data}(x)}\left[(D_1(x_i))^2\right]\right] \tag{8}$$

Loss Function in Illumination Transfer Network. In the IllumTransN, we transfer the illumination component of normal-light image to the generated reflection. In order to make the enhanced image with better visual perception and normal brightness, we train the IllumTransN by using the reflection components generated and normal-light images. The generator F can reconstruct the illumination characteristics. Therefore, our objective function of $L_I(F, D_2)$ is mainly composed of the illumination adversarial loss $L_{adv}(F, D_2)$, the color consistency loss $L_{col}(F, D_2)$, the content loss $L_{con}(F, D_2)$ and the light loss $L_{lig}(F, D_2)$. The $L_I(F, D_2)$ of is IllumTransN formulated as:

$$L_I(F, D_2) = \mu_{adv}L_{adv}(F, D_2) + \mu_{col}L_{col}(F, D_2) \\ + \mu_{con}L_{con}(F, D_2) + \mu_{lig}L_{lig}(F, D_2) \tag{9}$$

where μ_{adv}, μ_{col}, μ_{con} and μ_{lig} are regularization parameter. $L_{col}(F, D_2)$ is color loss to make the generated images to be close to the saturated color of normal-light images, $L_{con}(F, D_2)$ is content loss to retain the texture and structure of original low-light image, $L_{lig}(F, D_2)$ is light loss to minimize the distance of brightness between $F(G(LL))$ and NL, $L_{adv}(F, D_2)$ is adversarial loss to affects illumination transferring.

In the IllumTransN, the $L_{col}(F, D_2)$ is defined in RGB format rather than the converted color space. The ℓ_1 loss is used for the R channel and Huber Loss is used for the G and B channels. Thus, the $L_{col}(F, D_2)$ can be expressed as:

$$L_{col}(F, D_2) = E_{h_i \sim S_{data}(h)}, E_{l_i \sim S_{data}(l)}\left[\|R(h_i) - R(F(G(l_i)))\|_1 \right. \\ \left. + \|G(h_i) - R(F(G(l_i)))\|_H + \|B(h_i) - B(R(F(G(l_i))))\|_H\right] \tag{10}$$

where $R(\cdot)$, $G(\cdot)$ and $B(\cdot)$ represent three channels of the images in RGB format.

We adopt the high-level features maps in VGG19 to constrain content loss, which is defined as:

$$L_{con}(F, D_2) = \begin{cases} E_{l_i \sim S_{data}(l)}\left[\|VGG_k(G(l_i)) - VGG_k(F(G(l_i)))\|_1\right] & 0 \le t \le 5 \\ E_{h_i \sim S_{data}(h)}, E_{l_i \sim S_{data}(l)}\left[\|VGG_k(h_i) - VGG_k(F(G(l_i)))\|_1\right] & t > 5 \end{cases} \tag{11}$$

For $L_{lig}(F, D_2)$, we convert the image to HSV format. Since V channel represents the brightness, the Huber Loss is employed in $L_{lig}(F, D_2)$, which is expressed as:

$$L_{lig}(F, D_2) = E_{h_i \sim S_{data}(h)}, E_{l_i \sim S_{data}(l)}\left[\|V(h_i) - V(F(G(l_i)))\|_H\right] \tag{12}$$

The loss function of generator F can be expressed as:

$$L(F) = \mu_{adv}E_{l_i \sim S_{data}(l)}\left[((D_2(F(G(l_i))) - 1)^2\right] + \mu_{col}L_{col}(F, D_2)$$

$$+ \omega_{con} L_{con}(F, D_2) + \omega_{lig} L_{lig}(F, D_2) \tag{13}$$

Since the least square loss performs more stable and higher quality results during training, we also adopt the least square loss for the discriminator in IllumTransN to distinguish the synthesized image $F(G(l_i))$ from the normal-light image h. The loss function of the discriminator D_2 can be expressed as follows:

$$L(D_2) = \mu_{adv} \left[E_{h_i \sim S_{data}(h)} \left[(D_2(h_i) - 1)^2 \right] + E_{l_i \sim S_{data}(l)} \left[(D_2(F(G(l_i))))^2 \right] \right] \tag{14}$$

Fig. 5. Examples of images present in RAISE [31].

Fig. 6. Visual quality comparison of image decomposition by JieP, STAR and our proposed method. From left to right: input images, the results of JieP [18], STAR [19], and RetDecN.

3 Experiment

3.1 Experiment Setting

We use the same dataset as [12] which contains 1000 low/normal light image pairs from RAISE [31], including building, plants, people, landscape and nature, as shown in Fig. 5. We use 80% of these 1000 image pairs for training, and others for test. The resolution of training images is set to 256×256. We set $\omega_{adv} = 300$, $\omega_{col} = 10$, $\omega_{con} = 1.5$, $\mu_{col} = 150$, $\mu_{col} = 5$, $\mu_{con} = 1.5$, $\mu_{lig} = 3$ respectively. Our ProGAN are conducted on the Tensorflow framework. Before training, we utilize the JieP model to decompose low/normal light images to obtain its counterpart reflection components. Moreover, we validate our ProGAN on the LOL [12] and MEF datasets [32].

3.2 Experimental Results

Reflection Decomposition. In our ProGAN, the RefDecN can generate the reflection component of input image by generator G. We compare our reflection decomposition method with two traditional methods: JieP [18] and STAR [19]. As it shown in shown in Fig. 6, it can be clearly seen that the reflection components decomposed by JieP and STAR are with large artifact and color distortions. The reflection components decomposed by our method are with smaller artifact and less color distortions.

Low-light Image Enhancement. We compared our ProGAN with four state-of-the-arts methods, namely, JieP [18], STAR [19], KinD [13], RetinexNet [12] where the first two methods are Retinex-based methods, and the last two methods are deep learning methods. As shown in Fig. 7, the enhanced image by JieP and STAR in the extremely dark areas do not work well. The results of KinD have obvious boundary and edge in shaded areas. RetinexNet takes the closer results to the ground truth in term of color and texture, however, it will lead to image sharpening. Our ProGAN can outperform the other methods and generate the best results with rich details, color appearance and the brightness, especially in the extremely dark areas.

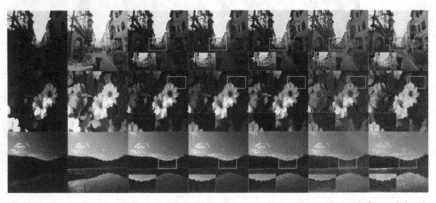

Fig. 7. Visual quality comparison of low-light image enhancement. From left to right: input images, ground truth, and enhanced result of JieP, STAR, KinD, RetinexNet and our ProGAN.

We also evaluate our proposed ProGAN on the dataset LOL and MEF. We use the metric which is NIQE for quantitivee comparision. The smaller the NIQE, the better the quality. As listed in Table 1, our proposed ProGAN outperforms other compared state-of-the-arts method. In addition, Table 2 lists average PSNR results for the test datasets of RAISE, which also demonstrate that our methods achieve the best results in comparison.

Fig. 8. Results of removing/changing components in the loss function of RefDecN. From left to right: without the color loss, using the ℓ_1 Loss and Huber Loss for the color loss built on RGB format, using the ℓ_1 Loss and Huber Loss for the color loss built on HSV format, our ProGAN.

Fig. 9. Results of removing/changing components in the loss function of IllumTransN. From left to right: ground truth, without the light loss, and using the loss function: $L_{lig}(F, D_2) = E_{h_i \sim S_{data}(h)}, E_{l_i \sim S_{data}(l)}, E_{y_i \sim S_{data}(y)}[F(G(l_i))/G(l_i) - h_i/y_i]$, our ProGAN.

Table 1. NIQE Results of RAISE, LOL and MEF by different LL image enhancement methods

Methods	Raise	Lol	MEF
Jiep [18]	4.1336	7.1633	3.1615
STAR [19]	3.9952	8.7662	3.2124
KinD [13]	4.1845	3.7065	3.3753
RetinexNet [12]	5.6138	10.2173	4.9047
Ours	**3.3059**	**3.0945**	**3.0183**

Table 2. Average PSNR(dB) results for the test dataset of RAISE by different methods

Method	JieP [18]	STAR [19]	KinD [13]	RetinexNet [12]	Ours
PSNR	15.56	17.30	16.97	16.95	17.36

3.3 Ablation Experiment

We perform the ablation experiment to study the role of color loss in RefDecN and that of light loss in IllumTransN. Figure 8 shows examples of ablations of our full loss function. As shown in Fig. 8b, without the color loss, the reflections are far from expectation. The reflections of the color loss built on channels of YUV format are more saturate color and less artifact than those of RGB and HSV format. Figure 9 shows results of our ProGAN outperforms other light losses in terms of color and brightness.

4 Conclusion

This paper presents a progressive GAN-based transfer network to realize low-light image enhancement. Our ProGAN includes reflection decomposing network (RefDecN) and illumination transferring network (IllumTransN) to preserve the structure of low-light image and reconstruct the illumination of normal-light image. The joint internal and external priors are integrated in RefDecN learning to generate the appropriate reflection with the structure, texture, content and color appearance of the object itself. The dedicated loss functions with adversarial loss, color consistency loss, content loss and light loss are designed to learn the mappings of these two GANs. Experiments results demonstrate our proposed RefDecN can decompose images to obtain the applicable reflections and our IllumTransN can generate the enhanced images with pleasant quality, saturate color and brightness, which further validates the superiority of our ProGAN over the competing methods. In the future work, we will focus on the light image enhanced for unpaired images and with extremely low-light.

Acknowledgments. This work was supported by the National Natural Science Foundation of China under Grant 61906009, the Scientific Research Common Program of Beijing Municipal Commission of Education KM202010005018, and the International Research Cooperation Seed Fund of Beijing University of Technology (Project No. 2021B06).

References

1. Pizer, S.M., Amburn, E.P., Austin, J.D., Cromartie, R., Zuiderveld, K.: Adaptive histogram equalization and its variations. Comput. Vis. Graph. Image Process. **39**(3), 355–368 (1987)
2. Zuiderveld, K.: Contrast limited adaptive histogram equalization. Graph. Gems **IV**, 474–485 (1994). https://doi.org/10.1016/B978-0-12-336156-1.50061-6
3. Jobson, D., Rahman, Z.U., Woodell, G.: Properties and performance of a center/surround retinex. IEEE Trans. Image Process. Publ. IEEE Signal Process. Soc. **6**, 451–462 (1997). https://doi.org/10.1109/83.557356
4. Rahman, Z., Jobson, D.J., Woodell, G.A.: Multi-scale retinex for color image enhancement. In: Proceedings of 3rd IEEE International Conference on Image Processing, vol. 3, pp. 1003–1006 (1996). https://doi.org/10.1109/ICIP.1996.560995
5. Jobson, D., Rahman, Z.-U., Woodell, G.: A multi - scale retinex for bridging the gap between color images and the human observation of scenes. IEEE Trans. Image Process. **6**, 965–976 (1997). https://doi.org/10.1109/83.597272

6. Yu, X.G., Li, H.L.: LIME: low-light image enhancement via illumination map estimation. IEEE Trans. Image Process. **26**(2), 982–993 (2017). https://doi.org/10.1109/TIP.2016.263 9450

7. Ren, X., Li, M., Cheng, W.-H., Liu, J.: Joint Enhancement and Denoising Method via Sequential Decomposition, pp. 1–5 (2018). https://doi.org/10.1109/ISCAS.2018.8351427

8. Lore, K.G., Akintayo, A., Sarkar, S.: LLNet: a deep autoencoder approach to natural low-light image enhancement. Pattern Recogn. **61**, 650–662 (2017)

9. Gharbi, M., Chen, J., Barron, J., Hasinoff, S., Durand, F.: Deep bilateral learning for real-time image enhancement. ACM Trans. Graph. (2017). https://doi.org/10.1145/3072959.3073592

10. Lv, F., Lu, F., Wu, J., Lim, C.: MBLLEN: Low-light Image/Video Enhancement Using CNNs. British Machine Vision Conference (BMVC) (2018)

11. Shen, L., Yue, Z., Feng, F., Chen, Q., Liu, S., Jie, M.: MSR-net:Low-light Image Enhancement Using Deep Convolutional Network. arXiv:1711.02488 [cs.CV] (2017)

12. Wei, C., Wang, W., Yang, W., Liu, J.: Deep Retinex Decomposition for Low-Light Enhancement. arXiv:1808.04560 (2018)

13. Zhang, Y., Zhang, J., Guo, X.: Kindling the Darkness: A Practical Low-light Image Enhancer, pp. 1632–1640 (2019). https://doi.org/10.1145/3343031.3350926

14. Jiang, Y., et al.: EnlightenGAN: deep light enhancement without paired supervision. IEEE Trans. Image Process. **30**, 2340–2349 (2021). https://doi.org/10.1109/TIP.2021.3051462

15. Chen, J., Liu, G., Chen, X.: AnimeGAN: a novel lightweight GAN for photo animation. In: Li, K., Li, W., Wang, H., Liu, Y. (eds.) ISICA 2019. CCIS, vol. 1205, pp. 242–256. Springer, Singapore (2020). https://doi.org/10.1007/978-981-15-5577-0_18

16. Barrow, H., Tenenbaum, J.: Recovering Intrinsic Scene Characteristics from Images (1978)

17. Olkkonen, M., Hansen, T., Gegenfurtner, K.: Color appearance of familiar objects: effects of object shape, texture, and illumination changes. J. Vis. **8**(5), 13 (2008). https://doi.org/10. 1167/8.5.13

18. Cai, B., Xu, X., Guo, K., Jia, K., Hu, B., Tao, D.: A Joint Intrinsic-Extrinsic Prior Model for Retinex, pp. 4020–4029 (2017). https://doi.org/10.1109/ICCV.2017.431

19. Xu, J., et al.: STAR: a structure and texture aware retinex model. IEEE Trans. Image Process. **29**, 5022–5037 (2020). https://doi.org/10.1109/TIP.2020.2974060

20. Yang, W., Wang, W., Huang, H., Wang, S., Liu, J.: Sparse gradient regularized deep retinex network for robust low-light image enhancement. IEEE Trans. Image Process. **30**, 2072–2086 (2021). https://doi.org/10.1109/TIP.2021.3050850

21. Ren, X., Yang, W., Cheng, W.-H., Liu, J.: LR3M: robust low-light enhancement via low-rank regularized retinex model. IEEE Trans. Image Process. **29**, 5862–5876 (2020). https://doi. org/10.1109/TIP.2020.2984098

22. Zhu, M., Pan, P., Chen, W., Yang, Y.: EEMEFN: low-light image enhancement via edge-enhanced multi-exposure fusion network. Proc. AAAI Conf. Artif. Intell. **34**, 13106–13113 (2020). https://doi.org/10.1609/aaai.v34i07.7013

23. Loh, Y.P., Chan, C.S.: Getting to know low-light images with the exclusively dark dataset. Comput. Vis. Image Understand. **178**, 30–42 (2019). https://doi.org/10.1016/j.cviu.2018. 10.010

24. Sasagawa, Y., Nagahara, H.: YOLO in the dark - domain adaptation method for merging multiple models. In: Vedaldi, A., Bischof, H., Brox, T., Frahm, J.-M. (eds.) ECCV 2020. LNCS, vol. 12366, pp. 345–359. Springer, Cham (2020). https://doi.org/10.1007/978-3-030-58589-1_21

25. Pizer, S.M., Johnston, R.E., Ericksen, J.P., Yankaskas, B.C., Muller, K.E.: Contrast-limited adaptive histogram equalization: speed and effectiveness. In: Proceedings of Conference on Visualization in Biomedical Computing, pp. 337–345 (1990)

26. Abdullah-Al-Wadud, M., Hasanul Kabir, M., Ali Akber Dewan, M., Chae, O.: A dynamic histogram equalization for image contrast enhancement. IEEE Trans. Consum. Electron. **53**(2), 593–600 (2007)

27. Wu, X., Liu, X., Hiramatsu, K., Kashino, K.: Contrast accumulated histogram equalization for image enhancement. In: 2017 IEEE International Conference on Image Processing (ICIP), pp. 3190–3194 (2017)

28. Mao, X., Li, Q., Xie, H., Lau, R., Zhen, W., Smolley, S.: Least Squares Generative Adversarial Networks, pp. 2813–2821 (2017). https://doi.org/10.1109/ICCV.2017.304

29. Chen, Y., Lai, Y., Liu, Y.: CartoonGAN: generative adversarial networks for photo cartoonization. IEEE/CVF Conf. Comput. Vis. Pattern Recogn. **2018**, 9465–9474 (2018)

30. Nguyen, D., Tien, D., Pasquini, C., Conotter, V., Boato, G.: RAISE - a raw images dataset for digital image forensics (2015). https://doi.org/10.1145/2713168.2713194

31. Ma, K., Zeng, K., Wang, Z.: Perceptual quality assessment for multi- exposure image fusion. IEEE Trans. Image Process. **24**(11), 3345 (2015)

32. Ying, Z., Li, G., Ren, Y., Wang, R., Wang, W.: A new image contrast enhancement algorithm using exposure fusion framework. In: Felsberg, M., Heyden, A., Krüger, N. (eds.) CAIP 2017. LNCS, vol. 10425, pp. 36–46. Springer, Cham (2017). https://doi.org/10.1007/978-3-319-646 98-5_4

Rethinking Shared Features and Re-ranking for Cross-Modality Person Re-identification

Na Jiang[1](✉), Zhaofa Wang[1], Peng Xu[1], Xinyue Wu[1,2](✉), and Lei Zhang[2]

[1] College of Information Engineering, Capital Normal University, Beijing, China
jiangna@cnu.edu.cn
[2] Beihang University, Beijing, China
zy2114208@buaa.edu.cn

Abstract. Cross-Modality Re-Identification (*CM-ReID*) between infrared images (*IR*) and color image is an extended task of person *ReID*, which is mainly responsible for retrieving the specified object at night or in dim environment. It remains challenging due to inter-camera and cross-modality. Targeting to solve these problems, this paper proposed a cross-modality ReID via shared features and re-ranking. It consists of a multi-branch network with attention mechanism and rethinking re-ranking strategy. The network explicitly leverages the global context block and cross-modality constraint to learn distinguished representations, which builds a retrieved bridge between IR and RGB by mining cross-modality shared space. The global context block can capture more context information from original image, and the cross-modality constraint (CrMC) can reduce the possibility of high-dimensional shared feature space. Besides, the improved re-ranking strategy is introduced to further optimize the initial results. Although the proposed method is simple, extensive experimental results demonstrate that it significantly outperforms the state-of-the-art approaches on *CM-ReID* datasets.

Keywords: Cross-modality · Person re-identification · Shared features · Improved re-ranking

1 Introduction

Person re-identification (ReID) with deep neural networks has progressed and achieved high performance in recent years [14,18,19], the aim of ReID is to determine whether this person has appeared in multiple non-overlapping cameras deployed at different locations. ReID is widely applied in intelligent video surveillance and criminal investigations. However, under dim light or night scenes, the existing Visible to Visible ReID [24,25,30] technology cannot capture the effective appearance features, which will still produce a large number of error retrieval. To overcome the perception limitations of a single visible camera, some visible (RGB) light surveillance cameras can automatically switch to infrared (IR) mode when the light is insufficient. Therefore, it is of great significance to study Cross-Modality Re-Identification (CM-ReID).

© Springer Nature Switzerland AG 2022
B. Þór Jónsson et al. (Eds.): MMM 2022, LNCS 13142, pp. 305–317, 2022.
https://doi.org/10.1007/978-3-030-98355-0_26

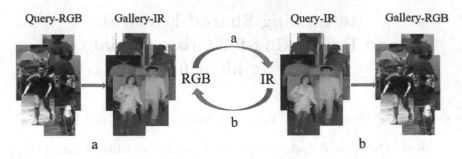

Fig. 1. There are two retrieval modes for CM-ReID. One is to use RGB as query and IR as gallery for retrieval, other is to use IR as query and RGB as gallery.

As shown in Fig. 1, there are two retrieval modes for CM-ReID: from IR to RGB and from RGB to IR. Compared with the Visible to Visible ReID, the CM-ReID faces the intra-modality and cross-modality discrepancies at the same time. To solve this problem, abundant works have been proposed, such as SENet [10], CBAM [22], CCNet [11], DANet [4] and so on. They greatly promoted the development of CM-ReID. In recently yeas, generative adversarial networks (GANs) which achieve outstanding performance in many computer vision task has been introduced into CM-ReID [17]. Such methods improve the performance of CM-ReID by generating cross-modality fake images to replace the original probe image. However, the quality of these fake images generated by transfer learning are not reliable, especially the fake RGB images generated from IR images. This kind of methods is highly dependent on the training sample pairs, and thus cannot be applied to large-scale monitoring scenarios. By analyzing the advantages and disadvantages of the existing methods, we put forward further improvements on the basis of a popular baseline [28].

In this paper, we design a two-stream network to learn distinguished representations for CM-ReID. Different from the existing two-stream frameworks, we introduce a global context block (GC) [1] into the shared structure. Under the supervision of Cross Entropy Loss (CE) and Triplet Loss with Batch Hard Mining (TH) [9], the network can better learn the cross-modality shared features between IR and RGB modes. Meanwhile, we design an up-sampling structure for each mode with reference to GANs, which can achieve the shared features more suitable for CM-ReID. Different from the idea of generating unreliable fake images, the design of up-sampling is mainly to introduce cross-modality constraint (CrMC). It can enhance the shared features learning suitable for CM-ReID and reduce the possibility of shared space. In addition, inspired by optimization strategies [5,6], we utilize an improved re-ranking in the test stage. It will adjust the initial retrieval order by the new k-query strategy and gallery-to-gallery similarity.

The main contributions can be summarized as follows.

1. Propose a cross-modality ReID method based on shared features learning, which realizes effectively person retrieval between IR images and RGB images.

2. Introduce and improve re-ranking to CM-ReID, which further improves performance with simple k-query strategy.
3. The proposed approach obtains the state-of-the-art Rank-1 and mAP on two popular CM-ReID datasets [15,23].

2   Related Work

CM-ReID is a promising research direction [12,27,29]. Most of the existing and outstanding methods are based on deep learning. According to the design motivation, they can be divided into two series: based on feature learning and based on image generation. The former usually uses the multi-branch networks to learn the shared and specific features under different modes, while the latter mainly utilizes GANs to generate fake images to replace the cross-modality probe images. They have been greatly fostered the development of CM-ReID, but there are still deficiencies in accuracy and practicability. In the section, therefore, we briefly review some representative works and analyze their existing problems.

2.1   Based on Feature Learning

Under different modalities, the features conducive to ReID are also different. The network usually pays more attention to texture and color in RGB mode. While in IR mode, it will focus on extracting shape and position. Only learning the specific feature of a particular modality cannot get the correct matching results through similarity measurement. Therefore, it is necessary to establish a cross-modality feature mapping space to learn distinguished and shared features. The representative works are as follows.

Wu et al. [23] propose a Deep zero-padding method so as to learn the information of specific domain more flexibly. At the same time, the first CM-ReID dataset SYSU-MM01 is established, which provide great convenience for the subsequent studies. Ye et al. [26] adopt two-stream network to extract the features of RGB and IR images, and propose Hierarchical Cross-modality Metric Learning. This method optimizes the feature representation by the joint training of contrastive loss and identity loss, and converts the data to the same feature space to calculate the distance between vectors. On this basis, Lu et al. [13] propose CM-ReID method with shared-specific feature learning. This method is first to extract shared and specific features simultaneously using two-stream convolutional structure, which significantly improves the ReID accuracy.

Inspired by them, this paper also focuses on feature learning. But the difference is that the network we designed synchronously learns shared and specific features, but only the shared features participate in similarity measurement. This can greatly reduce the correlation between specific features and shared features, and improve the discriminative power of the features extracted from two modalities for CM-ReID.

2.2 Based on Image Generation

With the success of GANs, a series of style transfer structures [7,16,32] are introduced into the task of CM-ReID. They are mainly responsible for generating fake images of RGB and IR from cross-modality real images, which effectively narrow the gap between different modalities by feature space transformation. The representative works are as follows.

Dai et al. [3] propose cmGAN, which is the first method to introduce GAN for training. It firstly extracts and processes the single-modality features of RGB and IR images, then extracts the shared features by generator and classifies the modalities by discriminator. Wang et al. [20] propose AlignGAN, which is also based on the idea of GAN. It consists of three modules: pixel alignment, feature alignment and joint discrimination. And these three modules perform maximum and minimum games during training. Choi et al. [2] propose a Hierarchical Cross-Modality Disentanglement (Hi-CMD) method, which automatically disentangles identification factors from visible-thermal images to reduce intra-modality and cross-modality discrepancies.

Compared with those methods based on feature learning, such methods are easier to achieve outstanding performance on closed-set because of the introduction of transfer learning. However, the methods based on image generation only convert the image style at the visualization-level. The fake contains a lot of identity noise, which will affect the final similarity measurement and cross-modality retrieval.

3   Our Proposed Method

In this section, we elaborate the framework of the proposed feature learning method for CM-ReID. As shown in Fig. 2, the framework explicitly leverages the global context (GC) block and cross-modality constraint (CrMC) to learn distinguished representations, which builds a retrieved bridge between IR and RGB by mining cross-modality shared feature space. The GC block facilitates the construction of shared feature space by capturing more context information. The cross-modality constraint module generates the fake images through the upsampling structure, and then calculates the Mean Squared Error Loss (MSE) to enhance the learning of low-level features of shared feature space. Besides, Cross Entropy Loss (CE) and Triplet Loss with Batch Hard Mining (TH) are used to supervise the shared feature learning, which can further improve shared feature representation. During the test stage, an improved k-query strategy considering inter-modality similarity is utilized to optimize the cross-modality similarity measure. More implementation details are explained below.

3.1   Shared Feature Learning

As shown in Fig. 2, our proposed network adopts a multi-branch network structure, which consists of a shared feature learning branch and two cross-modality constraint branches. The shared feature branch is refer to the classical ResNet50. But the difference is that we introduced GC block to improve it. For any pedestrian pictures with different modalities, the branch can extract the shared feature by GC block with the supervision of CE and TH.

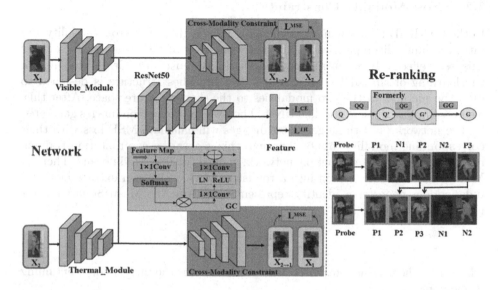

Fig. 2. The architecture of the proposed two-stream network with GC block has the supervision of CE, TH and MSE loss. In each branch, the input images are down-sampled and then up-sampled to generate fake images. Then, the features extracted from two modalities will be connected together and they will be used as the inputs of the ResNet50 backbone with GC block. In the testing stage, the new k-query strategy will make a contribution to retrieval performance. Q' is the set of the k nearest neighbors of the probe, and G' is the set of the k nearest neighbors of each probe in the Q' set.

As mentioned above, we optimize the traditional ResNet50 and introduce the global context (GC) block [1]. As the improvement of Non-Local (NL) [21] block, the GC block maintains the accuracy of NL block but with the less computation. Besides, it combines the Squeeze-Excitation (SE) block of channel-based attention mechanism, which can not only capture global spatial information with NL block, but also effectively expand the receptive field and adds useful semantic information. The detailed architecture of the GC block is illustrated as,

$$z_i = x_i + W_{v2}ReLU(LN(W_{v1}\sum_{j=1}^{N_p} \frac{exp\,(W_k x_j)}{\sum_{m=1}^{N_p} exp\,(W_k x_m)} x_j)) \tag{1}$$

where $exp\,(W_k x_j)/\sum_{m=1}^{N_p} exp\,(W_k x_m)$ is the weight of global attention pooling, and $W_{v2}ReLU(LN(W_{v1}(\cdot)))$ is the feature conversion function of the bottleneck layer. In order to obtain the lightweight advantage of SE block, the bottleneck layer conversion module is used to replace 1×1 convolution. A layer normalization (LN) is added in front of the ReLU to reduce the optimization difficulty, while the generalization is improved.

3.2 Cross-Modality Constraint

In the CM-ReID task, the most challenging issue is that both cross-modality and intra-modality discrepancies coexist between RGB and IR images. To address this issue effectively, we introduce cross-modality constraint (CrMC) to enhance the learning of shared features. And a two branches structure is designed to map the pictures in the two modalities to the shared feature space. After this, we up-sampling the features like UNet. Then we get the person images generated by the network, and these generated images will calculate MSE loss with their corresponding modality inputs. Through this generation confrontation training method, the feature extraction network, named Visible Module and Thermal Module, will be constrained into a robust network which can extract modality independent pedestrian identity representation. And the Mean Squared Error (MSE) Loss is defined as,

$$L_M = \frac{1}{N} \sum (x_i - y_i)^2 \tag{2}$$

where x_i is the forecast output of the model, and y_i is the target, both containing N elements.

3.3 Training and Testing

Training. During this stage, the shared features of pedestrian images in different modalities will be extracted by the Visible Module and the Thermal Module, and the features will be mapped to the same feature space. The features in this step will also generate fake images by up-sampling, and we use MSE Loss to constrain the Visible Module and the Thermal Module to enable them to extract identity information more effectively. After that, we use the improved ResNet50 with GC block to extract the shared features again. For the whole network, we still adopt Cross Entropy (CE) Loss and Triplet Loss with Batch Hard Mining (TH) to supervise the training process of our two-stream network. And they are defined as Eq. 3 and Eq. 4, respectively.

$$L_{TH} = \frac{1}{P \times K} \sum_{a \in \text{ batch}} \left(\max_{p \in A} d_{a,p} - \min_{n \in B} d_{a,n} + \alpha \right)_+ \tag{3}$$

$$L_{CE} = -y \log p - (1 - y) \log (1 - p) = \begin{cases} -\log p & y = 1 \\ -\log (1 - p) & y = 0 \end{cases} \tag{4}$$

In Eq. 3, for a training batch, P represents the number of pedestrian IDs and K denotes the number of different images with the same ID. Then the A

and the B represent the set of positive samples and the set of negative samples, respectively. And in Eq. 4, y means the same as Ground Truth(GT), p is the results of network prediction.

Testing. ReID ultimately belongs to the image retrieval problem. As one of the common methods to improve the accuracy in the field of image retrieval, the re-ranking algorithm does not need additional training samples, so it can be widely used in different initial sorting. Because of its advantages, we also use the re-ranking algorithm in the test stage, and adopt a new k-query strategy to improve it to make better use of the information both the same modality and the different modality.

Generally, finding the k-reciprocal nearest neighbors mainly depends on several matrices, including the distance matrix between Query (QQ), the distance matrix between Gallery (GG), the distance matrix between Query and Gallery (QG). Generally speaking, the probe only retrieves the k-reciprocal nearest neighbors in the QG matrix. But in our new k-query strategy, we also use the QQ matrix. For ease of illustration, here we assume that the Probe is IR image and the Gallery is RGB image, i.e. TV mode. Given an IR Probe as the index, we firstly find k IR nearest neighbors in the QQ matrix, and then use them as the index to find k RGB nearest neighbors in the QG matrix, which are the k nearest neighbors of the IR Probe in the RGB gallery. And then the RGB images retrieved above will be marked as a new Q. After that, we will find k RGB nearest neighbors of each query in the new Q according to the GG matrix. Finally, all RGB nearest neighbors found in the previous step will be regarded as the nearest neighbors set of the IR Probe.

Because the original distance contains important ordering information, it cannot be ignored. So, we jointly aggregate the original distance and Jaccard distance to revise the initial ranking list, the final distance d^* is defined as,

$$d^*(p,g_i) = (1 - \lambda)d_J(p,g_i) + \lambda d(p,g_i) \tag{5}$$

where λ is a hyperparameter according to experience. It is used to adjust the influence degree of the two distances on the final result. In this paper, λ value is 0.3, following [31].

4 Experiment

4.1 Implementation Details

This experiment is based on PyTorch framework. Experiments are carried out on NVIDIA GeForce GTX Titan X. During training, the batch size is set to 8, and we use the SGD optimizer with the initial learning rate of 0.1. The image size is cropped to a uniform 144×288. And the hyperparameters λ and k are set to 0.3 and 20.

4.2   Datasets and Evaluation Metrics

We use two available datasets (SYSU-MM01 [23] and RegDB [15]) for model evaluation. SYSU-MM01 is a popular CM-ReID dataset, which contains 491 identities collected by two IR cameras and four RGB cameras. There are two retrieval modes in this dataset: All-Search and Indoor-Search. RegDB is collected by dual camera systems. There are a total of 412 person IDs and 8,240 images. Each identity has 10 different IR images and 10 different RGB images. This dataset has two retrieval modes, TV-Search and VT-search.

In this paper, all the experiments follow the standard evaluation protocol in existing CM-ReID methods. Queries and galleries images are from different modalities. And then, the standard cumulative matching characteristics curve(CMC) and mean average precision(mAP) are adopted.

4.3   Comparison Experiment

In order to verify the effectiveness of our proposed method, we compare our proposed algorithm with the baselines as well as the state-of-the-art methods. Among them, we follow the traditional test method. That is to say, RegDB dataset only evaluates VT mode, while SYSU-MM01 dataset evaluates two retrieval modes. Specifically, VT mode means using RGB probe and IR gallery. In contrast, TV mode means using IR probe and RGB gallery. The experimental results are shown in Table 1.

Table 1. Comparative experiment

Method	RegDB		SYSU-MM01			
Mode	VT		TV-All-Search		TV-Indoor-Search	
Metric	Rank-1	mAP	Rank-1	mAP	Rank-1	mAP
Deep Zero-Padding (ICCV2017) [15]	–	–	14.80	15.95	20.58	26.92
HCML (AAAI2018) [26]	24.44	20.08	14.32	16.16	24.52	30.08
HSME (AAAI2019) [8]	50.85	47.00	20.68	23.12	–	–
AlignGAN (ICCV2019) [20]	56.30	53.40	42.40	40.70	45.90	54.30
Hi-CMD (CVPR2020) [2]	70.44	65.93	34.94	35.94	56.14	64.17
cm-SSFT (CVPR2020) [13]	72.30	72.90	61.60	63.20	70.50	62.0
Baseline (arXiv2020) [28]	85.85	81.72	49.89	48.96	53.87	58.58
Ours	**90.67**	**91.50**	**65.32**	**64.85**	**72.50**	**78.59**

Whether on RegDB or on SYSU-MM01, the proposed algorithm outperforms others on Rank-1 and mAP. Specifically, on RegDB, our method surpasses baseline by 4.82% on Rank-1 and 9.78% on mAP in VT mode. And our model surpasses the state-of-the-art method (cm-SSFT) on SYSU-MM01 by 3.72% on Rank-1 and 1.65% on mAP in All-Search setting. During the Indoor-Search setting, the model outperforms cm-SSFT by 2% on Rank-1 and 16.59% on mAP.

Overall, this comparison indicates the effectiveness of our proposed algorithm. This benefits from the learning of shared features and the use of re-ranking.

4.4   Ablation Experiments

To further analyze effectiveness of each component of the proposed algorithm, we perform an ablation study of our two-stream network. The experimental results of two datasets are shown in the following tables. And the best results for each index are marked in bold.

Table 2. Ablation experiments of RegDB

Method	RegDB			
Mode	VT-Search		TV-Search	
Metric	Rank-1	mAP	Rank-1	mAP
Baseline	85.85	81.72	85.10	80.40
+CrMC	86.11	81.76	85.31	81.21
+GC+CrMC	89.23	84.72	88.33	83.81
+GC+CrMC+(K-Re)	**90.80**	91.33	**90.00**	90.65
+GC+CrMC+(Our-Re)	90.67	**91.50**	89.88	**90.71**

Table 3. Ablation Experiments of SYSU-MM01

Method	SYSU-MM01							
Mode	TV-All		TV-Indoor		VT-All		VT-Indoor	
Metric	Rank-1	mAP	Rank-1	mAP	Rank-1	mAP	Rank-1	mAP
Baseline	49.89	48.96	53.87	58.58	57.87	44.25	60.89	46.29
+CrMC	50.04	49.53	54.90	63.13	60.13	44.40	64.820	46.26
+GC+CrMC	50.89	50.19	56.62	64.33	62.96	47.03	67.86	50.02
+GC+CrMC+(K-Re)	62.19	60.66	71.78	76.08	63.06	62.02	68.75	**68.73**
+GC+CrMC+(Our-Re)	**65.32**	**64.85**	**72.50**	**78.59**	**64.55**	**65.59**	**69.55**	67.48

As shown in the first rows of Table 2 and Table 3, the baseline [28] without our approaches only achieve about 85.85% Rank-1 and 81.72% mAP on RegDB, and 49.89% Rank-1 and 48.96% mAP on SYSU-MM01. Whether you use GC block or CrMC alone or both, it can be found that all indicators are improved to a certain extent. The third line adopts the original k-nearest neighbor method, and the fourth line adopts the improved re-ranking method in this paper. Although there is a small improvement in the RegDB, there is a significant improvement in the SYSU-MM01. This shows that in the case of sufficient data, the improved re-ranking will play a better role in retrieval.

4.5   Re-ID Visualization

To show the effectiveness of our algorithm, we visualize some ranking results of our CM-ReID method in Fig. 3. The images in the first column are query images. Green is the correct search result, while red is the wrong search result. In addition, we perform the two-way retrieval of IR $\rightarrow$ RGB and RGB $\rightarrow$ IR at the same time, which facilitates the comparison of visual effects.

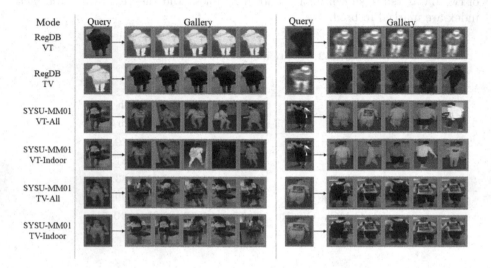

Fig. 3. This is the visualization of the retrieval results of our method. There are six retrieval patterns from the two datasets. And each pattern presents two sets of cross-modality retrieval.

5   Conclusion

In this paper, we propose a cross-modality re-identification method via shared features and re-ranking. Its contribution is focused on exploring feature learning module and re-ranking strategy to improve the person retrieval performance between IR and RGB modalities. The feature learning module explicitly leverages the global context block and cross-modality constraint to learn distinguished representations. The improved re-ranking with k-query strategy is introduced to further optimize the initial results. These steps together achieve the goal of improving the accuracy of CM-ReID. Although the proposed method is simple, it significantly outperforms the state-of-the-art approaches on RegDB and SYSU-MM01 datasets. In the future, we will continue to study person re-identification and pay attention to the generalization and efficiency.

Acknowledgements. This work was supported by the National Natural Science Foundation of China under Grant No.62002247, the Open Project Program of State Key Laboratory of Virtual Reality Technology and Systems, Beihang University (No. VRLAB2020A03), and the general project numbered KM202110028009 of Beijing Municipal Education Commission.

References

1. Cao, Y., Xu, J., Lin, S., Wei, F., Hu, H.: GCNET: non-local networks meet squeeze-excitation networks and beyond. In: Proceedings of the IEEE/CVF International Conference on Computer Vision Workshops (2019)
2. Choi, S., Lee, S., Kim, Y., Kim, T., Kim, C.: Hi-CMD: hierarchical cross-modality disentanglement for visible-infrared person re-identification. In: Proceedings of the IEEE/CVF Conference on Computer Vision and Pattern Recognition, pp. 10257–10266 (2020)
3. Dai, P., Ji, R., Wang, H., Wu, Q., Huang, Y.: Cross-modality person re-identification with generative adversarial training. In: IJCAI, vol. 1, p. 2 (2018)
4. Fu, J., et al.: Dual attention network for scene segmentation. In: Proceedings of the IEEE/CVF Conference on Computer Vision and Pattern Recognition, pp. 3146–3154 (2019)
5. Garcia, J., Martinel, N., Gardel, A., Bravo, I., Foresti, G.L., Micheloni, C.: Discriminant context information analysis for post-ranking person re-identification. IEEE Trans. Image Process. **26**(4), 1650–1665 (2017)
6. Garcia, J., Martinel, N., Micheloni, C., Gardel, A.: Person re-identification ranking optimisation by discriminant context information analysis. In: Proceedings of the IEEE International Conference on Computer Vision, pp. 1305–1313 (2015)
7. Ge, Y., et al.: FD-GAN: pose-guided feature distilling GAN for robust person re-identification. arXiv preprint arXiv:1810.02936 (2018)
8. Hao, Y., Wang, N., Li, J., Gao, X.: HSME: hypersphere manifold embedding for visible thermal person re-identification. In: Proceedings of the AAAI Conference on Artificial Intelligence, vol. 33, pp. 8385–8392 (2019)
9. Hermans, A., Beyer, L., Leibe, B.: In defense of the triplet loss for person re-identification. arXiv preprint arXiv:1703.07737 (2017)
10. Hu, J., Shen, L., Sun, G.: Squeeze-and-excitation networks. In: Proceedings of the IEEE Conference on Computer Vision and Pattern Recognition, pp. 7132–7141 (2018)
11. Huang, Z., Wang, X., Huang, L., Huang, C., Wei, Y., Liu, W.: CCNET: criss-cross attention for semantic segmentation. In: Proceedings of the IEEE/CVF International Conference on Computer Vision, pp. 603–612 (2019)
12. Li, D., Wei, X., Hong, X., Gong, Y.: Infrared-visible cross-modal person re-identification with an x modality. In: Proceedings of the AAAI Conference on Artificial Intelligence, vol. 34, pp. 4610–4617 (2020)
13. Lu, Y., et al.: Cross-modality person re-identification with shared-specific feature transfer. In: Proceedings of the IEEE/CVF Conference on Computer Vision and Pattern Recognition, pp. 13379–13389 (2020)
14. Luo, H., Jiang, W., Zhang, X., Fan, X., Qian, J., Zhang, C.: Alignedreid++: dynamically matching local information for person re-identification. Pattern Recogn. **94**, 53–61 (2019)

15. Nguyen, D.T., Hong, H.G., Kim, K.W., Park, K.R.: Person recognition system based on a combination of body images from visible light and thermal cameras. Sensors **17**(3), 605 (2017)
16. Qian, X., et al.: Pose-normalized image generation for person re-identification. In: Ferrari, V., Hebert, M., Sminchisescu, C., Weiss, Y. (eds.) ECCV 2018. LNCS, vol. 11213, pp. 661–678. Springer, Cham (2018). https://doi.org/10.1007/978-3-030-01240-3_40
17. Ronneberger, O., Fischer, P., Brox, T.: U-net: convolutional networks for biomedical image segmentation. In: Navab, N., Hornegger, J., Wells, W.M., Frangi, A.F. (eds.) MICCAI 2015. LNCS, vol. 9351, pp. 234–241. Springer, Cham (2015). https://doi.org/10.1007/978-3-319-24574-4_28
18. Sun, Y., Zheng, L., Yang, Y., Tian, Q., Wang, S.: Beyond part models: person retrieval with refined part pooling (and a strong convolutional baseline). In: Ferrari, V., Hebert, M., Sminchisescu, C., Weiss, Y. (eds.) ECCV 2018. LNCS, vol. 11208, pp. 501–518. Springer, Cham (2018). https://doi.org/10.1007/978-3-030-01225-0_30
19. Wang, C., Zhang, Q., Huang, C., Liu, W., Wang, X.: Mancs: a multi-task attentional network with curriculum sampling for person re-identification. In: Ferrari, V., Hebert, M., Sminchisescu, C., Weiss, Y. (eds.) ECCV 2018. LNCS, vol. 11208, pp. 384–400. Springer, Cham (2018). https://doi.org/10.1007/978-3-030-01225-0_23
20. Wang, G., Zhang, T., Cheng, J., Liu, S., Yang, Y., Hou, Z.: RGB-infrared cross-modality person re-identification via joint pixel and feature alignment. In: Proceedings of the IEEE/CVF International Conference on Computer Vision, pp. 3623–3632 (2019)
21. Wang, X., Girshick, R., Gupta, A., He, K.: Non-local neural networks. In: Proceedings of the IEEE Conference on Computer Vision and Pattern Recognition, pp. 7794–7803 (2018)
22. Woo, S., Park, J., Lee, J.-Y., Kweon, I.S.: CBAM: convolutional block attention module. In: Ferrari, V., Hebert, M., Sminchisescu, C., Weiss, Y. (eds.) ECCV 2018. LNCS, vol. 11211, pp. 3–19. Springer, Cham (2018). https://doi.org/10.1007/978-3-030-01234-2_1
23. Wu, A., Zheng, W.S., Yu, H.X., Gong, S., Lai, J.: RGB-infrared cross-modality person re-identification. In: Proceedings of the IEEE International Conference on Computer Vision, pp. 5380–5389 (2017)
24. Yang, Q., Yu, H.X., Wu, A., Zheng, W.S.: Patch-based discriminative feature learning for unsupervised person re-identification. In: Proceedings of the IEEE/CVF Conference on Computer Vision and Pattern Recognition, pp. 3633–3642 (2019)
25. Yang, W., Huang, H., Zhang, Z., Chen, X., Huang, K., Zhang, S.: Towards rich feature discovery with class activation maps augmentation for person re-identification. In: Proceedings of the IEEE/CVF Conference on Computer Vision and Pattern Recognition, pp. 1389–1398 (2019)
26. Ye, M., Lan, X., Li, J., Yuen, P.: Hierarchical discriminative learning for visible thermal person re-identification. In: Proceedings of the AAAI Conference on Artificial Intelligence, vol. 32 (2018)
27. Ye, M., Lan, X., Wang, Z., Yuen, P.C.: Bi-directional center-constrained top-ranking for visible thermal person re-identification. IEEE Trans. Inf. Forensics Secur. **15**, 407–419 (2019)
28. Ye, M., Shen, J., Lin, G., Xiang, T., Shao, L., Hoi, S.C.: Deep learning for person re-identification: a survey and outlook. IEEE Trans. Pattern Anal. Mach. Intell. (2021)

29. Ye, M., Wang, Z., Lan, X., Yuen, P.C.: Visible thermal person re-identification via dual-constrained top-ranking. In: IJCAI, vol. 1, p. 2 (2018)

30. Zheng, M., Karanam, S., Wu, Z., Radke, R.J.: Re-identification with consistent attentive siamese networks. In: Proceedings of the IEEE/CVF Conference on Computer Vision and Pattern Recognition, pp. 5735–5744 (2019)

31. Zhong, Z., Zheng, L., Cao, D., Li, S.: Re-ranking person re-identification with k-reciprocal encoding. In: Proceedings of the IEEE Conference on Computer Vision and Pattern Recognition, pp. 1318–1327 (2017)

32. Zhu, J.Y., Park, T., Isola, P., Efros, A.A.: Unpaired image-to-image translation using cycle-consistent adversarial networks. In: Proceedings of the IEEE International Conference on Computer Vision, pp. 2223–2232 (2017)

Adversarial Attacks on Deepfake Detectors: A Practical Analysis

Ngan Hoang Vo[1,2]([✉]), Khoa D. Phan[1,2], Anh-Duy Tran[1,2],
and Duc-Tien Dang-Nguyen[3,4]

[1] Faculty of Information Technology, University of Science,
Ho Chi Minh City, Vietnam
{vhngan,pdkhoa}@apcs.fitus.edu.vn, taduy@fit.hcmus.edu.vn
[2] Vietnam National University, Ho Chi Minh City, Vietnam
[3] University of Bergen, Bergen, Norway
ductien.dangnguyen@uib.no
[4] Kristiania University College, Oslo, Norway
ductien.dangnguyen@kristiania.no

Abstract. In this day and age, fake images can be easily generated using some of the state-of-the-art Generative Adversarial Networks (GANs), including Deepfake. These fake images, along with unfactual content, can pose a substantial threat to our society since they are indistinguishable from real ones by the human eye. Therefore, Deepfake detection has gained immense interest in academia and industry. In practice, most detection methods use simple deep neural networks (DNNs) as the backbone. However, they are vulnerable to adversarial examples. This work presents practical pipelines in both white-box and black-box attack scenarios that can fool DNN-based Deepfake detectors into classifying fake images as real. We show that adversarial attacks can be a real threat to Deepfake detectors, even in a black-box setting. We also analyze the transferability of the white-box attacks from one model to another. Then, defensive perspectives are considered based on the practical context.

Keywords: Deepfake · Deepfake detection · Adversarial attacks · Deep learning · GANs

1 Introduction

Deepfake is a mix of *deep learning* and *fake*. A Deepfake is a video, photo, or audio recording that seems real but has been manipulated using artificial intelligence (AI) [19]. The underlying technology can replace faces, manipulate facial expressions, synthesize faces, and synthesize facial attributes [2]. Generative Adversarial Networks (GANs) [26] are popular methods to create Deepfakes. Their impact on current politics, misinformation, and trust is discussed in several work [6,7]. Therefore, detecting Deepfakes is an essential task for media forensics and is currently receiving a lot of research attention due to the significance of

---

N. H. Vo and K. D. Phan—Equal contribution.

B. Þór Jónsson et al. (Eds.): MMM 2022, LNCS 13142, pp. 318–330, 2022.
https://doi.org/10.1007/978-3-030-98355-0_27

the threat. Usually, the detection of Deepfakes happens with various combined Convolutional Neural Network (CNN) architectures such as autoencoders (AEs) [13] due to the popularity of practical sources, which are usable for the training of Deepfake generators based on neural networks. As a result, those detectors are the most simple, popular, and widely used ones.

Unfortunately, Deepfake detectors have some weaknesses that can be revealed by adversarial attacks [22], which use images containing subtle perturbations generated by malicious optimization algorithms in order to fool classifiers. The robustness of the Deepfake detection model against perturbation can be evaluated through performing adversarial attacks on them. Currently, there are many methods of attack, but they are still in theory. Therefore, in the context of practicality, this paper explores hands-on attack approaches to test those detectors.

The key idea of our proposed method is to choose simple and practical detection methods then analyze hands-on adversarial attacks on them. We train simple but robust Deepfake detection models throughout the process then create adversarial images using those models. Finally, perturbed images are tested on the mentioned models. With that, each model's robustness and the effectiveness of the attack methods can be observed. We show that adversarial attacks can be a real threat to Deepfake detectors, even in a black-box setting. We also study the transferability of the attacks from one model to another. These sections are the foundation for a more in-depth approach to the theory, which is much harder and not just practicality as described. In this paper, the main contributions are (Table 1):

- Analyze the actual needs of the common Deepfake detectors and explore practical adversarial attacks to test those detectors.
- Create adversarial examples in white-box and black-box settings and use trained Deepfake detectors to classify them. Then, we examine the result.
- Experiment with tuning parameters on the adversarial attacks to improve the attack performance and the ability to transfer the adversarial images from one targeted model to another. We also suggest simple defensive approaches.

2   Background

2.1   Detecting Generated Images

The traditional forensics-based techniques evaluate pixel-level disparities. They provide explanatory indications for the detection and tell the differences between real and fake [18]. However, when photos or videos are altered by simple transformations, these works experience robustness difficulties. Most of the current Deepfake detection techniques use data-driven deep neural networks (DNNs) as the backbone, [15] such as autoencoders (AEs).

The first reason for this use comes from the fact that most Deepfakes are generated using AEs because of the Internet sources with different human faces. The datasets are usable for the training of Deefake generators based on neural networks. FakeApp [3] is an example o this autoencoder-decoder architecture.

As a result, there is a large set of data to train artifacts, so the neural networks are helpful for detecting Deepfakes. Second, there are many popular, large, and public datasets that help the training process of CNN-based Deepfake detectors. FFHQ [23], Diverse Fake Face Dataset (DFFD) [1], FaceForensic++ [24] are some examples of those datasets.

Based on this practical context, we are motivated to choose simple DNN architectures to experiment as Deepfake detectors, which are described in more detail in Sect. 4. However, many more robust and advanced Deepfake detectors are often hard to widely use in the real world.

2.2 Adversarial Attacks on Deepfake Detectors

Deep neural networks are known to be vulnerable to adversarial attacks. Adversarial attacks are methods that convert an image to a new indistinguishable one so that when the converted image is fed into a neural network classifier, it will be misclassified. The process can be done in many ways, both in white-box and black-box settings. Recently, other researchers have also been concerned over the effect of adversarial examples on Deepfake detectors and the security issues they present [12,21]. They mainly concern Deepfake videos detection, but the pipeline they used is a per-frame classifier. They cropped out the face in each video frame and input it into an image classifier to detect the Deepfake. They are concerned about both white-box and black-box attacks in their research. Their targeted models are the top models that were employed in the Deepfake Detection Challenge. In the work of Neekhara et al. [21], they propose a universal attack that can fool any detector it encounters in the black-box setting by transfer attack.

Despite being robust and powerful, the act of setting up and building those attacks seems to be time-consuming and unintelligible when it comes to practical scenarios. Therefore, simplicity and practicality are the most important criteria for choosing attack methods on white-box and black-box settings. The details of those methods are discussed in Sect. 4.

3   Analyzing Adversarial Attacks on Deepfake Detectors

3.1   Threat Model

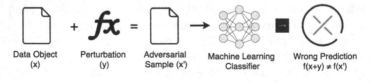

Fig. 1. Hat is adversarial attack?

The adversarial attacks task is to modify an image by adding perturbation to it so that the image is classified incorrectly by a victim Deepfake detection model. If the image is fake, the model to output must be a real label and vice versa. Our attack is considered successful if the modified image using adversarial attacks can successfully fool the detection model (Fig. 1). It is also crucial that the perturbation are kept at a minimum to be imperceptible to the human eye. To monitor the quality of the adversarial images, the Structural Similarity Index Measure (SSIM) are used. SSIM also mimics human perception. It measures structural information, which is the idea that the pixels have strong inter-dependencies when they are spatially close, while other metrics like Mean Squared Errors measure absolute errors. It makes the score higher when there are perturbations that stand out in the image.

The knowledge an attacker has about the targeted classifier (such as its parameters and architecture). The adversary's level of knowledge generally falls into one of three loosely defined categories: black-box, grey-box, and white-box attacks. An attack done by an adversary who knows more about the model than a black-box, but less than a white-box, is called a grey-box attack. In this work, we focus on white-box and black-box only. To create an adversarial example in white-box settings, most of the time, we utilize the gradient. With full access to the detection model, including the parameters, we can easily backpropagate to get the gradient of the image. In the black-box setting, there are two types of results, binary results, which the model only returns if the image is real or not, and probability score, in which the model returns the probability of the image to be fake. In black-box attacks of this work, probability score output are used.

In the remaining of the paper, we use the following notation:

- X is the image that we want to perturb
- ϵ is the maximum amount of changes to one pixel
- L is the model with a loss function.
- sign is the function to extract the sign of a number
- y_{true} is the true label of the image

3.2 White-Box Attacks

Fast Gradient Sign (FGS). FGS is the simplest method of creating adversarial images in this work. To create an adversarial image, the only work is to find the gradient of the image through backpropagation and add that gradient to the image instead of subtracting it. In a white-box setting, we have complete access to the model, which includes the preprocessing process, architecture, and parameters so getting the gradient is no issue.

$$X^{adv} = X + \epsilon sign(\nabla_X L(X, y_{true}))$$

Iterative Gradient Sign (IGS). IGS is an extension to the Fast Gradient Sign method. Just like FGS, the gradient are used to change the image, but instead of doing it just once, it is done multiple times with a smaller step size iteratively

[17]. To ensure the maximum changes to the image are within a boundary, we clip the pixel values of the results after each step.

$$X_0^{adv} = X, \ X_{N+1}^{adv} = clip_{X,\epsilon}(X_N^{adv} + \alpha sign(\nabla_X L(X_N^{adv}, y_{true})))$$

The obvious choice of loss function for these algorithms is the binary cross-entropy loss, for it is the same cost function that we used to train our detection models. However in [5,12,21] suggest that using the raw output of the model instead of using sigmoid can improve the effectiveness of the attack. Assuming negative output from the model is fake and positive output is real, the second loss function is:

$$L(X, y_{true}) = \begin{cases} X & \text{if } y_{true} = real \\ -X & \text{if } y_{true} = fake \end{cases}$$

In the experiment, both of the loss functions are used to compare the results.

Robust Iterative Gradient Sign (IGS w/aug). As our images go through the Internet, they can be affected by multiple sources of neutral perturbation like noise, compression. It is important that the adversarial images can withstand these kinds of perturbation [9,12]. To do that, some augmentations are added to the input to make the attacks more robust [4]. With t is the transformation of the input image.

$$X_0^{adv} = X, \ X_{N+1}^{adv} = clip_{X,\epsilon}(X_N^{adv} + \alpha sign(\nabla_X L(t(X_N^{adv}), y_{true})))$$

Deepfool. In the Deepfool paper [20], the authors observe that the robustness of a linear binary classification model for an image is equal to the distance between that image to the hyperparameter plane separating the two classes $F = \{x : w^T x + b = 0\}$. The minimal perturbation required to change the model decision corresponds to the orthogonal projection of the image to the separating plane. For the general binary classifier, the author linearized the model around the current input. The algorithm iteratively updates, and it stops when it changes the decision of the classifier.

3.3 Black-Box Attacks

Simple Black-Box Attacks (SimBA). The idea for this attack is to search for the adversarial image by changing it little by little until the decision of the classifier flips [11]. To achieve that target, the algorithm only needs to know the output probability of the model to access the difference each time the image is changed. The algorithm starts with an image x a set of directions $q \in Q$ picked uniformly at random. As we iterate through Q, either $x + \epsilon q$ or $x - \epsilon q$ is going to increase the output probability of our targeted label. So we update the image in that direction.

Natural Evolution Strategy (NES). In the white-box setting, we have full access to the model, and the only need is to backpropagate the gradient. However, in this attack, we try to estimate the gradient of the model through the black box setting [12,14,25]. To do that, first, a number of random noises is sampled around the image. For each of the samples, we add it to the image and feed it to the classifier to receive a probability score. Finally, all the noise sample is summed up weighted by the corresponding probability score. Now that having the estimated gradient of the image, we then create the adversarial image by using IGS.

3.4 Transfer Attacks

Prior works have suggested the possibility of transferring the attacks on one model to another [21]. The idea is there are common features on the image that models use to predict whether the image is fake or not. If an image is changed in a way that can deceive a detection model, it can also deceive other models because the common features that are used to tell if the image is fake or not have been adversarially changed. By augmenting the image before inputting it into the model, we can extract more general features to perturb therefore improve the transferability of the attacks.

4 Experimental Results

4.1 Experiment Setup

Deepfake Detectors on Unperturbed Data. Four deep convolutional neural networks are employed in the detection of Deepfake face images: a basic convolutional model, a model built with XceptionNet architecture and two EfficientNet models - one from version one and one from version two. These models are chosen because they were utilized in the top three entries in the Deepfake detection challenge hosted by Kaggle. The baseline model is a simple convolutional neural network with 4 convolution layers. All of the models were trained with binary cross-entropy loss and Adam optimizer with the initial learning rate of 0.001 for 15 epochs.

Dataset. The chosen dataset consists of 70,000 real images and 70,000 fake images from www.kaggle.com/xhlulu/140k-real-and-fake-faces. This dataset is chose because of its simplicity and the quality of its images. We want to keep the task of Deepfake detection simple and robust to better survey the effect of each of the surveyed adversarial attack methods on each of the detection models. The real images from our chosen dataset were taken from the Flickr-Faces-HQ Dataset(FFHQ) [16]. It has a lot of diversity in age, gender, ethnicity, and background. The dataset uses the real faces and StyleGan to generate the fake faces.

Evaluation Metrics. The model is evaluated based on two categories: accuracy and recall of the fake images. For evaluating adversarial attacks, the accuracy and recall score of the perturbed images are used. The lower the score is, the better the attacks are. Accuracy helps with seeing the overall performance of the detection model. The recall is to understand more about the inner working of the detecting process. Recall can show the percentage of the fake images that the model gets right. We keep track of the structural similarity index measure (SSIM) to compare attacks on their ability to keep the images from deviating from the original images too much. For black-box attacks, we take the mean of the number of times we queried the model. For white-box attacks, the images perturbed using a model are used and tested on other models to measure the transferability of the attacks.

Table 1. Accuracy of our detection models on unperturbed data

Model	Baseline	Xception	EfficientNetB3	EfficientNetv2s
Accuracy	79.95%	**99.15%**	98.05%	98.70%
Recall	93.35%	**98.65%**	98.30%	98.15%

4.2 White-Box Attacks

For the iterative gradient sign attacks using Binary Cross Entropy (BCE) and the model's output (lin) as loss, the maximum changes ϵ are set to 3/255, the learning rate α to 1/255, and the attacks are run for four iterations. We also employ an augmentation layer for the iterative gradient sign attacks. The augmentation includes a 3×3 Gaussian blur with sigma chosen at random in the range of (0.1;2) and Gaussian noise in the range of (−0.005; 0.005). For the fast gradient sign attack, we tested both 3/255 and 1/255 as ϵ.

Table 2. Results of our models on white-box adversarial examples. All methods bring the accuracy of all of the detection models down very low and shows that it is not hard to make adversarial examples in the white-box setting.

Attack	Baseline Acc	Baseline Rec	Xception Acc	Xception Rec	EfficientNet B3 Acc	EfficientNet B3 Rec	EfficientNet v2s Acc	EfficientNet v2s Rec
FGS(1/255)	**23.12%**	**46.25%**	6.10%	8.50%	0.05%	0.10%	2.23%	0.05%
FGS(3/255)	**48.38%**	**96.75%**	4.62%	8.65%	2.62%	5.25%	0.8%	0.25%
IGS(BCE)	0%	0%	4.3%	**8.6%**	0%	0%	0%	0%
IGS(BCE) w/aug	0%	0%	3.4%	**6.8%**	0%	0%	0%	0%
IGS(lin)	0%	0%	0.12%	**0.25%**	0%	0%	0%	0%
IGS(lin) w/aug	0.03%	0.05%	0.92%	**1.85%**	0%	0%	0%	0%
Deepfool	**5.70%**	**11.40%**	0.07%	0.15%	0.03%	0.05%	0.05%	0.10%

The results are shown in Table 2. Of all of the attacks, the iterative gradient sign with the output of the model as loss produces the best result. By introducing data augmentation into the attacks, we made it so that the attacks are more robust, and according to our results, it does not make a big difference in the final result. The baseline model seems to handle the FGS attack decently well. We suspect that is because of the simplicity of the model. It only learned the general features making it easily confused when seeing perturbation in the image. The recall score of the model on the FGS(3/255) attack images is 96.75%, while the accuracy is only 48.38% indicates that the model labeled almost every perturbed image as fake. Even though Deepfool did not get any model to 0%, it makes the biggest impact on the XceptionNet model.

4.3 Black-Box Attacks

For the Natural Evolution Strategies (NES) attack, a sample size n of 50 is used. The maximum changes are also set as $\epsilon = 3/255$ and learning rate as $\alpha = 1/255$ just like in the white-box attacks. The maximum number of iterations for NES is also set at 100, which set the cap for querying the model at 5000 times. For the Simple Black-box Attack, the maximum changes $\epsilon = 12/255$ and the maximum number of iterations at 10000.

Table 3. Results of our models on Black-box adversarial examples. The table shows that it is possible to create adversarial images even in black-box settings.

Attack	Baseline Acc	Rec	Xception Acc	Rec	EfficientNet B3 Acc	Rec	EfficientNet v2s Acc	Rec
SimBA	0%	0%	27%	50%	21%	34%	21%	36%
NES	10.2%	8%	30.25%	53.33%	20.8%	33.2%	25.71%	40.96%

Table 4. Black-box query count and SSIM. The attacks take on average a lot of query to run, the lowest is 982.

Attack	Baseline SSIM	QC	Xception SSIM	QC	EfficientNet B3 SSIM	QC	EfficientNet v2s SSIM	QC
SimBA	0.99	4211	0.99	8383	0.98	7134	0.99	6553
NES	0.96	982	0.97	1608	0.96	1055	0.97	1187

In Table 3, black-box results are shown and in Table 4, the SSIM score and the average query count it takes to run the attacks. Both attacks have very comparable results. However, SimBA took significantly more queries to get there. It can be observed that the XceptionNet model is the most resistant to the attacks, and the two EfficientNet models produced similar results to each other.

4.4 Transfer Attacks

In this section, we discuss the transfer attacks and our tuning of the parameters of the white box attacks to make them more transferable. Here we do not consider the Deepfool attack because it is too tailored to its target model to have much transferability. Because of the poor performance of the attacks on the baseline network and the tendency for it to classify every image as fake after a certain amount of perturbation, we also take it out in this part.

First, as it can be observed in the last part, using image augmentation before input to the model can improve the transfer attacks. So we tune the parameter of the augmentation up to observe the impact of it on the results. The image augmentation has two parts: blur and noise, so there have 3 parameters to change. That is the kernel size and sigma for the Gaussian Blur and the range for the noise. The IGS method with binary cross entropy loss is used for this experiment because it is the higher performing attack of the two attacks that have data augmentation.

Table 5. The results of tuning the augmentation of images before input to IGS with BCE loss. Increasing the augmentation to a point can have an impact on the performance of the attacks. The best white-box results are here, with all models having 0% detection rate.

Parameters	Target	Xception		EfficientNet B3		EfficientNet v2s	
		Acc	Rec	Acc	Rec	Acc	Rec
$KS = 5$	Xception	1.03%	2.05%	**56.57 %**	**62.9%**	10.8%	3.2%
$\sigma = (0.1; 2)$	EffNet B3	**39.12%**	**38.35%**	0%	0%	15.88%	2.75%
$noise = 0.01$	EffNet v2s	34.52%	33.10%	**61.98%**	**76.15%**	0%	0%
$KS = 5$	Xception	1.1%	2.2%	**57.5%**	**63.5%**	10.78%	3.1%
$\sigma = (0.1; 2)$	EffNet B3	**39.77%**	**39.3%**	0%	0%	16.3%	3%
$noise = 0$	EffNet v2s	34.52%	32.85%	**61.7%**	**74.8%**	0%	0%
$KS = 5$	Xception	0.62%	1.25%	**53.23%**	**60.8%**	9.38%	2%
$\sigma = (0.1; 2)$	EffNet B3	**35.58%**	**35.85%**	0%	0%	14.85%	2.4%
$noise = 0.05$	EffNet v2s	32.73%	32.95%	**61.62%**	**77.7%**	0%	0%
$KS = 5$	Xception	0%	0%	**43.55%**	**53.9%**	6.53%	0.25%
$\sigma = 5$	EffNet B3	**25.77%**	**28.85%**	0%	0%	14.65%	1.1%
$noise = 0.1$	EffNet v2s	26.35%	30.75%	**58.03%**	**79.35%**	0%	0%
$KS = 5$	Xception	0.15%	0.05%	**48.93%**	**56.45%**	13.03%	0.35%
$\sigma = 10$	EffNet B3	**56.7%**	**53.3%**	0.1%	0.1%	32%	4.85%
$noise = 0.4$	EffNet v2s	40.27%	49.05%	**66.05%**	**84.6%**	0%	0%

In Table 5, the reader can see the results of our experiment with tuning the image augmentation parameter. In general, it can be observed that changing the data augmentation can have a significant impact on the effectiveness of the adversarial images on one model to another without decreasing the performance of the attack on the targeted model. It can be seen that both the augmentation (blur and noise) have an effect on the outcome. As the intensity of the augmentation increased, we noticed that it increased the performance for some models but decreased for others. So each model should have a different augmentation point that is optimal.

Next, the perturbation of the attacks is increased, specifically the IGS attack with linear loss, as it is the best attack in the white-box attacks and the FGS attack because we suspect that the more general the adversarial image is, the more transferable it becomes. As increase the strength of the perturbation is increased, we detect a rise in the performance of the attack. However, as the SSIM score goes below 0.9, the perturbation starts to be visible for the naked eye and as it enters the 0.6 range, the perturbation is very pronounced, so we stop experimenting at that point.

In Fig. 2 and 3, the impact on the accuracy and recall rate of the attacked models as we increase the perturbation, which is indicated by the lowering of the SSIM. Both the IGS and FGS transfer attacks become better as the perturbation increases. The results from the IGS vary a lot more than the results from FGS indicate that IGS transfer attacks depend more on the target model than FGS. While the IGS attacks accuracy seems to decrease more if the perturbation is further increased, the FGS accuracy dipped hard first and hovered around 20%. We supposed that is because of the simplicity of the model, it only learned the general features making it easily confused when seeing perturbation in the image. It is noticeable that in general, the FGS transfer attacks have a significantly lower recall rate than the IGS ones.

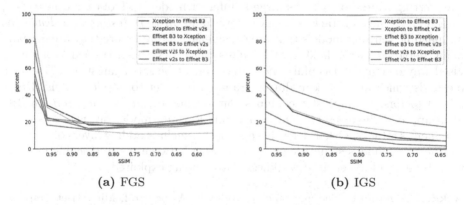

(a) FGS   (b) IGS

Fig. 2. Transfer attacks accuracy with increasing perturbation

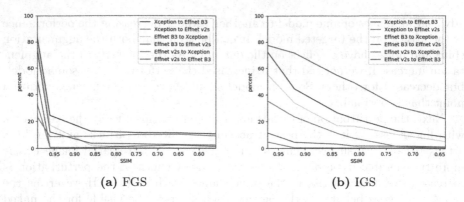

(a) FGS   (b) IGS

Fig. 3. Transfer attacks recall with increasing perturbation

5   Conclusion

Through the study of 4 white-box and 2 black-box adversarial attack methods, the best of our white-box method is the *Iterative Gradient Sign* with the accuracy is under 1% most of the time. For the black-box attacks, the *Natural Evolution Strategy* method is much better than the *Simple Black box Attack* as it takes substantially fewer queries to run. Moreover, white-box attacks can be performed when the detection model is deployed in client-side applications. Additionally, adversarial attacks pose a very practical threat to Deepfake detectors. Even in a black-box setting, attackers can still create adversarial images that are indistinguishable from the originals. We also showed the possibility of transferring white-box attacks targets different models to fool each other.

The adversarial attack is a clever way to do *pressure testing* and *debugging* on machine learning models that are considered *mature* before they are actually being deployed in the field [8]. Classifiers which have been trained in a supervised way on current Deepfake techniques cannot be safe against new Deepfake methods which are not seen during training. In order to develop robust Deepfake detectors, we suggest techniques comparable to *Adversarial Training* [10]. This approach involves training a machine learning model on instances of an opponent's attacks. Other defensive approaches include adding layers of randomization to a model's structure or extrapolating between many machine learning models to avoid adversarial weaknesses from being exploited.

Acknowledgement. The assistance provided by Assoc. Prof. Minh-Triet Tran was greatly appreciated. This work was supported by MediaFutures: Research Centre for Responsible Media Technology and Innovation, Norway, through the Centres for Research-based Innovation scheme, project number 309339.

References

1. http://cvlab.cse.msu.edu/dffd-diverse-fake-face-dataset.html
2. I never said that! High-tech deception of 'deepfake' videos, July 2018. https://www.cbsnews.com/news/i-never-said-that-high-tech-deception-of-deepfake-videos/
3. FakeApp 2.2.0 - download for PC free, March 2019. https://www.malavida.com/en/soft/fakeapp/#gref
4. Athalye, A., Engstrom, L., Ilyas, A., Kwok, K.: Synthesizing robust adversarial examples. In: International Conference on Machine Learning, pp. 284–293. PMLR (2018)
5. Carlini, N., Wagner, D.: Towards evaluating the robustness of neural networks. In: 2017 IEEE Symposium on Security and Privacy (SP), pp. 39–57. IEEE (2017)
6. Citron, D., Chesney, R.: Deepfakes and the new disinformation war, June 2020. https://www.foreignaffairs.com/articles/world/2018-12-11/deepfakes-and-new-disinformation-war
7. Vaccari, C., Chadwick, A.: Deepfakes and disinformation: exploring the impact of synthetic political video on deception, uncertainty, and trust in news (2020). https://journals.sagepub.com/doi/full/10.1177/2056305120903408
8. Dickson, B.: Adversarial attacks against machine learning systems - everything you need to know, June 2020. https://portswigger.net/daily-swig/adversarial-attacks-against-machine-learning-systems-everything-you-need-to-know
9. Dziugaite, G.K., Ghahramani, Z., Roy, D.M.: A study of the effect of JPG compression on adversarial images. arXiv preprint arXiv:1608.00853 (2016)
10. Goodfellow, I., Shlens, J., Szegedy, C.: Explaining and harnessing adversarial examples. CoRR arXiv:1412.6572 (2015)
11. Guo, C., Gardner, J., You, Y., Wilson, A.G., Weinberger, K.: Simple black-box adversarial attacks. In: International Conference on Machine Learning, pp. 2484–2493. PMLR (2019)
12. Hussain, S., Neekhara, P., Jere, M., Koushanfar, F., McAuley, J.: Adversarial Deepfakes: evaluating vulnerability of Deepfake detectors to adversarial examples. In: Proceedings of the IEEE/CVF Winter Conference on Applications of Computer Vision, pp. 3348–3357 (2021)
13. Goodfellow, I., Bengio, Y., Courville, A.: Deep Learning. MIT Press (2016). http://www.deeplearningbook. [org. 1, 2]
14. Ilyas, A., Engstrom, L., Athalye, A., Lin, J.: Black-box adversarial attacks with limited queries and information. In: International Conference on Machine Learning, pp. 2137–2146. PMLR (2018)
15. Juefei-Xu, F., Wang, R., Huang, Y., Guo, Q., Ma, L., Liu, Y.: Countering malicious Deepfakes: survey, battleground, and horizon. ArXiv arXiv:2103.00218 (2021)
16. Karras, T., Laine, S., Aila, T.: A style-based generator architecture for generative adversarial networks. In: Proceedings of the IEEE/CVF Conference on Computer Vision and Pattern Recognition, pp. 4401–4410 (2019)
17. Kurakin, A., Goodfellow, I., Bengio, S., et al.: Adversarial examples in the physical world (2016)
18. Li, H., Li, B., Tan, S., Huang, J.: Identification of deep network generated images using disparities in color components. Signal Process. **174**, 107616 (2020)
19. Metz, R.: The fight to stay ahead of Deepfake videos before the 2020 us election, June 2019. https://edition.cnn.com/2019/06/12/tech/deepfake-2020-detection/index.html

20. Moosavi-Dezfooli, S.M., Fawzi, A., Frossard, P.: DeepFool: a simple and accurate method to fool deep neural networks. In: Proceedings of the IEEE Conference on Computer Vision and Pattern Recognition, pp. 2574–2582 (2016)
21. Neekhara, P., Dolhansky, B., Bitton, J., Ferrer, C.C.: Adversarial threats to Deep-Fake detection: a practical perspective. In: Proceedings of the IEEE/CVF Conference on Computer Vision and Pattern Recognition, pp. 923–932 (2021)
22. Neekhara, P., Hussain, S.S., Jere, M., Koushanfar, F., McAuley, J.: Adversarial Deepfakes: evaluating vulnerability of DeepFake detectors to adversarial examples. In: 2021 IEEE Winter Conference on Applications of Computer Vision (WACV), pp. 3347–3356 (2021)
23. NVlabs: Nvlabs/FFHQ-dataset: Flickr-Faces-HQ dataset (FFHQ). https://github.com/NVlabs/ffhq-dataset
24. Rössler, A., Cozzolino, D., Verdoliva, L., Riess, C., Thies, J., Nießner, M.: Face-Forensics++: learning to detect manipulated facial images. In: 2019 IEEE/CVF International Conference on Computer Vision (ICCV), pp. 1–11 (2019)
25. Wierstra, D., Schaul, T., Glasmachers, T., Sun, Y., Peters, J., Schmidhuber, J.: Natural evolution strategies. J. Mach. Learn. Res. **15**(1), 949–980 (2014)
26. Xuan, X., Peng, B., Dong, J., Wang, W.: On the generalization of GAN image forensics. ArXiv arXiv:1902.11153 (2019)

Multi-modal Semantic Inconsistency Detection in Social Media News Posts

Scott McCrae$^{(\boxtimes)}$, Kehan Wang, and Avideh Zakhor

University of California, Berkeley, USA
{mccrae,wang.kehan,avz}@berkeley.edu

Abstract. As computer-generated content and deepfakes make steady improvements, semantic approaches to multimedia forensics will become more important. In this paper, we introduce a novel classification architecture for identifying semantic inconsistencies between video appearance and text caption in social media news posts. While similar systems exist for text and images, we aim to detect inconsistencies in a more ambiguous setting, as videos can be long and contain several distinct scenes, in addition to adding audio as an extra modality. We develop a multi-modal fusion framework to identify mismatches between videos and captions in social media posts by leveraging an ensemble method based on textual analysis of the caption, automatic audio transcription, semantic video analysis, object detection, named entity consistency, and facial verification. To train and test our approach, we curate a new video-based dataset of 4,000 real-world Facebook news posts for analysis. Our multi-modal approach achieves 60.5% classification accuracy on random mismatches between caption and appearance, compared to accuracy below 50% for uni-modal models. Further ablation studies confirm the necessity of fusion across modalities for correctly identifying semantic inconsistencies.

Keywords: Multi-modal · Social media · Forensics · Fusion

1 Introduction

There has been a great deal of attention on misinformation and deepfakes recently, especially with regards to the COVID-19 pandemic and 2020 US Presidential election. There are a variety of methods for detecting both manipulated media, such as Photoshopped images, and machine-generated data, such as images from generative adversarial networks (GANs) [2,10,11,26,28,34,35,41]. However, these tools tend to focus on a single modality, such as imagery, and look for clues that the image has been manipulated. While these tools are indisputably useful, we are interested in investigating multi-modal analysis, where we attempt to detect manipulations or misinformation using semantic clues from a variety of modalities.

The use of multiple modalities allows us to reason about the semantic content of each source. For instance, a caption describing an out-of-control protest would be inconsistent with a video of a candle-light vigil. On their own, neither modality

© Springer Nature Switzerland AG 2022
B. Þór Jónsson et al. (Eds.): MMM 2022, LNCS 13142, pp. 331–343, 2022.
https://doi.org/10.1007/978-3-030-98355-0_28

is manipulated, but together they represent an inconsistency. This can happen when an attacker attempts to misrepresent some original source. Furthermore, detecting video semantic inconsistencies is important so that attackers cannot evade deepfake detection by only producing video content.

Detecting caption and video inconsistency is challenging because of the abstract relationships among different modalities. The caption in social media posts is not always a literal description of its corresponding video. Our videos cover a wide range of styles and subjects, are not necessarily well-produced, and have imperfect automatically-generated transcripts with no audio descriptions. We hope to strike a balance between perceived human difficulty and the challenge of learning abstract associations between modalities from a small set of noisy data. We adopt a self-supervised random-swapping approach for generating inconsistencies, in line with the random non-matches generated in [3].

In this paper, we introduce a novel classification architecture for identifying semantic inconsistencies between video appearance and text caption in social media news posts. To analyze the semantic alignment of videos and captions, we need three main ingredients. First, we need pristine data as ground truth. Second, we need to extract semantic feature representations from each modality and its constituents, such as transcripts and named entities. Third, we need to jointly reason about semantic content. Each of these components are discussed in turn in the following sections.

2   Related Works

The capabilities of multi-modal systems have advanced rapidly in recent years. Research in multi-modal learning with text and imagery has demonstrated the efficacy of learning modality-specific embeddings [12]. New methods have been developed with the goal of leveraging transformers to jointly process text and imagery [18,21,31,32]. [24] adapts [37] to include text embeddings which are jointly learned with video embeddings, and is trained on a very large corpus of instructional videos [25]. [23] extends joint text and image transformer-based methods to process text and video clips. [19] employs cross-modal transformers with video frame and text embeddings for multi-modal learning. Recent research has shown promising results adapting transformer methods to process videos [6], opening the door to processing video clips which are longer than a few seconds.

A variety of methods have been introduced recently for detecting computer-generated content and semantic inconsistencies. [40] detects neural fake news by modeling a joint distribution over a news article's domain, date, authors, headline, and body. [34] demonstrates the relative ease of detecting GAN-generated images from a variety of state-of-the-art generators at the time of publication. [33] checks for consistency between a news article and its images and captions. [30] attempts to identify and attribute inconsistencies between images and their captions. [22] introduces and evaluates detection methods on a new dataset for the task of identifying semantic inconsistencies between images and captions.

We introduce a new system in the area of multi-modal semantics, reasoning with video appearance, rather than images, in addition to other modalities like caption and audio transcript. Specifically, we learn a shared semantic embedding for features extracted from video clips, captions, and transcripts. We then use a recurrent architecture to condense information from several video clips, and concatenate the condensed representation with facial recognition and named entity recognition features before making a final classification. In this manner, we can verify semantic consistency between a caption and a video using information on visual and textual semantics.

3   Motivation and Intuition

To study misinformation and multimedia forensics, we want to learn semantic relationships between video and text in real-world social media content. We opted to create our own dataset to study semantic consistency between many modalities. While there are several popular multi-modal datasets [1,4,5,17,25], datasets designed for tasks such as human activity recognition or video retrieval are not well-suited to our goal of analyzing inconsistent news in social media.

Instead, we aim to develop a method with capabilities similar to [3,22,33], extending semantic inconsistency detection to include videos rather than just text and imagery. Motivated by [12], we aim to learn a semantic embedding for each of the video appearance, caption, and transcript modalities in a social media post. Additionally, we include named entity verification methods inspired by [33]. Since automatic transcriptions may contain typos, we aim to verify names between captions and transcripts by learning a character-based embedding of names in each domain. We also perform facial recognition in an offline manner, by building a database of faces for every name identified in our dataset of captions, then comparing facial recognition features for frames in a video with the facial recognition features for names appearing in the accompanying caption. Our database of faces is collected via Google Images, and features are computed with [29], chosen for its high performance and relatively small feature dimension. We leverage models pre-trained on larger datasets in an effort to alleviate issues with the scale of our relatively small dataset. For instance, while [3] reports results on their full dataset and successively smaller versions, the smallest version reported on is an order of magnitude larger than our full dataset.

4   Method

4.1   System Architecture

We propose a multi-modal model with two stages of fusion, shown in Fig. 1. Our pipeline begins with data collection. Then, each modality undergoes a feature extraction step. Captions are passed directly to BERT [8] for feature extraction. Audio is transcribed using DeepSpeech (DS) [13], and then the transcription is passed to BERT. Both caption and transcript are run through a Named Entity Recognition (NER) step to extract the names of people. A separate embedding is learned for each of these text features.

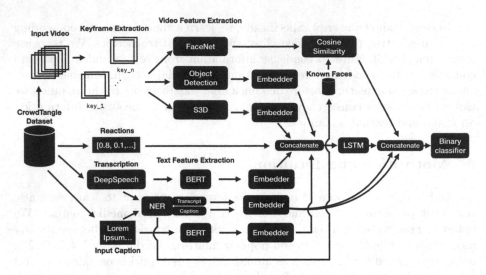

Fig. 1. Our semantic inconsistency detection architecture. Modality-specific feature extraction is run in parallel, and features representing the content of each modality are concatenated with facial verification features in order to perform classification.

Videos are split into clips and undergo several pre-processing steps, described in Sect. 4.3. We extract both activity recognition and object detection features for each clip, using [14] and [24] respectively, each of which have an additional learned semantic embedding. These embeddings are concatenated with the caption and transcript embeddings.

We also include normalized Facebook reactions to a post as a feature, which we hypothesize provide a measure of sentiment. Normalized reactions are concatenated with the clip, caption, and transcript embeddings. These features are passed to a Long Short-Term Memory (LSTM) [15] module to condense features at the clip level into a summary feature vector for the entire video. We opt to fuse modality features early, before the LSTM, due to the findings of [38].

We add facial verification and name verification features to the fused video, caption, and transcript feature before classification. With all features computed and fused, we make a binary classification using a learned multi-layer perceptron.

4.2   Dataset Design

We construct our dataset using raw data accessed via CrowdTangle (CT) [7], a public insights tool owned and operated by Facebook. The platform can surface public Facebook posts, including sources such as posts by celebrities and news outlets.

Using CT's historical data function, we downloaded all public Facebook posts which had videos in the last decade from the US General Media group, for a total of 647,009 posts. This list of organizations was curated by CT. It ranges from large, relatively non-partisan sources such as The Associated Press to smaller, more partisan sources such as Breitbart News.

While CT provides access to large amounts of Facebook posts, it has two limitations that impact this project. First, it does not provide labels for whether or not a post contains misinformation. Second, since it does not provide video files, they must be scraped from Facebook using other tools. Therefore, we used CT to source posts to scrape and used the open-source `youtube-dl` tool [39] to scrape video files. Due to this limitation, we were only able to scrape a sample of 4,651 videos.

Fig. 2. Example videos and captions from our dataset.

To construct a labelled dataset for multi-modal semantic alignment, we treat the original caption-video post pairs as pristine examples and randomly swap in new captions from other posts to generate inconsistent examples. Examples are shown in Fig. 2. In this manner, a pristine example features a real-world video, and associated modalities such as a transcript, and a real-world caption which were intended to relate to each other by the organization which posted them. We assume that pristine examples are semantically consistent across modalities, and that a random swap of caption would result in some amount of semantic mismatch between the new caption and the original video. In practice, half of the examples in our dataset are pristine and half are inconsistent.

We opt to perform swaps on real-world captions rather than creating inconsistencies by generating captions using large language models. This avoids reducing the problem of identifying semantic inconsistencies across modalities to detecting whether or not a caption is synthetically generated. Although some real news posts may include synthetically generated text, such as short reports on financial news [27], we do not attempt to filter out posts which might contain synthetic text. If such synthetic posts are present, they would not be correlated with semantic inconsistency labels due to our random swapping approach.

4.3   Video Pre-processing

After collecting video data, we standardize video formats for input to our system. Figure 1 illustrates how data flows through our model. Each video is transcoded to a constant resolution of 256 × 256 pixels and a constant frame rate of 10 frames per second, as in [25], using the FFmpeg utility [9].

Videos from Facebook have a wide range of video lengths, styles, and subjects. In our dataset, the minimum video length is 1 s, the maximum length is 14 h, and the mean is 8.5 min. To handle different video lengths, we adopt a keyframe-based approach. Each video is broken up into a sequence of 32-frame-long clips, with each clip beginning at a keyframe. The clip length was selected based on the recommended parameters of [25].

In practice, we identify keyframes as timestamps in a video where the FFmpeg [9] scene detection filter is triggered, with the scene detection threshold left at the default of 0.4. If no keyframes are detected, which might be the case with videos which are all one shot, we create placeholder keyframes every 32 frames. In this manner, we process as much of a video as possible, even if no keyframes are detected. We choose to use 16 keyframes per video, taking into account that 73% of videos in our dataset have at most 16 keyframes. We did not observe a significant difference in performance between using 8 or 16 keyframes.

Every video is transcribed with DS [13]. Before passing a video's audio stream into DS, we transcode it using FFmpeg to the PCM signed 16-bit little-endian format with a sample rate of 16 kHz, apply a highpass filter with cutoff 200 Hz, and apply a lowpass filter with cutoff 3 kHz. This approach allows us to transcribe the wide range of audio recordings scraped online with an encoding closely matching the training audio for [13]. Below is an excerpt from an example audio transcript with typos generated using DS:

> in ohio on tuesday minnesota senator amicable no time getting back on the campaign trail she picked off with a tour of new hampshire traveling to all ten counties and just thirty hours overcasting a wave of support after snagging the spotlight on tuesday night going head to head against fortune elizabeth warehouses not even the billionaire ...

While our transcripts are mostly correct, they tend to include misspelled names. In this case, misspelled names include "amicable" and "warehouses." The correct names are "Amy Klobuchar" and "Warren." These errors make it difficult to directly compare named entities in captions and transcripts.

4.4   Named Entity Verification

In this section we describe our approaches to verifying named entities using facial verification and text-based comparison of names in captions and transcripts. Our inclusion of named entity verification is motivated by the findings in [33] that named entities can provide strong signals around multi-modal inconsistency.

Facial Verification. We define facial verification in this context as checking whether or not people named in the caption of a video actually appear in the video. To accomplish this, we identify people in captions and build a database of representations for them. People are identified with the named entity recognition (NER) feature in the spaCy [16] natural language processing library. Using spaCy's `en_core_web_trf` language model, which implements RoBERTa [20], we run NER on all captions, and take all strings with the `PERSON` label as names of people. These strings are compiled into a set of people whose names appear in our dataset.

Once all names are identified, we compute a representation for each person. First, we query Google Images for the top 10 results for each name, and consider them ground-truth references for the visual appearance of each name. Having multiple images per name allows us to capture potentially diverse lighting conditions, poses, ages, and camera angles.

Once reference images are collected, we use FaceNet [29] to compute facial recognition features for each image, selected for its relatively small feature size. Figure 1 shows how FaceNet features are used in our model. At inference time, FaceNet features are computed for a video's keyframes. We then take the cosine similarity between the features for names appearing in the caption and the features for each keyframe in the video. In practice, these keyframe features are pre-computed for efficiency. The similarity scores are passed on to our model's classification head to be used alongside features from other modalities.

This approach to person identification has a few drawbacks. The reference images of named entities from Google Images are not manually curated, and multiple people can appear in one single reference image. Additionally, in some cases, an individual might be referenced first by their full name, i.e. "Alice Appleseed," and then only by their first name, "Alice." Our NER approach does not account for this, but it is less of a problem for well-known individuals who can often be uniquely identified by their first or last name, such as "Kanye West" and "Kanye," or "Nancy Pelosi" and "Pelosi."

Name Verification. We also compare names in captions to audio transcripts, which provides an extra signal and can alleviate the problem where an individual might be a topic of discussion, rather than a visual subject.

We find that many names in audio transcripts have spelling errors but high phonetic similarity with their corresponding names in the captions. Therefore, to achieve fuzzy name matching, we compute learnable, character-based embeddings for the names which appear in captions and/or transcripts.

Given a string representing a named entity, we convert each character to its lower-case ASCII numerical value and pad to a maximum length of 64 characters. In our dataset, 100% of strings identified as names have at most 64 characters. We then feed this vector into a 2-layer fully connected network, with hidden size 64 and output size 32. These name embeddings are then passed on to our classification head for use along with other modalities, as shown in Fig. 1.

By taking in the numerical values of each character of a name, our embedding can learn to match phonetic patterns in names, and the patterns in which DS generates vowels and consonants for sounds in names. Thus, the embedding is able to approximate a textual name to sound conversion.

4.5   Facebook Reactions

Since our data is collected from Facebook, we have access to the Facebook reactions for each post. In Facebook, users can react to a post with: Like, Love, Wow, Haha, Sad, Angry, and Care. We hypothesize that reactions can provide a coarse measure of the semantics of an entire post, considering all of its modalities.

We take the normalized reactions as an input feature, shown in Fig. 1. To normalize reactions, we divide the raw count of each reaction by the total number of reactions a post received, so the model can ignore a post's popularity.

4.6   Ensemble Feature Extraction

We adopt a uni-modal ensemble approach to multi-modal fusion, as shown in Fig. 1. To classify whether or not a post is inconsistent, we take as input a video, a transcript, the normalized reactions to the video's pristine post, and a caption. In addition to the named entity verification features described in Sect. 4.4, we compute features for the caption, transcript, and video clip inputs.

Both the audio transcript and caption are processed using a pre-trained BERT [8] language model, implemented by HuggingFace [36]. When using the language model, inputs are truncated to their first 1024 characters, and split into two sets of characters with length 512 to accommodate the language model's maximum input length. In our dataset, 60% of audio transcripts and 99.97% of captions have at most 1024 characters.

Videos are processed using both a video-understanding network and an object detection network. For video understanding, we use S3D-MIL-NCE (S3D) [24], and for object detection, we use a ResNet50 model [14]. S3D is run on the full 32-frame sequence in each of the video clips, split by keyframe, while ResNet is run on each keyframe. We use the mixed_5c output of S3D, as recommended.

4.7   Multi-modal Fusion

For each modality, we learn an embedding to a semantic latent space, as shown in Fig. 1. Each embedding function is implemented as a 2-layer fully connected network, mapping from the output feature space of a feature extraction network to a common 256-dimensional latent space. The learned semantic embeddings for video clips, transcripts, and captions are concatenated and passed through a Long Short-Term Memory (LSTM) [15] module to condense information from the clips into one summary feature vector. This fuses multi-modal content at the clip level, before the output of the LSTM is concatenated with named entity verification features. This fusion approach is motivated by the early fusion methods proposed in [38]. The final combined feature vector is passed to our classification network. Our classifier is a 3-layer fully connected network, with input size 1096, hidden layer sizes 512 and 128, and output size 2.

5   Experiments

5.1   Experimental Design

We train our model with the dataset described in Sect. 4. We optimize the binary cross-entropy loss function, where our model classifies caption, audio transcript, and video appearance tuples as either pristine or inconsistent.

We report classification accuracy for our experiments, computed as the percentage of examples correctly identified as either pristine or inconsistent in our balanced test set. Our data is split such that 15% of the examples are reserved for the test set, and the other 85% for training and validation.

5.2   Results and Ablation Studies

Table 1. Binary classification accuracy (%) of heavily multi-modal models

Modality or feature removed								
Model	Names & Faces	Caption	Names	Video	Transcript	Faces	Reacts	None
Full	49.8	54.2	52.4	54.7	57.0	56.9	57.4	58.3
No OD	49.9	51.5	54.8	56.5	59.5	59.6	**60.5**	**60.5**

Table 2. Best model confusion matrix (%)

	Predict pristine	Predict inconsistent
Pristine examples	51.0	49.0
Inconsistent examples	28.6	71.4

Table 3. Binary classification accuracy (%) of uni- and bi-modal models

Modalities used				
Caption & Video	Video	Caption	Faces	Names
49.6	49.8	49.9	51.7	**53.5**

We perform a variety of ablation experiments to characterize the impact of each modality on the accuracy of our model. The authors are not aware of directly comparable work which detects semantic inconsistencies in the modalities included here, nor directly applicable benchmarks. Results are shown in Table 1, with each modality removed one-by-one. Due to the fact that removing object detection features improved model performance, we perform one-by-one removal ablation studies again, with object detection features always removed. These experiments are referred to as "No OD" models in Table 1. "Removing" a modality refers to removing its features or embeddings from our classifier.

For instance, removing video appearance makes the semantic video embeddings inaccessible to our classifier, although facial verification is still performed.

As seen in Table 1, best performance is achieved by using all modalities, except object detection features, and reaches classification accuracy of 60.5%. Table 2 shows the confusion matrix for this model. We observe that the model is more accurate when classifying inconsistent examples. Specifically, it can correctly detect inconsistency 71% of the time, and detects consistency 51% of the time. Table 3 shows results for models using one or two modalities.

We observe that named entities are key to model accuracy, as seen in Table 1, further confirming the importance of named entities demonstrated in [33]. Without facial verification, classification accuracy decreases slightly to 59.6%. Without comparing names between captions and transcripts, classification accuracy falls to 54.8%. Without either consistency check, accuracy falls to 49.9%. We find that named entities are not the only useful information provided by captions. As seen in Table 1, when caption embeddings are removed, accuracy falls to 54.2% and 51.5%, with and without object detection (OD) features, respectively. Combining of semantic embeddings and named entity verification is the best use of the information in the caption modality.

We note that video embeddings from S3D are more important than OD embeddings from ResNet. In fact, removing OD embeddings improves accuracy, while removing S3D embeddings lowers accuracy. When OD embeddings are present, removing S3D embeddings leads to 3.8% lower accuracy, and without OD embeddings, removing S3D embeddings leads to 4% lower accuracy. It could be that S3D features contain much of the relevant OD feature information for our task. Additionally, OD features are not temporally aware. Furthermore, the ResNet50 model we take features from is trained for image classification, which may be too general to be useful for modelling abstract video semantics.

We observe that Facebook reactions do not seem to provide a useful signal.

Finally, we observe that multi-modal fusion is necessary for achieving the best possible accuracy. Removing any one of our modalities decreases performance, with the exception of reactions. No uni-modal model can perform better than random; accuracy for uni- and bi-modal models is shown in Table 3. Caption-only and video-only models achieve 49.9% and 49.8% classification accuracy, respectively, confirming that our dataset does not have linguistic or visual bias. A model combining caption and video clip embeddings achieves 49.6% accuracy, highlighting the importance of incorporating additional modalities and features. A model which solely compares named entities in captions and transcripts achieves 53.5% accuracy, and a model which compares named entities in captions with facial verification features achieves 51.7% accuracy. While named entities are important, they are not sufficient to achieve the best results.

6 Conclusion

We have introduced a novel multi-modal semantic inconsistency detection system for use in real-world social media posts. We demonstrate the importance of making use of modalities beyond video appearance and captions, including transcripts, facial verification, and fuzzy named entity comparison.

We observe that fusion across modalities is key to detecting semantic inconsistencies. We find that named entities provide strong signals for detecting inconsistency, and that verifying named entities using both language-based and visual methods is better than only using one. Semantic consistency checks cannot be fully explained by named entity verification, however, highlighting the need to consider semantic embeddings for language and video.

Future work could explore attributing and characterizing inconsistencies. Modules for explainable facial verification and author attribution could take steps towards addressing this. Our approach would likely benefit from more data, and we are interested in expanding data collection to other social networks. Increasing the size of our dataset might also allow for more challenging inconsistencies during training time.

References

1. Abu-El-Haija, S., et al.: YouTube-8M: a large-scale video classification benchmark. ArXiv arXiv:1609.08675 (2016)
2. Agarwal, S., et al.: Detecting deep-fake videos from appearance and behavior. In: 2020 IEEE International Workshop on Information Forensics and Security (WIFS), pp. 1–6 (2020)
3. Aneja, S., Bregler, C., Nießner, M.: COSMOS: catching out-of-context misinformation with self-supervised learning. ArXiv arXiv: 2101.06278 [cs.CV] (2021)
4. Antol, S., et al.: VQA: Visual Question Answering. In: International Conference on Computer Vision (ICCV) (2015)
5. Araujo, A., et al.: Stanford I2V: a news video dataset for query-by-image experiments. In: ACM Multimedia Systems Conference (2015)
6. Bertasius, G., Wang, H., Torresani, L.: Is space-time attention all you need for video understanding? arXiv: 2102.05095 (2021)
7. CrowdTangle Team: CrowdTangle. Facebook, CA, United States (2021)
8. Devlin, J., et al.: BERT: pre-training of deep bidirectional transformers for language understanding. arXiv: 1810.04805 [cs.CL] (2019)
9. FFmpeg Developers. Version 4.3.1 (2020). http://ffmpeg.org/
10. Guarnera, L., Giudice, O., Battiato, S.: DeepFake detection by analyzing convolutional traces. In: CVPR, June 2020
11. Güera, D., Delp, E.J.: DeepFake video detection using recurrent neural networks. In: 2018 15th IEEE International Conference on Advanced Video and Signal Based Surveillance (AVSS), pp. 1–6 (2018)
12. Habibian, A., et al.: Video2vec embeddings recognize events when examples are scarce. In: IEEE Transactions on Pattern Analysis and Machine Intelligence, pp. 2089–2103 (2017)
13. Hannun, A., et al.: Deep speech: scaling up end-to-end speech recognition. arXiv: 1412.5567 [cs.CL] (2014)
14. He, K., et al.: Deep residual learning for image recognition. arXiv: 1512.03385 [cs.CV] (2015)
15. Hochreiter, S., Schmidhuber, J.: Long short-term memory. Neural Comput. 9(8), 1735–1780 (1997). ISSN: 0899-7667

16. Honnibal, M., et al.: spaCy: industrial-strength natural language processing in Python (2020). https://doi.org/10.5281/zenodo.1212303
17. Kay, W., et al.: The kinetics human action video dataset. ArXiv arXiv:1705.06950 (2017)
18. Li, G., et al.: Unicoder-VL: a universal encoder for vision and language by cross-modal pre-training. arXiv: 1908.06066 [cs.CV] (2019)
19. Li, L., et al.: HERO: hierarchical encoder for video+language omni-representation pre-training. In: EMNLP, pp. 2046–2065. Association for Computational Linguistics, November 2020
20. Liu, Y., et al.: RoBERTa: a robustly optimized BERT pretraining approach. arXiv: 1907.11692 [cs.CL] (2019)
21. Lu, J., et al.: ViLBERT: pretraining task-agnostic visiolinguistic representations for vision-and-language tasks. arXiv: 1908.02265 (2019)
22. Luo, G., Darrell, T., Rohrbach, A.: NewsCLIPpings: automatic generation of out-of-context multimodal media. arXiv: 2104.05893 (2021)
23. Luo, H., et al.: UniVL: a unified video and language pre-training model for multi-modal understanding and generation. arXiv:2002.06353 (2020)
24. Miech, A., et al.: End-to-end learning of visual representations from uncurated instructional videos. In: CVPR (2020)
25. Miech, A., et al.: HowTo100M: learning a text-video embedding by watching hundred million narrated video clips. In: ICCV (2019)
26. Mittal, T., et al.: Emotions don't lie: an audio-visual deepfake detection method using affective cues. In: Proceedings of the 28th ACM International Conference on Multimedia, MM 2020, Seattle, WA, USA, pp. 2823–2832. Association for Computing Machinery (2020). ISBN: 9781450379885
27. Peiser, J.: The rise of the robot reporter. The New York Times, February, 2019
28. Popescu, A.C., Farid, H.: Exposing digital forgeries by detecting traces of resampling. IEEE Trans. Sig. Process. **53**(2), 758–767 (2005)
29. Schroff, F., Kalenichenko, D., Philbin, J.: FaceNet: a unified embedding for face recognition and clustering. In: 2015 IEEE Conference on Computer Vision and Pattern Recognition (CVPR) (2015)
30. Shekhar, R., et al.: FOIL it! Find One mismatch between Image and Language caption. In: Proceedings of the 55th Annual Meeting of the Association for Computational Linguistics (Volume 1: Long Papers), pp. 255–265. Association for Computational Linguistics, July 2017
31. Su, W., et al.: VL-BERT: pre-training of generic visual-linguistic representations. arXiv: 1908.08530 [cs.CV] (2020)
32. Tan, H., Bansal, M.: LXMERT: learning cross-modality encoder representations from transformers. In: Proceedings of the 2019 Conference on Empirical Methods in Natural Language Processing (2019)
33. Tan, R., Plummer, B.A., Saenko, K.: Detecting cross-modal inconsistency to defend against neural fake news. In: Empirical Methods in Natural Language Processing (EMNLP) (2020)
34. Wang, S., et al.: CNN-generated images are surprisingly easy to spot...for now. In: CVPR (2020)
35. Wang, S., et al.: Detecting photoshopped faces by scripting photoshop. In: ICCV, October 2019
36. Wolf, T., et al.: Transformers: state-of-the-art natural language processing. In: EMNLP: System Demonstrations, pp. 38–45. Association for Computational Linguistics, October 2020

37. Xie, S., et al.: Rethinking spatiotemporal feature learning: speed-accuracy trade-offs in video classification. arXiv: 1712.04851 [cs.CV] (2018)
38. Xu, H., et al.: Multilevel language and vision integration for Text-to-Clip retrieval. In: AAAI, vol. 33, no. 01, pp. 9062–9069, July 2019
39. youtube-dl. Version 2021.01.24.1 (2021). https://youtube-dl.org
40. Zellers, R., et al.: Defending against neural fake news. In: Advances in Neural Information Processing Systems, vol. 32 (2019)
41. Zhao, H., et al.: Multi-attentional deepfake detection. In: Proceedings of the IEEE/CVF Conference on Computer Vision and Pattern Recognition (CVPR), pp. 2185–2194, June 2021

EEG Emotion Recognition Based on Dynamically Organized Graph Neural Network

Hanyu Li[1,2], Xu Zhang[1,2(✉)], and Ying Xia[1,2]

[1] Department of Computer Science and Technology, Chongqing University of Posts and Telecommunitcations, Chongqing, China
s190201010@stu.cqupt.edu.cn, {zhangx,xiaying}@cqupt.edu.cn
[2] Chongqing Engineering Research Center of Spatial Big Data Intelligent Technology, Chongqing, China

Abstract. Emotion recognition based on EEG has a wide range of applications in the e-healthcare systems, especially it helps diagnose and treat a variety of mental illnesses such as depression. Due to individual differences between subjects and the non-stationary characteristic of EEG, traditional emotion recognition methods are difficult to achieve good performance. In this paper, we propose a dynamically organized graph neural network (DOGNN) for EEG-based emotion recognition. Unlike previous studies that require a fixed graph structure, the proposed DOGNN method can dynamically learn the intrinsic relationship between different electroencephalogram (EEG) channels based on frequency band information, and further, construct graph structure for every subject. We conduct extensive experiments on two open public datasets (SEED and SEED-IV). The experimental evaluation exhibits that the proposed method achieved better performance. In addition, we visualize the topographic maps for different frequency bands learned by the proposed model and the result is consistent with previous neuroscience studies. This demonstrates that our approach is capable of capturing more effective the frequency band and spatial features for EEG emotion recognition.

Keywords: EEG · Emotion recognition · Graph neural network · Graph construction

1 Introduction

Emotion is a psychophysiological process accompanied by complex neural processes and physiological changes, and reflects human thoughts, feelings, and behavior. Emotion recognition has always been a hot research topic in the academic and industrial domain, and has attracted the attention of many scholars. Especially in the medical field, emotion recognition plays an important role in the

Supplementary Information The online version contains supplementary material available at https://doi.org/10.1007/978-3-030-98355-0_29.

precaution, diagnosis, and treatment of various mental diseases, such as depressive disorder, schizophrenia. However, manual diagnosis is a time-consuming process that results in subjective interpretation and inter-observer variability, experts began to benefit from computer-assisted diagnosis. Under the condition of limited access to healthcare services and doctors, automation is undoubtedly beneficial which provides a wide range of services and less cost. Deep learning and machine learning provide exciting ways to pursue automated healthcare systems by extracting features from complex emotional information and training applicable models.

The required information for emotion recognition is obtained from subjects through collecting non-physiological signals such as human postures, facial expression, and speech; and other methods are a collection of physiological signals, like functional magnetic resonance imaging (fMRI) [1], functional near-infrared spectroscopy (fNIRS) [2], electroencephalogram (EEG) [3]. Compared with easily disguised non-physiological signals, emotion recognition based on physiological signals is more objective and reliable. Among these physiological signals, EEG has advantages of non-invasive, high temporal resolution, and low financial cost. So, EEG has a wide range of applications in emotion recognition.

In the past few years, machine learning methods and signal processing methods have been presented by a large number of studies for EEG emotion recognition. Emotion recognition methods usually consist of two parts, namely discriminative feature extraction and emotion classification. Generally, we can extract EEG features for emotion recognition from the time-domain and frequency-domain. Liu et al. [4]. Duan et al. [5] and Zheng et al. [7] divided the EEG signal into 5 frequency bands, and then extract EEG features, such as the differential entropy (DE), the power spectral density (PSD), the rational asymmetry (RASM), and the differential asymmetry (DASM) feature for each frequency band.

For the emotional classification problem, both machine learning and deep learning achieved high performance. Compared with traditional machine learning, deep learning generates new features from limited series of EEG features located in the training dataset, which saves a lot of time in mining the relationships between the EEG signals [6]. Convolutional neural network (CNN) is one of the most successful deep learning methods which had been widely used to deal with various classification problems. Yang et al. [8] proposed to construct a 3D representation feature by combining EEG signals from different frequency bands while retaining the spatial information between channels, and use CNN to classify. However, these traditional CNN methods can not capture complex neighborhood information as they analyze local information based on fixed connections (determined by convolution kernel), resulting in limited interpretability of the anatomical structures and analysis of functions.

Graph neural network (GNN) is another currently popular deep learning method that aims to build neural networks based on graph theory. Zhong et al. [9] proposed a regularized graph neural network (RGNN) which uses the biological topology among different brain regions to capture both local and global interchannel relations. Song et al. [10] proposed a novel dynamical graph convolutional neural networks (DGCNN) which dynamically learn the internal relationship between different EEG electrodes and express it in the form of an adjacency matrix.

Inspired by the above studies, in this paper we proposed a novel dynamically organized graph neural network (DOGNN) for EEG emotion recognition and evaluated the model on two publicly available datasets: SEED and SEED-IV. The main contributions of this paper can be summarized as follows: **1.** The DOGNN can dynamically organize the graph construction module according to interchannel connection and information for each frequency band. At the same time, we combine some biological knowledge to capture the relationship between local and global inter-channel relationships. Moreover, We combine cross-subject adversarial domain training to increase the generalization of the model. **2.** We analyze the emotional neuronal activities between channels from the perspective of frequency bands, and it turns out that, prefrontal and centro-parietal regions may be the most informative regions. Moreover, we note β, γ bands have a wider and deeper activation in the prefrontal region, which shows the β, γ bands may have more discriminative features for detecting negative emotions than the other frequency bands in the prefrontal region.

This article is structured as follows. In Sect. 2, the dataset information. Section 3, introduces feature extraction and our model in detail. In Sect. 4, we introduce the experimental setup, and the performance analysis of DOGNN. Finally, we summarize the paper in Sect. 5.

2   Emotional EEG Databases

We conduct extensive experiments on two open emotion recognition datasets, SEED [11] and SEED-IV [7]. In the SEED and SEED-IV datasets, there are 15 subjects (7 males and 8 females) in the experiments. Before collecting SEED and SEED-IV datasets, a series of different types of film clips were used as emotional stimulation materials. The SEED dataset includes three types of emotional stimulation materials (positive, neutral, negative) and The SEED-IV includes four types (happy, sad, fear, neutral). During the experiments, each subject watched film clips while his/her EEG signals were recorded at a sampling rate 1000 Hz with the ESI NeuroScan System, which had a 62-channel cap according to the 10–20 system. For the SEED and SEED-IV datasets, each subject has three experiments, and each experiment was performed at an interval of no less than one week. In addition, after the clip stimuli, the subjects were required to fill out a self-assessment to ensure that the subjects were evoked with the expected emotion.

The raw EEG data were down-sampled from 1000 Hz to 200 Hz. To further filter the noise and remove the artifacts, bandpass frequency filters of 0–75 and 1–75 Hz were applied to SEED and SEED-IV. After that, the filtered EEG signals of each channel are divided into 1-s and 4-s length segments without overlapping for SEED and SEED-IV datasets, respectively. The segments are attached with the label of the corresponding emotional labels. For the SEED datasets, each subject has 3394 data samples on the SEED dataset. For the SEED-IV dataset, each subject has three different experiments. Therefore, there are 851,832 and 822 data samples in the three experiments, respectively.

In studies of EEG emotion, researchers tended to extracted features as input data instead of using raw EEG time series. These two data sets provide five different EEG feature types including differential entropy (DE), power spectral density (PSD), differential asymmetry (DASM), differential caudality (DCAU), and rational asymmetry (RASM). A large number of previous studies have shown that the DE feature is more discriminative for emotion recognition [9,10].

In this paper, we use the DE feature as input for the model. The DE feature is extracted from the segment at the frequency band of δ (1–3 Hz), θ (4–7 Hz), α (8–13 Hz), β (14–30 Hz), and γ (31–50 Hz) and Specific definition of DE is as follows.

$$\mathrm{h}(x) = -\int_{-\infty}^{\infty} \frac{1}{\sqrt{2\pi\sigma^2}} e^{\frac{(x-\mu)^2}{2\sigma^2}} \log \frac{1}{\sqrt{2\pi\sigma^2}} e^{\frac{(x-\mu)^2}{2\sigma^2}} dx = \frac{\log 2\pi e \sigma^2}{2} \qquad (1)$$

where x is a time series that obeys the Gaussian distribution, that is, $x \sim N\left(\mu, \delta^2\right)$, and σ is the variance of x, and e is the Euler constant. Since the EEG had 62 channels, the feature dimension of each segment was $62 \times 5 = 310$.

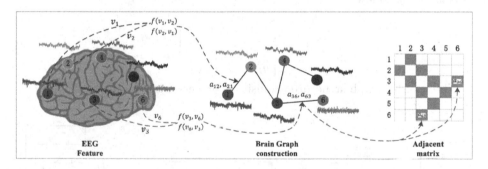

Fig. 1. This is an example of general brain construction functions. $f(v_i, v_j)$ is the distance function between different channels.

3   Method

Electrodes of EEG signals are irregularly distributed on the surface of the subject's brain. Therefore, EEG signals can be constructed as a graph representation that represents physical or functional connectivity across different brain regions. Here, the definition of the EEG signal on the connected graph is as follows:

$$\begin{aligned} G &= (\mathcal{V}, \mathcal{E}, A) \\ \mathcal{V} &= \{v_i \mid i = 1, \ldots, N\} \\ \varepsilon &= \{e_{ij} \mid v_i, v_j \in \mathcal{V}\} \\ A &= \{a_{ij}\} \end{aligned} \qquad (2)$$

where $\mathcal{V}$ represents the set of nodes with the number of N in the graph G, $\mathcal{E}$ denotes the set of edges connecting these nodes, $A \in R^{N \times N}$ is the adjacency matrix, describing the importance of connections between any two nodes in $\mathcal{V}$, and its elements a_{ij} denotes the adjacent connection weight between nodes v_i and v_j. Figure 1 demonstrates appliance example of the EEG signal in the brain graph structure.

In this paper, unlike many previous studies based on a predefined graph structure, we proposed a graph function to dynamically organize graphs of inter-channel relationships that according to input EEG emotion features in different frequency bands. The adjacent weight a_{kij} of the graph function corresponding to the k-th frequency band is defined by function $f(v_{ki}, v_{kj})$ as

$$a_{kij} = f(v_{ki}, v_{kj}) = \frac{\exp\left(\theta(v_{ki})\theta(v_{kj})^T\right)}{\sum_{i=1}^{N}\exp\left(\theta(v_{ki})\theta(v_{kj})^T\right)} \tag{3}$$

where $v \in R^{1 \times 1 \times F}$ is a feature vector of one frequency band of one node in $V \in R^{K \times N \times F}$, there are a total of N nodes (EEG channels) and K frequency bands (K=5), θ is the sigmoid activation function. The exponential function is a softmax activation function for normalization and obtains a bounded adjacent weight matrix. Therefore, the adjacent matrix $A_k(k = 1, \ldots, K)$ can be represented as follows:

$$A_k = \begin{bmatrix} a_{k11} & \cdots & a_{k1\,N} \\ \vdots & \ddots & \vdots \\ a_{kN1} & \cdots & a_{kNN} \end{bmatrix} \tag{4}$$

The specific graph structure acquisition process is shown in Fig. 2.

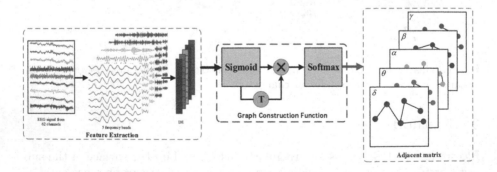

Fig. 2. The process of automatically constructing graph structure.

Neuroscience has discovered that the left and right hemispheres of the human brain are asymmetrical with emotional responses [12]. Besides, adding information about the asymmetry of neuronal activity between the left and right hemispheres to the model has a positive effect on emotion recognition in previous studies showing [9, 20]. To take advantage of the asymmetry between the hemispheres, we set the inter-channel relations in A_k to $[-1, 0]$ as follows:

$$A_{kjj} = -1 \times A_{kij} \tag{5}$$

where (i, j) is the index of channel pairs: (FP1, FP2), (AF3, AF4), (F5, F6), (FC5, FC6), (C5, C6), (CP5, CP6), (P5, P6), (PO5, PO6) and (O1, O2).

Spectral graph convolution is a popular signal processing method for graph data operation and has been successfully used for medical diagnosis [13]. Next, we applied spectral graph convolution in our model to process features. Let L denote the normalized graph Laplacian matrix and can be expressed as

$$L = I - D^{-\frac{1}{2}} A D^{-\frac{1}{2}} = U \Lambda U^T \tag{6}$$

where I is an identity matrix, D is the diagonal degree matrix with $D_{ii} = \sum_j A_{ij}$ ($A \in R^{N \times N}$ is our adjacent weight matrix A_k, note that we use the absolute values of A to compute the diagonal degree matrix D since A has negative entries), the columns of $U \in R^{N \times N}$ is the matrix of eigenvectors and constitute the Fourier basis, and $\Lambda \in R^{N \times N}$ is a diagonal matrix of its eigenvalues. The operation of spectral graph convolution can be defined as the multiplication of a signal $x \in R^n$ (a scalar for each node) with a filter Θ denoted by $\Theta *_G x$, can be expressed as

$$\Theta *_G x = \Theta(L)x = \Theta \left(U \Lambda U^T \right) x = U \Theta(\Lambda) U^T x \tag{7}$$

according to this definition, a graph signal x is filtered by a filter Θ with multiplication between Θ and graph Fourier transform $U^T x$ [14].

The outputs of the graph convolution layer of every frequency band were flattened and concatenated as a new feature vector. This new feature vector will be fed into classifier layers to predict emotional states. Considering EEG signals is the individual differences across subjects and the non-stationary characteristic of EEG, which hinder the generalization of trained classifiers among different subjects. To improve the generalization of model cross subjects, we apply a domain adversarial method [15] to reduce the discrepancies between source and target domain, i.e., training sets and testing sets, respectively. The domain adversarial method has two classifiers, i.e., an emotion label classifier and a domain classifier. The label classifier produces emotion label predictions of subjects according to the input, and the domain classifier learns a prediction of the corresponding domain. The loss function is defined as

$$\frac{1}{n_s} \sum_{i=1}^{n_s} L_y \left(C_y \left(p_i \right), y_i \right) + \frac{1}{n_s + n_t} \sum_{i=1}^{n_s + n_t} L_d \left(C_d \left(p_i \right), d_i \right) \tag{8}$$

where n_s and n_t is data sample number of source and target domain, respectively. $L_y \left(C_y \left(p_i \right), y_i \right)$ denotes the loss for the emotion label prediction $C_y \left(p_i \right)$ when the true label is y_i and p_i is the new feature vector that we get from the graph convolution layer. $L_d \left(C_d \left(p_i \right), d_i \right)$ is the loss for domain prediction $C_d \left(p_i \right)$ when the true domain is d_i. Base on the graph and domain adversarial method, we propose DOGNN as shown in Fig. 3.

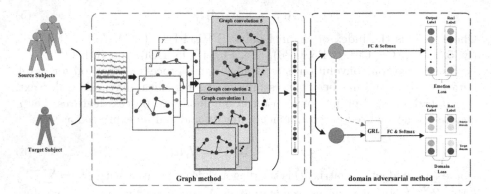

Fig. 3. This is the overall architecture of our DOGNN model. FC denotes the fully connected layer. GRL denotes the gradient reversal layer.

4   Experiments

4.1   Experiment Setup

To evaluate the effect of DOGNN, we conduct cross-subject emotion recognition in the SEED and SEED-IV. We adopted the leave-one-subject-out (LOSO) cross-validation strategy [16] to evaluate our proposed DOGNN. The DE features of 14 subjects in SEED/SEED-IV are used as the training dataset and the dataset of the remaining one subject is the testing dataset. Repeating this procedure to use the DE features of each subject as the testing dataset, using the mean accuracy (acc) and standard deviation (std) as the model's performance. Moreover, we implemented DOGNN using Pytorch on one Nvidia 1080Ti GPU. We optimize our model parameters with Adam. We empirically set 0.5 at the output fully connected layer, and batch size of 200.

4.2   Experiment Results

In this section, we validate the efficiency of our DOGNN model, we compared our model with the various existed representative methods of EEG emotion recognition in the past on both SEED and SEED-IV. The result is shown in Table 1. With the DE features, the DOGNN achieved averaged accuracy of 88.53% on the SEED dataset and 73.55% on the SEED-IV dataset. Our model is higher than the RGNN which is based on predefined and fixed graph structure on the SEED dataset. This shows based on fixed graph structure according to prior knowledge could not properly model the dynamic brain signals of different subjects in different emotional states with the data increasing. Moreover, the classification performance of our model is better than other baseline methods both in SEED and SEED-IV which shows the effectiveness of our DOGNN model in cross-subject emotion recognition.

Table 1. The mean accuracies (acc) and standard deviations (std) in SEED and SEED-IV for cross-subjects EEG emotion recognition experiment.

Method	SEED (acc/std)	SEED-IV (acc/std)
SVM	56.73/16.29	37.99/12.52
TCA [17]	63.64/14.88	56.56/13.77
SA [18]	69.00/10.89	64.44/09.46
DANN [19]	79.14/13.14	54.63/08.03
DAN [19]	83.81/08.56	58.87/08.13
DGCNN [10]	79.95/09.02	52.82/09.23
BiDANN-S [20]	84.14/06.87	65.59/10.39
A-LSTM [21]	72.18/10.85	55.03/09.28
R2G-STNN [22]	84.16/07.63	–
BiHDM [23]	85.40/07.53	69.03/08.66
MS-STM [24]	84.00/08.30	67.73/13.15
TANN [25]	84.41/08.75	68.00/08.35
RGNN [9]	85.30/06.72	**73.84**/08.02
Ours	**88.53**/05.67	73.55/10.19

4.3 Discussion

In this section, we discuss performance differences of the DOGNN model with different features. We discuss the performance of adding the prior knowledge of the asymmetry of the brain and which channel pairs have a positive effect on the model. Besides, we analyze important brain regions and inter-channel relations in the different frequency bands for emotion recognition.

Figure 4 shows five kinds of features' performance in our model, i.e., DE, PSD, DASM, DCAU, and RASM. We found that the DE feature has the best performance in emotion recognition, reaching 88.53%, followed by PSD, which shows that DE feature is more discriminated compared with other features. This finding is consistent with previous research [10].

Moreover, we compare the performance of 3 indexes of channel pairs in SEED and SEED-IV datasets. The indexes of channel pairs are shown in Fig. 5. As shown in Fig. 6, in the SEED-IV data set, adding indexes of channel pairs was better than not adding in the performance of emotion recognition. However, in the SEED dataset, this advantage decreased, indicating that when the dataset was small, the addition of prior knowledge about brain emotion had a positive impact on the classification effect.

To analyze the interchannel relationships of the different frequency bands in emotion recognition, we obtained five average adjacent matrixes which are composed of the corresponding frequency band information. We extracted the diagonal elements of five adjacent matrixes and transformed them into topographic maps for easy analysis, which is shown in Fig. 7. We note that the pre-

352   H. Li et al.

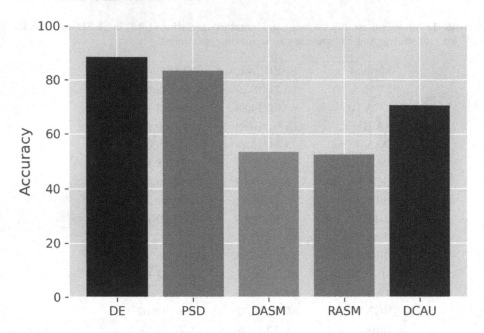

Fig. 4. The performance of different indexes of channel pairs.

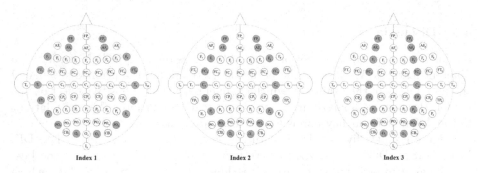

Fig. 5. These are 3 kinds of indexes. Index 1 includes (FP1, FP2), (AF3, AF4), (F7, F8), (FT7, FT8), (T7, T8), (TP7, TP8), (P7, P8), (PO7, PO8) and (O1, O2). Index 2 is our model's channel pairs. Index 3 includes (FP1, FP2), (AF3, AF4), (F3, F4), (FC3, FC4), (C3, C4), (CP3, CP4), (P3, P4), (PO5, PO6) and (O1, O2).

frontal and centro-parietal electrodes (e.g. F7, CPZ) have the largest weights in the topographic maps for all the frequency bands. Activation of the prefrontal and parietal regions was associated with both positive and negative emotions, consistent with previous research [26,27]. Moreover, in Fig. 7, we can see that activation of β, γ in the right-prefrontal region is stronger than δ, θ, α, indicating that, β, γ contains more discriminative information for negative emotion recognition.

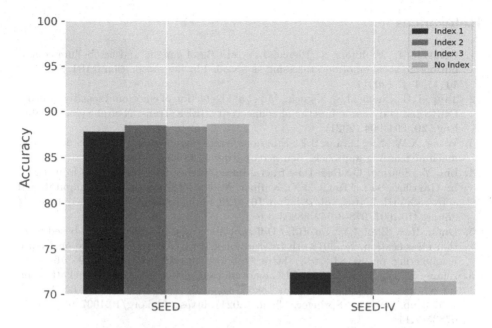

Fig. 6. The performance of different indexes of channel pairs.

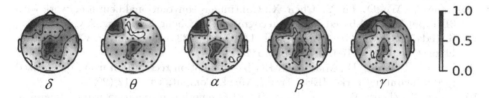

Fig. 7. The topographic maps learned by DOGNN

5 Conclusion

In this paper, we proposed a novel DOGNN method for cross-subject EEG signal emotion recognition. The DOGNN method combines some biological knowledge that can dynamically organize the graph construction module according to interchannel connection for each frequency band. Besides, to improve the generalization of the model, we apply a domain adversarial method to reduce the discrepancies across subjects. Our model outperform state-of-arts methods on SEED, and achieve good performance on SEED-IV.

Acknowledgments. This research is supported by National Natural Science Foundation of China (41571401), Chongqing Natural Science Foundation (cstc2019jscx-mbdxX0021), Major Industrial Technology Research and Development Project of Chongqing High-tech Industry (D2018-82).

References

1. Ceravolo, L., Frühholz, S., Pierce, J., et al.: Basal ganglia and cerebellum contributions to vocal emotion processing as revealed by high-resolution fMRI. Sci. Rep. **11**(1), 1–15 (2021)
2. Tang, T.B., Chong, J.S., Kiguchi, M., et al.: Detection of emotional sensitivity using fNIRS based dynamic functional connectivity. IEEE Trans. Neural Syst. Rehabil. Eng. **29**, 894–904 (2021)
3. Wang, X.W., Nie, D., Lu, B.L.: Emotional state classification from EEG data using machine learning approach. Neurocomputing **129**, 94–106 (2014)
4. Liu, Y., Sourina, O.: Real-time fractal-based valence level recognition from EEG. In: Gavrilova, M.L., Tan, C.J.K., Kuijper, A. (eds.) Transactions on Computational Science XVIII. LNCS, vol. 7848, pp. 101–120. Springer, Heidelberg (2013). https://doi.org/10.1007/978-3-642-38803-3_6
5. Duan, R.N., Zhu, J.Y., Lu, B.L.: Differential entropy feature for EEG-based emotion classification. In: 2013 6th International IEEE/EMBS Conference on Neural Engineering, pp. 81–84 (2013). https://doi.org/10.1109/NER.2013.6695876
6. Zhang, X., Du, T., Zhang, Z.: EEG emotion recognition based on channel attention for e-healthcare applications. In: Lokoč, J., et al. (eds.) MMM 2021. LNCS, vol. 12573, pp. 159–169. Springer, Cham (2021). https://doi.org/10.1007/978-3-030-67835-7_14
7. Zheng, W.L., Liu, W., Lu, Y., et al.: EmotionMeter: a multimodal framework for recognizing human emotions. IEEE Trans. Cybern. **49**(3), 1110–1122 (2018)
8. Yang, Y., Wu, Q., Fu, Y., Chen, X.: Continuous convolutional neural network with 3D input for EEG-based emotion recognition. In: Cheng, L., Leung, A.C.S., Ozawa, S. (eds.) ICONIP 2018. LNCS, vol. 11307, pp. 433–443. Springer, Cham (2018). https://doi.org/10.1007/978-3-030-04239-4_39
9. Zhong, P., Wang, D., Miao, C.: EEG-based emotion recognition using regularized graph neural networks. IEEE Trans. Affect. Comput. **14**, 1–12 (2020)
10. Song, T., Zheng, W., Song, P., et al.: EEG emotion recognition using dynamical graph convolutional neural networks. IEEE Trans. Affect. Comput. **11**(3), 532–541 (2018)
11. Zheng, W.L., Lu, B.L.: Investigating critical frequency bands and channels for EEG-based emotion recognition with deep neural networks. IEEE Trans. Auton. Ment. Dev. **7**(3), 162–175 (2015)
12. Tucker, D.M.: Lateral brain function, emotion, and conceptualization. Psychol. Bull. **89**(1), 19 (1981)
13. Ahmedt-Aristizabal, D., Armin, M.A., Denman, S., et al.: Graph-based deep learning for medical diagnosis and analysis: past, present and future. arXiv preprint arXiv:2105.13137 (2021)
14. Shuman, D.I., Narang, S.K., Frossard, P., et al.: The emerging field of signal processing on graphs: extending high-dimensional data analysis to networks and other irregular domains. IEEE Signal Process. Mag. **30**(3), 83–98 (2013)
15. Ganin, Y., Ustinova, E., Ajakan, H., et al.: Domain-adversarial training of neural networks. J. Mach. Learn. Res. **17**(1), 2096–3030 (2016)
16. Zheng, W.L., Lu, B.L.: Personalizing EEG-based affective models with transfer learning. In: Proceedings of the Twenty-Fifth International Joint Conference on Artificial Intelligence, vol. 7, pp. 2732–2738. AAAI Press, New York (2016). https://doi.org/10.5555/3060832.3061003

17. Pan, S.J., Tsang, I.W., Kwok, J.T., et al.: Domain adaptation via transfer component analysis. IEEE Trans. Neural Netw. **22**(2), 199–210 (2010)
18. Fernando, B., Habrard, A., Sebban, M., et al.: Unsupervised visual domain adaptation using subspace alignment. In: Proceedings of the IEEE International Conference on Computer Vision, pp. 2960–2967. IEEE (2013). https://doi.org/10.1109/ICCV.2013.368
19. Li, H., Jin, Y.-M., Zheng, W.-L., Lu, B.-L.: Cross-subject emotion recognition using deep adaptation networks. In: Cheng, L., Leung, A.C.S., Ozawa, S. (eds.) ICONIP 2018. LNCS, vol. 11305, pp. 403–413. Springer, Cham (2018). https://doi.org/10.1007/978-3-030-04221-9_36
20. Li, Y., Zheng, W., Zong, Y., et al.: A bi-hemisphere domain adversarial neural network model for EEG emotion recognition. IEEE Trans. Affect. Comput. **12**(2), 494–504 (2018)
21. Song, T., Zheng, W., Lu, C., et al.: MPED: a multi-modal physiological emotion database for discrete emotion recognition. IEEE Access **7**, 12177–12191 (2019)
22. Li, Y., Zheng, W., Wang, L., et al.: From regional to global brain: a novel hierarchical spatial-temporal neural network model for EEG emotion recognition. IEEE Trans. Affect. Comput. (2019)
23. Li, Y., Wang, L., Zheng, W., et al.: A novel bi-hemispheric discrepancy model for EEG emotion recognition. IEEE Trans. Cogn. Dev. Syst. **13**(2), 354–367 (2020)
24. Li, J., Qiu, S., Shen, Y.Y., et al.: Multisource transfer learning for cross-subject EEG emotion recognition. IEEE Trans. Cybern. **50**(7), 3281–3293 (2020)
25. Li, Y., Fu, B., Li, F., et al.: A novel transferability attention neural network model for EEG emotion recognition. Neurocomputing **447**, 92–101 (2021)
26. Quirk, G.J., Beer, J.S.: Prefrontal involvement in the regulation of emotion: convergence of rat and human studies. Curr. Opin. Neurobiol. **16**(6), 723–727 (2006)
27. Schutter, D.J.L.G., Putman, P., Hermans, E., et al.: Parietal electroencephalogram beta asymmetry and selective attention to angry facial expressions in healthy human subjects. Neurosci. Lett. **314**(1–2), 13–16 (2001)

An Unsupervised Multi-scale Generative Adversarial Network for Remote Sensing Image Pan-Sharpening

Yajie Wang[1], Yanyan Xie[2(✉)], Yanyan Wu[1], Kai Liang[2], and Jilin Qiao[2]

[1] Engineering Training Center, Shenyang Aerospace University, Shenyang, China
wangyajie@sina.com
[2] School of Computer Science, Shenyang Aerospace University, Shenyang, China

Abstract. Pan-sharpening of remote sensing images is an effective method to get high spatial resolution multi-spectral (HRMS) images by fusing low spatial resolution multi-spectral (LRMS) images and high spatial resolution panchromatic (PAN) images. Recently, many remote sensing images pan-sharpening methods based on convolutional neural networks (CNN) have been proposed and achieved excellent performance. However, two drawbacks still exist. On the one hand, since there are no ideal HRMS images as targets for learning, most existing methods require an extra effort to produce the simulated data for training. On the other hand, these methods ignore the local features of the original images. To address these issues, we propose an unsupervised multi-scale generative adversarial network method, which can train directly on the full-resolution images without down-sampling. Firstly, a multi-scale dense generator network is proposed to extract features from the original images to generate HRMS images. Secondly, two discriminators are used to protect the spectral information of LRMS images and spatial information of PAN images, respectively. Finally, to improve the quality of the fused image and implement training under the unsupervised setting, a new loss function is proposed. Experimental results based on QuickBird and GaoFen-2 data sets demonstrate that the proposed method can obtain much better fusion results for the full-resolution images.

Keywords: Remote sensing · Pan-sharpening · Unsupervised · Full-resolution images · Generative adversarial network

1 Introduction

The high spatial resolution multi-spectral (HRMS) images are used widely in remote sensing images research fields, such as environmental monitoring, road information extraction, and vegetation classification. However, due to the limitations of sensor technique and physical conditions, HRMS images are hard to get by a single sensor. So many remote sensing satellites, such as QuickBird, GaoFen-2, and WorldView3 usually carry two kinds of optical sensors to obtain two different images, namely high spatial resolution panchromatic (PAN) images, and low spatial resolution multi-spectral (LRMS)

© Springer Nature Switzerland AG 2022
B. Þór Jónsson et al. (Eds.): MMM 2022, LNCS 13142, pp. 356–368, 2022.
https://doi.org/10.1007/978-3-030-98355-0_30

images. The pan-sharpening aims to fuse information from PAN and LRMS images to generate images with high spatial and spectral resolution, simultaneously [1–3].

Up to now, various pan-sharpening methods have been proposed and can be roughly divided into four categories: component substitution (CS) methods, multiresolution analysis (MRA) methods, model-based optimization (MOP) methods, and deep learning-based methods. The CS method separates the LRMS image into spectral and spatial components through a spatial transform and replaces the spatial component with a PAN image to improve the spatial resolution of the multi-spectral image. It is easy to implement, but the fused image can suffer from severe spectral distortion [1, 2]. The CS methods include principal component analysis (PCA) [5] and Gram-Schmidt (GS) [6]. The MRA methods can overcome the problem of spectral distortion, but they can cause some spatial degradation [13], representative methods include wavelet transform [7] and Laplace pyramid transform [8]. The MOP methods implement pan-sharpening by establishing the relationship model between PAN images, LRMS images, and HRMS images, such as variational [9] and sparse representation [10] methods.

In recent years, convolutional neural networks (CNN) have been widely utilized in various research fields and achieved astonishing performance. To remote sensing images pan-sharpening, Masi et al. [11] first proposed a pan-sharpening method based on three-layer convolutional neural networks and obtained better results. The network architecture was original proposed for the super-resolution problem [24]. Then Yang et al. [12] presented a deep network architecture called PanNet, which incorporated the domain knowledge into the deep network architecture to improve fusion performance. Liu et al. [3] proposed a two-stream fusion network (TFNet) to solve the problem of generic pan-sharpening. Peng et al. [15] presented a novel pan-sharpening method based on a multi-scale dense network, which uses different size filters to extract features of the input images. Ma et al. [14] proposed an unsupervised generative adversity network for pan-sharpening (PAN-GAN). It can train directly on the original images. But PAN-GAN only uses a simple three-layer network structure in the generator, limiting its ability to solve complex problems.

Inspired by the multi-scale filtering network and the generative multi-adversity network, we propose an unsupervised multi-scale generative adversity network, which is trained on the original images without down-sampling to make full use of the spatial and spectral information of the original images. In this paper, different from the literature [14], we use a novel multi-scale dense generator network to extract features from PAN and LRMS images. Since we do not have reference images to calculated losses, the quality of the generated image can only be evaluated through the consistency difference between the generated HRMS image and the LRMS and PAN images. That is, to make the spectral information contained in the degraded HRMS image as close as possible to the LRMS image, the degraded spatial information is as close as possible to the PAN image. So we use two different discriminators to distinguish the degraded fusion image and the input original images. And affected by the unreferenced evaluation index, we use a new loss function to further improve the results of image fusion. Our contributions are summarized as follows:

– We propose a novel unsupervised multi-scale generative adversarial network architecture, which can be implemented on the original images without any preprocessing.

- We use the multi-scale features extraction network in the generator to extract rich, multi-scale features of the original images. And to reduce the parameters and optimize the network structure, dense networks are added to generator networks.
- We view quality with no reference (QNR) indexes [16], spectral loss, and spatial loss as a new loss function to optimize the proposed network.

The rest of this paper is organized as follows. Section 2 introduces the background of generative adversarial networks (GANs). Section 3 describes the details of our network architecture. Section 4 elaborates the loss function of the proposed method. In Sect. 5, the experimental results, evaluation, and comparisons are presented. The conclusion is given in Sect. 6.

2   Relate Work

In recent years, GANs have been widely used in various images generation tasks and achieved excellent results. GANs were proposed by Goodfellow et al. [18]. It consists of two parts: the generator and the discriminator. The main idea of GANs is to create a confrontation game between the generator and the discriminator. The generator G captures the distribution of real data and generates an approximate sample. The discriminator D distinguishes the generated sample from the real sample. But the stability of the original GANs is an important issue. Alec et al. introduced CNN to GANs and drops the pooling layer to improve the performance of GANs [20]. Arjovsky et al. proposed to use Wasserstein distance instead of the original GAN's cross-entropy loss function to increase the stability of the network [19]. Mao et al. proposed the least squares generative adversarial networks (LSGAN), which used the least square loss to replace the objective function of the original GANs to stabilize the training process [17]. In this paper, we use LSGAN as the basic GANs. The objective functions of LSGAN are defined as follows:

$$\min_{D} V_{LSGAN}(D) = \frac{1}{2}E_{x\sim P_{data}}(x)[(D(x) - b)^2] + \frac{1}{2}E_{z\sim P_z}(z)[(D(G(z)) - a)^2] \quad (1)$$

$$\min_{G} V_{LSGAN}(G) = \frac{1}{2}E_{z\sim P_z}(z)[(D(G(z)) - c)^2] \quad (2)$$

Where $D(\cdot)$ is the discriminator function; $G(\cdot)$ is the generator function; a and b represent labels of fake data and true data; c is the value of the fake data that the generator G wants discriminator D to believe. LSGAN collects samples x from the real distribution $P_{data}(x)$. The input of G is a random vector z generated by the prior distribution function $P_z(z)$. The data generated by the generator network is represented as G(z).

3   Unsupervised Multi-scale Generative Adversarial Network

3.1   Motivation and Overview of the Framework

At present, the pan-sharpening method based on deep learning has become a research hot spot. Different from the traditional remote sensing images fusion methods, deep learning-based methods focus on feature extraction, so it can obtain better HRMS images. However, the existing deep learning-based pan-sharpening methods have problems that cannot fully extract information on multiple scales of images and require reference images for training. Therefore, on the one hand, we use a multi-scale dense network in the generator to extract more information; on the other hand, we formulate the pan-sharpening problem as a multi-task problem, using two discriminators to implement the pan-sharpening under the unsupervised setting.

The framework of the proposed method is shown in Fig. 1. It includes the generator, spatial discriminator, and spectral discriminator. First, the PAN and the up-sampled LRMS images are stacked to form a 5-channel image as input of the generator to generate HRMS images. Then the spatial discriminator identifies the original PAN image and the average pooled HRMS image. The spectral discriminator identifies the original LRMS image and the down-sampled HRMS image. Each discriminator establishes an adversarial game with the generator to train separately, once these two discriminators cannot distinguish their inputs, the desirable HRMS image can be obtained.

3.2 Network Architecture of Generator

The generator network is designed based on the network framework of [15] and makes some improvements to protect more spectral and spatial information. It mainly includes four parts: shallow feature extraction layer, multi-scale feature extraction layer, global feature fusion layer, and image reconstruction layer. Figure 2 shows the architecture of our generator. First, different from the literature [15], the shallow feature extraction layer uses a 9×9 convolutional neural network to extract shallow features of the input images.

Second, the multiscale feature extraction layer uses three multiscale dense blocks (MDB) to extract more information from the shallow features. The network architecture of MDB is shown in Fig. 3. Each MDB contains four layers. The first three layers are the multiscale dense connected layer, and the last layer is a local feature fusion layer. Each multiscale dense connected layer has three convolution layers with the filter sizes of 3×3, 5×5, and 7×7, respectively.

Then the global feature fusion layer fuses all features extracted by the shallow feature extraction layer and multiscale feature extraction layer. It can reduce redundant information to a certain extent and learn the most significant information. The global feature fusion layer uses a 3×3 convolutional neural network.

Finally, the convolutional layer with 5×5 kernel and global residual learning are introduced to the image reconstruction to get the fused image.

To preserve more effective information and prevent gradient disappearance as the network deepens, some dense connections are added to the network. Dense connection means that the input of each layer is the result of the cascade of all the outputs of the previous layer. In addition, our generator network follows the deep convolutional generative adversarial network (DCGAN) rules [20]. Except for the last layer of the generator uses tanh and batch norm (BN) as the activation function, the rest layers of the generator all use rectified linear units (Relu) and BN as the activation function.

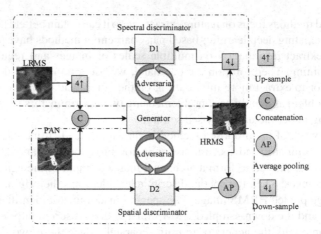

Fig. 1. The architecture of the proposed method

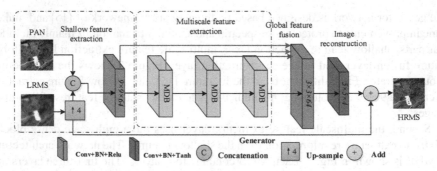

Fig. 2. The network architecture of the generator

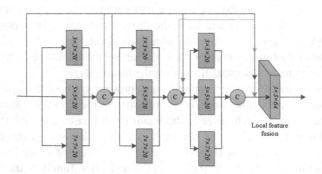

Fig. 3. The network architecture of the MDB

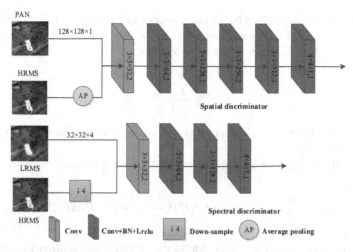

Fig. 4. The network architecture of the discriminator

3.3 Network Architecture of Discriminator

According to the characteristics of remote sensing image fusion, two different discriminators are used to solve the pan-sharpening problem. The network architecture of each discriminator is shown in Fig. 4. Both discriminators use a fully convolutional neural network as the underlying network. Since the resolution of the input images is different, spatial and spectral discriminators use different network layers. The spatial discriminator has six layers, except the filter size of the last layer is 4 × 4, the filter size of other layers is 3 × 3, and the extracted features in each layer are 16, 32, 64, 128, 256, and 1. The spectral discriminator has only four layers, and the structure is the same as the first four layers of the spatial discriminator. The discriminator network also follows the rules of DCGAN. The batch norm and leaky Relu are used as activation functions of each layer, except the first layer. The output of the discriminator is the classification results [14].

4 Loss Function

4.1 Loss Function of Generator

The loss functions of the generator include spatial loss, spectral loss, and QNR loss, as shown in Eq. 3.

$$L_g = L_{spatial} + L_{spectral} + L_{QNR} \tag{3}$$

Where L_g is the total loss of the generator, $L_{spatial}$ represents the spatial loss between the generated HRMS image and the original PAN image, $L_{spectral}$ represents the spectral loss between the generated HRMS image and the original LRMS image, L_{QNR} is the supplementary loss of the generator.

Since $l1$ loss function has a better performance in the pan-sharpening problem than the $l2$ loss function [21], $l1$ is used as a part of the loss function of the generator. The formula of the $l1$ loss function is shown as follows:

$$L1 = \frac{1}{N} \sum_{n=1}^{N} |x_n - y_n| \tag{4}$$

Where x and y refer to two kinds of images, and N represents the number of samples, $|\cdot|$ is the absolute value.

The spatial loss includes spatial adversarial loss and spatial information loss:

$$L_{spatial} = \omega \frac{1}{N} \sum_{n=1}^{N} (D_{spatial}(AP(I_f^n)) - d)^2 + \mu L1(\nabla AP(I_f^n), \nabla I_{pan}^n) \tag{5}$$

Where the first part on the right side is the spatial confrontation loss, the second part is the spatial information loss, ω is the parameter to balance the two losses, μ is the parameter used to balance the spectral loss and spatial loss, I_f^n represents the generated image; $AP(\cdot)$ is the average pooling operation, I_{pan}^n is the original PAN image; ∇ represents the high-pass filtering operation, extracts the high-frequency components of the fusion image and the PAN image, $D_{spatial}$ is the spatial discriminator, and d is the hyper-parameter.

The spectral loss includes spectral adversarial loss and spectral information loss. It is defined as follows:

$$L_{spectral} = \lambda \frac{1}{N} \sum_{n=1}^{N} (D_{spectral}(I_f^n) - c)^2 + L1(\downarrow I_f^n, I_{ms}^n) \tag{6}$$

Where the first part on the right side is the spectral confrontation loss, the second part is the spectral information loss, λ is the parameter to balance the two losses. $D_{spectral}$ is the spectral discriminator, $\downarrow$ represents the down-sampling, I_{ms}^n represents the original LRMS image, and c is the hyper-parameter.

Using the $l1$ loss function can optimize the quality of the fused image to a good level, but to further improve the spatial details and spectral quality of the fused image, the QNR is added to the loss function of the generator. QNR is widely used in the pan-sharpening problem, mainly including spatial distortion index D_s and spectral distortion index D_λ [16]. It is proposed based on the assumption that the spectral quality of the image does not change after fusion [2]. The loss function of QNR is defined as follows:

$$QNR = (1 - D_\lambda)(1 - D_S) \tag{7}$$

$$L_{QNR} = 1 - QNR \tag{8}$$

4.2 Loss Function of Discriminator

In this paper, the loss functions of LSGAN are used as the loss function of the spatial discriminator $D_{spatial}$ and the spectral discriminator $D_{spectral}$ [17]. The loss functions of discriminators are shown as follows:

$$D_{spectral} = \frac{1}{N} \sum_{n=1}^{N} (D_{spectral}(\downarrow I_f^n) - b)^2 + \frac{1}{N} \sum_{n=1}^{N} (D_{spectral}(I_{ms}^n) - a)^2 \qquad (9)$$

$$D_{spatial} = \frac{1}{N} \sum_{n=1}^{N} (D_{spatial}(AP(I_f^n)) - b)^2 + \frac{1}{N} \sum_{n=1}^{N} (D_{spatial}(I_{pan}^n) - a)^2 \qquad (10)$$

Where a and b represent the labels of the target image and the down-sampled HRMS image, $\downarrow I_f^n$ stands for the down-sampled HRMS image, I_{ms}^n and I_{pan}^n represent the LRMS and PAN images, respectively.

5 Experiments

5.1 Datasets

In this paper, QuickBird satellite images and GaoFen-2 satellite images are used to verify the effectiveness of the proposed method. The spatial resolution and wavelength range of the two satellite images are shown in Table 1. To accommodate the training and testing of the network, we crop the two remote sensing images into patches of size 128×128 to train and size 512×512 to test. Finally, The QuickBird data sets have 12,000 samples for training and 50 samples for testing; the GaoFen-2 data sets have 30,000 samples for training and 50 samples for testing.

Table 1. The spectral wavelength and spatial resolution of two data sets

Satellite	Spectral wavelength (nm)				Spatial resolution (m)	
	Red	Green	Blue	Nir	MS	PAN
QuickBird	630–690	520–600	450–520	760–890	0.6	2.4
GaoFen-2	630–690	520–590	450–520	770–890	0.8	3.2

5.2 Implement Details

The proposed model is implemented with Tensorflow 1.5 and trained on an RTX 2028TI. We use the Adaptive moment estimation (Adam) [24] method to optimize the weights of networks. The initial learning rate is 0.0001, the decay rate is 0.99, and the batch size is 8. According to literature [14] and experimental study, the hyper-parameters in Eqs. 5,

6, 9, and 10 are set as $\omega = 1e - 4$, $\lambda = 2e - 4$, $\mu = 100$, b is a random number ranging from 0.7 to 1.2, a is a number ranging from 0 to 0.3, c and d are a number ranging from 0.7 to 1.2.

To verify the superiority of the proposed model and compare it with other methods, we evaluate results under both Wald's protocol and full-resolution setting, respectively. Under Wald's protocol, the original PAN and LRMS images are degraded four times as the input images, the original LRMS images are regarded as the reference images. Five reference evaluation indexes are used to evaluate the proposed model and other models, including spectral angle mapping (SAM) [22], Quality index (Q4) [21], spatial correlation coefficient (SCC) [3], and erreur relative globale adimensionnelle de synthese (ERGAS) [3]. Under the full-resolution setting, since there are no ideal HRMS images as reference images, D_λ, D_s, and QNR are used as metrics to evaluate the quality of the fused images. When SCC, Q4, QNR are 1, SAM, ERGAS, D_λ, D_s are 0, the quality of the fused image is best. In this paper, we mainly research full-resolution images.

We compare the proposed method with several widely used pan-sharpening methods. The traditional methods have GSA [6], MTF-GLP [25], BDSD [4], and ATWT [6]. The supervised methods include PNN [11], PanNet [12], and PSMD-Net [15]. The unsupervised methods are Pan-GAN [14] and our proposed method. The traditional methods are implemented in MATLAB. The supervised and unsupervised methods are implemented in PyCharm.

5.3 Quantitative Comparison

Tables 2 and 3 show the average quantitative results of 50 test images from GaoFen-2 and QuickBird. The numbers in bold black represent the best performers on this metric. The first four metrics test the pan-sharpening images under the reduced-resolution setting. The later three metrics evaluate the pan-sharpening image under the full-resolution setting. From the two tables, we can view that our method obtains better average values on D_λ, D_s, and QNR, which is much better than all the other methods. However, on SCC, SAM, ERGAS, and Q4, our proposed method and Pan-Gan fall behind other CNN-based methods because they do not use the reference images to minimize the loss of the generated data and the label data in training. But our method also has better performance in all metrics in unsupervised methods. The results demonstrate that the proposed method has the powerful practical ability for full-resolution remote sensing images pan-sharpening.

5.4 Visual Comparison

Figures 5 and 6 show some representative fusion images from QuickBird and GaoFen-2 data sets. All the displayed images only contain the data of R, G, and B channels, and are obtained by the original LRMS and PAN images. In Figs. 5 and 6, (a) and (b) show the up-sampled LRMS image and PAN image, respectively. From Figs. 5 and 6, we can observe that all methods have enhanced the clarity of the image to varying degrees. However, the fused images of BDSD produce some color distortion; MTF-GLP and ATWT blur the results. And it can be observed that several deep learning-based methods also produce some spatial or spectral distortion. Among them, the results of Pan-GAN are similar to ours, but some missing spatial information is noticeable. Our method produces better results with less blurring and spectral distortions. The experimental results indicate that our proposed method can effectively preserve more spatial and spectral information in the full-resolution remote sensing images pan-sharpening.

Table 2. Average quality metrics of different methods on 50 satellite images from QuickBird

Method	SCC ↑	SAM ↓	ERGAS ↓	Q4 ↑	D_s ↓	D_λ ↓	QNR ↑
GSA	0.9197	8.7295	6.6957	0.9230	0.0565	0.0353	0.9102
BDSD	0.9328	10.046	8.5852	0.9130	0.0239	0.0366	0.9404
MTF_GLP	0.9302	8.6448	6.0102	0.9267	0.0418	0.0393	0.9205
ATWT	0.9235	7.4149	6.3250	0.8949	0.0654	0.0137	0.9218
PNN	0.9543	5.6535	4.6924	0.9427	0.0607	0.0361	0.9052
PanNet	**0.9576**	**5.5064**	**4.3109**	0.9432	0.0259	0.0236	0.9513
PSMD-Net	0.9482	5.6110	4.5623	**0.9453**	0.0641	0.0251	0.9125
Pan-Gan	0.9361	5.7405	4.7594	0.9347	0.0312	**0.0105**	0.9586
Proposed	0.9452	5.6942	4.6476	0.9420	**0.0205**	0.0116	**0.9681**

Table 3. Average quality metrics of different methods on 50 satellite images from GaoFen-2

Method	SCC ↑	SAM ↓	ERGAS ↓	Q4 ↑	D_s ↓	D_λ ↓	QNR ↑
GSA	0.6647	6.7000	10.6973	0.7911	0.2817	0.0366	0.6918
BDSD	0.6456	8.2215	11.2090	0.7692	0.0712	0.0463	0.8858
MTF_GLP	0.7252	6.1479	7.7845	0.8447	0.1681	0.2373	0.8120
ATWT	0.7218	6.5339	8.9857	0.8418	0.0991	0.0222	0.8809
PNN	0.8514	3.8514	4.6755	0.8503	0.0533	0.0179	0.9296
PanNet	**0.9135**	3.6618	4.4922	0.8784	0.0362	0.0287	0.9361
PSMD-Net	0.9089	**3.5687**	**4.4730**	**0.8869**	0.0308	0.0196	0.9502
Pan-Gan	0.8973	3.7186	4.6235	0.8692	0.0268	0.0143	0.9593
Proposed	0.9075	3.7963	4.5137	0.8712	**0.0256**	**0.0124**	**0.9623**

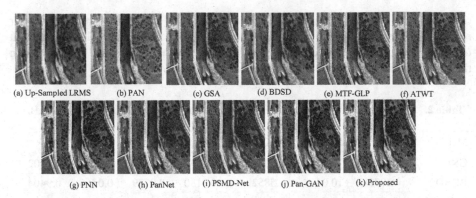

Fig. 5. Pan-sharpening results of different methods on the test image of QuickBird.

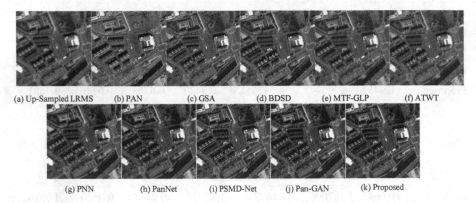

Fig. 6. Pan-sharpening results of different methods on the test image of GaoFen-2.

6   Conclusion

In this paper, we propose an unsupervised multi-scale generative adversarial network model for the pan-sharpening problem. The model consists of one generator and two discriminators to reduce both the spectral and spatial distortions. To preserve more spatial details and color characteristics to improve the performance of remote sensing images fusion, QNR is added to the loss function of the generator. The proposed method can be trained on either reduced-scale or full-scale images without ground truth and focuses on original PAN and LRMS images without any preprocessing step. The experiments on GaoFen-2 and QuickBird images demonstrate that our model obtains better evaluation metrics and preserves the spectral and spatial information well under the unsupervised setting. In the future, we will continue to study unsupervised methods and further improve the result of pan-sharpening.

References

1. Tian, X., Chen, Y., Yang, C., et al.: Variational pansharpening by exploiting cartoon-texture similarities. IEEE Trans. Geosci. Remote Sens. **60**, 1–6 (2021)

2. Luo, S., Zhou, S., Feng, Y., Xie, J.: Pansharpening via unsupervised convolutional neural networks. IEEE J. Select. Top. Appl. Earth Observ. Remote Sens. **13**, 4295–4310 (2020)
3. Liu, X., Wang, Y., Liu, Q.: Remote sensing image fusion based on two-stream fusion network. In: Schoeffmann, K., et al. (eds.) MMM 2018. LNCS, vol. 10704, pp. 428–439. Springer, Cham (2018). https://doi.org/10.1007/978-3-319-73603-7_35
4. Garzelli, A., Nencini, F., Capobianco, L.: Optimal MMSE PanSharpening of very high resolution multispectral images. IEEE Trans. Geosci. Remote Sens. **46**(1), 228–236 (2008)
5. Shahdoosti, H.R., Ghassemian, H.: Combining the spectral PCA and spatial PCA fusion methods by an optimal filter. Inf. Fusion. **27**, 150–160 (2016)
6. Vivone, G., et al.: A critical comparison among pansharpening algorithms. IEEE Trans. Geosci. Remote Sens. **53**(5), 2565–2586 (2014)
7. Jinju, J., Santhi, N., Ramar, K., Bama, B.S.: Spatial frequency discrete wavelet transform image fusion technique for remote sensing applications. Eng. Sci. Technol. Int. J. **22**(3), 715–726 (2019)
8. Aiazzi, B., Alparone, L., Barducci, A., Baronti, S., Pippi, I.: Multispectral fusion of multisensor image data by the generalized Laplacian pyramid. IEEE Int. Geosci. Remote Sens. Symp. **2**, 1183–1185 (1999)
9. Ballester, C., Caselles, V., Igual, L., Verdera, J., Rougé, B.: A variational model for P+ XS image fusion. Int. J. Comput. Vision **69**(1), 43–58 (2006)
10. Yu, X., Gao, G., Xu, J., Wang, G.: Remote sensing image fusion based on sparse representation. In: IEEE Geoscience and Remote Sensing Symposium, pp. 2858–2861 (2014)
11. Masi, G., Cozzolino, D., Verdoliva, L., Scarpa, G.: Pansharpening by convolutional neural networks. Remote Sens. **8**(7), 594 (2016)
12. Yang, J., Fu, X., Hu, Y., Huang, Y., Ding, X., Paisley, J.: PanNet: a deep network architecture for pan-sharpening. In: Proceedings of the IEEE International Conference on Computer Vision, pp. 5449–5457 (2017)
13. Wei, J., Xu, Y., Cai, W., Wu, Z., et al.: A two-stream multiscale deep learning architecture for pan-sharpening. IEEE J. Select. Top. Appl. Earth Observ. Remote Sens. **13**, 5455–5465 (2020)
14. Ma, J., Yu, W., Chen, C., Liang, P., Guo, X., Jiang, J.: Pan-GAN: an unsupervised pansharpening method for remote sensing image fusion. Inf. Fusion **62**, 110–120 (2020)
15. Peng, J., Liu, L., Wang, J., Zhang, E., Zhu, X., et al.: PSMD-Net: a novel Pan-Sharpening method based on a multiscale dense network. IEEE Trans. Geosci. Remote Sens. **59**(6), 4957–4971 (2021)
16. Alparone, L., Aiazzi, B., Baronti, S., Garzelli, A., Nencini, F., Selva, M.: Multispectral and panchromatic data fusion assessment without reference. Photogramm. Eng. Remote. Sens. **74**(2), 193–200 (2008)
17. Mao, X., Li, Q., Xie, H., Lau, R.Y., Wang, Z., Paul Smolley, S.: Least squares generative adversarial networks. In: Proceedings of the IEEE International Conference on Computer Vision, pp. 2794–802. (2017)
18. Goodfellow, I.J., et al.: Generative adversarial networks. arXiv preprint arXiv:1406.2661 (2014)
19. Arjovsky, M., Chintala, S., Bottou, L.: Wasserstein generative adversarial networks. In: International Conference on Machine Learning, pp. 214–223 (2017)
20. Radford, A., Metz, L., Chintala, S.: Unsupervised Representation Learning with Deep Convolutional Generative Adversarial Networks. arXiv preprint. arXiv:1511.6434 (2020)
21. Chen, J., Pan, Y., Chen, Y.: Remote sensing image fusion based on Bayesian GAN. arXiv:2009.09465 (2020)
22. Yuhas, R.H., Goetz, A.F., Boardman, J.W.: Discrimination among semi-arid landscape endmembers using the spectral angle mapper (SAM) algorithm. In: Proceedings of the Summaries 3rd Annual JPL Airborne Geoscience Workshop, vol. 1, pp. 147–149 (1992)

23. Dong, C., Loy, C., He, K., Tang, X.: Image super-resolution using deep convolutional networks. IEEE Trans. Pattern Anal. Mach. Intell. **38**(2), 295–307 (2016)
24. Kingma, D.P., Ba, J.: Adam: a method for stochastic optimization. arXiv preprint arXiv:1412.6980 (2014)
25. Aiazzi, B., Alparone, L., Baronti, S., Garzelli, A., Selva, M.: MTF-tailored multiscale fusion of high-resolution MS and Pan imagery. Photogramm. Eng. Remote. Sens. **72**(5), 591–596 (2006)

Leveraging Selective Prediction for Reliable Image Geolocation

Apostolos Panagiotopoulos, Giorgos Kordopatis-Zilos[✉],
and Symeon Papadopoulos

Information Technologies Institute, CERTH, 60361 Thessaloniki, Greece
{apanag,georgekordopatis,papadop}@iti.gr

Abstract. Reliable image geolocation is crucial for several applications, ranging from social media geo-tagging to media verification. State-of-the-art geolocation methods surpass human performance on the task of geolocation estimation from images. However, no method assesses the suitability of an image for this task, which results in unreliable and erroneous estimations for images containing ambiguous or no geolocation clues. In this paper, we define the task of image localizability, i.e. suitability of an image for geolocation, and propose a selective prediction methodology to address the task. In particular, we propose two novel selection functions that leverage the output probability distributions of geolocation models to infer localizability at different scales. Our selection functions are benchmarked against the most widely used selective prediction baselines, outperforming them in all cases. By abstaining from predicting non-localizable images, we improve geolocation accuracy from 27.8% to 70.5% at the city-scale, and thus make current geolocation models reliable for real-world applications.

Keywords: Image Localizability · Selective Prediction · Geolocation Estimation · Spatial Entropy · Prediction Density

1 Introduction

A great portion of the images daily uploaded on the Internet are from smartphones and therefore contain geotags, providing information for their geographic location. However, there are numerous cases, such as social media photos, where this information is missing. Therefore, the ability to estimate the geographic location of these images, known as *location estimation* or *geolocation*, is crucial for a number of applications ranging from social media mining to media verification. More formally, image geolocation is the process of inferring the GPS coordinates of the depicted picture based solely on its visual elements.

State-of-the-art approaches for geolocation employ the latest advances in Computer Vision, such as Convolutional Neural Networks (CNNs), to extract representations of the depicted scenes and utilize huge databases of images taken worldwide either for training a classifier [5–7] or for retrieval [2–4,11]. Classification solutions partition the earth into a set of geographic cells, and the images

© Springer Nature Switzerland AG 2022
B. Þór Jónsson et al. (Eds.): MMM 2022, LNCS 13142, pp. 369–381, 2022.
https://doi.org/10.1007/978-3-030-98355-0_31

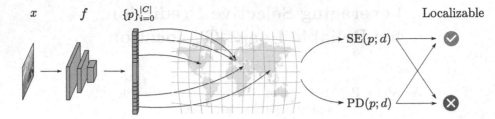

Fig. 1. Each image x is passed through a base geolocation model f, yielding a cell probability distribution $\{p\}_{i=1}^{|C|}$. Considering this distribution in the context of a world map, we measure whether our model's confidence is concentrated in a particular region or dispersed over globe through our selection functions $\text{SE}(p; d)$ and $\text{PD}(p; d)$, to assess the localizability of the input image.

are passed through a CNN to be classified into a single cell. Retrieval solutions compare the test images against the ones from a large-scale database in order to retrieve the most similar images and derive a single estimation by aggregating their locations. In both cases, performance is measured by the percentage of images localized within a certain distance d from their ground-truth location, denoted as *geolocation accuracy @ d km*.

Ongoing research focuses mainly on improving geolocation accuracy at different granularities (e.g. $d = 1, 25, 200, 750$ and 2500 km). However, contrary to most image classification datasets where images usually contain enough visual cues to be classified in a unique class, a good portion of images in geolocation datasets depict scenes with no apparent visual cues mapping to the image's location (e.g. indoor spaces, portraits). Such images could have been captured anywhere on the globe, and therefore attempting to localize them would most likely result in erroneous or unreliable estimations. Hence, we deem crucial for the reliability of geolocation systems to estimate not only the geolocation of input images but also their *localizability*.

In a general sense, we consider localizable the images that contain enough visual cues for their accurate geolocation. However, localizability is better approached considering a granularity scale (i.e. the range within which an image can be correctly placed from its true location) and a geolocation model (i.e. a mechanism that derives the image's location from its visual content). To this end, we introduce the problem of *image localizability detection*, building upon the foundation of *selective prediction* [12]. We propose a methodology that utilizes state-of-the-art geolocation systems to infer localizability at different scales. More precisely, we re-implement an image geolocation model [5] and, instead of interpreting the output probability distribution as pure categorical data and predicting the most probable location, we visualize the whole distribution on the world map. We then devise two novel selection functions, i.e. Spatial Entropy and Prediction Density, which measure cell probability dispersion and concentration over the globe, exploiting intrinsic proprieties of geolocation systems – unlike current state-of-the-art selection functions. We extensively evaluate our methodology on the two most widely used evaluation datasets, i.e. Im2GPS [2] and Im2GPS3k [11], and highlight the effectiveness of our proposed selection functions compared to state-of-the-art approaches in selective prediction. By discarding images considered non-localizable at city-scale, we boost the accuracy of our base geolocation model at city-scale from 27.8% to 70.5%, making it reliable for real-world applications. To the best of our knowledge, we are the first to propose the task of image localizability detection and leverage selective prediction to address it. Therefore, our work makes the following contributions:

- We introduce the problem of image localizability detection and frame it under a selective prediction framework. This formulation allows current classification models to infer localizability, and hence abstain from predicting non-localizable images.
- We propose two novel selection functions, specifically designed for geolocation, that outperform current state-of-the-art selection functions which do not consider spatial information.
- We extensively evaluate our methodology on the two most widely used datasets, achieving good separation between localizable and non-localizable images, and making current geolocation systems more reliable.

2   Related Work

This section gives an overview of some of the fundamental works that have contributed to geolocation estimation and selective prediction.

Geolocation Estimation: Hays and Efros [2] introduced the problem of planet-scale image location estimation. They used handcrafted features to retrieve images similar to a query image and infer its location based on theirs. Weyand et al. [5] took advantage of the deep learning advances and trained a Convolutional Neural Network (CNN) to extract features from images. Additionally, they formulated the geolocation problem as a classification task and divided the earth's surface, using Google's s2 geometry library,[1] to create a set of classes for the training and test images. More recent works modify the classification pipeline using a hierarchical partitioning of the earth [6], or novel loss functions [7]. Recently, a hybrid scheme called Search within Cell [8] was proposed, which combines a classification and retrieval approach for the final location estimation.

Selective Prediction: Works in this area focus on machine learning systems that are not only able to make predictions but also to know when to abstain from predicting. Although the field exists for several decades, it was not until recently that a unified formulation was introduced [12] and approaches regarding deep architectures were proposed by El-Yaniv and Wiener [15,16]. In [15], Softmax Response (the maximum output after the softmax layer) and MC-Dropout [13]

---

[1] https://s2geometry.io.

(a) A sunset picture in Hawaii   (b) A monument in Egypt

Fig. 2. Placing our model's cell probability distribution on a map illustrates its ability to associate visual *concepts* to locations.

were used as confidence functions, and an algorithm that finds the appropriate threshold given a desired risk was proposed. In [16], an algorithm for jointly training the classification network and the selection function was proposed.

3 Methodology

In this section, we present the proposed methodology for the selection of localizable images; this is illustrated in Fig. 1.

3.1 Geolocation Estimation

A geolocation model f takes as input an image $x \in \mathbb{R}^{H \times W \times 3}$ and returns the estimated GPS coordinates $\hat{y} \in \mathbb{R}^2$ of the location it was captured. Following the classification approach for geolocation, we first divide the earth's surface into a grid of geographic cells C, and then we employ a CNN, with $|C|$ outputs in the final layer, corresponding to the cells of the grid. For each input image x, the CNN creates a probability distribution over the grid of cells. The predicted location $\hat{y}$ is the mean coordinates of the cell with the highest probability.

Most geolocation approaches [5–7] consider only the cell with the highest probability, ignoring all the information provided by the cell probability distribution over the grid. We found that this probability distribution can provide valuable insights for the localizability of images. More precisely, a trained network has learned both to estimate the location of images and also to associate *concepts* with locations. For example, when the network is presented with the image of Fig. 2a, the probability of several cells nearby the sea is high. However, when presented with the image from Fig. 2b, all cells around Egypt are activated, since the image contains many visual cues that map to that area. Thus, even though it is challenging to predict the exact location of those images, the model generates *reasonable* estimates to candidate locations.

By inspecting the map, it is evident that the network is more confident for the estimation of Fig. 2b's location than Fig. 2a's since the probability distribution is more concentrated on a specific area. Thus, the estimation of the former can be considered more reliable than the latter. The spatial distribution of cells is essential information for the geolocation estimation problem, differentiating it from the general image classification task. Hence, our goal in this paper is to exploit this information to improve the reliability of the model's predictions.

3.2 Localizability

To develop and evaluate a methodology for image localizability, we have to associate all images in a dataset with ground-truth labels that indicate localizability. Moreover, labeling images as localizable or not is highly subjective and depends on the collection of images recognized by the prospective annotator. To address the former issue, we define localizability at a certain scale d (distance tolerance from the ground truth location). To address the latter issue, we approximate localizability in terms of our model's ability to infer location from the input image, i.e. we assess which images our employed model is able to predict correctly. Therefore, all images that our model is able to predict within a certain distance from their ground-truth location are labeled as localizable, and all other images are labeled as non-localizable.

More formally, given a geolocation estimation model f, the localizability of an image $x \in \mathbb{R}^{M \times N \times 3}$ at distance d is defined as:

$$\mathcal{L}_f(x;d) = \begin{cases} 1, & \text{if } \text{GCD}(f(x), y) < d \\ 0, & \text{otherwise} \end{cases} \tag{1}$$

where $\text{GCD}(\cdot, \cdot)$ is the Great Circle Distance between two locations, and y is the ground-truth location of x.

3.3 Selective Prediction

Predicting which images are localizable according to our model's geolocation capability can be formulated as a selective prediction scheme following the formulation in [12]. Here, we adapt their definitions to fit the needs of the geolocation estimation task. Our aim is to build a selective geolocation system (f, g) such that f is the base geolocation module, as described in Sect. 3.1, and g is the selection function. Then our selective geolocation system is defined as:

$$(f, g)(x;d) = \begin{cases} f(x;d), & \text{if } g(x;d) = 1 \\ abstain, & \text{if } g(x;d) = 0 \end{cases} \tag{2}$$

The selection function g is usually modeled based on a confidence function κ_f (which measures our model's confidence or uncertainty), a scale d and a tunable threshold θ. For κ_f measuring confidence, $g(x;d)$ is defined as follows:

$$g(x;d) = \begin{cases} 1, & \text{if } \kappa_f(x;d) \geq \theta \\ 0, & \text{if } \kappa_f(x;d) < \theta \end{cases} \tag{3}$$

Let $P(X, Y)$ be the distribution over $\mathcal{X} \times \mathcal{Y}$, where $\mathcal{X}$ is the image space and $\mathcal{Y}$ the coordinate space, characterizing the probability of image X being

374   A. Panagiotopoulos et al.

captured at geographical coordinates Y. Given an underlying distribution P, a confidence function κ_f and a scale d, varying the parameter θ determines the performance of our selective geolocation system, which can be expressed using coverage and risk, as follows:

Coverage is the mass probability of the non-rejected region in $\mathcal{X}$, and can be approximated given enough i.i.d. samples (x_i, y_i) from P as follows:

$$\phi_d(f, g) \triangleq \mathbb{E}_{P(X)}\left[g(x; d)\right] \approx \frac{1}{N}\sum_{i=1}^{N} g(x_i; d) \tag{4}$$

Risk is the expected percentage of the kept images that will be predicted outside a radius d, and can be approximated given enough i.i.d. samples (x_i, y_i) from P as follows:

$$R_d(f, g) \triangleq \mathbb{E}_{P(X,Y)}\left[l_d(f(x), y)\right] \approx \frac{\frac{1}{N}\sum_{i=1}^{N} l_d(f(x_i), y_i)g(x_i; d)}{\phi_d(f, g)} \tag{5}$$

where l_d is a loss function defined as:

$$l_d(l_1, l_2) = \begin{cases} 1, & \text{if } \mathrm{GCD}(l_1, l_2) > d \\ 0, & \text{if } \mathrm{GCD}(l_1, l_2) \leq d \end{cases} \tag{6}$$

3.4 Estimating Image Localizability

Our main goal in this work is to find good confidence functions and thresholds for the function g. For f, we employ a geolocation system similar to [5]; however, any geolocation system that tackles geolocation as a classification problem can be used.

Spatial Entropy (SE) measures the dispersion of cell probabilities around the globe. To calculate the $\mathrm{SE}(p; d)$ of the cell distribution $\{p\}_{i=0}^{|C|}$ at scale d, we initially select the most probable cell and merge all cells within distance d from it to form a super-cell. The probability of the super-cell derives from the sum of the cell probabilities of the individual cells. Then, we ignore all cells merged to the super-cell and find the next most probable cell from the remaining ones. Similarly, we merge it with its neighboring cells that are inside a radius d. This process is repeated until the cumulative probability of the super-cells accounts for the 90% of the total confidence.[2] We denote as $\{\bar{p}\}_{i=0}^{|C'|}$ the new probability distribution of the super-cells; hence, SE is defined as:

$$\mathrm{SE}(p; d) = -\sum_{i=0}^{|C'|} \bar{p}_i \log_2 \bar{p}_i \tag{7}$$

---

[2] We empirically found this to remove noise from cell distributions compared to considering cells accounting for 100% of the total confidence.

Higher Spatial Entropy indicates lower confidence; therefore, we devise the selection function g_{SE} as:

$$g_{SE}(x) = \begin{cases} 1, & \text{if } \text{SE}(p;d) \leq \theta_{SE} \\ 0, & \text{if } \text{SE}(p;d) > \theta_{SE} \end{cases} \tag{8}$$

where θ_{SE} is a tunable threshold.

Prediction Density (PD) measures the concentration of cell probability in a particular region instead of its dispersion around the globe. To calculate the $\text{PD}(p;d)$ of the cell distribution $\{p\}_{i=0}^{|C|}$ at scale d, we accumulate the model's cell probabilities in a radius d around the most probable cell, which can be considered as the model's confidence that an input image can be localized at scale d. This is formulated as follows:

$$\text{PD}(p;d) = \sum_{c \in C} p_c \cdot \mathbb{1} \left[\text{GCD}(c, \arg\max_{c' \in C} p_{c'}) \leq d \right] \tag{9}$$

where $\mathbb{1}$ is the indicator function. Higher Prediction Density denotes higher confidence; therefore, we devise the selection function g_{PD} as:

$$g_{PD}(x) = \begin{cases} 1, & \text{if } \text{PD}(p;d) \geq \theta_{PD} \\ 0, & \text{if } \text{PD}(p;d) < \theta_{PD} \end{cases} \tag{10}$$

where θ_{PD} is a tunable threshold.

4   Evaluation Set-up

4.1   Datasets

To train our geolocation model, we use the training split of the MediaEval Placing Task 2016 dataset (*MP-16 train*) [9], which is a subset of the Yahoo Flickr Creative Commons 100 Million (*YFCC100M*) [10]. It consists of 4,723,695 images posted on Flickr with their metadata, among which geographical coordinates. We also use the YFCC25k dataset from [6], composed of 25,600 randomly selected images from YFCC100M (excluding images from MP-16 train), for validation. Due to the unavailability of several images, we end up with a total of 23,007 images. Finally, for evaluation, we use the Im2GPS [2] and Im2GPS3k [11] datasets, provided by the original authors, consisting of 237 and 3,000 images, respectively.

4.2   Implementation Details

For the cell partitioning described, we adopt the fine partitioning from [6] and terminate cell splitting when each cell contains between 50 and 1,000 images from the MP-16 train. We discard all cells that end up with less than 50 photos. This results in 13,662 cells and 4,071,346 images for training. Although the

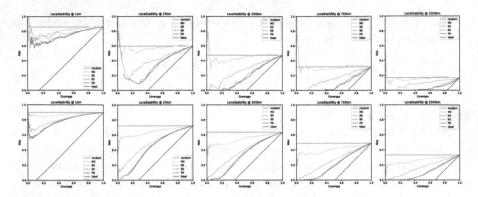

Fig. 3. Risk-Coverage curves for six selection functions on Im2GPS (top row) and Im2GPS3k (bottom row). Lower is better.

particular partitioning implementation could affect the geolocation estimation performance, we are primarily interested in the performance of our localizability methods, and hence we do not consider alternate partitionings.

For the geolocation model f, we use EfficientNet-B4 [1] as our backbone CNN and replace its last layer with a linear layer consisting of 13,662 neurons corresponding to our total number of cells. We replicate the pre-processing and training pipeline of Kordopatis et al. [8], and we do not use any further additions such as hierarchical partitioning [6] or the MvMF loss [7].

4.3   Competing Approaches

In Sect. 5, we compare our selection functions against two baseline runs (which serve to visualize selective performance limits) and two state-of-the-art methods in selective prediction, briefly described below:

Random selection function: randomly selects whether to predict $f(x)$ or abstain from providing a prediction, with an equal probability of 50%.

Ideal selection function: Selects images based on their ground-truth localizability values, prioritizing the images considered localizable.

Softmax Response (SR) [14]: Uses the maximum probability after the final softmax layer, i.e. the maximum cell probability, as confidence function. It has been employed for selective prediction in [15]. Note that this selection function cannot be intrinsically adapted for the different scales d.

Monte-Carlo Dropout (MC) [13]: Uses as confidence function the variance of the softmax response of multiple forward passes of an input image with dropout applied in the final layer. This is shown to be a good approximation of a Bayesian Neural Network with Gaussian parameter priors [13] and a state-of-the-art method in selective prediction [15]. Following [15] we use a dropout of 0.5. Note that again this selection function cannot be intrinsically adapted for the different scales d.

5   Experiments

5.1   Selective Geolocation Performance

We benchmark the selective prediction performance of the proposed selection functions g_{SE} and g_{PD} against the competing approaches. We evaluate them in both Im2GPS and Im2GPS3k at scales $d = 1$, 25, 200, 750 and 2500 km, which are the most widely reported scales and correspond to street, city, region, country and continent level granularity scales.

First, we present the Risk-Coverage (RC) curves for each dataset, illustrated in Fig. 3. These curves are obtained by computing the risk and coverage of each method for different values of the threshold θ. Both our selection functions achieve state-of-the-art performance, yielding lower risk at every coverage level in all datasets and scales. SE and PD perform similarly, with PD consistently outperforming SE by a small margin. Moreover, in coarser granularity scales, the performance gap between our selection functions and the competing SR and MC widens considerably, with our selection functions reaching close to the ideal. This can probably be attributed to their intrinsic adaptation to different scales. Finally, it is evident that RC curves on Im2GPS3k are smoother and more monotonous, which is expected due to its greater size and variety of images.

Although risk-coverage curves give a comprehensive insight of the selective prediction performance, we need to determine a specific threshold θ that separates localizable and non-localizable images given a selection function. To do so, we chose the θ value that corresponds to the coverage that equals the percentage of images f can successfully localize. We learn this value on the validation YFCC25K dataset for each selection function and each granularity scale. We call the risk and coverage at this threshold *Optimal Risk* (OR) and *Optimal Coverage* (OC) respectively. We also report the classification accuracy and the F1-score of the positive class.

Tables 1 and 2 display the results of the selection functions on the two evaluation datasets. We note that high accuracy in finer scales d is not indicative of good separation between localizable and non-localizable images due to the class imbalance; however, combined with F1-score, they provide useful insights. In particular, it is evident that the proposed SE and PD achieve better class separation than the SR and MC, with PD slightly surpassing SE. Moreover, in most cases, the selected threshold θ for our methods leads to lower risk and wider coverage compared to the competition.

Table 1. Selective prediction performance of our two selection functions against state-of-the-art on Im2GPS. We report the localizability accuracy and the F1-score as well as the optimal risk (OR) and coverage (OC) (for more details read Sect. 5.1). ↑ indicates that higher is better, and ↓ that lower is better.

	Acc ↑	F1 ↑	OR ↓	OC ↑
SR	74%	38%	71%	27%
MC	**83%**	23%	67%	5%
SE	76%	44%	67%	**28%**
PD	78%	**47%**	**64%**	27%

(a) $d = 1$ km

	Acc ↑	F1 ↑	OR ↓	OC ↑
SR	70%	66%	40%	49%
MC	62%	31%	53%	19%
SE	73%	72%	37%	**55%**
PD	**79%**	**77%**	**31%**	50%

(b) $d = 25$ km

	Acc ↑	F1 ↑	OR ↓	OC ↑
SR	70%	73%	31%	57%
MC	53%	36%	38%	25%
SE	76%	80%	29%	**67%**
PD	**78%**	**81%**	**26%**	64%

(c) $d = 200$ km

	Acc ↑	F1 ↑	OR ↓	OC ↑
SR	70%	79%	24%	74%
MC	49%	53%	28%	41%
SE	79%	86%	20%	**78%**
PD	**84%**	**88%**	**12%**	70%

(d) $d = 750$ km

	Acc ↑	F1 ↑	OR ↓	OC ↑
SR	82%	90%	14%	**88%**
MC	61%	74%	16%	62%
SE	85%	91%	10%	85%
PD	**87%**	**92%**	**8%**	85%

(e) $d = 2500$ km

Table 2. Selective prediction performance of our two selection functions against state-of-the-art on Im2GPS3k. We report the localizability accuracy and the F1-score as well as the optimal risk (OR) and coverage (OC) (for more details read Sect. 5.1). ↑ indicates that higher is better, and ↓ that lower is better.

	Acc ↑	F1 ↑	OR ↓	OC ↑
SR	84%	34%	70%	14%
MC	**87%**	7%	84%	3%
SE	85%	44%	64%	**16%**
PD	86%	**45%**	**62%**	15%

(a) $d = 1$ km

	Acc ↑	F1 ↑	OR ↓	OC ↑
SR	78%	62%	39%	29%
MC	70%	23%	58%	11%
SE	83%	72%	35%	**34%**
PD	**85%**	**74%**	**29%**	31%

(b) $d = 25$ km

	Acc ↑	F1 ↑	OR ↓	OC ↑
SR	76%	69%	33%	38%
MC	65%	35%	48%	18%
SE	80%	75%	31%	**43%**
PD	**82%**	**77%**	**26%**	40%

(c) $d = 200$ km

	Acc ↑	F1 ↑	OR ↓	OC ↑
SR	72%	74%	28%	53%
MC	57%	50%	37%	34%
SE	78%	80%	24%	**56%**
PD	**80%**	**81%**	**22%**	55%

(d) $d = 750$ km

	Acc ↑	F1 ↑	OR ↓	OC ↑
SR	70%	79%	25%	**73%**
MC	58%	65%	28%	53%
SE	78%	84%	18%	71%
PD	**80%**	**86%**	**16%**	70%

(e) $d = 2500$ km

5.2   Selective Geolocation Reliability

We present a quantitative and qualitative assessment of the performance of our selective models (f, g_{SE}) and (f, g_{PD}) compared to f.

We split both Im2GPS and Im2GPS3k into a localizable and a non-localizable subset using our selective models at city-scale. Table 3 displays the geolocation accuracies on these splits at all granularity scales, compared to the performance of the base model f without a selection scheme. For fine and medium granularity scales, our selective models achieve more than double the geolocation accuracy of the base model f, with only a tiny portion of localizable images rejected by our functions. In particular, prediction density increased the geolocation accuracy on Im2GPS3k from 27.8% to 70.5% by discarding non-localizable images, from which only 8.2% could have been successfully localized. This highlights

Table 3. Geolocation accuracies (%) when evaluating the whole dataset and the Localizable (L) and Non-Localizable (N) subsets. The percentage of images on (L) corresponds to the Optimal Coverage (OC) column of Tables 1 and 2.

	1 km	25 km	200 km	750 km	2500 km
f	14.3	40.5	52.7	68.3	83.1
$(f, g_{SE})^L$	24.4	62.6	74.0	86.2	91.6
$(f, g_{PD})^L$	27.1	69.5	79.6	89.8	94.0
$(f, g_{SE})^N$	1.9	13.2	26.4	46.2	72.6
$(f, g_{PD})^N$	1.6	11.7	26.0	47.0	72.6

(a) Im2GPS

	1 km	25 km	200 km	750 km	2500 km
f	10.1	27.8	36.5	51.0	66.8
$(f, g_{SE})^L$	24.6	65.3	77.4	86.9	92.6
$(f, g_{PD})^L$	26.6	70.5	80.8	89.1	94.1
$(f, g_{SE})^N$	2.7	8.4	17.7	35.0	55.6
$(f, g_{PD})^N$	2.6	8.2	15.3	32.3	54.5

(b) Im2GPS3k

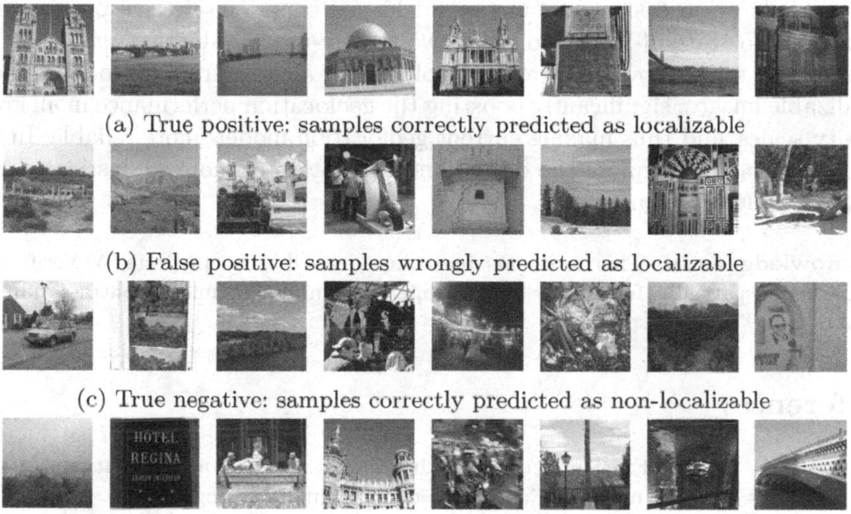

(a) True positive: samples correctly predicted as localizable

(b) False positive: samples wrongly predicted as localizable

(c) True negative: samples correctly predicted as non-localizable

(d) False negative: samples wrongly predicted as non-localizable

Fig. 4. Sample predictions of Prediction Density (PD) on randomly selected images of the Im2GPS3k dataset.

the reliability current image geolocation models can achieve using the selective prediction mechanisms presented.

Figure 4 depicts image samples randomly selected from Im2GPS3k for qualitative evaluation of our methodology. Images are grouped by their predicted and ground-truth localizability in (a) true positive, (b) false positive, (c) true negative and (d) false negative, using PD at city-scale as the selection function. True positive samples either depict landmarks or characteristic elements that hint at very specific locations (e.g. the Golden Gate Bridge). True negative samples contain mostly generic scenes that should not even be attempted to be localized. The two images with the car and the lights could have been localized if they were in our training dataset, but even in that case, a similar scene can easily exist in multiple cities. False positive samples contain enough visual cues to be worthy of geolocation, however not enough for the required granularity. Finally, all false negative samples besides the Edificio Meneses picture are not localizable and their correct geolocation by our geolocation model could be attributed to presence of very similar images in the train dataset.

6   Conclusions

In this paper, we introduced the problem of image localizability detection and used it as a foundation for reliable image geolocation. We adapted a selective prediction methodology to the context of geolocation and presented two novel selection functions, Spatial Entropy and Prediction Density, tailored to the needs of the geolocation task. Our functions achieved superior selective performance compared to state-of-the-art on the two widely-used evaluation datasets. We also demonstrated how they can be exploited to abstain from geolocating non-localizable images, significantly boosting the geolocation performance in all granularity scales, and thus making current geolocation models more reliable. In the future, we plan to explore the design and evaluation of more sophisticated and trainable selection functions.

Acknowledgments. This work has been supported by the projects WeVerify and MediaVerse, partially funded by the European Commission under contract number 825297 and 957252, respectively.

References

1. Tan, M., Le, Q.: EfficientNet: rethinking model scaling for convolutional neural networks. In: International Conference on Machine Learning (2019)
2. Hays, J., Efros, A.A.: IM2GPS: estimating geographic information from a single image. In: IEEE Computer Vision and Pattern Recognition (2008)
3. Hays, J., Efros, A.A.: Large-scale image geolocalization. In: Choi, J., Friedland, G. (eds.) Multimodal Location Estimation of Videos and Images, pp. 41–62. Springer, Cham (2015). https://doi.org/10.1007/978-3-319-09861-6_3
4. Kordopatis-Zilos, G., Popescu, A., Papadopoulos, S., Kompatsiaris, Y.: Placing images with refined language models and similarity search with PCA-reduced VGG features. In: MediaEval (2016)
5. Weyand, T., Kostrikov, I., Philbin, J.: PlaNet - photo geolocation with convolutional neural networks. In: Leibe, B., Matas, J., Sebe, N., Welling, M. (eds.) ECCV 2016. LNCS, vol. 9912, pp. 37–55. Springer, Cham (2016). https://doi.org/10.1007/978-3-319-46484-8_3
6. Müller-Budack, E., Pustu-Iren, K., Ewerth, R.: Geolocation estimation of photos using a hierarchical model and scene classification. In: Ferrari, V., Hebert, M., Sminchisescu, C., Weiss, Y. (eds.) ECCV 2018. LNCS, vol. 11216, pp. 575–592. Springer, Cham (2018). https://doi.org/10.1007/978-3-030-01258-8_35
7. Izbicki, M., Papalexakis, E.E., Tsotras, V.J.: Exploiting the earth's spherical geometry to geolocate images. In: Brefeld, U., Fromont, E., Hotho, A., Knobbe, A., Maathuis, M., Robardet, C. (eds.) ECML PKDD 2019. LNCS (LNAI), vol. 11907, pp. 3–19. Springer, Cham (2020). https://doi.org/10.1007/978-3-030-46147-8_1

8. Kordopatis-Zilos, G., Galopoulos, P., Papadopoulos, S., Kompatsiaris, I.: Leveraging EfficientNet and contrastive learning for accurate global-scale location estimation. In: ACM International Conference on Multimedia Retrieval (2021)
9. Larson, M., Soleymani, M., Gravier, G., Ionescu, B., Jones, G.J.: The benchmarking initiative for multimedia evaluation: MediaEval 2016. IEEE MultiMedia **24**(1), 93–6 (2017)
10. Thomee, B., et al.: YFCC100M: the new data in multimedia research. Commun. ACM **59**(2), 64–73 (2016)
11. Vo, N., Jacobs, N., Hays, J.: Revisiting IM2GPS in the deep learning era. In: IEEE International Conference on Computer Vision (2017)
12. El-Yaniv, R.: On the foundations of noise-free selective classification. J. Mach. Learn. Res. **11**(5), 1605–1641 (2010)
13. Gal, Y., Ghahramani, Z.: Dropout as a Bayesian approximation: representing model uncertainty in deep learning. In: International Conference on Machine Learning (2016)
14. Hendrycks, D., Gimpel, K.: A baseline for detecting misclassified and out-of-distribution examples in neural networks. In: International Conference on Learning Representations (2017)
15. Geifman, Y., El-Yaniv, R.: Selective classification for deep neural networks. In: Advances in Neural Information Processing Systems (2017)
16. Geifman, Y., El-Yaniv, R.: SelectiveNet: a deep neural network with an integrated reject option. In: International Conference on Machine Learning (2019)

Compressive Sensing-Based Image Encryption and Authentication in Edge-Clouds

Hongying Zheng, Yawen Huang, Lin Li, and Di Xiao$^{(\boxtimes)}$

College of Computer Science, Chongqing University, Chongqing 400044, China
xiaodi_cqu@hotmail.com

Abstract. Compressive sensing (CS) is often utilized to encrypt data on resource constrained terminals due to its lightweight and confidentiality. However, due to its low security level, it cannot meet the security requirements when interacting with the cloud in a complex cloud environment. Therefore, the more complex and higher security encryption computing is migrated to the edge device, and CS is combined as a new image data security transmission framework. In terms of image data confidentiality, lightweight encryption based on CS is implemented on the terminal, and then the data is clustered into central data and residual data by the proposed clustering algorithm at the edge, and the central data is further encrypted with high strength. In terms of image data integrity, hash algorithm based on CS is used to verify the correctness of the reconstructed data, and the redundancy of Reed-solomon code (RS) is used to improve the tampering recovery capability of data transmitted between edge devices and cloud. Simulation results and analysis verify the security and applicability of our transmission framework.

Keywords: Edge-clouds · Compressive sensing · Image encryption · Image authentication

1 Introduction

With the rapid development of network technology, users have higher requirements for computing resources. In order to cope with the changes of storage and computing demand, cloud computing emerges as the times require, bringing a huge change to the Internet industry [1–3]. Nowadays, the wide application of the Internet of things (IoT) in daily life generates huge amounts of data. At the same time, the slow development of network bandwidth cannot guarantee the efficiency of the server. In order to respond to users' data processing requests in real time, some capabilities of cloud are migrated to the edge devices, which is called edge-clouds computing [4].

However the transmission of large amount of image data on the edge-clouds will increase bandwidth burden and privacy leakage. Especially in the aspect of security, the necessary encryption methods are needed to ensure the confidentiality and integrity of the transmitted data [5]. As a low complexity encryption method, compressive sensing (CS) can compress and encrypt data simultaneously, especially when the terminal resource is limited. Nevertheless, the distance between the edge devices and the central cloud is

© Springer Nature Switzerland AG 2022
B. Þór Jónsson et al. (Eds.): MMM 2022, LNCS 13142, pp. 382–393, 2022.
https://doi.org/10.1007/978-3-030-98355-0_32

far away, and the low security level CS [9, 10] encrypted ciphertext is far from enough, therefore the strong encryption work can be migrated to the edge-clouds.

During data transmission, as shown in Fig. 1, two main tasks are firstly performed on the image data X in the resource constrained terminals: 1. X is compressed and encrypted by CS to generate measurements Y and then quantized as Q. 2. By taking advantage of the irreversibility of CS if it does not meet the reconstruction criteria, a measurement hash Y_{hash} is generated with X and then extracted as a message authentication code MAC, which is used to verify the correctness of the reconstructed image transmitted to the terminal. Next, after the quantized measurements Q and hash measurements MAC are uploaded to the edge devices, the strong encryption will be completed on the edge devices: Q is clustered into central data CEN and residual data RES, and the location information $Site$ is generated. Then, CEN and $Site$ which may leak most of the plaintext energy are encrypted by diffusion-permutation high strength encryption to generate the strongly encrypted central data E. In order to resist tampering attacks, Reed-Solomon code (RS) [22] is used to generate redundancy before uploading E to the cloud server, and a small part of strongly encrypted central data $\overline{E}$ is left on the edge devices. Then, the message authentication code $RMAC$ of most of the strongly encrypted central data $\hat{E}$ is generated by the keyed hash algorithm with modification localized capability in [19], which is used for tampering identification and location. In particular, the purpose of RS coding is to improve the recovery capability of tampering. Finally, $\hat{E}$, MAC and $RMAC$ are uploaded to the cloud server for storage. Since the image decryption and reconstruction are carried out in the edge devices which are more secure, the keys driving the encryption algorithms are exchanged and shared between the resource constrained terminals and the edge devices. The main contributions of our work are as follows:

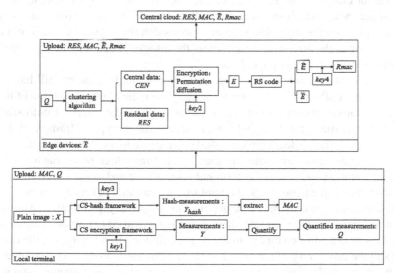

Fig. 1. Encrypted data transmission framework based on compressed sensing in edge-clouds

- In the resource constrained terminals, CS is used for lightweight encryption, and then the data is transmitted to the edge devices for high strength encryption. The two-layer encryption framework ensures the security of data transmission.
- In the process of edge high strength encryption, we propose a clustering algorithm based on compressed data. Only the central data and location information, which may leak plaintext energy, are encrypted by diffusion-permutation. It not only makes the ciphertext achieve a higher level of confidentiality, but also reduces the computational complexity of the encryption algorithm.
- In the process of decoding, to verify whether the data transmitted to the resource constrained terminals is correct, a hash algorithm based on CS is proposed, which robustness is very suitable for the authentication of CS reconstructed image.
- In order to resist the tampering attacks from edge devices to cloud servers, we utilize RS coding to encode the central data, which not only effectively resists the tamper attacks, but also improves the image tamper recovery accuracy.

2 Related Research

2.1 Background of Edge-Clouds

With the development of big data, cloud computing, as the center of centralized data processing, reduces the burden of terminals and improves the utilization of resources [6]. However, it is easy to cause network congestion and network delay due to the frequent interaction with terminals. In order to solve the problem of cloud computing in real-time response, edge-clouds are proposed as a new three-layer computing model. Some capabilities of cloud can be migrated to edge devices, including computing resources and storage capacity, which are more secure than cloud. There are two reasons why edge devices are more secure than cloud centers: One is that the physical address of the edge device is closer to the terminal, which limits the attacker's action; and the other is that users have control over most edge devices.

However, data transmission on edge cloud computing framework still has security problems. First of all, the cloud center is far away from the physical position of the edge devices, so the adversary is easy to steal and tamper with the data. Second, untrusted cloud service providers may grab data. In [7, 8], a three-layer encryption framework for edge computing is proposed to deal with untrusted service providers. Plaintext data is encoded by RS to generate redundant data and then divided into three parts. Each part cannot reconstruct plaintext and is stored in terminal, edge device and cloud server, respectively. The main encryption and decryption operations are carried out on edge devices, so that untrusted cloud service providers cannot obtain users' privacy information. Although the algorithm ensures that the plaintext information is not leaked to untrusted cloud service providers, there are still two threats to the edge computing framework: On the one hand, there is still the possibility of tampering in the transmission process; On the other hand, edge devices are still vulnerable to damage in the physical environment, which easily results in the loss of data stored in edge devices. Therefore, in edge computing, we need a secure transmission, which can resist tampering attacks and minimize the loss of users in the case of data loss.

2.2 Application Background of CS in Security

CS breaks the restriction of Nyquist sampling theorem that the sampling frequency must be more than twice the maximum frequency in order to reconstruct the signal. Since most of the signals $X \in R^n$ can be expressed as k-sparse signals under a certain kind of basis $\Psi: X = \Psi S$, the measurement matrix, which is unrelated to the Ψ, is used to sample the sparse signal S at a sampling frequency far lower than two times of the highest frequency to obtain measurements Y:

$$Y = \Phi X = \Phi \Psi S = \theta S. \tag{1}$$

Under the condition of satisfying RIP [11], the measurements have enough information to reconstruct the original signal X by solving the optimization problems.

CS as a method to reduce the sampling rate has attracted the attention of researchers in various fields. In the field of security, CS can be regarded as a traditional symmetric encryption scheme [12], which has been proved theoretically to be able to guarantee the computational security of the encryption process in the case of "one-time pad", but it cannot achieve Shannon's perfect secrecy, i.e., the attacker can infer the energy information of plaintext from the measurements with confidentiality [13].

The security level of CS encryption scheme is far from enough in many practical applications. Chen et al. proposed to introduce the 3-D cat map into the generation of measurement matrix, as well as into the subsequent replacement and diffusion of encryption work [14]. And in [15], Gong et al. proposed to use the hash value of the image encrypted by Arnold transform as the initial value of chaos to generate measurement matrix. The keys generated by different images are different, which can effectively resist the Chosen plaintext attack. In [16], Chai et al. proposed to used block compressive sensing (BCS) to measure the image, which prominently improves the efficiency of the algorithm in the experimental results. However, in these encryption schemes, the high complexity of reconstruction limits its application in resource constrained terminals.

In the cloud era, this problem has the potential to be well solved. However, if the untrusted cloud undertakes the reconstruction work, which will steal the plaintext information and bring great security risks to users. In order to prevent the outsourcing cloud from stealing plaintext information, Xie et al. [17] proposed that the receiver receives the ciphertext from the cloud center and transmits the ciphertext to the outsourcing decryption server (ODS) for decoding and reconstruction. In [18], the sparse basis after the secret primary transformation replaces the measurement matrix, which can be disclosed to the cloud as the secret matrix. However, only relying on primary transformation to encrypt sparse transformation cannot guarantee data security. In the case of real-time processing, it is proposed to hand over the reconstruction task to a more secure edge devices [19]. Although the reconstruction based on CS ciphertext is not our focus, it is necessary to show that our reconstruction and decryption work are carried out on edge devices. CS can not only be used as encryption system, but also can be used as a method to generate image hash value according to the fact that the measurement matrix cannot reconstruct plaintext without reconstruction conditions.

Algorithm 1 A clustering algorithm based on compressed data	Algorithm 3 A message authentication code extraction algorithm based on penalty authentication

Algorithm 1 A clustering algorithm based on compressed data

Input: Quantified measurements Q

Output: central data CEN, residual data RES, location map $Site$

1: Initialize $T = 8$, $Win(1,1) = Q(1)$, $Win_{First} = 1$, $Win_{Last} = 1$, $Win(1) = Q(1)$;
2: Reshape a two-dimensional matrix $Q_{M \times N}$ into a one-dimensional vector $Q_{(M \times N) \times 1}$;
3: **for** $k = 1$ to $M \times N$ **do**
4:     $Win(i) = Q(Win_{First} : Win_{Last})$;
5:     $M = \lfloor \text{mean}(Win(i)) \rfloor$;
6:     **for** $j = 1$ to $Win_{Last} - Win_{First} + 1$ **do**
7:         $R(i,j) = Win(i,j) - M$;
8:     **end for**
9:     **if** $R(i,:) < T$ **then**
10:         $Win_{Last} = Win_{Last} + 1$;
11:     **else**
12:         $Win(i,:) = Q(Win_{First} : Win_{Last} - 1)$;
13:         $CEN(i) = \lfloor \text{mean}(Win(i)) \rfloor$;
14:         $RES(i,:) = Win(i,:) - CEN(i)$;
15:         $Site = Win_{First}$;
16:         $Win_{First} = k$;
17:         $Win_{Last} = k$;
18:         $k = k - 1$;
19:         $i = i + 1$;
20:     **end if**
21: **end for**
22: **return** CEN, RES, $Site$;

Algorithm 3 A message authentication code extraction algorithm based on penalty authentication

Input: The hash measurements $Y_{hash_{M \times N}}$

Output: The message authentication code MAC

1: Initialize $Level_{3 \times 1} = 0$;
2: compute $Hash_{max} = \max(Y_{hash})$, $Hash_{min} = \min(Y_{hash})$, $Hash_{ave} = \text{mean}(Y_{hash})$;
3: Assign values to arrays $Level$:
    $Level[1] = (Hash_{ave} + Hash_{min})/2$;
    $Level[2] = Hash_{ave}$;
    $Level[3] = (Hash_{ave} + Hash_{max})/2$;
4: **for** $i = 1$ to M **do**
5:     **for** $i = 1$ to M **do**
6:         **if** $Hash_{min} \leq Y_{hash} \leq Level[1]$ **then**
7:             $MAC(i,j) = 0$;
8:         **else if** $Level[1] \leq Y_{hash} \leq Level[2]$ **then**
9:             $MAC(i,j) = 1$;
10:        **else if** $Level[2] \leq Y_{hash} \leq Level[3]$ **then**
11:            $MAC(i,j) = 2$;
12:        **else if** $Level[3] \leq Y_{hash} \leq Hash_{max}$ **then**
13:            $MAC(i,j) = 3$;
14:        **end if**
15:    **end for**
16: **end for**
17: **return** MAC;

3 Two-Layer Encryption Framework Based on Edge-Clouds Framework

3.1 Lightweight Encryption Algorithm on Resource Constrained Terminals

In resource constrained terminals, CS can be used to simultaneously compress and encrypt image data. This guarantees the low-intensity and low-computational complexity encryption of image data, although the CS-based information encryption systems only achieve computational security rather than perfect security. The lightweight encryption algorithm based on CS is as follows:

- Step 1: The measurement matrix Φ, as a $key1$ shared between the encoder and decoder, is generated by inputting initial value to one Gaussian PRNG (G-PRNG).
- Step 2: The sparse original image data X are linearly projected through the measurement matrix Φ to generate ciphertext sequence Y according to Eq. (1) of CS.
- Step 3: Calculate the maximum Y_{max} and minimum Y_{min} values of the measurements. Then the two dimensional vector Y consisting of measurements are quantified to the finite field $GF(2^n)$ by the following Eq. (2); the quantized measurements Q is recovered by inverse quantization by the following Eq. (3).

$$Q = 255 \times \lfloor (Y - Ymin)/(Ymax - Ymin) \rfloor, \tag{2}$$

$$Y = [Ymin + Q \times (Ymax - Ymin)]/255. \tag{3}$$

Algorithm 2 A strong encryption algorithm based on permutation and diffusion	Algorithm 4 An algorithm to improve the accuracy of tamper recovery
Input: central data CEN, location map $Site$	**Input:** High security ciphertext $E_{M \times 1}$
Output: High security ciphertext E	**Output:** Ciphertext on the cloud $\widehat{E}$, Ciphertext on the edge devices $\overline{E}$
1: Reshaping the CEN and $Site$ into the vector of $C_{2M \times 1}$;	1: Reshaping E into $B_{p \times q}$;
2: The input initial value x_0 is iterated $2M$ times by CCM to generate chaotic sequence $F_{2M \times 1}$;	2: Generate Vandermonde matrix $V_{r \times p}$;
3: the center data CEN is replaced to the corresponding position of the index sequence $F(1 : M)$ to get the corresponding sequence $E_{M \times 1}$;	3: Combine V and identity matrix $I_{p \times p}$ into coding matrix $C_{(p+r) \times p}$;
4: **for** $i = 1$ to M **do**	4: Converting C, V and B to finite fields
5: $\quad E(i) = mod(Emid(i) + F(M + i), 256)$;	5: **for** $j = 1$ to q **do**
6: **end for**	6: $\quad R(: j) = V \times B(:, j)$;
7: **return** E;	7: **end for**
	8: $\widehat{E} = R(1 : (p - 1), :)$
	9: $\overline{E} = R(p : (p + r), :)$
	10: **return** $\widehat{E}$, $\overline{E}$;

3.2 High Strength Encryption Algorithm on Edge Devices

Since edge devices are closer to the physical device, which makes the attack more difficult, the encrypted and quantized measurements can be transmitted to the edge devices to share the encryption responsibility for the resource limited terminal. Therefore, we try to balance the confidentiality and transmission burden, and propose a data clustering algorithm based on CS measurements with variable window size, which decomposes the measurements into center data with a large amount of energy and residual data with a small amount of energy. In addition, only a small part of the location map needs to be preserved, as shown in Algorithm 1.

In Algorithm 1, firstly, the threshold T is set. The value of threshold T determines the number of elements in each window and the amount of energy contained in residual data. Furthermore, when T is larger, the number of elements in each window is more, and the clustering effect is better, but the energy is larger, and vice versa. Next, put the window WIN on the measurements and slide it continuously for clustering. When a window ends, the start and end positions of the new window are both the end positions of the previous window, and slide backward one position: $Win_{Last} = Win_{First} = Win_{Last} + 1$; And the data of the end window needs to be recorded: central data CEN: $CEN(i) = \lfloor \text{mean}(Win(i)) \rfloor$, residual data RES: $RES(i, j) = Win(i, j)-CEN(i)$, and part of location map $Site$: $Site(i) = Win_{First}(i)$. Among them, Win_{First} and Win_{Last} are the start and end positions of the window Win on the quantized measurements Q respectively, i is the window index, and j is the element index in the window. Finally, the center data, residual data and part of location map of each window are output.

In order to elaborate our algorithm in detail, let us take one-dimensional vector $Q[8, 15, 25, 24, 27]$ as an example, as shown in Fig. 2. Then, we describe the process of traversing Q to illustrate how the algorithm clusters. In the initial state, Win_{First} and Win_{Last} point to the head of Q, that is, $Win_{First} = Win_{Last} = 1$; In the first iteration: $Win(1) = Q[8]$, and obviously in the window $R < T$, and Win_{Last} slides back one position: $Win_{Last} = Win_{Last} + 1 = 2$; In the second iteration: $Win(1) = Q[8, 15]$, $M = 11$, $R = [3, 4]$, therefore $R < T$ and then $Win_{Last} = 3$; In the third iteration: $Win(1) = Q[8, 15, 25]$, $M = 16$, $R = [8, 1, 9]$, therefore $R(1)$&$R(3) \geq T$ and then delete the last element of the window $Win(1) = Q[8, 15]$, record $CEN(1) = 11$, $RES(1,:) = [3, 4]$, $Site(1) = 1$ and set $Win_{First} = Win_{Last}$

= 3; In the fourth iteration: Add new window $Win(2) = Q[25]$, therefore $R < T$ and then $Win_{Last} = 4$; In the 5th iteration: $Win(2) = Q[25, 24]$, $M = 24$, $R = [1, 0]$, therefore $R < T$ and then $Win_{Last} = 5$; In the 6th iteration: $Win(2) = Q[25, 24, 27]$, $M = 25$, $R = [0, 1, 2]$, therefore $R < T$. And then $Win_{Last} = 5$. Since Q has all been traversed, and record $CEN(2)$ = 25, $RES(2,:) = [25, 24, 27]$, $Site(2) = 3$. Among them, M and R are the intermediate variables of the central data and residual data respectively, and the equation expressions are also the same.

It is obvious that the central data leaks most of the energy in the case of controlling the value of threshold, so we only need to further encrypt the central data to ensure the secure transmission of data (location information should also be strongly encrypted. Because the processing method is the same as the central data, we will not repeat it again). We use Logistic-Tent [20] cascade map(CCM) to generate chaotic sequences to encrypt the central data by diffusion and permutation and CCM is defined as follows:

$$x_{k+1} = \begin{cases} abx_k(1 - bx_k), & x_k < 0.5 \\ ab(1 - x_k)[1 - b(1 - x_k)] & x_k \geq 0.5 \end{cases}, \tag{4}$$

where parameters $a \in [3.57, 4]$ and $b \in (1, 2]$.

As shown in Algorithm 2, the Central data CEN and part of location map $Site$ are diffused and permuted by using two chaotic sequences, and the initial input parameters x_0 is regarded as the secret key $key2$ and shared between the encoder and decoder. Among them, Sequence E is obtained by diffusion process according to Eq. (5). When the data is downloaded to the edge devices, the high security ciphertext E needs to be decrypted through inverse diffusion according to Eq. (6).

$$E(i) = \mod(E_{mid}(i) + F(m + i), 256), \tag{5}$$

$$E_{mid}(i) = \mod(E(i) - F(m + i), 256). \tag{6}$$

After strong encryption of the measurements which are uploaded from the terminal to the edge devices, the residual data, which almost does not leak energy, is uploaded directly to the cloud; while the center data encrypted by diffusion-permutation needs to be processed by RS coding in order to improve the tampering recovery capability of image data. Please refer to Sect. 4 for details.

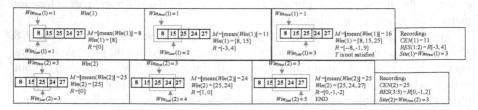

Fig. 2. Clustering with vector Y as an example

4 Double Security Message Authentication Method Based on Edge-Clouds Framework

4.1 Authentication of the Reconstructed Image Transmitted on Terminal

Because of the avalanche effect of traditional hashing algorithm, the decrypted plaintext data is very sensitive to changes during authentication. To overcome this limitation, we propose a message authentication code extraction algorithm based on penalty authentication, as shown in Algorithm 3, where its simple linear operation can be well adapted to resource-constrained terminals.

In Algorithm 3, first, Y_{hash} is divided into four levels: $[Hash_{min}, Level(1)]$, $[Level(1), Level(2)]$, $[Level(2), Level(3)]$, $[Level(3), Hash_{ave}]$. Among them, $Hash_{min}$, $Hash_{max}$ and $Hash_{ave}$ are the maximum, minimum and average values in Y_{hash} respectively, and the level calculation process is as follows:

$$\begin{cases} Level1 = (Hash_{ave} + Hash_{min})/2 \\ Level2 = Hash_{ave} \\ Level3 = (Hash_{ave} + Hash_{max})/2 \end{cases}, \tag{7}$$

Then, extract the $MAC(i,j)$ of each element $Y_{hash}(i,j)$ according to each level, as Eq. (8). Finally, MAC are obtained.

$$MAC(i,j) = \begin{cases} 0, Hash_{min} \le Y_{hash}(i,j) \le Level1 \\ 1, Level1 \le Y_{hash}(i,j) \le Level2 \\ 2, Level2 \le Y_{hash}(i,j) \le Level3 \\ 3, Level3 \le Y_{hash}(i,j) \le Hash_{max} \end{cases}, \tag{8}$$

When the decoder receives the reconstructed information, we use a penalty mechanism to authenticate the message authentication code. MAC and $\widetilde{MAC}$ are respectively generated by the original image during encoding and the reconstructed image during decoding on resource-constrained terminals. Accordingly, the punishment coefficient pub is determined according to the difference between $MAC(i,j)$ and $\widetilde{MAC}(i,j)$:

$$pub = \sum_{i=1}^{k} \left(MAC(i,j) - \widetilde{MAC}(i,j) \right). \tag{9}$$

The loss rate μ of the reconstructed image is determined by pub as $\mu = (pub/k) \times 100\%$. If the loss of the reconstructed image is less than the threshold value, it will pass the authentication; otherwise, it will not pass.

4.2 High Precision Tampering Recovery of the Encrypted Central Data on Edge-Clouds

In the process of central data uploading to the cloud server and downloading to the edge devices, the transmission distance is relatively long, which makes the central data vulnerable to tampering attacks by adversaries, so relatively accurate tampering recovery is essential. We introduce RS code [21] to improve the accurate recovery of tampering

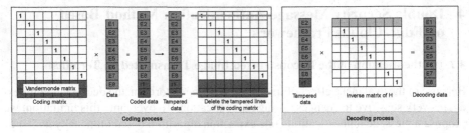

Fig. 3. RS coding and decoding process

and the RS coding process is shown in the Fig. 3. In encoding, the original data with m length is encoded into $m + r$ data by RS; in decoding, if the data length is greater than m, the original data can be completely recovered. In our work, we use the correction property of RS to improve the capability of accurate recovery of data tampering, and the details are shown in Algorithm 4.

In Algorithm 4, firstly, the high security ciphertext E is reconstructed into a matrix $B_{p \times q}$, where each block is $B(:, j)$, and the coding matrix is generated which is composed of identity matrix I and Vandermonde matrix V; Next, each block B is RS coded by the V to generate $R_{(p+r) \times q}$ with redundant data over the finite field 2^n; Finally, $\hat{E} = R(1:(p - 1),:)$ is uploaded to the cloud server, and $\overline{E} = R(p:(p + r),:)$ is saved on the edge device.

5   Experiment and Analyses

5.1   Data Storage and Security Analyses

The proposed two-layer encryption framework clusters the measurements of low-intensity encryption by a certain threshold on the edge devices to generate the central data, residual data and partial location information, which are all integers. It can avoid the generation of floating-point numbers, and greatly reduce the transmission pressure.

Let us take Lena of 256×256 as an example. The compression ratio is 0.5 and the quantization range is $[0, 255]$. If the threshold T is too large, the residual data will leak too much energy; but if it is too small, the clustering will be more decentralized. Therefore, we set the threshold $T = 8$ so that the binary code length of residual data can be exactly 3 bits. Lena is compressed and quantized into quantized measurements Q, which size is 128×256. The experimental results show that after the quantized measurements are preprocessed by our clustering algorithm, 2420 central data, 4840 location information and 128×256 residual data will be generated. The binary coding length of both the central data and location information is 8 bits, but the binary code plus symbol bit of the residual data only needs 4 bits. Therefore, in this example, the total length of binary codes of the unclustered elements Q is $128 \times 256 \times 8 = 262144$, but the total length of binary codes is: $(2420 + 4840) \times 8 + 128 \times 256 \times 4 = 189152$ after clustering.

In the aspect of data integrity, on the one hand, the robust *MAC* based on CS is used to ensure the correct transmission of reconstructed data; on the other hand, an improved data tampering recovery algorithm based on RS is proposed, which can resist tampering attacks in remote transmission.

5.2 Histogram Analysis

Histogram is an important statistical feature of image, which is often used to evaluate the performance of image encryption scheme. The best encryption algorithm is to make the ciphertext histogram distribution uniform and flat; the second best encryption algorithm is to make the ciphertext histograms of different images similar [15, 22]. Figure 4 shows the histograms of the central data and residual data. We can see that the central data histograms of different images after permutation-diffusion are uniform and flat, while the residual data histograms of different images are not flat, but they are similar. Therefore, when the attacker intercepts the encrypted central data and residual data, it is not feasible to obtain plaintext information through histogram statistics.

5.3 Image Recovery in Case of Edge Devices Damaged

As a kind of physical device, the edge devices have the risk to be damaged, and the additional information stored here may also be lost, which may cause the original data to be irrecoverable. However, the robustness of CS can solve this problem very well. Even if a part of the data is lost, a low-quality version can still be recovered. In the process of experiment, we discard the data stored in the edge, and reconstruct the image with only the ciphertext stored on the cloud server, as shown in Fig. 5.

5.4 The Recovery Capability of Tampered Image

We perform RS encoding on the central data transmitted to the cloud server at the edge devices to ensure accurate recovery of tampered data. During the experiment, we divide the data into blocks of m pixels, and each block generates r redundant elements. When the tampered data in each block does not exceed $r/(r + h)\%$, the image can be completely accurately recovered. In the case of setting the parameter $m = 8$, we set two groups of parameters of "$r = 2$" and "$r = 3$". At the same time, 5, 20, 30 and 50 data were randomly tampered within the central data. As shown in Table 1, take Lena as an example. Compared with [19], regardless of the number of tampering, the image reconstruction quality of our proposed schemes is significantly higher than the unimproved tampering recovery algorithm in [19].

(a)Central data of Lena   (b) Residual data of Lena   (c)Central data of Camera   (d)Residual data of Camera

Fig. 4. Histogram analysis

(a)PSNR of Lena:37.3806   (b)PSNR of Camera:31.8363   (c)PSNR of Lake:32.4144   (d)PSNR of Man:31.8363

Fig. 5. Reconstructed image with damaged edge nodes.

Table 1. Image reconstruction quality under different tampering numbers

	Redundant codes	Number of tampered data			
		5	20	30	50
Unimproved[19]	r = 0	38.5026	37.4063	36.5071	34.3238
Our Improved Method	r = 2	38.5610	37.8029	36.8734	34.3626
	r = 3	38.5610	38.2299	37.5648	34.4963

6 Conclusion

In this paper, we take advantage of the edge devices with computing resources and more secure features to enhance the security of image data transmission from resource constrained terminals to cloud servers. A two-layer encryption system is adopted, including lightweight encryption based on CS and high-strength encryption combined with clustering algorithm. And two verification systems are used: one is the robust compressed measurement hash function and the other is the tampering recovery algorithm with higher accuracy. For the transmission image data, our encryption scheme combined with edge computing not only improves the security level of the transmitted image data, but also reduces the computational complexity of high strength encryption through clustering algorithm. On the other hand, in terms of data integrity, the compressed measurement hash function has the advantages of lightweight and robustness, which is very suitable for irreversible CS data authentication; and the algorithm with higher tampering recovery accuracy is more effective in resisting the attacker's tampering with the data transmitted to the cloud server.

Acknowledgment. The work was supported by the National Key R&D Program of China (Grant No. 2020YFB1805400) and the National Natural Science Foundation of China (Grant No. 62072063).

References

1. Mell, P., Grance, T.: The NIST definition of cloud computing. Commun. ACM **53**, 1–23 (2011)
2. Dillon, T., Wu, C., Chang, E.: Cloud computing: issues and challenges. In: IEEE International Conference on Advanced Information Networking and Applications, pp. 27–33. IEEE (2010)

3. Tayade, D.: Mobile cloud computing: issues, security, advantages, trends. Int. J. Comput. Sci. Inf. Technol. **5**(5), 6635–6639 (2014)

4. Shi, W., Cao, J., Zhang, Q.: Edge computing: vision and challenges. IEEE Internet Things J. **3**(5), 637–646 (2016)

5. Chen, D., Zhao, H.: Data security and privacy protection issues in cloud computing. In: 2012 International Conference on Computer Science and Electronics Engineering, pp. 647–651. Hangzhou (2012)

6. Carcary, M., Doherty, E., Conway, G.: The adoption of cloud computing by Irish SMEs-an exploratory study. Electr. J. Inf. Syst. Evaluat. **17**, 3–14 (2014)

7. Wang, T., Zhou, J., Chen, X.: A three-layer privacy preserving cloud storage scheme based on computational intelligence in fog computing. IEEE Trans. Emerg. Top. Comput. Intell. **2**(1), 3–12 (2018)

8. Wang, T., Mei, Y., Jia, W.: Edge-based differential privacy computing for sensor–cloud systems. J. Parall. Distrib. Comput. **136**, 75–85 (2020)

9. Donoho, D.: Compressed sensing. IEEE Trans. Inf. Theory **52**(4), 1289–1306 (2006)

10. Candès, E., Wakin, M.: An introduction to compressive sampling. IEEE Signal Process. Mag. **25**(2), 21–30 (2008)

11. Baraniuk, R., Davenport, M., Devore, R.R.: A simple proof of the restricted isometry property for random matrices. Construct. Approx. **28**(3), 253–263 (2008)

12. Candes, E.J., Tao, T.: Near-optimal signal recovery from random projections: universal encoding strategies? IEEE Trans. Inf. Theory **52**(12), 5406–5425 (2006)

13. Bianchi, T., Bioglio, V., Magli, E.: Analysis of one-time random projections for privacy preserving compressed sensing. IEEE Trans. Inf. Forensics Secur. **11**(2), 313–327 (2016)

14. Chen, J., Zhang, Y., Qi, L.: Exploiting chaos-based compressed sensing and cryptographic algorithm for image encryption and compression. Opt. Laser Technol. **99**, 238–248 (2018)

15. Gong, L., Qiu, K., Deng, C.: An image compression and encryption algorithm based on chaotic system and compressive sensing. Opt. Laser Technol. **115**, 257–267 (2019)

16. Chai, X., Fu, X., Gan, Z., Zhang, Y., Lu, Y., Chen, Y.: An efficient chaos-based image compression and encryption scheme using block compressive sensing and elementary cellular automata. Neural Comput. Appl. **32**(9), 4961–4988 (2018)

17. Xie, D., Chen, F., Luo, Y.: One-to-many image encryption with privacy-preserving homomorphic outsourced decryption based on compressed sensing. Digit. Signal Process. **95**, 1051–2004 (2019)

18. Zhang, Y., Xiang, Y., Zhang, L.: Efficiently and securely outsourcing compressed sensing reconstruction to a cloud. Inf. Sci. **496**, 150–160 (2019)

19. Zhang, Y., Wang, P., Fang, L.: Secure transmission of compressed sampling data using edge clouds. IEEE Trans. Industr. Inf. **16**(10), 6641–6651 (2020)

20. Zhou, Y., Hua, Z., Pun, C.M.: Cascade chaotic system with applications. IEEE Trans. Cybern. **99**, 2168–2267 (2014)

21. Plank, J.S.: T1: erasure codes for storage applications. In: Proceedings of the 4th USENIX Conference on File and Storage Technologies, San Francisco, CA, pp. 1–74 (2005)

22. Pak, C., Huang, L.: A new color image encryption using combination of the 1D chaotic map. Signal Process. **138**, 129–137 (2017)

ECAS-ML: Edge Computing Assisted Adaptation Scheme with Machine Learning for HTTP Adaptive Streaming

Jesús Aguilar-Armijo(✉)[iD], Ekrem Çetinkaya[iD], Christian Timmerer[iD], and Hermann Hellwagner[iD]

Christian Doppler Laboratory ATHENA, Institute of Information Technology, Alpen-Adria-Universität Klagenfurt, Klagenfurt, Austria
{jesus.aguilar,ekrem.cetinkaya,christian.timmerer,
hermann.hellwagner}@aau.at

Abstract. As the video streaming traffic in mobile networks is increasing, improving the content delivery process becomes crucial, e.g., by utilizing edge computing support. At an edge node, we can deploy adaptive bitrate (ABR) algorithms with a better understanding of network behavior and access to radio and player metrics. In this work, we present ECAS-ML, Edge Assisted Adaptation Scheme for HTTP Adaptive Streaming with Machine Learning. ECAS-ML focuses on managing the tradeoff among bitrate, segment switches and stalls to achieve a higher quality of experience (QoE). For that purpose, we use machine learning techniques to analyze radio throughput traces and predict the best parameters of our algorithm to achieve better performance. The results show that ECAS-ML outperforms other client-based and edge-based ABR algorithms.

Keywords: HTTP Adaptive Streaming · Edge computing · Content delivery · Network-assisted video streaming · Quality of experience · Machine learning

1 Introduction

Video streaming traffic today represents a significant fraction of mobile network traffic. Therefore, it became very important to assure a good QoE to the video clients. HTTP Adaptive Streaming (HAS) became the *de facto* standard for video streaming. HAS divides the content into chunks or segments, each one encoded in different qualities, which allows adapting to changing network conditions. The ABR algorithm decides which segment on which quality level to request. We can classify ABR algorithms into four main categories: *(1)* client-based adaptation, *(2)* server-based adaptation, *(3)* network-assisted adaptation, and *(4)* hybrid adaptation [4]. The most popular category is client-based adaptation. It provides scalability because the ABR algorithm runs in each client device. However, client-based adaptation has the problem that a client is not aware of what other clients are requesting.

B. Þór Jónsson et al. (Eds.): MMM 2022, LNCS 13142, pp. 394–406, 2022.
https://doi.org/10.1007/978-3-030-98355-0_33

Edge computing brings storage and computing power closer to the clients [11]. At the edge computing node, we also have access to radio metrics using the Radio Network Information Service (RNIS) [8] as well as to clients' player metrics [1]. Hence, an edge-based adaptation scheme has more computing power, storage and valuable information to run the ABR algorithm and make better decisions than clients independently.

Recurrent neural networks (RNNs) [24] are the common neural network structures when it comes to working with sequential data. Their structure allows them to capture the temporal dependencies thanks to their internal memory system. Long short-term memory networks (LSTMs) [10] are a special type of RNNs in which the memory is extended.

In this work, we use machine learning techniques in an edge-based ABR mechanism to improve the QoE by managing the tradeoff among bitrate, segment switches, and stalls according to the current radio network conditions. LSTM is deployed to predict parameters for this tradeoff based on radio conditions. Furthermore, we compare the results against different client-based and edge-based ABR algorithms in diverse radio scenarios.

The main contributions of this paper are as follows:

- the ECAS-ML system, an on-the-fly edge-based adaptation scheme with machine learning;
- the ECAS-ML ABR adaptation algorithm that manages the tradeoff among bitrate, segment switches and stalls to improve the QoE;
- the consideration of the device's screen resolution in the ABR algorithm, as higher screen resolutions demand higher bitrate to maintain a good QoE;
- machine learning techniques (*i.e.,* parameter prediction using LSTM) to improve managing the tradeoff mentioned above according to the current radio network conditions;
- a comprehensive evaluation of the ECAS-ML performance, including a comparison with other state-of-the-art client-based and edge-based ABR algorithms.

The remainder of this paper is structured as follows. Section 2 discusses related work. In Sect. 3 we present the proposed ECAS-ML approach. Section 4 introduces the experimental setup we created to evaluate ECAS-ML. The results are described in Sect. 5. Finally, Sect. 6 concludes the paper and outlines future work.

2   Related Work

Although most of the ABR algorithm proposals are client-based, we can also find edge-based solutions.

In [5], Bhat *et al.* leverage the information of network conditions available in a software-defined network (SDN) to provide assistance to the video streaming delivery process, improving the final QoE of the clients. The adaptation algorithms of the video streaming clients remain unmodified. Furthermore, a better selection of caching strategies can lead to higher cache hit rates and, in consequence, an improvement of the content delivery process and QoE.

In [9], Fajardo *et al.* introduce a new element in the mobile network architecture called ME-DAF to support multimedia delivery. ME-DAF implements content awareness, client awareness, and network awareness using the capabilities of edge computing. However, it is unclear if this scheme can outperform other edge-based ABR algorithms.

Kim *et al.* [15] propose an Edge Computing Assisted Adaptive Streaming Scheme for Mobile Networks that focuses on optimizing QoE, fairness and resource utilization. Moreover, they design an optimization model and a greedy-based ABR algorithm. Their results outperform other existing edge-based solutions such as Prius [26].

Aguilar-Armijo *et al.* [2] propose EADAS, an edge-based mechanism consisting of *(i)* an adaptation algorithm and *(ii)* a segment prefetching scheme that supports the client-based ABR algorithm by improving its decisions on-the-fly. EADAS leverages edge capabilities such as the availability of player metrics, radio metrics and all clients' requests, as well as storage and computing power to improve the final QoE and fairness of the video streaming clients, outperforming other ABR solutions.

We can also find other work that combines edge-based approaches with machine learning techniques.

In [6], Chang *et al.* introduce an edge-based adaptive scheme that uses Q-learning techniques to select the adequate bitrate during the video streaming session in shared networks. Moreover, they consider radio metrics provided by the RNIS. The proposed scheme is evaluated against client-based algorithms such as buffer-based, rate-based and dashJS, but not against edge-based ABR algorithms.

Ma *et al.* [18] present Steward: Smart Edge based Joint QoE Optimization for Adaptive Video Streaming. Their mechanism optimizes the QoE and fairness under bandwidth bottlenecks using an edge-based ABR algorithm based on neural networks and reinforcement learning. In our understanding, the comparison with other ABR algorithms should also include edge-based algorithms and should be made with different radio network conditions.

3   The ECAS-ML System

3.1   System Architecture

We propose an edge-based adaptation mechanism for HAS named ECAS-ML. The system architecture of ECAS-ML is shown in Fig. 1. When a client sends a segment request to the video server, it is intercepted by the ECAS-ML mechanism located at the edge computing node. Next, the adaptation algorithm is executed on-the-fly and sends the modified segment request to the server. During the whole video streaming session, ECAS-ML requests radio information from the RNIS and machine learning techniques are used to predict the best set of parameters by analyzing the radio traces periodically to provide a better adaptation. When the segment is served, the edge computing node forwards it to the client.

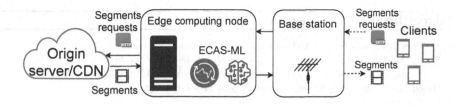

Fig. 1. ECAS-ML system architecture.

ECAS-ML is designed to be located on an edge node close to a base station in a cellular network. At this location, we have access to the necessary storage and computing power for running machine learning techniques. Moreover, we have access to radio metrics provided by the RNIS and to player metrics such as buffer size that are reported periodically by the clients using the HTTP POST protocol. This process was standardized by 3GPP [1].

3.2 ECAS Algorithm

There are four main factors that affect the QoE: bitrate, segment switches, stalls and screen resolution. There is a tradeoff among bitrate, segment switches and stalls where the improvement of one metric may degrade the others. For example, if we want to achieve a higher bitrate, it might be at the risk of possible stall events in case the radio throughput experiences fading.

Another factor that affects the QoE is the screen resolution of the device that is playing the video. The same bitrate leads to different QoE perceived by the user, *i.e.*, higher resolutions require higher bitrates to maintain a good QoE. This fourth factor is often ignored in state-of-the-art ABR algorithms. ECAS-ML considers the screen resolution in the QoE measurement as nowadays different devices with different resolutions are connected to the mobile networks consuming video streaming content (Table 1).

Table 1. Notation used in this paper.

Symbol	Definition
Q	Number of quality representations
N	Window size (number of segments)
L	Segment length (sec.)
$r_{s,t}$	Bitrate of the quality s of the segment number t (kbps)
$r'_{s,t}$	Bitrate score of the quality s of the segment number t (kbps)
$\overline{r}_{t..t-N}$	Mean bitrate of the last N+1 segments (kbps)
B	Current buffer level of the current client (sec.)
$B_{s,t+1}$	Predicted buffer level after requesting quality s of the segment number t+1 (sec.)
$dt_{s,t+1}$	Download time of quality s of the segment number t+1 (sec.)

Algorithm 1: ECAS-ML algorithm.

---

1 // This algorithm is executed for each segment request for each client
   Data: *switches_penalty_factor, stalls_penalty_factor, buffer_threshold_1, buffer_threshold_2, screen_resolution, est_throughput, Q, N, L, B,* $\overline{r_{t..t-N}}$
   Result: Quality index to request (*quality_to_request*)

2 $QoE\_score = 0$;

3 $quality\_to\_request = 0$;

4 $best\_score = 0$;

5 // For each quality index

6 **for** *s = 0, 1, 2, ... Q-1* **do**

7   **if** *screen_resolution == "240p"* **then**

8          $\beta = 8.17$;

9   **if** *screen_resolution == "360p"* **then**

10         $\beta = 3.73$;

11   **if** *screen_resolution == "480p"* **then**

12         $\beta = 2.75$;

13   **if** *screen_resolution == "720p"* **then**

14         $\beta = 1.89$;

15   **if** *screen_resolution == "1080p"* **then**

16         $\beta = 0.78$;

17   **if** *screen_resolution == "2160p"* **then**

18         $\beta = 0.5$;

19     $r'_{s,t+1} = r_{s,t+1} \times (1 - e^{-\beta \times r_{s,t+1} \times 0.001})$

20     $\overline{r_{t+1..t-N}} = \frac{(\overline{r_{t..t-N}} \times (N+1)) + r_{s,t+1}}{N+2}$

21     $switches\_penalty = |\overline{r_{t+1..t-N}} - r_{s,t+1}| \times switches\_penalty\_factor$

22     $dt_{s,t+1} = \frac{r_{s,t+1} \times L}{est\_throughput}$

23     $B_{s,t+1} = B + L - dt_{s,t+1}$

24   **if** $B_{s,t+1} < L \times buffer\_threshold\_1$ **then**

25   // Buffer in high risk area, we do not consider that quality

26         $QoE\_score = -inf$;

27   **else**

28   **if** $B_{s,t+1} < L \times buffer\_threshold\_2$ **then**

29   // Buffer in medium risk area

30             $b\_dif = L \times buffer\_threshold\_2 - B_{s,t+1}$
               $stalls\_penalty = b\_dif \times \overline{r_{t+1..t-N}} \times stalls\_penalty\_factor$
               $QoE\_score = r'_{s,t+1} - switches\_penalty - stalls\_penalty$;

31   **else**

32   // Buffer in low risk area

33             $QoE\_score = r'_{s,t+1} - switches\_penalty$;

34   **if** *s == 0* **then**

35         $best\_score = QoE\_score$;

36   **if** *QoE_score > best_score* **then**

37         $best\_score = QoE\_score$;

38         $quality\_to\_request = s$;

39 **return** *quality_to_request*;

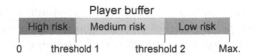

Fig. 2. ECAS-ML buffer areas.

ECAS-ML was designed to manage the tradeoff among bitrate, segment switches and stalls and to consider the screen resolution in order to maximize the final QoE perceived by the user. For that purpose, we introduce four variables in our algorithm:

- *Switches penalty factor*, an integer number that controls the segment switches. A high switches penalty factor indicates we prioritize reducing segment switches during the video streaming session.
- *Stalls penalty factor*, an integer number that controls the stalls. The higher the stalls penalty factor, the fewer stalls will occur during the video streaming session.
- *Buffer threshold 1*, an integer number that delimits the high-risk area of the buffer. A long high-risk area means more conservative segment requests, therefore, fewer stalls and lower mean bitrate.
- *Buffer threshold 2*, an integer number that delimits the low-risk area of the buffer. ECAS-ML focuses on maintaining the buffer in the medium-risk and low-risk areas, in order to keep the video streaming session stable. The different buffer areas are shown in Fig. 2.

For each segment request of each user, Algorithm 1 is executed. The algorithm evaluates all the different qualities and assigns each one of them a QoE score. Finally, it would request the segment quality with the highest QoE score.

For each segment quality, the process to assign a QoE score is the following:

- **Phase 1** *(lines 7 to 19)*: First, it considers the device's screen resolution to calculate the bitrate score $r'_{s,t+1}$. We use the equations and β values shown in [3] as a baseline for our algorithm. The beta value models the curve that relates bitrate and Mean Opinion Score (MOS). We obtain and include beta values for 1080p and 2160p resolutions according to our experiments.
- **Phase 2** *(lines 20 to 23)*: This phase of the algorithm calculates: *(1)* the mean bitrate of the last $N + 1$ segments plus the segment quality we are evaluating ($\overline{r_{t+1..t-N}}$); *(2)* the switches penalty; *(3)* the download time for the segment quality we are evaluating using the estimated throughput based on the radio and backhaul throughput available at the RNIS ($dt_{s,t+1}$); and *(4)* the estimated player buffer size after receiving the quality we are evaluating ($B_{s,t+1}$).
- **Phase 3** *(lines 24 to 33)*: In this phase, different lines of code are executed depending on the estimated buffer size and the buffer thresholds. We differentiate three risk areas: *High risk:* there is a high risk of a stall if we request this quality, so its QoE score is set to the minimum which means we do not

consider that quality. *Medium risk:* there is a medium risk of a stall in future requests, so we apply a switches penalty and a stall penalty proportionally to the difference between the estimated buffer size and threshold 2. *Low risk:* we consider there is no risk of stalls in the following segment request and only the switches penalty is applied.

– **Phase 4** *(lines 34 to 38)*: Finally, if the QoE score of the quality we are evaluating is better than the previous best QoE score, we update the quality to request and the best score to beat.

3.3   Parameter Prediction with Machine Learning

The machine learning part of ECAS-ML is designed to process sequential data since radio traces consist of the throughput over time. We model this problem as predicting the most suitable parameters for the given radio trace, thus a regression problem.

RNNs are known to work well with sequential data. One downside of RNNs is short-term memory. If the input sequence is long, RNNs usually fail to utilize the early stage information to later stages. To address this issue LSTM [10] is proposed.

The memory structure in LSTM consists of three gates (*i.e.*, input, forget, and output). When new input arrives, these gates can be used to perform three different actions: *(1)* use the incoming information (input gate); *(2)* delete the information (forget gate); and *(3)* use the incoming information to impact the output (output gate). This structure allows LSTM to remember the input for a longer time; thus, enabling the LSTM to exploit the dependencies when the temporal delay is higher.

RNNs have one common drawback, which is the exploding gradients problem, and we used gradient clipping [20] to address this issue. Moreover, Huber loss [13] with $\Delta = 1$ is used as the loss function as it is known to work better against exploding gradients compared to mean absolute error (MAE). Also, it combines the advantages of both mean squared error (MSE) and MAE losses.

We use an LSTM-based approach to predict parameters since LSTMs are known to exploit long-term dependencies effectively [7]. The proposed structure is illustrated in Fig. 3. The proposed model takes the throughput over time as an input and predicts the optimal set of parameters for the given input vector. The input vector length increases as the streaming session continues and new parameters are predicted periodically.

The ML model takes a radio trace as input which is the throughput per second, and predicts a vector with four values (*i.e.*, *switch penalty, stall penalty, threshold 1,* and *threshold 2*). The input vector ($V_{t,s}$) definition for a given trace (t) and second (s) is given in Eq. 1.

$$V_{t,s} = [T_{t,1}, T_{t,2}, T_{t,3}, ..., T_{t,s}] \tag{1}$$

where ($T_{t,s}$) is the throughput in second s for the radio trace t. Each value in the input vector is the throughput per second from the beginning of the streaming

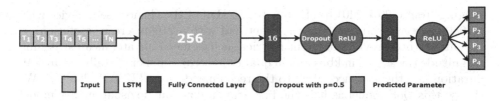

Fig. 3. Structure of the proposed LSTM-based model. The numbers inside the boxes indicate the output feature size. T_N is the throughput value at the Nth second in the radio trace.

session until the current second. By following this approach, it is possible to utilize the ML model in the very early stages of the streaming session as the minimum length of the input vector is five (*i.e.*, five seconds of the radio trace). Moreover, as the streaming continues, the ML model has more reliable data to predict, thus resulting in a better set of parameters.

Since the radio trace lengths can vary, the input size of the model should be adaptive. The ML model in ECAS-ML is designed to work with variable length traces. One common approach to follow in those situations is padding the input to match the maximum sequence length in the dataset. However, using zero padding is not suitable for our use case as the throughput can actually be zero from time to time. Thus, we did not apply any padding; instead, we trained the network with a single radio trace (*i.e.*, batch size 1) at a time.

4   Experimental Setup

To test our proposed scheme ECAS-ML, we developed a Python-based edge computing and video streaming simulator that supports edge mechanisms, real radio traces and video streaming datasets. Its architecture consists of a video streaming server, an edge computing node, a base station and multiple clients. We consider the latency and the throughput between each path of the network to simulate the content delivery. The testbed follows the procedure explained in Sect. 3.1. Periodically, the edge computing node collects player and radio information to perform the adaptation decisions.

To compare performance, we implement three client-based ABR algorithms that follow three different approaches: throughput-based ABR (TBA [19]), buffer-based ABR (BBA [12]), and hybrid-based ABR (SARA [14]). Moreover, we implement three edge-based ABR algorithms: Greedy-Based Bitrate Allocation (GBBA) [15], EADAS [2], and our proposed scheme ECAS-ML.

We use the *Big Buck Bunny*[1] video from the streaming dataset [17]; it must be noted that similar results were obtained with other videos. We choose two second segments and bitrate levels of [50, 100, 150, 200, 250, 300, 400, 500, 600, 700, 900, 1200, 1500, 2000, 2500, 3000, 4000, 5000, 6000, 8000] kbps in resolutions

---

[1] http://ftp.itec.aau.at/datasets/DASHDataset2014/BigBuckBunny/2sec/.

ranging from (320 × 240) to (1920 × 1080). Half of the clients use a device with a 1080p screen resolution, and the other half with a 2160p screen resolution.

Our testbed provides different metrics such as mean bitrate, mean switching magnitude (measured in kbps and in quality indices), number of stalls, mean stall duration and the QoE according to the recommendation ITU-T P.1203 [23]. We choose this QoE model as it is the first standardized audiovisual quality model for HAS and it has been widely trained and validated.

For the radio traces, our simulator uses real radio traces from a 4G dataset [22] with different mobility patterns. This dataset consists of 5 trace categories, and each category contains a different number of radio traces (*i.e.*, *bus (16)*, *car (53)*, *pedestrian (31)*, *static (15)*, and *train (20)*). There are 135 radio traces in total, and we removed 6 from the dataset since they were causing an imbalance in the dataset due to being too long. In the end, we used 121 traces for training and 8 for testing. Since each category has a different number of traces, we picked one trace from *bus* and *static* and two from *car, pedestrian*, and *train* for testing.

For each radio trace in the training set, input vectors are extracted from the fifth second until the end of the trace. These vectors are then shuffled randomly and used for training the model. We used 136, 466 input vectors in total for training and 10, 015 for testing. We needed the optimal set of parameters as labels for input vectors in the training dataset. These parameters were found by applying a brute force approach in the simulation.

Pytorch [21] is used as the machine learning framework. The LSTM model is trained with Adam [16] as the optimizer with the learning rate of $5e - 6$, and Huber loss [13] with $\Delta = 1$ as the loss function. Dropout [25] is applied after each layer to prevent overfitting. The ECAS-ML model is trained for 50 epochs with a gradient clipping applied to prevent the exploding gradients problem.

5   Results

5.1   ECAS Performance Evaluation

We compare the performance of ECAS-ML to other client-based and edge-based ABR algorithms as explained in Sect. 4.

Table 2. ECAS performance evaluation.

	BBA	TBA	SARA	GBBA	EADAS	ECAS-ML
Mean bitrate (kbps)	1314	2700	2700	2732	2668	2772
Mean switching magnitude (kbps)	325	921	633	991	958	1113
Mean switching magnitude (quality index)	1.02	4.00	3.14	3.32	4.14	4.21
Number of stalls	0	246	65	97	22	16
Mean stall duration (ms)	0	1107	1427	3153	2407	2523
QoE score (ITU-T P.1203 mode 0)	3.25	3.05	2.86	3.07	3.41	3.65

In Table 2 we show the mean metrics of the eight clients during the video streaming session. ECAS-ML has the highest mean switching magnitude, which decreases the QoE, but also the highest mean bitrate and a low number of stalls. The tradeoff among bitrate, segment switches and stalls is successfully managed as ECAS-ML achieves a high QoE, outperforming other client-based and edge-based algorithms. More concretely, ECAS-ML improves over the QoE of *BBA* by 12.31%, of *TBA* by 19.67%, of *SARA* by 27.6,2%, of *GBBA* by 18.89%, and of *EADAS* by 7.04%.

TBA, *SARA* and *GBBA* have a high number of stalls since their algorithms are not conservative enough for sudden drops in the radio throughput as they occur in the real 4G traces we used to conduct these experiments. Even with a high mean bitrate, this high number of stalls decreases the final QoE.

5.2 Buffer Behavior

We show the behavior of the buffer size over time in Fig. 2. This simulation was made with one user with a car mobility pattern with the setup explained in Sect. 4. The value of the first buffer threshold is 3 and the value of the second buffer threshold is 6, therefore, as the segment duration is 2 s, the buffer areas are as follows:

- High-risk area: from 0 s to 6 s.
- Medium-risk area: from 6 s to 12 s.
- Low-risk area: from 12 s to 20 s (maximum buffer size) (Fig. 4).

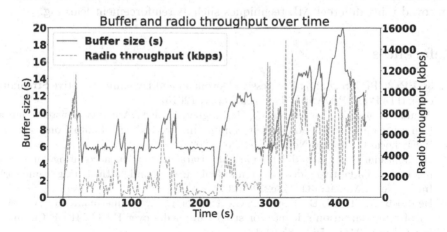

Fig. 4. Buffer size and radio throughput over time.

ECAS-ML provides the best quality possible while maintaining the buffer level above the first threshold, set at 6 s, and considering the segment switches penalty. Even in highly variable conditions such as the radio throughput traces used in this simulation, ECAS-ML prevents many stalls by avoiding the high-risk area where stalls occur more frequently. The second buffer threshold is not as critical as the first one, as it delimits the medium-risk and low-risk areas. If the buffer is in the low-risk area, it will not face any stalls penalty, just the switching penalty. Hence it would tend to request higher qualities as long as the radio throughput is high enough, and it will return to the medium-risk area if the radio throughput drops.

Determining proper values of both buffer thresholds is key for the adequate performance of ECAS-ML. If the first threshold is set too low, sudden radio throughput drops may lead to stall events that degrade the QoE. On the other hand, if the first threshold value is too high, the behavior would be too conservative, and we may not leverage all the network's resources.

6   Conclusions and Future Work

In this work, we present ECAS-ML, an edge-based adaptation scheme for HAS. ECAS-ML focuses on achieving the best QoE managing the tradeoff among bitrate, segment switches and stalls. For this purpose, the ECAS-ML algorithm includes four variables: switches penalty factor, stalls penalty factor and two buffer thresholds. ECAS-ML also considers the device's resolution in its algorithm, as higher resolutions demand higher bitrates to achieve a good QoE. ECAS-ML utilizes an LSTM model to predict the optimal set of parameters for the given status of the radio trace. Results show that ECAS-ML outperforms other ABR algorithms: client-based (BBA, TBA and SARA) and edge-based ones (GBBA and EADAS). In future work, the parameter prediction part of ECAS-ML can be improved using different ML techniques such as reinforcement learning.

References

1. 3GPP: 3GPP TS 26.247. Progressive Download and Dynamic Adaptive Streaming over HTTP (3GP-DASH). Technical report (2015)
2. Aguilar-Armijo, J., Timmerer, C., Hellwagner, H.: EADAS: edge assisted adaptation scheme for HTTP adaptive streaming. In: Proceedings of 46th Conference on IEEE Local Computer Networks (LCN) (2021)
3. Belmoukadam, O., Jawad Khokhar, M., Barakat, C.: On accounting for screen resolution in adaptive video streaming: QoE-driven bandwidth sharing framework. Int. J. Netw. Manage 31(1), e2128 (2021)
4. Bentaleb, A., Taani, B., Begen, A.C., Timmerer, C., Zimmermann, R.: A survey on bitrate adaptation schemes for streaming media over HTTP. IEEE Commun. Surv. Tutor. 21(1), 562–585 (2018)
5. Bhat, D., Rizk, A., Zink, M., Steinmetz, R.: SABR: network-assisted content distribution for QoE-driven ABR video streaming. ACM Trans. Multimedia Comput. Commun. Appl. (TOMM) 14(2s), 1–25 (2018)

6. Chang, Z., Zhou, X., Wang, Z., Li, H., Zhang, X.: Edge-assisted adaptive video streaming with deep learning in mobile edge networks. In: 2019 IEEE Wireless Communications and Networking Conference (WCNC), pp. 1–6. IEEE (2019)
7. Chung, J., Gulcehre, C., Cho, K., Bengio, Y.: Empirical evaluation of gated recurrent neural networks on sequence modeling. In: NIPS 2014 Workshop on Deep Learning (2014)
8. ETSI: Mobile Edge Computing (MEC); Radio Network Information API. Technical report. Accessed: October 2020
9. Fajardo, J.O., Taboada, I., Liberal, F.: Improving content delivery efficiency through multi-layer mobile edge adaptation. IEEE Netw. **29**(6), 40–46 (2015)
10. Hochreiter, S., Schmidhuber, J.: Long short-term memory. Neural Comput. **9**(8), 1735–1780 (1997). https://doi.org/10.1162/neco.1997.9.8.1735
11. Hu, Y.C., Patel, M., Sabella, D., Sprecher, N., Young, V.: Mobile edge computing-a key technology towards 5G. ETSI White Paper **11**(11), 1–16 (2015)
12. Huang, T.Y., Johari, R., McKeown, N., Trunnell, M., Watson, M.: A buffer-based approach to rate adaptation: evidence from a large video streaming service. ACM SIGCOMM Comput. Commun. Rev. **44**(4), 187–198 (2014)
13. Huber, P.J.: Robust estimation of a location parameter. In: Breakthroughs in Statistics, pp. 492–518. Springer, Cham (1992). https://doi.org/10.1007/978-1-4612-4380-9_35
14. Juluri, P., Tamarapalli, V., Medhi, D.: SARA: segment aware rate adaptation algorithm for dynamic adaptive streaming over HTTP. In: Proceedings of IEEE International Conference on Communication Workshops (ICCW), pp. 1765–1770 (2015)
15. Kim, M., Chung, K.: Edge computing assisted adaptive streaming scheme for mobile networks. IEEE Access **9**, 2142–2152 (2021)
16. Kingma, D.P., Ba, J.: Adam: a method for stochastic optimization. In: 3rd International Conference on Learning Representations (ICLR) (2015)
17. Lederer, S., Müller, C., Timmerer, C.: Dynamic adaptive streaming over HTTP dataset. In: Proceedings of 3rd ACM Multimedia Systems Conference, pp. 89–94 (2012)
18. Ma, X., Li, Q., Chai, J., Xiao, X., Xia, S.T., Jiang, Y.: Steward: smart edge based joint QoE optimization for adaptive video streaming. In: Proceedings of 29th ACM NOSSDAV Workshop, pp. 31–36 (2019)
19. Nguyen, D.V., Le, H.T., Nam, P.N., Pham, A.T., Thang, T.C.: Adaptation method for video streaming over HTTP/2. IEICE Commun. Express **5**(3), 69–73 (2016)
20. Pascanu, R., Mikolov, T., Bengio, Y.: On the difficulty of training recurrent neural networks. In: International Conference on Machine Learning, pp. 1310–1318. PMLR (2013)
21. Paszke, A., et al.: PyTorch: an imperative style, high-performance deep learning library. In: Advances in Neural Information Processing Systems, pp. 8024–8035 (2019)
22. Raca, D., Quinlan, J.J., Zahran, A.H., Sreenan, C.J.: Beyond throughput: a 4G LTE dataset with channel and context metrics. In: Proceedings of 9th ACM Multimedia Systems Conference, pp. 460–465 (2018)
23. Robitza, W., et al.: HTTP adaptive streaming QoE estimation with ITU-T Rec. P.1203 - open databases and software. In: Proceedings of 9th ACM Multimedia Systems Conference, Amsterdam (2018). https://doi.org/10.1145/3204949.3208124
24. Rumelhart, D.E., Hinton, G.E., Williams, R.J.: Learning representations by back-propagating errors. Nature **323**(6088), 533–536 (1986)

25. Srivastava, N., Hinton, G., Krizhevsky, A., Sutskever, I., Salakhutdinov, R.: Dropout: a simple way to prevent neural networks from overfitting. J. Mach. Learn. Res. **15**(1), 1929–1958 (2014)
26. Yan, Z., Xue, J., Chen, C.W.: Prius: hybrid edge cloud and client adaptation for HTTP adaptive streaming in cellular networks. IEEE Trans. Circuits Syst. Video Technol. **27**(1), 209–222 (2016)

Fast CU Depth Decision Algorithm for AVS3

Shiyi Liu[1,2]($\boxtimes$), Zhenyu Wang[1,2]($\boxtimes$), Ke Qiu[1,2]($\boxtimes$), Jiayu Yang[1,2]($\boxtimes$), and Ronggang Wang[1,2]($\boxtimes$)

[1] National Engineering Laboratory for Video Technology,
Peking University Shenzhen Graduate School, Shenzhen, China
{shy_liu11,qiuke,jiayuyang}@pku.edu.cn, {wangzhenyu,rgwang}@pkusz.edu.cn
[2] Pengcheng Laboratory, Shenzhen, China

Abstract. The third generation of Audio Video Coding Standard (AVS3) achieves more than 20% coding performance improvement compared with the previous video coding standards, HEVC and AVS2. AVS3 adopted a more flexible CU partition scheme, which brings promising coding efficiency but makes the computational complexity much higher than HEVC and AVS2. In this paper, we propose fast algorithms for CU partitioning based on the CU depth. The spatial neighboring depth information is used to predict a QT depth range of current CU, according to which the partition tree can be befittingly pruned. On this basis, we predict a proposed BET (BT and EQT) depth to further skip some partitions. The threshold to skip partition processes is decided from statistics. The experimental results show that the combination of the proposed methods can achieve 22.07% time-saving with 0.57% BDBR loss under Random Access configuration and 45.17% complexity reduction with 0.50% BDBR loss under All Intra configuration.

Keywords: AVS3 · QT · BET · Fast algorithm

1 Introduction

The third generation of Audio Video coding Standard (AVS3) is the advanced video compression standard developed by the AVS working group of China to improve video coding efficiency. The baseline profile was finalized on March 9, 2019, which saves 23.52% bit-rate compared with AVS2 [1] and 22% bit-rate with HEVC [2]. However, the improved coding efficiency benefit from new coding tools is at the cost of a much higher computational complexity. The encoding time of AVS3 is twice that of AVS2 and seven times as long as HEVC [3].

As widely recognized, block partitioning is the most time-consuming module in the hybrid video coding framework due to the recursive hierarchy and the rate-distortion optimal (RDO) process. In the hierarchical unit representation framework that consists of coding unit (CU), prediction unit (PU), and transformation unit (TU), CU splits recursively as a basic unit at the top level while

© Springer Nature Switzerland AG 2022
B. Þór Jónsson et al. (Eds.): MMM 2022, LNCS 13142, pp. 407–418, 2022.
https://doi.org/10.1007/978-3-030-98355-0_34

predict and transform should be decided on that basis. Moreover, each combination of PU and TU type in every CU node contains a complete RDO process, and the optimal CU size and mode are selected and signaled by minimizing a Lagrangian RD cost,

$$J = D + \lambda \cdot R, \tag{1}$$

where D represents the distortion between original and reconstructed pixel values and R specifies the number of bits required that weight with a constant Lagrange multiplier λ. As a result, the CU splitting procedure increases encoding complexity signally, thus pruning the CU partition tree can decrease encoding complexity effectively.

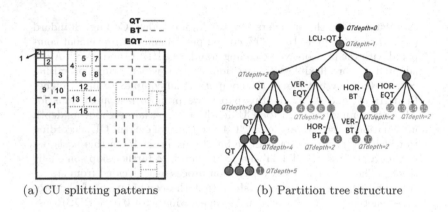

(a) CU splitting patterns   (b) Partition tree structure

Fig. 1. Illustration of CU partitioning structure in AVS3.

Compared with AVS2 and HEVC, the CU splitting structure is more flexible in AVS3. In the first place, AVS3 adopts multiple tree types by introducing nested binary-tree (BT) and extended quad-tree (EQT) [4] in addition to quad-tree (QT). Figure 1(a) demonstrates the CU splitting patterns of QTBT plus EQT partition structure in AVS3. BT in horizontal and vertical directions splits a CU into two symmetric rectangular parts, while EQT in the two directions may produce two narrow sub-CUs on the upper and lower edge and two sub-CUs with the same shape as their parent. Particularly, BT and EQT can apply to the leaf nodes of all partition types in the partitioning tree, while QT is not allowed to split the sub-CUs of BT or EQT in AVS3. In addition to the multiple tree structure, AVS3 also expands the largest CU (LCU) size from 64×64 to 128×128, and the smallest CU (SCU) size is 4×4. Figure 1(b) shows the sub-tree structure of the first QT node with $QTDepth = 1$ while mapping to Fig. 1(a) of AVS3. When LCU is split by QT recursively, the QT depth increases until reaching the allowed maximum QT depth. As a result of the multiple tree structure and the larger LCU size, the number of possible CU sizes increases exponentially. Given that all the allowed partition types and splitting depths are evaluated by the

RDO process to determine the best CU size, the computational complexity of the AVS3 encoder surges accordingly. Therefore, it's fairly necessary to optimize CU partition to promote the real applications of AVS3.

In this paper, we propose depth-based algorithms using very close spatial information to optimize the CU partition process. The spatial neighboring SCU depth information is first utilized to predict the optimal QT depth and prune the partition tree. Furthermore, an BET (BT and EQT) depth of the neighboring SCUs is proposed to predict the BT and EQT depth and skip the RDO process of some partitions. The algorithms can work under both Random Access (RA) configuration and All Intra (AI) configuration. Experiment results show that the proposed approach can reduce remarkable encoding time with negligible performance loss for both inter and intra coding.

The rest of the paper organizes as follows. The review of related work presents in Sect. 2. Section 3 describes the proposed depth-based fast method for CU partitioning. Experimental results and analysis are in Sect. 4. Finally, Sect. 5 concludes this paper.

2   Related Work

As the more flexible CU partition structure is adopted in the advanced video coding standards, numerous fast approaches have been proposed to reduce its adverse impact on coding complexity increasing. To address the CU partition mode decision problem in the encoding process, most fast methods develop based on statistics. However, in recent years, more and more learning-based fast algorithms have emerged. [17] explored a fast encoding approach based on Convolutional Neural Networks to partly substitute classical heuristics-based encoder speed-ups by a systematic and automatic process. [18] proposed a fast intra-encoding platform for AVS2. The platform uses numerous speedup methods, including code optimization, single-instruction multiple-data acceleration, and fast algorithms for almost all the time-consuming modules. However, the drawbacks of such learning-based fast methods are apparent. First, finding effective features for decisions requires professional domain understandings and is very time-consuming. Second, there is complexity overhead to extract features and to learn the optimum hyper-plane with an online learning mode. Finally, the speed-up performance of the learning-based method relies heavily on the training data [20].

On the contrary, the statistical approaches usually also achieve efficient speed-up performance requiring very limited complexity overhead in implementation. [7] explored the RD costs and distortion characteristics of sub-CUs for HEVC. In [8], the texture complexity of an inter CU was evaluated based on the coding information of the co-located CU to terminate CU splitting in HEVC. [9] listed 13 fast strategies for CU partitioning using the splitting topology and RD cost characteristics for the upcoming *Versatile Video Coding* (VVC). For AVS3, [22] reduced intra mode search progress by rough mode search and share candidates. In [11], the texture direction is studied to prune the AVS3 intra CU partition tree. To save the inter encoding complexity, [10] calculated a texture difference metric and [19] utilized the optimal results of BT to skip QT and EQT, which achieved remarkable time-savings in the early reference software of AVS3.

Among the statistical approaches, spatial correlation is widely used to save encoding time. [5] studied the complexity of local texture for intra CU to reduce the depth searches in AVS2. In [6], the depth information correlation between spatio-temporal adjacent CUs was used to skip some depths in HEVC. [21] utilized neighboring LCU depth information to speed up VVC intra coding.

However, the fast methods for AVS2 and HEVC can not deal with the multiple CU partition trees in AVS3 since the depth of BT and EQT is different from the CU depth in the partition tree that only contains QT. The fast methods for VVC can hardly work on EQT due to the different splitting structures. Moreover, the introduction of multiple CU partition types and more inter-prediction tools makes the fast algorithm for CU partition in inter-frame coding more complicated and difficult. On top of the fast methods for VVC and AVS3, the spatial correlation of neighboring LCUs or CUs can hardly be used to optimize the complexity in inter coding.

3   The Proposed Method

Since the texture and motion information of neighboring CUs are similar due to spatial correlation in video content, the splitting depth of neighboring CUs may also close to each other. Based on the CU partition scheme in AVS3 described in Sect. 1, the partition of a CU can be divided into two processes, including recursive QT splitting and recursive BET splitting. Therefore, the acceleration methods of this paper predict the QT depth and BET depth respectively using the spatial neighboring depth information to prune the CU partition tree.

3.1   QT Depth Prediction

On account that all partition types can apply to the leaf nodes of QT, the RDO search of QT is very time-consuming. Considering that the spatial correlation decrease with the increase of distance in natural images, we predict the optimal QT depth of the current CU by using the QT depths of neighboring SCUs instead of neighboring CU or LCU. The CU partition tree can be pruned by skipping some unlikely QT depths in the encoder.

In the proposed method, a QT depth searching range for the current CU is derived from the nearest neighboring CUs. As is shown in Fig. 2, up to six adjacent SCUs at the top and left of the current CU are considered, which are consistent with SKIP/DIRECT motion candidates. We calculate the maximal and minimal QT depth of the neighboring SCUs, which generate the predicted QT depth range. The RDO process will only search the optimal QT depth of the current CU within this range. More specifically, we skip BT and EQT when the current QT depth is smaller than the predicted minimal QT depth and perform CU splitting using QT directly to compare with non-split. On the contrary, if

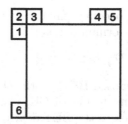

Fig. 2. Positions of neighboring reference SCUs.

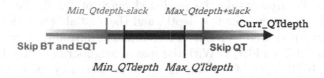

Fig. 3. The predicted range of QT depth.

the current QT depth is larger than the predicted maximum QT depth, QT is skipped and other partition types will be checked as usual.

To improve the accuracy of prediction, we introduce some restrictions. In particular, when the current CU is out of the boundary or at the edge of the picture, some neighboring CUs are not available. In this case, the prediction of QT depth may be inaccurate. Hence, this method will be disabled if there are less than two available neighboring SCUs in Fig. 2. Furthermore, on account that the spatial correlation may discontinue, a slack variable is used to reduce the compression loss introduced by misestimation. With the slack variable, the predicted optimal QT depth range can be expanded, as Fig. 3 shows. A smaller depth range leads to more time saving but larger compression performance loss, while a larger depth range will cause less encoding time-saving at the cost of less compression efficiency loss. The slack variable is decided in Sect. 3.3.

3.2 BET Depth Prediction

According to the CU partition scheme of AVS3, once a CU is split by BT or EQT, QT is not allowed to split the offspring anymore, the recursive BT and EQT partitions cost much complexity. When the spatial neighboring QT depths are very similar, the splitting depth generated by BT and EQT may also spatially close. In this part, we predict a BET splitting depth of the current CU, and some partitions beyond the predicted BET depth are skipped.

For the QT nested BT plus EQT partitioning structure of AVS3 illustrated in Fig. 1, a BET depth is proposed to express the CU splitting depth generated by BT and EQT. From the perspective of the CU area becoming smaller after splitting, BT makes the area of the sub-CU become half of the original, and the EQT makes the area of the sub-CU become a quarter of the original. We consider the extent that CU becomes smaller to express the CU depth of BT and EQT. The BET depth is formulated as (2),

$$D_{BET} = D_{QT} * 2 - log_2(w) - log_2(h),\qquad(2)$$

where D_{BET} denotes the proposed BET depth, D_{QT} represents the QT depth. w and h denote the width and height of CU, respectively. EQT increases the BET depth by 2 and BT increases the BET depth by 1. On the other hand, QT does not affect BET depth. When a CU is only split by QT recursively, BET depth remains 0 until BT or EQT is applied.

In the middle area within the predicted range of Fig. 3, the predicted QT depth is close to the current QT depth, and the spatial correlation of the proposed BET depth is used to reduce the complexity introduced by the recursive RDO process of BT and EQT. With the spatial neighboring SCUs demonstrated in Fig. 2, the BET depth of the current CU is predicted by calculating the average BET depth of all available neighboring BET depths. When the predicted BET depth is small, the RDO process will not search the EQT partition as it leads to the BET depth increment by 2.

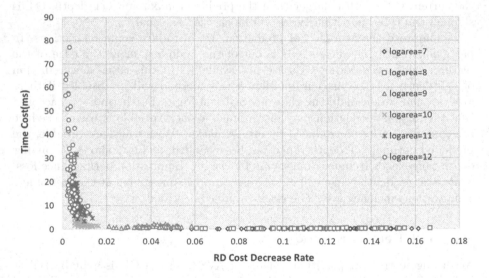

Fig. 4. The scatter plot of the RD Cost and encoding time influenced by EQT.

To reduce the prediction error, we disable the BET prediction in some situations. Since CU splits recursively, the effect of the fast algorithm has a strong correlation with CU size. The scatter diagram shown in Fig. 4 demonstrates the impact of EQT on RD cost and encoding time when EQT is selected as the optimal partition mode among different CU sizes. In convenience, CU size is represented by taking the logarithm of the CU area,

$$logarea = log_2(w) + log_2(h).\qquad(3)$$

According to Fig. 4, the EQT decision process of CUs with a larger size costs more encoding time while decreasing less RD Cost. In particular, when CUs with a *logarea* larger than 10 skip the decision process of EQT, much encoding time is saved, only increasing less than 2% RD Cost. On the contrary, skipping the EQT decision process of CUs with *logarea* less than 10 cannot save much encoding time but increase much RD Cost, which may lead to large compression efficiency loss. Therefore, we propose that CUs with *logarea* less than 10 are not allowed to either predict BET depth or skip EQT.

3.3 Threshold Decisions

In this part, we decide the slack variable of the QT depth prediction method and the BET depth threshold of the BET depth prediction method statistically.

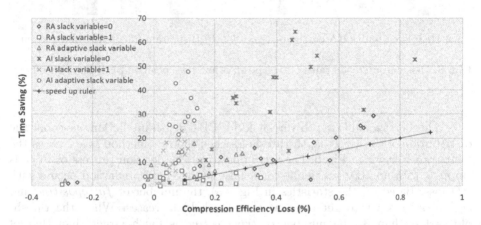

Fig. 5. The scatter plot of the compression efficiency loss and time-saving with different slack variables.

We introduce three mechanisms of slack variable and select the optimal one under RA and AI configurations through statistics of testing. In addition to setting the slack variable 0 and 1, an adaptive slack variable mechanism is designed to reduce the performance loss induced by misprediction and improve the encoding time-saving. To be more specific, when the predicted maximum QT depth equals the predicted minimum QT depth, we use a slack variable of 1 and otherwise 0. Figure 5 demonstrates the compression efficiency loss and the time-saving of the three mechanisms under RA and AI configurations. Each point represents the test result of a sequence. Since a large slack variable leads to large efficiency loss but more time-saving, it may be hard to evaluate the three mechanisms. For convenience, we propose a speed-up ruler to evaluate the trade-off between compression efficiency loss and time-saving. The ruler stipulates that the ratio of time-saving and compression efficiency loss is 25, as shown by the straight line in Fig. 5. We consider that more result points above the ruler, better the corresponding mechanism of the slack variable. When all the result points are above the ruler, more time-saving, better the corresponding mechanism. It can be seen that under RA configuration, only the adaptive slack variable mechanism is above the ruler, while under AI configuration, most points far exceed expectations, and setting the slack variable 0 can save more encoding time.

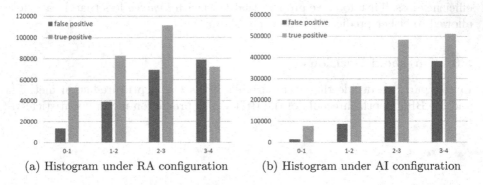

(a) Histogram under RA configuration   (b) Histogram under AI configuration

Fig. 6. Distribution histograms of true positive and false positive BET depth threshold.

To get a reasonable depth threshold for BET depth prediction, we count the distribution of the BET depth threshold when the fast method is active, as the histograms shown in Fig. 6. For a true positive, the decision process of EQT is skipped with no RD loss, while for a false positive, misprediction occurs with RD loss. Based on the statistics in Fig. 6(a), the number of $falsepositive$ and $truepositive$ start to get close as the threshold increases. When the threshold is less than 3, the number of $truepositive$ is much larger than that of $falsepositive$. By contrast, the number of $truepositive$ is always larger than that of $falsepositive$ under AI configuration, as shown in Fig. 6(b). When the threshold is larger than 3, more than 40% positive samples are $falsepositive$, which may lead to large compression efficiency loss. Consequently, the BET depth threshold to skip EQT is set 3 under both RA and AI configurations.

4   Experimental Results

The proposed method is carried out on the reference software of AVS3, High-Performance Model (HPM) [12], and the open-source platform of AVS3, uAVS3e [13] under the common test condition of AVS3 [14]. More specifically, video sequences are tested for 2 s under RA configuration and 10 s with a downsampling ratio of 8 under AI configuration at four QP values of 27, 32, 38, and 45. The test platform is Intel(R) Xeon(R) Gold 6154 CPU@3.00 GHz. The performance of the proposed fast methods is evaluated by measuring the trade-off between the coding performance in terms of Bjøntegaard delta bit rate (BDBR) [15] at Y

Table 1. Experimental results on HPM-4.0.

Sequences		QT depth prediction method				QT&BET depth prediction method			
		RA		AI		RA		AI	
		BDBR	TS	BDBR	TS	BDBR	TS	BDBR	TS
UHD-4K	Tango2	0.05%	4.69%	0.25%	21.48%	0.86%	26.88%	0.68%	39.53%
	ParkRunning3	0.16%	15.52%	0.17%	22.38%	0.62%	37.76%	0.32%	39.13%
	Campfire	0.00%	10.35%	0.09%	16.53%	0.59%	36.55%	0.35%	35.40%
	DaylightRoad2	0.03%	2.98%	0.17%	8.66%	0.98%	23.89%	0.86%	29.22%
1080P	Cactus	0.17%	6.95%	0.31%	32.16%	0.74%	27.61%	0.46%	44.89%
	BasketballDrive	0.08%	5.65%	0.24%	17.68%	0.74%	26.76%	0.60%	36.53%
	MarketPlace	0.07%	3.48%	0.16%	21.19%	1.02%	22.75%	0.36%	38.11%
	RitualDance	0.04%	3.50%	0.27%	20.63%	0.81%	29.35%	0.53%	40.71%
720P	City	−0.07%	4.36%	0.30%	41.13%	0.53%	19.22%	0.38%	48.13%
	Crew	0.07%	2.77%	0.28%	19.25%	0.97%	21.34%	0.61%	38.27%
	vidyo1	0.04%	1.56%	0.15%	8.93%	0.82%	19.22%	0.58%	35.29%
	vidyo3	0.08%	1.38%	0.12%	8.60%	0.71%	19.73%	0.50%	33.45%
Overall		0.06%	5.79%	0.21%	20.87%	0.78%	25.67%	0.52%	37.92%

component where a positive value indicates the performance loss, and encoding time saving (TS), as shown in (4),

$$TS = \frac{T_{anchor} - T_{proposed}}{T_{anchor}} \times 100\% \tag{4}$$

where T_{anchor} denotes the anchor encoding time, and $T_{proposed}$ represents the test encoding time.

The experimental results of the proposed depth-based methods on HPM-4.0 are given in Table 1. In particular, the slack variable used in the QT depth prediction method is set 0 under AI configuration and set adjustable under RA configuration. By comparison, we can find the QT depth prediction method proposed in section III-A saves 5.79% encoding time with 0.06% BDBR under RA configuration and 20.87% time with 0.21% BDBR loss under AI configuration. After introducing the BET depth prediction method on top of QT depth prediction, the joint depth prediction fast algorithm saves 25.67% encoding time with 0.78% BDBR loss under RA configuration and 37.92% complexity with 0.52% BDBR under AI configuration.

uAVS3e is the open-source encoder for the baseline profile of AVS3 but is much faster than the baseline due to the adoption of many fast algorithms. By the end of June 2020, uAVS3e has achieved nearly 50 times encoding speed-up with 1.81% BDBR loss for Y component but nearly 5% comprehensive BDBR gain compared with HPM-4.0. For key coding modules, uAVS3e utilizes a wave-front parallel coding scheme (WPP), frame-level parallel algorithms, and assembly instruction optimization. Moreover, in the development and optimization process of uAVS3e, Class B(1920×1080), C(832×480), D(416×240), and E(1280×720) of the HEVC test sequences [16] are used.

Table 2. Experimental results on uAVS3e.

Sequences		QT depth prediction method				QT&BET depth prediction method			
		RA		AI		RA		AI	
		BDBR	TS	BDBR	TS	BDBR	TS	BDBR	TS
Class B 1080P	Kimono	0.13%	4.16%	0.05%	1.41%	0.98%	24.04%	0.36%	23.30%
	ParkScene	0.24%	11.06%	0.27%	37.46%	0.52%	29.52%	0.32%	44.58%
	BasketballDrive	0.18%	5.54%	0.17%	10.97%	0.78%	24.13%	0.48%	27.27%
	Cactus	0.03%	9.41%	0.27%	34.54%	0.55%	23.56%	0.36%	42.96%
	BQTerrace	−0.01%	8.91%	0.26%	36.96%	0.33%	19.59%	0.30%	44.38%
Class C 480P	BasketballDrill	0.20%	6.50%	0.85%	52.82%	0.61%	20.48%	0.87%	54.80%
	BQMall	0.18%	9.00%	0.39%	45.49%	0.69%	25.88%	0.43%	50.57%
	PartyScene	0.13%	17.84%	0.46%	64.38%	0.41%	29.84%	0.46%	64.61%
	RaceHorsesC	0.27%	13.26%	0.53%	54.39%	0.62%	28.19%	0.54%	55.79%
Class D 240P	BasketballPass	0.34%	4.90%	0.68%	31.73%	0.83%	18.27%	0.81%	36.07%
	BQSquare	0.29%	13.75%	0.45%	60.97%	0.78%	24.94%	0.49%	62.24%
	BlowingBubbles	0.04%	9.01%	0.40%	45.37%	0.39%	17.74%	0.41%	48.44%
	RaceHorses	0.08%	14.34%	0.51%	49.75%	0.45%	22.54%	0.53%	52.41%
Class E 720P	FourPeople	0.14%	3.01%	0.38%	30.87%	0.76%	15.51%	0.52%	40.28%
	Johnny	−0.02%	2.89%	0.44%	14.79%	0.26%	12.35%	0.70%	30.37%
	KristenAndSara	−0.29%	2.46%	0.19%	15.56%	0.17%	13.69%	0.37%	30.93%
Overall		**0.12%**	**7.77%**	**0.39%**	**37.50%**	**0.57%**	**22.07%**	**0.50%**	**45.17%**

Table 3. Comparison with experimental results of other methods on uAVS3e.

Fast methods	RA		AI	
	BDBR	TS	BDBR	TS
The proposed QT depth prediction method	0.12%	7.77%	0.39%	37.50%
The proposed QT&BET prediction method	0.57%	22.07%	0.50%	45.17%
The fast method to skip EQT in [19]	1.00%	29.27%	0.45%	18.17%
Depth prediction using neighboring CU depth information [6]	0.10%	4.45%	0.01%	2.04%
Depth prediction using neighboring LCU depth information [21]	1.98%	18.91%	0.56%	29.76%

We implemented our depth-based proposed methods on uAVS3e and Table 2 shows the simulation performance. It is worth mentioning that since the fast algorithms in [11] [22] have been integrated into uAVS3e, the proposed fast methods are developed and tested based on them. The results show that the proposed fast approaches keep effective on top of other adopted fast methods. The QT depth prediction method reduces 7.77% encoding time at the cost of 0.12% BDBR under RA configuration and 37.50% encoding complexity with only 0.39% BDBR loss under AI configuration. The joint algorithm achieves 22.07% time-saving with 0.57% BDBR loss under RA configuration and 45.17% complexity-reducing with 0.50% performance loss under AI configuration. The QT depth prediction fast method has been adopted by uAVS3e, and the BET depth fast algorithm is also on the proposal agen

For comparison, we also implemented some other fast algorithms on uAVS3e. The experimental results are listed in Table 3. First, we use the optimal partition depths of QT and BT and early skip EQT according to the algorithm in [19]. The experimental results show that it saves more encoding time but with much BDBR loss under RA configuration. Under AI configuration, it achieves less BDBR but with only 18.17% time-saving. Moreover, we use the spatial depth information of neighboring CUs of the same size as the current CU and neighboring LCUs to prune the partition tree. The results show that the information from neighboring CUs is very limited and it can only save little encoding time. The spatial correlation of neighboring LCUs is not strong enough to achieve a good trade-off between time-saving and BDBR loss under RA configuration. Therefore, using very close spatial information from neighboring SCUs is more effective and can save much encoding time on top of many other fast algorithms that exist in uAVS3e.

5   Conclusion

Compared with AVS2 and HEVC, AVS3 promotes compression efficiency significantly but costs much higher encoding complexity due to the more flexible CU partition structure. This paper proposes fast CU partition methods based on CU depth. The spatial neighboring depth information is used to predict a QT depth range and skip some partitions. Furthermore, a BET depth is proposed to represent the splitting depth generated by BT and EQT in AVS3. When the current QT depth is within the predicted QT depth range, the algorithm predicts the BET depth to skip EQT for large CUs. We test our fast algorithms on the baseline profile of AVS3 reference software, HPM-4.0, and the open-source encoder platform of AVS3, uAVS3e. The experimental results show that our depth-based methods can achieve remarkable time-savings with negligible BDBR loss on HPM-4.0 under both RA and AI configurations. Although there have been some fast algorithms in uAVS3e, our methods provide 22.07% time-saving with 0.57% BDBR loss under RA configuration and 45.17% time-saving with 0.50% BDBR loss under AI configuration.

Acknowledgements. Thanks to the National Natural Science Foundation of China 62072013 and 61902008, Shenzhen Research Projects of JCYJ20180503182128089 and 20180608 0921419290, Shenzhen Cultivation of Excellent Scientific and Technological Innovation Talents RCJC20200714114435057.

References

1. Gao, W., Ma, S.: An overview Of AVS2 standard. Adv. Video Coding Syst. **22**, 35–49 (2014)
2. Sullivan, G.J., Ohm, J.R., Han, W.J., Wiegand, T.: Overview of the high efficiency video coding (HEVC) standard. IEEE Trans. Circ. Syst. Video Technol. **22**(12), 1649–1668 (2013)
3. Fan, K., et al.: Performance and computational complexity analysis of coding tools in AVS3. In: 2020 IEEE International Conference on Multimedia & Expo Workshops (ICMEW), pp. 1–6 (2020)

4. Wang, M., et al.: Extended quad-tree partitioning for future video coding. In: 2019 Data Compression Conference (DCC), pp. 300–309 (2019)
5. Li, J., Luo, F., Zhou, Y., Wang, S., Wang, M., Ma, S.: Content based fast intra coding for AVS2. In: 2017 IEEE Third International Conference on Multimedia Big Data (BigMM), pp. 94–97 (2017)
6. Zhang, Y., Wang, H., Li, Z.: Fast coding unit depth decision algorithm for inter-frame coding in HEVC. In: 2013 Data Compression Conference (DCC), pp. 53–62 (2019)
7. Tan, H.L., Liu, F., Tan, Y.H., Yeo, C.: On fast coding tree block and mode decision for high-efficiency video coding (HEVC). In: 2012 IEEE International Conference on Acoustics, Speech and Signal Processing (ICASSP), pp. 825–828 (2012)
8. Ahn, S., Lee, B., Kim, M.: A novel fast CU encoding scheme based on spatiotemporal encoding parameters for HEVC inter coding. IEEE Trans. Circuits Syst. Video Technol. **25**(3), 422–435 (2015)
9. Wieckowski, A., Ma, J., Schwarz, H., Marpe, D., Wiegand, T.: Fast partitioning decision strategies for the upcoming versatile video coding (VVC) standard. In: 2019 IEEE International Conference on Image Processing (ICIP), pp. 4130–4134 (2019)
10. Yuan, H., Gao, W.: Inter-frame coding optimization and fast algorithm based on texture difference metric M5684. In: AVS3-P2, August 2020
11. Wu, T., Liu, S., Wang, Z., Wang, R., Wang, R.: Fast CU partition decision algorithm for AVS3 intra coding. IEEE Access **9**, 7540–7549 (2021)
12. https://gitlab.com/avs3software/hpm
13. https://github.com/uavs3/uavs3e
14. Chen, J.: AVS3-P2 common test conditions v5.0, N2617. In: AVS3-P2, December 2018
15. Bjontegaard, G.: Calculation of average PSNR differences between RD-curves. In: ITU-T VCEG-M33, April 2001
16. Bossen, F.: Common test conditions and software reference configurations. In: Joint Collaborative Team on Video Coding (JCTVC), JCTVC-B300, March 2012
17. Franck, G., Racape, F., Jaiswal, S., Bordes, P., Leannec, F.L., Francois, E.: CNN-based driving of block partitioning for intra slices encoding. In: 2019 Data Compression Conference (DCC), pp. 162–171 (2019)
18. Kui, F., Wang, R., Wang, Z., Li, G., Gao, W.: IAVS2: a fast intra-encoding platform for IEEE 1857.4. IEEE Trans. Circ. Syst. Video Technol. **27**(12), 2726–2738 (2017)
19. Wang, M., et al.: Fast coding unit splitting decisions for the emergent AVS3 standard. In: 2019 Picture Coding Symposium (PCS), pp. 1–5 (2019)
20. Yun, Z., Kwong, S., Wang, S.: Machine learning based video coding optimizations: a survey. Inf. Sci. **506**, 395–423 (2020)
21. Chen, J., Chiu, Y., Lee, C., Tsai, Y.: Utilize neighboring LCU depth information to speedup FVC/H.266 intra coding. In: 2019 International Conference on System Science and Engineering (ICSSE), pp. 308–312 (2019)
22. Wu, S., Wang, Z., Cai, Y., Wang, R.: Fast mode decision algorithm for intra encoding of the 3rd generation audio video coding standard. In: Lokoč, J., et al. (eds.) MMM 2021. LNCS, vol. 12572, pp. 481–492. Springer, Cham (2021). https://doi.org/10.1007/978-3-030-67832-6_39

MEViT: Motion Enhanced Video Transformer for Video Classification

Li Li[1,2] and Liansheng Zhuang[1(✉)]

[1] University of Science and Technology of China, Hefei 230026, China
`lili1234@mail.ustc.edu.cn`, `lszhuang@ustc.edu.cn`
[2] Peng Cheng Laboratory, Shenzhen 518000, China

Abstract. Due to the advantages in extracting the long-range dependencies, self-attention based transformers are widely used to model the spatio-temporal features for video classification, which achieves competitive performance compared to 3D CNNs. To reduce the computational complexity, existing methods divide the frames into patches and factorize the spatial and temporal domains. However, most existing methods globally connect the patches at the same position in different frames to extract the temporal features, and ignore the patch motion due to video objects moving, which might hurt the performance of transformers. This paper proposes a novel architecture called Motion Enhanced Video Transformer (MEViT) for video classification, which captures patch motion information via a new module named Motion self-attention. Different from existing self-attention operation on the temporal dimension, motion self-attention globally connects the query patch and the neighborhood patches in other frames along the temporal dimension when modelling the patch temporal dependencies. Furthermore, this paper also discusses how attention blocks are stacked and how to use the spatio-temporal feature to get the classification feature. Experiments on popular public datasets (including Kinetics-400/600 and Something-Something-v2) demonstrate that our MEViT model outperforms existing dominant video transformer models.

Keywords: Video classification · Video transformer · Motion self-attention

1 Introduction

Video understanding has many real-world applications, including behavior analysis, video retrieval, and human-robot interaction. One of the most important tasks in video understanding is video classification, which is to produce a label

---

This work was supported in part by Next Generation AI Project of China No. 2018AAA0100602, in part to Dr. Liansheng Zhuang by NSFC under contract No. U20B2070 and No. 61976199, and in part to Dr. Houqiang Li by NSFC under contract No. 61836011. Li Li is with the School of data science.

© Springer Nature Switzerland AG 2022
B. Þór Jónsson et al. (Eds.): MMM 2022, LNCS 13142, pp. 419–430, 2022.
https://doi.org/10.1007/978-3-030-98355-0_35

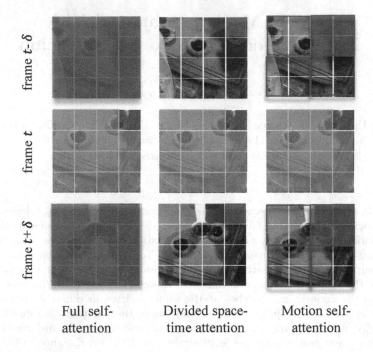

Fig. 1. Visualization of the different self-attention schemes. Each video clip is viewed as a sequence of frame-level patches which contain 16×16 pixels. For illustration, we use blue to represent the query patch, and use non-blue to display the self-attention spatio-temporal neighborhood under each scheme. Patches without color are not used for self-attention calculation of blue patch. (Color figure online)

that is relevant to the video given its frames. There are at least two challenges in video classification to overcome: how to represent the spatio-temporal information in a video and how to use the spatio-temporal information for classification. Spatio-temporal information contains two aspects: spatial information such as objects in the frame and temporal information such as correlations in different frames which is important for video classification. Previous methods used convolutional and recurrent operations to gather the information from the given video. Both convolutional and recursive operations process a local neighborhood, either in space and time; thus long-range correlation can be captured only when these operations are repeated and the signal is gradually propagated through the data.

However, there is an important defect in existing divided space-time attention, which might hurt the performance of transformer models. Current divided space-time attention concatenates the query patch and the patches located at the same position in other frames as shown in Fig. 1 with the assumption that these patches are well-aligned so that they can jointly model the motion information of some part in video. Nevertheless, due to video object moving or video camera moving, there always exist patch motions, which lead to the misalignment between the query patch and those patches from the other frames. The misalignment may violate the performance of temporal features extracted by self-attention. Obviously, we should consider the neighbor patches from a different frame when doing self-attention, so that we can capture the relative patch motion. Inspired by this insight, this paper proposes a novel model named Motion Enhanced Video Transformer (MEViT), which can capture the motion information. MEViT divides each frame into non-overlapping patches. Several adjacent patches make up one block. Self-attention in time dimension is calculated on the same spatial block in different frames, which is named Motion self-attention. To avoid the computing cost, MEViT does not use space-time attention to jointly learn the spatial information and time information in all layers. Instead, it calculates spatial features first and then the spatio-temporal features as done in [27]. Experiments on public datasets including Kinects-400/600 and Something-something-v2 demonstrate its effectiveness.

The main contributions are summarized as follows:

- This paper proposes a new architecture named Motion Enhanced Video Transform for video classification, which can better extract temporal features for videos.
- Motion self-attention scheme is introduced to model the long-range patch dependencies, which can better capture the patch motion information due to video object moving or video camera moving.
- Extensive experiments on public datasets including Kinects-400/600 and Something-something-v2 show that our proposed MEViT outperforms state-of-the-art video transformers.

2   Related Works

Early works on video classification used hand-crafted features to encode appearance and motion information [15,22]. With the success of CNNs in image classification [14], the model for video classification is dominated by deep learning which can be broadly classified into two categories: 2D-based and 3D-based approaches. The 2D-based approaches [12,16] process each frame independently to extract frame-based features, which are then modeled by some kind of temporal model performed at the end of the network. The 3D-based approaches [8,9] are considered as the current state-of-the-art since they can typically learn stronger temporal models via 3D convolutions. However, they also incur higher computational and memory costs. To alleviate this, some works attempt to improve their efficiency via factorising convolutions across spatial and temporal dimensions or using grouped convolutions [8,21,27].

Recently, transformer-based architectures also showed promising results on large scale image classification [6]. The Vision Transformer (ViT) demonstrated the pure transformer network which is similar to the application in NLP can also obtain state-of-the-art results on ImageNet [5]. ViT has inspired a lot of follow-up work in the field of computer vision. We notice that there are many parallel methods that can extend ViT to other tasks in computer vision [3,4,11,26], and improve its data efficiency [19].

Vision transformer architectures, derived from [6], were extended through time dimension for video classification [1,2]. Because performing full space-time attention is computationally prohibitive, their main focus is on reducing computation cost via temporal and spatial factorization. In TimeSformer [2], the authors apply spatial and temporal attention in an alternating manner reducing the complexity of calculating attention weights. In a similar fashion, ViViT [1] explores several methods of space-time factorization. In addition, they also proposed to adapt the patch embedding to 3D data. Our work proposes a similar approximation to full self-attention which is also efficient. To this end, we restrict full self-attention to Motion self-attention which not only extracts the temporal features of patches from the same spatial location in other frames, but also extracts the neighborhood around that location in other frames. And this paper discusses the stacking mode of attention blocks and how to use spatio-temporal features for video classification.

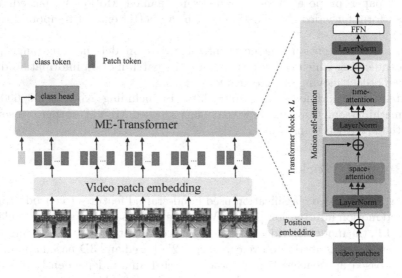

Fig. 2. Diagram of our model. The input clips is linearly projected into the patch embedding, and add the position embedding. The patches and the class token are fed into the transformer.

3   Our Method

The architecture of our model is shown in Fig. 2. It consists of the following modules: video patch embedding module, Motion Enhanced Video Transformer, Motion self-attention module, and the class embedding module.

Video Patch Embedding. The input of the model is a video clip which contains T frames sampling from the video $X \in R^{T \times H \times W \times 3}$, where H and W are the height and width of a frame. Following the ViT approach, each frame of the input X is parted into N non-overlapping patches with the size $P \times P$. And then, the patch is reshaped into a flatten vector $x_{(p,t)} \in R^{3 \times P^2}$, with p denoting the spatial locations and t denoting the index of frames. Then the vector $x_{(p,t)}$ is linearly projected into the an embedding patch token $z_{(p,t)}^{(0)} \in R^d$:

$$z_{(p,t)}^{(0)} = Ex_{(p,t)} + e_{(p,t)}^{pos}, \tag{1}$$

where $e_{(p,t)}^{pos}$ is the positional embedding and E is the trainable matrix. In order to use the transformer for video classification, a learnable vector $z_{(0,0)}^{(0)}$ named class token which represents the embedding of the classification is added in the first position of the sequence of patch tokens. The place of class token added into the transformer influences the accuracy of recognition, and we talk about the class embedding later.

Motion Enhanced Video Transformer (MEViT). Transformer consists of L encoding blocks with A heads. At each block $l \in \{1, ..., L\}$ and each head $a \in \{1, ..., A\}$, each patch token or class token is projected into query, key, and value vector by the preceding block:

$$q/k/v_{(p,t)}^{(l,a)} = W_{Q/K/V}^{(l,a)} LN\left(z_{(p,t)}^{(l-1)}\right),$$

$$(p,t) \in \{(p,t)| \begin{matrix} p' = 1, ..., N \\ t' = 1, ..., T \end{matrix}\} \cup \{(0,0)\} \tag{2}$$

where LN is the LayerNorm, and d_h is hidden dim of each head. W_Q, W_K, W_V are learnable weights for embedding vector query, key, and value matrices.

The weights of self-attention are computed via dot-product. The self-attention weights $\alpha_{(p,t)}^{(l,a)} \in R^{NT+1}$ for query patch $q_{(p,t)}^{(l,a)}$ are given by

$$\alpha_{(p,t)}^{(l,a)} = SM\left(\frac{q_{(p,t)}^{(l,a)^T}}{\sqrt{d_h}} \cdot \left[k_{(0,0)}^{(l,a)} \{k_{(p',t')}^{(l,a)}\}_{\begin{matrix} p' = 1, ..., N \\ t' = 1, ..., T \end{matrix}}\right]\right), \tag{3}$$

where SM denotes the softmax activation function. The attention weights are used as coefficients in a weighted sum over the values for each attention head:

$$s_{(p,t)}^{(l,a)} = \alpha_{(0,0)}^{(l,a)} v_{(0,0)}^{(l,a)} + \sum_{t'=1}^{T} \sum_{p'=1}^{N} \alpha_{(p,t),(p',t')}^{(l,a)} v_{(p',t')}^{(l,a)}. \tag{4}$$

These outputs from attention heads are concatenated and passed through embedding matrix W_O and the feed-forward network (FFN):

$$z'^{(l)}_{(p,t)} = W_O \begin{bmatrix} s^{(l,1)}_{(p,t)} \\ \vdots \\ s^{(l,A)}_{(p,t)} \end{bmatrix} + z^{(l-1)}_{(p,t)},$$

$$z^{(l)}_{(p,t)} = FFN\left(LN\left(z'^{(l)}_{(p,t)}\right)\right) + z'^{(l)}_{(p,t)}. \tag{5}$$

The full self-attention (3) is computed by joint space and time dimension which incurs high computational cost. A reduction in computation can be achieved by disentangling the spatial and temporal dimensions. When the attention weight is computed over one dimension, the computational cost is significantly reduced. In the case of space-attention, only $N+1$ query-key comparisons are made, using exclusively keys from the same frame as the query:

$$\alpha^{(l,a)space}_{(p,t)} = SM\left(\frac{q^{(l,a)^T}_{(p,t)}}{\sqrt{d_h}} \cdot \left[k^{(l,a)}_{(0,0)}\{k^{(l,a)}_{(p',t)}\}_{p'=1,\dots,N}\right]\right). \tag{6}$$

The baseline time-attention proposed by TimeSformer [2] which uses of the patches from the same location as the query patch in the different frames:

$$\alpha^{(l,a)time}_{(p,t)} = SM\left(\frac{q^{(l,a)^T}_{(p,t)}}{\sqrt{d_h}} \cdot \left[k^{(l,a)}_{(0,0)}\{k^{(l,a)}_{(p,t')}\}_{t'=1,\dots,T}\right]\right) \tag{7}$$

The full self-attention is approximated by divided space-time attention via space-attention (6) and time-attention (7).

Motion Self-attention. To extract the motion information, we need to care about not only the patches from the same location in different frames, but also the neighborhood around the location in other frames. Each frame is parted to non-overlapping blocks and each block contains $M \times M$ patches. The self-attention in time dimension is calculated by including the patch from the same spatial block in different frames:

$$\alpha^{(l,a)time}_{(p,t)} = SM\left(\frac{q^{(l,a)^T}_{(p,t)}}{\sqrt{d_h}} \cdot \left[k^{(l,a)}_{(0,0)}\{k^{(l,a)}_{(p',t')}\} \begin{matrix} p' \in B \\ t' = 1,\dots,T \end{matrix}\right]\right), \tag{8}$$

where B is the block which query patch p belongs to. The Motion self-attention uses the (8) as the time-attention layer. The model has L Motion self-attention blocks, each block has (8) and (6) orderly.

Classification Embedding. The final clip embedding is obtained from the class token of final block:

$$y = LN\left(z_{(0,0)}^{(L)}\right) \in R^d. \tag{9}$$

The class token has two purposes: guiding the self-attention learning between patches and aggregating overall information to the linear classifier [20]. Recent works have shown that separating two approaches is beneficial to the classification. We will test whether this method influences the accuracy in video classification. In our model, there are two stages: self-attention stage which updates the spatio-temporal feature of patch tokens and class-attention stage which only updates the class token. In class-attention layer, we only update the class token embedding and keep the features of patch token consistent. First, the query vectors for class token and the key/value vectors for patch tokens are calculated, and then the weight of attention and outputs of each class-attention head are calculated:

$$q_{(0,0)}^{(l,a)} = W_Q^{(l,a)} LN\left(z_{(0,0)}^{(l-1)}\right),$$

$$k/v_{(p,t)}^{(l,a)} = W_{K/V}^{(l,a)} LN\left(z_{(p,t)}^{(l-1)}\right),$$

$$\alpha_{(0,0)}^{(l,a)} = SM\left(\frac{q_{(0,0)}^{(l,a)^T}}{\sqrt{d_h}} \cdot \left[k_{(p',t')}^{(l,a)}\right]\begin{matrix}p' = 1, ..., N \\ t' = 1, ..., T\end{matrix}\right), \tag{10}$$

$$s_{(0,0)}^{(l,a)} = \sum_{t'=1}^{T} \sum_{p'=1}^{N} \alpha_{(0,0),(p',t')}^{(l,a)} v_{(p',t')}^{(l,a)}.$$

Then, we use the (5) to calculate the $z_{(0,0)}^{(l)}$ as the output of class-attention layer.

To summarize, our model has some Motion self-attention blocks(SA), and each Motion self-attention block is composed of space-attention layer and time-attention layer orderly in Fig. 2.

4 Experiment

4.1 Experiment Setup

Datasets. We trained and evaluated the proposed models on the two widely used datasets. The Kinetics [13] dataset contains short clips sampled from YouTube. The version of the datasets used in this paper contains approximately 260k clips for Kinetics-400 and 375k clips for Kinetics-600. The SSv2 [10] dataset consists of about 220k short videos, with a length between 2 and 6 s that picture humans performing pre-defined basic actions with everyday objects. Because the backgrounds and objects of the videos are consistent in different action classes, this dataset often needs stronger temporal modeling (Fig. 3).

Network Architecture. Most of the experiments were performed using the MEViT-B/16 (L = 12, h = 12, d = 768, P = 16). For the space-attention module in the Motion self-attention, we use the pre-trained weights from ImageNet. For the time-attention layers, the block size varies from 1 to 14.

Training and Inference. For training phase, we resize the smaller dimension of each frame to a value $\in [256, 320]$, and take a random crop of size 224×224 from the same location for all frames of the same video. In the inference phase, we give the accuracy results for 1×3 views (only 1 temporal clip and 3 spatial crops) not the popular approach of using up to 10 temporal clips and 3 spatial crops. The models are implemented by pytorch, and were trained on a DGX-v1 server.

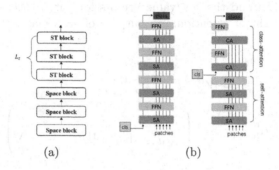

(a)   (b)

Fig. 3. The number of blocks using time-attention layer and model with class-attention layers. Space block represents the Motion self-attention only having the space-attention, and ST block represents the Motion self-attention block.

4.2   Ablation Studies

This subsection shows our proposed model with Motion self-attention can better learn the spatio-temporal features. And, we explore the importance of class token and class-attention layers. Then, we test the top-heavy transformer which uses only space-attention layers in the early transformer blocks.

Effect of the Motion Self-attention. We conduct the experiment to show the proposed Motion self-attention scheme has better performance. Table 1 shows the accuracy of our model using the Motion self-attention varying size M from 1 to 7. First, performance of our proposed Motion self-attention is superior to the origin divided space-time attention when the block size equal to 1. Second, model with Motion self-attention the block size M = 2 has the best performance. Compared to the origin divided space-time attention when block size is equal to 1, our model (M = 2) gets a bigger receptive field with more patches in the other frames in time dimension. The accuracy drops when the block size is bigger than 2, because the attention weights is calculated by more patches which might be noise.

Effect of Class-Attention Layers. For fair comparison, the total number of layers is fixed to 12. The inserted-layer i is the place where the class token is inserted into our model, i.e., our model has i self-attention blocks and $(12 - i)$ class-attention blocks. From the Table 2, we find that the architecture contains 11 self-attention blocks and 1 class-attention block gets the best performance. There is no benefit in copying the class embedding information of the class-attention block back to the patch embedding of the self-attention blocks in front process. If we keep 12 self-attention blocks, we find our model can achieve better performance by adding only one class-attention block which needs more parameters.

Table 1. Effect of the block size of motion self-attention.

Block size	Top-1	Top-5
1	78.6	93.0
2	**80.2**	**93.6**
3	80.0	93.2
7	77.6	92.8
14	77.9	92.8

Table 2. Effect of class-attention layers.

SA+CA	Inserted-layer	Top-1
9+3	9	79.4
10+2	10	80.3
11+1	11	**80.5**
12+1	12	80.6

Depth of Time-Attention Layer. Some works found that extracting the spatial information and temporal information independently is useful for video classification. We talk about the top-heavy model which keeps only the space-attention layer in the front Motion self-attention blocks, so the model has only L_t blocks with time-attention layer in Fig. 3a. The accuracy of using different numbers of time-attention layers is shown in Table 3. From the result, we can see the model with no time-attention layer has the worst performance, and model with $L_t = 8/12$ time-attention layers has the best performance. It's obvious that our model is significantly superior to the space-only attention model. Space-only attention model focuses on the spatial information and ignores the temporal information. In this situation, video classification task is regarded as object recognition. But, the first four blocks with no time-attention layer get higher accuracy. In the front block, the model calculates the attention weights from the patches in the same frame would be less affected by noise from the other frames.

Table 3. Effect of L_t. L_t denotes the number of block with the time-attention layer in our model architecture.

L_t	0	2	4	8	12
Top-1	75.6	77.5	77.9	**80.3**	80.2

4.3   Comparison with State-of-the-Art

Based on our ablation studies in the previous section, we compare to the current state-of-the-art for all mentioned datasets using our model. Our model use eleven SA layers and one CA layer, and the self-attention layers contains four space-attention layers. The results are shown in the Tables 4, 5 and 6. Unless otherwise stated, we report the results using the 1×3 views for all datasets.

For the Kinetics-400, our model training with 16 frames achieves the best performance but only using one temporal crops in the inference in the Table 4. Compared to the state-of-the-art convolution model X3D-XXL, our model brings about 0.7% gains on Top-1 accuracy, and compared to transformer-based methods, our model brings about 0.5% gains. Similarly, our model has great improvement on the Kinetics-600 in Table 5. On the SSv2, our model also matches the state-of-the-art created by the ViViT-L.

Table 4. Comparison on the Kinetics-400 dataset.

Method	Top-1	Top-5	Views
blVNet [7]	73.5	91.2	3×3
TEA [16]	76.1	92.5	10×3
TSM-R101 [17]	76.3	–	10×3
I3D NL [25]	77.7	93.3	10×3
CorrNet-101 [23]	79.2	–	10×3
LGD-R101 [18]	79.4	94.4	–
SlowFast [9]	79.8	93.9	10×3
X3D-XXL [8]	80.4	94.6	10×3
TimeSformer-L [2]	80.7	94.7	10×3
ViViT-L/16 $\times$ 2 [1]	80.6	94.7	4×3
Our model	80.6	**94.7**	1×3
Our model(16$\times$)	81.1	**94.9**	1×3

Table 5. Comparison on the Kinetics-600 dataset.

Block size	Top-1	Top-5
AttentionNAS [24]	79.8	94.4
LGD-R101 [18]	81.5	91.6
SlowFast [9]	81.8	92.5
X3D-XL [8]	81.9	–
TimeSformer [2]	82.4	93.3
ViViT-L/16 $\times$ 2 [1]	82.5	–
Our model (16$\times$)	**85.6**	**95.2**

Table 6. Comparison on the SSv2 dataset.

Block size	Top-1	Top-5
TRN [28]	48.8	77.6
SlowFast [9]	61.7	–
TimeSformer [2]	62.5	–
TSM [17]	63.4	88.5
TEA [16]	65.1	–
blVNet [7]	65.2	90.3
ViViT-L/16 $\times$ 2 [1]	65.4	89.8
Our model (16$\times$)	**65.7**	**90.5**

5   Conclusion

This paper presented Motion Enhanced Video Transformer (MEViT) for video classification. Compared to existing video transformers, our model can better model the temporal features and achieve state-of-the-art performance in the video recognition datasets including Kinetics-400/600 and SSv2. It uses the proposed Motion self-attention scheme to capture the long-range patch dependencies, which considers the patch motion due to video object moving. Future efforts will be devoted to combine our approaches with other transformer architectures besides the standard ViT. Finally, we will apply our model in long-time video recognition.

References

1. Arnab, A., Dehghani, M., Heigold, G., Sun, C., Lučić, M., Schmid, C.: ViViT: a video vision transformer (2021)
2. Bertasius, G., Wang, H., Torresani, L.: Is space-time attention all you need for video understanding? (2021)
3. Carion, N., Massa, F., Synnaeve, G., Usunier, N., Kirillov, A., Zagoruyko, S.: End-to-end object detection with transformers. In: Vedaldi, A., Bischof, H., Brox, T., Frahm, J.-M. (eds.) ECCV 2020. LNCS, vol. 12346, pp. 213–229. Springer, Cham (2020). https://doi.org/10.1007/978-3-030-58452-8_13
4. Chen, C.F., Fan, Q., Panda, R.: CrossViT: cross-attention multi-scale vision transformer for image classification (2021)
5. Deng, J., Dong, W., Socher, R., Li, L.J., Li, K., Fei-Fei, L.: ImageNet: a large-scale hierarchical image database. In: 2009 IEEE Conference on Computer Vision and Pattern Recognition, pp. 248–255. IEEE (2009)
6. Dosovitskiy, A., et al.: An image is worth 16 × 16 words: transformers for image recognition at scale (2020)
7. Fan, Q., Chen, C.F.R., Kuehne, H., Pistoia, M., Cox, D.: More is less: learning efficient video representations by big-little network and depthwise temporal aggregation. In: Wallach, H., Larochelle, H., Beygelzimer, A., d' Alché-Buc, F., Fox, E., Garnett, R. (eds.) Advances in Neural Information Processing Systems, vol. 32. Curran Associates, Inc. (2019). https://proceedings.neurips.cc/paper/2019/file/3d779cae2d46cf6a8a99a35ba4167977-Paper.pdf
8. Feichtenhofer, C.: X3D: expanding architectures for efficient video recognition. In: Proceedings of the IEEE/CVF Conference on Computer Vision and Pattern Recognition (CVPR), June 2020
9. Feichtenhofer, C., Fan, H., Malik, J., He, K.: SlowFast networks for video recognition. In: Proceedings of the IEEE/CVF International Conference on Computer Vision (ICCV), October 2019
10. Goyal, R., et al.: The "something something" video database for learning and evaluating visual common sense. In: Proceedings of the IEEE International Conference on Computer Vision, pp. 5842–5850 (2017)
11. Heo, B., Yun, S., Han, D., Chun, S., Choe, J., Oh, S.J.: Rethinking spatial dimensions of vision transformers (2021)
12. Karpathy, A., Toderici, G., Shetty, S., Leung, T., Sukthankar, R., Fei-Fei, L.: Large-scale video classification with convolutional neural networks. In: Proceedings of the IEEE conference on Computer Vision and Pattern Recognition, pp. 1725–1732 (2014)

13. Kay, W., et al.: The kinetics human action video dataset. arXiv preprint arXiv:1705.06950 (2017)
14. Krizhevsky, A., Sutskever, I., Hinton, G.E.: ImageNet classification with deep convolutional neural networks. In: Pereira, F., Burges, C.J.C., Bottou, L., Weinberger, K.Q. (eds.) Advances in Neural Information Processing Systems, vol. 25. Curran Associates, Inc. (2012). https://proceedings.neurips.cc/paper/2012/file/c399862d3b9d6b76c8436e924a68c45b-Paper.pdf
15. Laptev, I.: On space-time interest points. Int. J. Comput. Vision **64**(2), 107–123 (2005)
16. Li, Y., Ji, B., Shi, X., Zhang, J., Kang, B., Wang, L.: Tea: temporal excitation and aggregation for action recognition. In: Proceedings of the IEEE/CVF Conference on Computer Vision and Pattern Recognition, pp. 909–918 (2020)
17. Lin, J., Gan, C., Han, S.: TSM: temporal shift module for efficient video understanding. In: Proceedings of the IEEE/CVF International Conference on Computer Vision (ICCV), October 2019
18. Qiu, Z., Yao, T., Ngo, C.W., Tian, X., Mei, T.: Learning spatio-temporal representation with local and global diffusion. In: Proceedings of the IEEE/CVF Conference on Computer Vision and Pattern Recognition (CVPR), June 2019
19. Touvron, H., Cord, M., Douze, M., Massa, F., Sablayrolles, A., Jégou, H.: Training data-efficient image transformers & distillation through attention. In: International Conference on Machine Learning, pp. 10347–10357. PMLR (2021)
20. Touvron, H., Cord, M., Sablayrolles, A., Synnaeve, G., Jégou, H.: Going deeper with image transformers. arXiv preprint arXiv:2103.17239 (2021)
21. Tran, D., Wang, H., Torresani, L., Feiszl, M.: Video classification with channel-separated convolutional networks. In: Proceedings of the IEEE/CVF International Conference on Computer Vision (ICCV), October 2019
22. Wang, H., Kläser, A., Schmid, C., Liu, C.L.: Dense trajectories and motion boundary descriptors for action recognition. Int. J. Comput. Vision **103**(1), 60–79 (2013)
23. Wang, H., Tran, D., Torresani, L., Feiszli, M.: Video modeling with correlation networks. In: Proceedings of the IEEE/CVF Conference on Computer Vision and Pattern Recognition (CVPR), June 2020
24. Wang, X., et al.: AttentionNAS: spatiotemporal attention cell search for video classification. In: Vedaldi, A., Bischof, H., Brox, T., Frahm, J.-M. (eds.) ECCV 2020. LNCS, vol. 12353, pp. 449–465. Springer, Cham (2020). https://doi.org/10.1007/978-3-030-58598-3_27
25. Wang, X., Girshick, R., Gupta, A., He, K.: Non-local neural networks. In: Proceedings of the IEEE Conference on Computer Vision and Pattern Recognition, pp. 7794–7803 (2018)
26. Wu, H., et al.: CVT: introducing convolutions to vision transformers (2021)
27. Xie, S., Sun, C., Huang, J., Tu, Z., Murphy, K.: Rethinking spatiotemporal feature learning: speed-accuracy trade-offs in video classification. In: Proceedings of the European Conference on Computer Vision (ECCV), September 2018
28. Zhou, B., Andonian, A., Oliva, A., Torralba, A.: Temporal relational reasoning in videos. In: Proceedings of the European Conference on Computer Vision (ECCV), pp. 803–818 (2018)

CDeRSNet: Towards High Performance Object Detection in Vietnamese Document Images

Thuan Trong Nguyen[1,2(✉)], Thuan Q. Nguyen[1,2], Long Duong[1,2],
Nguyen D. Vo[1,2], and Khang Nguyen[1,2]

[1] University of Information Technology, Ho Chi Minh, Vietnam
{18521471,18521470}@gm.uit.edu.vn, {longdp,nguyenvd,khangnttm}@uit.edu.vn
[2] Vietnam National University, Ho Chi Minh, Vietnam

Abstract. In recent years, document image understanding (DIU) has received much attention from the research community. Localizing page objects (tables, figures, equations) in document images is an important problem in DIU, which is the foundation for extracting information from document images. However, it has remained many challenges due to the high degree of intra-class variability in page document. Especially, object detection in Vietnamese image documents has still limited. In this paper, we propose CDeRSNet: a novel end-to-end trainable deep learning network to solve object detection in Vietnamese documents. The proposed network consists of Cascade R-CNN with the deformable convolution backbone and Rank & Sort (RS) Loss. CDeRSNet detects objects varying in scale with high detection accuracy at a higher IoU threshold to localize objects that differ in scale with detection accuracy at high quality. We empirically evaluate CDeRSNet on the Vietnamese image document dataset - UIT-DODV with four classes of objects: table, figure, caption, and formula. We achieved the best performance on the UIT-DODV dataset with 79.9% in terms of mAP, which is higher 5.4% than current results. In addition, we also provide a comprehensive evaluation and insightful analysis of CDeRSNet. Finally, we demonstrate CDeRSNet outperformance over state-of-the-arts models in object detection such as GFocal, GFocalV2, VFNet, DetectoRS on the UIT-DODV dataset. Code can be available at: https://github.com/trongthuan205/CDeRSNet.git.

Keywords: Object detection · CDeRSNet · RSLoss

1 Introduction

In recent decades, traditional paper documents have been digitized and stored on electronic devices. Since then, electronic documents have been increasingly widely used in the economy, life, and society. Electronic documents have many remarkable advantages over paper documents, such as quick sharing, cost-saving organization, and reduced burden on the economy. However, in order to quickly

© Springer Nature Switzerland AG 2022
B. Þór Jónsson et al. (Eds.): MMM 2022, LNCS 13142, pp. 431–442, 2022.
https://doi.org/10.1007/978-3-030-98355-0_36

and accurately search for electronic documents in an archive containing millions of documents, besides the title search, it is also required to know the content of the document page. This is one of the Industry 4.0 trends [2]. Document Image Understanding (DIU) [15,22] is the automatic process of extracting useful information from an image document page. DIU combines image analysis and pattern recognition techniques to process and extract the information from image documents. It refers to the logical and semantic analysis of image documents to extract information that humans can understand and simultaneously train machine learning models to recognize the necessary information.

Documents are not only texts consisting of simple characters but also objects such as images, drawings, diagrams, formulas, tables, etc. The detection of objects in image documents is one of the problems that receive significant attention from the research community in Document Analysis and Recognition [10,13]. For the object detection problem on an image document, the detector gets an image document page as input then returns the object's locations (if any) in the image. The problem has many challenges arising from external factors such as tilt, blur, noise, illumination, and occlusion, etc., which are inevitable. In addition, the internal factors of the structure and layout in the different templates pose many challenges for the detector. Internal factors mainly include complex layouts (single-column and multi-column pages) and the diversity of objects (font style, font size, and content format). Page objects detection in the document images helps to locate the objects in the document, which is a prerequisite for discovering the content of the document page. Understanding the contents of these objects will help applications in many ways, such as summarizing the content of documents, searching for scientific documents based on the description or content of the object.

Almost previous research on page object detection [1,6,14,18,19] still has many limitations related to the quality of the bounding boxes prediction. In this paper, we propose CDeRSNet: a novel end-to-end trainable deep learning network to solve object detection on the Vietnamese scientific papers dataset - UIT-DODV [6]. The proposed network consists of Cascade R-CNN [3] with the deformable convolution network [5] backbone and Rank & Sort (RS) Loss [12]. CDeRSNet detects objects varying in scale with high detection accuracy at a higher IoU threshold to localize objects that differ in scale with detection accuracy at high quality.

We summarize our contributions as follows:

- We propose CDeRSNet: a novel end-to-end trainable deep learning network to solve page object detection in Vietnamese documents. CDeRSNet achieved 79.9% on the mAP metrics, which is 5.4% higher than current results on the Vietnamese scientific papers dataset - UIT-DODV
- We provide an empirical evaluation and demonstrated CDeRSNet superior performance over state-of-the-art models in object detection such as GFocal [9], GFocalV2 [8], VFNet [20], and DetectoRS [16] on the UIT-DODV dataset.

2 Related Work

2.1 Object Detection

Zhang et al. [20] proposed VarifocalNet to learn an Iou-aware Classification Score (IACS) as a joint representation of object presence confidence and localization accuracy. In addition, Zhang et al. also introduced Varifocal Loss to train a dense object detector to predict the IACS and propose a new star-shaped bounding box feature representation for IACS prediction and bounding box refinement. Qiao, Chen, and Yuille [16] proposed the Recursive Feature Pyramid, which incorporates extra feedback connections from Feature Pyramid Networks into the bottom-up backbone layers, presenting Recursive Feature Pyramid and Switchable Atrous Convolution at the macro and micro levels and then combined results in DetectoRS. Li et al. [8] improved Focal Loss V2 (GFocal LV2) from Generalized Focal Loss (GFocal) [9]. GFocal V2 introduced a completely novel and different perspective to perform Localization Quality Estimation based on the learned distributions of the four parameters of the bounding box.

2.2 Object Detection in Documents Images

Traditional Methods: Cesarini et al. [4] proposed a new table detection method by detecting horizontal and vertical lines. Gatos et al. [7] proposed a strategy to reduce the mistakes of the candidate area then added intersect points detection.

Deep Learning Based Methods: In 2018, Vo et al. [19] combined outputs of two object detectors - Fast R-CNN and Faster R-CNN to exploit the advantages of the two models before applying bounding box regression to increase performance in page object detection. In 2020, Prasad et al. [14] proposed CascadeTabNet by incorporating HRNet as the backbone for Cascade R-CNN to achieve high-resolution representations. Agarwal, Mondal, and Jawahar [1] proposed CDec-Net includes a multi-stage extension of Mask R-CNN with the dual backbone. In 2021, Dieu et al. [6] leverage CascadeTabNet along with the fused loss function to efficiently parse the Vietnamese paper documents.

3 CDeRSNet: Cascade Deformable Rank Sort Network

In general, deep learning models in Sect. 2.2 have attained higher effectiveness than the traditional method, but these models have limitations. Firstly, all object detection models in document images use a CNN as a backbone for feature extraction. However, most of these CNNs were initially designed for image classification in the Imagenet dataset. Therefore they may not be enough effectiveness and robustness to be applied directly to extract features on document images. Secondly, previous detectors used IoU thresholds to determine positives or negatives. The commonly used IoU threshold is 0.5, which leads to noise detection (low quality) and often degrades the performance for a higher threshold.

In this paper, we approach the above problems based on Cascade R-CNN with Deformable Convolution Network (DCN) as the backbone. Besides, we handle issues related to IoU through Dynamic Training and RS Loss.

3.1 Cascade R-CNN

The success of Cascade R-CNN is demonstrated in two main aspects: stepwise improvement of the predictions and adaptive processing of the training distributions. In previous object detection methods, the models calculated the IoU scores to determine the positives and negatives for bounding box predictions. However, these detectors are often trained at a low IoU threshold (e.g., 0.5 - a relatively sensitive threshold), leading to noisy detections. On the other hand, object detection accuracy decreases due to the scarcity of positive regions when suddenly increasing to the higher IoU threshold. Cai and Vasconcelos [3] proposed Cascade R-CNN to solve this problem, which is a multi-stage object detection architecture. Cascade R-CNN consists of a sequence of detectors trained with increasing IoU thresholds to be more sequentially selective against false positives. Furthermore, detectors leverage the output of the previous detector as a good distribution for training higher quality detectors in the next stage. Each regressor is optimized for the bounding boxes distribution generated by the earlier rather than the initial distribution.

3.2 Deformable Convolutional Networks

The ResNeXt architecture is a standard convolutional network used as the backbone in deep learning object detection methods. In ResNeXt, the receptive fields at each neuron are similar and fixed (e.g.: 3×3 or 5×5). Although regular convolutions work well at lower-level layers, they do not operate robustly to capture features at higher-level layers due to arbitrary scales and high transformations. DCN allows grids to deform based on a trainable offset. In regular convolution, samples are taken on the input feature map x using regular grid R, defined by:

$$y(p_0) = \sum_{p_n \in R} w \times (p_n) \times x(p_0 + p_n) \tag{1}$$

Whereas in a deformable convolution, for each location p_0 on the output feature map y incremented by a learnable offset $\triangle p_n$ such that $\{\triangle p_n | n = 1, ..., N\}$, where $N = |R|$, is given by:

$$y(p_0) = \sum_{p_n \in R} w \times (p_n) \times x(p_0 + p_n + \triangle p) \tag{2}$$

DCN is operated on grid R, but for each point incremented by a learnable offset $\triangle p$. The transformation is used to generate $2N$ number of feature maps corresponding to $N2D$ offsets $\triangle p_n$ (x-direction and y-direction for each offset). DCN allows each neuron to change its receptive field based on the previous feature map and makes the convolution operation arbitrary scales and high transformations.

3.3 Dynamic Training

Object detection often represents the ground-truth as bounding boxes in the image. Therefore, for the proposed regions, there is an ambiguity in determining the positive areas. Labels are often assigned by calculating the IoU score between prediction and ground-truth then matching with a predefined IoU threshold. In order to achieve high-quality object detection, we need to train the model with a higher IoU threshold. However, as mentioned in [3], it is impractical to increase the IoU threshold because positive patterns can degrade. In addition, Zhang et al. [21] observed that changing different IoU thresholds continuously during training resulted in a significant increase in positive regions. Based on this observation, Dynamic Label Assignment (DLA) is a branch used in Dynamic R-CNN to adjust the IoU threshold based on the distribution during training. With this flexibility, DLA can limit the scarcity of positive labels at the start of training and leverage from training at high IoU thresholds. DLA built upon the formula:

$$label = \begin{cases} 1 & maxIoU(b, G) \geq T_{now} \\ 0 & maxIoU(b, G) < T_{now} \end{cases} \tag{3}$$

where T_{now} stands for the current IoU threshold, DLA automatically updates the T_{now} based on the statistics of proposals to fit this distribution change. In practice, DLA computes the largest $K_I th$ in each batch value then updates T_{now} at each C iteration using the mean of them to enhance the robustness of the training.

3.4 Rank and Sort Loss

In recent years, object detection's performance has improved with auxiliary head (e.g., centerness, IoU, mask-IoU). However, Li et al. [9] found that using continuous IoU predictions to supervise the classifier performed better than using an auxiliary head. Rank and Sort (RS) Loss is designed based on this idea. RS Loss is considered a ranking-based loss function to train object detection or segmentation. In order to supervise the classifiers of visual detection tools by considering the localization qualities of the prediction (e.g., IoU), RS Loss decomposes the problem into two tasks:

- Ranking: rank each positive higher than all negatives
- Sorting: sort the s_i logits in descending order of constant label y_i based on the IoUs

RS Loss demonstrated some significant success from prioritizing the positives during the training process. The detector with RS Loss does not need an auxiliary head due to its ranking-based nature. In addition, RS Loss can handle extremely imbalanced data without any sampling heuristics. RS Loss is calculated based on a 3-step algorithm at [11] with the loss function defined as follows:

$$L_{ij} = \begin{cases} (l_R(i) - l_R^*(i))p_R(j|i) & i \in P, j \in N \\ (l_S(i) - l_S^*(i))p_S(j|i) & i \in P, j \in P \\ 0 & otherwise \end{cases} \tag{4}$$

where the error is calculated on $i \in P$ and $j \in N$ with P, N being the set of positive and negative samples, respectively. The ranking $p_R(j|i)$ and sorting probability mass function $p_S(j|i)$ uniformly distribute the ranking and sorting errors on i respectively on the samples that caused the error.

3.5   CDeRSNet: Cascade Deformable Rank Sort Network

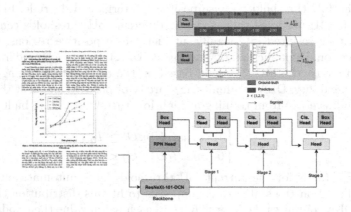

Fig. 1. CDeRSNet model architecture

The CDeRSNet model architecture is illustrated in Fig. 1. The architecture strategy of the CDeRSNet is similar to the Cascade R-CNN. Instead of using backbone ResNeXt-101 as Cascade R-CNN, CDeRSNet performs with the backbone ResNeXt-101-DCN to help extract features in document images at a higher level efficiently. In addition, each training stage of the CDeRSNet is similar to Cascade R-CNN. However, we add RS Loss to the Classification Head branch and uses the GIoU [17] loss function in the Bounding Box branch to improve the localization quality of the IoU-based predictions.

4   Experimental and Discussion

4.1   Implementation Details

We implement CDeRSNet in Pytorch using the MMDetection[1] framework. We use 2× GPU RTX 2080 Ti with 12 GB memory for our experiments. We use pre-trained ResNeXt-101-64 × 4d-DCN with Carafe FPN as the network head. In addition, we also reference the source code of Dynamic R-CNN [2] and RS Loss[3] provided by Zhang et al. and Oksuz et al., respectively. We train CDeRSNet with document images multi-scale with 7 different scales (3 smaller scales,

[1] https://github.com/open-mmlab/mmdetection.
[2] https://github.com/hkzhang95/DynamicRCNN.
[3] https://github.com/kemaloksuz/RankSortLoss.

original scale, and 3 larger scales), while testing with single-scale is (1333, 800). CDeRSNet is trained on 36 epochs with 0.012 as an initial learning rate and learning rate decay at 27 and 33 epoch. We use 0.001 as a warmup schedule for the first 500 iterations.

4.2 Dataset and Evaluation Metric

Dataset: We perform experiments on the UIT-DODV dataset. The dataset includes 2,394 images, with 1,440 images are for training, 234 images for validation, and 720 images for testing. We summarized the number of objects on the UIT-DODV dataset in Table 1.

Table 1. Statistical number of objects on the UIT-DODV dataset

	Table	Figure	Caption	Formula
Training	1,029	1,143	2,106	1,349
Testing	548	678	1,174	330
Validation	149	212	334	83
Total	1,726	2,033	3,614	1,762

Evaluation Metrics: We report experimental results based on the mAP score.

4.3 Experimental Results

The experimental results in Table 2 show that CDeRSNet reached the outperformance with an impressive mAP up to 79.9%. Besides, we also achieved 76.5% with Cascade R-CNN was conducted by training dynamic IoU at the first stage with the same configuration. Although RS Loss and Dynamic Training demonstrated impressive results, the model combined achieved 79.0% - lower than CDeRSNet 0.9%. In general, training with backbone ResNeXt-101-DCN and multi-scale helped exploit better features that create a foundation for further improvements.

Table 2. Experimental results on Cascade R-CNN with Dynamic Training and RSLoss on the UIT-DODV dataset

Method	Backbone	Table	Figure	Formula	Caption	AP@.50	AP@.75	mAP
Cascade R-CNN	ResNeXt-101	94.4	83.3	46.3	73.1	88.4	81.5	74.3
Cascade R-CNN	ResNeXt-101-DCN	95.2	85.0	47.3	74.6	88.1	82.6	75.5
Cascade R-CNN + Dynamic	ResNeXt-101-DCN	94.9	85.2	50.7	75.2	89.1	84.0	76.5
Cascade R-CNN + Dynamic + RSLoss	ResNeXt-101-DCN	96.2	87.6	56.3	76.0	**92.4**	86.8	79.0
CDeRSNet	**ResNeXt-101-DCN**	**96.4**	**88.7**	**58.1**	**76.3**	92.3	**87.2**	**79.9**

4.4 Experimental Analysis

Figure 2 illustrates the Top-4 effectiveness models in Table 2. We can observe the most improvement in the semantic object - Formula (yellow box), the most challenging object and accounts for the least number on the UIT-DODV dataset. For document images with the double-column page, as shown in Fig. 2, the detector tends to overfit with the objects fixed to one-side. For example, in Fig. 2a, the formula extended to both sides leads to the prediction results are two boxes with the intersection of both boxes at the borderline. Since the ground-truth of the mentioned object is a single bounding box from the combination of two prediction boxes, another case appears that one of these two boxes has a lower IoU (possibly false positive) than with the distribution of the training data. It is why the positive region with a low IoU value was removed when we trained with dynamic IoU, as shown in Fig. 2b. We solved these problems with RS Loss (as in Figs. 2c, 2d). Due to the ranking of positives higher than negative and the sorting positives together helps to bring about a higher confidence score. The higher confidence score is compatible with Non-Maximum Suppression (NMS) and contributes to the increased performance of AP. However, the combined RS Loss and Dynamic didn't achieve performance as expected (lower than CDeR-SNet 0.9%). Because sorting affected the dynamic distribution that makes IoU no longer accurate and reflects the proposed box distribution at that time.

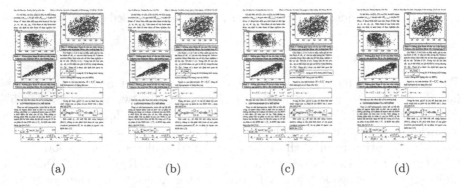

    (a)   (b)   (c)   (d)

Fig. 2. Illustration of the Top-4 effectiveness models: (a) Cascade R-CNN + DCN, (b) Cascade R-CNN + DCN + Dynamic, (c) Cascade R-CNN + DCN + Dynamic + RS Loss, (d) CDeRSNet - (blue box: figure, red box: caption, and yellow box: formula) (Color figure online)

    We illustrated some good prediction cases are presented in Fig. 3. CDeRSNet inherited the success from RS Loss when leveraged absolutely the success of RS Loss with imbalanced data. Specifically, the Formula (yellow box) account for the least number on UIT-DODV dataset had a significant improvement due to the positive priority. In addition, CDeRSNet also predicted better in another semantic object - Caption while remaining the good prediction in Table and Figure compared to an existing model. We compared the AP of each class between CDeRSNet and the state-of-the-art model in Table 3 to prove the effectiveness of our model.

Fig. 3. Exemplary of good prediction cases on CDeRSNet model (green box: table, blue box: figure, red box: caption, and yellow box: formula) (Color figure online)

Although CDeRSNet had high performance, it still has some limitations. We observed that the wrongly predicted boxes come from the locations where the same object appears close to each other (the box with the same color in Fig. 4). Specifically, the boxes tend to overlap, which is caused by NMS did not work well. We explained that RS Loss provides a higher confidence score. Therefore it also requires NMS to be considered carefully instead of using the default value of R-CNN or Cascade R-CNN models is 0.005.

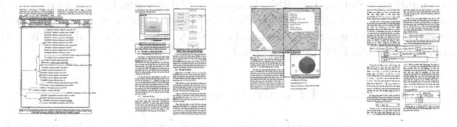

Fig. 4. Exemplary of bad prediction cases on CDeRSNet model (green box: table, blue box: figure, red box: caption, and yellow box: formula) (Color figure online)

4.5 Comparision with State-of-the-arts

We conducted experiments on the state-of-the-art models on object detection, and the best model has been published on the UIT-DODV dataset compared with CDeRSNet. We trained four models: GFocal, GFocalV2, VFNet, DetectoRS, with the best effectiveness model provided by MMDetection. The results reported in Table 3 show that CDeRSNet gave a superior performance on the UIT-DODV dataset. In addition, we compared CDeRSNet with the best model

Table 3. Comparison with state-of-the-arts on the UIT-DODV dataset

Method	Table	Figure	Formula	Caption	AP@.50	AP@.75	mAP
GFocalV2	7.83	66.2	78.0	34.3	69.2	49.4	46.7
GFL	94.0	83.6	45.0	61.9	89.4	77.0	71.1
CascadeTabNet + Fused Loss [6]	94.3	83.0	47.5	73.0	89.1	81.6	74.5
Faster R-CNN + ResNeXt-101-DCN + RS Loss	95.4	85.8	52.3	67.8	92.1	81.8	75.3
VFNet	95.1	85.7	52.8	75.1	92.4	83.5	77.2
DetectoRS	96.1	85.5	54.5	76.5	92.0	85.2	78.1
CDeRSNet (Ours)	**96.4**	**88.7**	**58.1**	**76.3**	**92.3**	**87.2**	**79.9**

on UIT-DODV dataset. CDeRSNet improved up to 5.4% on the mAP. As mentioned in Sect. 4.4, the Formula received the most significant improvement, with AP increasing to 10.6%. We also experimented with the baseline using RS Loss, which achieved the best performance on the MS COCO dataset. In this model, Oksuz et al. used Faster R-CNN with ResNeXt-101-DCN as the backbone and RS Loss. Compared to this baseline, CDeRSNet is still higher than 4.6%, which means this baseline with RS Loss didn't work as effectively as CDeRSNet on the UIT-DODV dataset.

On the other hand, the state-of-the-art model for the object detection problem that achieves the closest results to the model we use is DetectoRS, with the mAP score is 78.1%. Although GFocalV2 is a new object detection model that was proposed at the CVPR 2021 conference, it received only reached 46.7%. In general, we reached the most significant success with CDeRSNet in improving the performance on the semantic object (Caption, Formula). Thanks to deformable convolution, CDeRSNet extracted high-level features from document images robustly. In addition, CDeRSNet also leveraged RS Loss to handle imbalanced data and resolve the problem related to the low-quality prediction in both four classes on the UIT-DODV dataset.

5 Conclusion and Future Work

In this paper, we proposed CDeRSNet - a novel end-to-end deep learning model for object detection in document images on the Vietnamese research paper dataset UIT-DODV. CDeRSnet achieved 79.9% in terms of mAP, which is 5.4% higher than current results on the UIT-DODV dataset. In addition, CDeRSNet also attained outperformance over state-of-the-art models for page object detection on the UIT-DODV dataset. This result is the foundation for us to develop other problems in DIU, such as Table Structure Recognition or Caption Extraction on image documents in the future.

Acknowledgment. This research is funded by the University of Information Technology – Vietnam National University Ho Chi Minh City under grant number D1-2021-32. We express our sincere thanks to UIT-Together Research Group, Multimedia Communications Laboratory (MMLab), Faculty of Information Science and Engineering – University of Information Technology – Vietnam National University – Ho Chi Minh City, for supporting my team in this research process.

References

1. Agarwal, M., Mondal, A., Jawahar, C.V.: CDeC-Net: composite deformable cascade network for table detection in document images. arXiv: 2008.10831 [cs.CV] (2020)
2. Alcácer, V., Cruz-Machado, V.: Scanning the industry 4.0: a literature review on technologies for manufacturing systems. Eng. Sci. Technol. Int. J. **22**(3), 899–919 (2019)
3. Cai, Z., Vasconcelos, N.: Cascade R-CNN: delving into high quality object detection. In: 2018 IEEE/CVF Conference on Computer Vision and Pattern Recognition, pp. 6154–6162 (2018). 2018.00644, https://doi.org/10.1109/CVPR
4. Cesarini, F., Marinai, S., Sarti, L., Soda, G.: Trainable table location in document images. In: Object Recognition Supported by User Interaction for Service Robots, vol. 3, pp. 236–240. IEEE (2002)
5. Dai, J., et al.: Deformable convolutional networks. arXiv: 1703.06211 [cs.CV] (2017)
6. Dieu, L.T., Nguyen, T.T., Vo, N.D., Nguyen, T.V., Nguyen, K.: Parsing digitized Vietnamese paper documents. In: Tsapatsoulis, N., Panayides, A., Theocharides, T., Lanitis, A., Pattichis, C., Vento, M. (eds.) CAIP 2021. LNCS, vol. 13052, pp. 382–392. Springer, Cham (2021). https://doi.org/10.1007/978-3-030-89128-2_37
7. Gatos, B., Danatsas, D., Pratikakis, I., Perantonis, S.J.: Automatic table detection in document images. In: Singh, S., Singh, M., Apte, C., Perner, P. (eds.) ICAPR 2005. LNCS, vol. 3686, pp. 609–618. Springer, Heidelberg (2005). https://doi.org/10.1007/11551188_67
8. Li, X., et al.: Generalized focal loss V2: learning reliable localization quality estimation for dense object detection. arXiv: 2011.12885 [cs.CV] (2020)
9. Li, X., et al.: Generalized focal loss: learning qualified and distributed bounding boxes for dense object detection. CoRR abs/2006.04388 arXiv: 2006.04388 [cs.CV] (2020)
10. Li, Y., et al.: Rethinking table structure recognition using sequence labeling methods. In: Lladós, J., Lopresti, D., Uchida, S. (eds.) ICDAR 2021. LNCS, vol. 12822, pp. 541–553. Springer, Cham (2021). https://doi.org/10.1007/978-3-030-86331-9_35
11. Oksuz, K., Cam, B.C., Akbas, E., Kalkan, S.: A ranking based, balanced loss function unifying classification and localisation in object detection. arXiv preprint arXiv:2009.13592 (2020)
12. Oksuz, K., Cam, B.C., Akbas, E., Kalkan, S.: Rank & sort loss for object detection and instance segmentation. arXiv preprint arXiv:2107.11669 (2021)
13. Peng, S., Gao, L., Yuan, K., Tang, Z.: Image to LaTeX with graph neural network for mathematical formula recognition. In: Lladós, J., Lopresti, D., Uchida, S. (eds.) ICDAR 2021. LNCS, vol. 12822, pp. 648–663. Springer, Cham (2021). https://doi.org/10.1007/978-3-030-86331-9_42

14. Prasad, D., Gadpal, A., Kapadni, K., Visave, M., Sultanpure, K.: CascadeTabNet: an approach for end to end table detection and structure recognition from image-based documents. arXiv: 2004.12629 [cs.CV] (2020)
15. Qiao, L., et al.: LGPMA: complicated table structure recognition with local and global pyramid mask alignment. In: Lladós, J., Lopresti, D., Uchida, S. (eds.) ICDAR 2021. LNCS, vol. 12821, pp. 99–114. Springer, Cham (2021). https://doi.org/10.1007/978-3-030-86549-8_7
16. Qiao, S., Chen, L.-C., Yuille, A.: DetectoRS: detecting objects with recursive feature pyramid and switchable atrous convolution. arXiv: 2006.02334 [cs.CV] (2020)
17. Rezatofighi, H., et al.: Generalized intersection over union: a metric and a loss for bounding box regression. In: Proceedings of the IEEE/CVF Conference on Computer Vision and Pattern Recognition, pp. 658–666 (2019)
18. Vo, N.D., Nguyen, K., Nguyen, T.V., Nguyen, K.: Empirical evaluation of state-of-the-art object detection methods for document image understanding. In: Fundamental and Applied IT Research Conference, pp. 180–184 (2017). https://doi.org/10.15625/vap.2017.00022
19. Vo, N.D., Nguyen, K., Nguyen, T.V., Nguyen, K.: Ensemble of deep object detectors for page object detection. In: Proceedings of the 12th International Conference on Ubiquitous Information Management and Communication, pp. 1–6 (2018)
20. Zhang, H., Wang, Y., Dayoub, F., Sünderhauf, N.: VarifocalNet: an IoU-aware dense object detector. arXiv: 2008.13367 [cs.CV] (2021)
21. Zhang, H., Chang, H., Ma, B., Wang, N., Chen, X.: Dynamic R-CNN: towards high quality object detection via dynamic training. In: Vedaldi, A., Bischof, H., Brox, T., Frahm, J.-M. (eds.) ECCV 2020. LNCS, vol. 12360, pp. 260–275. Springer, Cham (2020). https://doi.org/10.1007/978-3-030-58555-6_16
22. Zhang, P., et al.: VSR: a unified framework for document layout analysis combining vision, semantics and relations. In: Lladós, J., Lopresti, D., Uchida, S. (eds.) ICDAR 2021. LNCS, vol. 12821, pp. 115–130. Springer, Cham (2021). https://doi.org/10.1007/978-3-030-86549-8_8

Demonstration Papers

Making Few-Shot Object Detection Simpler and Less Frustrating

Werner Bailer[✉]

Joanneum Research, Graz, Austria
`werner.bailer@joanneum.at`

Abstract. Few-shot object detection is useful in order to extend object
detection capabilities in media production and archiving applications
with specific object classes of interest for a particular organization or
production context. While recent approaches for few-shot object detection have advanced the state of the art, they still do not fully meet
the requirements of practical workflows, e.g., in media production and
archiving. In these applications, annotated samples for novel classes are
drawn from different data sources, they differ in numbers and it may
be necessary to add a new class quickly to cover the requirements of a
specific production. In contrast, current frameworks for few-shot object
detection typically assume a static dataset, which is split into the base
and novel classes. We propose a toolchain to facilitate training for few-
shot object detection, which takes care of data preparation when using
heterogeneous training data and setup of training steps. The toolchain
also creates annotation files to use combined data sets as new base models, which facilitates class-incremental training. We also integrated the
toolchain with an annotation UI.

Keywords: Few-shot learning · Object detection · Data preparation ·
Annotation tool · Incremental training

1 Introduction

Few-shot object detection is useful in order to extend object detection capabilities in sourcing (e.g., annotation of feeds of raw material) or archiving with
specific object classes of interest for a particular organization or production context. If the object class of interest is not covered by a publicly available dataset
(or license conditions do not permit the use of such a dataset), the labeling
of a large amount of training samples is typically not feasible. Few-shot object
detection enables training with an amount of samples that can be labeled by a
single user with acceptable effort. While the resulting classifier is likely to achieve
lower performance than one trained on a thousands of samples, it may still enable
detection of otherwise uncovered classes. In addition, detection results (possibly
in combination with object tracking) can be used to mine data for retraining a
classifier on a larger set.

© Springer Nature Switzerland AG 2022
B. Þór Jónsson et al. (Eds.): MMM 2022, LNCS 13142, pp. 445–451, 2022.
https://doi.org/10.1007/978-3-030-98355-0_37

While recent approaches for few-shot object detection have advanced the state of the art, they still do not fully meet the requirements of practical workflows, e.g., in media production and archiving. In these applications, annotated samples for novel classes are drawn from different data sources, they differ in numbers and it may be necessary to add a new class quickly to cover the requirements of a specific production. In contrast, current frameworks for few-shot object detection typically assume a static dataset, which is split into the base and novel classes. In this paper, we propose a training toolchain that extends the widely used approach "Frustratingly simple few-shot object detection" by Wang et al. [6] in order to facilitate the training of few-shot learning models and enable class-incremental training. In addition, we integrate the toolchain with an annotation user interface (UI). The tools described in this paper are available as open source software.

In Sect. 2 we provide more details about the motivation of this work and the choice of the few-shot learning framework. In Sect. 3 we present the toolchain and discuss its integration with the annotation UI in Sect. 4. Section 5 concludes the paper.

2   Motivation and Context

This work focuses on few-shot object detection, serving use cases in annotating incoming material in media production or for archiving. We can observe three main aspects, where the setup of benchmarking problems (and thus the methods described in literature, as well as the existing implementations) deviate from the practical requirements of using few-shot object detection in media use cases:

- The typical setup of the problem is posed as n-way k-shot, i.e. a problem with n classes and k samples per shot. However, in practice the number of samples per class that are provided may differ.
- There is no fixed predefined dataset, but the set of base classes will contain a mixture of third party and maybe own data for some classes, while the novel classes are mined from own or third party media content (e.g., web sites). Thus the concept of a dataset is fluid, and the available data will evolve over time.
- Classes may need to be added incrementally, which requires creating balanced training sets, but approaches should aim to keep the training effort low. This again means that there is no fixed notion of a dataset, but it needs to be updated on the fly.

Taking these aspects into consideration, we decided to focus on metric or contrastive rather than meta-learning type of approaches. In addition, we are interested to use a framework, which can be applied to object detection as well as segmentation. Methods of interest are thus Karlinsky et al. [3], which uses FPN to create an object detection pipeline using metric learning. Classification is done using a different method for pretrained classes, while few-shot learning is done with FPN (in the DCN variant) instead. Singh et al. [5] propose to train a generic object detector on ImageNet, sampling positive and negative candidate regions. This approach is suitable for generic object detection, beyond the originally trained classes. An approach based on meta-features and learning reweighting of those features is proposed by Kang et al. [2]. A recent work [6] applies fine-tuning only to region proposal and classification layers on a data set consisting of many base class and few new class samples while fixing the feature extraction part of the network, using Faster R-CNN [4] as a backbone. It has been shown that it can outperform meta-learning approaches [6].

We are interested in a framework that can potentially also be used with single-stage detectors and extended to support segmentation. We thus use the work of Wang et al. [6] as the basis of our work. This work proposes a two-stage fine-tuning (TFA) approach. A backbone model such as Faster R-CNN is trained on the base classes using a standard training approach. Then the last layer of the model is extended to include the novel classes, and the new weights are randomly initialized. Fine-tuning of the model is performed by training with a dataset formed from k samples from each of the base classes, and the samples of the novel classes. Both the classification and bounding box regression branch are trained using this balanced dataset, but the feature extraction part of the model is not updated. In addition, the fine-tuning step uses a cosine similarity based classifier, which results in improved accuracy for the novel classes and lower decrease for the base classes compared to an FC-based classifier. As an alternative to randomly initializing the new weights, a separate training step for the last layer can be performed with the new classes, and the results can be used to initialize the weights of the novel classes in the combined model.

3   Training Toolchain

We have extended the framework of Wang et al. [6] with a tool that dynamically generates datasets and drives the training process. The tool aims to facilitate the training process and to enable incremental training. The code of training toolchain is available at https://github.com/wbailer/few-shot-object-detection.

3.1   Facilitating Training

We aim to drive the few-shot training process by the available data in the process, so that few-shot training can be deployed as a service to be integrated in a media analysis toolchain. The expected input to such a service are a set of samples and corresponding annotations, as well as a small configuration file, which describes the base model to be used, the data locations and whether all or just some classes of the new data shall be used for training. The user may supply separate datasets for training and validation, or the tool can create splits at a defined ratio. The samples and annotations may be entirely user supplied (i.e., manually annotated), or may result from a semi-automatic process. Such a process may use weakly supervised object detection and tracking, where the user only coarsely identifies the object in one frame and provides a class label, but the bounding boxes (or masks) are determined automatically by segmenting the object throughout a sequence.

In particular, the tool covers the following steps:

- Determine the base and novel classes from the provided annotations. For both the base and novel classes only a subset of classes may be actually used in the training. This provides more flexibility in the process, and is also required to support incremental training without splitting the source annotation files.
- Determine how many instances are available, and set up the k-shot n-way problem accordingly, with $k = \min(k_1, \ldots, k_n)$.
- If needed, create the training and validation splits of the dataset.
- Prepare model structures for novel only training and fine-tuning of the combined base+novel model by adjusting the layer sizes to match the number of classes in the different sets. This includes scaling up the number of classes arbitrarily, which goes beyond the current functionality of the framework, that assumes a split of fixed number of classes.
- If the number of samples strongly varies, set up multiple training problems to make best use of the data. This is implemented by specifying a factor q, which causes a split if half of the classes have q times more samples than the one with the fewest samples, i.e., $\mathrm{median}(k_1, \ldots, k_n) \geq q \ \min(k_1, \ldots, k_n)$.

The tool currently supports annotations in COCO format[1]. However, this does not mean that COCO is required as a base model, as long as the annotations are provided in this format. The training tool has been tested with a pretrained base model containing 60 COCO classes (from the model zoo provided by the authors of the few-shot learning framework[2]), and adding a subset of 20 novel classes selected from the LVIS dataset. This example training configuration is provided with the code (under `configs/custom_datasets`).

3.2 Towards Incremental Training

The proposed tool can also be used for incremental training of new classes. The training tool provides as additional output the dataset annotation files that are required to use the resulting model as a base model. Similar to the splitting of the training step in case of unequal number of samples, also different incremental training steps can use different values for k. These files can be directly used as base models in the next training iteration.

However, due to the two-stage fine-tuning (TFA) approach in the framework, the fine-tuning step is run for all classes, including the base classes and of novel classes from previous iterations. This step is typically computationally more expensive than the training process for novel classes, in particular, if the number of classes in an incremental training step is small. Thus the runtime saving in incremental training will be less than the fraction of the added classes to all

---

[1] https://cocodataset.org/#format-data.
[2] https://github.com/ucbdrive/few-shot-object-detection/blob/master/docs/ MODEL_ZOO.md.

novel classes. A recent paper proposes to avoids running this fine-tuning step after incremental training [1], but at the expense of training an instance feature embedding, and requiring access to these features at inference stage.

4   Integration with Annotation UI

In order to facilitate the creation of the necessary annotations and configuration files, we decided to integrate the proposed toolchain with an annotation UI. We chose the open source tool MakeSense[3] as a basis. It is a rather lightweight tool written using TypeScript and React, that runs in the browser and does not require image upload to a server. The tool supports point, line, rectangle and polygon annotations, and can export them in common formats, including COCO. A screenshot of an example project is shown in Fig. 1.

Fig. 1. Example of annotating samples for few-shot annotation.

When creating a new project, we have added a dialog that collects the basic information about the few-shot training task (see Fig. 2). Then the user selects the set of images to work on, and defines the labels for the novel classes. The base model is selected from a fixed set of preconfigured base models, as the model file, the annotation files and the subset of included classes need to match. Models resulting from few-shot training and used as base models for incremental training can be added here (in the current version, this step is not automated and needs to be done manually).

Once the user is done with the annotation, the configuration for few-shot training can be exported. This export will store the annotation file (which is split into the training and validation sets automatically), the script calling for the toolchain described in Sect. 3 and the configuration file needed by this script.

---

[3] https://www.makesense.ai/.

Fig. 2. Dialog for configuring few-shot training.

The user needs to set via environment variable or in this script the location of the local installation of the few-shot learning framework. As the annotation UI runs in the browser, it cannot directly start the training toolchain, this would require running a local server that could be called from the TypeScript code, and would then run the training tool. However, starting the script manually is probably easier than requiring the installation of an additional component.

The modified version of the annotation tool is available at https://github.com/wbailer/make-sense.

5 Conclusion

In this paper, we have proposed a toolchain to facilitate training for few-shot object detection, which takes care of data preparation when using heterogeneous training data and setup of training steps. The toolchain also creates annotation files to use combined data sets as new base models, which facilitates class-incremental training. We integrated the toolchain with an annotation UI, allowing the user to perform the necessary configuration and annotation in the browser. Both the toolchain extending a widely used few-shot learning framework and the extended annotation UI are available as open source software.

Acknowledgments. This work has received funding from the European Union's Horizon 2020 research and innovation programme, under grant agreement n° 951911 AI4Media (https://ai4media.eu) and from the program "ICT of the Future" of the Austrian Federal Ministry of Climate Action, Environment, Energy, Mobility, Innovation and Technology (BMK).

References

1. Ganea, D.A., Boom, B., Poppe, R.: Incremental few-shot instance segmentation. In: Proceedings of the IEEE/CVF Conference on Computer Vision and Pattern Recognition, pp. 1185–1194 (2021)

2. Kang, B., Liu, Z., Wang, X., Yu, F., Feng, J., Darrell, T.: Few-shot object detection via feature reweighting. In: Proceedings of ICCV (2019)
3. Karlinsky, L., et al.: RepMet: Representative-based metric learning for classification and few-shot object detection. In: Proceedings of CVPR (2019)
4. Ren, S., He, K., Girshick, R., Sun, J.: Faster R-CNN: towards real-time object detection with region proposal networks. In: Advances in Neural Information Processing Systems, pp. 91–99 (2015)
5. Singh, B., Li, H., Sharma, A., Davis, L.S.: R-FCN-3000 at 30 fps: decoupling detection and classification. In: Proceedings of CVPR (2018)
6. Wang, X., Huang, T., Gonzalez, J., Darrell, T., Yu, F.: Frustratingly simple few-shot object detection. In: International Conference on Machine Learning, pp. 9919–9928. PMLR (2020)

PicArrange - Visually Sort, Search, and Explore Private Images on a Mac Computer

Klaus Jung[✉], Kai Uwe Barthel, Nico Hezel, and Konstantin Schall

HTW Berlin, University of Applied Sciences - Visual Computing Group,
Wilhelminenhofstraße 75, 12459 Berlin, Germany
klaus.jung@htw-berlin.de
https://visual-computing.com

Abstract. The native macOS application PicArrange integrates state-of-the-art image sorting and similarity search to enable users to get a better overview of their images. Many file and image management features have been added to make it a tool that addresses a full image management workflow. A modification of the Self Sorting Map algorithm enables a list-like image arrangement without loosing the visual sorting. Efficient calculation and storage of visual features as well as the use of many macOS APIs result in an application that is fluid to use.

Keywords: Content-based image retrieval · Exploration · Image browsing · Visualization · CNNs · Image sorting

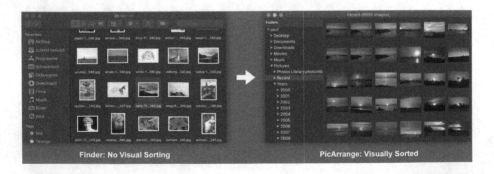

Fig. 1. Exploring a folder with 6695 images using macOS Finder and PicArrange

1 Introduction

In many situations, people need to view and navigate through large amounts of images. This includes searching for appropriate images on the Internet or

B. Þór Jónsson et al. (Eds.): MMM 2022, LNCS 13142, pp. 452–457, 2022.
https://doi.org/10.1007/978-3-030-98355-0_38

finding images from stock agencies. Visual similarity search helps to identify images that meet the search requirements. In most cases such systems are used to access images from a database using a web browser. However, with high-quality cameras built into smartphones the number of personal images keeps increasing, even if people are not professional photographers. Typically images are arranged as thumbnails sorted by file name or creation date. Surprisingly, visual image search is not integrated into common computer operating systems. Moreover, image lists only show images contained in a single folder of the file system. Figure 1 compares the display of images using the macOS' Finder and the proposed PicArrange application.

This paper introduces PicArrange, a native application highly integrated into the macOS to seamlessly work with images on the computer's file system. Here "file system" includes attached files storage as well as network shares or cloud drives. However, the focus is put to deal with private images without transferring any image data to a server for analysis purpose. PicArrange can display visually sorted images from several folders at the same time, making it easy to find duplicate images or finding the best looking image from a certain category. All analysis is done locally by calculating and storing the visual feature vectors for the displayed images to keep data privacy. By compressing the feature vectors, the amount of stored analysis data is reduced to a minimum, enabling PicArrange to handle hundreds of thousands of images simultaneously.

2   Related Work

Many web-based image management systems offer the possibility to find "similar images", such as Google Images , Pixabay[1], Pexels[2], Adobe Stock[3], and others. In many cases, similarity search is based on tagged keywords, some systems use visual comparison or a combination of both. In most cases, the algorithms used are not published. A few systems use a visually sorted arrangement of the presented images. Wikiview[4] [2] uses Self-Sorting Maps (SSM) [5] for visual sorting to allow browsing of Wikimedia Common images. Picsbuffet[5] [1] can be used to explore images from Pixabay, Fotolia, and IKEA.

Operating systems like macOS, iOS, or Windows nowadays do some analysis on local images using machine learning approaches for image classification and identi-fication. On macOS and iOS, the images need to be part of Apple's Photo Library to be analysed. Most visibly, faces found in the images are related to certain persons in a semi-automatic approach. Depending on the amount of images, the analysis takes hours or days. It does not work for images from the file system that have not been imported into the Photo Library. Kiano[6] uses Apple's Photo Library API

---

[1] https://pixabay.com.
[2] https://www.pexels.com.
[3] https://stock.adobe.com.
[4] https://wikiview.net.
[5] https://picsbuffet.com/pixabay.
[6] https://visual-computing.com/project/kiano.

to display images visually arranged similar to Picsbuffet. ImageX[7] [3] is a multi-platform, Java-based application that allows to visually explore and search images from the file system of Linux, Windows, and Mac operating systems.

3 PicArrange

The presented demo application PicArrange differs from the applications mentioned in Sect. 2 in several aspects. It is neither web-based nor does it rely on a web service for image analysis. Compared to ImageX, it is not platform independent, which might be a disadvantage at first sight. However, PicArrange is designed to integrate into macOS as much as possible, offering features more than just image sorting (see Sect. 3.4), thus addressing users that need a complete workflow in image management and want to retain to the look and feel of a native application, using interaction methods to which they are already accustomed. Performance, i.e. fast processing times, is also a requirement that led to the decision to use native APIs as much as possible.

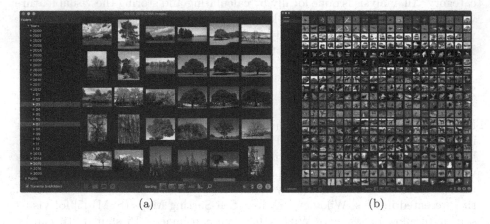

(a)   (b)

Fig. 2. Viewing images from multiple folders (a) and with many columns (b)

The most visible difference compared to ImageX, Kiano, or Picsbuffet is the arrangement of sorted images. Whereas these applications display an endless map of visually sorted images that topologically represents a torus, PicArrange uses a "linear" column-based layout (Fig. 2). This adopts the presentation style of the Finder application. A map that is almost square in size and repeats endlessly at the edges is a good approach to get an overview of a huge amount of images. Visual sorting benefits from many places in both dimensions to arrange similar images nearby. But in most cases, exploring private images on the local file system the users do not display thousands of images at once. A list of images with a small number of columns ensures that the user knows when he or she has

---

[7] https://visual-computing.com/project/imagex.

seen all images in that folder because the list simply has an end. Nevertheless, visually sorting images in this layout leads to an improved visualization (see Sect. 3.2 and Fig. 1).

Unlike the Finder, PicArrange can display images from multiple folders at once (Fig. 2 (a)). It is also possible to include images from the subfolders of a folder, so that all images of the subtree of this folder are displayed. This allows the user to get an overview of the images, even when they are arranged in a complex folder structure.

A short introduction to PicArrange with many screenshots can be found at https://visual-computing.com/project/picarrange/help. The application is available in the App Store[8].

3.1 Feature Calculation

For a good compromise between processing time, sorting quality, and storage size of feature vectors, PicArrange computes features using the MobileNetV3 CNN [4]. The pretrained network is modified in such a way that activations before the fully connected layer are passed to a compression network integrated to the model. This network reduces the data to 64 dimensions and can be seen as an alternative to Principal Component Analysis. Converted to Apple's CoreML API, image features can be calculated in a single step using the GPU processing power of the Mac computer.

When displaying only small thumbnails, details of the image content cannot be perceived. The subjective quality of a visually sorted image arrangement is increasingly influenced by the colors of the images compared to their content (compare Fig. 2 (a) with (b)). For this reason, we calculate a second feature vector not using a neural network. It calculates its values from color histograms, edge histograms, and a frequency analysis. Finally, a weighted combination of CNN and non-CNN features is used, with CNN features given a higher weight in PicArrange's similarity search (content is more important than color) compared to the visually sorted image arrangement. The optimal weighting for the visual search was determined using mean average precision calculations, and for visual sorting the weighting was adjusted to provide a good subjective viewing experience of the sorted images.

3.2 Image Arrangement

Self-Organizing Maps (SOM) or Self-Sorting Maps (SSM) arrange images on a grid of $N \times M$ positions. Within these algorithms, border processing at the grid's boundaries is needed. When creating a seamless map of endless repeated images on a torus, calculations in the vicinity of the borders need to wrap around grid positions. The last images of a row is followed by the first image of that row. For PicArrange's list with a few columns this would require that the last images of a row need to be similar to the first one. Such a restriction is not necessary and

---

[8] Download PicArrange from https://apps.apple.com/app/picarrange/id1530678223.

Fig. 3. Border (red) of 28 images placed on 5 × 6 positions (Color figure online)

would make it more difficult for the algorithm to find good places for the images in such a narrow grid. Thus, a border processing of constant continuation is used within PicArrange's image sorting process.

Most applications using SOM or SSM show holes or duplicate images at certain map positions if the number of images is not a multiple of the number of columns N. Holes can be easily created by padding the unsorted array with duplicate images carrying a flag "do not show in final result". However, the holes will be at "random" positions of the sorted array. An application used to explore images in the file system should not show duplicates unless there are duplicate files. So both options do not meet the user's expectation of a list without duplicates and without holes, expect at the last positions of the last row. To achieve this goal, PicArrange uses a modified constant continuation border processing where the border is not simply a rectangle, but the shape around images filling up $N \times M$ positions in scanline order (Fig. 3).

3.3 Similarity Search

Similarity search is implemented by selecting a query image and sorting all images of the list by their feature vector's L2-distance to the feature vector of the query image. To improve the usability of the application, other things can also be done. Searching for similar images can be an iterative process where the user identifies images from the first result that fit the expectation even better than the query image. Often there is the need to use more than just one image for the query. https://visual-computing.com/project/picarrange/help/? p=12 shows screenshots for an iterative search looking for windmills and towers. When multiple images are used as query, the result images are sorted by the smallest distance to one of the query images.

3.4 Integration into MacOS

The main features apart from image sorting and similarity search are listed below. They have been implemented by using many of Apple's APIs.

– Use drag & drop into the Finder to copy images to any other folder.
– Delete selected image files.
– Show image files in Finder or open them with macOS' Preview application.
– Open images with any macOS application registered to view or edit images.
– Sort images by creation date, modification date, file name, or file size.

- View images from multiple folders at once.
- Display images of all macOS-supported image file formats, including camera manufacturers' RAW formats.
- Display videos and first pages of PDF documents as well.
- Display image file information.
- Support for attached storage devices, network shares, and iCloud folders.
- Filter displayed images by criteria like file name, creation date, modification date, or size.
- PicArrange also has a build-in single image viewer with zoom, full screen and slideshow.

Processing time depends on the time used for traversing the file system, acquiring thumbnails from the OS, feature calculation, and image sorting. For a set of 5300 typical digital camera images (JPEG) on the local SSD, the total processing time is about 340 s (64 ms per image) including feature calculation (Intel i7-6820HQ, Radeon Pro 455 2 GB). For a second run on the same set, PicArrange uses its stored feature vectors. The processing time reduces to 1.7 s (0.32 ms per image).

4   Conclusion

This demo presents a highly integrated viewer for images and videos on a macOS file system that allows users to explore and process all their images. Using CNN-based image features and optimized image sorting, users benefit from improved visualization and image search without sacrificing familiar functionality.

References

1. Barthel, K.U., Hezel, N., Mackowiak, R.: Imagemap - visually browsing millions of images. In: He, X., Luo, S., Tao, D., Xu, C., Yang, J., Hasan, M.A. (eds.) MultiMedia Modeling, pp. 287–290. Springer International Publishing, Cham (2015). https://doi.org/10.1007/978-3-319-14442-9_30
2. Barthel, K.U., Hezel, N., Schall, K., Jung, K.: Real-time visual navigation in huge image sets using similarity graphs. In: Proceedings of the 27th ACM International Conference on Multimedia. MM '19, Association for Computing Machinery, New York, NY, USA, pp. 2202–2204 (2019). https://doi.org/10.1145/3343031.3350599
3. Hezel, N., Barthel, K.U.: Dynamic construction and manipulation of hierarchical quartic image graphs. In: Proceedings of the 2018 ACM on International Conference on Multimedia Retrieval. ICMR '18, Association for Computing Machinery, New York, NY, USA, pp. 513–516 (2018). https://doi.org/10.1145/3206025.3206093
4. Howard, A., et al.: Searching for mobilenetv3. In: ICCV, pp. 1314–1324. IEEE (2019). https://doi.org/10.1109/ICCV.2019.00140
5. Strong, G., Gong, M.: Self-sorting map: an efficient algorithm for presenting multimedia data in structured layouts. Trans. Multi. **16**(4), 1045–1058 (2014). https://doi.org/10.1109/TMM.2014.2306183

XQM: Search-Oriented vs. Classifier-Oriented Relevance Feedback on Mobile Phones

Kim I. Schild[1], Alexandra M. Bagi[1], Magnus Holm Mamsen[1], Omar Shahbaz Khan[1], Jan Zahálka[2], and Björn Þór Jónsson[1](✉)

[1] IT University of Copenhagen, Copenhagen, Denmark
bjth@itu.dk
[2] Czech Technical University, Prague, Czech Republic
jan.zahalka@cvut.cz

Abstract. In today's media-rich and mobile-dominated society, an important research direction in multimedia retrieval concerns scaling multimedia interfaces down to mobile phones. We present XQM, an interactive learning app for images on Android mobile phones, with two different interface variants: (a) a search-oriented interface, which emphasises finding a particular image rapidly; and (b) a classifier-oriented interface, which emphasises helping users to build the interactive classifier.

Keywords: Interactive learning · Relevance feedback · Mobile devices

1 Introduction

Interactive learning has recently seen revival as a vital interaction paradigm for media collections, alongside the traditional browsing, filtering and searching paradigms. In interactive learning, user and system collaborate to build an interactive classifier to model the user's information need: the system shows the user media items that its current classifier suggests might be relevant, the user then gives feedback to the system on some or all of those media items, and the system uses that feedback to improve the classifier [9,18]. This process continues until the classifier satisfies the user's information need, either by finding a specific media item or by identifying a class of media items.

Recent work has focused on scalability of the interactive learning process, with Exquisitor, the state of the art, capable of interactively suggesting images from the YFCC100M collection in less than 0.3 s using a single CPU core [7]. Most of today's media are created using mobile phones and many mobile owners today carry around collections of thousands of images. While mobile media browsers have many modern features, including filtering based on automatically generated semantic labels, and many studies have proposed various learning apps for mobile phones (e.g., [3,5,12]), we are not aware of mobile apps supporting interactive learning. This suggests another research direction for scaling interactive learning, namely *scaling down* to the mobile phone.

© Springer Nature Switzerland AG 2022
B. Þór Jónsson et al. (Eds.): MMM 2022, LNCS 13142, pp. 458–464, 2022.
https://doi.org/10.1007/978-3-030-98355-0_39

To study interactive learning on mobile devices, we have recently proposed XQM, a mobile approach for interactive learning shown in Fig. 1. In this demonstration we focus on adapting the interface of interactive learning to

(a) the small screen of the mobile device and (b) the mobile interaction paradigm of swiping and pressing. We present two modes of interaction within XQM, which differ mainly in their approach to working with the user to build the interactive classifier:

- *Search-oriented* mode, aiming to find a media item satisfying the user's information need as rapidly as possible.
- *Classifier-oriented* mode, aiming to clearly present the current output of the classifier at any time.

As a fully-fledged mobile system for exploring image collections supported by an intelligent model, XQM joins the broader family of multimedia analytics systems [2,11,14,17].

(a) Initial screen   (b) Classifier result

Fig. 1. The goal of interactive learning is to propel users from an initial set of suggestions to an interactive classifier that captures their information need.

2   XQM Architecture

Currently, the two interaction modes are implemented as two separate Android apps for technical reasons. Figure 2 shows the common architecture of both modes of XQM. Consider first the off-line *data processing phase* of the app. When new images are saved to DCIM storage, they are sent to a server for semantic feature extraction. The server returns the most prominent semantic features found in the image and then stores them in a SQLite feature database. XQM uses a server instead of on-device processing since (a) state-of-the-art semantic classifiers would rapidly drain the charge from the mobile phone, and (b) lightweight semantic classifiers for mobile phones are not competitive in terms of quality [10]. We note, however, that since the app is a research prototype, this process is currently initiated by the user and images can be processed in batches to improve performance. Furthermore, we have developed a script to install new image collections, along with their feature vectors, for evaluation purposes.

Turning to the on-line *interactive exploration phase*, XQM implements a traditional interaction loop, where the system builds an interactive classifier over the semantic feature space, based on relevance feedback from the user [7,13,16]. In each round of interaction, the user is shown the images most relevant to the current classifier, and allowed to give positive and negative feedback on those

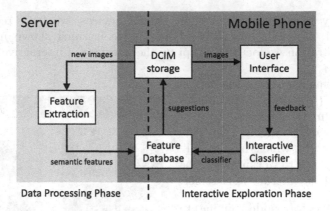

Fig. 2. Architecture of the XQM interactive learning app.

images. This feedback is then used to build a better classifier, and retrieve the next batch of the most relevant images. Once the user has found an image, it can be shared via the traditional sharing methods of the mobile phone. In the classifier-oriented app, the resulting classifier can be saved and revisited later.

XQM is implemented in Java and Kotlin. In keeping with the state of the art [7], XQM builds a Linear SVM classifier [6], using the libSVM library [4]. Note that the library requires at least one positive and one negative example; until these are provided, the user is shown random images. The semantic feature extractor is ImageNet Shuffle [8] a deep neural network using the ResNeXt-101 architecture [15]. There are some minor differences in the "look and feel" of the two interfaces, and in non-essential functionality, such as sharing images. The main differences between the search-oriented and classifier-oriented variants of XQM lie in the way that (a) the relevant images are shown to the user, and (b) the user communicates the feedback to the system, described below.

3   Search-Oriented Interface

The left side of Fig. 1 shows the initial *home screen* of the search-oriented interface. Each exploration session starts by presenting 6 random images from the collection—the largest number of images that can be displayed on the mobile screen in adequate resolution. If the user finds positive or negative examples, she can swipe the images right for positive and left for negative judgment. Tapping an image shows a larger view of the image and metadata, which allows the user to inspect the image in detail and swipe left or right to give judgment.

Once an image has been swiped off the screen, the interactive classifier is trained and the image replaced by the highest-ranked image (or, if the interactive classifier is missing either a positive or a negative example, a random image is used). The user can repeat this process as desired, until she finds one or

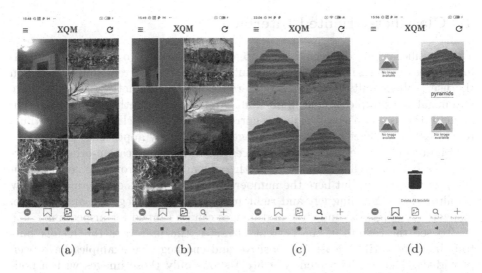

(a)   (b)   (c)   (d)

Fig. 3. Classifier-oriented interface: (a) labeling a positive example; (b) labeling a negative example; (c) classifier result; and (d) saving the classifier.

more of the target images. Once she is confident in the current results, but the screen does not contain a target image, she can press the *fast forward* button to load the screen with the six highest rated images by the classifier. This feature can be used to rapidly seek target images that are distinguished from similar images only by details not captured by the semantic labels. If the user feels that the classifier is only partially satisfactory and wants to add different kinds of positive (or negative) examples, she can press a *random* button to get six random images from the collection. Once these random images are swiped, they are again replaced by the images ranked by the classifier.

Due to its focus on retrieval of target images, the search-oriented interface never shows the same image twice to the user in the home screen, but it does allow the user to revisit previously seen images. She can also revisit the positive and negative examples by tapping on the corresponding buttons at the bottom of the home screen, and from those screens remove images from the positive or negative lists, which impacts the classifier in the next interaction round.

We evaluated the search-oriented interface variant with novice users, who were asked to find instances of specific classes of images. The results indicate that the search-oriented interface succeeds in its goal of implementing interactive learning on a mobile device. Despite some variance in approach and performance, the users were overwhelmingly able to find relevant example images [1].

Overall, the emphasis of the interface design in the search-oriented interface is to facilitate finding *specific* target images as efficiently as possible. While this is appropriate for retrieval-oriented interactions, novice users noted that they felt unsure of what the system was actually doing under the hood. And since the interface hides previously seen images, they had no means to inspect the current output of the interactive classifier. This inspired the classifier-oriented interface.

4   Classifier-Oriented Interface

The classifier-oriented interface aims to add transparency to the classifier building process, in turn improving overall interface clarity and reducing pressure on the user. This results in two main differences in the interaction. First, positive and negative examples are not immediately replaced, but rather labelled as such. Second, the user can view the entire current output of the classifier at any time, regardless of whether the resulting images have already appeared on screen.

Figure 3 illustrates the working process with the classification-oriented interface. As before, each session starts with random images from the collection in the *pictures* screen, but here the number of random images can be increased by scrolling down. Swiping left and right judges images as negative and positive, respectively (Fig. 3(a) and (b)), and images can be tapped for inspection.

To see the results of the current classifier, the user taps the *results* button (inactive until at least one positive and one negative examples have been provided). The results screen (Fig. 3(c)) shows only those images with a non-negative classifier score; if many images are returned, scrolling down loads more examples. The user can then refine the classifier by labeling the images in the results screen, either as positives to re-inforce the model, or negatives to refine the model. As before, the images are labeled as examples, rather than replaced, and to refresh the output of the classifier, the user taps the results button again.

The user can also return to the *pictures* screen, which is then refreshed with a new set of random images that can further supply the classifier with positive examples. In this manner, the user can alternate between finding new examples in the pictures screen, and refining the classifier in the results screen. The focus is thus on building the interactive classifier, which can be stored for future use (Fig. 3(d)) by saving the lists of positive and negative examples under a custom name. The stored classifiers thus provide re-entry points to the dataset.

We have conducted a preliminary evaluation of the two interface variants with novice users, where they were asked to find instances of general classes of images. The results indicate that (a) there were no noticeable differences in the ability to complete the assigned tasks, but (b) that novice users preferred the classification-oriented approach. In particular, users rated the classification-oriented interface higher on learnability and satisfaction.

5   Conclusion

XQM is an early mobile phone implementations of interactive learning over multimedia data. The demonstration app features two interaction modes, each with a distinct niche: the search-oriented mode suitable for looking for specific items, and the classifier-oriented mode that leans more towards explainability. Both modes produce relevant results and assist users in the intelligent exploration of their mobile multimedia collections.

Acknowledgments. This work was supported by a PhD grant from the IT University of Copenhagen, and by the European Regional Development Fund project Robotics for Industry 4.0, CZ.02.1.01/0.0/0.0/15 003/0000470.

References

1. Bagi, A.M., Schild, K.I., Khan, O.S., Zahálka, J., Jónsson, B.Þ.: XQM: interactive learning on mobile phones. In: Proceedings of International Conference on Multi-Media Modeling (MMM). Springer, Prague, Czech Republic, pp. 281–293 (2021)
2. Barthel, K.U., Hezel, N., Schall, K., Jung, K.: Real-time visual navigation in huge image sets using similarity graphs. In: Proceedings of the ACM Multimedia. Nice, France (2019)
3. Bonis, M.D., Amato, G., Falchi, F., Gennaro, C., Manghi, P.: Deep learning techniques for visual food recognition on a mobile app. In: Choros, K., Kopel, M., Kukla, E., Sieminski, A. (eds.) Proceedings of the International Conference on Multimedia and Network Information Systems (MISSI). Wrocław, Poland, pp. 303–312 (2018)
4. Chang, C., Lin, C.: LIBSVM: a library for support vector machines. ACM Trans. Intell. Syst. Technol. **2**, 1–27 (2011)
5. Choe, D., Choi, E., Kim, D.K.: The real-time mobile application for classifying of endangered parrot species using the CNN models based on transfer learning. Mobile Inf. Syst. 1–13 (2020)
6. Cortes, C., Vapnik, V.: Support-vector networks. Mach. Learn. **20**(3), 273–297 (1995)
7. Khan, O.S., et al.: Interactive learning for multimedia at large. In: Jose, J., et al. (eds.) Advances in Information Retrieval. ECIR 2020. LNCS, vol. 12035. Springer, Cham (2020). https://doi.org/10.1007/978-3-030-45439-5_33
8. Mettes, P., Koelma, D.C., Snoek, C.G.: The ImageNet shuffle: reorganized pre-training for video event detection. In: Proceedings of ACM International Conference on Multimedia Retrieval, pp. 175–182 (2016)
9. Pingen, G.L.J., de Boer, M.H.T., Aly, R.B.N.: Rocchio-based relevance feedback in video event retrieval. In: Proceedings of MultiMedia Modeling (MMM), pp. 318–330 (2017)
10. Samangouei, P., Chellappa, R.: Convolutional neural networks for attribute-based active authentication on mobile devices. In: IEEE International Conference on Biometrics Theory, Applications and Systems (BTAS), pp. 1–8 (2016)
11. Strezoski, G., Groenen, I., Besenbruch, J., Worring, M.: Artsight: an artistic data exploration engine. In: Proceedings of ACM Multimedia. Seoul, South Korea (2018)
12. Tran, V., Pham, V., Nguyen, H.: Design a learning model of mobile vision to detect diabetic retinopathy based on the improvement of mobilenetv2. Int. J. Digital Enterprise Technol. (IJDET) (2021)
13. Tronci, R., Murgia, G., Pili, M., Piras, L., Giacinto, G.: Imagehunter: a novel tool for relevance feedback in content based image retrieval. In: Proceedings of Workshop on New Challenges in Distributed Information Filtering and Retrieval, pp. 53–70 (2013)
14. Worring, M., Koelma, D., Zahálka, J.: Multimedia pivot tables for multimedia analytics on image collections. IEEE Trans. Multimed. **18**(11), 2217–2227 (2016)
15. Xie, S., Girshick, R., Dollar, P., Tu, Z., He, K.: Aggregated residual transformations for deep neural networks. In: Proceedings of CVPR (2017)

464   K. I. Schild et al.

16. Zahálka, J., Worring, M.: Towards interactive, intelligent, and integrated multimedia analytics. In: Proceedings of IEEE VAST, pp. 3–12 (2014)
17. Zahálka, J., Worring, M., Van Wijk, J.J.: II-20: intelligent and pragmatic analytic categorization of image collections. IEEE Trans. Visual. Comput. Graph. **27**(2), 422–431 (2021)
18. Zhou, X., Huang, T.: Relevance feedback in image retrieval: a comprehensive review. Multimed. Syst. **8**, 536–544 (2003)

MoViDNN: A Mobile Platform for Evaluating Video Quality Enhancement with Deep Neural Networks

Ekrem Çetinkaya$^{(\boxtimes)}$ [iD], Minh Nguyen [iD], and Christian Timmerer [iD]

Christian Doppler Laboratory ATHENA, Institute of Information Technology,
Alpen-Adria-Universität Klagenfurt, Klagenfurt, Austria
{ekrem.cetinkaya,minh.nguyen,christian.timmerer}@aau.at

Abstract. This is to inform you that corresponding author has been identified as per the information available in the Copyright form.Deep neural network (DNN) based approaches have been intensively studied to improve video quality thanks to their fast advancement in recent years. These approaches are designed mainly for desktop devices due to their high computational cost. However, with the increasing performance of mobile devices in recent years, it became possible to execute DNN based approaches in mobile devices. Despite having the required computational power, utilizing DNNs to improve the video quality for mobile devices is still an active research area. In this paper, we propose an open-source mobile platform, namely **MoViDNN**, to evaluate DNN based video quality enhancement methods, such as super-resolution, denoising, and deblocking. Our proposed platform can be used to evaluate the DNN based approaches both objectively and subjectively. For objective evaluation, we report common metrics such as execution time, PSNR, and SSIM. For subjective evaluation, Mean Score Opinion (MOS) is reported. The proposed platform is available publicly at https://github.com/cd-athena/MoViDNN.

Keywords: Super resolution · Deblocking · Deep neural networks · Mobile devices

1 Introduction

The computational power of mobile devices has increased significantly in recent years. With the increasing RAM capacity, CPU power, and, more importantly, the introduction of powerful GPUs, mobile devices have become powerful enough to execute complex tasks, which can only be done with stationary computers until recently. This steep improvement in mobile devices has also increased the number of studies that focus on utilizing deep neural networks in mobile devices [4,5,8,9,11].

Video content has become predominant in mobile data traffic. It is estimated to occupy 77% by 2026 [2]. Moreover, mobile devices are being mainly used

© Springer Nature Switzerland AG 2022
B. Þór Jónsson et al. (Eds.): MMM 2022, LNCS 13142, pp. 465–472, 2022.
https://doi.org/10.1007/978-3-030-98355-0_40

for watching online video content. For example, more than 70% of watch time on YouTube are from mobile devices [12]. However, video streaming through mobile broadband suffered unstable and low quality due to severe throughput fluctuations [10].

With the increasing number of studies for improving video quality in mobile devices using DNNs, tools to evaluate proposed methods have become an important issue. In this paper, we propose **MoViDNN**, A **Mo**bile Platform for Evaluating **Vi**deo Quality Enhancement with **D**eep **N**eural **N**etworks. The contribution of this paper is two-fold:

(i) **DNN Based Video Quality Enhancement Evaluation Platform for Mobile Devices:** We provide a platform to apply different machine learning-based approaches to improve video quality and examine their performance in mobile devices with some key objective metrics, including Peak Signal-to-Noise Ratio (PSNR), Structural Similarity Index Measure (SSIM), and execution time. To achieve general results, we apply those approaches for videos belonging to various categories such as animation, sport, movie, *etc.*.

(ii) **Subjective Test Platform:** We design a subjective test environment to subjectively evaluate how much improvement in the video quality is perceived by the viewer. The DNN-applied and original videos in the **DNN test** are shown one-by-one randomly on the screen. The viewer is supposed to assess the quality of the videos on a scale of 1 (bad) to 5 (excellent).

The remainder of this paper is organized as follows. Section 2 provides an overview of related work. Section 3 describes the overall structure and capabilities of our proposed app, followed by implementation details in Sect. 4. Finally, conclusions and future work are given in Sect. 5.

2   Related Work

Numerous DNN based enhancement techniques are proposed for images and videos for super-resolution, denoising, and deblocking tasks.

Shi *et al.* [13] proposes ESPCN, which utilizes a sub-pixel convolution layer to provide a real-time image and video super-resolution method. In ESPCN, all intermediate feature layers are extracted in the low-resolution (LR) space. In the last layer, final LR features are upscaled with the sub-pixel convolution layer in which an array of upscaling filters are learned.

Liu *et al.* [8] proposed EVSRNet for the Mobile AI 2021 challenge [4]. The proposed network consists of residual blocks [3] and a sub-pixel convolution layer which is used at the end to upscale the input. Since the execution time of the network was essential for the challenge, they used neural architecture search (NAS) to determine the optimal hyperparameters for the network.

Zhang *et al.* [16] propose DnCNN, which utilizes residual connections and a CNN for image denoising. DnCNN was the first CNN-based denoising approach that can outperform traditional methods. A single model can be used for different applications such as JPEG deblocking and with varying degradation factors.

Evaluation of DNN performance for mobile devices has gotten attention in recent years thanks to the steep improvement in mobile device capabilities [5].

AI Benchmark Mobile [5][1] is a platform that is proposed to evaluate the performance of mobile devices for executing DNNs. It provides various computer vision tests, including object recognition, image deblurring, and image super-resolution. AI benchmark focuses on the performance of mobile devices for the execution of DNNs instead of evaluating the performance of proposed DNN methods. Therefore, it is not a suitable platform for assessing DNN based video enhancement methods for mobile applications. Moreover, subjective testing is not possible to do with this platform.

Liu *et al.* [9] investigated an mobile application called ZoomSR for evaluating deep learning-based, on-device SR networks. ZoomSR comprises of two tasks for the participants: *(i)* image task, and *(ii)* reading task. In the former task, the tested images are examined in terms of their quality. In the latter task, the tested images are assessed how hard their text is to be read. Both tasks use a 7-point Likert scale from 1 to 7. Different from this work, our app focuses on evaluating the machine learning-based video enhancement networks in improving video quality and the assessment scale if from 1 to 5, which is commonly used in video quality assessment [6, 14, 15].

3   MoViDNN: A Mobile Platform for Evaluating Video Quality Enhancement with Deep Neural Networks

The proposed platform is implemented as an Android application and is described in this section.

3.1   Application Structure

Figure 1 shows the MoViDNN architecture comprising two main components: (a) *DNN Test*, and (b) *Subjective Test*. The *DNN Test* component is responsible for applying DNNs for the input videos from *Original Videos* and save the resulting videos into *DNN-applied Videos*. Moreover, a CSV (comma-separated values) file of corresponding objective metrics (*i.e.*, execution time, PSNR, and SSIM) is saved. The *Subjective Test* component provides an environment to evaluate the quality of videos subjectively by asking the viewers to rate their experience of watching those videos to get the Mean Opinion Score (MOS) and saving MOS in *Results*.

3.2   DNN Test

The DNN test of the proposed platform is used to evaluate DNN based video enhancement approaches (*i.e.*, super-resolution, denoising, and deblocking) for mobile devices.

---

[1] https://ai-benchmark.com/download.html.

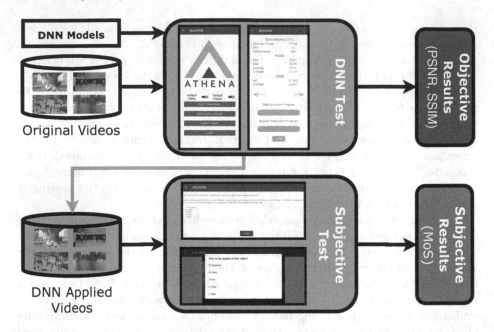

Fig. 1. MoViDNN architecture.

Due to the limited computing power of mobile devices, it is essential to apply quantization for the DNN models before using them, as the DNNs are computationally expensive approaches. By applying quantization, it is possible to reduce both the DNN model size and the running time, thus, making them suitable for mobile platforms.

Since 10 s of video is suitable for subjective testing [14], we limit the length of videos to 10 s to reduce the processing on the mobile device. Frames from the input video are extracted in the display order and stored in the local storage temporarily. Afterward, each frame is passed to the DNN in the same order, and the output frame is saved temporarily again. Finally, the resulting frames are concatenated together and converted to a video for the subjective test.

In the final screen of the DNN test, the objective metrics for the given video are displayed. We report PSNR *(minimum, maximum, average* and *y-PSNR)*, SSIM *(all* and *y-SSIM)*, and DNN execution time *(time per frame in milliseconds, frames per second (FPS),* and *total frame count)*.

3.3 Subjective Test

The proposed application provides a platform for a subjective test to examine deep learning-based SR and deblocking networks. The subject watches multiple videos, including original and DNN-applied ones generated from the DNN test session. The videos are played in a 1920 × 1080 pixel (Full HD) area. Our application randomly selects either DNN-applied videos or original ones. When each video is played completely, the subject is asked to rate the experience of watching that video using one of the five levels of the following scale: (1) Bad, (2) Poor, (3) Fair, (4) Good, (5) Excellent. The scores of the tested videos in every single subjective test are stored in a CSV file.

4   Implementation Details

The proposed platform is implemented as a standalone Android application. Tensorflow-lite [1] is used as the DNN framework in the application.

We provide a Github repository[2] that can be used to convert existing DNN models to mobile compatible versions using Tensorflow [1] as the backend. Once a network is quantized and converted to a *tensorflow-lite* version, it can be evaluated in the platform.

The proposed application comes with three DNN models, namely, ESPCN [13], EVSRNet [8], and DnCNN [16]. Multiple videos in [7] with different content genres (*e.g.*, movie, sports, natural scene, architecture) are included as well. MoViDNN will automatically update the list of available networks and videos once additions are made.

5   Conclusions and Future Work

In this paper, we introduced **MoViDNN** to evaluate DNN-based video quality enhancement methods in mobile devices. **MoViDNN** can be used for both objective and subjective evaluation. For objective evaluation, PSNR, SSIM, and execution time are calculated and reported. For subjective evaluation, MOS is calculated for each test video. We include several state-of-the-art DNNs in the context of super-resolution and deblocking in the demonstration. Moreover, we provide a Github repository that can be used to convert and evaluate additional DNNs with **MoViDNN**. Finally, a real-world demonstration of the **MoViDNN** can be seen in the provided video[3].

As future work, we plan to improve the subjective test part of **MoViDNN** by including a crowdsourcing option. Moreover, extending the platform to support additional DNN based video quality enhancement methods such as video frame interpolation can also be done.

Acknowledgment. The financial support of the Austrian Federal Ministry for Digital and Economic Affairs, the National Foundation for Research, Technology and Development, and the Christian Doppler Research Association, is gratefully acknowledged. Christian Doppler Laboratory ATHENA: https://athena.itec.aau.at/.

---

[2] https://github.com/cd-athena/MoViDNN/tree/main/TFLite_Quantization.
[3] https://www.youtube.com/watch?v=MzeEsNRlVv0.

A   Running the Application

After installing the application, make sure you give the permission of allowing management of all files.

A.1   DNN Test

Steps for evaluating a new DNN structure are as following:

1. Use the Github repository to quantize and convert the DNN model into a *tensorflow-lite* model.
2. Place the quantized network into the allocated folder in the mobile device storage.
3. Place the desired input video to the allocated folder in the mobile device storage. This step is optional as we provide several test sequences in the application by default.
4. Click on **DNN TEST** button in the home screen (see Fig. 2a).
5. Pick the DNN model, the accelerator (CPU, GPU, NNAPI), and the videos in the DNN configuration page of the application and start the evaluation process as illustrated in Fig. 2b.
6. Wait for the process to be completed, which will take some time (Fig. 2c).
7. Once the DNN test is completed as in Fig. 2d, a subjective test can be run for the new DNN structure.

A.2   Subjective Test

Steps for running a subjective test are as following:

1. Click on **SUBJECTIVE TEST** button in the home screen (see Fig. 2a).
2. Pick the DNN models and the videos in the Subjective configuration page of the application as illustrated in Fig. 3a. Click **NEXT** button.
3. Read carefully the instruction of subjective test about how to rate the experience of watching the video. Click **START** button (see Fig. 3b).
4. To play a new video, click **CONTINUE** button and watch the whole video. Rate the quality of the video when a pop-up is shown. Here, 5 means excellent, and 1 means bad. The pop-up screen is shown in Fig. 3c.
5. Repeat the previous step for other videos until the Subjective test is finished.
6. Click **HOME** button to return to the home screen of the app or **AGAIN** button for another participant doing the subjective test (see Fig. 3d).

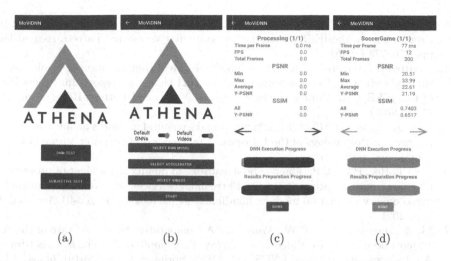

Fig. 2. DNN test UI of MOVIDNN. *(a)* Home screen, *(b)* Network, accelerator and video selection, *(c)* Processing, *(d)* Complete process.

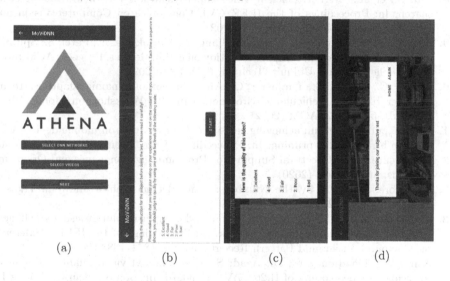

Fig. 3. Subjective test UI of MOVIDNN. *(a)* Network and video selection, *(b)* Subjective Instruction, *(c)* Video assessment, *(d)* End of a test.

References

1. Abad, M., Agarwal, A., Paul Barham, E.B., Chen, Z., Citro, C., et al.: TensorFlow: large-scale machine learning on heterogeneous systems (2015). www.tensorflow. org/

2. Ericsson: mobile data traffic outlook. www.ericsson.com/en/mobility-report/data forecasts/mobile-traffic-forecast Accessed 22 Sept 2021

3. He, K., Zhang, X., Ren, S., Sun, J.: Deep residual learning for image recognition. In: Proceedings of the IEEE conference on computer vision and pattern recognition, pp. 770–778 (2016)
4. Ignatov, A., Romero, A., Kim, H., Timofte, R.: Real-time video super-resolution on smartphones with deep learning, mobile ai 2021 challenge: report. In: Proceedings of the IEEE/CVF Conference on Computer Vision and Pattern Recognition, pp. 2535–2544 (2021)
5. Ignatov, A., et al.: Ai benchmark: running deep neural networks on android smartphones. In: Proceedings of the European Conference on Computer Vision (ECCV) Workshops, p. 0 (2018)
6. ITU-T: Rec. P.1203. Parametric bitstream-based quality assessment of progressive download and adaptive audiovisual streaming services over reliable transport - video quality estimation module. handle.itu.int/11.1002/ps/P1203-01 Accessed 26 Aug 2021
7. Li, Z., Duanmu, Z., Liu, W., Wang, Z.: A Comparative Study of State-of-the-Art Video Encoders on 4K Videos. In: Karray, F., Campilho, A., Yu, A. (eds.) Image Analysis and Recognition. LNCS, vol. 11662. Springer, Cham (2019). https://doi.org/10.1007/978-3-030-27202-9_14
8. Liu, S., et al.: Evsrnet: efficient video super-resolution with neural architecture search. In: Proceedings of the IEEE/CVF Conference on Computer Vision and Pattern Recognition, pp. 2480–2485 (2021)
9. Liu, X., Li, Y., Fromm, J., Wang, Y., Jiang, Z., Mariakakis, A., Patel, S.: SplitSR: an end-to-end approach to super-resolution on mobile devices. Proceed. ACM Interact. Mobile Wearable Ubiquit. Technol. 5(1), 1–20 (2021)
10. Müller, C., Lederer, S., Timmerer, C.: An evaluation of dynamic adaptive streaming over HTTP in vehicular environments. In: 4th Workshop on Mobile Video (MoVid), pp. 37–42. ACM (2012)
11. Niu, W., et al.: Patdnn: achieving real-time dnn execution on mobile devices with pattern-based weight pruning. In: Proceedings of the Twenty-Fifth International Conference on Architectural Support for Programming Languages and Operating Systems, pp. 907–922 (2020)
12. Omnicore: YouTube by the Numbers: Stats, Demographics and Fun Facts. . Accessed 6 Sep 2021
13. Shi, W., et al.: Real-time single image and video super-resolution using an efficient sub-pixel convolutional neural network. In: Proceedings of the IEEE Conference on Computer Vision and Pattern Recognition, pp. 1874–1883 (2016)
14. Song, W., Tjondronegoro, D., Azad, S.: User-centered video quality assessment for scalable video coding of H.264/AVC standard. In: Boll S., Tian Q., Zhang L., Zhang Z., Chen Y.P.P. (eds.) Advances in Multimedia Modeling. LNCS, vol. 5916. Springer, Heidelberg (2010). https://doi.org/10.1007/978-3-642-11301-7_9
15. Tran, H.T., Nguyen, D., Thang, T.C.: An open software for bitstream-based quality prediction in adaptive video streaming. In: Proceedings of the 11th ACM Multimedia Systems Conference, pp. 225–230 (2020)
16. Zhang, K., Zuo, W., Chen, Y., Meng, D., Zhang, L.: Beyond a gaussian denoiser: residual learning of deep cnn for image denoising. IEEE Trans. Image Process. 26(7), 3142–3155 (2017)

DataCAP: A Satellite Datacube and Crowdsourced Street-Level Images for the Monitoring of the Common Agricultural Policy

Vasileios Sitokonstantinou[1,2]([✉]) [iD], Alkiviadis Koukos[1], Thanassis Drivas[1], Charalampos Kontoes[1], and Vassilia Karathanassi[2]

[1] Institute for Space Applications and Remote Sensing, National Observatory of Athens, BEYOND Centre of EO Research and Satellite Remote Sensing, I. Metaxa and Vas. Pavlou Street, Penteli, 15236 Athens, Greece
vsito@noa.gr
[2] Laboratory of Remote Sensing, National Technical University of Athens, 9 Heroon Polytechniou Street, Zographos, 15790 Athens, Greece

Abstract. Recently, massive amounts of satellite images are becoming available. The automated and efficient management, knowledge extraction and visualisation of these big earth data can enable the timely and comprehensive decision making in a number of operational scenarios. In this work, we demonstrate DataCAP that combines the Open Data Cube (ODC) technology on Satellite Image Time-series (SITS), with Machine Learning (ML) pipelines and crowdsourced street-level images to assist in the monitoring of the Common Agricultural Policy (CAP). DataCAP offers a suit of processing tools to simply and intuitively search, store and analyse radar and optical satellite images, along with visualisation tools that combine satellite and street-level imagery for the visual verification of algorithmic decisions.

Keywords: Data cube · Sentinel-1 · Sentinel-2 · Geo-tagged street-level pictures · Satellite image time-series

1 Introduction

The Common Agricultural Policy (CAP) is transitioning to a new era, namely the CAP 2020+ reform, in which the current operating model is set to be simplified and improved significantly. This will be achieved by leveraging big satellite data and advanced ICT technologies that will ultimately form the so-called Area Monitoring System (AMS). The AMS is expected to fully automate and optimize the administration and control system of the CAP [3]. Until now, Paying Agencies (PAs), the implementation bodies of the CAP, have to inspect at least

Supported by the ENVISION (No. 869366) and the CALLISTO (No. 101004152) projects, which have been funded by EU Horizon 2020 programs.

5% of farmers' declarations, performing field visits or visual inspections on very high resolution satellite images. However, these methods are non-exhaustive, time-consuming, complex, and reliant on the skills of the inspector [8]. Recently, several solutions have emerged towards the development of a comprehensive AMS, taking advantage of Earth Observation (EO) data and Machine Learning (ML) techniques to systematically monitor the agricultural land over very large areas [8].

The backbone of all these solutions is the Copernicus program, specifically its Sentinel-1 (S1) and Sentinel-2 (S2) satellite missions. The S1 twin satellites are equipped with radar sensors, which capture useful information for the detection of mowing, grazing and harvest events. The S2 twin satellites are equipped with optical sensors, which capture multi-spectral images of the optical and near-infrared parts of the spectrum. The exploitation of S2 data enables crop type mapping, crop growth predictions and a plethora of other crop monitoring applications. The Sentinel data are freely available and characterized by high revisit frequency (6 d for S1 and 5 d for S2) and high spatial resolution (10–60 m), which are key features for an AMS.

In order to extract knowledge from Satellite Image Time-Series (SITS), and thereby make decisions on CAP compliance, ML algorithms are employed. In an AMS, SITS are combined with the parcel geometries (vector data) from the Land Parcel Identification System (LPIS) that has attached, for each parcel, the declared crop type label [8]. Two of the most common ML tasks, found in literature, are crop type classification and grassland mowing detection [2,6,7]. AMS can significantly improve the controls and reduce the administrative burden for PAs, however they are not equipped to manage big satellite data. For this reason, Analysis Ready Data (ARD) and multidimensional datacubes are key building blocks for such systems [5]. EO datacubes organise the data in such a way that anyone can intuitively exploit them. An EO datacube is an array of four dimensions; including longitude, latitude, time, and variable [1].

Having said that, EO-derived information is not panacea. Sentinels' spatial and temporal resolution limitations make it difficult to confidently decide on special scenarios, such as when we have small and narrow parcels, or broad crop type categories, or cloudy scenes. Therefore, EO data and EO-driven information needs to be accompanied by timely in-situ observations [2]. Typical in-situ data collection methods are expensive, time-consuming and therefore cannot provide continuous data streams. However, crowdsourced street-level images or images at the edge constitute an excellent alternative source [2].

In this work, we demonstrate DataCAP, an AMS module that comprises a Sentinel datacube, ML pipelines for crop classification and grassland mowing detection, and street-level images retrieved from the Mapillary API. DataCAP offers easy and efficient searching, storing, pre-processing and analyzing of big EO data, but also visualisation tools that combine satellite and street-level imagery for verifying algorithmic decisions. DataCAP comprises two components (Fig. 1), the data management component (Sect. 2) and the visualisation component (Sect. 3).

2 Data Management Component

DataCAP's Data Management Component (DMC) is an automated module that searches, harvests (Fig. 1 A) and pre-processes Sentinel data (Fig. 1 B), which are then indexed as ARD in its datacube (Fig. 1 C). This way, DataCAP offers easy and fast spatiotemporal data querying on SITS. The code for DataCAP DMC, including instructions on how to set up the datacube that facilitates it, can be found at https://github.com/Agri-Hub/datacap. DataCAP also enables the combination of satellite ARD with other data, including vector data for object-based image analysis, labelled data for supervised learning and crowdsourced street-level imagery for visual verification of ML outputs. The repository additionally includes two demo jupyter notebooks, showcasing the functionalities of DataCAP's DMC in the context of two CAP monitoring scenarios. Nevertheless, it should be noted that DataCAP is generic and can find applications in multiple other domains that leverage big satellite data and crowdsourced street-level images. Some indicative examples are land use/land cover change detection and burnt area mapping.

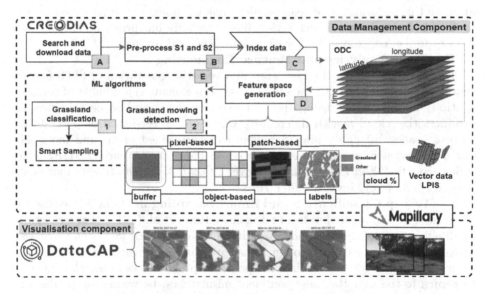

Fig. 1. DataCAP architecture: data management and visualisation components

DataCAP's datacube has been built on the Open Data Cube (ODC) software. ODC has been developed by Geoscience Australia (GA) and is supported by the Committee of Earth Observation Satellites (CEOS) [4]. ODC provides a user-friendly Python API, which loads data into Xarray data structures. This structure simplifies the management of multidimensional arrays, enabling the slicing of data on each of the dimensions of the cube. Currently, our datacube contains time-series of S1 and S2 ARD (2017) over Netherlands (6,375 km^2).

A - Search and Download The S1 and S2 data products are automatically harvested and downloaded from the CreoDIAS API[1]. The user can request Sentinel products within a specified time window over the area of interest, along with other user defined parameters such as the maximum allowed cloud coverage. The metadata of each GET response is stored in a PostgreSQL/PostGIS database in order to have full control and geo-spatial querying capabilities over the products that have been downloaded.

B - Pre-processing The downloaded products are then processed to ARD. The output of this step returns time-series of i) S1 backscatter coefficient and coherence products, ii) S2 atmospherically corrected multi-spectral imagery; along with a scene classification product that includes clouds, dark pixels etc.

C - Index to ODC The ARD are automatically loaded into the datacube, triggering a batch process whenever a new image is downloaded and preprocessed. ODC provides two methods for loading data, indexing or ingesting. The indexing method stores only the metadata of each product in the database, while having the actual data products in a file system. On the other hand, the ingestion method stores the data in both. According to ODC documentation[2] Cloud Optimized Storage formats combined with GDAL or other software improve the performance of reading files, making indexing the preferred choice.

The indexing is done using YAML files, which are blueprints for storing each data type (i.e. coherence, backscatter, multi-spectral images).

D - Data Analytics and Feature Engineering

DataCAP assists on the fast, easy and versatile generation of SITS feature spaces (Fig. 1 D) to feed ML pipelines. Users can execute i) a number of complex spatio-temporal queries using the LPIS (vector data) and scene classification products (i.e. cloud mask); ii) create pixel-based, object-based or patch-based feature spaces; iii) apply inward buffers to avoid mixed pixels and more. For our two downstream tasks, we generated an *object-based (mean)* S1/S2 time-series, from *01/03/2017 - 31/10/2017* over *Utrecht, Netherlands*, with max cloud coverage *>85%* and inward buffer *10 m*.

E - 1 Crop Classification and Smart Sampling In DataCAP we use the crop classification algorithm from Sitokonstantinou et al. (2018) that we slightly modified for mapping grasslands over Utrecht, Netherlands [8]. Then the classification results are passed through the smart sampling algorithm from [6]. The smart sampling algorithm utilizes the posterior probabilities of the classification to return to the user the most confident mismatches, between crop predictions and farmer declarations, for further visual inspection through DataCAP's Visualisation component.

E - 2 Grassland Mowing Event Detection DataCAP leverages the Sen4CAP[3] grassland mowing detection algorithm. The algorithm calculates vegetation index time-series trends and identifies abrupt drops. If the drops are

---

[1]   https://finder.creodias.eu/.
[2]   https://datacube-core.readthedocs.io/en/latest/ops/ingest.html.
[3]   http://esa-sen4cap.org/.

larger than a pre-defined threshold then they are characterized as a mowing event.

3 Visualisation Component

DataCAP's visualisation component is demonstrated at http://62.217.82.91/. This demo GUI is structured based on the two downstream tasks presented earlier and enables the verification of the ML outputs via means of visual inspection. The interface offers two types of visualisations, i) time-series of S1 and S2 images and ii) crowdsourced street-level images.

Using the API of the crowdsourcing platform Mapillary, we automatically download all available street-level images over the area and time window of interest. Then, each downloaded image is matched with the corresponding LPIS object(s) it illustrates. We annotate images that are taken either towards the windshield direction (Case 1) or the window direction (Case 2).

We use Eqs. 1 and 2 to move the initial geo-location coordinates (lat_1, lon_1) to new coordinates (lat_2, lon_2) that are $d = 10\,m$ away in the direction of angle θ. For Case 1, we set $\theta = compass\_angle + 45^\circ$ for the right half of the image and $\theta = compass\_angle - 45^\circ$ for left half. For Case 2 we set $\theta = compass\_angle$.

$$lat_2 = \arcsin\left(\sin lat_1 \cdot \cos \frac{d}{R}\right) + \cos lat_1 \cdot \sin \frac{d}{R} \cdot \cos \theta) \tag{1}$$

$$lon_2 = lon_1 + \arctan\left(\sin \theta \cdot \sin \frac{d}{R} \cdot \cos lat_1, \cos \frac{R}{d} - \sin lat_1 \cdot \sin lat_2\right), \tag{2}$$

where R is the radius of the Earth. If the new coordinates of an image fall within any parcel geometry, then we match the parcel(s) label with that image. The code and the produced annotated street-level images are open.

Visual Inspection of Parcels to Verify ML Results. One can select the flagged parcels according to the smart sampling algorithm, and can verify if the farmer declaration or ML prediction was correct. This is done by inspecting parcel-focused time-series of S1 and S2 images, with an adjustable buffer around the parcel. The time-series reveal the crop growth for each parcel, thus allowing to distinguish between different crop types. In the same manner, visual inspection of the time-series of grassland parcels can reveal sudden changes in the vegetation cover, thus indicating mowing events. Finally, the street-level images offer a very high resolution complementary information to finalise the decision.

4 Conclusion

In this demo paper, we presented DataCAP, a data handling and visualisation module for the monitoring of the CAP. DataCAP consists of i) a back-end component that helps collect and prepare satellite ARD to feed pertinent ML pipelines, and ii) a front-end component that utilizes the satellite ARD and street-level images to help verify the ML outputs. The demonstrated solution is scalable, extendable and reproducible. DataCAP's code and produced annotated datasets are open, encouraging the data science community to exploit them in similar or other pertinent domains and applications.

References

1. Appel, M., Pebesma, E.: On-demand processing of data cubes from satellite image collections with the gdalcubes library. Data **4**(3) (2019). www.mdpi.com/2306-5729/4/3/92 https://doi.org/10.3390/data4030092
2. D'Andrimont, R., Lemoine, G., Van der Velde, M.: Targeted grassland monitoring at parcel level using sentinels, street-level images and field observations. Remote Sens. **10**(8) (2018). /www.mdpi.com/2072-4292/10/8/1300 https://doi.org/10.3390/rs10081300.
3. Devos, W., Lemoine, G., Milenov, P., Fasbender, D.: Technical guidance on the decision to go for substitution of otsc by monitoring (2018)
4. Killough, B.: Overview of the open data cube initiative. In: IGARSS 2018–2018 IEEE International Geoscience and Remote Sensing Symposium, pp. 8629–8632 (2018). https://doi.org/10.1109/IGARSS.2018.8517694
5. Picoli, M.C., et al.: Cbers data cube: a powerful technology for mapping and monitoring brazilian biomes. ISPRS Ann. Photogramm. Remote Sens. Spatial Inf. Sci. **3**, 533–539 (2020)
6. Rousi, M., et al.: Semantically enriched crop type classification and linked earth observation data to support the common agricultural policy monitoring. IEEE J. Selected Topics Appl. Earth Observ. Remote Sens. **14**, 529–552 (2020)
7. Sitokonstantinou, V., et al.: A sentinel based agriculture monitoring scheme for the control of the cap and food security. In: Eighth International Conference on Remote Sensing and Geoinformation of the Environment (RSCy2020). International Society for Optics and Photonics, vol. 11524, p. 1152407 (2020)
8. Sitokonstantinou, V., et al.: Scalable parcel-based crop identification scheme using sentinel-2 data time-series for the monitoring of the common agricultural policy. Remote Sens. **10**(6), 911 (2018)

A Virtual Reality Reminiscence Interface for Personal Lifelogs

Ly-Duyen Tran[1]([⊠]), Diarmuid Kennedy[1], Liting Zhou[1], Binh Nguyen[2,3], and Cathal Gurrin[1]

[1] Dublin City University, Dublin, Ireland
ly.tran2@mail.dcu.ie
[2] AISIA Research Lab, Ho Chi Minh City, Vietnam
[3] Vietnam National University, Ho Chi Minh University of Science, Ho Chi Minh City, Vietnam

Abstract. Letters, diaries, postcards, photo albums, home videos, and lifelogs! These are artefacts of our personal history, they represent how we cherish and preserve memories, re-engage with our past and share our experiences with others. In this demonstration paper, we explore an Virtual Reality (VR) approach to help people reminisce about the past through lifelogs. Our user study found that most participants enjoyed the experience, although for some, the VR environment was overwhelming.

Keywords: Lifelogging · Virtual Reality · Multimedia

1 Introduction

Sharing life experiences allows individuals to form connections both across memories and with other people [7]; such memory connections support the discovery of meaning from the past that may have gone unrecognised; and shared memories could help individuals to feel alive, loved, and cared for. An example of traditional reminiscing activities could be storytelling, flipping through photo albums, or sharing recorded videos with contacts on social media. While technologies such as Google Photos can present collages of captured photos in various ways, what they do not capture are memories that have not been expressly captured, whose significance only becomes evident with the passage of time. For example, the first moment that we meet our significant other is unlikely to be on a traditional photo album. Lifelogging offers us the ability to look back to our past experiences in a more thorough and more authentic way.

Due to the growing popularity of wearable technologies and improved storage capabilities, lifelogging has become more accessible to many. According to the 5R's defined by Sellen and Whittaker [9], lifelogs are valuable for human memory-related processes defined by their 5R's: recollecting, reminiscing, retrieving, reflecting and remembering intentions. Although lifelogging has attracted many works from the research community in recent years, the majority of them

© Springer Nature Switzerland AG 2022
B. Þór Jónsson et al. (Eds.): MMM 2022, LNCS 13142, pp. 479–484, 2022.
https://doi.org/10.1007/978-3-030-98355-0_42

focus on retrieval; few of them address what happens *after* retrieving the needed information. In this demonstration, we focus on the challenge of *reminiscing* using lifelog data.

With Virtual Reality (VR) Head Mounted Displays (HMDs) becoming more available, this medium offers some advantages compared to other media due to its ability to facilitate an immersive experience. Thus, research has explored on how VR could aid reminiscence [4,12]. In this demonstration paper, we explore an VR approach to help people relive past events in an immersive way using a conventional lifelog collection captured by wearable cameras. Specifically, we describe how the prototype is designed in Sect. 3 and the details of our user study in Sect. 4.

2   Related Works

In 1945, Vannevar Bush described a blueprint of a personal information system called *Memex* [2]. This system, *Memex*, was described as an in-depth extension of an individual's memory. Bush's vision has inspired MyLifeBits [6], a Microsoft Research project started by Gordon Bell in 2001, which has helped lifelogging attract more attention from the research community. Lifelogs contain large amounts of data gathered from different streams of information such as photos taken from wearable cameras, geo-location, biometrics data, food diaries, or social media activities. While showing great potential in various domains [1,5,10], lifelogging poses many practical challenges, such as effectively searching through large archives of lifelog data. Virtual Reality has been used in the task of lifelog retrieval [3,11] and has been shown to be a viable method of navigating through multimedia archives. However, as the objectives of such systems are to retrieve lifelog photos in a fast and accurate manner, there is little attention to reminiscence factors such as optimising the sharing of data with others, surprising, or provoking emotions in users.

3   System Prototype Design

The idea of this prototype was inspired from various science fiction works, for example, *Doctor Who*'s Time Vortex, which describes a medium which the Doctor used to travel through time and space. The user explores lifelog photos in a VR environment designed to be a time vortex. Revisiting lifelog photos in this case is analogous to traveling back in time. The prototype system is built using lifelogs captured by wearable cameras. All lifelog photos in the VR space are represented as a rectangular floating object, as seen in Fig. 1, which has been arranged in 12 columns forming a 'vortex'. The user navigates through different years following a looping path inside. Each photo appears in small 'memory' fragments which are gradually united into a whole photo. As the users move forward in the vortex, more 'memories'/photos are uncovered.

The user enters the visualisation at the latest year in the lifelog (in our case 2020). In the vortex, the user can choose to move forward or backward. As they

Fig. 1. A shot of lifelog images in the VR Interface prototype.

move forward, they go back through time, year by year, seeing images and videos (called memories) from that year temporally organised and selected for relevance (some assumed information need) or memorability. The year they are currently viewing is displayed in the middle of the vortex in front of the user. When they want to watch the montage of the current memory, the vortex will dissolve and disappear, leaving a large screen in space playing the required video (in this case, a stop-motion video of wearable camera images). After the video stops, the user is transported back to the vortex for further exploration.

4   User Study

In order to judge how attractive the VR lifelog interface was, we devised a small user study. For this study, the memorable events for the vortex were manually chosen by the lifelogger (just one per year for the demo), but these could be automatically chosen by a lifelog management system. The list of events are shown in Table 1.

Table 1. Events chosen in this prototype.

Year	Event description
2012	Being on a plane going on holiday
2013	Christmas shopping with family
2014	Giving lectures in China
2015	Driving up a volcano in Iceland with friends
2016	Having lunch with family
2017	My wedding day
2018	A Queen concert in Dublin
2019	Christmas Day with family
2020	Building the floor of a new house with a friend

4.1   Experimental Procedure

In all, 9 participants agreed to participate in our study. The participants represented a variety of backgrounds including computer science (6), engineer (1), chemistry (1), and web design (1). Out of these, 5 users did not know the lifelogger personally and have little to no prior knowledge of lifelogging.

For the participant to interact with the interface, we used an Oculus Quest 2 HMD. Each user was given an approximate time of 10 min for the experience. After getting used to the control of the system, the participants were asked to explore the VR space freely and find at least one memorable detail from the list above. Upon completion, participants were asked to rate the demonstration based on the short version of the User Experience Questionnaire (UEQ-S) proposed by Schrepp et al. [8]. We also presented open questions for comments and suggestions.

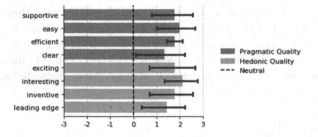

Fig. 2. UEQ-S results with 95% confident interval. Each criteria was rated on a scale of −3 to 3, with 0 being neutral.

4.2   UEQ-S Results

Despite different backgrounds, most participants provided better than neutral ratings on the criteria provided, which are *supportive, easy, efficient, clear, exciting, interesting, inventive,* and *leading edge*. The mean scores are shown in Fig. 2. The *interesting* factor achieved the best score at 2.1. Meanwhile, the *clear* factor was the lowest at 1.3. This is due to one participant being concerned about the lack of textual context of the events causing considerable difficulty in understanding. It is worth noting that in an anticipated use of lifelogs, that it would be the lifelogger themselves who would be exploring the lifelog in the VR system, so such concerns are unlikely to arise in a real-world application.

Based on Schrepp et al.'s process, the scores were transformed and categorised into two categories: pragmatic quality (*supportive, easy, efficient,* and *clear*) and hedonic quality (*exciting, interesting, inventive* and *leading edge*). Figure 3 illustrates the relative quality of the system compared to other products in a benchmark dataset provided by the original authors. The score for Pragmatic Quality falls into the Good category, which is in the range of 25%

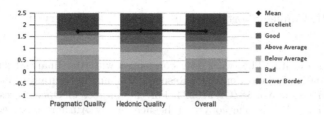

Fig. 3. UEQ-S benchmarks. The line represents the mean results for this prototype.

best results. Hedonic Quality and Overall scores fall into the Excellent category, which is in the range of the 10% best results.

4.3   Feedback

Most of the participants found the vortex visualisation in VR interesting. According to one participant, '*it was like a dream*'. An interesting observation is more than half of the participants thought that the field trip in Iceland in 2015 was the most interesting memory; they were amazed at the scenery. The second popular choice was the lifelogger's wedding day, for which one user expressed his feeling: '*it made me tear up*'.

On the other hand, some criticised the visualisation being overwhelming and causing dizziness. One participant noted the interface '*requires the user to move their head around frequently, hence it is easy to miss an event if they are not aware of it*'. Another commented '*it can be a bit overwhelming to have some many pictures around you it is sometimes tempting to focus more on the pictures in front [instead of where you are standing]*'.

5   Conclusions and Future Work

As lifelogging becomes more accessible to many, it is important to explore different ways a lifelogger could reminisce on past events and share them with others. In this paper, we developed a VR prototype for viewing past events using personal lifelogs, focusing on the reminiscent factor of Sellen and Whittaker's 5R's [9]. The prototype received generally good responses from participants in our user study. However, there are potential improvements in future work. For example, the vortex in this prototype could be redesigned to help with orientation and reduce the number of photos shown at a single time. Incorporating textual descriptions for each event is necessary for the understanding of lifelogs. Other information such as heart rate could also be used to illustrate the importance of an image and potentially help guiding the user's focus. Another way we can utilise this interface is to integrate a lifelog search engine for choosing events.

This work was featured in a short film called Eternal Memory by Diarmuid Kennedy with the involvement of a Ballymun Community Group, the Setanta Strings Ensemble. The film was officially selected for Montreal Independent Film

Festival 2021, Cannes Short Film Festival 2021, and Kerry International Film Festival 2021.

Acknowledgements. This work was conducted with the financial support of the Science Foundation Ireland Centre for Research Training in Digitally-Enhanced Reality (d-real) under Grant No. 18/CRT/6224. For the purpose of Open Access, the author has applied a CC BY public copyright licence to any Author Accepted Manuscript version arising from this submission.

References

1. Aizawa, K., Maruyama, Y., Li, H., Morikawa, C.: Food balance estimation by using personal dietary tendencies in a multimedia food log. IEEE Trans. Multimedia **15**(8), 2176–2185 (2013)
2. Bush, V., et al.: As we may think. Atlantic Mon. **176**(1), 101–108 (1945)
3. Duane, A., Gurrin, C., Huerst, W.: Virtual reality lifelog explorer: lifelog search challenge at ACM ICMR 2018. In: Proceedings of the 2018 ACM Workshop on The Lifelog Search Challenge, pp. 20–23 (2018)
4. D'Cunha, N.M., et al.: A mini-review of virtual reality-based interventions to promote well-being for people living with dementia and mild cognitive impairment. Gerontology **65**(4), 430–440 (2019)
5. Gelonch, O., et al.: Acceptability of a lifelogging wearable camera in older adults with mild cognitive impairment: a mixed-method study. BMC Geriatr. **19**(1), 110 (2019)
6. Gemmell, J., Bell, C., Lueder, R.: Mylifebits: a personal database for everything. Commun. ACM **49**, 89–95 (2006)
7. Haight, B.: Sharing life stories: acts of intimacy. Generations **25**(2), 90–92 (2001)
8. Schrepp, M., Hinderks, A., Thomaschewski, J.: Design and evaluation of a short version of the user experience questionnaire (UEQ-S). Int. J. Interact. Multimedia Artif. Intell. **4**, 103 (2017)
9. Sellen, A.J., Whittaker, S.: Beyond total capture: a constructive critique of lifelogging. Commun. ACM **53**(5), 70–77 (2010)
10. Signal, L., et al.: Kids'Cam: an objective methodology to study the world in which children live. Am. J. Prev. Med. **53**(3), e89–e95 (2017)
11. Spiess, F., et al.: Exploring intuitive lifelog retrieval and interaction modes in virtual reality with VITRIVR-VR. In: Proceedings of the 4th Annual on Lifelog Search Challenge, LSC 2021, pp. 17–22. Association for Computing Machinery, New York (2021)
12. Tsao, Y.C., Shu, C.C., Lan, T.S.: Development of a reminiscence therapy system for the elderly using the integration of virtual reality and augmented reality. Sustainability **11**(17), 4792 (2019)

Video Browser Showdown 2022

Efficient Search and Browsing of Large-Scale Video Collections with Vibro

Nico Hezel[✉], Konstantin Schall, Klaus Jung, and Kai Uwe Barthel

HTW Berlin, University of Applied Sciences - Visual Computing Group,
Wilhelminenhofstraße 75, 12459 Berlin, Germany
nico.hezel@htw-berlin.de
http://visual-computing.com/

Abstract. In this paper, we present the newest version of our interactive video browser tool *Vibro*. For this iteration, we focused on improving the user interface to enable a more accessible temporal search, upgrading the shot-detection algorithm, replacing a keyword-based search with rich text input, and reducing query times by applying a graph-based approximate nearest neighbor search method. With these extensive updates, we feel well-equipped to handle the huge amounts of data coming our way in the next VBS competitions and achieve competitive results in the contest.

Keywords: Content-based video retrieval · Exploration · Visualization · Image browsing · Visual and textual co-embeddings

1 Introduction

The Video Browser Showdown (VBS) [13] represents a competition where participants have to solve a variety of tasks using their interactive video browsing systems. The three main categories are *visual Known-Item Search* (v-KIS), *textual Known-Item Search* (t-KIS) and *Ad-Hoc Video Search* (AVS). For both KIS tasks, the goal is to find one exact segment that matches the given description and for AVS, as many suiting segments as possible have to be submitted. At the next VBS, the V3C1 dataset [4] (containing 7475 video files and 1000 h of video content) is combined with the V3C2 dataset (9760 videos and 1300 h), doubling the amount of video material in comparison to previous years. Even though advances in deep learning for multimedia content analysis have led to better visual feature vectors [5], improved automatic keywording of images [1] and better visual and textual co-embeddings [6,14], browsing and finding specific items in large video collections still remains a very challenging task.

After participating in several VBS competitions, we have identified some key criteria of previous winners. Most successful systems [9] have exploited the chronological order of different scenes in a video, therefore we believe that supporting temporal queries is very important. In addition, systems that allowed

© Springer Nature Switzerland AG 2022
B. Þór Jónsson et al. (Eds.): MMM 2022, LNCS 13142, pp. 487–492, 2022.
https://doi.org/10.1007/978-3-030-98355-0_43

to view many images helped to get a better overview of the results and enabled a more efficient browsing experience [12]. Furthermore we observed that the newest developments for co-embeddings of visual and textual data [14] led to exceptional results for textual query searches. Lastly, as the size of the data has more than doubled, we strongly believe that video browsing tools can benefit from approximate nearest neighbor techniques [2,16], which greatly increase search speed for a small trade-off in accuracy.

With these criteria in mind, we upgraded our previous system in several aspects. First, we cleaned up the user interface (Fig. 1) by removing some rarely used components and optimizing others for temporal search. Second, we introduced an improved shot-detection algorithm. Third, we replaced the previously used keyword propagation mechanism [11] for textual search by introducing a CLIP model [14], which allows rich text input in contrast to the previous keyword based search. Finally, we updated our internal data structure to an image graph optimized for approximate nearest neighbor search and efficient exploration of neighbors nodes.

2 Video Preprocessing

As a preprocessing step, all frames of a video are aggregated into three levels of abstraction. On the first level, only one frame per second is stored, all others are ignored. These frames are then subsequently merged into keyframes by analyzing their visual appearance with a handcrafted low-level feature, based on color and edge histograms, and frequency analysis, with a total of 50 dimensions. For this second step, the first frame of a video is selected as the keyframe. All subsequent frames are compared with their previous frame and the last keyframe. If in either case the similarity falls below a threshold, the current frame becomes a new keyframe. This procedure is repeated until the end of the video. The threshold was set to only filter out near-duplicates. Next, the keyframes are grouped into shots. Here we utilize a combination of the low-level features and high-level CNN features obtained from a ResNet152 [8] with DARAC-Pooling [15]. The same algorithm as in the previous step is used, only with a higher threshold, since the goal is to only merge semantically similar keyframes here. For the V3C1 dataset, consisting of 7475 videos with a total of 1000 h, this preprocessing results in over 3.5 million frames, 1.3 million keyframes and 700k shots. Compared to the baseline shot-segmentation provided in the dataset, which consists of around 1 million shots [4], we save about 30% shots with this procedure.

3 Navigation and Visualization

Figure 1 shows an overview of the current interface. Part A is reserved for query formulation. A detailed explanation of all available options and their underlying methods can be found in Sect. 4. In part B, the top 4000 results of the current query are visualized in a 2D-sorted map by applying an optimized SSM [3]. This process takes a fraction of a second. Search queries can be formulated for two

Fig. 1. Revised user interface for the current version of *Vibro* (Color figure online)

different shots (tab-buttons at the top of part A) and the displayed results change when these shots are switched. Furthermore, these two queries are combined in a temporal search, and its results are presented in part C as a list of five consecutive shot-frames. The video containing the selected frame (green border) is displayed in part D using a video player or a list of all keyframes. Additionally, a new query image can be chosen from anywhere by double-clicking any of the visible frames. In combination with the visually sorted view, this allows a fast navigation to the desired video frame. Even though all searches are performed on keyframe-level, only shot-level images are shown in each part of the UI to reduce the number of images. We also employ a hierarchical image similarity graph [10] for exploration of the entire video collection ("Global Map" button in part C). In practice, the presented tool *Vibro* is capable of locating searched video frames by either finding an exact image by search, browsing and exploration or by defining two vague concepts and combing them with a temporal search.

The designed system performs quite well in the KIS-tasks, but its usage is too slow for AVS-tasks. The current AVS-scoring scheme rewards systems that can send a large variety and number of frames in a short period of time. Therefore, we designed a separate user interface for this part of the competition. After selecting one image from the main UI a pure image-based search can be triggered by the AVS "Start" button at the bottom of part A. The best 20 images are displayed on a separate UI. Now the user marks all positive frames and sends them to the evaluation server. Furthermore the submitted frames are used in a relevance feedback loop. Together with the initial image and other positive frames they form a multi-image query to produce the next 20 results.

4 Search Modalities

Vibro allows queries of three modalities, namely sketch, text and image-by-example. In addition, the search results of these three methods are combined with adjustable weights into a single result list, which is then displayed on the user interface.

Sketches and Images. In sketch-based search, queries can be formulated either by drawing in the blank canvas, or by selecting an example image from any part of the user interface and modifying its appearance using the provided drawing tools. In order to enable this functionality, we extract two different feature vectors from all keyframes. First, the low-level feature vector (already used for video preprocessing) and a second 768-dimensional high-level CNN feature vector obtained from the ResNetx16 used in the visual part of the CLIP model [14]. The first feature is used to obtain the visual appearance (color and shape layouts) and is recomputed if an image was modified, whereas the second describes the semantic content and is only computed once. Both of them are also used in image-by-example queries, which can be triggered by selecting one of the presented shot-frames or by dragging an image from an online source onto the canvas. For a pure sketch query on a blank canvas, only the low-level features are used.

Rich Text. The third possible search input is text. In previous years we employed a keyword propagation mechanism, where a large corpus of annotated images was used to suggest keywords for unknown images by nearest neighbor search [11]. Even though the results for single keyword queries were satisfying, the quality deteriorated as more words were suggested. For example, an image showing a person riding on a horse in the mountains can only be described by the three keywords "person; horse; mountain". With this approach, the information on the interaction between these objects is missing. To overcome this limitation we integrated CLIP [14], a co-embedding model which encodes rich text input and images into a shared vector space. Now, we can not only process keyword based queries but also rich text inputs, which more accurately describe the desired frame.

Fusion of Modalities. Since the low-level feature only consists of 50 dimensions, we can perform a full linear search in under 100 ms on the entire dataset. In this case we obtain a similarity score for each keyframe and remember their value for potential score fusing. However, text and image queries are accelerated by a graph-based approximate nearest neighbor search algorithm (Sect. 5), where each query yields exactly 4000 results ordered by a descending similarity score. Since text and image features share one embedding space, only a single graph is needed. In order to fuse the search results of the low- and high-level visual features we use a weighted average of their scores where the initial weight $\alpha \in [0,1]$ is set to 0.5 and can be changed with a slider. If a text query is used with a sketch or an image query, we perform a separate graph-based search with the text embedding and combine both similarity scores with a second user adjustable weight $\beta \in [0,1]$.

Temporal Queries. For two different timestamps any of the described multi-modal queries can be performed and the similarity scores of the keyframes are obtained for each of them. In order to enable a temporal search we rank consecutive sequences of keyframes from a single video according to the probability that the sequence contains content from the first query-tab followed by content from the second. The similarity score from the first timestamp of each frame is combined with the highest score of the second timestamp for all subsequent frames within a given time range. The final result is then sorted by these sums of similarity scores.

5   Graph-Based Nearest Neighbor Search

The time needed to search an entire image collection depends on the number of images and the complexity of the similarity calculation between the query and a database image. The latter is influenced by the size of the feature vector and the formula for the similarity calculation. Since features cannot be compressed infinitely and the number of images in most datasets keeps increasing, there has been a move towards approximate nearest neighbor searches [2]. Such methods do not take all the data into account; depending on the algorithm, some image features are omitted or heavily quantized. The resulting inaccuracy is traded for a computational speedup by one or two magnitudes.

In the case of VBS, more and more videos have been added to the dataset over the years and teams are using more sophisticated methods to achieve better search results. In the past, we reduced our CNN features without PCA whitening [7] to 64 dimensions and quantized them in bytes. These features performed almost 10% worse than high-dimensional features with PCA whitening in a content-based image retrieval system. The latter, in turn, are not compressible and therefore cannot be used in an interactive system as it takes too long to search millions of images. We have redesigned our internal graph data structure to produce excellent results for approximate nearest neighbor search. Compared to a full search, the results are over 99% identical and can be computed 20 times faster. Our new graph is more efficient than the best state-of-the-art approaches [16] while requiring less memory and can more efficiently provide similar neighbors for interactive exploration. The graph is constructed in less than 2 h using the high-level features of the CLIP model and is faster than a full-scan search for result lists up to 32000 elements.

References

1. Asano, Y.M., Rupprecht, C., Vedaldi, A.: Self-labelling via simultaneous clustering and representation learning. In: ICLR. OpenReview.net (2020)
2. Aumüller, M., Bernhardsson, E., Faithfull, A.: ANN-benchmarks: a benchmarking tool for approximate nearest neighbor algorithms. Inf. Syst. **87**, 101374 (2020)
3. Barthel, K.U., Hezel, N.: Visually Exploring Millions of Images using Image Maps and Graphs, chap. 11, pp. 289–315. Wiley, Hoboken (2019)

4. Berns, F., Rossetto, L., Schoeffmann, K., Beecks, C., Awad, G.: V3C1 dataset: an evaluation of content characteristics. In: ICMR 2019 Proceedings of the 2019 on International Conference on Multimedia Retrieval (2019)
5. Cao, B., Araujo, A., Sim, J.: Unifying deep local and global features for image search. arXiv pp. arXiv-2001 (2020)
6. Chen, Y.-C., et al.: UNITER: UNiversal image-TExt representation learning. In: Vedaldi, A., Bischof, H., Brox, T., Frahm, J.-M. (eds.) ECCV 2020. LNCS, vol. 12375, pp. 104–120. Springer, Cham (2020). https://doi.org/10.1007/978-3-030-58577-8_7
7. Gordo, A., Almazán, J., Revaud, J., Larlus, D.: Deep image retrieval: learning global representations for image search. In: Leibe, B., Matas, J., Sebe, N., Welling, M. (eds.) ECCV 2016. LNCS, vol. 9910, pp. 241–257. Springer, Cham (2016). https://doi.org/10.1007/978-3-319-46466-4_15
8. He, K., Zhang, X., Ren, S., Sun, J.: Deep residual learning for image recognition. In: Proceedings of the IEEE Conference on Computer Vision and Pattern Recognition, pp. 770–778 (2016)
9. Heller, S., et al.: Towards explainable interactive multi-modal video retrieval with Vitrivr. In: Lokoč, J., et al. (eds.) MMM 2021. LNCS, vol. 12573, pp. 435–440. Springer, Cham (2021). https://doi.org/10.1007/978-3-030-67835-7_41
10. Hezel, N., Barthel, K.U.: Dynamic construction and manipulation of hierarchical quartic image graphs. In: Proceedings of the 2018 ACM on International Conference on Multimedia Retrieval, ICMR 2018, pp. 513–516. Association for Computing Machinery, New York (2018)
11. Hezel, N., Schall, K., Jung, K., Barthel, K.U.: Video search with sub-image keyword transfer using existing image archives. In: Lokoč, J., et al. (eds.) MMM 2021. LNCS, vol. 12573, pp. 484–489. Springer, Cham (2021). https://doi.org/10.1007/978-3-030-67835-7_49
12. Kratochvíl, M., Veselý, P., Mejzlík, F., Lokoč, J.: SOM-hunter: video browsing with relevance-to-SOM feedback loop. In: Ro, Y.M., et al. (eds.) MMM 2020. LNCS, vol. 11962, pp. 790–795. Springer, Cham (2020). https://doi.org/10.1007/978-3-030-37734-2_71
13. Lokoč, J., et al.: Is the reign of interactive search eternal? Findings from the video browser showdown 2020. ACM Trans. Multimedia Comput. Commun. Appl. **17**(3), 1–26 (2021)
14. Radford, A., et al.: Learning transferable visual models from natural language supervision. CoRR abs/2103.00020 (2021)
15. Schall, K., Barthel, K.U., Hezel, N., Jung, K.: Deep aggregation of regional convolutional activations for content based image retrieval. In: 2019 IEEE 21st International Workshop on Multimedia Signal Processing (MMSP), pp. 1–6. IEEE (2019)
16. Wang, M., Xu, X., Yue, Q., Wang, Y.: A comprehensive survey and experimental comparison of graph-based approximate nearest neighbor search. Proc. VLDB Endow. **14**(11), 1964–1978 (2021)

Multi-modal Interactive Video Retrieval with Temporal Queries

Silvan Heller[1]($\boxtimes$)(iD), Rahel Arnold[1](iD), Ralph Gasser[1](iD), Viktor Gsteiger[1](iD), Mahnaz Parian-Scherb[1](iD), Luca Rossetto[2](iD), Loris Sauter[1](iD), Florian Spiess[1](iD), and Heiko Schuldt[1](iD)

[1] Department of Mathematics and Computer Science, University of Basel, Basel, Switzerland
{silvan.heller,rahel.arnold,ralph.gasser,viktor.gsteiger, mahnaz.parian-scherb,florian.spiess,heiko.schuldt}@unibas.ch
[2] Department of Informatics, University of Zurich, Zurich, Switzerland
rossetto@ifi.uzh.ch

Abstract. This paper presents the version of vitrivr participating at the Video Browser Showdown (VBS) 2022. vitrivr already supports a wide range of query modalities, such as color and semantic sketches, OCR, ASR and text embedding. In this paper, we briefly introduce the system, then describe our new approach to queries specifying temporal context, ideas for color-based sketches in a competitive retrieval setting and a novel approach to pose-based queries.

Keywords: Video Browser Showdown · Interactive video retrieval · Content-based retrieval

1 Introduction

The Video Browser Showdown (VBS) is an annual evaluation campaign for interactive video retrieval systems [9], with its 11th iteration happening in 2022. At VBS, system operators are tasked with finding relevant items within a large video collection. In the 2022 installment – for the first time – both the first and second shard of the V3C Dataset [13] are being used, resulting in approximately 2'300 h of video. vitrivr is an open-source, multi-modal multimedia retrieval system which has participated in the VBS several times, including last year's installment [5]. A plethora of query modalities are supported by the system [4], notable in a competitive setting are color and semantic sketches, OCR, ASR, and text embedding [14]. The retrieval model is discussed in [7], and details on the storage layer can be found in [3]. Built as a general-purpose tool for multimedia retrieval, vitrivr is also used in other contexts such as lifelog retrieval [6].

In this paper, we present the version of vitrivr we plan to participate with at VBS 2022. Our focus for this participation lies on the improvements we have made to temporal queries, new ideas for making color sketches useful in a competitive setting and a novel approach to pose-based queries.

© Springer Nature Switzerland AG 2022
B. Þór Jónsson et al. (Eds.): MMM 2022, LNCS 13142, pp. 493–498, 2022.
https://doi.org/10.1007/978-3-030-98355-0_44

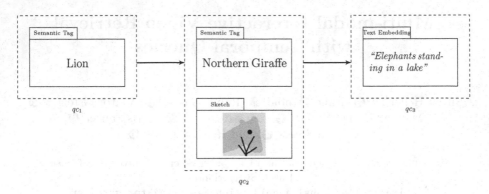

Fig. 1. A multi-modal temporal query consisting of three query containers (dashed, qc_1, qc_2 and qc_3), each with different modalities. This is a formulated query for "Shots of first a lion (semantic tag), followed by a giraffe (semantic tag) whose head is visible while eating a branch (sketch) concluded by a shot of *Elephants standing in a lake* (text embedding)". The temporal order is given through the order of query containers.

The remainder of this paper is structured as follows: Sect. 2 shows our algorithm for temporal queries, Sect. 3 introduces new ideas for color sketches, Sect. 4 discusses our approach to pose-based queries, and Sect. 5 concludes.

2   Temporal Queries

A temporal query as illustrated in Fig. 1 consists of multiple, ordered similarity sub-queries of various and possibly different modalities and time distances between the sub-queries. The results of the sub-queries are then aggregated and scored according to the order of the query containers and the specified time distances. For notation purposes, we define a video V which is segmented into a list of segments $S = \langle s_1, s_2, ...s_m \rangle$. Given a temporal query TQ and its list of query containers $TQ = \langle qc_1, ..., qc_n \rangle$, with each query container being a possibly multi-modal query, each query container is executed separately. The result is then a set RS of scored segments per container, i.e. $RS_i = \langle \langle s_f, s_g, ..., s_l \rangle, qc_i \rangle$, with a segment possibly appearing in multiple elements of the result set if it is a suitable result for multiple containers.

The aggregation process creates sequences of segments where sequences with more and higher scored result segments from multiple query containers are preferred for each object. A temporal sequence TS is defined as an ordered list of segment-container tuples $TS = \langle \langle s_i, qc_a \rangle, \langle s_j, qc_b \rangle, ..., \langle s_z, qc_n \rangle \rangle$. We have experimented with different algorithms, and will describe the current scoring algorithm utilised by vitrivr here:

1. For each tuple $\langle s_i, qc_a \rangle$ within the flattened list of results, temporal sequence candidates are constructed. Segments are appended to a temporal sequence

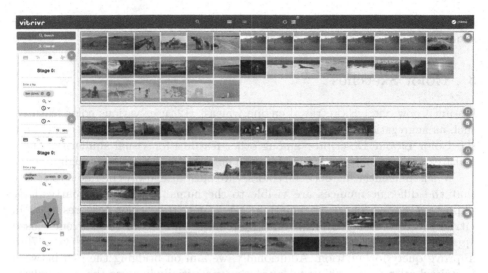

Fig. 2. The improved Temporal Scoring View of vitrivr with a temporal distance query and two toggled results.

if they follow the ordering specified by the user, i.e., for $TS = \langle s_1, qc_i \rangle$, only tuples $\langle s_x, qc_j \rangle$ with $j > i$ are considered.

2. Scores are aggregated within a sequence TS (with the first element $\langle s_i, qc_a \rangle$) with a decay function. For a given time difference t between two elements, all segments except the first $(TS \setminus \langle s_i, qc_a \rangle)$ have their score multiplied with $adj(t) = e^{-|l \cdot (t-m)|}$, with l being the penalty of being not at the user-specified distance (we use $l = 0.1$), and $m \leq 0$ being the time to the next segment as defined by the temporal query. Items that are within the perfect time distance receive no penalty on their score.

3. After normalizing the score with respect to the number of sub-queries (3 in our example), the highest-scoring sequences are selected.

In Fig. 2, we show a screenshot of vitrivr's user interface. The query containers are on the left, with the additional temporal distance between the first and the second query container. Additionally, results are grouped by video and their visibility can be interactively toggled by the user if they do not fulfill the search criteria. The evaluation [11] of the VBS competition in 2020 showed that frequent use of temporal queries increases the performance of retrieval systems. Different systems at VBS employ different scoring and aggregation algorithms. In the VIRET system [8], temporal aggregation is evaluated for each modality separately. VIREO [10] displays two canvases to the user to input two object-sketch queries at the timestamp t and t' with $t < t'$. The similarity is then determined between a video and the two queries. SomHunter [15] uses a fixed number of three adjacent temporal queries. Visione also introduced temporal querying for the 2021 version of their retrieval system [1]. They employ a similar strategy to the VIRET system with the possibility to provide two queries that should occur within a certain threshold of time.

3   Color Sketches

Up until now, vitrivr's retrieval engine Cineast [12] uses various color features, such as aggregation based features (histogram, median, and average color), and the Color Layout Descriptor among other features for visual similarity. These features are grouped into categories with empirically determined weights.

When differentiating between colors, care must also always be taken to ensure that the different nuances are visible to the human eye. This is particularly important during query formulation. We (fine-) tune color features used in vitrivr's retrieval engine based on a systematic analysis of the currently used approaches. We expect color sketches in combination with staged querying [7] to improve query formulation. Additionally, we aim on bridging the gap between perceived color input and actual extraction, potentially limiting the color palette drastically.

4   Pose-Based Queries

As an addition to vitrivr, we include a pose-based query mode to search and find human-specific poses using the detailed location of detected body parts. The new feature module captures joint information, which is provided by the human 2D pose estimation framework OpenPose [2]. This algorithm localizes human body parts such as shoulders, ankles and knees from video frames. We use the 18 key-points model and the joint location coordinates together with the part affinity field information and store it in a 3 channel feature vector, which is used for finding specific poses.

On the user interface side, a new mode for query formulation based on pose is added. This new mode allows the user to describe the pose they are searching for using a canvas with a skeleton consisting of 18 key-points. Individual joints can be moved to specify the approximate pose of a person. To simplify lookup for common poses, a selection of preset configurations is provided.

During retrieval, the coordinates of the query are compared to stored features in the database. To measure the similarity, we use normalized coordinates to cover the instances in different locations of the frame. Normalization is done by determining the center of mass for each identified skeleton and then moving the origin of the coordinate system to that center of mass. In addition to the coordinates, we also consider the distances between joints to minimize the perspective effects (Fig. 3).

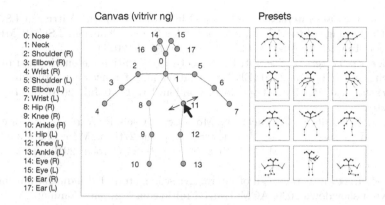

Fig. 3. Sketching mechanism for posed-based queries. Users can either adjust the skeletton's joints individually using their mouse or select a preset pose from a list.

5 Conclusion

In this paper, we presented the version of vitrivr with which we plan to participate at VBS 2022. Both temporal queries and staged querying using color sketches have shown promising results in past iterations of VBS, and pose-based queries as yet another modality could be interesting for challenging Visual KIS tasks or AVS tasks.

Acknowledgements. This work was partly supported by the Swiss National Science Foundation, project "Participatory Knowledge Practices in Analog and Digital Image Archives" (contract no. CRSII5_193788).

References

1. Amato, G., et al.: VISIONE at video browser showdown 2021. In: Lokoč, J., et al. (eds.) MMM 2021. LNCS, vol. 12573, pp. 473–478. Springer, Cham (2021). https://doi.org/10.1007/978-3-030-67835-7_47
2. Cao, Z., Hidalgo, G., Simon, T., Wei, S., Sheikh, Y.: OpenPose: realtime multi-person 2D pose estimation using part affinity fields. IEEE Trans. Pattern Anal. Mach. Intell. **43**(1), 172–186 (2021)
3. Gasser, R., Rossetto, L., Heller, S., Schuldt, H.: Cottontail DB: an open source database system for multimedia retrieval and analysis. In: MM 2020: The 28th ACM International Conference on Multimedia, Virtual Event / Seattle, WA, USA, 12–16 October 2020, pp. 4465–4468. ACM (2020)
4. Gasser, R., Rossetto, L., Schuldt, H.: Multimodal multimedia retrieval with vitrivr. In: Proceedings of the 2019 on International Conference on Multimedia Retrieval, ICMR 2019, Ottawa, ON, Canada, 10–13 June 2019, pp. 391–394. ACM (2019)
5. Heller, S., et al.: Towards explainable interactive multi-modal video retrieval with Vitrivr. In: Lokoč, J., et al. (eds.) MMM 2021. LNCS, vol. 12573, pp. 435–440. Springer, Cham (2021). https://doi.org/10.1007/978-3-030-67835-7_41

6. Heller, S., et al.: Interactive multimodal lifelog retrieval with Vitrivr at LSC 2021. In: Proceedings of the 4th Annual on Lifelog Search Challenge, LSC@ICMR 2021, Taipei, Taiwan, 21 August 2021, pp. 35–39. ACM (2021)

7. Heller, S., Sauter, L., Schuldt, H., Rossetto, L.: Multi-stage queries and temporal scoring in Vitrivr. In: 2020 IEEE International Conference on Multimedia & Expo Workshops, ICME Workshops 2020, London, UK, 6–10 July 2020, pp. 1–5. IEEE (2020)

8. Lokoc, J., Kovalcík, G., Soucek, T., Moravec, J., Cech, P.: A framework for effective known-item search in video. In: Proceedings of the 27th ACM International Conference on Multimedia, MM 2019, Nice, France, 21–25 October 2019, pp. 1777–1785. ACM (2019)

9. Lokoč, J., et al.: Is the reign of interactive search eternal? Findings from the video browser showdown 2020. ACM Trans. Multimedia Comput. Commun. Appl. **17**(3) (2021)

10. Nguyen, P.A., Wu, J., Ngo, C.-W., Francis, D., Huet, B.: VIREO @ video browser showdown 2020. In: Ro, Y.M., et al. (eds.) MMM 2020. LNCS, vol. 11962, pp. 772–777. Springer, Cham (2020). https://doi.org/10.1007/978-3-030-37734-2_68

11. Rossetto, L., et al.: Interactive video retrieval in the age of deep learning - detailed evaluation of VBS 2019. IEEE Trans. Multim. **23**, 243–256 (2021)

12. Rossetto, L., Giangreco, I., Schuldt, H.: Cineast: a multi-feature sketch-based video retrieval engine. In: 2014 IEEE International Symposium on Multimedia, ISM 2014, Taichung, Taiwan, 10–12 December 2014, pp. 18–23. IEEE Computer Society (2014)

13. Rossetto, L., Schuldt, H., Awad, G., Butt, A.A.: V3C – a research video collection. In: Kompatsiaris, I., Huet, B., Mezaris, V., Gurrin, C., Cheng, W.-H., Vrochidis, S. (eds.) MMM 2019. LNCS, vol. 11295, pp. 349–360. Springer, Cham (2019). https://doi.org/10.1007/978-3-030-05710-7_29

14. Spiess, F., et al.: Multi-modal video retrieval in virtual reality with vitrivr-vr. In: Jónsson B., et al. (Eds.): MMM 2022, LNCS 13142, pp. 499–504. Springer, Heidelberg (2022)

15. Veselý, P., Mejzlík, F., Lokoč, J.: SOMHunter V2 at video browser showdown 2021. In: Lokoč, J., et al. (eds.) MMM 2021. LNCS, vol. 12573, pp. 461–466. Springer, Cham (2021). https://doi.org/10.1007/978-3-030-67835-7_45

Multi-modal Video Retrieval in Virtual Reality with vitrivr-VR

Florian Spiess[1]([✉])(iD), Ralph Gasser[1](iD), Silvan Heller[1](iD),
Mahnaz Parian-Scherb[1](iD), Luca Rossetto[2](iD), Loris Sauter[1](iD),
and Heiko Schuldt[1](iD)

[1] Department of Mathematics and Computer Science, University of Basel,
Basel, Switzerland
{florian.spiess,ralph.gasser,silvan.heller,mahnaz.parian-scherb,
loris.sauter,heiko.schuldt}@unibas.ch
[2] Department of Informatics, University of Zurich, Zurich, Switzerland
rossetto@ifi.uzh.ch

Abstract. In multimedia search, appropriate user interfaces (UIs) are
essential to enable effective specification of the user's information needs
and the user-friendly presentation of search results. vitrivr-VR addresses
these challenges and provides a novel Virtual Reality-based UI on top of
the multimedia retrieval system vitrivr. In this paper we present the version of vitrivr-VR participating in the Video Browser Showdown (VBS)
2022. We describe our visual-text co-embedding feature and new query
interfaces, namely text entry, pose queries and temporal queries.

Keywords: Video browser showdown · Virtual reality · Interactive
video retrieval · Content-based retrieval

1 Introduction

User interaction plays an important role in multimedia search, although it is
often underestimated. This concerns, on the one hand, the as precise and natural
as possible specification of the information need for the search and, on the other
hand, the presentation of, and ideally also the interaction with the search results.
Virtual Reality (VR) based user interfaces (UIs) allow for innovative solutions
to both phases: queries can be specified more naturally than in desktop UIs,
and the VR-based results display goes way beyond a traditional 2D layout and
allows users to immersively explore their search results.

These advantages are explored by vitrivr-VR, which combines a VR-based
user interface with the vitrivr stack[1], an open-source multimedia retrieval system. One way to evaluate the effectiveness of novel retrieval systems is through
evaluation campaigns like the Video Browser Showdown (VBS) [10], in which
other VR systems, such as EOLAS [16], also participate.

This paper describes the version of vitrivr-VR with which we plan to participate in the VBS 2022. We focus on the changes that have resulted directly

---

[1] https://www.vitrivr.org/.

© Springer Nature Switzerland AG 2022
B. Þór Jónsson et al. (Eds.): MMM 2022, LNCS 13142, pp. 499–504, 2022.
https://doi.org/10.1007/978-3-030-98355-0_45

from lessons learned during the previous participation of vitrivr-VR in the VBS 2021 [14], which was vitrivr-VR's first appearance. We expect our improvements to help cope with the large VBS'22 dataset, the premiere usage of the combined first two shards (V3C1 and V3C2) of the V3C dataset [12].

For query specification, we have improved the speech-to-text transformation for text queries. This is backed by a more advanced visual-text co-embedding compared to the VBS'21 version of vitrivr-VR. We also add support for temporal queries to the vitrivr-VR query interface, i.e., users can specify several subqueries with temporal dependencies. Finally, vitrivr-VR also supports pose queries, to allow querying for specific body poses.

The paper is structured as follows: Sect. 2 introduces vitrivr-VR and Sect. 3 describes our visual-text co-embedding feature. Section 4 describes new interfaces for query formulation in VR, including text entry, temporal queries, and pose queries, and Sect. 5 concludes.

2   vitrivr-VR

vitrivr-VR is an experimental, virtual reality multimedia retrieval system prototype based on the open-source vitrivr stack. The full stack of vitrivr-VR consists of three main parts:

Cottontail DB [4] is a column store used in the vitrivr stack to store extracted multimedia features and metadata and perform Boolean as well as similarity queries. Cineast [11] is the retrieval engine and feature extractor at the core of the vitrivr stack. It facilitates both query processing and feature transformation during online retrieval as well as offline feature extraction phases. Additionally, Cineast is responsible for score fusion, result set reconstruction, and temporal scoring. The retrieval model is described further in [6]. vitrivr-VR is the experimental, VR-based user interface facilitating fully-immersive query formulation and results exploration in virtual reality, the newest iteration of which we describe in this paper. Within the vitrivr stack, it is an alternative to the conventional, web-based two-dimensional user interface vitrivr-ng.

vitrivr-VR is developed in Unity[2] with C# for the HTC Vive Pro and Valve Index, and communicates with Cineast using the RESTful API provided through its OpenAPI specifications. To interface with VR hardware, vitrivr-VR uses the Unity OpenXR plugin[3].

The user interface components of vitrivr-VR can be categorized into three main categories: i.) query formulation (see more details in Sect. 4), ii.) result set exploration, and iii.) media item inspection. The query modalities currently supported through query formulation are concept, text, Boolean, and geo-spatial queries.

Result set exploration is facilitated through a cylindrical, rotatable results display as seen in Fig. 1, which supports both a media segment and a media object centered view. In the media segment centered view, each media segment

---

[2] https://unity.com/.
[3] https://docs.unity3d.com/Packages/com.unity.xr.openxr@latest.

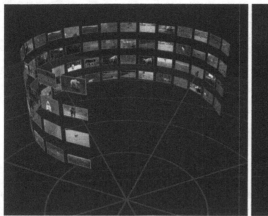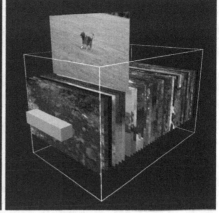

Fig. 1. Screenshots of the vitrivr-VR system; cylindrical results view (left) and video segment view (right).

result (shots in the case of videos) is displayed ordered by similarity score in a grid around the cylindrical display. The media object centered view displays only a configurable number of the top scoring segments for each media object and presents them with increasing distance from the cylindrical display with decreasing score. Segments from each media object occupy only a single grid position in the cylindrical display, ordered by score.

Media item inspection is done through the *media segment inspector* and the *media object segment view.* The media segment inspector pops out of the result view when a result is selected, can be freely moved and placed around the virtual space and persists even when the result set is cleared. It allows the selected media segment to be inspected in detail, i.e. in the case of video viewing the source video segment, as well as metadata such as detected concepts. The media object segment view is a temporally ordered, interactive 3D representation of a media object's segments, which can be accessed from the media segment inspector. It displays the segments inside a box, allowing users to quickly 'riffle' through them and select a segment for closer inspection in the media segment inspector. To increase precision for media objects containing large numbers of segments, a handle allows users to scale the box similar to pulling out a drawer.

3   Visual-Text Co-embedding

The visual-text co-embedding feature, inspired by approaches such as [3, 7], works as shown in Fig. 2. For each video segment, each video frame is first transformed individually by a pre-trained visual feature encoder, and then aggregated and embedded into a joint co-embedding space by an embedding network trained by us. The textual embedding path works analogously except no pooling is needed. For VBS'21, mean pooling was used for visual feature aggregation. We

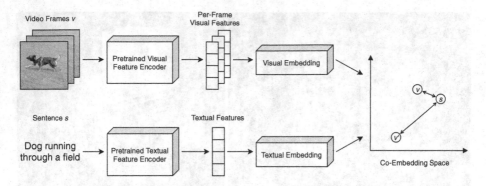

Fig. 2. The visual-text co-embedding as implemented in vitrivr. The objective is to minimize the distance between a video segment v and a matching query sentence s in the co-embedding space, while maximizing the distance to unrelated videos v'.

have improved the visual feature aggregation for VBS'22 to take the temporal context of video frames into account.

As a visual feature encoder, we use the output of the second to last layer of InceptionResNetV2 [15] trained on ImageNet [2] using average pooling through the Keras implementation[4]. As a textual feature encoder we use the Universal Sentence Encoder [1] with weights provided through TensorFlow Hub[5]. Disregarding visual feature aggregation, our visual and textual embedding networks both consist of the same network architecture: a fully connected layer with 1024 units and ReLU activation followed by a dropout layer with rate 0.2 and another fully connected layer with 256 units, which represent the final embedding space. To arrive at the final co-embedding, the output is normalized to the unit hypersphere.

Similar to [3], we perform the training using a bi-directional, pairwise triplet hard loss as seen in Eq. 1, where v is a visual sample, s is a corresponding textual sample, v' and s' are non-matching visual and textual samples, d is the Euclidean distance in the co-embedding space, and α is a configurable margin parameter.

$$l_{PTH}(v,s) = \max_{s'}\left[\alpha + d(v,s) - d(v,s')\right]_+ + \max_{v'}\left[\alpha + d(v,s) - d(v',s)\right]_+ \quad (1)$$

During training, only the visual and textual embedding networks are trained; the pretrained visual and textual feature encoders remain fixed to greatly reduce required training resources. The networks are trained on a mixture of captioned video and image datasets consisting of Flickr30k [19], Microsoft COCO [9], MSR-VTT [18], TextCaps [13], TGIF [8], and VaTeX [17].

[4] https://keras.io/api/applications/inceptionresnetv2.
[5] https://tfhub.dev/google/universal-sentence-encoder/4.

4 VR Query Formulation

Based on our experience from the previous instance of the VBS, we integrated a offline speech-to-text solution utilizing Mozilla DeepSpeech[6] and implemented interfaces to make the existing temporal query modalities and new pose query modalities accessible from VR.

Temporal Queries: Previously, vitrivr-VR did not allow the specification of temporal context during query formulation. Utilizing the same temporal query logic recently added to the vitrivr stack [5], we have implemented a temporal query interface in VR. It allows the specification of temporal context of query terms by grabbing and reordering them in 3D space.

Pose Queries: Leveraging the intuitive 3D manipulation options in VR, vitrivr-VR supports a new query-by-pose feature. To formulate a pose query, a life size, mannequin-like pose representation can be manipulated by grabbing and rotating joints. The adjusted pose representation is framed using a virtual camera and projected onto a canvas to create a pose query.

5 Conclusion

In this paper we present the state of the vitrivr-VR system, with which we plan to participate in the VBS 2022. We describe our system, our visual-text co-embedding feature, changes to our speech-to-text method, and our new temporal and pose query formulation interfaces.

Acknowledgements. This work was partly supported by the Swiss National Science Foundation (project "Participatory Knowledge Practices in Analog and Digital Image Archives", contract no. CRSII5_193788).

References

1. Cer, D., et al.: Universal sentence encoder. CoRR (2018)
2. Deng, J., Dong, W., Socher, R., Li, L., Li, K., Li, F.: ImageNet: a large-scale hierarchical image database. In: Conference on Computer Vision and Pattern Recognition (2009)
3. Faghri, F., Fleet, D.J., Kiros, J.R., Fidler, S.: VSE++: improving visual-semantic embeddings with hard negatives. In: British Machine Vision Conference 2018 (2018)
4. Gasser, R., Rossetto, L., Heller, S., Schuldt, H.: Cottontail DB: an open source database system for multimedia retrieval and analysis. In: International Conference on Multimedia (2020)
5. Heller, S., et al.: Multi-modal interactive video retrieval with temporal queries. In: International Conference on Multimedia Modeling (2022)

---

[6] https://github.com/mozilla/DeepSpeech.

6. Heller, S., Sauter, L., Schuldt, H., Rossetto, L.: Multi-stage queries and temporal scoring in vitrivr. In: International Conference on Multimedia & Expo Workshops (2020)
7. Li, X., Xu, C., Yang, G., Chen, Z., Dong, J.: W2VV++: fully deep learning for ad-hoc video search. In: International Conference on Multimedia (2019)
8. Li, Y., Song, Y., Cao, L., Tetreault, J.R., Goldberg, L., Jaimes, A., Luo, J.: TGIF: A new dataset and benchmark on animated GIF description. In: Conference on Computer Vision and Pattern Recognition (2016)
9. Lin, T.-Y., et al.: Microsoft COCO: common objects in context. In: Fleet, D., Pajdla, T., Schiele, B., Tuytelaars, T. (eds.) ECCV 2014. LNCS, vol. 8693, pp. 740–755. Springer, Cham (2014). https://doi.org/10.1007/978-3-319-10602-1_48
10. Lokoč, J., et al.: Is the reign of interactive search eternal? Findings from the video browser showdown 2020. In: ACM TOMM (2021)
11. Rossetto, L., Giangreco, I., Schuldt, H.: Cineast: a multi-feature sketch-based video retrieval engine. In: IEEE International Symposium on Multimedia (2014)
12. Rossetto, L., Schuldt, H., Awad, G., Butt, A.A.: V3C - a research video collection. In: International Conference on Multimedia Modeling (2019)
13. Sidorov, O., Hu, R., Rohrbach, M., Singh, A.: TextCaps: a dataset for image captioning with reading comprehension. In: Vedaldi, A., Bischof, H., Brox, T., Frahm, J.-M. (eds.) ECCV 2020. LNCS, vol. 12347, pp. 742–758. Springer, Cham (2020). https://doi.org/10.1007/978-3-030-58536-5_44
14. Spiess, F., Gasser, R., Heller, S., Rossetto, L., Sauter, L., Schuldt, H.: Competitive interactive video retrieval in virtual reality with vitrivr-VR. In: Lokoč, J., et al. (eds.) MMM 2021. LNCS, vol. 12573, pp. 441–447. Springer, Cham (2021). https://doi.org/10.1007/978-3-030-67835-7_42
15. Szegedy, C., Ioffe, S., Vanhoucke, V., Alemi, A.A.: Inception-v4, inception-resnet and the impact of residual connections on learning. In: AAAI Conference on Artificial Intelligence (2017)
16. Tran, L., et al.: A VR interface for browsing visual spaces at VBS2021. In: International Conference on Multimedia Modeling (2021)
17. Wang, X., Wu, J., Chen, J., Li, L., Wang, Y., Wang, W.Y.: Vatex: a large-scale, high-quality multilingual dataset for video-and-language research. In: International Conference on Computer Vision (2019)
18. Xu, J., Mei, T., Yao, T., Rui, Y.: MSR-VTT: a large video description dataset for bridging video and language. In: Conference on Computer Vision and Pattern Recognition (2016)
19. Young, P., Lai, A., Hodosh, M., Hockenmaier, J.: From image descriptions to visual denotations: new similarity metrics for semantic inference over event descriptions. Trans. Assoc. Comput. Linguistics **2**, 67–78 (2014)

Video Search with Context-Aware Ranker and Relevance Feedback

Jakub Lokoč[(✉)], František Mejzlík, Tomáš Souček, Patrik Dokoupil, and Ladislav Peška

Department of Software Engineering, Faculty of Mathematics and Physics, Charles University, Prague, Czech Republic
{jakub.lokoc,ladislav.peska}@matfyz.cuni.cz

Abstract. Interactive video search systems effectively combine text-image embedding approaches and smart user interfaces allowing various means of browsing in intermediate result sets. In this paper, we combine features from VIRET and SOMHunter systems into a novel approach for segment based interactive video retrieval. Based on our SOMHunter log analysis and VIRET tool performance in known-item search tasks, we focus on two specific features – a combination of context-aware ranking by text queries and Bayesian-like relevance feedback approach for refining scores using promising candidates.

Keywords: Interactive video retrieval · Relevance feedback · Deep learning

1 Introduction

The Video Browser Showdown (VBS) competition represents a great opportunity to annually benchmark interactive video search systems in a fair competition with challenging search tasks [12] (summarized in Table 1). The last ten years of the competition revealed that state-of-the-art systems need effective search initialization as well as more advanced browsing capabilities to quickly analyze and refine candidate sets. These recommendations are then reflected by participating systems[1] that combine ranking models with interactive user interfaces.

In this work, we combine approaches used by SOMHunter and VIRET systems at VBS 2021. Based on our analysis of actually used features by SOMHunter users, we restrain from cumulative style of development. Instead, we select just a limited set of features from SOMHunter [17] and use them to enhance context-aware ranker tested previously by the VIRET tool [14]. Our motivation is to design a simple system and interface for the new tool for VBS 2022, which we denote as *Context-aware Video Hunter*, or simply *CVHunter*.

---

[1] Regular participants are e.g. vitrivr [3], VIRET [14], Vireo [18], SOMHunter[17], HTW [4], VERGE [2], Exquisitor [5], VISIONE [1], diveXplore [8], VideoGraph [16].

© Springer Nature Switzerland AG 2022
B. Þór Jónsson et al. (Eds.): MMM 2022, LNCS 13142, pp. 505–510, 2022.
https://doi.org/10.1007/978-3-030-98355-0_46

Table 1. Summary of task types used at VBS 2021.

Textual known-item search task (T)	
Duration: 420 s	**Number of tasks:** 5
Example task: T_8 asking to find "A young man sitting outdoors and eating ... ... He wears a dark T-shirt and silver headphones ... ... It is evening, trees are visible behind him (out of focus)."	
Visual known-item search task (V)	
Duration: 300 s	**Number of tasks:** 21
Example task: V_7 showing roughly 20s long target video segment 	
Ad-hoc video search task (A)	
Duration: 300 s	**Number of tasks:** 10
Example task: A_9 asking to find shots showing a sign with text (readable)	

2 SOMHunter Performance Revision

SOMHunter [6,7] was designed as a light-weight system presenting ranked set of representative video frames (based on a text query), allowing relevance feedback actions and exploration/exploitation browsing options. Search models in SOMHunter are based on the W2VV++ approach [9,13], allowing text-image search and image-image similarity with the same set of features. For VBS 2021, the SOMHunter engine [17] supported two new features – localized text queries and query relocation. We remind that localized queries allow users to place a free-form text query on a canvas, while the relocation component enables selection of an example image instead of the original text query. The CollageHunter system [10] relying on the SOMHunter engine used a variant of localized queries utilizing images (instead of text query) found with the help of external engines. In the rest of this section, we analyze queries in our VBS 2021 logs to determine the effectivity of the aforementioned new features.

Figure 1 shows performance analysis of localized collage queries and relocation. Either the top ranked frame from the searched target scene or video is considered in the corresponding ranked result set (variants SCENE and VIDEO in graphs). The left graph for collage queries compares positioned queries PQ with a variant of the same queries, where the positioning was ignored UQ (evaluated after the competition). The curves show the number of found items up to a given rank R, assuming either the best ranked frame from the searched scene or whole video. The results show that query image localization on a canvas can improve results in some cases, but for the price of nontrivial implementation efforts (e.g., extraction and management of descriptors of all utilized image cuts).

We hypothesize that the performance is affected by the size of image cuts and the fixed regular partitioning of image cuts introducing additional noise. Furthermore, users (under competition stress) often used an example image spread

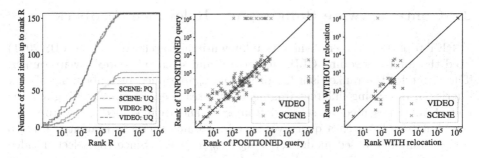

Fig. 1. Left: number of found items up to a rank r when using (PQ) or ignoring (UQ) positions of query images. Middle: scatter plot of ranks when using or ignoring positions of query images. Right: scatter plot showing the effect of query relocation. Queries taken from VBS2021 logs. The performance drop for SCENE for $Rank > 100$ is caused by presentation filters [11] considering just three top ranked frames from each video. Unknown ranks in scatter plots depicted at the position 10^6.

across the whole canvas. Although the middle graph in Fig. 1 shows that particular query attempts may bring an interesting improvement over the version without query localization, the average performance gain is not dazzling and so we decided to restrain from sub-image representations in CVHunter. We note that values above the diagonal mean a better rank when using positioned queries. Unknown values of ranks are depicted at coordinate 10^6, for cases where all correct frames were filtered by the presentation filter (i.e., show just a limited number of frames from each video).

Regarding localized text queries found in SOMHunter logs, their number is too low to make conclusions. Furthermore, the few found queries did not show a promising result, compared to our preliminary offline experiment performed before VBS 2021. We note that SOMHunter users could decide at VBS 2021 to search with a standard textbox option located above the canvas (unlike users of CollageHunter). The low number of performed localized text queries further supports our decision to not consider this concept in the next iteration of VBS.

The right graph in Fig. 1 presents the effect of query relocation, where users could "replace" the query vector obtained from a text query, especially for more complex temporal queries. In order to find another vector, a sorted image map was dynamically computed for the neighbourhood of the original query vector. Although example image based browsing is a standard tool offered by image search engines, our logs from VBS 2021 do not show a notable effect achieved by query relocations conveniently enabling example image selection.

To sum up our analysis, both localized queries and query relocation added to SOMHunter in 2021 extended a set of search options and allowed to try more search strategies to improve ranking. On the other hand, the overall effect observed from our logs was not overwhelming. In order to keep our new system simple, we skip both features and focus on context-aware ranking strategies. To refine results, we plan to keep also approaches for relevance score updates.

3   Context-Aware Ranking and Relevance Feedback

VIRET tool [14] (winner of the visual known-item search category at VBS 2021) used the joint-embedding CLIP model [15] and so-called context-aware ranker. The input for the ranker is a list of vectors v_{q_i} obtained by embedding of text queries q_i describing different fragments of a searched scene. Assuming a video collection represented by selected frames f_j and their embedded vectors v_{f_j}, the similarity between a query vector and a frame vector is evaluated using a cosine similarity based model $s_{ij} = \sigma_{cos}(v_{q_i}, v_{f_j}) + 1$. Since the selected video frames are temporally ordered, the context-aware ranker can operate on vectors $VS_i = < s_{i,1}, \cdots, s_{i,k} >$ for each q_i, where k is the number of indexed frames.

The implementation of the context-aware ranker for VBS 2021 used a sliding window of a fixed size c. For each window position t, the method finds maximum score $m_{i,t}$ from $s_{i,t}, \cdots, s_{i,(t+c)}$ in each vector VS_i. The score for the window segment is then computed as the product of max scores $m_{i,t}$ for all queries q_i.

Since context-aware ranking reduces demands on exact temporal ordering specification of searched fragments (unlike temporal queries), users can just fill query parts q_i into the query text box. We plan to preserve this feature also in CVHunter. However, we plan to extend the model by the relevance feedback approach implemented previously by SOMHunter. In other words, once the context-aware ranker sorts window-based segments, the next interactive search step could be selection of likes for displayed segment images. Since we assume one resulting segment per display line, the likes can be selected for different text query parts q_i in one iteration (e.g., a like for a cat and a like for a dog when searching for a sequence showing both animals occurring in a row). Figure 2 depicts an overview of the approach.

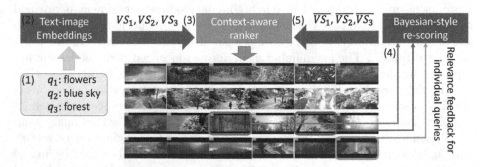

Fig. 2. Overview of the proposed search mechanism: Users can formulate several text queries (1), which are projected to a shared text-image space and relevance of individual frames w.r.t. sub-queries is calculated (2). Relevance score vectors are then combined via context-aware ranker (3). Based on the presented results, users may select particular images as relevant for individual sub-queries (4). This relevance feedback is then utilized to update respective relevance vectors and re-order the list of results.

A straightforward option to integrate relevance feedback actions is to update score vectors VS_i after obtaining likes bound to particular query parts q_i. This approach extends the feedback loop adopted by SOMHunter by considering likes for different query parts and maintenance of multiple relevance score vectors. Once users click the rescore button, the sliding window approach can be used again to recalculate the overall scores.

Regarding the joint-embedding model for text query parts, CVHunter currently supports both W2VV++ and CLIP approaches. However, the system can be easily updated with any state-of-the-art joint-embedding approach available at the time of competition.

4   Conclusions

This paper revisits design decisions in our previous interactive video search system SOMHunter and presents a new system called CVHunter for participation at VBS 2022. The new version combines context-aware ranking of video segments from our another tool VIRET (version from VBS 2021) with relevance feedback actions targeting frames belonging to different query parts.

Acknowledgements. This paper has been supported by Czech Science Foundation (GAČR) project 19-22071Y, Charles University grant SVV-260588, and by Charles University Grant Agency (GA UK) project number 1310920.

References

1. Amato, G., et al.: VISIONE at video browser showdown 2021. In: Lokoč, J., et al. (eds.) MMM 2021. LNCS, vol. 12573, pp. 473–478. Springer, Cham (2021). https://doi.org/10.1007/978-3-030-67835-7_47

2. Andreadis, S., et al.: VERGE in VBS 2021. In: Lokoč, J., et al. (eds.) MMM 2021. LNCS, vol. 12573, pp. 398–404. Springer, Cham (2021). https://doi.org/10.1007/978-3-030-67835-7_35

3. Heller, S., et al.: Towards explainable interactive multi-modal video retrieval with vitrivr. In: Lokoč, J., et al. (eds.) MMM 2021. LNCS, vol. 12573, pp. 435–440. Springer, Cham (2021). https://doi.org/10.1007/978-3-030-67835-7_41

4. Hezel, N., Schall, K., Jung, K., Barthel, K.U.: Video search with sub-image keyword transfer using existing image archives. In: Lokoč, J., et al. (eds.) MMM 2021. LNCS, vol. 12573, pp. 484–489. Springer, Cham (2021). https://doi.org/10.1007/978-3-030-67835-7_49

5. Khan, O.S., et al.: Exquisitor at the video browser showdown 2021: relationships between semantic classifiers. In: Lokoč, J., et al. (eds.) MMM 2021. LNCS, vol. 12573, pp. 410–416. Springer, Cham (2021). https://doi.org/10.1007/978-3-030-67835-7_37

6. Kratochvíl, M., Veselý, P., Mejzlík, F., Lokoč, J.: SOM-hunter: video browsing with relevance-to-SOM feedback loop. In: Ro, Y.M., et al. (eds.) MMM 2020. LNCS, vol. 11962, pp. 790–795. Springer, Cham (2020). https://doi.org/10.1007/978-3-030-37734-2_71

7. Kratochvíl, M., Mejzlík, F., Veselý, P., Souček, T., Lokoč, J.: SOMHunter: lightweight video search system with SOM-guided relevance feedback. In: Proceedings of the 28th ACM International Conference on Multimedia, MM 2020. ACM (2020)

8. Leibetseder, A., Schoeffmann, K.: Less is more - diveXplore 5.0 at VBS 2021. In: Lokoč, J., et al. (eds.) MMM 2021. LNCS, vol. 12573, pp. 455–460. Springer, Cham (2021). https://doi.org/10.1007/978-3-030-67835-7_44

9. Li, X., Xu, C., Yang, G., Chen, Z., Dong, J.: W2VV++ fully deep learning for ad-hoc video search. In: Proceedings of the 27th ACM International Conference on Multimedia, pp. 1786–1794 (2019)

10. Lokoč, J., Bátoryová, J., Smrž, D., Dobranský, M.: Video search with collage queries. In: Lokoč, J., et al. (eds.) MMM 2021. LNCS, vol. 12573, pp. 429–434. Springer, Cham (2021). https://doi.org/10.1007/978-3-030-67835-7_40

11. Lokoč, J., et al.: A W2VV++ case study with automated and interactive text-to-video retrieval. In: Proceedings of the 28th ACM International Conference on Multimedia, MM 2020. Association for Computing Machinery, New York (2020)

12. Lokoč, J., et al.: A task category space for user-centric comparative multimedia search evaluations. In: International Conference on Multimedia Modeling (2022)

13. Mettes, P., Koelma, D.C., Snoek, C.G.M.: Shuffled ImageNet banks for video event detection and search. ACM Trans. Multimedia Comput. Commun. Appl. (TOMM) **16**(2), 1–21 (2020)

14. Peška, L., Kovalčík, G., Souček, T., Škrhák, V., Lokoč, J.: W2VV++ BERT model at VBS 2021. In: Lokoč, J., et al. (eds.) MMM 2021. LNCS, vol. 12573, pp. 467–472. Springer, Cham (2021). https://doi.org/10.1007/978-3-030-67835-7_46

15. Radford, A., et al.: Learning transferable visual models from natural language supervision (2021)

16. Rossetto, L., et al.: VideoGraph – towards using knowledge graphs for interactive video retrieval. In: Lokoč, J., et al. (eds.) MMM 2021. LNCS, vol. 12573, pp. 417–422. Springer, Cham (2021). https://doi.org/10.1007/978-3-030-67835-7_38

17. Veselý, P., Mejzlík, F., Lokoč, J.: SOMHunter V2 at video browser showdown 2021. In: Lokoč, J., et al. (eds.) MMM 2021. LNCS, vol. 12573, pp. 461–466. Springer, Cham (2021). https://doi.org/10.1007/978-3-030-67835-7_45

18. Wu, J., Nguyen, P.A., Ma, Z., Ngo, C.-W.: SQL-like interpretable interactive video search. In: Lokoč, J., et al. (eds.) MMM 2021. LNCS, vol. 12573, pp. 391–397. Springer, Cham (2021). https://doi.org/10.1007/978-3-030-67835-7_34

Exquisitor at the Video Browser Showdown 2022

Omar Shahbaz Khan[1,2(✉)], Ujjwal Sharma[2], Björn Þór Jónsson[1],
Dennis C. Koelma[2], Stevan Rudinac[2], Marcel Worring[2], and Jan Zahálka[3]

[1] IT University of Copenhagen, Copenhagen, Denmark
`omsh@itu.dk`
[2] University of Amsterdam, Amsterdam, Netherlands
[3] Czech Technical University in Prague, Prague, Czech Republic

Abstract. Exquisitor is the state-of-the-art large-scale interactive learning approach for media exploration that utilizes user relevance feedback at its core and is capable of interacting with collections containing more than 100M multimedia items at sub-second latency. In this work, we propose improvements to Exquisitor that include new features extracted at shot level for semantic concepts, scenes and actions. In addition, we introduce extensions to the video summary interface providing a better overview of the shots. Finally, we replace a simple keyword search featured in the previous versions of the system with a semantic search based on modern contextual representations.

Keywords: Interactive learning · Video browsing · Multimodal representation learning · Semantic search

1 Introduction

The Video Browser Showdown (VBS) is a live interactive video retrieval challenge, in which researchers participate with their retrieval tools to solve interactive tasks. VBS holds significant importance to researchers developing exploration and search tools for multimedia collections, as it is an opportunity to test their techniques in a realistic setting. Furthermore, the event leads to better insight in interactive retrieval, thus inspiring new methods, systems and further research [7]. This year's edition expands the video collection from 7,475 video clips (~1,000 h) [14] to 17,235 video clips (~2,300 h) [13].

Exquisitor is a prototype interactive learning system for large-scale media exploration, and has participated in the last two editions of VBS, where it performed adequately [3,4]. It uses user relevance feedback at its core, which builds a semantic classifier on the fly to find relevant items for the information need represented in the tasks. In addition to the single classifier, Exquisitor can build more classifiers and merge their result sets using various relational operators [4], with each classifier also having options for applying metadata filters. These multiple classifiers allow Exquisitor to deal with task descriptions that have a temporal nature, which are common in VBS. The need is evident by

© Springer Nature Switzerland AG 2022
B. Þór Jónsson et al. (Eds.): MMM 2022, LNCS 13142, pp. 511–517, 2022.
https://doi.org/10.1007/978-3-030-98355-0_47

looking at systems that generally do well in VBS, which incorporate modules for addressing temporal queries [6,8,10,15].

Previously, Exquisitor relied on video segmentation provided with the VBS collection and represented each segment with semantic features extracted from a corresponding keyframe. The keyframes are presented to the user during the interactive learning sessions, whose relevance judgment is used to build the semantic classifier(s) deployed for producing new suggestions. To determine whether the correct video segment has been found, the user can browse the video in Exquisitor's video summary view to fully compare the video content with the task description. As the provided segments are of arbitrary length, the features extracted from a single keyframe may not include information about the entire segment, especially since Exquisitor uses a compression scheme that reduces the number of features used to describe a keyframe [17]. The video summary interface of Exquisitor is also affected by the pre-defined shot structure, which makes it difficult to get an overview of the video, especially those with longer shots.

Additionally, the keyword search for finding initial positives, in its current form, is too restrictive, as it only uses available ImageNet concepts as search terms. These concepts do not always match the descriptions of tasks and make it difficult for the user to determine the right concepts.

In this paper, we introduce improvements to Exquisitor with additional features at shot level based on semantic concepts, actions and scenes. Furthermore, we conduct our own shot boundary detection that ensures shots are between 1–10 s. In addition, we introduce extensions to the video summary interface providing a better overview of the shots. Lastly, the keyword search used to find initial positive items for the user relevance feedback process, has been replaced with a semantic search based on modern contextual representations.

2   Exquisitor

Exquisitor is the state-of-the-art large-scale interactive learning approach capable of handling collections with over 100 million images [5,11]. The system consists of a web-based user interface and an interactive learning server.

Exquisitor Interface: Figure 1 shows the user interface of Exquisitor which allows the user to provide feedback to the systems suggestions based on the current classifier. Initially, arbitrary suggestions are presented. When a user hovers over a keyframe 4 buttons appear that allow, labeling it positive, negative, submitting the segment to the VBS evaluation server or ignoring it. The user can get new suggestions from the current model by pressing the "Next" button marking all current segments as viewed and at any point during the interactive session view these already seen segments through the "History" button. Additionally, at this screen the user can also apply metadata filters such as video level filters (categories and tags), and keyframe level filters (number of faces present, dominant color and amount of text present). In addition, the user can directly search for a specific video using its id, which opens the video summary view.

Fig. 1. Exquisitor's interface for building semantic classifiers.

At the top of the screen the user can add more classifiers, which opens a new similar screen to Fig. 1 in a new tab, to define multiple classifiers for different temporal concepts. The returned items from the classifiers can be merged using the merge view, which are ranked using classifier ranking operations [4]. The user can view the merge results to find the relevant segment or continue improving the classifiers. Depending on the collection size, the interface can directly retrieve the videos using local paths, but if space requirement is higher than the available local storage, a web-server is used to serve the videos instead.

Exquisitor Server: Exquisitor combines cluster-based indexing with an efficient compressed data representation containing the most important features extracted from each shot per modality [1,17]. Given Exquisitor's scalability, the expanded VBS dataset is of no concern to the core relevance feedback performance. The underlying model used for interactive multimodal learning in Exquisitor is a linear SVM, which is trained based on user relevance judgments on presented video segments. The hyperplane formed by the SVM is used for extracting k-farthest clusters from the index, as the intention is to present the user with the items for which the classifier is most confident. From this point a late fusion step in the form of rank aggregation is performed to get the top r suggestions to present the user with. Additionally, the server allows multiple users and handle keyword search requests.

Interactive Learning and VBS: There are three different task types presented at VBS: Textual and Visual Known-Item-Search (KIS), and Ad-hoc Video Search (AVS). The goal of the KIS task is to find a single video segment in one specific video. The description is provided textually or through a visual snippet with audio. For the AVS task the goal is to find as many video segments matching the textual description in any video.

Within Exquisitor, semantic classifiers are built through user relevance feedback to bring forth the correct segment(s). The tasks have a time limit—KIS tasks end after 1 correct submission from the team, whereas AVS tasks allows submissions until the time has run out.

3   Improving Segment Representations

Exquisitor uses features extracted from the keyframes of video segments. Since video segments are of arbitrary size, more information is lost for longer segments as the keyframe may not fully cover it. Furthermore, as the information is based on entities, queries related to actions are difficult to represent with the classifier.

The length of provided video segments can be longer than 30 s but also shorter than 1 s. The longer segments may contain the relevant sequence which the representative keyframe is not highlighting [12]. The shorter segments cause an issue of segment overload, where no major change is happening in multiple continuous short segments, which would benefit from merging them together and improving the browsing experience.

Inspired by [16], we process the videos with our own video shot boundary detection method to provide less coarse segments, while still being slightly over segmented for addressing subtle changes. A post process step is performed on the segments that ensures a lower and upper bound of 1 s and 10 s respectively, to avoid excessively short or long segments. The first 7,475 videos in the collection corresponds to the previous years' collection which had 1,087,657 segments. With our approach this is reduced to 992,455 segments, a reduction of 8.7%. For the entire collection with 17,235 videos, this results in 2,285,514 segments. We extract semantic concepts [9], actions [2] and scenes [18] from the segments. These are treated as separate modalities within Exquisitor and are combined through rank aggregation during the retrieval process.

4   UI Extensions

Video Summary: The new shots are easier to view and process for a user. However, viewing is not always ideal as tasks are time dependent. Therefore, we now show up to 5 uniformly sampled thumbnails from the shot, so the user can rapidly determine whether it is relevant or not. Figure 2 shows the new video summary view. In addition to the shot thumbnails, the video player has been updated to show the entire video file instead of the shot file.

Keyword Search: The keyword search feature of Exquisitor is used to find initial positive examples for the user relevance feedback process. Originally it used a mapping of 12,988 assigned semantic concepts from ImageNet [9]. However,

Fig. 2. The new video summary view with every shot having up to 5 thumbnails.

these concepts may not necessarily align with the user's vocabulary making it difficult to find the right concept. Restricting users to a limited set of search terms may result in users spending more time locating the appropriate search terms instead of actually searching. To avoid this, we replace the current keyword search with a semantic search that accepts natural language queries, using all available features, allowing users to search without being constrained by the limited set of search terms available from metadata.

5 Conclusions

This work presents a series of incremental improvements to Exquisitor. We extract features based on semantic concepts, actions and scenes at shot level. These features are used within Exquisitor as separate modalities and are combined through rank aggregation. We use our own using a shot boundary detection method that ensures they have an upper and lower bound on the duration. Furthermore, we replace the keyword search with semantic search allowing the use of natural language queries. These changes permit Exquisitor to more efficiently explore video collections while being transparent to the user.

Acknowledgments. This work was supported by a Ph.D. grant from the IT University of Copenhagen and by the European Regional Development Fund (project Robotics for Industry 4.0, CZ.02.1.01/0.0/0.0/15 003/0000470).

References

1. Guðmundsson, G.Þ., Jónsson, B.Þ., Amsaleg, L.: A large-scale performance study of cluster-based high-dimensional indexing. In: Proceedings of International Workshop on Very-large-scale Multimedia Corpus, Mining and Retrieval (VLS-MCM), Firenze, Italy (2010)
2. Hara, K., Kataoka, H., Satoh, Y.: Can spatiotemporal 3D CNNs retrace the history of 2D CNNs and ImageNet? In: Proceedings of the IEEE Conference on Computer Vision and Pattern Recognition (CVPR), pp. 6546–6555 (2018)
3. Jónsson, B.Þ, Khan, O.S., Koelma, D.C., Rudinac, S., Worring, M., Zahálka, J.: Exquisitor at the video browser showdown 2020. In: Ro, Y.M., et al. (eds.) MMM 2020. LNCS, vol. 11962, pp. 796–802. Springer, Cham (2020). https://doi.org/10.1007/978-3-030-37734-2_72
4. Khan, O.S., et al.: Exquisitor at the video browser showdown 2021: relationships between semantic classifiers. In: Lokoč, J., et al. (eds.) MMM 2021. LNCS, vol. 12573, pp. 410–416. Springer, Cham (2021). https://doi.org/10.1007/978-3-030-67835-7_37
5. Khan, O.S., et al.: Interactive learning for multimedia at large. In: Jose, J.M., et al. (eds.) ECIR 2020. LNCS, vol. 12035, pp. 495–510. Springer, Cham (2020). https://doi.org/10.1007/978-3-030-45439-5_33
6. Kratochvíl, M., Veselý, P., Mejzlík, F., Lokoč, J.: SOM-Hunter: video browsing with relevance-to-SOM feedback loop. In: Ro, Y.M., et al. (eds.) MMM 2020. LNCS, vol. 11962, pp. 790–795. Springer, Cham (2020). https://doi.org/10.1007/978-3-030-37734-2_71
7. Lokoč, J., et al.: Interactive search or sequential browsing? A detailed analysis of the video browser showdown 2018. ACM TOMM 15(1), 1–18 (2019)
8. Lokoč, J., Kovalčík, G., Souček, T.: VIRET at video browser showdown 2020. In: Ro, Y.M., et al. (eds.) MMM 2020. LNCS, vol. 11962, pp. 784–789. Springer, Cham (2020). https://doi.org/10.1007/978-3-030-37734-2_70
9. Mettes, P., Koelma, D.C., Snoek, C.G.: The ImageNet shuffle: reorganized pretraining for video event detection. In: Proceedings of the 2016 ACM on International Conference on Multimedia Retrieval, ICMR 2016, pp. 175–182. Association for Computing Machinery, New York (2016)
10. Nguyen, P.A., Wu, J., Ngo, C.-W., Francis, D., Huet, B.: VIREO @ video browser showdown 2020. In: Ro, Y.M., et al. (eds.) MMM 2020. LNCS, vol. 11962, pp. 772–777. Springer, Cham (2020). https://doi.org/10.1007/978-3-030-37734-2_68
11. Ragnarsdóttir, H., et al.: Exquisitor: breaking the interaction barrier for exploration of 100 million images. In: Proceedings of ACM Multimedia, Nice, France (2019)
12. Rossetto, L., Giangreco, I., Gasser, R., Schuldt, H.: Competitive video retrieval with vitrivr at the video browser showdown 2018-final notes. arXiv preprint arXiv:1805.02371 (2018)
13. Rossetto, L., Schoeffmann, K., Bernstein, A.: Insights on the V3C2 dataset. CoRR arXiv:2105.01475 (2021)
14. Rossetto, L., Schuldt, H., Awad, G., Butt, A.A.: V3C – a research video collection. In: Kompatsiaris, I., Huet, B., Mezaris, V., Gurrin, C., Cheng, W.-H., Vrochidis, S. (eds.) MMM 2019. LNCS, vol. 11295, pp. 349–360. Springer, Cham (2019). https://doi.org/10.1007/978-3-030-05710-7_29

15. Sauter, L., Amiri Parian, M., Gasser, R., Heller, S., Rossetto, L., Schuldt, H.: Combining Boolean and multimedia retrieval in vitrivr for large-scale video search. In: Ro, Y.M., et al. (eds.) MMM 2020. LNCS, vol. 11962, pp. 760–765. Springer, Cham (2020). https://doi.org/10.1007/978-3-030-37734-2_66

16. Yuan, J., et al.: Tsinghua University at TRECVID 2004: shot boundary detection and high-level feature extraction. In: TRECVID. Citeseer (2004)

17. Zahálka, J., Rudinac, S., Jónsson, B.Þ., Koelma, D.C., Worring, M.: Blackthorn: large-scale interactive multimodal learning. IEEE TMM **20**(3), 687–698 (2018)

18. Zhou, B., Lapedriza, A., Khosla, A., Oliva, A., Torralba, A.: Places: a 10 million image database for scene recognition. IEEE Trans. Pattern Analy. Mach. Intell. **40**, 1452–1464 (2017)

Videofall - A Hierarchical Search Engine for VBS2022

Thao-Nhu Nguyen[1(✉)], Bunyarit Puangthamawathanakun[1], Graham Healy[1],
Binh T. Nguyen[2,3], Cathal Gurrin[1], and Annalina Caputo[1]

[1] Dublin City University, Dublin, Ireland
thaonhu.nguyen24@mail.dcu.ie
[2] AISIA Research Lab, Ho Chi Minh City, Vietnam
[3] Vietnam National University, Ho Chi Minh University of Science,
Ho Chi Minh City, Vietnam

Abstract. In this paper, we introduce a multi-user hierarchical video search tool called VIDEOFALL. Our objective, in the Video Browser Showdown (VBS) 2022, is to explore if VIDEOFALL interactive video retrieval under time constraints is a useful approach to take, given the overhead of requiring multiple users. It is our conjecture that combining different skills of normal users can support a master user to retrieve target videos efficiently. The system is designed on top of the CLIP pre-trained model and the video keyframes are embedded into a vector space in which queries would also be encoded to facilitate retrieval.

Keywords: Video Browser Showdown · Interactive video retrieval · Hierarchical engine · Multi-user search engine

1 Introduction

The motivation for VIDEOFALL is that each individual has distinct abilities and skills that can uniquely inform the retrieval process for the video retrieval challenge. Hence, our conjecture is that combining the efforts of multiple users into one collaborative searching tool could be an interesting approach for the VBS.

In this paper, we propose VIDEOFALL, a hierarchical interactive video search engine that enables multiple users to interact simultaneously, all with the aim of finding potentially relevant pieces of video content from a large archive. We utilise a pre-trained Contrastive Language-Image Pre-training (CLIP) model [4] as the backbone of the retrieval approach, which supports a group of users to search using various techniques, such as colour, OCR or textual descriptions. Afterward, upon finding a potentially relevant item, those users pass it onto a master user for final review before selecting it as submittable or not. The master user will consequently handle the higher-level task of validating all non-overlapping results from the database and sending back the final result to the server.

© Springer Nature Switzerland AG 2022
B. Þór Jónsson et al. (Eds.): MMM 2022, LNCS 13142, pp. 518–523, 2022.
https://doi.org/10.1007/978-3-030-98355-0_48

2   Related Research

The Video Browser Showdown (VBS), an annual competition in the Multimedia Modeling Conference (MMM) since 2012, is known for supporting a live experimental comparison between video retrieval systems. All competitors are required to resolve two main types of tasks: Known-Item search (KIS) and Ad-hoc Video Search (AVS). AVS simulates the scenario of finding as many correct scenes as possible from the given description. Meanwhile, KIS is concerned with locating just one specific scene fitting with the provided description. There are two subtasks of KIS including (1) visual KIS, where the clip containing the target scene will be displayed and (2) textual KIS with an increasingly detailed query description being shown.

There have been a number of notable relevant approaches taken during the most recent VBS challenges. The third release of VISIONE [1] allowed user to query by combining different types of representations including text, objects, colour, visual examples, and their spatial relationships. For each specific type of information, different AI-based techniques were separately employed in order to extract as many features as possible. SOM-Hunter [9] has proven to be a high-performing system in which the scenes were ranked and visualized on high-dimensional data by using a self-organising map (SOM). Aside from employing the traditional bag-of-words model for describing objects, SOM-Hunter also enabled seeking targets by multiple text queries to capture the positional relationships between objects; a user had the ability to specifically describe objects or events in a sub-region of the whole scene. While most of the teams have designed traditional 2D retrieval systems, vitrivr-VR [3] introduced an interactive Virtual-Reality-based engine that co-embedded text and video into the same high-dimensional space. Additional information from Optical Character Recognition (OCR) and Automatic Speech Recognition (ASR) were also attached to that 3D feature space. Users could use both textual and speech-to-text queries in order to retrieve the target frame. Then, the result was presented in a 2D scrolling list according to the ranked list of scenes. Different from vitrivr-VR, the main goal of EOLAS [8] - another VR system first introduced last year - was to explore the latent feature space where all frames were embedded. Based on the cosine distance between encoded vectors, the group of videos would be visualized on the wide and surrounding 3D view in the virtual environment. As a result, user was able to directly interact with the system.

There are a few multiple-user system that have developed before. Schoeffmann et al. [7] provided a collaborative search system in which each individual user received a specific view from the web interface. The authors used Feature Map, a similarity-based map of keyframes, as their main interface. Furthermore, all users shared the same synchronized view of inspection actions in a cooperative heatmap. Then, the collaborative retrieved results would be re-ranked to finalise the submittable result. Unlike Schoeffmann's system [7], ours primarily utilise the distinct point of view to explore different aspects of one event. Therefore, we provide all normal users the same UI. The final result is only submitted by the master user after evaluating all possible frame received from the unique normal users.

3   An Overview of VIDEOFALL

In general, the search engine of VIDEOFALL consists of two fundamental components: (1) the indexer, where all keyframes extracted from the given videos are encoded to latent space using the CLIP image encoder; and (2) the retrieval engine, in which the input query is also embedded and then ranked based on the cosine distance. Meanwhile, the User Interface (UI) is designed to ease multiple-user access. Figure 1 indicates the VIDEOFALL workflow overview, while the User Interaction flow and the UI protocols of the system are illustrated in Fig. 2 and Fig. 3 respectively.

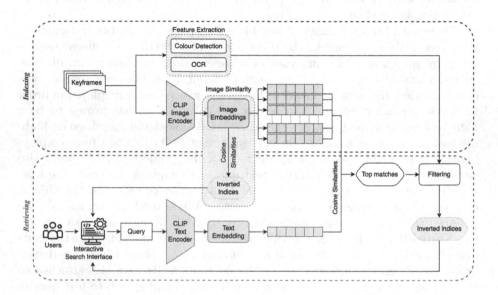

Fig. 1. VIDEOFALL workflow

3.1   Source Data

This year's competition will combine two parts of the Vimeo Creative Commons Collection dataset (V3C) [6], which is comprised of V3C1 [2] and V3C2 [5]. These two extensive collections of videos, with different topic categories ranging from Arts, Fashion, Technology to Food, were already segmented into shots represented by pre-extracted keyframes. We did not alter the provided shot boundaries or keyframes. The dataset details are presented on Table 1.

3.2   System Overview

As shown in Fig. 1, the overall system consists of two main stages: indexing and retrieving. At indexing time, colour and OCR are extracted from the original keyframes in order to support retrieving in the next stage.

Table 1. Dataset details

Name	No. videos	No. keyframes	No. hours of content	Size (TB)
V3C1	7475	1,082,659	1,000	1.3
V3C2	9760	1,425,454	1,300	1.6
Total	**17,235**	**2,508,113**	**2,300**	**2.9**

Feature Extraction. Our goal is to determine the globally dominant colour of one frame which would be used as a filter to narrow the search space. That colour would belong to one of the 32 basic colour bins on the palette. Thinking of each pixel as a data point in 3D space, we apply the KMeans clustering algorithm to the set of points. The colour has the nearest distance to the group's center point value would be assigned as the label of that group. The denser the group is, the more that colour dominates the frame. After that, both the top 5 densest groups in ascending order and the extracted OCR will be combined as metadata to support queries.

Indexing. We will leverage the pre-trained CLIP model [4] from OpenAI corporation, which aims to make connections between the visual and textual representations. CLIP text and image encoders will be trained on the full-sentence description of the image instead of just one label, resulting in a deeper understanding of the dataset. Furthermore, training on a couple of large-scale datasets (e.g. ImageNet, Youtube-BB, ObjectNet, ...) supports the model learning various aspects of images. In VIDEOFALL, the CLIP image encoder will be exploited to convert all keyframes into feature vectors in a latent space.

Retrieval. Once users input a textual query, it will be fed into the pre-trained text encoder to be encoded into a single vector having the same dimension as the image embedding above. The pairwise cosine distances between all image text pairs are computed before being ranked for later use. Then, we will get the ranked list of the top-most fitting images to the description. The same process is applied to the image embedding vectors to create an inverted index of similar images. These indices enable the direct retrieval of relevant images given a sample scene, also known as image similarity.

3.3 User Interface

We have introduced two simple UIs for two main phases in user interaction. The UI for the first phase, illustrated in Fig. 3a, is designed to be easily accessible for the searches performed by normal users. For each task, users translate the provided topic description into the query for the UI. After obtaining the list of matching images in reverse order of relevance to the query, this is refined to remove overlapping images among users. At this stage, the users have 2 options,

522   T.-N. Nguyen et al.

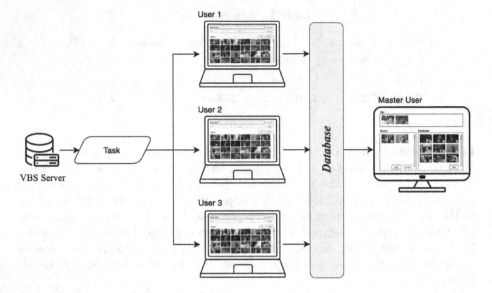

Fig. 2. The user interaction flow

either add an image to the Review list for validation by the master user in the next stage, or put an image in the Star list if they find the correct shot. In the second phase, the UI (Fig. 3b) is developed specifically for the master user who will take responsibility for reviewing candidates and generating the final submission. From the Review list, the master user can use visual similarity to find similar images to any image in the Review list, or they can just directly sumbit from the Star list. It is noteworthy that the master user can submit the final results at any time.

Fig. 3. The two user interface protocols: (a) UI for the normal users and (b) UI for the master user.

4   Conclusion

In this paper, we have introduced a multi-user interactive system, VIDEOFALL, built on top of the CLIP model. We decided to make a multi-user system because different people can bring different skillsets to the retrieval process. VIDEOFALL aims at capturing the wide range of users' understandings of the queries and the aggregation of their searching may help the team to find required content faster and more effectively.

Acknowledgments. This research was conducted with the financial support of Science Foundation Ireland under Grant Agreement No. 18/CRT/6223, and 13/RC/2106_P2 at the ADAPT SFI Research Centre at DCU. ADAPT, the SFI Research Centre for AI-Driven Digital Content Technology, is funded by Science Foundation Ireland through the SFI Research Centres Programme.

References

1. Amato, G., et al.: VISIONE at video browser showdown 2021. In: Lokoč, J., et al. (eds.) MMM 2021. LNCS, vol. 12573, pp. 473–478. Springer, Cham (2021). https://doi.org/10.1007/978-3-030-67835-7_47
2. Berns, F., Rossetto, L., Schoeffmann, K., Beecks, C., Awad, G.: V3C1 dataset: an evaluation of content characteristics. In: Proceedings of the 2019 on International Conference on Multimedia Retrieval, ICMR 2019, pp. 334–338. Association for Computing Machinery, New York (2019). https://doi.org/10.1145/3323873.3325051
3. Heller, S., et al.: Towards explainable interactive multi-modal video retrieval with vitrivr. In: Lokoč, J., et al. (eds.) MMM 2021. LNCS, vol. 12573, pp. 435–440. Springer, Cham (2021). https://doi.org/10.1007/978-3-030-67835-7_41
4. Radford, A., et al.: Learning transferable visual models from natural language supervision. CoRR arXiv:2103.00020 (2021)
5. Rossetto, L., Schoeffmann, K., Bernstein, A.: Insights on the V3C2 dataset. CoRR arXiv:2105.01475 (2021)
6. Rossetto, L., Schuldt, H., Awad, G., Butt, A.A.: V3C - a research video collection. CoRR arXiv:1810.04401 (2018)
7. Schoeffmann, K., et al.: Collaborative feature maps for interactive video search. In: Amsaleg, L., Guðmundsson, G.Þ, Gurrin, C., Jónsson, B.Þ, Satoh, S. (eds.) MMM 2017. LNCS, vol. 10133, pp. 457–462. Springer, Cham (2017). https://doi.org/10.1007/978-3-319-51814-5_41
8. Tran, L., et al.: A VR interface for browsing visual spaces at VBS2021. In: Lokoč, J., et al. (eds.) MMM 2021. LNCS, vol. 12573, pp. 490–495. Springer, Cham (2021). https://doi.org/10.1007/978-3-030-67835-7_50
9. Veselý, P., Mejzlík, F., Lokoč, J.: SOMHunter V2 at video browser showdown 2021. In: Lokoč, J., et al. (eds.) MMM 2021. LNCS, vol. 12573, pp. 461–466. Springer, Cham (2021). https://doi.org/10.1007/978-3-030-67835-7_45

IVIST: Interactive Video Search Tool in VBS 2022

Sangmin Lee, Sungjune Park, and Yong Man Ro$^{(\boxtimes)}$

Image and Video Systems Lab, School of Electrical Engineering,
KAIST, Daejeon, South Korea
{sangmin.lee,sungjune-p,ymro}@kaist.ac.kr

Abstract. This paper presents the details of the proposed video retrieval tool, named Interactive VIdeo Search Tool (IVIST) for the Video Browser Showdown (VBS) 2022. In order to retrieve desired videos from a multimedia database, it is necessary to match queries from humans and video shots in the database effectively. To boost such matching relationship, we propose a multi-modal-based retrieval scheme that can fully utilize various modal features of the multimedia data and synthetically consider the matching relationships between modalities. The proposed IVIST maps human-made queries (*e.g.*, language) and features (*e.g.*, visual and sound) from the database into a multi-modal matching latent space through deep neural networks. Based on the latent space, videos with high similarity to the query feature are suggested as candidate shots. Prior knowledge-based filtering can be further applied to refine the results of candidate shots. Moreover, the user interface of the tool is devised in a user-friendly way for interactive video searching.

Keywords: Video Browser Showdown · Interactive video retrieval · Multi-modal matching

1 Introduction

The Video Browser Showdown (VBS) is a video retrieval challenge held at the International Conference on MultiMedia Modeling (MMM) [12,15] annually from 2012. In VBS, there are three searching scenarios to be evaluated: visual known-item search (visual KIS), textual known-item search (textual KIS), and ad-hoc video search (AVS). For KIS, participants need to search a specific instance, given a single video clip (visual KIS) or descriptions explaining a video clip (textual KIS). For AVS, a general description is provided to search as many target videos as possible [5,10]. With these scenarios, participants try to find desirable videos and shots from datasets [1,13,14] with thousands of videos as fast as possible by using their own video retrieval tool.

In this paper, we introduce an enhanced version of Interactive VIdeo Search Tool (IVIST) for VBS 2022. It is needed to match queries from humans and

---

S. Lee and S. Park—Both authors have contributed equally to this work.

© Springer Nature Switzerland AG 2022
B. Þór Jónsson et al. (Eds.): MMM 2022, LNCS 13142, pp. 524–529, 2022.
https://doi.org/10.1007/978-3-030-98355-0_49

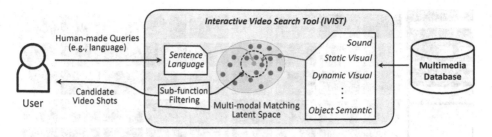

Fig. 1. Concept of the proposed IVIST. It effectively matches human-made queries and videos in multimedia database by exploiting multi-modal capability.

videos in the database effectively for retrieving desired videos from a multimedia database. We propose a multi-modal-based retrieval method that fully exploits various modal features of multimedia data and integrally take into account the matching relationships between modalities. The relationship between each modality can be complemented with each other through the multi-modal scheme. The proposed IVIST maps human-made queries (*e.g.*, language) and features (*e.g.*, visual and sound) from the database into a multi-modal matching latent space through deep neural networks. Video shots that are similar to the query feature are presented as candidate video shots for users. Further, there are several sub-functions such as place recognition, similar shot finding, and video category searching to refine candidate video shots for efficient video searching.

The following sections are described as follows: Section 2 describes the overall framework of IVIST, Sect. 3 introduces the main functions of IVIST, and Sect. 4 concludes the paper.

2   Overall Framework

IVIST is composed of the front-end, back-end, and database. For the front-end, ReactJS is adopted to build the user interface, and it takes and sends input queries to the back-end server. In addition, it displays the results acquired from the back-end. For the back-end, Flask is deployed to play an intermediate role between the front-end and database. To store the meta-data, MongoDB is adopted because it supports quick searching capability and flexible schema.

The overall architecture is shown in Fig. 1. Through the user interface, users can send human-made queries such as language-based scene description. Then, the most relevant results are obtained and sent back to the user interface by using multi-modal matching latent space. The candidate shots are obtained by measuring the feature similarity. The candidate shots can be further refined by adopting other sub-functions such as place detection. The user interface of IVIST is depicted in Fig. 2. The searching functions are visualized in the left side bar to be controlled intuitively, and the retrieval results are displayed for user convenience to find the desirable video shots.

Fig. 2. The user interface of IVIST. It present various candidate video shots for user-made query.

3 Retrieval Functions

In VBS 2022, IVIST adopts main multi-modal retrieval function and sub-functions for refining candidate shots. The sub-functions includes the existing functions used in the previous VBS (*i.e.,* object detection, scene-text recognition, dominant-color finding, and place recognition) and the newly augmented functions (*i.e.,* similar image searching, and video category searching).

3.1 Multi-modal Retrieval Function

Users can send a language query which describes a certain video clip, so that the model find the corresponding target video shots. To this end, we construct multi-modal matching latent space by training the deep networks to be aware of the correspondence among multi-modalities. Transformer-based extractor [18] which can effectively recognize sequential information is adopted to obtain latent feature of the language query. Various modalities (*e.g.,* sound, static visual, and dynamic visual) from multimedia database are encoded and fused through deep neural networks such as the transformer and mapped into the constructed latent space. In the multi-modal matching latent space, we can obtain candidate video shots through comparison with the query feature. The extracted query feature is compared with the stored video shot features to find the video shots which are close to the input query mostly. In addition, obtained candidate video shots can be further filtered by applying sub-functions such as place detection, similar image searching, and video category searching for efficient and user-friendly video searching. The model is trained with datasets with internet videos [2,11,19].

Fig. 3. The retrieval examples by querying the video category 'surf'.

3.2 Candidate Filtering Function

For object detection, IVIST adopts the object detection model, named HTC [4]. HTC is built upon Cascade R-CNN [3] and is trained with 91 classes of MS-COCO dataset [9]. For scene-text searching, PixelLink [6] and ASTER [16] are deployed for scene-text detection and scene-text recognition. Given the cropped images which are detected by PixelLink and supposed to contain scene-text, ASTER could recognize which scene-text exists in the image. Dominant-color finding is a function to filter the images depending on their dominant colors. For example, when the user tries to find the shot where a airplane in flying in the sky, the user could filter the images which consist of the sky blue color dominantly at the first. For place recognition, IVIST adopts VGG-16 [17] and ResNet-152 [8] to recognize the places [20].

In the case that the retrieval results contain video shots which look similar with the target video shot (but not the exact target video shot that the users need to find), it would be convenient to use the similar video shots and find the target video by using the image similarity. To this end, first, IVIST extracts image features via ResNet [8] pretrained on ImageNet [7]. Note that, the key frames are used to extract image features. Then, for each image, the image similarity between other images from different videos is calculated, and the image list could be obtained in the order of the image similarity (having top-K similar images). Therefore, when the users select an image which looks similar with the target video shot and send an image query, IVIST could retrieve the video shots which are top-K similar images with the query image. Finally, it would be easier for the users to find the desirable video shots by using similar image searching.

For visual KIS, textual KIS, and AVS, the video category could be a helpful method to find desirable video shots. For example, when the users try to find the video shots which contain bride and groom, the users could filter the videos which have a 'wedding' category. Similarly, if the users need to retrieve the video shots described as 'A man is surfing.', the users could select a 'surf' category to filter out the videos among the thousands of video datasets as shown in Fig. 3. To this end, IVIST exploits the video category description provided by [1] to store the metadata in the database and use it for the desirable video retrieval.

4   Conclusion

This paper introduces the IVIST, a video retrieval tool for VBS 2022, focusing on improving multi-modal matching capabilities. By storing the various features in the database, IVIST could find the desirable video shots by sending a human-made language query describing the video shots. By exploiting multi-modal retrieval function and sub-functions for candidate filtering, the users are able to find the target video shots more efficiently. Moreover, the user interface of IVIST becomes more intuitive and user-friendly for interactive video searching.

References

1. Berns, F., Rossetto, L., Schoeffmann, K., Beecks, C., Awad, G.: V3c1 dataset: an evaluation of content characteristics. In: International Conference on Multimedia Retrieval, pp. 334–338 (2019)
2. Caba Heilbron, F., Escorcia, V., Ghanem, B., Carlos Niebles, J.: ActivityNet: a large-scale video benchmark for human activity understanding. In: IEEE/CVF Conference on Computer Vision and Pattern Recognition, pp. 961–970 (2015)
3. Cai, Z., Vasconcelos, N.: Cascade R-CNN: delving into high quality object detection. In: IEEE/CVF Conference on Computer Vision and Pattern Recognition, pp. 6154–6162 (2018)
4. Chen, K., et al.: Hybrid task cascade for instance segmentation. In: IEEE/CVF Conference on Computer Vision and Pattern Recognition, pp. 4974–4983 (2019)
5. Cobârzan, C., et al.: Interactive video search tools: a detailed analysis of the video browser showdown 2015. Multimedia Tools Appl. **76**(4), 5539–5571 (2016). https://doi.org/10.1007/s11042-016-3661-2
6. Deng, D., Liu, H., Li, X., Cai, D.: Pixellink: detecting scene text via instance segmentation. In: AAAI Conference on Artificial Intelligence, vol. 32 (2018)
7. Deng, J., Dong, W., Socher, R., Li, L.J., Li, K., Fei-Fei, L.: ImageNet: a large-scale hierarchical image database. In: IEEE/CVF Conference on Computer Vision and Pattern Recognition, pp. 248–255. IEEE (2009)
8. He, K., Zhang, X., Ren, S., Sun, J.: Deep residual learning for image recognition. In: IEEE/CVF Conference on Computer Vision and Pattern Recognition, pp. 770–778 (2016)
9. Lin, T.-Y., et al.: Microsoft COCO: common objects in context. In: Fleet, D., Pajdla, T., Schiele, B., Tuytelaars, T. (eds.) ECCV 2014. LNCS, vol. 8693, pp. 740–755. Springer, Cham (2014). https://doi.org/10.1007/978-3-319-10602-1_48

10. Lokoč, J., et al.: Interactive search or sequential browsing? A detailed analysis of the video browser showdown 2018. ACM Trans. Multimed. Comput. Commun. Appl. **15**(1), 1–18 (2019)
11. Miech, A., Zhukov, D., Alayrac, J.B., Tapaswi, M., Laptev, I., Sivic, J.: Howto100M: learning a text-video embedding by watching hundred million narrated video clips. In: IEEE/CVF International Conference on Computer Vision, pp. 2630–2640 (2019)
12. Rossetto, L., et al.: Interactive video retrieval in the age of deep learning-detailed evaluation of VBS 2019. IEEE Trans. Multimedia **23**, 243–256 (2020)
13. Rossetto, L., Schoeffmann, K., Bernstein, A.: Insights on the v3c2 dataset. arXiv preprint arXiv:2105.01475 (2021)
14. Rossetto, L., Schuldt, H., Awad, G., Butt, A.A.: V3C – a research video collection. In: Kompatsiaris, I., Huet, B., Mezaris, V., Gurrin, C., Cheng, W.-H., Vrochidis, S. (eds.) MMM 2019. LNCS, vol. 11295, pp. 349–360. Springer, Cham (2019). https://doi.org/10.1007/978-3-030-05710-7_29
15. Schoeffmann, K.: Video browser showdown 2012–2019: a review. In: International Conference on Content-Based Multimedia Indexing, pp. 1–4. IEEE (2019)
16. Shi, B., Yang, M., Wang, X., Lyu, P., Yao, C., Bai, X.: ASTER: an attentional scene text recognizer with flexible rectification. IEEE Trans. Pattern Anal. Mach. Intell. **41**(9), 2035–2048 (2018)
17. Simonyan, K., Zisserman, A.: Very deep convolutional networks for large-scale image recognition. arXiv preprint arXiv:1409.1556 (2014)
18. Vaswani, A., et al.: Attention is all you need. In: Advances in Neural Information Processing Systems, pp. 5998–6008 (2017)
19. Xu, J., Mei, T., Yao, T., Rui, Y.: MSR-VTT: a large video description dataset for bridging video and language. In: IEEE/CVF Conference on Computer Vision and Pattern Recognition, pp. 5288–5296 (2016)
20. Zhou, B., Lapedriza, A., Khosla, A., Oliva, A., Torralba, A.: Places: a 10 million image database for scene recognition. IEEE Trans. Pattern Anal. Mach. Intell. **40**(6), 1452–1464 (2017)

VERGE in VBS 2022

Stelios Andreadis[✉], Anastasia Moumtzidou, Damianos Galanopoulos,
Nick Pantelidis, Konstantinos Apostolidis, Despoina Touska,
Konstantinos Gkountakos, Maria Pegia, Ilias Gialampoukidis,
Stefanos Vrochidis, Vasileios Mezaris, and Ioannis Kompatsiaris

Information Technologies Institute/Centre for Research and Technology Hellas,
Thessaloniki, Greece
{andreadisst,moumtzid,dgalanop,pantelidisnikos,kapost,destousok,
gountakos,mpegia,heliasgj,stefanos,bmezaris,ikom}@iti.gr

Abstract. This paper presents VERGE, an interactive video search
engine that integrates multiple retrieval methodologies and also combines
them with reranking and fusion techniques. Moreover, a user interface,
implemented as a Web application, enables users to formulate queries,
view the top retrieved shots and watch the respective videos, before submitting a shot to a VBS task, all in an efficient and easy manner.

1 Introduction

VERGE is an interactive video search engine that provides a multitude of
retrieval capabilities along with a friendly and simple user interface (UI) for submitting queries and viewing the top results. With a long-standing participation
in the Video Browser Showdown (VBS) competition [17], VERGE is constantly
reformed in order to better tackle the competition's "Ad-Hoc Video Search"
(AVS) and "Known Item Search - Visual/Textual" (KIS-V, KIS-T) tasks. This
year, existing search modalities are improved, e.g. visual similarity and face
detection, others are extended, e.g. to more concepts and activities, while novel
concept-based late fusion techniques are introduced. Moreover, the VERGE UI
has been adapted accordingly to support all the different search approaches.

The paper is structured as follows: Sect. 2 presents the overall framework
of the VERGE engine, Sect. 3 continues with the detailed description of the
retrieval components, Sect. 4 illustrates the UI and some usage scenarios, and
Sect. 5 concludes with the future work.

2 The VERGE Framework

As depicted in Fig. 1, the VERGE framework consists of three layers. The first
layer contains the various retrieval modalities that are applied on the competition's datasets, i.e. V3C1 and V3C2 [16], and in most cases their results are
prestored in a database. The second layer refers to the services that can accept
queries and respond with the top results, i.e. the most relevant shots/videos.
The third layer is the Web Application UI that allows users to formulate their
queries, calls the services and visualises the retrieved results.

© Springer Nature Switzerland AG 2022
B. Þór Jónsson et al. (Eds.): MMM 2022, LNCS 13142, pp. 530–536, 2022.
https://doi.org/10.1007/978-3-030-98355-0_50

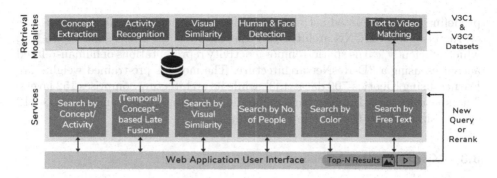

Fig. 1. The VERGE framework

3 Retrieval Modalities

3.1 Concept-Based Retrieval

This module annotates each keyframe with a pool of concepts, which comprises 1000 ImageNet concepts, a selection of 300 concepts of the TRECVID SIN task [14], 500 event-related concepts, 365 scene classification concepts, 580 object labels, 30 style-related concepts as well as 22 sports classification labels. To obtain the annotation scores for the 1000 ImageNet concepts, we used an ensemble method, averaging the concept scores from three pre-trained models that employ different DCNN architectures, i.e. the EfficientNet-B3, EfficientNet-B5 [19] and InceptionResNetV2. To obtain scores for the subset from the TRECVID SIN task, we trained and employed two models based on the EfficientNet-B1 and EfficientNet-B3 architectures on the official SIN task dataset. For the event-related concepts we used the pre-trained model of Event-Net [9]. Regarding the extraction of the scene-related concepts, we utilized the publicly available VGG16 model, fine-tuned on the Places365 dataset [23]. Object detection scores were extracted using models pre-trained on the established MS COCO and Open Images V4 datasets, with 80 and 500 detectable objects, respectively. For the style-related concepts we employed the pre-trained models of [20]. To label sports in video frames, we constructed a custom dataset with Web images from sports and utilized it to train a model of the EfficientNetB3 architecture. Finally, to offer a cleaner representation of the concept-based annotations we employed various text similarity measures between all concepts' labels. After manual inspection of the text analysis results we formed groups of very similar concepts for which we create a common label and assign the max score of its members.

3.2 Spatio-Temporal Activity Recognition

This module aims to extract human-related activities for each shot to enable filtering functionalities using the labels of the activities. A sorted list of 700 predefined human-related activities and the corresponding prediction scores are extracted using a DCNN architecture. Specifically, a 3D-CNN, similarly to [10], which efficiently learns spatio-temporal activity representations of human-related activities using a 3D-ResNet architecture. The model's pre-trained weights are learned using Kinetics-700 dataset [3], while its architecture comprises 152 layers. The spatio-temporal dimensions of the model's input correspond to 112×112 spatial size with 16 frames temporal duration.

3.3   Visual Similarity Search

This module retrieves visually similar content using DCNNs and two approaches will be tested. The first one uses a 1024 vector from a fine-tuned GoogleNet architecture [15] and an IVFADC index database vector that is created with these vectors [11]. The second one involves the use of a new Bayesian-based image retrieval method [13]. As input, we use the visual features extracted from the fc-7 layer of VGG-16 for each shot. Then, we compute the semantic affinities of them, transform them into a probability distribution and project them in the Hamming space via minimizing the Kullback-Leibler divergence. Next, Bayesian regression is used for learning the projection of visual features to the learnt hash codes. For achieving fast retrieval, we use k-NN on GPU [8] between hash codes.

3.4   Human and Face Detection

This module aims to detect and count humans and human faces in each frame shot, so that the user can easily distinguish the results of single-human or multi-human activities. The detection can be performed in crowd-center scenes, where partial occlusions among humans or between humans and objects are possible to occur. To deal with this, a dataset named CrowdHuman [18] is selected, which includes annotations for the humans and their corresponding faces. Using this dataset, an optimal, in terms of speed and accuracy, object detector YoloV4 [1] is fine-tuned, intended to extract the detected human silhouettes and faces, making it possible to count the total number of them.

3.5   Text to Video Matching Module

The text to video matching module inputs a complex free-text query along with a set of video shots and returns a ranked list with the most relative video shots w.r.t. to the input textual query. For this, we utilize the attention-based dual encoding network presented in [6]. This network is trained to transform video-caption samples into a new joint embedding space. In this embedding space, a straightforward comparison between free-text queries and video or image instances is feasible. The network consists of two similar sub-networks [4] in parallel, one for the video shot and one for the natural language sentence. Each sub-network consists of multiple levels of encoding, i.e. using mean-pooling, attention-based [6], bi-GRU sequential model, and CNN layers. Following the state-of-the-art approach [4–6], the improved marginal ranking loss [5] is used to train the entire network. Following [7], we effectively combine the results delivered from multiple trained models. Regarding the training data, we use a combination of four large-scale video caption datasets: MSR-VTTT [22], TGIF [12], ActivityNet [2] and Vatex [21]. The ResNet-152 deep network trained on the ImageNet-11k dataset is used as initial video shot representation.

3.6   Concept-Based Late Fusion

This module combines two or more visual concepts (Sect. 3.1) and generates a sorted list of shots using a late fusion approach. First, separate lists of shot probabilities for each concept are created. Then, the intersection at shot level of the concepts is computed, which is reranked by an objective function that respects the principle that the higher the concept probabilities or the more relevant the shots are, the higher their scores are. To achieve this, we compute the difference of the concept probabilities for all possible concept pairs and then we apply the inverse exponential function to them.

3.7   Temporal Late Fusion

This module incorporates two or more visual concepts (Sect. 3.1) and generates a sorted list of unique videos using a late fusion approach. At first, for each concept a separate list of shot probabilities is created. Then, the intersection of concepts per video is computed and only the first valid ordered tuple of each video is kept. Those shots are reranked through an objective function, which preserves the concept-based late fusion principles (Sect. 3.6) and also favours the ordering of the concepts by using a weighting function.

4   User Interface and Interaction Modes

The VERGE UI (Fig. 2) is provided as a Web application that allows its users to easily make queries, view the results, watch the corresponding videos and submit their selection during the VBS contest. The main characteristics that we aim for the UI to have are compactness (minimum usage of space for maximum functionality), intuitiveness (when a user sees it, they know exactly what to do), and efficiency (the speed of using it is not frustrating).

The VERGE interface contains three basic parts: the dashboard menu on the left, the results panel in the center, and the filmstrip on the bottom. The *dashboard menu* includes a countdown timer, indicating the remaining time for submission during an active VBS task, an undo button to return to the previous results, a switch button to select between a new query and reranking, and, finally, the search modules. The first search option is a text input field, where the user is able to describe with free text query what they are looking for (Sect. 3.5). The second option offers a long list of concepts and activities (Sects. 3.1, 3.2) that the user can search with scrolling or autocomplete. Multiple selection is

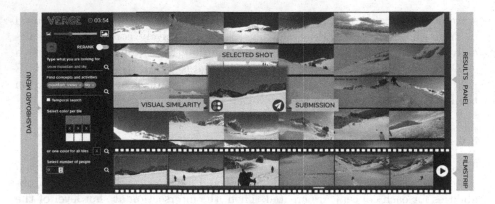

Fig. 2. The VERGE user interface

supported for late fusion (Sect. 3.6) and a checkbox can activate temporal fusion (Sect. 3.7). The third option is search by color, where the user is able to paint certain tiles of the image to be sought in a 3×3 grid. The fourth option is to retrieve shots with a set number of people appearing in them (Sect. 3.4). The top retrieved shots of all search modalities are visualised in the *results panel* in a grid view. Hovering over a shot shows two additional buttons: one for applying the fifth and final retrieval method, i.e. visual similarity (Sect. 3.3), and another one for submitting a shot to a contest task. When a shot is clicked, the *filmstrip* is updated with all the frames of the video it belongs to, while the button on the right can play the video in a popup.

To illustrate the usability of VERGE in the VBS contest, we discuss briefly here some cases that tackle actual queries of VBS 2021. For an AVS task that requests shots of "two women walking and talking", the user can fuse the concept "female_person" with the activities "walking" and "talking", and then rerank by setting the desired number of people to two. For a KIS-V task that shows a snow mountain and the sky, the user can search by color, painting the top tiles light blue and the bottom tiles white, and when a relevant image appears, they can apply visual similarity in order to get more results and find the specific shot (Fig. 2). Finally, for a KIS-T task that reads "a hand opening the window of a mountain hut", the user can use this exact sentence for free-text search and the expected shot can be found within the top twenty results.

5 Future Work

While a constant goal is to improve the developed retrieval algorithms both in terms of performance and time efficiency, the experience of VBS 2022 will drive the next modifications in the available search options as well as the VERGE UI.

Acknowledgements. This work has been supported by the EU's Horizon 2020 research and innovation programme under grant agreements H2020-825079 Mind-Spaces, H2020-780656 ReTV, and H2020-832921 MIRROR.

References

1. Bochkovskiy, A., Wang, C.Y., Liao, H.Y.M.: YOLOV4: optimal speed and accuracy of object detection. arXiv preprint arXiv:2004.10934 (2020)
2. Caba Heilbron, F., et al.: ActivityNet: a large-scale video benchmark for human activity understanding. In: Proceedings of IEEE CVPR 2015, pp. 961–970 (2015)
3. Carreira, J., Noland, E., Hillier, C., Zisserman, A.: A short note on the kinetics-700 human action dataset. arXiv preprint arXiv:1907.06987 (2019)
4. Dong, J., Li, X., Xu, C., Ji, S., He, Y., et al.: Dual encoding for zero-example video retrieval. In: Proceedings of IEEE CVPR 2019, pp. 9346–9355 (2019)
5. Faghri, F., Fleet, D.J., et al.: VSE++: improving visual-semantic embeddings with hard negatives. In: Proceedings of BMVC 2018 (2018)
6. Galanopoulos, D., Mezaris, V.: Attention mechanisms, signal encodings and fusion strategies for improved ad-hoc video search with dual encoding networks. In: Proceedings of ACM ICMR 2020 (2020)
7. Galanopoulos, D., Mezaris, V.: Hard-negatives or Non-negatives? A hard-negative selection strategy for cross-modal retrieval using the improved marginal ranking loss. In: Proceedings of IEEE/CVF ICCVW 2021 (2021)
8. Garcia, V., Debreuve, E., Barlaud, M.: Fast K nearest neighbor search using GPU. In: Proceedings of ACM ICMR 2008. ACM (2008)
9. Guangnan, Y., Yitong, L., Hongliang, X., et al.: EventNet: a large scale structured concept library for complex event detection in video. In: Proceedings of ACM MM 2015 (2015)
10. Hara, K., et al.: Can spatiotemporal 3D CNNs retrace the history of 2D CNNs and ImageNet? In: Proceedings of IEEE CVPR 2018 (2018)
11. Jegou, H., et al.: Product quantization for nearest neighbor search. IEEE Trans. Pattern Anal. Mach. Intell. 33(1), 117–128 (2010)
12. Li, Y., Song, Y., Cao, L., Tetreault, J., et al.: TGIF: a new dataset and benchmark on animated GIF description. In: Proceedings of IEEE CVPR 2016 (2016)
13. Lin, Z., Ding, G., Hu, M., Wang, J.: Semantics-preserving hashing for cross-view retrieval. In: Proceedings of IEEE CVPR 2015 (2015)
14. Markatopoulou, F., Moumtzidou, A., Galanopoulos, D., et al.: ITI-CERTH participation in TRECVID 2017. In: Proceedings of TRECVID 2017 Workshop, USA (2017)
15. Pittaras, N., Markatopoulou, F., Mezaris, V., Patras, I.: Comparison of fine-tuning and extension strategies for deep convolutional neural networks. In: Amsaleg, L., Guðmundsson, G.Þ, Gurrin, C., Jónsson, B.Þ, Satoh, S. (eds.) MMM 2017. LNCS, vol. 10132, pp. 102–114. Springer, Cham (2017). https://doi.org/10.1007/978-3-319-51811-4_9
16. Rossetto, L., Schuldt, H., Awad, G., Butt, A.A.: V3C – a research video collection. In: Kompatsiaris, I., Huet, B., Mezaris, V., Gurrin, C., Cheng, W.-H., Vrochidis, S. (eds.) MMM 2019. LNCS, vol. 11295, pp. 349–360. Springer, Cham (2019). https://doi.org/10.1007/978-3-030-05710-7_29
17. Schoeffmann, K., Lokoč, J., Bailer, W.: 10 years of video browser showdown. In: Proceedings of ACM MM 2021, pp. 1–3 (2021)
18. Shao, S., Zhao, Z., Li, B., Xiao, T., Yu, G., et al.: CrowdHuman: a benchmark for detecting human in a crowd. arXiv preprint arXiv:1805.00123 (2018)
19. Tan, M., Le, Q.V.: EfficientNet: rethinking model scaling for convolutional neural networks. arXiv preprint arXiv:1905.11946 (2019)

20. Tan, W.R., et al.: Ceci n'est pas une pipe: a deep convolutional network for fine-art paintings classification. In: 2016 IEEE ICIP, pp. 3703–3707. IEEE (2016)
21. Wang, X., et al.: VATEX: a large-scale, high-quality multilingual dataset for video-and-language research. In: Proceedings of IEEE/CVF ICCV 2019, pp. 4581–4591 (2019)
22. Xu, J., Mei, T., et al.: MSR-VTT: a large video description dataset for bridging video and language. In: Proceedings of IEEE CVPR 2016, pp. 5288–5296 (2016)
23. Zhou, B., Lapedriza, A., et al.: Places: a 10 million image database for scene recognition. IEEE Trans. PAMI 40(6), 1452–1464 (2017)

AVSeeker: An Active Video Retrieval Engine at VBS2022

Tu-Khiem Le[1(✉)], Van-Tu Ninh[1], Mai-Khiem Tran[2,3,4], Graham Healy[1], Cathal Gurrin[1], and Minh-Triet Tran[2,3,4]

[1] Dublin City University, Dublin, Ireland
tukhiem.le4@mail.dcu.ie, tu.ninhvan@adaptcentre.ie
[2] University of Science, VNU-HCM, Ho Chi Minh City, Vietnam
[3] John von Neumann Institute, VNU-HCM, Ho Chi Minh City, Vietnam
[4] Vietnam National University, Ho Chi Minh City, Vietnam

Abstract. Exploring video clips in a vast collection of videos is a difficult task. It is necessary to provide an efficient system for users to express the information need for sought events in that video collection. Thus, we propose to develop AVSeeker – an active video retrieval engine – to assist users in finding appropriate moments in videos with two main query types: textual descriptions and visual examples. The main characteristic of AVSeekeris that we change the retrieval engine from a passive system to an active one, which narrows the search space by gaining clues from users through an interactive relevance feedback manner. The AVSeeker is based on the LifeSeeker system from the annual Lifelog Search Challenge with the addition of an interactive relevance feedback via concept recommendation, enriched temporal concepts, and query-by-sketch functionality.

Keywords: Video retrieval system · Interactive relevance feedback retrieval system · Query by sketch

1 Introduction

Retrieving items from a large multimedia collection (known-item search) is a nontrivial problem and many research benchmarking challenges have been established to progress the domain. The Video Browser Showdown (VBS) [13] is one such challenge for video retrieval, which is held annually to evaluate different interactive video search engines. It is a live competition that provides a fair and accurate comparison of many interactive video retrieval system. In the VBS, a query can be in the form of a text in which new information is extended gradually to mimic the human's information seeking process, or in the form of a short video so that users can formulate the query themselves.

In this work, we present the Active Video Seeker (AVSeeker) - an interactive video search engine - with the core infrastructure inherited from our interactive lifelog retrieval system (LifeSeeker [8,9]), which competed in the Lifelog Search

© Springer Nature Switzerland AG 2022
B. Þór Jónsson et al. (Eds.): MMM 2022, LNCS 13142, pp. 537–542, 2022.
https://doi.org/10.1007/978-3-030-98355-0_51

Challenge (LSC) [5] for several years. AVSeeker is further enhanced with new relevant feedback search mechanism using concept recommendation and visual similarity search using sketch.

The main contributions of this paper are: (1) AVSeekeris introduced which incorporates a novel search mechanism in which the system actively suggests a list of relevant concepts related to the queries to refine the retrieval results rather than having the system passively return paginated candidate results in response to the user input; (2) A new temporal concept enrichment profess is proposed which enriches the concepts extracted from a video clip by integrating action/activity recognition; (3) A new query-by-sketch mechanism is described, which allows a user to retrieve the images by sketching the scene, which can help to bridge the limitation in the number of available visual concepts from the concept detectors.

2   Related Work

The most recent edition of the Video Browser Showdown (VBS) was in 2021 and we will now introduce some of the notable systems that participated in 2021. Vitrivr [6], achieved the highest score in the challenge. The authors of the system inherited some video pre-processing techniques of its predecessor [12] to enrich the metadata of the video for efficient retrieval, including Optical Character Recognition (OCR), Automatic Speech Recognition (ASR), concept enrichment using Faster-RCNN model pre-trained on the Openimages V4 dataset. Additionally, the system was also enhanced with the temporal querying mechanism and an efficient index structure for similarity search, including text and image search, which were claimed to increase the overall score of the searched results.

The video search engine from the SOMHunter team [7] also provided the same mechanisms of both temporal query and image search, however, with a different implementation. However, their main contribution was a customised relevance feedback mechanism to be used with self-organising maps (SOMs) [7] where users provided positive and negative examples for better localization of the exact result. The keywords of example frames were also used as a basis for keyword refinement after the relevance feedback process. This proposed feature showed its efficiency in VBS'20 by achieving the highest score in the competition.

For AVSeeker, we also integrated some typical features of such state-of-the-art interactive video retrieval systems, and propose a new interactive video retrieval technique via user feedback through concept suggestions to narrow the searching corpus. The description of our system is discussed detailed in Sect. 3.

3   AVSeeker – An Active Video Retrieval System

AVSeeker is developed based on our current lifelog retrieval system, which is LifeSeeker 2.0 [9], by directly extending the system to support video search. The main differences between the two retrieval system are discussed in Sects. 3.2, 3.3, and 3.4.

3.1 LifeSeeker – An Overview of Our Predecessor Retrieval System

LifeSeeker is an interactive retrieval system designed for the LSC challenge that emphasises on still-image search based on a given text query. The LSC dataset contains a collection of lifelog images in the first person perspective and the challenge requires the search engine to find one image which matches the query as quickly and accurately as possible. LifeSeeker operates on a free-text-search mechanism in which the system matches a given text query with a set of lifelog images. This was achieved by converting the text query and images into the same vector space and compare the similarity between the query's vector and the images' vectors. The images in the dataset were processed by multiple detectors to extract visual concepts, including objects [1], scene categories and scene attributes [18], and scene texts [2], for matching with the text query. An Elasticsearch [4] server was deployed to aid the process of indexing and retrieving the relevant images. Additionally, a Bag-of-Words matching mechanism was also implemented and served as a extra option for searching. Lastly, LifeSeeker also provided a visual similarity search function so that the user can retrieve the images which share the similar scene and structure.

Apart from inheriting the LifeSeeker's core functionality, we introduce our first video search prototype AVSeeker that is customised for the video search task. Given the differences between the LSC and VBS datasets (video keyframes and not lifelog images), AVSeeker is further enhanced with new search mechanisms described in detail in the following sections.

3.2 Active Video Search via Relevance Feedback Mechanism Using Concept Recommendation

We inherit the idea of the Akinator[1] application, which is a game trying to guess of which characters or objects the player is thinking, using a series of questions generated by the machine and obtaining corresponding multiple choice answers from the user. Based on this guessing game, we try to transform our passive search system into an active retrieval engine that supports the user during the searching process. In conventional passive search systems, the user needs to think of relevant concepts related to the information needed based on the description of the query, which depends heavily on the ability of the user and ultimately relies too much on the user to know which concepts are likely to assist in finding relevant content. In contrast, for an active retrieval engine, the mutual interaction between the user and the retrieval engine is more important. In AVSeeker, the system acts as an assistant for the user during the searching progress by suggesting related concepts to the query based on an initial input given by the user to narrow the set of relevant items.

In detail, the process of active video search via relevance feedback mechanism using concept recommendation follows three steps as follows:

1. At first, the user inputs some initial concepts that are best described the scene into the text search box, which is the conventional approach.

---

[1] https://en.akinator.com.

2. The system follows a concept pre-processing pipeline to retain important concepts (e.g. objects, animals, environment) and inputs them into ConceptNet[2] [14] to enhance the general context-understanding of the concepts (e.g. location, type, usage, related terms) for the construction of concept suggestion. An initial ranked list of relevant items which are related to corresponding concepts is returned to the user.
3. A list of scene-relevant concept is recommended to the user to gather the user feedback. Thereby, the result set is then quickly narrowed to a smaller set of relevant scenes.

3.3 AVSeeker's Extended Features from LifeSeeker

In LifeSeeker, we already have the mechanism to retrieve events based on concept matching. The more accurate concepts that can be extracted from the visual data, the better the performance. With each video clip, in addition to the information in the still image, we can also exploit information about the motion between the image frames. For instance, a video of a car running on a busy street and the other one with a car running on a highway can be distinguished via the movement trajectory of the vehicle. Additionally, other videos related to human understanding can also be recognized via the detection of the actions of the characters in the video. In this way, we find more concepts from a video clip for our search engine to work on. To achieve this, we apply the solution of finding objects based on their visual features and especially movement trajectories to the algorithm proposed by Nguyen et al. [11]. Furthermore, we employ the solutions from Vo et al. in [15,16] for finding action proposals, then we classify those candidates into known activities. This is similar to the process of detecting objects from images: we obtain a region proposal for an object, then we classify the region into known objects from training data.

3.4 Visual Similarity Search by Sketch

In the VBS challenge, the queries are not only expressed in text, but they also can be given as a visual example. For these queries, we integrate conventional visual similarity search approaches including Bag-of-Features model using Scaled-Invariant-Feature-Transform (SIFT) [10] and Speeded-up Robust Features (SURF) [3], region-based color clustering, Nearest-Neighbor search of the latent space representation of video frames. Additionally, we also integrate a Query-by-Sketch function into the AVSeeker by extending previous work in [17]. Once the user finishes a sketch and submits to the AVSeeker server, a pre-trained model extended from [17] is employed to adapt the sketch features to the video frame domain for similarity mapping. This process returns a ranked-list of videos in descending order of Euclidian distance in the latent space of the sketch feature.

---

[2] https://conceptnet.io/.

4 Conclusion

In this paper, we introduce our initial work of an active video retrieval – the AVSeeker – competing in VBS 2022. The AVSeeker inherits most of the features from its predecessor lifelog retrieval engine – LifeSeeker, and enhances the user interaction for large-scaled visual data search by proposing a concept-recommendation system which plays a role of an interactive relevance feedback to improve the precision of the search result. The AVSeeker also supports Query-by-Sketch function for queries that require visual similarity search.

Acknowledgement. This work was supported by the ADAPT Centre (Grant 13/RC/ 2106; 13/RC/2106_P2) and Insight Centre for Data Analytics (Grant SFI/12/RC/ 2289_P2) funded by Science Foundation Ireland Research Centres Programme and co-funded by the European Regional Development Fund.

References

1. Anderson, P., et al.: Bottom-up and top-down attention for image captioning and visual question answering. In: CVPR (2018)
2. Baek, Y., Lee, B., Han, D., Yun, S., Lee, H.: Character region awareness for text detection. In: Proceedings of the IEEE Conference on Computer Vision and Pattern Recognition, pp. 9365–9374 (2019)
3. Bay, H., Ess, A., Tuytelaars, T., Gool, L.V.: Speeded-up robust features (SURF). Comput. Vis. Image Underst. **110**, 346–359 (2008)
4. Gormley, C., Tong, Z.: Elasticsearch: The Definitive Guide, 1st edn. O'Reilly Media Inc., Sebastopol (2015)
5. Gurrin, C., et al.: Introduction to the third annual lifelog search challenge (LSC 2020). In: Gurrin, C., Jónsson, B.Þ., Kando, N., Schöffmann, K., Chen, Y.P., O'Connor, N.E. (eds.) Proceedings of the 2020 on International Conference on Multimedia Retrieval, ICMR 2020, Dublin, Ireland, 8–11 June 2020, pp. 584–585. ACM (2020). https://doi.org/10.1145/3372278.3388043
6. Heller, S., et al.: Towards explainable interactive multi-modal video retrieval with Vitrivr. In: Lokoč, J., et al. (eds.) MMM 2021. LNCS, vol. 12573, pp. 435–440. Springer, Cham (2021). https://doi.org/10.1007/978-3-030-67835-7_41
7. Kratochvíl, M., Veselý, P., Mejzlík, F., Lokoč, J.: SOM-hunter: video browsing with relevance-to-SOM feedback loop. In: Ro, Y.M., et al. (eds.) MMM 2020. LNCS, vol. 11962, pp. 790–795. Springer, Cham (2020). https://doi.org/10.1007/978-3-030-37734-2_71
8. Le, T.K., et al.: Lifeseeker: interactive lifelog search engine at LSC 2019. In: Proceedings of the ACM Workshop on Lifelog Search Challenge, LSC 2019, pp. 37–40. Association for Computing Machinery, New York (2019). https://doi.org/10.1145/3326460.3329162
9. Le, T.K., et al.: Lifeseeker 2.0: interactive lifelog search engine at LSC 2020. In: Proceedings of the Third Annual Workshop on Lifelog Search Challenge (2020)
10. LoweDavid, G.: Distinctive image features from scale-invariant keypoints. Int. J. Comput. Vis. **60**(2), 91–110 (2004)

11. Nguyen, T., Tran-Le, B., Thai, X., Nguyen, T.V., Do, M.N., Tran, M.: Traffic video event retrieval via text query using vehicle appearance and motion attributes. In: IEEE Conference on Computer Vision and Pattern Recognition Workshops, CVPR Workshops 2021, virtual, 19–25 June 2021, pp. 4165–4172. Computer Vision Foundation/IEEE (2021). https://doi.org/10.1109/CVPRW53098.2021.00470

12. Sauter, L., Amiri Parian, M., Gasser, R., Heller, S., Rossetto, L., Schuldt, H.: Combining boolean and multimedia retrieval in vitrivr for large-scale video search. In: Ro, Y.M., et al. (eds.) MMM 2020. LNCS, vol. 11962, pp. 760–765. Springer, Cham (2020). https://doi.org/10.1007/978-3-030-37734-2_66

13. Schoeffmann, K., Lokoc, J., Bailer, W.: 10 years of video browser showdown. In: Chua, T., et al. (eds.) MMAsia 2020: ACM Multimedia Asia, Virtual Event/Singapore, 7–9 March 2021, pp. 73:1–73:3. ACM (2020). https://doi.org/10.1145/3444685.3450215

14. Speer, R., Chin, J., Havasi, C.: Conceptnet 5.5: an open multilingual graph of general knowledge. In: AAAI (2017)

15. Vo, K., Yamazaki, K., Truong, S., Tran, M., Sugimoto, A., Le, N.: ABN: agent-aware boundary networks for temporal action proposal generation. IEEE Access **9**, 126431–126445 (2021). https://doi.org/10.1109/ACCESS.2021.3110973

16. Vo-Ho, V., Le, N., Yamazaki, K., Sugimoto, A., Tran, M.: Agent-environment network for temporal action proposal generation. In: IEEE International Conference on Acoustics, Speech and Signal Processing, ICASSP 2021, Toronto, ON, Canada, 6–11 June 2021, pp. 2160–2164. IEEE (2021). https://doi.org/10.1109/ICASSP39728.2021.9415101

17. Yuan, J., et al.: Shrec 2018 track: 2D scene sketch-based 3D scene retrieval. In: 3DOR@Eurographics (2018)

18. Zhou, B., Lapedriza, A., Khosla, A., Oliva, A., Torralba, A.: Places: a 10 million image database for scene recognition. IEEE Trans. Pattern Anal. Mach. Intell. **40**(6), 1452–1464 (2017)

VISIONE at Video Browser Showdown 2022

Giuseppe Amato(iD), Paolo Bolettieri(iD), Fabio Carrara(iD), Fabrizio Falchi(iD),
Claudio Gennaro(iD), Nicola Messina(✉)(iD), Lucia Vadicamo(iD),
and Claudio Vairo(iD)

ISTI-CNR, Via G. Moruzzi 1, 56124 Pisa, Italy
{giuseppe.amato,paolo.bolettieri,fabio.carrara,fabrizio.falchi,
claudio.gennaro,nicola.messina,lucia.vadicamo,claudio.vairo}@isti.cnr.it

Abstract. VISIONE is a content-based retrieval system that supports various search functionalities (text search, object/color-based search, semantic and visual similarity search, temporal search). It uses a full-text search engine as a search backend. In the latest version of our system, we modified the user interface, and we made some changes to the techniques used to analyze and search for videos.

Keywords: Content-based video retrieval · Video search · Information search and retrieval · Surrogate text representation

1 Introduction

In the last years, we witnessed an explosive growth in the amount of multimedia data present on the web. Nowadays, the pervasive use of social networks and cameras for surveillance applications generates a tremendous amount of multimedia content, which must be indexed for being efficiently browsed and retrieved. Visual data, in the past, were indexed using manual annotations. In high-data regimes, manual labeling is not feasible, so many techniques have been developed to search images or videos based on their content. In this paper, we describe VISIONE, a content-based video retrieval system for efficient and effective video search, which employs state-of-the-art deep learning techniques to extract visual content from videos at different levels of abstraction—from colors to high-level semantics. It employs a special textual encoding of the visual features and off-the-shelf full-text search tools for indexing all the different descriptors. With this expedient, on the one hand, we improve storage utilization by using the same data structure to store diverse multi-modal data; on the other, we exploit the scalability of off-the-shelf text search engines.

In this paper, we aim at describing the latest version of VISIONE for participating to the Video Browser Showdown (VBS) [10,17]. The first version of the tool [1,2] and the second [3] participated in previous editions of the competition, VBS 2019 and VBS 2021, respectively. VBS is an international video search competition that is held annually since 2012 and comprises three tasks, consisting

© Springer Nature Switzerland AG 2022
B. Þór Jónsson et al. (Eds.): MMM 2022, LNCS 13142, pp. 543–548, 2022.
https://doi.org/10.1007/978-3-030-98355-0_52

of visual and textual known-item search (KIS) and ad-hoc video search (AVS) [10,17]. Starting with VBS 2022, the V3C1 dataset [6] will be extended by V3C2 [18], obtaining a grand total of 17,235 video files and 2,300 h of video content. It is clear that the competition is becoming every year more and more challenging.

By analyzing the issues and the failure cases of VISIONE at previous VBS editions, we improved the tool in several ways, as described in the next section.

2   System Overview

VISIONE integrates the following search functionalities:

- **spatial object-based search**: the user can draw simple bounding-boxes on a canvas to specify the objects (along with their spatial locations) appearing in a target video scene.
- **spatial color-based search**: similar to object-based search, the user can draw simple bounding-boxes to specify the colors (along with their spatial locations) that appear in a target scene.
- **free text search**: the user can provide a textual description, in natural language, of a video scene.
- **visual similarity search**: the user can use an image (selected from the results of a previous search or from the web) as a query to search for video keyframes *visually* similar to it.
- **semantic similarity search**: the user can select an image from a search results list to retrieve video keyframes that are *semantically* similar to it.
- **temporal search**: the above search features can be used to simultaneously search for two different scenes that are temporally close in a video clip.

One of the main characteristics of our system is that all the features extracted from the video keyframes, as well as from the user query, are transformed into textual encodings so that an off-the-shelf full-text search engine is employed to support large-scale indexing and searching (see [3] for further details).

While the object/color and similarity search functionalities have been present in VISIONE since its first version [1], the text search and the temporal search were introduced last year [3]. The semantic similarity search (Sect. 2.1), although not initially foreseen in the second release of VISIONE [3], was included in the system as a test functionality a few weeks before the last VBS competition (June 2021). Since our team users gave positive feedback on this new feature, we decided to integrate it into this year's system as well. In addition, some techniques used for extracting dominant colors, objects, and visual features have been modified since just before the last VBS competition, as described in Sect. 2.2. We would like to note that VISIONE used to support a *keyword search* (query by scene tags) that has been removed from the system this year for two main reasons: on the one hand to improve the usability of the system (having too many search options could be confusing especially for novice users); on the other because we noticed that during the last competition this tool was rarely used in favor of the textual search that gives the possibility to use more detailed descriptions of a target scene than a list of tags. Finally, looking forward to VBS 2022, the user interface has been redesigned as described in Sect. 2.3.

Fig. 1. Qualitative results on GeM and TERN features for image-to-image retrieval on a sample image query.

2.1 Semantic Image Retrieval

In the last version of VISIONE, we employed multi-modal features extracted using a recently proposed architecture called TERN (Transformer Encoder Reasoning Network) to support the text-to-visual retrieval [11,12]. We recently observed that the visual features—the ones extracted from the visual path of TERN—carry very-high level semantics and are therefore good candidate descriptors for performing *semantic* content-based image retrieval (S-CBIR). This is reasonable, as the multi-modal contrastive learning used in TERN generates a space in which images with similar textual descriptions are close together.

The mainstream CBIR research is developed and evaluated in instance-retrieval scenarios, which do not require a deep semantic understanding to be solved. This is the case for the R-MAC [8] or GeM [16] descriptors. They cannot embed high-level semantics and entity-entity relationships, as they are more sensible to simple object classes and to very specific low-level patterns. Differently, the supervision with textual embeddings in TERN have the side effect of creating highly-semantic visual features, which can account for actions, object attributes, and relationships between multiple actors in the scene. We qualitatively compare the GeM versus the TERN features for a simple query image in Fig. 1. As we can notice, the GeM features can retrieve low-level matching images, like images with persons or with similar patterns in the background. Instead, the TERN descriptors can correctly capture the concept of *dancing people*.

Having very different natures, in VISIONE we incorporated both the GeM and TERN descriptors, covering both the instance and semantic retrieval needs.

2.2 Changes to Some Features Used in VISIONE

Compared to the last system description [3], we have modified and/or integrated some features used by our system for object, color, similarity, and text search. We used VarifocalNet [21], which is a dense object detector, instead of YOLOv3 [15], and we replaced R-MAC features [8], previously used to assess visual similarity, with features extracted using GeM [16]. Moreover, we significantly revised the color palette and the extraction of colors used for our color-based search. Previously, as indicated in [2,3], we used a color palette consisting of 32 colors, and we classified the color of each image pixel using a k-nearest neighbor

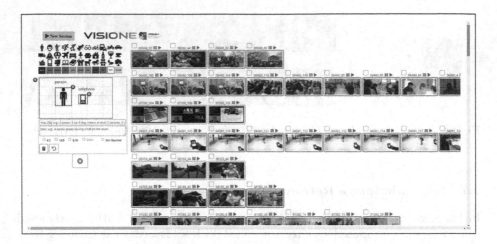

Fig. 2. New user interface. (Color figure online)

search between the actual pixel color and the colors in our palette. Nevertheless, many studies in the field of anthropology, visual psychology, and linguistics pointed out that some colors appear more memorable than others and that some basic color terms are used consistently and with consensus in different languages [5,7,19]. In particular, a set of 11 basic color terms (*white, black, red, green, yellow, blue, brown, purple, pink, orange, and gray*) are often used as universal color categories. Thus we decided to restrict our palette to these basic colors. To this purpose, we employed two *chip-based color naming* approaches [4,20] that, through the use of Probabilistic Latent Semantic Analysis and a parametric fuzzy model, respectively, provide ready-to-use hash tables to map RGB values to color names. We use both models to assign color terms to each pixel and then calculate the dominant colors for each of the 7×7 image cells. Finally, taking inspiration from [13] we are deploying in our system the CLIP features [14], aggregated through time, for text-to-video retrieval. In fact, with the increased dataset size, we need to better understand fine-grained actions. This aims to increase the discriminative power of the system—and in turn enhance the performance on textual-KIS and AVS tasks—by using state-of-the-art cross-modal features and leveraging the temporal domain.

2.3   New User Interface

From the analysis of the system logs collected in the last VBS, we realized that in some KIS tasks we were not able to submit the correct answer even though there was a keyframe of the target video (but not of the right shot) in the first positions of our result list. Therefore, we modified our user interface to improve the visualization and browsing of the results. In particular, inspired by other systems participating at VBS (e.g., [9,13]) we decided to place the search interface side by side with the browsing interface (respectively on the left and right of the GUI) and to display the search results by grouping those from the same video on a single row (Fig. 2). Now, the results from the same video can be inspected by moving horizontally in the browsing interface, those of different videos by moving vertically. In comparison to the previous interface—limited to only a total of 600 keyframes not grouped by video—this change allows us to set a maximum number of results for each video, enabling the browsing of a greater number of results. In addition, other minor adjustments have been made in the GUI, such as the possibility to add two or more canvas and text boxes for temporal queries (in the old interface the double canvas was fixed) and to display some details or select some search options when hovering the mouse over a result.

3   Conclusions and Future Work

In this paper, we presented the latest version of the VISIONE system for participating at the next edition of VBS. In particular, to improve the results visualization and browsing, we redesigned the interface taking inspiration from other VBS systems. We used the already deployed TERN features to perform semantic CBIR, and we replaced some color, similarity, and text search features to align with the current state-of-the-art in image and video retrieval. We plan to further improve the system by mixing TERN and CLIP features to obtain highly-semantic features for text-to-video retrieval. Furthermore, we plan to develop a system to manually weight different portions of the text to have finer control over the text queries.

Acknowledgements. This work was partially funded by AI4Media - A European Excellence Centre for Media, Society and Democracy (EC, H2020 n. 951911); AI4EU project (EC, H2020, n. 825619); AI4ChSites, CNR4C program (Tuscany POR FSE 2014-2020 CUP B15J19001040004).

References

1. Amato, G., et al.: VISIONE at VBS2019. In: Kompatsiaris, I., Huet, B., Mezaris, V., Gurrin, C., Cheng, W.-H., Vrochidis, S. (eds.) MMM 2019. LNCS, vol. 11296, pp. 591–596. Springer, Cham (2019). https://doi.org/10.1007/978-3-030-05716-9_51
2. Amato, G., et al.: The VISIONE video search system: exploiting off-the-shelf text search engines for large-scale video retrieval. J. Imaging **7**(5), 76 (2021)
3. Amato, G., et al.: VISIONE at video browser showdown 2021. In: Lokoč, J., et al. (eds.) MMM 2021. LNCS, vol. 12573, pp. 473–478. Springer, Cham (2021). https://doi.org/10.1007/978-3-030-67835-7_47
4. Benavente, R., Vanrell, M., Baldrich, R.: Parametric fuzzy sets for automatic color naming. JOSA A **25**(10), 2582–2593 (2008)
5. Berlin, B., Kay, P.: Basic Color Terms: Their Universality and Evolution. University of California Press, Berkeley (1991)

6. Berns, F., Rossetto, L., Schoeffmann, K., Beecks, C., Awad, G.: V3C1 dataset: an evaluation of content characteristics. In: Proceedings of the 2019 on International Conference on Multimedia Retrieval, pp. 334–338. Association for Computing Machinery (2019)
7. Boynton, R.M., Olson, C.X.: Salience of chromatic basic color terms confirmed by three measures. Vision. Res. **30**(9), 1311–1317 (1990)
8. Gordo, A., Almazan, J., Revaud, J., Larlus, D.: End-to-end learning of deep visual representations for image retrieval. Int. J. Comput. Vision **124**(2), 237–254 (2017)
9. Heller, S., et al.: Towards explainable interactive multi-modal video retrieval with vitrivr. In: Lokoč, J., et al. (eds.) MMM 2021. LNCS, vol. 12573, pp. 435–440. Springer, Cham (2021). https://doi.org/10.1007/978-3-030-67835-7_41
10. Lokoč, J., et al.: Is the reign of interactive search eternal? Findings from the video browser showdown 2020. ACM Trans. Multimed. Comput. Commun. Appl. **17**(3), 1–26 (2021)
11. Messina, N., Amato, G., Esuli, A., Falchi, F., Gennaro, C., Marchand-Maillet, S.: Fine-grained visual textual alignment for cross-modal retrieval using transformer encoders. arXiv preprint arXiv:2008.05231 (2020)
12. Messina, N., Falchi, F., Esuli, A., Amato, G.: Transformer reasoning network for image-text matching and retrieval. In: 2020 25th International Conference on Pattern Recognition (ICPR), pp. 5222–5229. IEEE (2021)
13. Peška, L., Kovalčík, G., Souček, T., Škrhák, V., Lokoč, J.: W2VV++ BERT model at VBS 2021. In: Lokoč, J., et al. (eds.) MMM 2021. LNCS, vol. 12573, pp. 467–472. Springer, Cham (2021). https://doi.org/10.1007/978-3-030-67835-7_46
14. Radford, A., et al.: Learning transferable visual models from natural language supervision. arXiv preprint arXiv:2103.00020 (2021)
15. Redmon, J., Farhadi, A.: YOLOv3: an incremental improvement. CoRR abs/1804.02767 (2018)
16. Revaud, J., Almazan, J., Rezende, R., de Souza, C.: Learning with average precision: training image retrieval with a listwise loss. In: International Conference on Computer Vision, pp. 5106–5115. IEEE (2019)
17. Rossetto, L., et al.: Interactive video retrieval in the age of deep learning - detailed evaluation of VBS 2019. IEEE Trans. Multimedia **23**, 243–256 (2020)
18. Rossetto, L., Schoeffmann, K., Bernstein, A.: Insights on the V3C2 dataset. arXiv preprint arXiv:2105.01475 (2021)
19. Sturges, J., Whitfield, T.A.: Salient features of munsell colour space as a function of monolexemic naming and response latencies. Vision. Res. **37**(3), 307–313 (1997)
20. Van De Weijer, J., Schmid, C., Verbeek, J., Larlus, D.: Learning color names for real-world applications. IEEE Trans. Image Process. **18**(7), 1512–1523 (2009)
21. Zhang, H., Wang, Y., Dayoub, F., Sunderhauf, N.: VarifocalNet: an IoU-aware dense object detector. In: Conference on Computer Vision and Pattern Recognition, pp. 8514–8523. IEEE, June 2021

Reinforcement Learning-Based Interactive Video Search

Zhixin Ma[1]([✉]), Jiaxin Wu[2], Zhijian Hou[2], and Chong-Wah Ngo[1]

[1] School of Computing and Information Systems, Singapore Management University, Singapore, Singapore
zxma.2020@phdcs.smu.edu.sg, cwngo@smu.edu.sg
[2] Department of Computer Science, City University of Hong Kong, Hong Kong, China
{jiaxin.wu,zjhou3-c}@my.cityu.edu.hk

Abstract. Despite the rapid progress in text-to-video search due to the advancement of cross-modal representation learning, the existing techniques still fall short in helping users to rapidly identify the search targets. Particularly, in the situation that a system suggests a long list of similar candidates, the user needs to painstakingly inspect every search result. The experience is frustrated with repeated watching of similar clips, and more frustratingly, the search targets may be overlooked due to mental tiredness. This paper explores reinforcement learning-based (RL) searching to relieve the user from the burden of brute force inspection. Specifically, the system maintains a graph connecting shots based on their temporal and semantic relationship. Using the navigation paths outlined by the graph, an RL agent learns to seek a path that maximizes the reward based on the continuous user feedback. In each round of interaction, the system will recommend one most likely video candidate for users to inspect. In addition to RL, two incremental changes are introduced to improve VIREO search engine. First, the dual-task cross-modal representation learning has been revised to index phrases and model user query and unlikelihood relationship more effectively. Second, two more deep features extracted from Slow-Fast and Swin-Transformer, respectively, are involved in dual-task model training. Substantial improvement is noticed for the automatic Ad-hoc search (AVS) task on the V3C1 dataset.

Keywords: Reinforcement learning · Query understanding · Feature enhancement · Interactive video retrieval

1 Introduction

Concept-based [8,11] and concept-free [2,13] search paradigms have enabled text-to-video search with either few keywords or a short sentence as query. Despite tremendous progress in this topic since the advancement in cross-modal representation learning, there are still various factors hindering effective video search. These factors can be attributed to system limitations such as the inability to model out-of-vocabulary query terms and user search intention, due to user because of

© Springer Nature Switzerland AG 2022
B. Þór Jónsson et al. (Eds.): MMM 2022, LNCS 13142, pp. 549–555, 2022.
https://doi.org/10.1007/978-3-030-98355-0_53

ambiguous query, or dataset bias for having several large clusters of shots with similar background scenes. In general, user-machine interaction is required to pave a way to resolve ambiguity or misinterpretation. Nevertheless, the current VIREO systems [8,14] fall short in dealing with any of these factors effectively. Specifically, the interaction is one-way, where the user interactively refines the query in a trial-and-error manner, while the system only responses to the current refined query by ignoring the search history and video browsing pattern.

Fig. 1. The retrieval result for a known-item visual query using the query terms: snow mountain, tree, sun. The shot on the right shows the search target. User has to manually inspect the search list to locate the search target.

In VBS 2021 [9], there are several snow-relevant queries, e.g., "There are snow covered mountains outside the hut.". Due to the limited query terms that can be expressed for these queries, most returned shots are snow landscapes. Figure 1 shows the result retrieved by VIREO search engine [14] for a visual known-item query. The query searches for a snow mountain scattered with trees on a sunny day. Due to the lack of distinctive terms to textually describe the visual scene, the returned shots are similar to each other with snow mountains and sunlight. As a consequence, a user has to exhaustively browse through the rank list, which is tiring and time-consuming especially when the ground-truth shot is ranked low in the list. Hierarchical clustering of shots for browsing could be a promising solution, which has been extensively explored in various VBS systems [1,10]. However, in the case when the shots are highly similar in terms of semantics and color-texture statistics, clustering may not be able to properly capture the subtle changes among shots. Relevance feedback, such as adopted by [12], is effective in distinguishing positive and negative examples but cannot adequately recommend satisfactory results when "the devil is in the details". This is not mentioning the fact that known-item-search involves only one true positive and relevance feedback is not always directly applicable to this task.

This paper aims to address the challenge as illustrated in Fig. 1 as a sequential search problem with AI planning. Inspired by [5], we extend the idea of lookahead inference from single video to a video collection. Specifically, in [5], an RL agent learns to locate the moment of interest in a video by interactively moving to the left or right of the current clip under navigation. Similarly but more broadly, our idea is to explore RL to provide a navigation path within and across videos such that user can identify the search target as rapidly as possible. The path is planned in advanced through learning and dynamically updated during search depending on user feedback. Given a rank list, user starts by clicking a shot for browsing. In a normal situation, a user will have few reactions upon watching a shot: video fast forward or backward browsing, retreat by picking another shot for browsing, or restart the search by refining query terms. The current VIREO search engine is considered passive because no learning is conducted to understand user browsing patterns and subsequent queries are treated independently. Reinforcement learning provides a mechanism to address both issues. First, a graph is constructed to connect the candidate shots with edges modeling their transition probabilities. With this graph, the user navigation path is traced with a long-term reward indicating the deviation from an optimal path. Second, a subsequent query is regarded as feedback of the current recommendation and is leveraged to adjust the navigation path. In other words, the search engine provides recommendations by actively tracking, memorizing, and learning-from-mistakes. The core engine of VIREO is based on the dual-task neural model that embeds cross-modal features in an interpretable latent space [13]. Several incremental changes are made to improve the core engine, aiming to reduce the sensitivity of query expression and enhance the underlying video representation. For example, the queries "A protest camp on a public square" and "Protest tents on a public square" express the same information need, but the return results can vary largely. In the current situation, user has to attempt multiple queries in the trial-and-error manner until reaching a satisfactory result. The improvement made is by decoding the embedded query into a list of canonical query terms for search. More concretely, two queries expressing the same information need are expected to be decoded with similar canonical terms such that their results do not vary arbitrarily. Other improvements made include training of dual-task model with a new unlikelihood loss function such that exclusive concepts (e.g., indoor versus outdoor) will not be decoded simultaneously to describe shot or query content.

2   Reinforcement Learning Based Interaction

The interaction between user and system is modelled as a graph traversing problem, where the graph provides video navigation paths for model-based reinforcement learning with Markov Decision Process. Precisely, an agent predicts the next navigation by either moving to the left or right of the current video or jumps to a shot of a new video, depending on the user feedback. To lay a skeleton for path navigation, we build a graph connecting all the shots in a video corpus, e.g., TVR and DiDeMo. For each shot, edges are established to link the preceding and succeeding shots, and the shots of other videos whose similarity is larger than an empirical threshold. The similarity is based on the average cosine similarity of both the semantic concepts and visual embeddings. The edge encodes the semantic difference between two shots. Specifically, we take the top-50 concepts in the shots and embed the difference in concepts as the edge representation.

The edges principally provide the information deviated from a shot. During the interactive search, a user can provide feedback such as "this is not a red rock mountain" or "the man should hold microphone" for the shot under navigation. The user feedback will be encoded together with the clip currently under browsing as well as the history of query as the representation for a new state. The agent then takes action a by selecting an edge from the current shot that best captures the feedback based on policy π. The policy network π_θ is implemented as a multi-layer perceptron. The corresponding shot will then be prompted to users for browsing.

The agent network is trained by simulation, similar to the idea of relative captioning [4]. Specifically, given a query, a list of candidate shots and the target shot, the network simulates the move at each step by receiving feedback. The simulated feedback is a concept randomly picked from the current or target shot. The concept is either an unwanted concept not present in the target or a missing concept not in the current shot. With this information, the agent receives a reward indicating whether a chosen path is optimal. We define the path optimality based on the shortest distance from the current shot to the target shot. If the selected edge is along the shortest path, the agent will receive a positive reward. We sample the starting nodes and trajectories (i.e., the shortest path) $\tau = (s_1, a_1, s_2, a_2, ...)$ from the graph. Each trajectory is divided into i.i.d. state-action pairs: $\{(s_i, a_i)\}$. We learn the policy using supervised learning by minimizing the loss function $L(a, \pi_\theta(s))$, which is the cross-entropy loss. Given the current policy and the simulated feedback, the value of taking an action can be computed by look-ahead policy based on the actor-critic algorithm [7]. During online search, the system needs extra computation time to encode query and video browsing history. Nevertheless, the time incurred is negligible for involving only encoding of the current feedback and video under browsing with the history observed so far. Overall, the interactive system still runs in real-time. Additional memory space is required to store the graph whose size is controllable depending on the number of edges that is allowed for a shot.

3   Query Understanding

The VIREO search engine is based on the dual-task model [13] to provide the initial search result. The model has only one decoder that interprets the semantic concepts underlying a video embedding. During retrieval, the query terms are matched directly with the decoded concepts for cosine similarity measure. As a consequence, the retrieval result changes depending on the query terms as well as how a query is phrased. During search, user often needs to interactively refine the query until reaching a satisfactory result before browsing. The refinement usually involves addition of new concepts, removal of the existing concepts upon seeing the search results, and rephrasing the original query. To relieve the user from these trial-and-error attempts, the dual-task model is revised to have two decoders. The second decoder interprets the query embedding with relevant semantic concepts. The decoded concepts are usually richer than the original set

Table 1. Comparing different query processing schemes for concept-based AVS search.

Concept selection	IACC.3 dataset			V3C1 dataset	
	tv16	tv17	tv18	tv19	tv20
Word2Vec	0.143	0.137	0.092	0.098	0.206
Direct [13]	0.152	0.132	0.090	0.096	0.173
Expand	0.183	0.243	0.142	0.139	0.260

Table 2. Incremental contributions of each feature enhancement for AVS search.

	Appearance feature		Motion feature	V3C1 dataset	
	ResNet, ResNeXt	Swin-Tranformer	SlowFast	tv19	tv20
L1	✓			0.184	0.262
L2		✓		0.172	0.258
L3	✓	✓		0.203	0.278
L4	✓		✓	0.185	0.306
L5		✓	✓	0.182	0.293
L6	✓	✓	✓	**0.207**	**0.325**

of query terms, covering subtle keywords overlooked by the user. For example, the subtle concepts decoded for the query "two or more men at a beach scene" are: sand, shore, ocean. These concepts are indirectly relevant and not likely to be included as query terms especially by novice users. Overall, the modification makes the search result relatively insensitive to query expression and is able to improve the search performance of automatic AVS. We empirically compare this method, which we call "Expand", to direct matching [13] and word2vec which consider only the original query terms. As shown in Table 1, the new methods significantly outperform the other methods across five different query sets. Despite using only concepts for AVS, the result has indeed surpassed the results of concept-free search [2].

Two other incremental improvements made includes enriching the current concept vocabulary with phrases and use of unlikelihood loss function to retrain the dual-task model. The dual-task model [13] considers only single words for training. We retrain the model using the phrases parsed from the video captions of the training datasets. In addition, the video decoder in the dual-task model treats each term independently. As the result, the potential "conflict" such as generating outdoor and indoor concepts, night and day concepts simultaneously is not resolved. We modify the unlikelihood loss function to explicit penalize the decoder when conflicting concepts are being fired by the decoder.

VIREO search engine [14] considers only appearance features (ResNet and ResNeXt) for video representation learning. The current system cannot effectively handle action-oriented query such as people clapping. We enhance the features with Swin-Transformer [6] and SlowFast [3], which are the state-of-the-art image and video classifiers, respectively. Table 2 shows the improvement introduced by different features. L1 shows the baseline performance with appearance features only. After appending Swin-Transformer feature, L3 improves 32 out of 50 queries. The queries "one or more picnic tables outdoors" and "a person wearing a backpack" gain the largest increase in average precision. When further appending slowfast feature, L6 improves 28 out of 50 queries. The queries which contain verbs, like "group of people clapping" and "one or more persons exercising in a gym", benefit from additional motion information.

4   Conclusion

We have presented one new feature, based on reinforcement learning, for VIREO search engine to particularly address the issue of "mental tiredness" in interactive search. Specifically, the engine recommends navigation path for user to browse, while dynamically adjusting the path based on feedbacks provided by user. Together with query understanding to smooth out result sensitivity, this two-way system-user interaction is expected to reduce unnecessary trial-and-error querying and exhaustive browsing from the user side. A user study will be conducted in the near future to investigate the degree in which the new feature can cut short the interactive search time and improve user experience. We have also introduced system improvements such as using unlikelihood loss function and state-of-the-art deep features for enhancing the performance of dual-task model. Although the effect of these changes is yet to be studied in VBS 2022, noticeable improvement has been obtained for TRECVid AVS automatic search.

Acknowledgment. This research was supported by the Singapore Ministry of Education (MOE) Academic Research Fund (AcRF) Tier 1 grant.

References

1. Barthel, K.U., Hezel, N., Mackowiak, R.: Navigating a graph of scenes for exploring large video collections. In: International Conference on Multimedia Modeling (2016)
2. Dong, J., et al.: Dual encoding for zero-example video retrieval. In: CVPR (2019)
3. Feichtenhofer, C., Fan, H., Malik, J., He, K.: Slowfast networks for video recognition. In: Proceedings of the IEEE/CVF ICCV (2019)
4. Guo, X., Rennie, S., Wu, H., Tesauro, G., Cheng, Y., Feris, R.S.: Dialog-based interactive image retrieval. In: Advances in Neural Information Processing Systems (2018)
5. He, D., Zhao, X., Huang, J., Li, F., Liu, X., Wen, S.: Read, watch, and move: reinforcement learning for temporally grounding natural language descriptions in videos. In: AAAI (2019)
6. Liu, Z., et al.: Swin transformer: hierarchical vision transformer using shifted windows. arXiv preprint arXiv:2103.14030 (2021)
7. Mnih, V., et al.: Asynchronous methods for deep reinforcement learning. In: 33rd International Conference on Machine Learning, ICML 2016 (2016)

8. Nguyen, P.A., Ngo, C.W.: Interactive search vs. automatic search: an extensive study on video retrieval. ACM Trans. Multimedia Comput. Commun. Appl. **17**(2), 1–24 (2021). https://doi.org/10.1145/3429457
9. Schoeffmann, K., Lokoč, J., Bailer, W.: 10 years of video browser showdown. In: Proceedings of the 2nd ACM International Conference on Multimedia in Asia (2021)
10. Schoeffmann, K., Taschwer, M., Boeszoermenyi, L.: The video explorer: a tool for navigation and searching within a single video based on fast content analysis. In: Proceedings of the first annual ACM SIGMM on Multimedia systems (2010)
11. Ueki, K., Hori, T., Kobayashi, T.: Waseda_meisei_softbank at trecvid 2019: ad-hoc video search. In: TRECVID (2019)
12. Veselý, P., Mejzlík, F., Lokoč, J.: Somhunter V2 at video browser showdown 2021. In: International Conference on Multimedia Modeling (2021)
13. Wu, J., Ngo, C.W.: Interpretable embedding for ad-hoc video search. In: Proceedings of the 28th ACM International Conference on Multimedia (2020)
14. Wu, J., Nguyen, P.A., Ma, Z., Ngo, C.W.: SQL-like interpretable interactive video search. In: International Conference on Multimedia Modeling (2021)

UIT at VBS 2022: An Unified and Interactive Video Retrieval System with Temporal Search

Khanh Ho[1,2]([✉]), Vu Xuan Dinh[1,2], Hong-Quang Nguyen[1,2], Khiem Le[1,2], Khang Dinh Tran[1,2], Tien Do[1,2], Tien-Dung Mai[1,2], Thanh Duc Ngo[1,2], and Duy-Dinh Le[1,2]

[1] University of Information Technology, Ho Chi Minh City, Vietnam
{19520624,18521662,18521297,19521689,18520896}@gm.uit.edu.vn,
{tiendv,dungmt,thanhnd,duyld}@uit.edu.vn
[2] Vietnam National University, Ho Chi Minh City, Vietnam

Abstract. This paper introduces our multimedia retrieval system for the Video Browser Showdown 2022 competition. The system was built for interactive retrieval task in a large video collection by focusing on four fundamental methods. First, we allow users to search by object features such as position and color. Secondly, our system also supports searching by text instances appearing in video segments. Next, we support searching by visual-textual association. And finally, the system can also search for videos containing a specific audio category. Moreover, we extend our framework to support temporal queries for all of the mentioned features.

Keywords: Video retrieval · Interactive video search · Temporal search

1 Introduction

Video Browser Showdown (VBS) is an annual competition aiming at the study of efficient multimedia retrieval systems for large-scale video collections. Participants in the competition are encouraged to develop an interactive retrieval tool to locate the exact video segment from an extensive database within a few minutes. The main challenge of these tasks is the ever-growing size of the video collection over time. For example, in the VBS 2022 competition, the total video duration has doubled with the addition of the second shard of the V3C dataset [13], up to 2300 h in video content. A more efficient way to represent and lookup data is needed for such extensive video collection.

With a database such large, a single filter might not be sufficient to locate a specific video. Previous works have shown that using a multi-modal query might be efficient for large-scale retrieval tasks [4,8]. For this reason, we introduce a multimedia retrieval system for the Video Browser Showdown 2022 competition. Our system relies on four fundamental features to perform retrieval. First, we allow users to search by object features such as position and color. This is

© Springer Nature Switzerland AG 2022
B. Þór Jónsson et al. (Eds.): MMM 2022, LNCS 13142, pp. 556–561, 2022.
https://doi.org/10.1007/978-3-030-98355-0_54

achieved by first indexing and retrieving the results produced by a state-of-the-art object detection method. Secondly, our system also supports searching by text instances appearing in video segments using PP-OCR [2] and Elasticsearch. In addition, we also support filtering videos containing a specific audio category using PANN [6] and searching by visual-textual association via CLIP [10]. Not only that, but we also extend our framework to support temporal queries for all of the mentioned features. Each of the functionalities above is indexed in a separated database, allowing them to be retrieved independently and merged later.

In the following sections, we will present more details about each feature in the proposed system. Section 2 introduces the general system framework along with four supported features, namely retrieval by object features, retrieval by text instances, visual-textual association and audio classification. Section 3 discusses the practical use of our system and how users can utilize the system efficiently for different retrieval tasks.

2 Proposed System

2.1 System Overview

Similar to many preexisting works in previous VBS iterations [14,15], our system consists of two processing stages, namely offline processing and online processing.

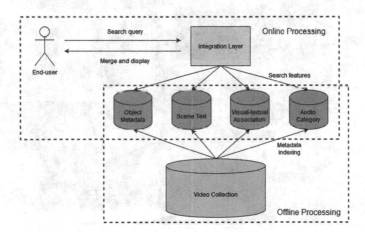

Fig. 1. Overview of our interactive video retrieval system with two processing stages and four search features.

In the offline processing stage, we computed features of video segments in V3C1 and V3C2 beforehand, then indexed them into corresponding databases for later uses. As the total number of videos in the two collections is enormous, indexing every frame in each video is expensive and impractical. However, we may not have sufficient information to represent the whole video segment if too few are indexed. Following the application of TransNetV2 [16] in VIRET's system [9], we also utilized this shot boundary detection method to split the video segment into multiple shorter ones, then indexed them instead.

The next stage is online processing, where end-users need to perform retrieval tasks on site. In the online processing stage, users can interact with the system through a visual interface. We support four kinds of query: object features, scene text, visual-textual association, and audio classification. In order to keep user queries simple and easy to use, we designed each feature to work independently, then merged their returned results. In other words, user queries can contain multiple search features; each feature operates in a separate database and returns its query result independently. After receiving results from different features, the system will attempt to merge them into a list of suitable videos, which will be displayed on the user interface. We noticed that human is excellent at perceiving colors, so instead of displaying the video on user interface, we only display their key-frames based on colors. To achieve this, frames are sampled from the video segments produced by TransNetV2, and then clustered based on their color histogram.

The general workflow of our system is illustrated in Fig. 1. More details about each search feature in our proposed system will be further explored in the following sections.

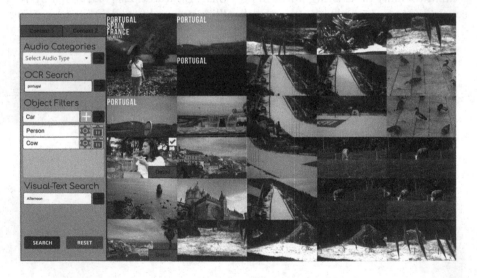

Fig. 2. Screenshot of the main user interface.

2.2   Object Search

Searching by object features is a prominent feature in our retrieval system. Previous works have explored this approach in their system [4,12]. We incorporated an object searching feature into the system to look up videos based on object position and color in keyframes. The feature also supports temporal queries for searching objects throughout the video segments. Our system allows users to append a list of object groups that appears in the video. Each object group consists of information about its quantity, object type, position, and dominant color. The object position can be determined by splitting the video frame into a 3×3 grid, and the user gets to choose in which cells the object appears. For dominant color, we use clustering algorithms to find which color is most visually recognized in the keyframe, i.e., appears most frequently.

In the object detection task, we used a pre-trained Faster-RCNN model [11] on the Visual Genome dataset [7]. The dataset has a wide variety of predefined classes for common objects in real-life images. After localizing objects in video keyframes, we determined their dominant color, then indexed their features into an SQL-like database.

2.3 Scene Text Search

According to several studies on both shards of the V3C dataset [1,13], many text instances exist in the videos. Thus this information might be suitable for large-scale querying. With scene text search, the system will return all video segments containing the text user entered. Studies have shown that many text instances in the video collection are English [1,13]; we utilize PaddleOCR [2] to perform text detection and text recognition for each video frame, then save the text information for later indexing. With Elasticsearch, we can search for text instances in an extensive database efficiently.

2.4 Visual-Textual Association

During video retrieval tasks with the absence of objects and text instances, searching by concepts might be helpful. For the visual-textual association feature, the system allows users to enter a description for a specific scene, and the target video will be returned. To perform this, we use Contrastive Language-Image Pre-training (CLIP) [10] for a zero-shot visual-textual association model. After computing the visual features of video frames, we indexed them using Faiss [5] for efficient retrieval.

2.5 Audio Category

Audio is a crucial component in videos. To take advantage of audio information, we built a search feature based on audio categories in videos. From video segments partitioned from the original collection, audio signals are extracted and fed into PANNS [6], a video tagging method, to determine audio categories presented in the video. The PANNs model provided by the original authors was pre-trained on the AudioSet dataset [3], which supports over 600 categories of sound organized hierarchically. From the AudioSet ontology, we took the 36 most common audio categories and indexed them into an SQL-like database for later queries.

2.6 Finalizing Query and Temporal Search

In practice, each of the query above is performed independently, and then the system will proceed to merge their results. To this end, we simply find the intersection between the results, and we expect each query will narrow down the search space for the user. The merged results can be ranked using the average similarity score of each query. Note that each query use a different metrics for computing similarity score, so we normalize them to the same scale of 0 to 1.

Next, we approach the temporal search feature in a brute-force manner. Suppose the user wants to search a video where event A occurs before event B. We will perform two queries searching for event A and event B, respectively. Let $\{a_0, a_1, \ldots, a_n\}$ be the timestamps where event A happens and $\{b_0, b_1, \ldots, b_m\}$ be the timestamps where event B happens in a video, we will brute-force all (a_i, b_j) pairs such that $a_i \leq b_j$. Our experiments showed that the returned results are narrow enough to be brute-forced efficiently.

3 System Demonstrations

The user interface offers easy-to-use features and mainly relies on user textual inputs (Fig. 2). To search by object features, the user can add object instances into the list presented on the left-hand side. Our system currently supports querying by object count, object position, and object dominant color.

For the visual KIS task, searching by text instances and audio categories might produce better results than the other features. However, we cannot fully utilize the mentioned features for tasks with less visual information, such as textual KIS and AVS tasks. In this case, searching by semantic concepts using visual-textual association might be more suitable.

4 Conclusion

This paper introduced our multimedia retrieval system for interactive video search in VBS 2022 with four key features: searching by object features, by scene text, by visual-textual association, and by audio category. Our system is suitable for retrieval tasks in the competition, and can be efficiently used by both expert and novice users. However, the system still exists limitations and can be further improved in the future. Currently our main limitation is Type-II error, where the video being looked for is eliminated if too many queries are used at once. Moreover, our system is more expensive compared to other systems, as the CLIP module utilizes GPUs parallelization for text query embedding. We aim to address this concern by caching common queries and remove the need of using GPUs.

Acknowledgement. This research is funded by University of Information Technology - Vietnam National University Ho Chi Minh City under grant number D1-2022-01.

References

1. Berns, F., et al.: V3C1 dataset: an evaluation of content characteristics. In: Proceedings of the 2019 on International Conference on Multimedia Retrieval, pp. 334–338 (2019)
2. Du, Y., et al.: PP-OCR: a practical ultra lightweight OCR system. arXiv preprint arXiv:2009.09941 (2020)
3. Gemmeke, J.F., et al.: Audio set: an ontology and human-labeled dataset for audio events. In: 2017 IEEE International Conference on Acoustics, Speech and Signal Processing (ICASSP), pp. 776–780. IEEE (2017)
4. Heller, S., et al.: Towards explainable interactive multi-modal video retrieval with Vitrivr. In: Lokoč, J., et al. (eds.) MMM 2021. LNCS, vol. 12573, pp. 435–440. Springer, Cham (2021). https://doi.org/10.1007/978-3-030-67835-7_41
5. Johnson, J., Douze, M., Jégou, H.: Billion-scale similarity search with GPUs. arXiv preprint arXiv:1702.08734 (2017)
6. Kong, Q., et al.: PANNs: large-scale pretrained audio neural networks for audio pattern recognition. IEEE/ACM Trans. Audio Speech Lang. Process. **28**, 2880–2894 (2020)
7. Krishna, R., et al.: Visual genome: connecting language and vision using crowdsourced dense image annotations. Int. J. Comput. Vision **123**(1), 32–73 (2017)
8. Le, N.-K., Nguyen, D.-H., Tran, M.-T.: An interactive video search platform for multi-modal retrieval with advanced concepts. In: Ro, Y.M., et al. (eds.) MMM 2020. LNCS, vol. 11962, pp. 766–771. Springer, Cham (2020). https://doi.org/10.1007/978-3-030-37734-2_67
9. Lokoč, J., Kovalčík, G., Souček, T.: VIRET at video browser showdown 2020. In: Ro, Y.M., et al. (eds.) MMM 2020. LNCS, vol. 11962, pp. 784–789. Springer, Cham (2020). https://doi.org/10.1007/978-3-030-37734-2_70
10. Radford, A., et al.: Learning transferable visual models from natural language supervision. arXiv preprint arXiv:2103.00020 (2021)
11. Ren, S., et al.: Faster R-CNN: towards real-time object detection with region proposal networks. Adv. Neural. Inf. Process. Syst. **28**, 91–99 (2015)
12. Ressmann, A., Schoeffmann, K.: IVOS - the ITEC interactive video object search system at VBS2021. In: Lokoč, J., et al. (eds.) MMM 2021. LNCS, vol. 12573, pp. 479–483. Springer, Cham (2021). https://doi.org/10.1007/978-3-030-67835-7_48
13. Rossetto, L., Schoeffmann, K., Bernstein, A.: Insights on the V3C2 dataset. arXiv preprint arXiv:2105.01475 (2021)
14. Rossetto, L., et al.: Interactive video retrieval in the age of deep learning. Detailed evaluation of VBS 2019. IEEE Trans. Multimedia **23**, 243–256 (2020)
15. Rossetto, L., et al.: On the user-centric comparative remote evaluation of interactive video search systems. IEEE MultiMedia **28**(4), 18–28 (2021)
16. Soucek, T., Lokoc, J.: TransNet V2: an effective deep network architecture for fast shot transition detection. CoRR abs/2008.04838, arXiv: 2008.04838 (2020)

V-FIRST: A Flexible Interactive Retrieval System for Video at VBS 2022

Minh-Triet Tran[1,2,3]($\boxtimes$) (iD), Nhat Hoang-Xuan[1,3]($\boxtimes$),
Hoang-Phuc Trang-Trung[1,2,3], Thanh-Cong Le[1,2,3], Mai-Khiem Tran[1,2,3],
Minh-Quan Le[1,3], Tu-Khiem Le[4], Van-Tu Ninh[4], and Cathal Gurrin[4] (iD)

[1] University of Science, VNU-HCM, Ho Chi Minh City, Vietnam
`tmtriet@fit.hcmus.edu.vn`, `hxnhat18@apcs.fitus.edu.vn`,
`{tthphuc,ltcong,tmkhiem,lmquan}@selab.hcmus.edu.vn`,
[2] John von Neumann Institute, VNU-HCM, Ho Chi Minh City, Vietnam
[3] Vietnam National University, Ho Chi Minh City, Vietnam
[4] Dublin City University, Dublin, Ireland
`tukhiem.le4@mail.dcu.ie`, `tu.ninhvan@adaptcentre.ie`, `cathal.gurrin@dcu.ie`

Abstract. Video retrieval systems have a wide range of applications across multiple domains, therefore the development of user-friendly and efficient systems is necessary. For VBS 2022, we develop a flexible interactive system for video retrieval, namely V-FIRST, that supports two scenarios of usage: query with **text descriptions** and query with **visual examples**. We take advantage of both visual and temporal information from videos to extract concepts related to entities, events, scenes, activities, and motion trajectories for video indexing. Our system supports queries with keywords and sentence descriptions as V-FIRST can evaluate the semantic similarities between visual and textual embedding vectors. V-FIRST also allows users to express queries with visual impressions, such as sketches and 2D spatial maps of dominant colors. We use query expansion, elastic temporal video navigation, and intellisense for hints to further boost the performance of our system.

Keywords: Video retrieval · Interactive system · Sketch retrieval · Color histogram matching · Human-object interaction · Image and video captioning · Moving entity trajectory

1 Introduction

With the rising prevalence of mobile and wearable devices, the amount of image and video data generated has been growing extensively in size. When a user wants to search for some specific items, the idea of browsing through the entire collection quickly becomes infeasible when there are weeks or months worth of data. We note that users often have in mind a picture of what they are searching for. This rough image can be easy to recall, but hard to describe in terms of words, for example, "the picture is mostly blue and green". If they are fortunate

© Springer Nature Switzerland AG 2022
B. Þór Jónsson et al. (Eds.): MMM 2022, LNCS 13142, pp. 562–568, 2022.
https://doi.org/10.1007/978-3-030-98355-0_55

enough, e.g., with the presence of some prominent objects, they can successfully describe the scene with a sentence and use it as a query. However, many times visual information can be difficult to be expressed effectively with words. In those cases, it is helpful to be able to utilize different forms of expressions than textual queries alone.

It would be difficult for users to search for a certain event in a huge amount of video clips. This is a challenging task to create an efficient video retrieval system that can support both accuracy and ease of use. Therefore, the Video Browser (VBS [9]) challenge has been organized for many years to encourage researchers worldwide to develop and enhance retrieval systems for video clips.

For VBS 2022, we propose and develop V-FIRST, a **F**lexible **I**nteractive **R**etrieval **S**ys**T**em for **V**ideos. Our system allows the user to specify various visual cues such as the global color histogram of the image, local prominent color patches, and a sketch of the sought scene. As visual information does not have a simple expression such as a sentence or clause, our system is made up of many retrieval modalities that utilize different visual aspects of the videos, and the user may choose to specify some, or all of them to assist with retrieval. With sufficient usage and feedback, over time, we can evaluate the compatibility of each modality with each specific use case and give recommendations to users based on that.

Our system is based on FIRST [13,15], which was a system used for retrieving images from lifelog, however, we have carefully extended it to accommodate for video retrieval. The first notable addition is temporal information, which was not present in images. Our system supports activity recognition and action proposal [16,17]. Second, our system enhances the captioning ability of images by utilizing optical character recognition (OCR) and extending the set of defined concepts. This enables better semantic similarity between the embeddings of the (textual) query, the generated caption, and the image itself. Third, apart from descriptive language, we support the inclusion of visual impressions, such as global color histogram, prominent color patches, and sketches of the video. Finally, we aim to integrate intellisense, a simple context-based suggestion system that asks the user some questions that would quickly reduce the set of possible answers to the query. This allows our system to actively assist the user in the retrieval process, instead of being passive and completely relying on the user's ability to generate effective queries.

We also implement query expansion in our system based on visual similarity/dissimilarity by allowing the user to specify scenes that are close to the sought scene or are irrelevant. Those samples then act as positive/negative samples and can be used as an input for the next query. Furthermore, our system allows temporal exploration of the retrieved results in both directions, as a means for the user to continue searching in the time dimension or to simply verify the correctness of the retrieved videos.

2   Related Work

The Video Browser Showdown (VBS [9]) competition serves as a benchmark of interactive video retrieval systems that are held annually. In the 2021 edition, vitrivr [3] managed to achieve the best score. This system is an example of a multimodal system, in which they allow users to search using pre-defined concepts and a rough color sketch of the scene. Other advanced features include temporal search, which is searching for concepts appearing in a specific order, and semantic sketching, where users essentially input a sketch of the scene's semantic segmentation result. Notably, all of these input methods are based on the same list of pre-defined concepts.

Traditional methods implement some subset of the features mentioned and attempt to enhance them in different ways. IVOS [7] and VISIONE [1] both enhance their retrieval performance by allowing users to specify the location of objects, in addition to normal queries. SOMHunter [4] upgrades object localization to concept localization by allowing clauses (e.g., woman eating) to be localized. Also, both SOMHunter [4] and VISIONE [1] supports temporal query by allowing users to input two queries instead of one.

VideoGraph [8] deviates by using Wikipedia to generate a knowledge graph that allows the user to search using semantically related concepts, e.g., they can search for "engine" and find scenes with cars and motorbikes. For input methods, aside from typical keyboard and mouse, vitrivr-VR [11] and EOLAS [12] utilize Virtual Reality to allow users to have an immersive view of the results. These systems use interaction within the virtual environment as a replacement for complex text queries.

3   V-FIRST- A Flexible Interactive Retrieval System for Video

3.1   System Overview

Figure 1 shows the overview structure of our proposed system, V-FIRST, which is developed from our current lifelog retrieval systems FIRST [13,15]. Thanks to the flexible architecture of FIRST, we can easily enhance and integrate new features for video clip retrieval into our system.

We develop two sets of query processing modules to support two types of query scenarios with text descriptions and visual examples. For queries with text descriptions, our system allows users to search with visual concepts, activities, motion of entities, and with free-text descriptions (see Sect. 3.2). For queries with visual examples, we support searching with sketches and spatial maps of colors (see Sect. 3.3).

We also develop additional functions to assist users. With Query Expansion, the system can use a result candidate as a positive or negative example for result refinement. We also assist users in quickly exploring a video clip with a flexible timeline to verify past or future events from an initial moment. We also develop a preliminary intellisense function to provide context-based hints to users to quickly refine the result. Finally, our system also allows users to combine different functions to perform a complex search or refine their search results.

3.2   Query Processing with Text Descriptions

For each video clip, we extract visual concepts [2,10] related entities appearing in each video shot, an equal-sized sequence of frames. We also capture the scene attributes and categories [18], and scene texts [6] from a video shot for indexing.

Besides useful information from each still image, we also take advantage of temporal information from video clips. We use action proposal detection [16,17] to find potential meaningful activities in a video clip, then classify these proposals for known activity categories.

Object movement can be useful information for retrieval. We develop the idea by Nguyen et al. [5,6] for traffic video event retrieval from text description into our system for general video cases. We evaluate the similarity between the trajectories of main entities in a video clip with the text description to find appropriate video clips having a certain event about object movement.

To further bridge the gap between text and visual information, we generate captions for main shots in a video clip so that we can evaluate the similarity between an input text query phrase with generated captions. Based on the simple idea of utilizing multiple input branches, including OCR features and object features, into transformer architecture and using a copy mechanism to generate captions, we implement a graph neural network to learn the relationship between OCR features and object features as another input branch. In this way, we successfully integrate a useful captioning module for our solution that can exploit spatial relationships between objects and scene texts.

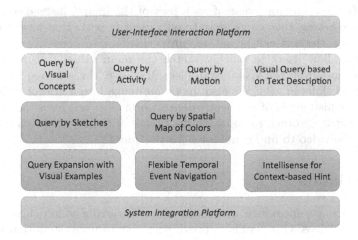

Fig. 1. System overview of our query system.

To provide users with a natural way to search with free text, we employ our Self-Attention based Joint Embedding Model (SAJEM [14]) in our retrieval system. In this way, our system encodes both a text query and a photo/sequence of photos into an embedding space to measure their similarity.

3.3   Query Processing with Visual Examples

In the Known-Item Search setting of VBS, we are given a dataset of video clips. We are presented with a query video, and our task is to use our system to find that clip. To express which data we want to retrieve, we need a query. Perhaps the most popular form of one is a textual sentence, which is used by Google, the most popular search engine. This form of expression is useful if our information need is simple enough to be parsed into a short sentence. For example, we might describe a picture in terms of the main objects and their interactions. However, what if the picture cannot be well described using words?

We can build a text-based system, and try to describe the query clips one by one. Another approach is searching based on visual cues (e.g., colors). This visual-based approach is content-agnostic and has the potential to outperform text-based approaches in certain circumstances. It is also more complicated to implement, since, unlike language, there are many ways to represent visual cues, and finding an efficient scheme to use and to search is challenging.

With a visual example, instead of describing that example in text and reusing the existing solutions in Sect. 3.2, we develop some preliminary utilities to assist users in describing the visual impressions from the example, such as global color histogram, prominent color patches, and sketches of the video.

We represent the query as a $m \times n$ grid, where each cell contains the main color. When the grid is overlaid on images being searched, the color of each cell represents the (expected) dominant color in that cell. This way, the user can specify the dominant color of each part of the image, instead of the whole image. Even better, they can choose to only identify parts that have a relatively uniform color, the rest can be left as "unspecified".

We also allow users to quickly sketch the main visual features that they remember most from the visual examples. Of course, this way requires the user to have good skills in arts. We also divide an image into a grid of cells, and we estimate the histogram of gradient orientation in each cell from the sketch. We use asymmetric distance to compare the fitness of the input sketch query with frames in the video to find candidates for the query.

4   Conclusion

In this paper, we introduce our solution for retrieving video clips in a large collection of videos. Our goal is to provide an easy-to-use system that can assist users in expressing their query needs in a flexible way. Therefore we provide two sets of utilities to handle queries in text description mode and queries with visual examples. These two scenarios correspond to the Ad-hoc Video Search (AVS) and Known-Item Search (KIS) of the VBS challenge.

We take advantage of the flexible architecture of our retrieval system to integrate different components for query processing. For a query with text description, users can search with visual concepts related to entities, scene attributes and categories, activities, scene-text, and even in free-text format. For a query with visual examples, users can define a draft 2D map of dominant colors or sketch out main visual features to find candidate images from the dataset. Query Expansion and Flexible Video Navigation assist users in further exploring potential results from an initial candidate. We also integrate a preliminary intellisense feature to automatically ask users questions to quickly refine the candidate list.

Acknowledgement. The team would like to thank Vinh-Hung Tran, Trong-Thang Pham for the enhanced captioning module; Trong-Tung Nguyen and Huu-Nghia Nguyen-Ho for the human-object interaction module; Tien-Phat Nguyen and Ba-Thinh Tran-Le for the moving trajectory retrieval method.

Hoang-Phuc Trang-Trung, Thanh-Cong Le, and Mai-Khiem Tran were funded by Vingroup Joint Stock Company and supported by the Domestic Master/ PhD Scholarship Programme of Vingroup Innovation Foundation (VINIF), Vingroup Big Data Institute (VINBIGDATA), code VINIF.2020.ThS.JVN.03, VINIF.2020. ThS.JVN.05, and VINIF.2020.ThS.JVN.06, respectively.

The work was funded by Gia Lam Urban Development and Investment Company Limited, Vingroup and supported by Vingroup Innovation Foundation (VINIF) under project code VINIF.2019.DA19.

References

1. Amato, G., et al.: VISIONE at video browser showdown 2021. In: Lokoč, J., et al. (eds.) MMM 2021. LNCS, vol. 12573, pp. 473–478. Springer, Cham (2021). https://doi.org/10.1007/978-3-030-67835-7_47

2. Anderson, P., et al.: Bottom-up and top-down attention for image captioning and visual question answering. In: CVPR (2018)

3. Heller, S., et al.: Towards explainable interactive multi-modal video retrieval with Vitrivr. In: Lokoč, J., et al. (eds.) MMM 2021. LNCS, vol. 12573, pp. 435–440. Springer, Cham (2021). https://doi.org/10.1007/978-3-030-67835-7_41

4. Kratochvíl, M., Veselý, P., Mejzlík, F., Lokoč, J.: SOM-hunter: video browsing with relevance-to-SOM feedback loop. In: Ro, Y.M., et al. (eds.) MMM 2020. LNCS, vol. 11962, pp. 790–795. Springer, Cham (2020). https://doi.org/10.1007/978-3-030-37734-2_71

5. Liu, Y., Chen, H., Shen, C., He, T., Jin, L., Wang, L.: AbcNet: real-time scene text spotting with adaptive Bezier-curve network. In: Proceedings of the IEEE/CVF Conference on Computer Vision and Pattern Recognition (CVPR), June 2020

6. Nguyen, N., et al.: Dictionary-guided scene text recognition. In: Proceedings of the IEEE/CVF Conference on Computer Vision and Pattern Recognition (CVPR), pp. 7383–7392, June 2021

7. Ressmann, A., Schoeffmann, K.: IVOS - the ITEC interactive video object search system at VBS2021. In: Lokoč, J., et al. (eds.) MMM 2021. LNCS, vol. 12573, pp. 479–483. Springer, Cham (2021). https://doi.org/10.1007/978-3-030-67835-7_48

8. Rossetto, L., et al.: VideoGraph – towards using knowledge graphs for interactive video retrieval. In: Lokoč, J., et al. (eds.) MMM 2021. LNCS, vol. 12573, pp. 417–422. Springer, Cham (2021). https://doi.org/10.1007/978-3-030-67835-7_38

9. Schoeffmann, K., Lokoc, J., Bailer, W.: 10 years of video browser showdown. In: Chua, T., et al. (eds.) MMAsia 2020: ACM Multimedia Asia, Virtual Event/Singapore, 7–9 March 2021, pp. 73:1–73:3. ACM (2020)

10. Tan, M., Pang, R., Le, Q.V.: EfficientDet: scalable and efficient object detection. In: 2020 IEEE/CVF Conference on Computer Vision and Pattern Recognition (CVPR), pp. 10778–10787 (2020)

11. Tran, D., et al.: A VR interface for browsing visual spaces at VBS2021, pp. 490–495 (2021)

12. Tran, L.-D., et al.: A VR interface for browsing visual spaces at VBS2021. In: Lokoč, J., et al. (eds.) MMM 2021. LNCS, vol. 12573, pp. 490–495. Springer, Cham (2021). https://doi.org/10.1007/978-3-030-67835-7_50

13. Tran, M., et al.: FIRST - flexible interactive retrieval system for visual lifelog exploration at LSC 2020. In: Gurrin, C., et al. (eds.) Proceedings of the Third ACM Workshop on Lifelog Search Challenge, LSC@ICMR 2020, Dublin, Ireland, 8–11 June 2020, pp. 67–72. ACM (2020)

14. Trang-Trung, H., Le, H., Tran, M.: Lifelog moment retrieval with self-attention based joint embedding model. In: Cappellato, L., Eickhoff, C., Ferro, N., Névéol, A. (eds.) Working Notes of CLEF 2020 - Conference and Labs of the Evaluation Forum, Thessaloniki, Greece, 22–25 September 2020. CEUR Workshop Proceedings, vol. 2696. CEUR-WS.org (2020). http://ceur-ws.org/Vol-2696/paper_60.pdf

15. Trang-Trung, H., et al.: Flexible interactive retrieval system 2.0 for visual lifelog exploration at LSC 2021. In: Gurrin, C., et al. (eds.) Proceedings of the 4th Annual on Lifelog Search Challenge, LSC@ICMR 2021, Taipei, Taiwan, 21 August 2021, pp. 81–87. ACM (2021)

16. Vo, K., Yamazaki, K., Truong, S., Tran, M., Sugimoto, A., Le, N.: ABN: agent-aware boundary networks for temporal action proposal generation. IEEE Access **9**, 126431–126445 (2021)

17. Vo-Ho, V., Le, N., Yamazaki, K., Sugimoto, A., Tran, M.: Agent-environment network for temporal action proposal generation. In: IEEE International Conference on Acoustics, Speech and Signal Processing, ICASSP 2021, Toronto, ON, Canada, 6–11 June 2021, pp. 2160–2164. IEEE (2021)

18. Zhou, B., Lapedriza, A., Khosla, A., Oliva, A., Torralba, A.: Places: a 10 million image database for scene recognition. IEEE Trans. Pattern Anal. Mach. Intell. **40**, 1452–1464 (2017)

diveXplore 6.0: ITEC's Interactive Video Exploration System at VBS 2022

Andreas Leibetseder[(✉)] and Klaus Schoeffmann

Klagenfurt University, Institute of Information Technology (ITEC),
Klagenfurt, Austria
{aleibets,ks}@itec.aau.at

Abstract. Continuously participating since the sixth Video Browser Showdown (VBS2017), diveXplore is a veteran interactive search system that throughout its lifetime has offered and evaluated numerous features. After undergoing major refactoring for the most recent VBS2021, however, the system since version 5.0 is less feature rich, yet, more modern, leaner and faster than the original system. This proved to be a sensible decision as the new system showed increasing performance in VBS2021 when compared to the most recent former competitions. With version 6.0 we reconsider shot segmentation, map search and introduce new features for improving concept as well as temporal context search.

Keywords: Video retrieval · Interactive video search · Video analysis

1 Introduction

The recurring team competition Video Browser Showdown [7,8,12,14] (VBS) aims at improving the quick interactive search of large video databases, in particular V3C1 and V3C2 [1,13]. Several competing teams develop custom retrieval systems using a known dataset in order to solve several types of tasks within a short time frame at an international live event: visual and textual Known Item Search (KIS) for retrieving specific unique items and Ad-hoc Video Search (AVS) for finding multiple items with a certain characteristic. Moreover, the developed systems typically are used by persons familiar with them (experts) as well as inexperienced users (novices). The diveXplore system [4–6,11,15,16] annually participates in these competitions since VBS2017, ever growing in complexity. With version 5.0 [6] we, therefore, decided to refactor the system optimizing its responsiveness and speed, while reducing its features, achieving the 12th rank out of 18 teams in VBS2021. In version 6.0 of the system, we aim at improving its underlying shot segmentation as well as its capabilities of temporal search. In the following we detail the system and describe its improvements for VBS2022.

2 diveXplore 6.0

2.1 Architecture

The interactive retrieval system diveXplore operates on metadata and pre-processed features extracted from video keyframes, i.e. representative frames

B. Þór Jónsson et al. (Eds.): MMM 2022, LNCS 13142, pp. 569–574, 2022.
https://doi.org/10.1007/978-3-030-98355-0_56

belonging to custom-segmented consecutive video scenes. It is built in a modular fashion and based on web-technologies enabling a user to issue combinable queries in two different modes: shot and map search. Figure 1 illustrates the system's main components grouped by type: preprocessing, back and front end.

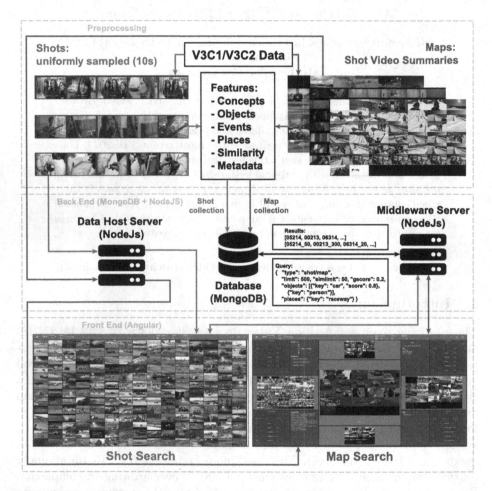

Fig. 1. diveXplore architecture

Generally, both of the diveXplore's search modes rely on its custom shot segmentation of uniformly sampling the source datasets into ten-second scenes. However, they differ in their targeted amount of data: shot search is concerned with features belonging to individual shot keyframes, while map search operates on a video basis: results are matched by feature frequency in all shots of particular videos. Additionally, this mode includes similarity search among video summary images (maps), which is determined via calculating their feature vector similarities. Table 1 lists and briefly describes all of our utilized deep features.

Table 1. diveXplore features

Type	Model	Ref.	Description
Concepts	Inception v3	[17]	1000 ImageNet categories
Objects	YOLO v4	[2]	80 MS COCO categories
Events	Moments in Time	[9]	304 Moments in Time action events
Places	Places365	[18]	365 individual places
Similarity (map)	Inception v3	[17]	Based on last fully connected (FC) layer

Most extracted deep features, i.e. concepts, objects and places, are extracted from shot keyframes, yet, action events require temporal context and are therefore determined using the full ten-second segments. In addition to hosting shots, maps and videos on a Node.js (https://nodejs.org) data host server, we store shot as well as map feature collections on a MongoDB (https://mongodb.com) database, which is accessible using a middleware Node.js query server. As portrayed in Fig. 1, queries as well as responses are formulated via POST request containing a JSON body, which allows for complex query combinations in both modes based on features and confidence thresholds. In this manner, the search interface can be deployed rather easily as it is possible to host and share all of the underlying data through dedicated, potentially more powerful servers.

2.2 Interface

As depicted the front end part of Fig. 1, diveXplore includes two different interfaces accommodating shot and map search mode. Despite displaying results quite differently, both share the same search bar (top blue area), which enables entering a series of combinable search terms. E.g., for creating a database request similar to the one shown in Fig. 1, a user enters the following list of search terms in a bash-like manner: '--objects car (0.8), person --places raceway'. Since entering many search terms this way could be tedious, the system offers smart autocompletion functionalities: besides listing available concepts and their shortcuts, as a user starts typing the autocompletion bar is updated to contain all relevant terms together with their concept categories. It even includes the frequency and example images of the suggested search concepts, as is in Fig. 2a demonstrating autocomplete with the example input 'car'.

For result display (cf. Fig. 1), shot search offers a simple, traditional view: it displays a grid of shots ordered by most to least relevant. This mode is useful for quickly scanning a large variety of shots regardless of the videos they originate from, which, for instance, is convenient for AVS tasks. The map view, however, offers a novel way of result browsing. By navigating aforementioned video summary maps, a user is able to quickly overview a video's complete content. Only one map is inspected at any given moment and all the information in the corner areas always correspond to that map, which is the largest one centered in the middle of the screen. The other maps are previews of the previous and next maps for two exploration modes: horizontal navigation traverses the list

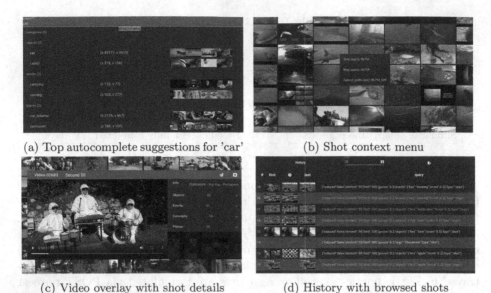

(a) Top autocomplete suggestions for 'car'   (b) Shot context menu

(c) Video overlay with shot details   (d) History with browsed shots

Fig. 2. diveXplore interface components

of result videos from highest to lowest rank according to feature frequency and vertical navigation enables a user to view similar videos to currently selected horizontal map. We've made it as easy as possible to switch from map to shot search – a single click suffices for issuing the current query using the respective other mode in a new browser tab. Also, as shown in Fig. 2b, the system implements convenience context menus to search for a shot in each available mode. Furthermore, the system provides the user with a video preview feature that can be activated by selecting any shot. As demonstrated in Fig. 2c, this overlay not only includes general information such as video description and tags but also its topmost objects, concepts, events and places. This video browser enables submitting much more precise timestamps for KIS tasks compared to simply submitting shot keyframes. Finally, diveXplore offers an extensive history feature (cf. Fig. 2d) which not only precisely records the issued queries color-coded by their type, it also stores shot thumbnails according to the user's browsing activity, i.e. first, last and longest inspected shot.

2.3   Improvements

Our system improvements are listed in Table 2. Although not having a big impact on AVS search, the rather long 10 s shot segmentation seems to greatly impede KIS tasks – seemingly simple tasks could not be found, even after the assigned search time. This especially happens in case the targeted video segments are very short. Therefore, we reduce the keyframe sampling interval to one-second for VBS2022. Furthermore, since merely using feature frequency for map retrieval

Table 2. System improvements impacting front end (fe) and back end (be)

Improvement	Impact	Description
1s segmentation	be, fe	Improving KIS performance
Alternative map search	be	Improving map retrieval accuracy
OCR, STT	be	New search features (e.g. [3,10])
Temporal search	be, fe	Improving result precision

seems to have detrimental effects on some queries, we explore alternative ways to match those features to improve result accuracy. Additionally, we introduce useful and proven successful features such as Optical Character Recognition (OCR) and Speech-to-Text (STT). Lastly, while temporal events are useful to retrieve activities, the system requires more sophisticated means for temporal context search, which also will include single keyframe-based features.

3   Conclusion

We introduced diveXplore 6.0 as a competing system at VBS2022. While some features proved to be helpful since refactoring the system, we continue this process by reducing the shot sampling interval, improving map search, adding proven useful features and offering sophisticated temporal concept search.

Acknowledgments. This work was funded by the FWF Austrian Science Fund under grant P 32010-N38.

References

1. Berns, F., Rossetto, L., Schoeffmann, K., Beecks, C., Awad, G.: V3C1 dataset: an evaluation of content characteristics. In: Proceedings of the 2019 on International Conference on Multimedia Retrieval, pp. 334–338. ACM (2019)
2. Bochkovskiy, A., Wang, C.Y., Liao, H.Y.M.: YOLOV4: optimal speed and accuracy of object detection. CoRR abs/2004.10934 (2020). https://arxiv.org/abs/2004.10934
3. Kay, A.: Tesseract: an open-source optical character recognition engine. Linux J. **2007**(159), 2 (2007)
4. Leibetseder, A., Kletz, S., Schoeffmann, K.: Sketch-based similarity search for collaborative feature maps. In: Schoeffmann, K., et al. (eds.) MMM 2018. LNCS, vol. 10705, pp. 425–430. Springer, Cham (2018). https://doi.org/10.1007/978-3-319-73600-6_45
5. Leibetseder, A., Münzer, B., Primus, J., Kletz, S., Schoeffmann, K.: diveXplore 4.0: the ITEC deep interactive video exploration system at VBS2020. In: Ro, Y.R., et al. (eds.) MMM 2020. LNCS, vol. 11962, pp. 753–759. Springer, Cham (2020). https://doi.org/10.1007/978-3-030-37734-2_65

6. Leibetseder, A., Schoeffmann, K.: Less is more - diveXplore 5.0 at VBS 2021. In: Lokoč, J., Skopal, T., Schoeffmann, K., Mezaris, V., Li, X., Vrochidis, S., Patras, I. (eds.) MMM 2021. LNCS, vol. 12573, pp. 455–460. Springer, Cham (2021). https://doi.org/10.1007/978-3-030-67835-7_44

7. Lokoc, J., Bailer, W., Schoeffmann, K., Muenzer, B., Awad, G.: On influential trends in interactive video retrieval: video browser showdown 2015–2017. IEEE Trans. Multimedia **20**, 3361–3376 (2018). https://doi.org/10.1109/TMM.2018.2830110

8. Lokoč, J., et al.: Interactive search or sequential browsing? A detailed analysis of the video browser showdown 2018. ACM Trans. Multimedia Comput. Commun. Appl. **15**(1), 29:1–29:18 (2019). https://doi.org/10.1145/3295663

9. Monfort, M., et al.: Moments in time dataset: one million videos for event understanding. IEEE Trans. Pattern Anal. Mach. Intell. **42**(2), 502–508 (2020). https://doi.org/10.1109/TPAMI.2019.2901464

10. Povey, D., et al.: The Kaldi speech recognition toolkit. In: IEEE 2011 Workshop on Automatic Speech Recognition and Understanding, No. CONF. IEEE Signal Processing Society (2011)

11. Primus, M.J., Münzer, B., Leibetseder, A., Schoeffmann, K.: The ITEC collaborative video search system at the video browser showdown 2018. In: Schoeffmann, K., et al. (eds.) MMM 2018. LNCS, vol. 10705, pp. 438–443. Springer, Cham (2018). https://doi.org/10.1007/978-3-319-73600-6_47

12. Rossetto, L., et al.: Interactive video retrieval in the age of deep learning - detailed evaluation of VBS 2019. IEEE Trans. Multimedia **23**, 243–256 (2021). https://doi.org/10.1109/TMM.2020.2980944

13. Rossetto, L., Schoeffmann, K., Bernstein, A.: Insights on the V3C2 dataset. arXiv preprint arXiv:2105.01475 (2021)

14. Schoeffmann, K.: A user-centric media retrieval competition: the video browser showdown 2012–2014. IEEE MultiMedia **21**(4), 8–13 (2014). https://doi.org/10.1109/MMUL.2014.56

15. Schoeffmann, K., Münzer, B., Leibetseder, A., Primus, J., Kletz, S.: Autopiloting feature maps: the deep interactive video exploration (diveXplore) system at VBS2019. In: Kompatsiaris, I., Huet, B., Mezaris, V., Gurrin, C., Cheng, W.-H., Vrochidis, S. (eds.) MMM 2019. LNCS, vol. 11296, pp. 585–590. Springer, Cham (2019). https://doi.org/10.1007/978-3-030-05716-9_50

16. Schoeffmann, K., et al.: Collaborative feature maps for interactive video search. In: Amsaleg, L., Guðmundsson, G.Þ, Gurrin, C., Jónsson, B.Þ, Satoh, S. (eds.) MMM 2017. LNCS, vol. 10133, pp. 457–462. Springer, Cham (2017). https://doi.org/10.1007/978-3-319-51814-5_41

17. Szegedy, C., Vanhoucke, V., Ioffe, S., Shlens, J., Wojna, Z.: Rethinking the inception architecture for computer vision. In: Conference on Computer Vision and Pattern Recognition, pp. 2818–2826. IEEE (2016). https://doi.org/10.1109/CVPR.2016.308

18. Zhou, B., Lapedriza, A., Khosla, A., Oliva, A., Torralba, A.: Places: a 10 million image database for scene recognition. IEEE Trans. Pattern Anal. Mach. Intell. **40**(6), 1452–1464 (2018). https://doi.org/10.1109/TPAMI.2017.2723009

CDC: Color-Based Diffusion Model with Caption Embedding in VBS 2022

Duc-Tuan Luu[1,2,3,4]([✉]), Khanh-An C. Quan[1,2,3,4], Thinh-Quyen Nguyen[1,4],
Van-Son Hua[1,4], Minh-Chau Nguyen[1,4], Minh-Triet Tran[2,3,4],
and Vinh-Tiep Nguyen[1,4]

[1] University of Information Technology, VNU-HCM, Ho Chi Minh City, Vietnam
tuanld@uit.edu.vn
[2] University of Science, VNU-HCM, Ho Chi Minh City, Vietnam
[3] John von Neumann Institute, VNU-HCM, Ho Chi Minh City, Vietnam
[4] Vietnam National University, Ho Chi Minh City, Vietnam

Abstract. With the rapid development of the internet and technology, the amount of information that people need to store is exploding. This leads to a burden on search engines which are required to qualify the need of seeking items within seconds or even less. Therefore, information retrieval tasks are getting more and more attention in the research community. Video Browser Showdown (VBS) is one of the annual competitions where researchers can evaluate and compare their works with others on the provided benchmarks. Given a query, which can be in form of a text or a short video, the system is supposed to return the video that is closely relevant to the information in the query. In this work, we introduce CDC: a video browser system using our proposed Color-based Diffusion model and the Caption embedding method inherited from the current state-of-the-art visual-language model (Oscar). To the best of our knowledge, Oscar is currently holding the best performance in cross-modal vision-language modeling, while the color-based feature with diffusion helps enhance the searching process.

Keywords: Word embedding · Color-based embedding · Diffusion

1 Introduction

Nowadays, the amount of visual and textual information has become immense, making difficult challenges for current search engines. There are two main types of search tasks: the known-item search (KIS) where users search for one particular scene in a given annotation-free multimedia collection and the Adhoc Video Search (AVS) where no known information is given beforehand. Many attempts have been made to increase the performance of retrieval systems. Along with scientific researches, the annual VBS competition is the place where different video search engines have the chance to compare interactively with each other. In this year's challenges, text and other related information are given as search queries.

© Springer Nature Switzerland AG 2022
B. Þór Jónsson et al. (Eds.): MMM 2022, LNCS 13142, pp. 575–579, 2022.
https://doi.org/10.1007/978-3-030-98355-0_57

In this work, we present the Color-based Diffusion model with Caption embedding for video browser (CDC). Our proposed method inherited from the current state-of-the-art Oscar [6] for visual-language retrieval with decoupled diffusion technique [10] on color-based features for enhanced video searching.

2   Related Work

In 2021, an improved version of [9] in VBS'20 named after Vitrivr [2] managed to achieve the highest score in the 2021 VBS competition. The proposed system inherited some typical features for video pre-processing techniques to enrich the metadata of the video for efficient retrieval, including Automatic Speech Recognition (ASR), Optical Character Recognition (OCR) and concept enrichment using Faster-RCNN model [8] pre-trained on the Openimages V4 dataset [4]. Besides, there are also a temporal querying mechanism and an efficient index structure for similarity search including text and image search were added to the system. The addition contributed to increase the overall score of the searched results.

SOMHunter team [5] also constructed a video search engine with the key idea of temporal query and image search. Nevertheless, the main point of [5] is the customised feedback mechanism. The system will use the self-organising maps (SOMs) along with the positive and negative examples from the users to produce the best result. After the relevance feedback process, the keywords of exemplary frames were also used as a basis for keywords refinement. In the competition, the proposed framework in [5] proved its efficiency in VBS'20 by achieving the highest score among other competitors. Following the similar approach, other teams including HTW [1], Exquisitor [3] and CollageHunter [7], who also achieved considerably good results in the VBS challenge since 2018, utilized the idea of building an interactive video search engine.

In our work, we inherited some typical features of previous state-of-the-art [6] with word embedding techniques to narrow down the searching corpus. We also made use of color-based features with the efficient diffusion method [10] for our system in the task of known-item search. The description of our detailed system is discussed in Sect. 3.

3   CDC: Color-Based Diffusion Model with Caption Embedding

3.1   AVS – Adhoc Video Search

Ad-hoc Video Search is an important property in this challenge since the range of the queries are unlimited. Both visual and textual information have a close relation and can enrich the search space. To achieve the highest recall of each concept, we aim to leverage different object detectors for the image captioning task. Currently, Oscar [6] is the state-of-the-art visual-language model. It represents each input image-text pair as a Word-Tag-Image triple, where Word is the sequence of word embeddings of the text, Tag is the word embedding sequence of the object tags (in text) detected from the image, and Image is the set of region vectors of the image. In Oscar, the detected object tags are used as anchor points in the process of learning the alignments between images and texts, employed in multi-layer self-attention Transformers for the task of understanding contextual cross-modal representation. The overview of Oscar [6] is shown in Fig. 1.

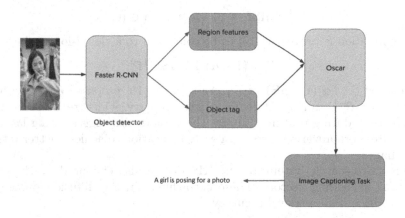

Fig. 1. The overview of Oscar [6]

Moreover, in our video search system, we also take the advantage of the word embedding techniques to reduce the text search space by removing the concepts or words that have similar meaning with each other. We also perform indexing the extracted concepts (as done in Apache Lucene) for fast retrieval.

3.2 KIS - Known Item Search

Apart from the pre-defined concepts, color scheme also plays an important role in the image representation. In this task, we use our color-based encoding method to obtain the images' local features. Then, the system follows the diffusion method introduced in [10] to retrieve the result using the color embedding space. In this task, we define a database as $\chi = \{\mathbf{x}_1, \ldots, \mathbf{x}_n\} \subset \mathbb{R}^d$ where each $\mathbf{x}_i$ is a feature vector. The query is denoted as $\mathcal{Q} = \{\mathbf{q}_1, \ldots, \mathbf{q}_m\} \subset \mathbb{R}^d$. The entire set is defined as $\bar{\chi} = \{\mathbf{q}_1, \ldots, \mathbf{q}_m, \mathbf{x}_1, \ldots, \mathbf{x}_n\}$, and we denote i-th element in $\bar{\chi}$ as $\bar{\chi}_i$. Follows [10], the graph construction of the affinity matrix is then defined as $\mathbf{A} = (a_{ij}) \in \mathbb{R}^{(n+m)\times(n+m)}$, where each element is obtained by

$$a_{ij} = \begin{cases} s(\bar{\chi}_i, \bar{\chi}_j) & i \neq j, \bar{\chi}_i \in \mathrm{NN}_k(\bar{\chi}_j), \bar{\chi}_j \in \mathrm{NN}_k(\bar{\chi}_i) \\ 0 & \text{otherwise} \end{cases}, \qquad (1)$$

In the next step, the stochastic matrix $\mathbf{S}$ is calculated by

$$\mathbf{S} = \mathbf{D}^{-1/2}\mathbf{A}\mathbf{D}^{-1/2}. \qquad (2)$$

where $\mathbf{D}$ is the diagonal degree matrix with each diagonal element d_{ii} in $\mathbf{D}$ is defined as $\sum_{j=1}^{n+m} a_{ij}$.

Next, the random walk algorithm is performed. For the t-th step of random walk, the state is recorded in a vector $\mathbf{f}^t = [\mathbf{f}_q^{t\top}, \mathbf{f}_d^{t\top}]^\top \in \mathbb{R}^{n+m}$, where $\mathbf{f}_q^t \in \mathbb{R}^m$, $\mathbf{f}_d^t \in \mathbb{R}^n$. We set the initial state to be a m-hot vector where $\mathbf{f}_q^0 = \mathbf{1}_m$, $\mathbf{f}_d^0 = \mathbf{0}_n$. The random walk iterates the following step:

$$\mathbf{f}^{t+1} = \alpha\mathbf{S}\mathbf{f}^t + (1-\alpha)\mathbf{f}^0, \quad \alpha \in (0,1). \tag{3}$$

The iteration is proved in [10] to be converged to a closed-form solution:

$$\mathbf{f}^* = (1-\alpha)(\mathbf{I} - \alpha\mathbf{S})^{-1}\mathbf{f}^0. \tag{4}$$

Denoted $(1-\alpha)(\mathbf{I} - \alpha\mathbf{S})$ as $\mathcal{L}_\alpha$, Yang et al. [10] proposed an algorithm to approximate $\mathcal{L}_\alpha^{-1}$ and maintain its sparse property, which reduces the heavy computations during runtime. Finally, the authors also suggest using late truncation after normalization instead of early truncation to achieve better retrieval performance.

Our video search system for the KIS task is also enhanced by the guided concepts' embedding vectors. These extra filters in the diffusion process will increase the system retrieval accuracy.

4   Conclusion

In this paper, we briefly introduce our work of a video retrieval system in the competition of Video Browser Showdown 2022. For the task of Adhoc Video Search, our system inherits the work of Oscar [6] model, which is state-of-the-art in cross-modal visual-language modeling. We enhance the power of searching in the Known Item Search task by proposing a color-based feature with the efficient diffusion method [10]. Besides, caption embeddings are used in both tasks for better search systems and cross-modal understanding.

Acknowledgement. Duc-Tuan Luu was funded by Vingroup Joint Stock Company and supported by the Domestic Master/ PhD Scholarship Programme of Vingroup Innovation Foundation (VINIF), Vingroup Big Data Institute (VINBIGDATA), code VINIF.2020.ThS.JVN.09

Khanh-An C. Quan was funded by Vingroup Joint Stock Company and supported by the Domestic Master/ PhD Scholarship Programme of Vingroup Innovation Foundation (VINIF), Vingroup Big Data Institute (VINBIGDATA), code VINIF.2020.ThS.JVN.07

This research is funded by University of Information Technology - Vietnam National University Ho Chi Minh City under grant number D1-2022-02.

References

1. Barthel, K.U., Hezel, N., Jung, K.: Fusing keyword search and visual exploration for untagged videos. In: Schoeffmann, K., et al. (eds.) MMM 2018. LNCS, vol. 10705, pp. 413–418. Springer, Cham (2018). https://doi.org/10.1007/978-3-319-73600-6_43

2. Heller, S., et al.: Towards explainable interactive multi-modal video retrieval with Vitrivr. In: Lokoč, Jakub, et al. (eds.) MMM 2021. LNCS, vol. 12573, pp. 435–440. Springer, Cham (2021). https://doi.org/10.1007/978-3-030-67835-7_41
3. Khan, O.S., et al.: Exquisitor at the video browser showdown 2021: relationships between semantic classifiers. In: Lokoč, J., et al. (eds.) MMM 2021. LNCS, vol. 12573, pp. 410–416. Springer, Cham (2021). https://doi.org/10.1007/978-3-030-67835-7_37
4. Krasin, I., et al.: OpenImages: a public dataset for large-scale multi-label and multi-class image classification (2016)
5. Kratochvíl, M., Veselý, P., Mejzlík, F., Lokoč, J.: SOM-hunter: video browsing with relevance-to-SOM feedback loop. In: Ro, Y.M., et al. (eds.) MMM 2020. LNCS, vol. 11962, pp. 790–795. Springer, Cham (2020). https://doi.org/10.1007/978-3-030-37734-2_71
6. Li, X., et al.: OSCAR: object-semantics aligned pre-training for vision-language tasks. In: Vedaldi, A., Bischof, H., Brox, T., Frahm, J.-M. (eds.) ECCV 2020. LNCS, vol. 12375, pp. 121–137. Springer, Cham (2020). https://doi.org/10.1007/978-3-030-58577-8_8
7. Lokoč, J., Bátoryová, J., Smrž, D., Dobranský, M.: Video search with collage queries. In: Lokoč, J., et al. (eds.) MMM 2021. LNCS, vol. 12573, pp. 429–434. Springer, Cham (2021). https://doi.org/10.1007/978-3-030-67835-7_40
8. Ren, S., He, K., Girshick, R.B., Sun, J.: Faster R-CNN: towards real-time object detection with region proposal networks. IEEE Trans. Pattern Anal. Mach. Intell. **39**, 1137–1149 (2015)
9. Sauter, L., Amiri Parian, M., Gasser, R., Heller, S., Rossetto, L., Schuldt, H.: Combining Boolean and multimedia retrieval in vitrivr for large-scale video search. In: Ro, Y.M., et al. (eds.) MMM 2020. LNCS, vol. 11962, pp. 760–765. Springer, Cham (2020). https://doi.org/10.1007/978-3-030-37734-2_66
10. Yang, F., Hinami, R., Matsui, Y., Ly, S., Satoh, S.: Efficient image retrieval via decoupling diffusion into online and offline processing. In: The Thirty-Third AAAI Conference on Artificial Intelligence, Honolulu, Hawaii, USA, 2019, pp. 9087–9094. AAAI Press (2019)

ViRMA: Virtual Reality Multimedia Analytics at Video Browser Showdown 2022

Aaron Duane$^{(\boxtimes)}$ and Björn Þór Jónsson

IT University of Copenhagen, Copenhagen, Denmark
{aadu,bjth}@itu.dk

Abstract. In this paper we describe the first iteration of the ViRMA prototype system, a novel approach to multimedia analysis in virtual reality, that is inspired by the M^3 data model. In this model, media is mapped into a multidimensional space, based on its metadata. ViRMA users can then interact with the media collection by dynamically projecting the metadata space to the 3D virtual space, through a variety of interactions, and exploring the resulting visualisations.

Keywords: Virtual reality · Human-computer interaction · Multimedia analytics

1 Introduction

In recent years, increasing emphasis has been placed on interactive analysis by users in various multimedia application domains, as it has become clear that to satisfy diverse and dynamic information needs, effective collaboration between human and machine is necessary [4]. This calls for combining sophisticated multimedia analysis, scalable data management, and interactive visualisation into a single system that supports the user's interactive analysis of a media collection [7].

At the same time, hardware for interacting with data in virtual reality has been improving rapidly, and has reached the point where quality interactions are possible with affordable hardware. Past research has suggested that VR is highly valuable due to its immersive quality, the degree to which it projects stimuli onto the sensory receptors of users, and that it will lead to more natural and effective human-computer interfaces [5]. In this paper we present the first iteration of the ViRMA (Virtual Reality Multimedia Analysis) prototype.

The foundation for the ViRMA prototype is the M^3 model [1] which is in turn based on the merging of concepts from business intelligence, such as analytical processing (OLAP), multidimensional analysis (MDA), and faceted browsing. ViRMA intends to utilise a visualisation paradigm which relies explicitly on the effective representation of multimedia data in 3D virtual space. With the ViRMA prototype, we aim to consider the impact of collection scale on VR interfaces to multimedia analytics, and use interactive competitions such as VBS and LSC [2] as a platform to evaluate our approach.

© Springer Nature Switzerland AG 2022
B. Þór Jónsson et al. (Eds.): MMM 2022, LNCS 13142, pp. 580–585, 2022.
https://doi.org/10.1007/978-3-030-98355-0_58

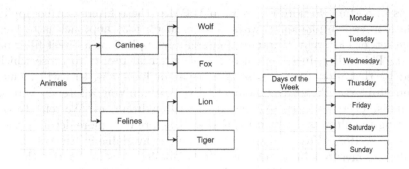

Fig. 1. Example of a hierarchy (left) and a tagset (right)

2   The VBS Dataset and M³

The M³ data model (pronounced "emm-cube") considers multimedia objects to reside in a multi-dimensional metadata space, and then provides support for exploring that space via operations to project it down to 3D space. In the context of the VBS collection, the media objects are extracted keyframes, taken from the collection's video sequences, which results in a dataset of several million images. In addition to the metadata already provided in the video collection, we have extracted semantic features from these keyframes using the ImageNet Shuffle [3], a deep neural network using the ResNeXt-101 architecture [6]. For each of the 1 million images, the 5 highest-scoring concepts are retained as tags, resulting in several thousand unique tags. Since the tags extracted by ImageNet Shuffle directly correspond to a subset of the WordNet database, we created a large hierarchy containing every distinct tag using the WordNet Python API.

3   System Description

The core components of ViRMA system can be described as falling under two main categories; components which support the generation of user queries, and components which support the visualisation and exploration of the data produced by these queries. We refer to these categories respectively as *query generation* and *data projection* within the context of the ViRMA system. In this section we will describe each of the components in these categories and how the user might interact with them in order to complete a typical VBS task.

3.1   Query Generation

To begin, the metadata extracted from the VBS collection is organised semantically into tags, tagsets, and hierarchies (see Fig. 1). These serve the underlying M³ model but, from the perspective of the user, these serve as potential filters which can be applied to their current query or browsing state.

It is important to note that within ViRMA, these filters can be applied to the data in two fundamental ways. The most obvious approach is to locate a tag, tagset, or hierarchy of interest, and simply apply it as a direct filter on the dataset. This will reduce the entire set of potential results to those which are tagged by that filter. In the case of a tagset or hierarchy, this will include all of their children. The other fundamental way of applying a filter in ViRMA, is to visualise it on a spatial axis in the virtual environment. We refer to this as projecting the filter as a dimension and will explore it in more detail in the *data projection* section. With so many potential filters available in ViRMA, including the different methods by which they can be applied, it is imperative that a user can effectively navigate and browse this metadata before deciding which are most appropriate to use and how they should be applied.

Browsing or searching for a tagset is comparatively straightforward as each tagset only contains a single group of semantically associated tags. Hierarchies, however, can contain any number of tags at varying depths of association and can quickly become cumbersome to navigate when searching for a specific tag or tagset in the hierarchy. One option is to restrict the depth and complexity of hierarchies so they are easier to navigate, but this reduces the utility of the hierarchy once it is projected as a dimension in the virtual space. To maintain the benefits of more semantically detailed hierarchies and yet mitigate their associated detriments, we introduced the concept of a *dimension explorer* to the ViRMA system which we will now describe.

Dimension Explorer. The dimension explorer is a dedicated user interface element which can be opened at any time within the virtual space. Once loaded, it is populated with a list of all tagsets and all hierarchies (at their topmost level) which are currently available for the dataset. From this list, the user can drill down into any tagset or hierarchy and their children before deciding to apply them as either a direct filter or project them as a dimension in the virtual space. When viewing the contents of a hierarchy in the dimension explorer, the user's depth in the hierarchy is contextualised by also displaying it's parent and children, if any exist.

As has been noted, in situations with deep or complex hierarchies, this approach can become tedious when the user cannot locate a specific tag or tagset they are searching for. To address this, the dimension explorer contains a search input which enables the user to search for specific tags or tagsets within their respective hierarchies. Selecting this search input will open a virtual keyboard which the user can interact with inside the virtual space using their wireless controllers. By submitting whole or partial tag names, the dimension explorer is loaded with any matching or related tags and tagsets whilst continuing to visually preserve their context within the hierarchy. This empowers the user to select whatever depth of a hierarchy that is appropriate for their current query or browsing state to be applied as a direct filter or to be projected into the virtual space.

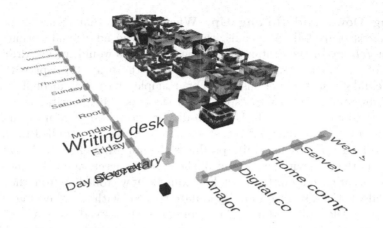

Fig. 2. A browsing state with three projected dimensions

3.2 Data Projection

Now that we have established the primary interaction mechanism by which a user can apply filters to the target dataset, we can begin to explore how this data is visualised within ViRMA's virtual environment. As previously stated, we refer to the concept of applying a filter as a visible dimension in the virtual space as *data projection*. This is to draw a distinction between data or metadata which can be visualised as a dimension on a spatial axis in the environment and data or metadata which can be visualised in other contexts, such as within the dimension explorer. If we consider all the data and metadata organised by the M^3 model as existing in a multi-dimensional space, projecting dimensions in the ViRMA system is the equivalent of taking a specific slice of that multi-dimensional space and mapping it to the three spatial dimensions available in our virtual environment.

Slicing and Dicing. When the user first loads into the ViRMA system, the virtual environment is empty and the only interactive elements present are those necessary to support initial query generation, such as the dimension explorer. We refer to the virtual environment within ViRMA as the projection space. Upon selecting a filter the user wishes to project as a dimension, and choosing which axis the user wants to map the dimension to (i.e. X: left/right, Y: up/down, or Z: in/out), the projection space is populated with the relevant axis and a representation of the data along that axis (see Fig. 2).

In the context of the M^3 model, projecting more than one dimension is referred to as *dicing* the multi-dimensional space and, from the perspective of the user, provides a data representation that conveys groups of images containing the various alcoholic drinks on each day of the week. The user can continue slicing and dicing the multi-dimensional space by projecting to the remaining third spatial dimension with any appropriate filter that suits their query.

Drilling Down and Rolling Up. When a tagset that exists as part of a hierarchy is projected to an axis, the user has the additional option to *drill down* or *roll up*. In the context of drilling down, this would involve drilling into a child of the current tagset and re-populating the projection space with that child's children on the axis instead. For example, with the "alcohol" tagset, a user might want to drill into "spirits" on the axis. The "spirits" tagset might contain children such as "whiskey", "vodka" or "rum" and upon drilling down, they would replace the parent tagset which was previously applied to the axis.

For rolling up, this naturally produces the opposing effect and involves re-populating the axis with the parent of the current tagset, and subsequently any siblings of that parent on that level. For example, if we rolled up from the children of the "alcohol" tagset, we would populate the axis with the "beverage" tagset, and will see "alcohol" and any of its siblings, such as "soda", "tea" or "coffee" now on the axis. Drilling down and rolling up can be accomplished easily in the ViRMA system by targeting a specific axis with one of the wireless controllers and selecting the appropriate contextual action which is displayed to the user.

Pivoting. Once a dimension has been applied to an axis in the projection space, it is important to understand that this dimension can be removed from the axis in two fundamentally different ways. The first method is the user can simply clear the dimension entirely, and all filters that were associated with the dimension are removed from the browsing state, increasing the amount of potential results in the current query. The second method is to replace the dimension on an axis whilst maintaining that dimension's filters on the browsing state. This is referred to as *pivoting* in the context of the M^3 model and is the equivalent of using the dimension explorer to apply a number of tags or tagsets as direct filters before projecting a different tagset as a dimension to one of the axes in the projection space. It is imperative that this concept is effectively conveyed to the user in the ViRMA system as it is fundamental in the user's understanding of the current browsing state within the projection space.

Cell and Timeline Exploration. Once the user has sufficiently refined their query using the aforementioned techniques, it is likely that they will want to explore the image contents of an individual cell in the data projection space. This can be accomplished at any time by pointing one of the wireless controllers at the relevant cell and selecting the contextual option that appears. This will temporarily reload the projection space with all of the images contained in that cell. Furthermore, while browsing a cell's contents, if the user wishes to view any individual result in the context of the wider lifelog, they can select the image via a contextual interaction and it will load a timeline above the cell's contents displaying the image as it appeared in the lifelog. The user can then scroll left in this list to move backwards in time and right to move forwards in time. Finally, the user may return to the original projection space by selecting the appropriate button on either controller.

4   Conclusion

The ViRMA system prototype is the first iteration of a novel virtual reality multimedia analysis platform based on the M^3 model. In this paper we have attempted to describe the system with respect to its underlying data model. It is our hope that we can evaluate our approach via VBS 2022 to serve as a benchmark against other multimedia analytics systems.

Acknowledgement. This work was supported by MCSA-IF grant 893914.

References

1. Gíslason, S., Jónsson, B.Þ, Amsaleg, L.: Integration of exploration and search: a case study of the M^3 model. In: Kompatsiaris, I., Huet, B., Mezaris, V., Gurrin, C., Cheng, W.-H., Vrochidis, S. (eds.) MMM 2019. LNCS, vol. 11295, pp. 156–168. Springer, Cham (2019). https://doi.org/10.1007/978-3-030-05710-7_13
2. Gurrin, C., et al.: Introduction to the fourth annual lifelog search challenge, LSC'21. In: Proceedings of ACM ICMR, Taipei, Taiwan (2021)
3. Mettes, P., Koelma, D.C., Snoek, C.G.: The ImageNet shuffle: reorganized pre-training for video event detection. In: Proceedings of ACM ICMR, pp. 175–182 (2016)
4. Seebacher, D., Häußler, J., Stein, M., Janetzko, H., Schreck, T., Keim, D.A.: Visual analytics and similarity search: concepts and challenges for effective retrieval considering users, tasks, and data. In: Proceedings of SISAP, pp. 324–332. Springer, Cham (2017). https://doi.org/10.1007/978-3-319-68474-1_23
5. Slater, M., Wilbur, S.: A Framework for Immersive Virtual Environments (FIVE): speculations on the role of presence in virtual environments. Presence 6(6), 603–616 (1997)
6. Xie, S., Girshick, R., Dollar, P., Tu, Z., He, K.: Aggregated residual transformations for deep neural networks. In: Proceedings of CVPR (2017)
7. Zahálka, J., Worring, M.: Towards interactive, intelligent, and integrated multimedia analytics. In: Proceedings of VAST, pp. 3–12 (2014)

Author Index

Printed in the United States
by Baker & Taylor Publisher Services

Printed in the United States
by Baker & Taylor Publisher Services